Java Programming Today

MIGUEL VARGAS MARTIN

Barbara Johnston

Albuquerque Technical Vocational Institute

PEARSON

Prentice
Hall

Upper Saddle River, New Jersey
Columbus, Ohio

Library of Congress Cataloging-in-Publication Data
Johnston, Barbara.
    Java programming today / Barbara Johnston.
        p. cm.
    Includes bibliographical references and index.
    ISBN 0–13–048623–X (alk. paper)
    1. Java (Computer program language)   2. Object-oriented programming (Computer
science) I. Title.

   QA76.73.J38J64 2004
   005.13′3—dc22
                                                                2003058017

Editor in Chief: Stephen Helba
Assistant Vice President and Publisher: Charles E. Stewart, Jr.
Assistant Editor: Mayda Bosco
Production Editor: Alexandrina Benedicto Wolf
Design Coordinator: Diane Ernsberger
Cover Designer: Ali Mohrman
Cover art: Frank Gonzales
Production Manager: Matt Ottenweller
Marketing Manager: Ben Leonard

This book was set in Times Roman by GTS Companies. It was printed and bound by R.R. Donnelley &
Sons Company. The cover was printed by Phoenix Color Corp.

Java is a registered trademark of Sun Microsystems, Inc.
Windows 98 and Windows XP are trademarks of Microsoft Corporation.
All other product names and company names mentioned herein are the property of their respective owners.

Pearson Prentice Hall™ is a trademark of Pearson Education, Inc.
Pearson® is a registered trademark of Pearson plc
Prentice Hall® is a registered trademark of Pearson Education, Inc.

Pearson Education Ltd.
Pearson Education Singapore Pte. Ltd.
Pearson Education Canada, Ltd.
Pearson Education—Japan

Pearson Education Australia Pty. Limited
Pearson Education North Asia Ltd.
Pearson Educación de Mexico, S.A. de C.V.
Pearson Education Malaysia Pte. Ltd.

10 9 8 7 6 5 4 3 2 1
ISBN 0–13–048623–X

Preface

Java Programming Today is written for the individual interested in learning to write computer programs in Java. You may be

- a college student planning to become a professional programmer,
- a community college student working towards an associate's degree in programming or web scripting,
- a mainframe programmer working for a company that is converting the company's software to a web-based environment using databases and Java Server Pages,
- an employee interested in becoming a programmer at your company, or
- a retired individual interested in learning to write programs for fun.

Whatever your situation, if you are ready to learn computer programming, *Java Programming Today* is for you. This text provides the software tools and covers all the basics in an easy-to-read, conversational style. Each Java concept is illustrated with example code and diagrams that the reader will find helpful and informative.

Java Programming Today Is for Beginning Programming Students

Java Programming Today assumes that the reader has never learned a programming language. We start at the beginning with a discussion of programming languages. The reader should have basic computer skills and be able to navigate through the various directory (or folder) structures on the computer.

Learning Java and object-oriented programming techniques as a first computer programming language is a wonderful advantage for today's programmer. The world of programming is rapidly becoming object-oriented. Many colleges and universities recognize this and are moving their first programming courses to Java. Students acquiring the object-oriented train of thought as their first language start thinking in terms of classes and objects—a most important mindset!

Java Programming Today Is Light on Math and Heavy on Java Concepts

Readers of *Java Programming Today* are not expected to have taken any math courses recently. It is true that many programming applications require rigorous mathematics, but the only skills we need here are addition, subtraction, multiplication, and division.

The author's philosophy is to provide Java students and instructors with "All of the stuff you need and none of the stuff you don't need." To understand Java, students must understand object-oriented programming and how Java interacts with the computer's operating system. To this end, this text presents the language fundamentals as well as complex topics such as stacks and heaps, and packaging and classpaths. In the real world, it is common to have several programmers work on one project. Therefore, it is necessary for programmers to separate their code into packages. How to incorporate the packages and tell Java where to find them is a practical task indeed!

Java Programming Today Is Packed with Example Code

Java Programming Today presents a wealth of Java program examples that illustrate various object-oriented concepts, as well as the right way to code and the wrong way to code. Troubleshooting sections illustrate pitfalls and poor style along with error-prone techniques. Seeing code written the wrong way is as informative as seeing code written the right way. Most people need to see many examples, and *Java Programming Today* has many. Each chapter has complete sample programs that illustrate new concepts as well as practice programs. Every program example in the text is found on the text's CD. The inside back cover of the text includes a program reference guide for a number of Java classes and sample programs.

Java Programming Today Offers Java Flexibility for Teaching

Java Programming Today presents the core Java language in the first nine chapters. Sun Microsystem's Java 2 Software Development Kit Standard Edition (J2SDK SE) is included on the text's CD, along with jEdit, a Java source code editor from the jEdit development group. The reader can install the Java environment and the jEdit editor and start writing Java programs in Chapter 2. There are four Advanced Topics chapters that present important material, including exception handling, input/output, Java archive files (JARs), packages, and classpaths. These items should be taught in an introductory Java course, but due to time constraints they may be omitted. The instructor may wish to have his or her students incorporate the various advanced topics such as error handling and creating JAR files early in the course and these chapters will provide reference to the core chapters. Six appendixes provide the information for installing and getting started using the Java environment and jEdit editor; an introduction to bits and bytes;

hexadecimal notation; Unicode; and IDEs. Nested classes are explained and found in supplemental material. Lastly, the Java debugging program is illustrated using sample programs from the text.

Java Programming Today Helps the Reader Build Java Programs from Scratch

Java Programming Today presents Java programs that are built from scratch, meaning that we use a text editor (jEdit or Microsoft's Notepad) to write each line of Java code. The Java file is saved on the hard disk. We then use the MS-DOS Prompt Window (Command Prompt) to enter the Java command needed to run these programs using Sun's J2SDK.

It is necessary to learn how to write code from scratch, because programmers must learn the purpose of each line of code, where the files must be located, and the underlying system requirements for the Java environment. But writing Java programs from scratch can be a time-consuming and tedious task!

Java Integrated Development Environments (IDEs) provide ease of use and allow for rapid code development, generating many lines of source code with a few mouse clicks. Some IDEs provide tools for working with databases and building Web applications. This is necessary in today's development arena. The tradeoff is that there is a learning curve for a programmer to become efficient with IDEs. IDEs build the code a certain way, which may or may not be the best way. Also, IDEs sometimes create their own directory structure and place the files where they want them. A programmer developing Java programs solely through an IDE may never understand what the code is doing nor the "software magic" that is performed by the development tool. We do not cover any specific development tool in this text. Appendix E provides a list of popular IDEs. Many of them are free for the Java developer to download and use.

Java Programming Today Uses a Unique Approach for Teaching Java

Java Programming Today uses a unique approach for introducing beginning programmers to the language and object-oriented programming principles. It's fun to have fun, and we have fun as soon as possible. Programming students, like many other students, are visual learners. The sooner they can see a concept in action, the better they learn. *Java Programming Today* has the beginning programmer using message boxes in Chapter 2 and painting text, graphics, and images in JApplets and JFrames in Chapter 3! Giving students the painting tools early on helps them to visualize programming concepts.

Object-oriented methodologies and programming concepts are complicated. Most people find them difficult to grasp at first. In *Java Programming Today*, instead of presenting these concepts formally, the readers are given enough information for a general understanding without overwhelming them. For example, Chapter 2 presents the idea of needing a Plumber (class), using the Yellow Pages to find a plumber (Don and Donna's Plumbing Service), and Donna comes to the house (she is a plumber object). Donna performs plumber tasks (methods) such as stopping the leak and fixing the faucet. The reader certainly can grasp this concept: classes are job descriptions, objects are persons performing the job, and the actual tasks are methods. In Chapter 2, we begin importing classes and calling both static and nonstatic methods.

Chapter 1 presents an overview of the language, and Chapter 2 introduces the language fundamentals, including keywords, operators, primitive data types, Strings, and arithmetic. We use Java's JOptionPane class, which allows students to gather data from the user via an input message box and display program output in a message box. This is much more fun than making calls to the console window using the System.out.println() method.

Chapter 3 introduces the reader to class hierarchy concepts. Although it is not a formal presentation of inheritance, we discuss how the class Object is the root class for all classes. It is important to get the reader thinking about inheritance and the notion that classes inherit methods and data from their superclasses. To assist the reader in learning this concept, we build an inheritance tree of job tasks. We begin with employees (all have names, tax ID numbers, work, and get a paycheck) and branch several layers for Airline and Hospital Employees ending at airline pilots (fly the plane, talk to the tower) and coronary care nurses (operate heart monitors, know heart medicines). We then see several examples of how Java subclasses inherit their methods from the superclasses.

Using these class hierarchy concepts, Chapter 3 introduces the JApplet and JFrame classes, examining the inheritance trees for both JApplet and JFrame. Applet and Web browser interaction is also covered. We see how our classes, by extending the JApplet or JFrame classes, gain the ability to be a JApplet or a JFrame. This allows the programmer to build fun programs incorporating methods from Java's Graphics class into the paint() method.

Chapter 4 presents control statements and loops, and Chapter 5 presents Arrays. Because we have developed JApplets and JFrames, the reader is able to build interesting programs and have fun designing the output by setting colors, showing images, and drawing graphical figures. One tool provided in this text is a pause method that allows the programmer to pause the program for a given number of milliseconds. By incorporating the pause method in nested *for* loops and drawing routines, the beginning programmer can watch the progress of the program. The reader can also build simple animated program.

Chapters 6 and 7 present object-oriented concepts, writing classes and methods, static methods, and instantiating our own anonymous classes within another class. Chapter 7 also presents the concept of interfaces and specific listeners, which give us the ability to incorporate buttons, sliders, and other graphic user interface (GUI) components into our programs. We build simple interfaces in this chapter. Chapter 8 covers how to build a GUI for a program. This GUI discussion includes controls, layout managers, panels, menus, and threads. Many coding examples present the how-tos for commonly used GUI controls. Chapter 9 presents the details of inheritance, including writing superclasses and subclasses. Abstract classes, interfaces, and polymorphism are presented as well.

The Advanced Topics chapters cover exception handling, Java I/O, Java archive files, packages, and classpaths nested classes, IDEs, and debugging. With the current emphasis on XML and Web application programming, the I/O chapter offers the basics for reading and writing data files—a needed task when writing XML-based applications.

Java Programming Today Provides All Necessary Software

Java Programming Today includes one CD that contains all of the example programs found in the text. The CD includes Sun Microsystems' J2SDK SE, and jEdit, an open source Java text editor distributed by the jEdit organization. Appendices provide installation instructions and use for these packages. In short, the CD contains everything the reader needs to get going with Java!

Java Programming Today Motto: Seeing Is Believing!

Java Programming Today's unique approach of introducing fun to write programs early on and its style and layout offer both beginning programming students and their instructors a wonderful tool for learning Java. Beginning Java programming students at Albuquerque's Technical Vocational Institute created several examples that illustrate the type and quality of programs beginning Java students can write. Examples are included throughout the text.

Java Programming Today Was Test-Driven by Students

Java Programming Today uses the same well-liked style found in the author's first text, *C++ Programming Today*. The C++ text is becoming a classroom favorite for C++ instructors because of its readability, clarity, methods of instruction, easily understood programming problems, depth of subject matter, and wonderful textbook design. *Java Programming Today* follows this lead and presents the nuts and bolts of the Java language and object-oriented concepts in a way that beginning programmers can easily grasp. Once again, the author (a faculty member at Albuquerque Technical Vocational Institute, New Mexico's largest community college) enlisted her students' assistance during the text's development. True to form, these students (the intended audience for this text) offered invaluable insight and information for this book.

Java Programming Today's Style Is a Classroom Favorite!

Java Programming Today's text design makes ultimate use of its color layout by incorporating colors to assist the reader throughout the text. The rainbow-colored tabs delineate the chapters, making it easy for the reader to find material in the text.

Highlighting bad code in red, and providing a light background and line numbers for good code help beginning programmers to see how code should be written and aid the classroom instructor in illustrating pertinent topics. The text uses red lights, yellow lights, green lights, and troubleshooting icons for emphasis; margin glossary entries for new terms; recommendation sections; and consistent color coding in figures. Actual program input and output windows are shown for all examples.

Java Programming Today's Supplements Make a Complete Package for Java Instructors

Java Programming Today offers the following ancillaries:

- Instructor's Manual containing PowerPoint slides of all the figures in the text and solutions to chapter questions and programming problems (ISBN 0-13-048624-8).

- TestGen, a computerized test bank (ISBN 0-13-048795-3).

- Companion Website at www.prenhall.com/johnston.

- Online Course Support: If your program is offering your digital electronics course in a distance-learning format, please contact your local Prentice Hall sales representative for a list of product solutions.

Acknowledgments

There are so many people to thank. First and foremost, I'd like to thank my immediate and extended family. These folks tolerated the long hours and lack of sense of humor as Crabzilla worked on this project. The time and energy required for a person to write a text is extraordinary, affecting all those around her. Thank you all for your patience and support.

Very special thanks go to Steve Parratto, fellow faculty member at Albuquerque Technical Vocational Institute and resident Java guru. Steve took me under his wing in his Java courses. Our boss, Paul Quan, Computer Technologies Program Director, allowed me to coteach with Steve and arranged my schedule to ensure that I was teaching Java throughout the development of this text. Steve patiently fielded questions from me in the lab, office, hallway, parking lot, on the phone, and via email. Steve is a continual source of support and is the main cheerleader for this text. Scott Bing, another TVI Java instructor, also fielded questions, reviewed material, and offered his perspective on teaching Java. Steve and Scott reviewed chapter drafts for content and flow. Scott's wife, Paula Bing, assisted with careful proofreading of several chapters. Many thanks to Steve, Scott, Paul, and Paula.

Three TVI Java programming students are my gold-star support team: Marc Benstein, Mia Boyd, and Gina Woodhouse. Marc, Mia, and Gina were students in Steve Parratto's Java courses and tutors in the department's Tech Center. They cheerfully volunteered to help me with this text. Their tasks included helping to outline chapters and individual chapter content, reading the material for clarity and correctness, assisting in organization of material, writing and running sample programs, offering ideas for chapter problems, and keeping me sane throughout the project.

After we outlined a chapter, Marc and Mia would forge ahead developing sample programs with only vague directions from me, such as "I need a program that has x, y, and z, and demonstrates q." Marc and Mia's influence is reflected in the unique and fun material found in this text. Marc developed the marcsPause() method in response to a request from me to pause a Java program and keep it simple, sweetie. His ideas for Java programs demonstrate the depth of this wonderful language. Marc will always be my main JavaGuy, and I wish him success in his career as a Java programmer. I am thrilled to have Mia's help on this text. She assisted with my first C++ text, and as usual, her insights into learning Java were invaluable to me. She also brings her wonderful sense of humor to the text, which includes her Coconut Estimator, Java Affirmations, and Sally's Seaside Shell Shack programs. Gina joined the Java gang once the writing was underway. Her eagle-eye proofreading skills caught many subtle errors and she pointed out areas that needed clarification and double-checked sample programs. Gina is responsible for JavaAnts at your picnic. I can't thank Marc, Mia, and Gina enough for all their hard work and dedication to this project.

The Technologies department at TVI supported me in this writing effort with words of encouragement, scheduling, and enthusiasm for the project. This department is led by Dr. Don Goodwin, Dean, and Steve Benavidez, Associate Dean. My Director Paul Quan and the E100 Lab support team, including Todd Edgel, Cheryl Brinkley, and Gary Johnson, were always helpful to the faculty and students. Thanks to the TVI students who contributed work to this text: Stephanie Chelius, David Talley, Edna Cardenas, Tim Wright, and Melissa Macpherson.

The text's cover design is based on the *C++ Programming Today* cover by Frank Gonzales. Frank's traffic light icons are also featured. Many thanks to my friend Nancy Koschmann Seemann, who once again waded through the page proofs of this book. Nancy provided a fresh set of eyes for proofreading the entire text at the final stage of production.

I would like to thank the following reviewers for their invaluable feedback: Scott Bing and Steve Parratto, Albuquerque Technical Vocational Institute, NM; Toni Black, University of New Mexico; Robert Borns, Purdue University, IN; Phillip Davis, Del Mar College, TX; Jack Gumaer, Northen Michigan University; Bill Liu, DeVry University, CA; and Lawrence Osborne, Lamar University, TX.

I am grateful to my editorial team at Prentice Hall. Assistant Editor Mayda Bosco is helpful and encouraging and keeps all of our ducks in a row. Charles Stewart, VP and Publisher, always offers positive comments, and I appreciate his insight and clear direction for the intended goals of this text. Special thanks to Production Editor Alex Wolf and her team, who handled the details of turning a manuscript into a finished text.

Barbara Johnston

Contents

█ Contents

6
Writing and Using Our Own Java Classes   286

7

More on Classes and Implementing Interfaces   368

It's fun to have fun! 369

8

Java Graphical User Interface Construction   438

Have a drink or prime the pump? 439

9

Inheritance and Interfaces   554

We're on the home stretch!   555

ADVANCED TOPICS

10

Exception Handling   628

Got Bugs?   629

11

Java Input/Output   670

Reading and Writing   671

12
JAR Files   710

13
Packages, Classpaths, and JARs   728

Appendices

Java Programming Today

1

An Overview of Java and Software Development

CHAPTER OBJECTIVES

Introduce this text to the reader.

Present an overview of the Java language.

Illustrate the concept of a computer programming language.

Explain Java bytecode and Java Virtual Machine (JVM).

Demonstrate how Java is a cross-platform programming language.

Help the beginning programmer start to think about all aspects of building software.

Welcome!

You are about to embark on a wonderful journey. Learning to write computer programs with the Java programming language will bring you a wonderful sense of accomplishment. When you become an efficient Java developer, technical career doors will open for you and many programming paths will become available. Java is a cornerstone in today's programming environment. Whether you are writing web-based applications, controllers for robots, implementing elegant user interfaces, building graphics for games or interfacing into databases, Java is where it all starts.

But beware! Programming—in any language—is not for everyone. Ahead in the journey are speed bumps, potholes, clear-air turbulence, and fog. A successful programmer uses many skills, including logical thinking and troubleshooting. At times, success seems to depend on just plain luck. If you are already familiar with another programming language and are now learning Java, you are aware of all these factors. If Java is your first programming language, you will find these pearls of wisdom to be true soon enough.

Software Developer Skill Set

Aside from learning Java, there are several other skills a student must learn to be a successful software developer and to contribute fully to a development or maintenance job. A few of these skills are listed in Table 1-1.

A software developer must also be a student of other fields. For any software job, the developer needs to become knowledgeable regarding the activities concerning the software while working closely with non-software experts on a project. For example, to write an inventory control and tracking system for an international company, the software team must have a good idea of all aspects of the business. Software developers are not expected to be experts in everything, but they should expect to keep learning new things long after school is out.

software development skill set
the necessary skills a person should possess to become a successful programmer

▌ TABLE 1-1
A software developer's skill set.

Skill	Where It Is Used
Documentation	All software needs to be documented well and be easy to read. Documentation describes what the program is doing, the logic that is used, how the user interacts with the program, and any special methods used to solve the problems. You should write your software assuming it will be used for years to come. Can someone read your software and know what you were doing?
Communication	Software developers must be able to communicate with team members, customers, and end users. Software projects often go through several design stages. Formal design and requirements documents are written before any code is built.
Quick learners	Software developers often work with experts in other fields who need to have software written. The software developer must gain some level of understanding of the new concepts before he or she is able to build the software. Often programming requires the use of mathematics, and the programmer should be familiar with mathematical concepts.
Debugging	It is vitally important to learn debugging skills when developing software. Debuggers aid in finding problems in software.
Troubleshooting	Debugging "broken" code is common. Good analysis/troubleshooting skills are invaluable.
Testing	Always think about how to test your software. Are you covering all the cases? Testing is one of the most important aspects of software development, but it is the one most often neglected.

A Few Details Concerning This Text

The goal of this text is to introduce the beginning programmer to the Java language and to ensure that the reader grasps the fundamental concepts of how this wonderful language works behind the scenes. Once these vital ideas are firmly in hand, the programmer may venture into wide open spaces and has the option to travel many programming paths.

Concepts, Order of Presentation   Chapter 1 presents an overview of the Java language without any specific code examples. At the end of Chapter 1, the reader is directed to Appendix A, *Getting Started with Java*, to install the Java software and write and run short Java application and applet programs. Chapter 2 presents language basics, including primitive variables, data types, operators, naming conventions and rules, and arithmetic. A simple concept of a class is presented, as are primitive wrapper classes. Application programs demonstrating these concepts can be written by the reader. Chapter 3 introduces Java's class hierarchy and inheritance in a general way so that the reader gains a feel for extending classes. We present the concept of a Java applet to demonstrate how classes inherit items from other classes. Later in the chapter, we build Java applets by extending JApplet and Java applications that extend JFrame. We are then able to perform drawing within a window.

Chapter 4 describes control statements and loops. Chapter 5 presents array concepts and references Advanced Topics Chapter 11, *Java Input/Output*. Chapter 6 helps us to write our own classes and methods and to build programs that contain many of our own classes. Chapter 7, *More on Classes and Implementing Interfaces*, presents several topics pertinent to classes and user interface concepts. Applying these concepts allows the programmer to add graphical user interface controls, such as buttons, combo boxes, and sliders to their programs. We build simple user interfaces to demonstrate these concepts. Chapter 8 presents a detailed discussion of the various user interface components and how to include and implement them in a Java program. These controls include buttons, sliders, combo boxes, menus, and panels. A formal discussion of inheritance concepts, as well as abstract classes and interfaces, is found in Chapter 9. In this chapter we write our own superclasses, subclasses, and interfaces.

Supporting appendices cover installing the Java Development Kit[1] from Sun Microsystems, and installing and using a Java editor, jEdit.[2] Scattered throughout the examples we use many of the useful classes found in Java, such as Vectors, Collections, Pattern, and Matcher. The reader is encouraged to explore the Advanced Topics chapters and appendices and apply these programming concepts to his or her programs.

Throughout these chapters, object-oriented ideas are presented with just enough detail to aid the reader in grasping Java concepts without overwhelming him or her with advanced concepts. Also, the reader is encouraged to learn how to use the standard documentation for the Java software. We frequently reference this documentation. The programs in these chapters gradually become more sophisticated, illustrating object-oriented methods in greater detail.

Once the beginning Java programmer is comfortable using classes, whether written by the programmer or given to him or her, as well as abstract classes and interfaces, he or she is ready to take on any Java topic!

Accompanying CD with This Book

One compact disk (CD) is included with this book. This CD contains all of the source code for the example programs in this text. The programs are organized into chapter

---

[1] Java^{TM} 2 Software Development Kit, Standard Edition Version 1.4.1 (J2SDK). Java is a registered trademark of Sun Microsystems, Inc.

[2] jEdit is an open source software program developed by a worldwide team lead by Slava Pestov. www.jedit.org.

and appendix folders. Java software includes the Java 2 Software Development Kit Standard Edition (J2SDK SE) from Sun Microsystems, which the reader should install on his or her personal computer. We include the J2SDK for a Microsoft Windows based machine, but other operating system J2SDKs are available from java.sun.com. A Java source code editor program, jEdit, is also found on the CD. Appendix A, *Getting Started with Java*, presents the instructions for installing the J2SDK. Appendix B, *jEdit, a Java Source Code Editor*, introduces the jEdit editor. This editor is a general purpose source code editor that provides a nice environment for entering and editing source code.

Appendix E, *Java Integrated Development Environments*, presents information on Java integrated development environments. The reader is encouraged to explore the websites listed in this appendix. Once the reader has become comfortable with Java, he or she should download an IDE such as the latest version of JBuilder® Personal from Borland® Corporation's web site, www.borland.com.[3] JBuilder is an **integrated development environment (IDE)** that contains a code editor, a program interface design tool, Java documentation, project management tools, and a debugger. The IDE provides the Java programmer with a complete development environment for Java. There are many different Java IDE packages available, we present a list of them in Appendix E. The reader may search the World Wide Web for "Java IDEs" to see a current list of such tools.

integrated development environment (IDE)

a complete development environment containing a code editor, a design tool, compiler, project management tools, and documentation

Two Ways to Build Java Programs

The Java programs in *Java Programming Today* are built "from scratch," meaning that we use a text editor (such as jEdit) to write each line of Java code. The Java file is saved on the hard disk. We then use the MS-DOS Prompt Window (Command Window) to enter—via the keyboard—the Java command needed to run these programs using Sun's J2SDK.

In Appendix E, we reference several IDEs. The integrated development environment allows the Java programmer to quickly lay out window designs by using graphical interface controls such as buttons, sliders, and check boxes, and it generates the necessary source code. Running the Java program is accomplished with a push of a button.

It is necessary for the Java programmer to learn both ways of writing Java programs. By writing code from scratch, the programmer not only learns the purpose of each line of code but also learns where these files must be located, the underlying system requirements for the Java environment, and how the computer is able to find and work with these files. But writing Java programs from scratch can be a time consuming and tedious task!

An IDE provides ease of use and allows for rapid code development generating many lines of source code with a few mouse clicks. This is necessary in today's

---

[3] JBuilder® and Borland® are registered trademarks of Borland, copyright 1994–2002, Borland Software Corporation.

development arena. The tradeoff is that many IDEs build the code a certain way, which may or may not be the best way. Also, the IDE may create its own directory structure and it places the files where it wants them. A programmer developing Java programs solely through an IDE may never understand either what the code is doing or the "software magic" that is performed by the development tool. If the programmer were given Java code to incorporate into a program, short of incorporating it into an IDE, that programmer would not know how this task is accomplished.

There is more to becoming a Java programmer than simply writing Java code! It is important to "look under the hood" and see the components that make this "Java automobile" run. *Java Programming Today* guides the Java programmer through building programs from scratch. In the later chapters we write larger Java programs and the reader may wish to build the same programs in an IDE to fully understand both techniques. Table 1-2 summarizes the pros and cons of the two approaches to learning Java programming.

Program Examples, Output, Errors, and Warnings   This book also includes a wide variety of program examples—from ten-liners to medium sized programs. There are complete programs, and the reader is welcome to use them as starting points for further expansion. You will find examples of code that are written incorrectly and hence do not build and execute. Sometimes seeing code

TABLE 1-2
Pros and cons for learning to write Java programs from scratch *v.* using an IDE such as JBuilder.

	From Scratch	IDE Tool
Pros	Learn the nuts and bolts of how Java programs are constructed.	Easy to get going and write Java programs.
	Write all the code and know where all the code pieces belong on the system.	No need to worry about environment setup and configuration because the IDE sets it up for the programmer. Interface builder generates Java code, making development proceed quickly.
	Programmer gains a complete knowledge of how Java and the computer environment work together.	
Cons	Difficult, due to setting up the environment on the computer. Programmer needs to understand some operating system fundamentals.	Generates source code.
		Some code may look different from how you are accustomed to seeing it. Program components are organized according to how the IDE wants them.
	All code is hand-typed, making program development tedious.	Difficult to integrate prewritten code into the IDE.

written the wrong way is more informative than seeing code written the right way. The associated error and warning messages for the erroneous code are presented as well.

Johnston's Rules for Programmers

As a team member of a commercial firm engaged in building and developing software, I am acquainted with technology skills needed in the marketplace. And as a member of the faculty of a technical and vocational community college, I have learned ways to help students master these skills. Teaching beginning programming students for many years has brought an understanding of the trial and tribulations that the new student encounters.

A common theme for all these students is their belief in a set of rules we develop at the beginning of each programming course. We refer to them as either the "Nine Commandments for Programmers" or the "Johnston Rules for Programmers." They are:

Keep your cool (don't get mad).

Work when you are rested (don't program when you are tired).

KISS your software (keep it simple, sweetie).

Give help/get help.

Study and know the rules for the language (syntax).

Learn the development environment and tools.

Understand the problem you are trying to solve.

Build and test your software in steps.

Save early/save often (back up your computer programming files often).

A tenth rule might emphasize, "Patience, patience." You can apply this maxim immediately, for several topics need to be covered before we reach the core of the Java language. Read on, and principles which now seem disjointed will come together shortly.

1.1
What is Java?

platform independent
a language that is able to run on a variety of computers or other hardware devices without being rebuilt on each machine

Java is a computer programming language developed in the early 1990s by Sun Microsystems. Originally named "Oak," then renamed "Java" in 1995, its initial purpose was to provide a language for embedded consumer electronic applications. The idea behind the Oak/Java language was to make it **platform independent**, meaning it could be used for building software and embedding it into consumer electronic devices such as microwave ovens, washing machines, and remote controls. The programming language for these electronic components must be able to work on a variety of hardware. Other languages, such as C++, would not work for these electronic devices because it must be built specifically for each computer processing unit (CPU) or controller. Because there are many different types of CPUs and electronic controllers, languages such as C++ were not viable solutions to this problem. Java was designed to meet this new challenge.

During this time, the World Wide Web (WWW) was emerging, and it too needed platform independent programs. The Internet is a distributed network of diverse computers, operating systems, and CPUs. Programs that were to be on the Internet would have to run on many types of computers. Java designers switched gears. The problem of writing platform independent programs so that users on various machines and operating systems could run the same program became their primary concern. The designers changed the primary focus of Java's purpose from consumer electronics to Internet programming.

Java was released to the public in 1995. As Java capabilities expand, it provides new, exciting tools for WWW developers. Java allows programmers to make web pages more interactive with animation, graphics, video, and audio. Soon, Java became the language of choice for businesses and information processing needs, because Java's platform independence frees businesses from being tied to one type of machine.

Java is the primary language for writing programs that reside on the Internet (the WWW) and for Intranet applications. An Intranet is an internal, trusted network located within a business or corporation. For example, a large corporation with many offices situated around the world can run Intranet networks that are secure—meaning they are free from outside sources or intrusions. Corporate data may be shared between offices in a seamless fashion thanks to Java programs.

The Java language is based on the C and C++ languages and its syntax (its code grammar) is the C and C++ syntax. Java designers removed many of the complex C and C++ components, leaving a concise and well designed computer language. When Java was released, a huge population of C and C++ programmers quickly embraced the Java language.

Java is a highly **portable language**, meaning that it runs on many types of hardware. Java programs can run on all types of computers, and thanks to the way Java is designed, Java programs can run on other hardware such as cell phones, Personal Data Assistants (PDAs), embedded processors, microprocessors, and smart cards (credit cards that have a microprocessor and memory). Java programs can be moved from one computer operating system to another, with minimal (or no) reworking required. Anyone who has ever had to upgrade a computer operating system or moved from one type of computer to another can appreciate the great portability feature of Java.

portable language
programs are written on one type of machine but are also able to run on many other types of computer hardware without rewriting or rebuilding

What is a Programming Language?

Java is a **computer programming language**. What does this mean? A computer language allows a programmer to write instructions or commands that form a computer program. The programmer must build the program—we will cover these

computer programming language
allows a programmer to write instructions or commands that form a computer program, commands make the computer perform tasks

steps in great detail later—and run or execute it. When a program is run, the commands found in the program make the computer perform tasks. For example, these tasks can include opening a window on the screen where you enter numbers into boxes in the window. These boxes are called edit fields. You may choose an arithmetic operation (add, subtract, multiply, or divide) by selecting a radio button. Pressing the OK button makes the program perform the chosen operation on your numbers. Your answer can be shown in a new window. Figures 1-1 and 1-2 illustrate these concepts.

Figure 1-1
Computer programmers write programs in a computer programming language, such as Java. The programs allow programmers to write instructions that the computer will perform when the program is executed.

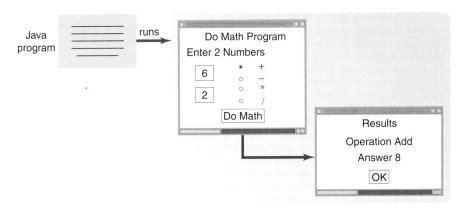

## 1

Figure 1-2
Computer programs run and issue commands to the computers, making the computers perform the programmer's desired tasks.

The types of instructions found in a computer program are as numerous as the possible tasks that a computer can perform. Computer programs can instruct the computer to perform mathematical calculations, read and display a digital image from a file, write information to a file, manipulate program data, and access records from a database. Programs can also play a sound clip, respond to a mouse click, or drive a motor on an assembly line. The fly-by-wire controls for modern aircraft receive their instructions from a computer that is running a program.

Over the past 40 years, there have been many different programming languages, including BASIC, COBOL, FORTRAN, C, C++, and Pascal. Just as we humans have many spoken languages with proper ways to speak and write the language (English, French, German, Chinese, etc.), each of these computer languages has its own rules for writing and using the language as well. Table 1-3 illustrates several written languages asking the question, "How are you?" Table 1-4 illustrates computer programming language instructions for writing the question, "How are you?"

TABLE 1-3
Spoken languages have grammar rules.

Language	How are you?
English	How are you?
German	Wie geht's Dir?
French	Comment va tu?
Spanish	¿Como estas?

TABLE 1-4
Computer programming languages also have grammar rules.

Language	How are you?
BASIC	PRINT "How are you?"
FORTRAN	WRITE(6,35)
	35 FORMAT('HOW ARE YOU?')
C	printf("How are you?");
C++	cout << "How are you? " ;
Java	System.out.println("How are you?");

1.2
The Big Java Picture, Java Source Code, Bytecode, and JVM

There are several steps that a programmer must take in order to write a Java program, and we cover these steps in great detail beginning in Appendix A and Chapter 2. Before we venture down the road of keywords, semicolons, and braces, it is important for the beginning programmer to understand how the Java code that he or she writes in a program turns into something that a computer can execute.

First, the programmer must use an editing program, such as jEdit or Microsoft's Notepad,[4] and he or she must type the Java instructions using the software, then save it into a file. The lines of Java instructions are known as **source code** or **lines of source code**. The file that contains these instructions, or source code, is known as a **source code file**. In Java, this file must be saved with a *.java* file extension. A **text-based file** is a data file of characters without any special formatting symbols, and the file is saved in a textual—not binary—format on a computer. Microsoft's Notepad, and the jEdit editor are examples of text-based file editors. It is not advisable to use a word processing program, such as Microsoft's Word,[5] for source code, because these programs automatically save the file in a binary format including special formatting characters in the file.

The following is a short Java program that was written in Microsoft's Notepad. In Java, the file name must be the same as the class name. In this short program, our class is named "JLove" (see the line—public class JLove) and we have saved this file as *JLove.java*.

source code or lines of source code

program instruction code written using the rules for the language

source code file

file containing lines of Java instructions

text-based file

data file of characters without any specific formatting symbols, Notepad is a text-based file editor

---

[4] Microsoft's Notepad is a registered trademark of Microsoft Corporation. All rights reserved.

[5] Microsoft Word is a registered trademark of the Microsoft Corporation. All rights reserved.

```
//File:  JLove.java
//A complete Java program
public class JLove
{
        public static void main(String args[] )
        {
                System.out.println("I Love Java!!! ");
        }
}
```

The next step in building a Java program is to have the **Java compiler** read the *JLove.java* source code file. A compiler's job is to read the Java source code and check that the grammar, or **syntax**, is correct. The Java language has grammar or syntax rules that specify the way the lines of source code must be written. We begin learning these rules in Chapter 2. If there are no syntax errors in our source code, the Java compiler writes a Java **bytecode** file that is named with the *.class* extension. (For our example above, the Java compiler writes a *JLove.class* file.) Figure 1-3 illustrates the source code bytecode relationship.

Once the bytecode file is produced, we are ready to run our Java program. The Java bytecode is read by the **Java Virtual Machine (JVM)**. The JVM is a separate program that reads the bytecode found in the class file and translates the commands into "native" instructions for the computer's processor. The Java *.class* file does not "talk to" the computer's processor directly. The Java Virtual Machine "talks to" the processor, "telling it" what tasks to perform. Java is said to be an **interpreted language**, because running a Java program involves having the JVM read and interpret the Java bytecode and issue the appropriate processor instructions. Figure 1-4 shows how the JVM interprets the bytecode and issues processor commands.

There are JVM programs written for different computer platforms. The JVM is **machine dependent**, meaning that it must be built specifically for the type of computer on which it is to run. If you are running a Windows machine, you must have a

Java compiler
reads the *.java* source code file and checks for syntax errors, if error-free, it writes the .class file of bytecode

syntax
grammatical rules for writing a computer language

bytecode
contained in a file with a *.class* extension, it is read by the JVM and translated into "native" instructions for the computer's processor

Java Virtual Machine (JVM)
a program that reads bytecode and translates the commands into "native" instructions for the computer's processor

interpreted language
the JVM reads and interprets Java bytecode, issuing the appropriate processor instructions

machine dependent
a program that must be built specifically for the type of computer on which it is to run

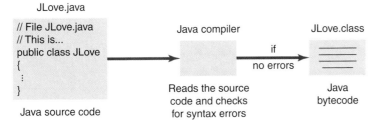

Figure 1-3
The Java compiler reads the *JLove.java* source code and checks it for syntax errors. If there are no errors, the compiler writes the *JLove.class* bytecode file. Bytecode always has the *.class* extension.

Figure 1-4
The Java Virtual Machine reads the *JLove.class* bytecode and issues appropriate commands for the computer's processor. In this case, the JVM is for a Pentium processor.

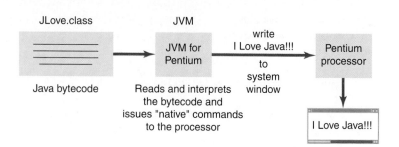

JLove.class

Java bytecode

JVM

JVM for Pentium

Reads and interprets the bytecode and issues "native" commands to the processor

write I Love Java!!! to system window

Pentium processor

I Love Java!!!

Windows JVM, because that JVM translates the Java bytecode into Windows processor commands. If you have a Sun Microsystems UltraSPARC Workstation,[6] you must have a JVM for this Sun platform, as it must translate the bytecode into UltraSPARC processor commands. There are many JVMs available for personal computers, Macintosh[7] computers, and other platforms. You, the beginning Java programmer, do not have to worry about the JVM as you work through the material in this text. When you install the J2SDK that comes with the text, it has a JVM that it uses.

Java is a Platform Independent Language

platform independent or cross platform

you can write a Java program on one machine and run it on any machine

One of the many advantages of the Java language is that it produces Java programs that are **platform-independent** or **cross-platform**. This means that you can write your Java program on one machine and run it on any machine! (In Java references, often times you see the acronym WORA, which stands for *Write Once Run Anywhere*.) Because the Java language is used extensively for WWW applications, Java programs need to be able to run on any type of computer. Key to this independence is the fact that the Java bytecode is interpreted by the JVM and the Java designers chose international standards for the character and numeric formats so that the Java programs behave consistently from one machine to another. We present more on the standards in Chapter 2.

Figure 1-5 illustrates how a Java program can be written on one machine and run by JVMs on many other types of computers. In this figure, we write a Java program that has two edit fields for numbers, radio buttons to select an arithmetic operation, and a "Do Math" button. The answer is presented in a separate window. The program is compiled on one machine and the bytecode can be interpreted by other computers' JVMs. This process is what makes Java a cross-platform language, unlike C++.

C++ is not a Platform Independent Language

If you write a computer program in C++, you must go through similar programming steps. First, you write the C++ source code in a text-based file and name

---

[6] Ultra SPARC Workstation is a registered trademark of Sun Microsystems, Inc.

[7] Macintosh is a registered trademark of Apple Computer, Inc. All rights reserved.

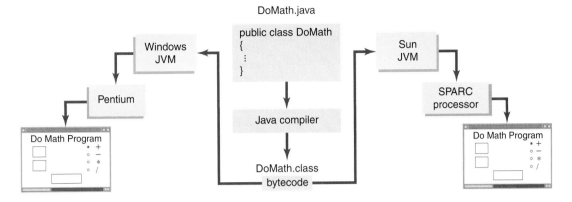

Figure 1-5
Java is a cross-platform language. Java source code written and compiled on one machine can then be run on any machine that has a JVM.

the file with a *.cpp* extension. A C++ compiler reads the C++ source, and it produces object code if there are no errors. This object code is then linked with the appropriate libraries and an executable file is produced. This executable file can be run—and it "talks to" the computer's processor directly, issuing the appropriate commands. Figure 1-6 illustrates this process.

For a C++ programmer to run his or her program on a Windows machine *and* a Sun workstation, he or she must go through the compile and link stages on both

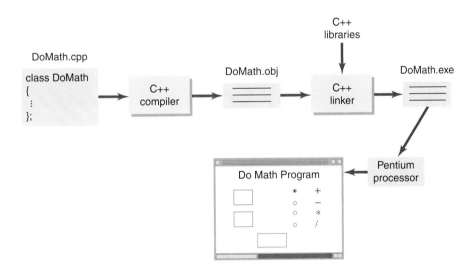

Figure 1-6
A C++ program must be compiled and linked on its target machine because the C++ executable file "talks to" the processor directly.

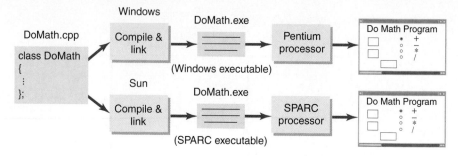

Figure 1-7
Standardized C++ source code is machine independent, but it must be built on every machine on which it is to be executed (i.e., machine dependent).

machines. C++ source code is machine independent, as long as the programmer follows the standardized rules for the language syntax and design, but the C++ executable file is machine dependent. This means that the C++ source code can be exactly the same on the Windows and Sun computers, but the build process must be repeated on both machines. Figure 1-7 shows how C++ source code is machine independent, but the executable program is not.

1.3
Why Do Programmers Love Java?

Aside from Java's portability from machine to machine, the Java language provides a wide variety of useful and powerful tools. There are many Java libraries providing the software developer with items for building robust and wonderful applications. The programmer can find all the user interface components available, such as buttons, check boxes, sliders, menus, edit fields, and commonly used dialog boxes ready to go. The language contains prebuilt software for mathematical functions, multimedia, graphics, file handling, database, security, networking, animation, and a wealth of error handling routines.

A visit to Sun Microsystems' http://www.java.sun.com website shows the Java programmer many of the **Application Programming Interfaces (APIs)** that can be incorporated into a Java program. APIs are existing classes with ready to use code, and include Java™ Speech, Java™ Telephony, Java™ Electronic Commerce Framework, and even an API for Robots (Java™ Technology Robotics Development Kit).[8]

Java is based on the C and C++ languages. Java benefits from many of the C and C++ features, including a large number of **operators** in C++. In Java there are symbols, that are part of the language, that instruct the language to perform certain

Application Programming Interfaces (APIs)
set of class libraries

operators
symbols that instruct the language to perform certain actions such as + add, − subtract, etc.

_____

[8] Java and all Java-based marks are registered trademarks of Sun Microsystems, Inc.

actions. For example, the "+" symbol adds numbers and the "*" symbol multiplies numbers. There are basic decision and control structures so that a program may branch to different code statements or loop over statements.

The Java language is completely **object-oriented**, and requires programmers to write their code as **classes**. Programmers have grown to love object-oriented programming, and we will spend time discussing this programming concept and techniques. In fact, object-oriented programming has now become the standard methodology for newer programming languages. Classes contain **methods**, which are discrete code sections that perform specific tasks. For now, think of a class as a "job description," and a method as a "task" that a person performing that job can do. Java's naming conventions state that class names begin with capital letters. With this in mind, we will capitalize our classes as we discuss them. For example, we can describe the job of an Electrician, and one of the many tasks an Electrician can perform is to fix wires.

Because Java is an object-oriented language, it provides the programmer with the ability to create new classes from existing classes. This programming action is known as **inheritance**—which is a powerful feature of the language. The concept of inheritance is exactly as you expect. Children inherit characteristics, behaviors, and properties from parents. With classes, the same idea applies. New, customized classes can be created from existing classes. Using our Electrician example, we can create a new type of Electrician, called an AutomotiveElectrician, by inheriting the Electrician properties. We present more on inheritance in Chapter 2 and later chapters.

In addition, an entire group of classes can be grouped into a **package**, thus enabling the classes to be organized and handled in a logical manner. For example, if your program contains many complicated mathematical calculations, it is possible to organize these calculations into separate classes and place the classes into a "calculator" package. This action helps keep your program from becoming too large and unwieldy. We will cover these concepts in great detail in this text.

One last consideration that should be mentioned is the way in which Java handles memory management. Java is conservative in the way it handles memory. All objects are references, and objects are passed by reference. Also, the language does not allow programs to access array data beyond what is declared. This built in limitation eliminates many nasty array problems that can crop up in other languages. Lastly, Java provides garbage collection as part of the language. Java's garbage collection services attempt to release memory and "clean up" after itself once program components are no longer needed. We discuss garbage collection in several places in this text. Garbage collection is first demonstrated in a sample program in Chapter 2.

object-oriented
a programming technique that requires programmers to write their code as classes

classes
can be thought of as a job description

methods
discrete code sections that perform specific tasks

inheritance
new classes can be built by inheriting characteristics, behaviors, and properties from "parent" classes

package
a technique that allows a group of classes to be organized and bundled into a single unit or group

Three Types of Java Programs

A Java program can be written in three different forms, and hence executed in three different ways. These three types of programs are Java applications, Java applets, and Java servlets. There are specific rules that the programmer must follow for each type of program. A **Java application** is a stand-alone program that can be run from the command line on a computer. The **Java applet** is a program that runs in a web browser. Typically, an applet is downloaded from a "server" onto the "client" machine, then run in the client's web browser program, such as Internet Explorer.[9]

The third type of program is a **Java servlet**. A servlet resides and runs on a web server. A servlet program responds to a request from a client. For example, a Java servlet could be on a utility company's web server. A utility customer could visit the company's website and request his or her utility usage for the last year. The servlet then accesses the appropriate database, retrieves the customer's information, and posts that information to the user. Servlets and Java Server Pages (JSPs) are an advanced topic and are not covered in this text, except for the brief discussion that follows. Several references for Java servlets and other advanced topics are found in the text's bibliography.

In *Java Programming Today*, we present the core concepts of the Java language, including applications and applets. The beginning Java programmer should understand that this text will take him or her on a journey through the language fundamentals, explaining the "hows" and the "whys" of Java, and will have you write many Java programs while learning these concepts. Once you are finished with this text, you are ready to venture out into the Java world—and whether you write robot controls, web based database applications, or controls for cell phones, the language fundamentals we cover in this text are applicable in the advanced world. After all, whether you are writing simple programs in Chapter 3, or a web based servlet, it's still just Java!

Figure 1-8 presents a diagram of the Java language and relates the material covered by this text to the entire field of Java. Because Java is a programming language, there are the basic concepts that all languages have, including data types, primitives, operators, control statements, loops, and arrays. Understanding object-oriented concepts is key to understanding Java. There are many Java libraries

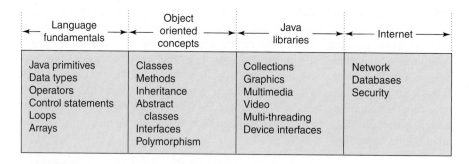

Figure 1-8
The Java world.

---

[9] Internet Explorer is a registered trademark of the Microsoft Corporation.

available to the Java programmer. Beyond that, there are networking, database, and security tools for developing software for the Internet.

Think of your learning experience in this text as if we are teaching you the fundamentals of flying an airplane. We explain the physics of flight, aircraft components, the purpose of the rudder, flaps, and the ailerons. We have you practice what you've learned by flying several different types of planes. Once you have finished with our flight school, you are ready to fly anything because, after all, flying airplanes is the same idea whether you are in a single engine Cessna or Boeing 737. (Of course, there must be special training for whichever type of aircraft you choose to fly.)

A Brief Aside About Servlets and JSP

It is important to have a brief discussion about Java servlets. A servlet is a program that resides on a server machine, and is executed on the server when a user browses a web page corresponding to that servlet. This is different from an applet that is downloaded onto the user's machine and executes on the user's computer. This ability to have Java programs run on the server side of the web is a powerful and useful feature.

There are servlets and JSPs (Java Server Pages). Servlets provide a way for a browser to initiate and run a program residing on a server. The server may access a database, run a calculation, and send appropriate output back to the user's browser. This output may be in Hyper Text Markup Language (HTML) format. Java Server Pages are used extensively in e-commerce systems, including popular online stores. Database access from a servlet requires you to use the Java Database Connectivity (JDBC) library. Java provides many libraries of prewritten, ready to go code so the programmer is free to write portable Java code that runs anywhere—and the software is not tied to any particular hardware or software vendor.

Java Server Pages (JSPs) have been modeled on ColdFusion technology.[10] JSP and Microsoft's Active Server Pages (ASP) allow the programmer to embed programming statements, scripts, and other components into a web page on the server. When a server gets a request from a browser, the JSP sends HTML code to the browser. This HTML code may have been dynamically produced by the JSP. Information that changes rapidly, such as stock quotations, weather data, or flight information, can be handled via a JSP on the web so that web data can be updated quickly.

Java Server Pages (JSPs) allow the programmer to embed programming statements into a web page on the server

Java Programming Today does not present a detailed discussion of servlets and JSP technology. (This material can easily fill another text.) It is important for beginning Java programmers to be familiar with the servlet and JSP technology, as more than likely learning this material will be the next destination on your Java training path.

---

[10] ColdFusion technology was invented by the Allaire Company of Boston, Mass.

1.4
Software Construction Techniques: An Overview

Your Dream House

Imagine that you are having your dream house built, and you have hired a contractor. The first day on the job the contractor shows up at your vacant lot and drops off piles of lumber, bags of cement, and rolls of wires. He leans the roll of your new living room carpeting against a tree. He stacks the windows on top of each other in the back, has the sheet-rock, electrical fixtures, plumbing items, and doorknobs lying on the dirt. Then he asks you where you want the kitchen. Moreover, he brings his crew to the site of the new house, and they are asking each other how to use the tools, reading how-to books, and looking at the wires and electrical outlets, wondering how they hook together.

Sounds silly? This scenario should never happen! The contractor has a blueprint of your house, and he knows what you want. He knows how much lumber and cement and wire to have on hand and doesn't have items delivered until it is the right time to use or install them. His builders know how to use equipment properly and understand construction techniques. The contractor knows there is a certain order in which things must happen. He makes sure the cement is dry before putting up the frame!

Building software and building houses take similar approaches. Before you start hammering two-by-fours together on your house frame, or writing your classes and methods, you must know what you want to build. What are the requirements and what is the program supposed to do? Just as the contractor builds your house in logical steps, software must be built in logical steps, too.

As students first start learning to program, they often make common mistakes with disastrous results. A student who would never build a house without a blueprint may sit down at the computer and start building software without a plan. Just as a contractor never will put on the roof until he is sure the walls are strong enough to hold it, students never should hook together complicated software modules without testing each piece.

How Not to Program

It is important to learn how to crawl before walking, and to walk before running, and much of this text covers the Java fundamentals of crawling and walking. In watching babies learn to crawl, walk, and run, adults sometimes have to let them fall a few times. There are all sorts of lessons awaiting beginning Java programmers. However, just as a responsible parent will keep a watchful eye on the toddler, it is only right to provide beginning programmers with a few pointers.

The following chapters of this book provide troubleshooting information concerning the language. Table 1-5 describes many steps to avoid while programming. I have compiled this table after watching many, many beginning programmers tackle programming assignments in the wrong way.

Troubleshooting: What Is Wrong with My Program?

If your car does not start, what do you do? You follow a logical set of steps to determine the problem. Is your battery dead? Do you have enough fuel? Is there a loose wire? Tracking down a software problem also involves asking simple questions and examining the program to find the error.

"What is wrong with my program?" This common phrase is heard in computer labs everywhere. The computer is unforgiving at times and does exactly what you tell it. Many mistakes can be avoided if a student will learn and follow the "nine commandments of programming" and to develop the good habits listed under the "Do" column in Table 1-5. Also read Appendix F, *Troubleshooting and Debugging*, and learn to use the jdb debugging tool.

TABLE 1-5
Don'ts and Do's for Programmers

Don't	Do
Don't go directly to the computer, start typing in code, and assume you will be able to figure out the program as you go along.	Do write down on paper what you need to do.
Don't avoid testing the easy stuff.	Do simple methods may seem obviously correct. Spending five minutes checking a two-line method may save you hours of work later.
Don't depend on the compiler to ensure that your code is written correctly. The compiler will allow code to compile but will result in run-time errors.	Do understand every single line of code you enter into your program.
Don't avoid comments in your code. You will be amazed how something that seems so clear is not clear a few days later.	Do write simple, clear comments explaining your program logic.
Don't type in your entire program before compiling. Often one or two errors will result in many compiler errors.	Do build your program in steps, stopping and testing each step as you go.
Don't type in random braces if your program won't compile.	Do indent your code and line up your braces.
Don't get mad! When you find yourself getting frustrated with the program, it's time to leave it alone for a while. Go get a soft drink or coffee, take a walk, do the dishes.	Do work on your program when you are rested and it is quiet. Programming requires concentration, and interruptions often cause you to lose your train of thought.
Don't wait to start your program until the last moment, even if you do work well under pressure.	Do plan to work on your program over the course of several days. This strategy will give you time to rethink problems and refine the work as needed.

■ REVIEW QUESTIONS AND PROBLEMS

To Do:

Proceed to Appendix A, *Getting Started with Java,* and install the J2SDK SE on your Windows machine. You may install the jEdit software (see Appendix B) so that you have a Java friendly text editor. Set your computer's path so that you are able to write, compile, and run the sample programs from Appendix A.

Review Questions

1. Who invented the Java language?

2. What language was the basis for Java?

3. What are the three types of Java programs?

4. What is the purpose of the Java Virtual Machine?

5. Describe what an IDE is and how a programmer would use one.

6. What is the difference between source code and bytecode?

7. Why is it beneficial for the Java programmer to know how to build Java programs "from scratch?"

8. What is the job of the Java compiler?

9. Why is it important to learn to use all the tools in your development environment?

10. Name three skills that programmers must have, besides just writing software.

11. What is the difference between platform dependent and platform independent languages?

12. Why is Java called an interpreted language?

13. What is a syntax error? When would a Java programmer see a syntax error?

14. Why would a word processing program, such as Microsoft Word, not be a good editor for a Java programmer?

15. Why should a programmer plan his or her program "on paper" before the code is entered into the computer?

Just for Fun! Java Scavenger Hunt

Visit the http://www.java.sun.com website, and see if you can find the answers to these questions. Although we haven't covered the material yet, this exercise introduced you to Sun Microsystems' Java site and to many Java concepts.

16. When was the "Java 2" name announced? Who made the announcement (which company)?

17. What makes the 2 in Java 2? (Where does the 2 come from? How is the name Java 2 different from Java 1?)

18. What does it mean when it says that companies are supporting the JavaPhone API?

19. Name four companies who support the JavaPhone API.

20. How can Java help the TV industry?

21. The Java 2 Platform Standard Edition is available for what systems from this website?

22. In the Java 2 Platform, Standard Edition v. 1.4.1 API Specifications, look up the String class. What class is it derived from?

23. How many String constructor methods are there?

24. What does the String method "equals" do?

25. What types of classes are found in the Package java.awt? What is the general purpose for this package?

2

Getting Started with Java Applications

KEY TERMS AND CONCEPTS

algorithm
case sensitive
class definition line
classes and objects
class constructors
code style and indention
comment
comment styles
compiler
constructors
declarations
escape sequence
final
identifier
identifier naming rules
java Java interpreter
javac Java compiler
Java keywords
Java statements
keywords
method
main method
method signature
new keyword
operators and precedence of
    operations
packages
primitive data types
programming terminology
syntax
variables and their values
whitespace characters

CHAPTER OBJECTIVES

Show how to begin designing software by developing a step by step approach (an algorithm) to a solution.

Introduce new terminology and software construction fundamentals.

Describe a simple example illustrating classes, objects, and methods.

Present a general format for a Java application program.

Show *javac* compiler commands and *Java* interpreter commands, as well as errors from the Java compiler.

Understand Java primitive data types and how to declare and use Java primitives.

Explore the various Java operators and how these operators are used in a Java program.

Illustrate the correct and incorrect ways of coding arithmetic and algebraic expressions in Java.

Introduce the java.lang package and demonstrate how to use String, System, Math, and primitive wrapper classes.

Present how to use classes and how to use static methods.

Import Java packages and classes and create Java objects via the new keyword and class constructors.

Introduce the four icons to the reader:

 Good Programming Practice!

 Be Cautious!

 Stop! Do Not Do This!

 Troubleshooting Tip

The Big Picture

Computer programs and programming languages take many forms. There are programs that operate on mainframe computers maintaining airline reservations for hundreds of flights and thousands of travelers. Banking, insurance, and tax records can also be found on mainframes. Programs running on personal computers provide people with application tools for bookkeeping, mathematical calculations, computer design packages, and image processing. Computer programs run on microprocessor controlled assembly lines. Now, using the Internet, you can access your bank account, shop for anything, see your property tax record, and research any topic of interest. Personal computers sitting on your desk allow you to watch movies, perform professional word processing, or make your own greeting cards—thanks to powerful and easy to use programs.

The software developers (programmers) who write these programs follow the same production steps. Such procedures involve taking an idea, determining all the necessary behaviors and actions, writing the software instructions, building the program according to the structure required by the language, and testing it to ensure the end results are what were desired. The majority of this text involves learning how to write the Java language software instructions—but it is important to keep the big picture in mind.

2.1
Programming Fundamentals

The first order of business for a programmer-wannabe is to understand that programming requires problem-solving skills. If you enjoy getting into the details of how to make something work, you have chosen the right career. Programmers are often presented with a problem or some sort of desired end result. ("Could you just make the computer do this?") The programmer must understand the problem or the goal and then come up with a plan of how to achieve it. Recognize that this plan will not be problem-free.

Algorithm Design

algorithm

process or set of rules followed to solve a problem

Building and testing your software in steps is an essential habit for a software developer. Something else must be mentioned while we're on the topic of software construction, and that is algorithm development. An **algorithm** is a process or a set of rules or steps to follow for solving a problem. It is important that you create a set of steps that solves the problem before you sit down and start entering source code.

Let's look at a few examples. Suppose you had to write a program that reads lines of text from a data file. Your program should count the number of times the word *sheep* is found. How will you solve this problem? There are several approaches you can take. Figure 2-1 illustrates one. You can read each line of text into your program and then search the line letter by letter for the letter "s." If you find an "s," check the next letter to see if it is an "h." If that letter is an "h," check the next for

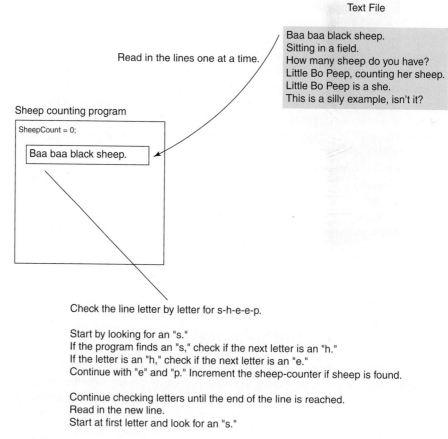

Text File

Read in the lines one at a time.

Baa baa black sheep.
Sitting in a field.
How many sheep do you have?
Little Bo Peep, counting her sheep.
Little Bo Peep is a she.
This is a silly example, isn't it?

Sheep counting program

SheepCount = 0;

Baa baa black sheep.

Check the line letter by letter for s-h-e-e-p.

Start by looking for an "s."
If the program finds an "s," check if the next letter is an "h."
If the letter is an "h," check if the next letter is an "e."
Continue with "e" and "p." Increment the sheep-counter if sheep is found.

Continue checking letters until the end of the line is reached.
Read in the new line.
Start at first letter and look for an "s."

Figure 2-1
Algorithm for counting the word *sheep* in lines of text.

"e," and so on. If you find the five letters you need, increment a sheep-counter. This scheme of checking the letters is an algorithm. (There are, of course, other algorithms for counting sheep.)

What steps are needed for determining the total surface area of a cylinder? (Yes, math problems are everywhere in programming.) Pop the top of your favorite tasty beverage and refresh yourself as we examine how to determine how much wrapping paper it would take to cover the beverage can. Look at Figure 2-2. We need to know two pieces of information: the cylinder's radius and height. We break

We need to know the radius of the cylinder.

A TASTY BEVERAGE

We need to know the height.

If we examine the can as three parts, we can find the total area.

Total surface area of our "tasty beverage" cylinder = area of top PI * R * R + area of bottom PI * R * R + Rectangular area of the center part of the cylinder = top circumference * height = PI * diameter * height = PI * 2 * R * height

Figure 2-2
Algorithm for determining the surface area of a cylinder.

the cylinder into three separate pieces: the top, side, and bottom portions. Using the radius and height, we can calculate the total surface area.

Steps to Programming Success

How do you become a good problem solver? Problem solving requires one to be methodical and careful. Let's create our own problem-solving algorithm with basic steps to aid us in understanding the problem and reaching a solution. In general, these steps are as follows.

Step 1: Read the problem statement.   Make sure you understand everything about the problem and what it is that you are being asked to do. Do not worry about *how* you are going to solve the problem; just understand *what* is the problem and the desired results.

Step 2: Plan your solution.   What are the main components of your problem? List them. What are the steps that you must take to reach your programming goal? Think through each of the steps and develop a plan for each one. It is not necessary to lay out every detail at this stage, but major aspects must be considered. You can write out a plan in a diagram (called a flow diagram) or describe your plan in short phrases (known as pseudocode).

Step 3: Test.   As you work toward your solution, identify items that can be individually tested and develop a plan to test the entire program. How will you know that your program is working correctly? Just because you are getting answers from the software doesn't mean that your answers are correct! Always think about testing your software while you are designing and building it.

Step 4: Implement the planned solution.   Now's the time to start typing. Once you have clearly defined steps in mind, and on paper, too, it is time to begin writing the program components. Test your software whenever possible. Expect to encounter programmatic details you hadn't thought of. Minor changes may be written as you go. You may need to revisit step 3 and develop more of the solution away from the computer. (*Note:* To enter the program and run it requires that you be familiar with the Java language and program steps.)

Step 5: Got bugs?   Most of us usually have bugs in our new software. The important thing is that you know that your program is not working correctly. If you know you have a problem, you are halfway to the correct solution. The best way to stomp on a software bug is to start at a point where you see the bug and work backward. Place print statements, have your program show you intermediate results, or use the debugging tool and watch what the code is doing. After all, you know what the code *should* be doing.

Step 6: Document what you have written.   Documentation involves writing comments in your source code that explain what you did.

Practice: How to Give a Cat a Bath   A practical example is useful in learning a new concept. Our practical example is to problem solve and determine how to give a cat a bath. Your cat needs a good shampoo and rinse because he's been hanging out under the car. He sleeps on your pillow—your sheets are filthy.

1. Read the problem statement many times. The cat needs to be bathed. The cat is dirty and shampoo must be used to remove the grease.

2. Plan your solution. The main components are the cat, the sink, water, and shampoo. Fill the sink with warm water and place the cat into the sink. Shampoo must be rubbed into the cat's fur and the cat must be scrubbed until clean. Then rinse all the shampoo off the cat. The cat is then towel-dried. Drain the sink and clean the area. Bandages may be needed afterward. It is safe to expect that the ten-pound cat will have the strength of a 150-pound man and possess eighteen sharp claws. Figure 2-3 illustrates this solution in both pseudocode and flow diagram.

3. Test. How will we know our cat-bathing program is working? Our program will be a success if (a) the cat becomes clean and is not injured in the process, (b) the kitchen is intact when we are finished, and (c) we are not visiting the emergency room afterward.

4. and 5. Implement the planned solution and correct bugs. (a) Prepare the sink area by clearing it of all items that may be knocked into the sink. (b) Obtain shampoo, towels, thick leather gloves, and a strong, able-bodied assistant. (c) Run warm water into the sink in preparation for inserting the cat. (d) Coax the cat from under the car. (*Note:* Fetching the cat from under the car is a different problem and is not addressed here.) (e) Put the cat into the sink. (f) Obtain the wet cat from under the couch. (g) Holding the cat firmly, place the cat into the sink again. (h) Gently pour water over the cat and rub in the shampoo. (i) Rinse. (j) Stand back and on the count of three, you and the able-bodied assistant let go of the wet cat and quickly step away from the sink. (k) Apply bandages to able-bodied assistant and yourself, if necessary.

6. Document. Write the list of steps for bathing the cat and add any bits of information that the next cat-bather will find useful.

Rule of Thirds

Many professional software developers profess that a programming project timeline should be divided into three parts. The **rule of thirds** states that the first third of the project time should be spent on program specifications and requirements, planning the user interface, and creating the necessary algorithms and test plans. The middle block of time is spent actually entering the program into the computer and testing each piece. The last block of time is reserved for system integration and testing. This period is used for testing the overall system and ensuring that the software performs as required.

It is especially important for beginning programming students to recognize the rule of thirds and to spend time studying the language and the programming

rule of thirds
theory stating that software project time should be divided into three parts: designing, writing, and implementing/testing

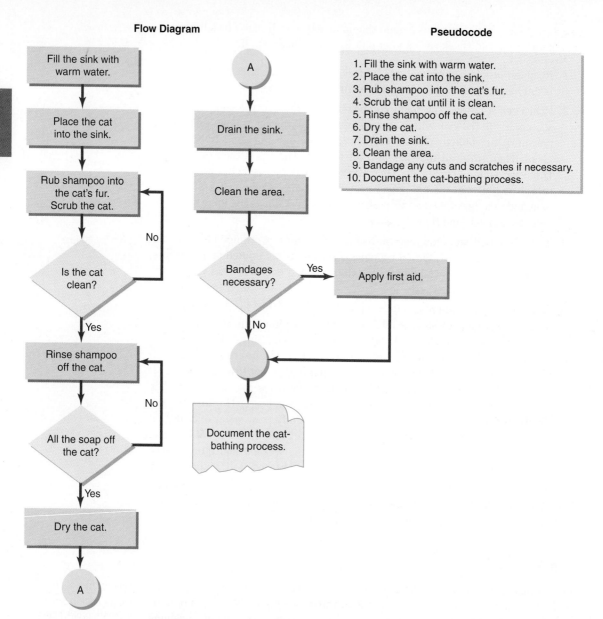

Figure 2-3
Pseudocode and flow diagram for bathing a cat.

problem. At this stage of your programming career, entering the Java statements and getting the program to run is the challenge, since you are new to the language. A misplaced semicolon can cost a new programmer hours (or days).

Try to avoid the temptation of doing all your thinking about your program at the keyboard. Get away from the computer, go to your favorite hangout, and put your thoughts on paper as you treat yourself to a snack.

How to Program

Table 2-1 provides a formal summary of the steps required for designing, building, testing, and integrating a software project. These steps are applicable for beginning Java programming assignments as well as large, multi-team programming efforts. Let's keep the big picture in mind here—it is necessary to make the program work, make it work correctly, and then make it work better.

TABLE 2-1
Summary of software development steps.

Development Concept	Task at Hand	Do
Concept validation	Getting started	Understand program's job and all requirements. Make a list!
Preliminary design	Blueprint	Identify logical steps for building the program. Identify objects and how objects will relate to each other. Find good stopping points. Decide how you will test each step.
Secondary design	Refine the blueprint	Write out the program framework. Write the complicated individual modules on paper first. Do this away from the computer!
Interface requirements	Fitting the parts together	If you are working on a team or on a large program, decide how all the parts will fit together and interact. Write down the interfaces so there is no confusion.
Prototype	Start construction	Build your program in steps. Set up a framework and test to make sure that it works. Don't continue until it all works correctly.
Functional testing	Test as you go	You may build test routines for sections of your code. You can control input/output and ensure that routines work properly.
Module integration	Integrate in steps	Integrate working sections in pieces. If sections have been tested individually, this task should be straightforward.
System integration and testing	Run the program from beginning to end	Once it is integrated, run the program through all the various cases.

Terminology and Project Construction

Part of learning any new skill involves learning new terminology. Computer programmers seem to have developed their own language. (RAM is not a male sheep, a bug is not an insect, surfing is not performed on the ocean, and a mouse is not a little mammal.) Table 2-2 presents several programming terms and phrases and their meaning.

▌ TABLE 2-2
Common programming terms and phrases.

Term	Meaning
API	Application Programming Interface. A set of customized libraries and routines used by programmers for certain tasks. APIs provide the necessary code to interface to and control hardware and software, such as Java™ Telephony, Java™ Speech, and Java™ Technology Robotics Development Kit.
bug	General catch all word meaning that the program is not running correctly.
bytecode	The contents of the class file produced by the Java compiler. The Java source code contained in the *.java* file is translated into bytecode contained in the *.class* file.
class	A basic component of an object-oriented programming language (i.e., Java or C++). A class can be thought of as a "job description" that has characteristics and behaviors.
code	This can refer to the textual-based phrases written in Java that represent a program (or portion of a program). Code can refer to a single line, such as a line of code or the entire program. Also, it can refer to program file contents such as source code, bytecode, or executable code.
compiler	Actual software program (such as Sun Microsystems J2SDK's Java compiler, javac) that reads Java statements contained in the *.java* file. It checks that the statements are written with the correct syntax. The Java compiler produces bytecode contained in the *.class* file.
debugger	A tool in the software development package (such as Sun Microsystems J2SDK or Borland's JBuilder) which allows the programmer to run the program a step at a time and examine program portions. A debugger is used to track down bugs.
executable class file	The bytecode file that the JVM reads and interprets. The JVM produces the processor instructions based on the commands in this class file.
method	A discrete block of code contained in a class, that performs a specific task.
object	An instance of a class. An object is a program component that performs the "job tasks" that are described in the class.
source code	Same as *code*.
syntax	The rules that dictate the correct way in which the language words and symbols are put together so that they have meaning to the Java language. It may be thought of as the "grammar" and "punctuation" rules for the computer language.

A Brief Introduction to Classes, Objects, and Methods

Java is an **object-oriented language**. This means that all Java programs are built using **objects**, and objects are instances of **classes**. It is easy to think of a class as a "job description." The job description contains the data and tasks that are performed by someone doing that job. The object is the actual "person" who is performing that job. **Methods** can be thought of as the various tasks performed by the object and are defined by the class. Java's naming convention requires classes to be capitalized. Method names must begin with a lower case letter, and subsequent words should be capitalized. Methods are indicated with a set of () following the name. We follow these conventions in our discussion.

Let's look at a few simple examples. What is the job description of a plumber? This job description can be characterized by asking, "What data does the plumber know?" and "What tasks can a plumber perform?" We can write a class description for a Plumber, including listing the data and tasks a Plumber can accomplish. One should also consider class properties when thinking about classes and job descriptions. What properties would a good Plumber possess? Plumber objects should have long fingers and be physically fit and flexible, because they need to crawl under sinks and reach into small compartments. Being strong and having a good back is also a plus for a plumber.

If you come into your kitchen, and find water spraying in the air where your sink faucet used to be, what do you do? You quickly reach for the phone book and look up "Plumbers." You know what type of professional you need to help with your ankle deep water. "Plumbers" are an example of a class. By reaching for the phone and dialing "Don and Donna's Plumbing Service," you are asking for an instance of a Plumber to come to your home. Donna, the Plumber object, arrives promptly. Donna stopTheLeak() and installANewFaucet(). Donna performs some of the various methods of the Plumber. (Let's not forget your tasks either. You, as the homeowner object must perform the tasks of writingTheCheck() to Donna and dryTheFloor().)

The entire world is object-oriented! Take a field trip down to your favorite fast food or campus area restaurant and list the "jobs" that are being performed. There are counter people taking orders, cooks in the back preparing the food, and bus boys and girls cleaning tables and floors. Each of these "jobs" can be described in a class definition. The counter people taking orders are all instances of the CounterWorker class. These CounterWorker objects are performing the tasks (methods) described by the class definition.

As we begin to explore and to learn Java, we must use the three terms—class, object, and method. Think of a class as a job description (Plumber). An object is an instance of the class, such as a person performing the job described by the class, (Donna). Methods are job tasks [stopTheLeak(), installANewFaucet()]. As we proceed through this text, we will learn all of the nuts and bolts of writing and using Java classes. For now, keep Plumbers and restaurant workers in mind as examples of classes, objects, and methods.

object-oriented language

all Java programs are built using objects

object

an instance of a class

class

think of a class as a "job description"

method

tasks are performed by the object and defined by the class

2

2.2
General Format of a Java Program

A Java program consists of several basic components, whether the program consists of a few lines of code or is large and complicated. To get us started, let's examine the JLove application program from Appendix A. By now, you should have worked through Appendix A, *Getting Started with Java*. This Appendix covers installing the Sun Microsystems J2SDK, writing and running a short application and applet program. If you have not studied Appendix A, you should do so as you read the remainder of this chapter.

The JLove (I Love Java!!!) Program

In our first program (the same one we wrote in Appendix A), we write I Love Java!!! in the MS-DOS Prompt command window. Figure 2-4 shows the output from this short program. Now let's examine the program, line by line.

The source code for our first Java program is shown in Program 2-1.

```
//Program 2-1    Getting Started with Java.
//This is our first program.
//File:  JLove.java


public class JLove
{
     public static void main(String args[] )
     {
          System.out.println("I love Java!!! ");
     }
}
```

```
C:\JPT>java JLove
I love Java!!!
```

Figure 2-4
The java command executing the JLove program from the folder C:\JPT. The output from the JLove program is "I Love Java!!!"

Comments

The first three lines in the example are comment lines.

```
//Program 2-1    Getting Started with Java.
//This is our first program.
//File:  JLove.java
```

Comment lines are written into the source file by the programmer in order to convey information concerning the code—information such as filenames, titles, data types, exceptions (possible errors), or explanations about what the software is doing. The compiler ignores all comment lines in a program. Comment lines may be placed anywhere in the source code. There are three ways to write comments in Java. The first two commenting techniques are from the C and C++ languages. These comments, that start with double forward slashes (//), are especially convenient for one line comments.

comment

lines in the source file that convey information concerning the code and are ignored by the compiler

```
//This is one way to write a comment.
//The compiler ignores everything from the double forward slashes
//to the end of the line (when it encounters a return/end of line character).
```

This comment below (shown in red, indicating "bad code") is written incorrectly. There must be two slashes // on each line.

```
//This comment is written correctly, but the following two lines are not.
To use the two forward slash style of commenting, the slashes must
be on each line.
```

A second, correct way to write a comment, by using /* and */ symbols, is as follows:

```
/* Here is another way to write a comment.
The compiler ignores everything in between the
beginning slash-star and the ending star-slash    */
```

This comment style is convenient for writing comments with multiple lines, because it needs only the /* at the start and the */ at the end of the comments lines. We could have written the first three lines of our JLove program like this:

```
/*Program 2-1   Getting Started with Java.
  This is our first program.
  File:  JLove.java                    */
```

The third way to write comments in Java source code uses the /** and */ symbols, and is a Java specific commenting technique. This commenting format is required by the javadoc utility program from Sun's J2SDK. This utility program prepares program documentation by reading source code and pulling out the comments within /** and */. The reader should refer to the javadoc utility documentation to learn the details for using the /** and */ comment and documentation generating tools found in Java. In this text, we will use the first two commenting styles in our examples.

One Last Comment on Comments The comments that you write in your Java source code should explain your thought process and logic, and describe important points concerning your code. You should not explain the Java language itself. (In theory, anyone reading your code would know Java and would not need you to explain the language to them.) Also, the comment line itself should be offset from the code, so that it is easy to see. This is an example of a poorly written comment:

```
System.out.println("I love Java!!!"); //Write I Love Java to console window
```

This comment, aside from being placed too close to the source code, is stating the obvious. Any programmer reading this code knows that we are writing "I Love Java" to the console window. It does not tell the reader why we are writing this phrase. In the line below, the comment is offset from the source line and explains why the phrase is needed in the program.

```
System.out.println("Write Total Value");        //report results
```

Try to ensure that your comments help the reader understand what you are writing, instead of wasting space and effort explaining the obvious.

Class Definition

The next line:

```
public class Jlove
```

class definition

the first line of a programmer-defined class

class

a Java keyword used in defining a class

public

a Java keyword and access specifier (See Chapters 6 and 9)

is the **class definition** line for the JLove class. The class definition line is the first line of a programmer-defined class. Every Java program must contain at least one programmer-defined class definition. The term **class** is a keyword (reserved word with special meaning to the language) in Java and must be followed by the name of the class. In this example, our programmer-defined class is JLove. For now, we always create our class definitions with the keyword **public**, and we will explain its meaning in later chapters.

One very important Java fact is that the source code file name must be the same name as the class name with a *.java* extension. In Program 2-1, the class name is JLove and the source code file must be named *JLove.java*. Figure 2-5 shows the relationship between the class definition line and its associated filename.

> **Special Note:** Older versions of Notepad tack on a ".txt" extension when you perform the initial save operation. This action results in the JLove.java file being saved as JLove.java.txt. Newer versions of Notepad, such as with XP, do not write this default extension. Be sure to check how your version of Notepad saves its files. (Better yet, install and use jEdit!) There is a way to suppress the addition of .txt. Put the filename and extension in quotes when saving, such as "JLove.java."

Notice the opening brace after the class definition line and the closing brace on the very last line of the program. The code is indented within the braces.

```
public class JLove
{
        public static void main(String args[] )
        {
                System.out.println("I love Java!!! ");
        }
}
```

In Java, the open and close braces are used to enclose blocks of code, and you must have a closing brace for every opening brace. There must be an opening brace after the class definition line, and a closing brace at the end of the class. Indenting the code within the braces makes the program easy to read. More guidance on the indention and coding style appears in the next section. Note that there is a set of opening closing braces after the public static void main line as well.

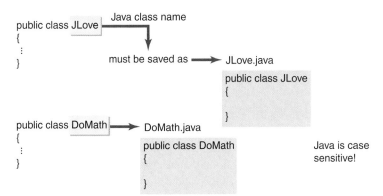

Figure 2-5
The source code file must be named using the class name and *.java* extension.

The main() Method

The line:

```
public static void main(String args[] )
```

is a method definition line for the JLove's main() method. A **method** is a block of code that performs certain tasks and can return information if necessary. When we refer to a method in *Java Programming Today*, we place the () beside the name to indicate that it is a method and not a variable, for example, main(). Methods allow the programmer to write discrete blocks of code in a logical manner.

The **method definition line** contains return information, the method name, and input information within the parentheses. In our JLove program, this method's name is "main," the return information is "void" (returns nothing), and the input

method
a block of code that performs certain tasks and can return data if necessary

method definition line
contains return type, method name, and input information

information is "String args[]." The "public static" refers to accessibility, and we will cover methods in greater detail in later chapters.

Java application programs must have a main() method and often contain many other methods as well. (Java applets, as a rule, do not have a main() method.) When the JVM begins to run a Java application, it looks for the main() method, because it is the starting point for the program.

Java Statements

Java statement

a line of Java code that issues a command or performs an operation

Java methods have a set of opening and closing braces enclosing the lines of source code, known as statements. A **Java statement** is part of the program that issues a command or commands to be executed. It specifies an action that must occur. The JLove main method:

```
public static void main(String args[] )
{
        System.out.println("I love Java!!! ");
}
```

contains one Java statement:

```
System.out.println("I love Java!!! ");
```

This statement is written according to Java language rules and ends with a semicolon. Many, but not all, statements in Java end with a semicolon. We will learn how to write many types of Java statements.

The System.out.println() statement is a Java command that instructs the computer to write the string of text enclosed in quotation marks to the command window. The println() method issues a "newline" character automatically, so that the next line of text is written on the following line in the command window. The System.out.print() method does not issue the newline command.

How's the Weather? Our second Java program contains several System.out. println() and System.out.print() statements, and both types of comment styles. The Java source code in Program 2-2 (file *Weather.java*) writes several weather related statements to the command window. The output from this program is shown in Figure 2-6.

Note, the line numbers outside the box (such as 1) are provided for the reader's convenience and SHOULD NOT be entered in the Java source code file.

```
1    /* Program 2-2    How's the weather? Our second Java program.
2        This program writes a few weather-related statements to the screen. */
3
4    //File:  Weather.java
```

```
5
6    public class Weather
7    {
8        public static void main(String args[] )
9        {
10       // Weather information
11            System.out.println(" We really need rain! ");
12            System.out.println(" The river is almost dry. ");
13            System.out.print(" We might hit 100 degrees today.");
14            System.out.print(" Where is the ice cream? ");
15       }
16   }
```

```
C:\JPT>
C:\JPT>javac Weather.java

C:\JPT>java Weather
 We really need rain!
 The river is almost dry.
 We might hit 100 degrees today. Where is the ice cream?
C:\JPT>
```

Figure 2-6
The javac compiler and java commands required to compile and run the weather
program contained in the *Weather.java* source code file. The file must be named
Weather.java.

In the command window in Figure 2-6, we see the rain and dry river statements on separate lines, because they are written by println(). After println() has
written the text, it issues a newline command. The 100 degree and ice cream statements are found on one line, because they are written by the print() method, which
does not issue newline commands after writing text to the window.

Escape Sequences   As a general rule, Java takes the string of text enclosed in
quotation marks in the System.out.println() or System.out.print() and displays what
it receives. In this statement:

```
System.out.println("I Love Java!!!");
```

the double quotes (" ") indicate the start and end of the string that is to be printed.

    An **escape sequence** is created when the backslash (\) is combined with cer-
tain characters inside the string, telling Java to "escape from" the normal way to
write the output. For example, combining the backslash with the letter *n* tells Java
to go to a new line before it prints "I Love Java!!!"

```
System.out.println("\n  I Love Java!!! ");
```

escape sequence
a backslash (\)
combined with a
character issues
printing directives such
as "\n go to a new line"

TABLE 2-3
Escape sequences in Java (partial list).

Escape sequence	Purpose
\n	New line. Places the screen cursor on the next line.
\r	Carriage return. Places the screen cursor at the beginning of the current line (not the next line). Any characters written after \r will overwrite existing characters.
\t	Tab. Advances the screen cursor to the next tab stop.
\\	Backslash. Required in the string in order to see a backslash character.
\"	Double quote. Required in the string in order to see a quotation character.

Escape sequences dictate different commands when the program is writing output. For instance, when the output needs to write a double quotation mark, we use the \" escape sequence.

Table 2-3 gives a partial list of Java escape sequence. It is important to note that these escape sequences are used only in output statements (such as string outputs, println(), and print()) and not in input statements. Program 2-3 demonstrates the use of escape sequences. The output from this program is seen in Figure 2-7.

```
1   //Program 2-3 Demonstrate Escape Sequences in Java
2   //File:  DemoEscSeq.java
3
4   public class DemoEscSeq
5   {
6      public static void main(String args [] )
7      {
8            //how to see quotation marks
9            System.out.println(" \"Do you see the quote marks?\"");
10
11           //how to see a \ in the output
12           System.out.println(" Do you see the backslash?->\\");
13
14           //how to move down 2 lines
15           System.out.println("\n\n Look! I've skipped 2 lines!");
16
17           //write a new statement with print
18           System.out.print(" I know I'm really going to love Java.");
19
```

```
20          //now overwrite part of the previous line
21          System.out.println("\rOverwrite the previous line.");
22
23      }
24  }
```

```
C:\JPT>javac DemoEscSeq.java

C:\JPT>java DemoEscSeq
 "Do you see the quote marks?"
 Do you see the backslash?->\


 Look! I've skipped 2 lines!
 Overwrite the previous line.love Java.

C:\JPT>
```

Figure 2-7
The javac compiler and java commands required to compile and run the Escape
Sequences demonstration program. The source code file must be named
DemoEscSeq.java.

Whitespace Characters and Coding Style in Java

Whitespace characters are spaces, carriage returns, linefeeds (the *Enter* key), tabs, vertical tabs, and form feeds. The Java compiler, for the most part, ignores whitespace characters. Why is this important to the Java programmer? It means that the compiler allows the programmer to write his or her code in a wide variety of styles and formats. The compiler is very particular about the syntax, of course, but style is up to the programmer.

> **whitespace characters**
> spaces, carriage returns, linefeeds (the *Enter* key), tabs, vertical tabs, and form feeds

Unlike the COBOL or FORTRAN languages, which have restrictions as to what data must be in which column and the length of source code lines, Java statements can be written in virtually any format. For example, our JLove program can be written like this:

```
//Program 2-4 JLove with bad style
//File: JLoveBadStyle
public class JLoveBadStyle {
public static void main(String args[] )   {
System.out.println("I love Java!!! ");    }  }
```

This program compiles, runs without error, and produces the same output as our first JLove program, but is hard to read the source code. In the following bad style example, the comment lines are jammed against the source lines and the code is not indented, which renders the entire program illegible.

```
//Another example of bad coding style
//File: JLoveBadStyle
public class JLoveBadStyle  //this code is hard to read
{
public static void main(String args[] )  //the code is not indented
{
System.out.println("I love Java!!! "); //write I love Java to the screen
} //end of main method
} //end of class definition
```

Always write your Java code so that it is easy to see the lines of source code, and so that the comments explain important details in your code. Use indention to offset blocks of code.

Many Java programmers and Java editing tools use a slightly different style in which the opening brace is placed on the same line of code instead of placing it on the next line, such as:

```
//A different Java coding style.
//The opening brace is found on the same line instead of a new line.

public class JLove {
    public static void main(String args[] ) {
        System.out.println("I love Java!! ");
    }
}
```

The closing braces are located on separate lines, and should be aligned vertically with the associated opening statement. The statements within the class definition and within the main method are indented. This style is acceptable and common-place in Java programming. In *Java Programming Today*, we show the opening and closing braces on separate lines and have the braces aligned vertically—making it easy to see where blocks of code begin and end.

Language Syntax, and Compiler Errors

Java's flexible indention and whitespace style gives the programmer leeway in the lay-out of his or her code. But this flexibility does not mean that you may write Java state-ments in just any old way. Java must be written with correct **syntax**. What do we mean by a syntax rule? A syntax rule is a grammatical rule for writing the language. If Java requires the word "class" to be in lower case letters, then to use a capital letter (Class) or all caps (CLASS) would cause a syntax error. If the code requires () symbols to be used, then a syntax error is issued if the programmer uses { }, < >, or [ ]. The name of a variable cannot have a space in it. If you try to name a variable "big dog," you have a syntax error, it must be named "bigdog," or better yet, "bigDog."

syntax

grammatical rules for writing the language

The source code in Program 2-5 contains several syntax errors and does not compile. Can you spot the syntax errors? Figure 2-8 shows the compiler error messages generated by this code:

```
1   //Program 2-5 Writes a poem to the command window.
2   File: Poem.java
3
4   //This code contains 3 syntax errors. Can you find them?
5
6   public class Poem
7   {
8     public static void main(String args[] )
9     {
10          System.out.println(" Roses are red \n Violets are blue ")
11          System.out.println(" Java is a fun language ");
12          system.out.println(" Hope you like it too!");
13     }
14  }
```

```
C:\JPT>
C:\JPT>javac Poem.java
Poem.java:2: 'class' or 'interface' expected
File: Poem.java
^
Poem.java:10: ';' expected
             System.out.println(" Roses are red \n Violets are blue ")
                                                                      ^
Poem.java:12: package system does not exist
             system.out.println(" Hope you like it too!");
                 ^
3 errors

C:\JPT>
```

Figure 2-8
The javac compiler output showing the problems it finds with the *Poem.java* file.

The javac Java compiler attempts to explain what it believes the three errors to be, tells you the line number, and places a "^" at the appropriate location in the source code line. In order to track down these three errors, we must examine the referenced lines. Let's tackle the easy error first. The error on line 10 is:

Poem.java:10: ';' expected
        System.out.println(" Roses are red \n Violets are blue ") ^

The tenth line is:

```
System.out.println(" Roses are red \n Violets are blue ")
```

The compiler is telling the programmer that it is expecting to see a semicolon after the parenthesis, and it writes a ^ symbol to indicate where it is expected. Ah ha! You say, we are missing a semicolon at the end of our println statement. Yes! The next error is on line 12:

Poem.java:12: package system does not exist
**   system.out.println(" Hope you like it too!");**
         ^

This error is a little tougher than the first error. The compiler is referencing a println statement, but telling you that a package does not exist. Wait a minute, you think, the word "system" should be capitalized. Right you are! We meant the line to read:

```
System.out.println("Hope you like it too!");
```

but we mistyped the first character. But what is Java telling us about a package? As we shall soon see, Java packages are referenced in lower case letters. When we wrote our line using lower case letters, Java assumed that system.out was a package.

The first error we see in this code is cryptic and does not give us many clues where to look. The error on line 2 reads:

Poem.java:2: 'class' or 'interface' expected
File: Poem.java

When we look at line 2, we see:

```
File: Poem.java
```

Whoops. This line was supposed to be a comment line, telling the reader that the name of this file is *Poem.java*. We meant to type the line using double slashes to indicate that it is a comment:

```
//File: Poem.java
```

Try as he or she may, the beginning Java programmer (and even more advanced programmers) may not understand what the compiler is saying. The Java programmer must know the syntax rules of the language, and he or she needs to be able to quickly recognize problems with semicolons or capitalization.

Program 2-6 is another example of Java source code that contains compiler errors. The errors are shown in Figure 2-9.

```
1   //Program 2-6 Write statements about bugs to the command window.
2   //File: javabugs.java
3
```

```
4   //This code contains 2 compiler errors. Can you find them?
5
6   public class JavaBugs
7   {
8      public static void main(String args[] )
9      {
10            System.out.println(" Java bugs are annoying. );
11            System.out.println(" They can make you quite mad. ");
12      }
13   }
```

```
C:\JPT>
C:\JPT>javac javabugs.java
javabugs.java:10: unclosed string literal
              System.out.println(" Java bugs are annoying. );
                                 ^
javabugs.java:11: ')' expected
              System.out.println(" They can make you quite mad. ");
                                                                  ^
javabugs.java:6: class JavaBugs is public, should be declared in a file named Ja
vaBugs.java
public class JavaBugs
       ^
3 errors

C:\JPT>
```

Figure 2-9
The javac compiler output showing the problems it finds with the file *javabugs.java*.
What should the file be named?

Compilers do the best they can to determine syntax errors. However, as you will soon learn, compilers cannot read your mind. In Program 2-6, the file is saved as *javabugs.java* and the class definition is JavaBugs. This bug is being described by the compiler's remarks for line 6:

javabugs.java:6: class JavaBugs is public, should be declared in a file named JavaBugs.java
public class JavaBugs

The Java source file must be named exactly as the class definition name followed by a *.java* extension. There are two other errors on lines 10 and 11. Line 10 is missing a quotation mark. This line:

```
System.out.println(" Java bugs are annoying. );
```

is missing the quotation marks after the term "annoying." This error propagates to the next line too, because Java assumes that the following line is still contained within the quotation marks. It is a common occurrence to have a compiler report problems on the line above and/or below the actual trouble line.

> **Important!** *The programmer must take the time to learn the correct syntax and environment rules for Java to be able to quickly spot compiler errors.*

2.3
Programs and Data

Balls and Sticks!

Imagine that you get a job at a gymnasium and are in charge of the equipment room. This gym supports many different sporting activities including golf, tennis, racquetball and squash, baseball, softball, basketball, and medicine ball. Medicine balls are big leather balls weighing anywhere between two and sixty pounds. One game of medicine ball involves two people tossing the ball back and forth.

Gym members come to your equipment room to check out whatever type of equipment is required for their sport. This room is a busy place, and when you see the equipment room, you find 200 loose balls rolling around on the floor. Bats, golf clubs, and racquets are piled in a corner. How do you find one golf ball in all that clutter?

Let's assume that your storage room is large enough so that you can build shelves along the walls. You need to have each piece of equipment contained in its own slot on a shelf. (If the bats, clubs, and racquets stick out a bit, that's okay.) Let's also assume that there is a variety of shelf containers and slot fixtures that easily attach on the shelf. These shelf containers come in various sizes, from golf-ball small to medicine-ball large. You order the shelving material and container fixtures. The next day (of course, you ordered on-line and paid the next-day shipping fee), you set up your shelves. Then you adjust your shelf containers and slot fixtures so that each ball and each stick fits nicely in its own slot. You must keep track of all your bats, balls, clubs, and racquets; you name each slot and container with a unique name, and you know the address (location) of each.

Now, think of each ball and stick as a single piece of program data. Data come in different sizes and types. Programs need "containers" to store all the program data. You, as the programmer, need to determine how many "containers" are required, select the appropriate types of containers, and give each container a name. The details of where the containers are located are handled by the operating system—you do not have to worry about that.

As you are designing your program and thinking through the logical steps, you must also ask yourself what types of data the program will handle. Will the program need "containers" for numeric data or textual data? How many different containers are required in the program? What level of accuracy (number of decimal places) is required? A bookkeeping program needs only two or three decimal places; on the other hand, an airborne radar system requires twenty decimal places.

2.4
Keywords, Primitive Types, and Identifiers in Java

The Java language has been designed with components from the C and C++ languages, including many of the same keywords (or reserved words), data types, and naming rules. The operators in Java are those from C++, and Java operators have the same order of operations as C++. The Java language requires that all executable code be contained within a class—which differs from C and C++. C++ allows you to write classes, but it is not mandatory. The remainder of this chapter explores these fundamental programming concepts. We will start to learn about classes and objects in Chapter 3.

Shelves = Memory, Types of Containers = Primitive Types, Labels = Variable Names

A programmer must designate the type of data container (primitive type) and name (variable) for each piece of data in the program. When the program executes, physical memory in the computer system is set aside for each piece of data. You may think of memory in your computer as gymnasium storage shelves. Selecting the appropriate type of container to place on the shelf is analogous to specifying a primitive type in your program. Remember that there are different types of containers that hold different types of data. Placing the label on the container and giving the variable a name serve similar purposes because you know the name of the container or variable.

To understand the different primitive types and the range of values they may hold, we need to introduce the concept of a **byte**. A byte is the basic unit of computer memory. The byte consists of eight **bits**. A bit is a unit of data that exists in one of two states. We often refer to a bit as being either a 1 or a 0.

byte
basic unit of computer memory, consisting of eight bits

Figure 2-10 illustrates how the number of bits dictates the number of unique bit combinations. Every value stored in memory must be represented by a unique bit pattern. A 1-byte storage container can have only 2^8, or 256 unique bit combinations. Figure 2-11 takes this concept a bit further. If a data type reserves two bytes, then there are sixteen bits for storage. Four bytes result in thirty-two bits of storage space. Examining the possible combinations show how reserving more bytes results in a larger number of combinations, hence, larger values and a wider range of values may be stored. If the concept of bits and bytes is new to you, or you would like a review, read Appendix C, *Bits, Bytes, Hexadecimal Notation, and Unicode*[TM].

bit
a unit of data that exists in one of two states, it is either a 1 or a 0

Java Keywords

The Java language has many reserved words, known as **keywords**. These keywords have specific meaning for the language and may not be used by the programmer as

keyword
reserved words that have specific meaning for the language

Bits	Possible Bit Combinations	Unique Values	
1	0	0	The number of unique values can be calculated by 2^n, where n = number of bits.
	1	1	2^1 = 2 combinations
2	00	0	
	01	1	2^2 = 4 combinations
	10	2	
	11	3	
3	000	0	
	001	1	
	010	2	2^3 = 8 combinations
	011	3	
	100	4	
	101	5	
	110	6	
	111	7	
8	00000000	0	
	00000001	1	2^8 = 256 combinations
	⋮	⋮	
	11111111	255	

Figure 2-10
Number of bits dictates the number of unique combinations.

Bytes	Bits	Possible Combinations	Signed Range	Unsigned Range
1	8	256	−128 to 127	0 to 255
2	16	65,536	−32,768 to 32,767	0 to 65,535
4	32	4,294,967,296	−2,147,483,648 to 2,147,483,647	0 to 4,294,967,295

2^8 = 256 combinations
2^{16} = 65,536 combinations
2^{32} = 4,294,967,296 combinations

Figure 2-11
More bytes equals a larger range of values.

identifiers (that is, names for classes, methods, or variables). Each keyword has specific syntax and actions associated with it. For example, our JLove application program uses four keywords: *public, class, static,* and *void.* The two keywords—*switch* and *case*—might be popular variable names in electronics or inventory

TABLE 2-4
Java keywords.

Keywords	Category and use
boolean, char, byte, int, long, short, double, float, strictfp, void	Primitive data types in Java.
new, this, super	Used with Java objects.
if, else, switch, case, break, default	Selection statements.
for, continue do, while	Iteration statements.
return, throw	Transfer control statements.
try, catch, finally, assert	Exception statements.
synchronized	Thread statements.
static, abstract, final, private, protected, public	Modify declarations.
class, instanceof, throws, native, transient, volatile, extends, interface, implements, package, import	Miscellaneous.
const, goto	Reserved for possible use.

2

programs. However, Java reserves these two words for its own use. The keyword *switch* is a conditional statement and *case* is a label. Table 2-4 shows the Java keywords divided into categories according to their use.

Primitive Data Types

If you are writing a banking program, it probably uses a variety of data including name and address information, account balance, deposit and withdraw amounts, account numbers, personal identification numbers, and transaction references. The money data needs to be numeric, while the name and address information must be textual (or character) data. It is important to have decimal place accuracy for the money to keep track of pennies, but our transaction references can be whole numbers.

The Java language provides eight built-in data types known as **primitive types** or **primitives** for the programmer's use. A primitive data type is a non-object type of "container" that can hold a specific kind of program data. Think of it this

primitive types or primitives

non-object containers that hold a specific kind of program data, such as "int" or "float"

Primitive data types in Java.

Type	Size in bytes	What kind of data it can hold (and special notes)
boolean	1 (8 bits)	Used for true/false conditions. Stores a true or false value. In Java, a boolean type is not based on integers and cannot be compared to 0 or 1.
byte	1 (8 bits)	A signed quantity used to hold generic 8-bit values, work with data files, or save storage space. Range: -128 to $+127$
char	2 (16 bits)	A printable character. A char is unsigned, integer based, and should hold only character or bit data. Can accommodate characters from any language, not just alphabet based language. ISO Unicode character set.
short	2 (16 bits)	A signed whole number. Range: $-32,768$ to $+32,767$
int	4 (32 bits)	A signed whole number. Range: $-2,147,483,648$ to $+2,147,483,647$
long	8 (64 bits)	A signed whole number. Range: -2^{63} to $+(2^{63} - 1)$
float	4 (32 bits)	A signed number with approximately 6–7 digits of decimal precision. A float is a single precision number, and should be used to minimize storage requirements. There is no speed enhancement. (IEEE 754 Standard) Range: $-3.4E^{38}$ to $+3.4E^{38}$ (huge numbers) $+/- 1.4E - 45$ (fractional numbers)
double	8 (64 bits)	A signed number with approximately 13–14 digits of precision. Exact accuracy depends on size of number. (IEEE 754 Standard) Range: $-1.7E^{308}$ to $+1.7E^{308}$ (huge numbers) $+/- 4.9E - 324$ (fractional numbers)

way: For each piece of data in your program, you must specify the appropriate type of container that must be used. For example, a customer's name needs to be stored as text, money information must be stored in either a float or a double in order to maintain the decimal portion, and transaction numbers can be stored as integers. Table 2-5 lists the primitive data types provided by Java.

Java language designers demonstrated forward thinking and planned for maximum code portability across platforms when they adopted the ISO Unicode Standard[1]

---

[1] The International Standards Organization Unicode format specifies the exact size and range.

for character data and IEEE 754 Standard[2] for floating point and double valued primitive types. Unlike other languages that do not specify exact size and ranges for the data, Java's incorporation of these standard formats ensures that program data is stored consistently across platforms.

Primitive Data Type Declarations in Java

A **variable** is an actual location in memory that has been set aside for use by the program; it is referenced by a specific name. Variables contain **values** that may be modified by the program. The program must **declare** a variable by stating the type of data it is to contain and give the variable a name. In Java, you may be declaring primitive data type variables, such as int, float, double, or declaring (creating) an instance of a class, which is an object. Declaration statements are typically performed once in a method or class, and then the variable (either primitive or object) is ready to be used as needed. (***Special note:*** the concept of that variable scope is discussed later.)

A variable declaration statement must have a data type and variable name. The basic format is:

```
data_type variable_name;
```

For example, in our banking program, the money, count, and check number variables could be declared in this way:

```
//Declaration of variables for banking program
float balance;
float deposit;
float withdraw;
int transactionType;
int checkNumber;
```

In these statements, we set up three floating point variables—balance, deposit, and withdraw—and two integer variables—transactionType and checkNumber. When you run this program, five separate memory locations are reserved (one location for each variable). It is valid to have several variables and one data type on one line, such as:

```
//Declaration of variables for banking program
float balance, deposit, withdraw;
int transactionType, checkNumber;
```

variable

an actual location in memory that holds program data and is referenced by a specific name

values

data that are held in variables

declare

the action taken by a programmer to create a variable by stating the data type and variable name

---

[2] The Institute of Electrical and Electronic Engineers (a professional engineering organization) wrote the IEEE 754 Standard, which describes how floating point numbers (numbers with decimal precision) are stored in 32- and 64-bit format.

It is good practice for the Java programmer to assign initial values into variables when he or she declares program components. Depending on where the variable is declared, Java may or may not initialize the values or require the variable to be initialized before it is used. (Nonmember or local scope primitives and objects must be initialized before use.) We cover variable initialization and scope issues in detail later in this text. For our previous banking example, we can initialize the variables in the following manner:

```
//Declare and initialize the variables for banking program
float balance = 0.0, deposit = 0.0, withdraw = 0.0;
int transactionType = 1, checkNumber = 1000;
```

Identifier Naming Rules in Java

In Java, an **identifier** is the name provided by the programmer for a programmer-defined package, object, method, or variable. Specific rules for naming identifiers are listed below. It is always a great idea to use descriptive names for your program items.

- The first character of a name must be a letter, an underscore (_), or a dollar sign ($).
- A letter can be A–Z, a–z, or any of the tens of thousands of Unicode letters from any of the major languages in the world. (It is best to stick with the ASCII character set A–Z, and a–z, because using complex characters may present editing and maintenance problems.)
- Names may contain numbers (0–9), dollar signs ($), or underscores (_).
- Names cannot contain spaces or any other symbols, such as ~ ! @ # % ^ & * ( ) − + = \ | ' ".
- Keywords cannot be used as variable names.
- Identifers may be any length.

Table 2-6 shows examples of valid and invalid variable names.

Upper and Lower Case Sensitive

Another Java feature is that the language recognizes the difference between upper case and lower case letters. Whether the words that you enter are Java keywords, prewritten Java classes and methods, or programmer named identifiers, Java distinguishes between the capitalized and noncapitalized words. It makes a difference to the Java compiler if you type the word *class*, *Class*, or *CLASS*. The word "class" is a keyword and has specific meaning to Java. "Class" and "CLASS" are two different words, and are not recognized as keywords. The Java compiler sees the variables *total*, *Total* and *TOTAL* as three separate variables. The Java interpreter knows to look for the "main" method when it first begins to execute a Java application

TABLE 2-6

Valid and invalid variable names.

Variable name	Good or bad?	If invalid, why?
`balance`	valid	Not applicable
`transaction amount`	invalid	Contains a space
`convert_2_#`	invalid	Cannot contain a # symbol
`_myMoney`	valid	Not applicable
`4temperature`	invalid	Cannot start with number
`break`	invalid	Cannot be a keyword
`myAuto`	valid	Not applicable
`%_of_grade`	invalid	Cannot contain a % symbol

program. The program must contain a main() method (main is not a keyword). However, the Java compiler does not know what a Main() or MAIN() method is, unless the programmer creates his or her own methods with these names.

Final Variables

We introduce the concept of a "final" variable now, and use it throughout the text in many programming examples. Java provides the **final** keyword so that the programmer may designate that a variable cannot be modified. For example, if we have a program that uses constant values, such as a pay rate or conversion factor, we do not want our values to be changed by the program. We use the "final" keyword in the declaration to make these variable values constant.

final
variables whose values cannot be changed

```
final float PAYRATE = 13.25;
final int EGGS_IN_A_DOZEN = 12;
```

The "final" variables may be initialized two ways. The value may be assigned when the variable is declared, as shown above. Or the value can be assigned in the class constructor method. Class constructors are covered in Chapter 6.

Java Naming Conventions

The Java Language Specification[3] describes naming conventions for Java programmers to follow when they write their source code. (Recall that a convention is a

---

[3] Gosling, J., B. Joy, and G. Steel. 1996. *The Java Language Specification*. Addison-Wesley. (http://java.sun.com/docs/books/jils/)

customary practice or suggested way of doing something and not a strict requirement.) Java programmers should use these naming conventions as these conventions help to make the code readable, avoid name conflicts, and results in
"standard" looking Java code.

Java naming conventions propose that class names should be descriptive
nouns or noun phrases. The name starts with a capital letter and uses a capital letter
for each word in the class name, such a JOptionPane, SecurityManager, and Math.
Names for methods (methods are the tasks that are defined in a class) are verb or
verb phrases. Method names begin with a lower case letter, and have capital letters
for each word in the identifier name, such as getHeight(), setOutput(), and
showMessageDialog().

Programmers are encouraged to make their names for variables short yet
descriptive. The names may be a series of lower case letters and do not need to be
complete words or phrases. This convention helps make variables easy to spot in
your program. If the variable name is a string of words, the first letter is lower case,
and the subsequent words use initial capitalization. Examples of variable names are
height, len (for length), userName, streetAddress, str (for a string), and hyp (for
hypotenuse). Variables that are final should be written entirely in capital letters such
as PAYRATE and EGGS_IN_A_DOZ. Single letter variable names are discouraged
unless the variable is used as a loop index. (We cover loops in Chapter 4.) One of
your primary goals as a Java programmer is to write descriptive code and that
includes how you name your variables, methods, and classes. Table 2-7 contains
sample names of classes, methods, and variables following this convention.

TABLE 2-7
Java naming convention examples for classes and identifiers.

Class names	Method names ( ) indicates it is a method	Variable names
ClassName	methodName( )	primitiveInt
DecimalFormat	applyPattern( )	size
NoBugs	stompCockroach( )	percent
CalculateTemperature	setHighTemp( )	_highT
JOptionPane	showMessageDialog( )	output
CustomCircle	getCustomSine( )	outputString

Java Strings

Now is a good time to introduce the Java String class, as we need String objects in
order to fully investigate Java operators. Remember that a class is a "job description." As the name implies, the job of the String class is to provide the Java

programmer with a way to work with text or character data. The String class comes complete with many tools (methods) for handling character data.

To create a String object, the Java programmer writes a declaration statement just like he or she does for primitive data types. Here we declare a String variable named vacationSpot and assign it the phrase "Cocoa Beach, Florida."

```
String vacationSpot;
vacationSpot = "Cocoa Beach, Florida";
```

Strings in Java have built in support for **concatenation** (hooking strings together) by using the "+" operator. For example, we can concatenate two string variables or concatenate a phrase contained within quotation marks. In Program 2-7, we write information to the command window by concatenating phrases and String variables. The output is seen in Figure 2-12.

concatenation

hooking strings together

```
1   //Program 2-7  Demonstrate String concatenation
2   //File:  StringCatDemo.java
3
4   public class StringCatDemo
5   {
6      public static void main( String args[])
7      {
8            String favoriteCourse = "Java Programming";
9            String bestStudent, output;
10           bestStudent = "Hannah White";
11           output = "\nCourse: " + favoriteCourse +
12                 " Top student: " + bestStudent;
13
14           System.out.println(output);
15
16   //You can break up long phrases using the +
17           String gettysburgAddress;
18
19           gettysburgAddress = "Four score and seven years ago"
20           + "\n our fathers brought forth on this continent, "
21           + "a new nation, \n conceived in liberty and dedicated"
22           + "\n to the proposition that all men are created equal.";
23
24           System.out.println("\n A Lincoln's famous speech: \n " +
25                 gettysburgAddress);
26      }
27   }
```

```
C:\JPT>
C:\JPT>javac StringCatDemo.java

C:\JPT>java StringCatDemo

Course: Java Programming Top student: Hannah White

A Lincoln's famous speech:
Four score and seven years ago
our fathers brought forth on this continent, a new nation,
conceived in liberty and dedicated
to the proposition that all men are created equal.

C:\JPT>
```

Figure 2-12
The javac and java commands to compile and execute the program contained in the StringCatDemo.java file.

2.5
Operators in Java

operators

symbols that represent certain instructions or commands, such as + for addition or * for multiplication

The Java language has many operators; this provides wonderful flexibility for the programmer. **Operators** are symbols that represent certain instructions or commands. A simple addition example shows the arithmetic operator + and the assignment operator =.

```
//Operator Example Addition
//Declare three variables, assigning values into x, and y
int x = 4, y = 7, sum;
sum = x + y;
```

A second example shows temperature conversion using four operators, =, /, *, and +:

```
//Operator Example Temp Conversion
double fTemp, cTemp = 78.2;
fTemp = 9.0/5.0 * cTemp + 32.0;
```

Table 2-8 is a complete listing of all the Java operators.

precedence of operations

the rules that govern which operation is performed first, which second, etc.

Operators and Precedence of Operations

Precedence of operations (or priority of operations) in Java simply means which operation is performed first, which second, and so on in a program statement. A program statement may contain many Java operators, such as multiplication,

TABLE 2-8
Java operators. The higher the priority, the higher the precedence.

Priority	Symbol	Purpose	Associativity
16	( ) [ ] .	parentheses, array subscript, and member selection	left to right
16	var++ var−−	post-fix increment/decrement	right to left
15	++var −−var	pre-fix increment/decrement	left to right
14	~	flip the bits of an integer	right to left
14	!	logical not (reverse a boolean)	right to left
14	−var +var	arithmetic plus, negation (these are not addition, subtraction)	right to left
13	(primitive type or object name)	creation or casting operator	right to left
12	* / %	multiply, divide, modulus	left to right
11	+ −	addition, subtraction	left to right
10	<< >> >>>	left and right bitwise shift	left to right
9	instanceof < <= > >=	relational operators	left to right
8	== !=	same as, not the same as	left to right
7	&	bitwise AND	left to right
6	^	bitwise exclusive or	left to right
5	|	bitwise inclusive or	left to right
4	&&	conditional AND	left to right
3	||	conditional OR	left to right
2	? :	ternary conditional operator	right to left
1	= *= /= %= += −= <<= >>= >>>= &= ^= |=	assignment operators	right to left

addition, assignment, etc. There must be a convention for the Java language to follow in order to obtain a consistent result.

Let's look at the temperature conversion example again.

```
fTemp = 9.0/5.0 * cTemp + 32.0;        //operator example
```

▌ TABLE 2-9

Java Operators. The four operators in the temperature conversion formula have precedence rankings of 12, 11, and 1. Multiplication and division have the higher precedence and are performed first.

Priority	Symbol	Purpose	Associativity
12	* / %	multiply, divide, modulus	left to right
11	+ −	addition, subtraction	left to right
1	= *= /= %= += −= <<= >>= >>>= &= ^= |=	assignment operators	right to left

In this expression, there are four operators: =, /, *, and +. Can you locate these four operators in the Java operator table? Table 2-9 shows a portion of the Java operator table. The multiplication and division operators have a priority ranking of 12, the addition priority ranking is 11, and the assignment ranking is 1. This means that because the multiplication (*) and division (/) operators have the higher priority, they will be performed before the addition and assignment operators.

When this program statement executes, the multiplication and division operations are performed before the addition and assignment; but which one gets carried out first? Do we divide 9.0 by 5.0 and then multiply by the value in cTemp? Or do we multiply 5.0 by cTemp and then use it as 9.0's divisor? The answer to this question is found in the operators' **associativity**. For the arithmetic operators, the associativity is "left to right," meaning that the operator on the left *in the expression* gets performed first. Reading the statement from left to right, we encounter the division operator first, so the computer divides 9.0 by 5.0 and then multiplies by the value in the cTemp variable. The addition is done next. The assignment operator finishes by placing the result from the calculations into fTemp.

associativity

when operators have the same precedence and are in the same statement, the associativity dictates which operation is performed first

The use of a set of parentheses changes the order of operations.

```
fTemp = 9.0/5.0 *(cTemp + 32.0);   //Operator Example Temp Conversion and ()'s
```

The operations inside the parentheses are executed first, following the precedence of operations. In this statement, the addition is performed first. Next, the division occurs, followed by the multiplication and assignment. Coding the temperature conversion formula in this manner produces an incorrect result.

Figure 2-13 illustrates several equations written in Java. Based on the precedence and associativity of the operators, arrows indicate the order that each calculation is performed.

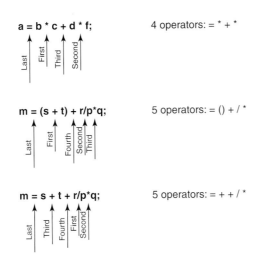

a = b * c + d * f;	4 operators: = * + *
m = (s + t) + r/p*q;	5 operators: = () + / *
m = s + t + r/p*q;	5 operators: = + + / *

Figure 2-13
Precedence and associativity of operators.

Assignment Operator (=)

In Java, the assignment operator takes the value on the right side of the assign operator (=) and places it in the variable on the left side. This code shows three assignment statements; the value of 7 is placed in the size variable, the numeric value 1534.34 is placed in balance, and the value of *y* placed into *x*.

```
size = 7;
balance = 1534.34;
x = y;
```

It is illegal (that is, it will not compile) if you place the value on the left side of the assign operator and the variable on the right side, like this:

```
7 = size;                 //THIS IS INCORRECT!
1534.34 = balance;        //CANNOT ASSIGN LIKE THIS!
```

It is possible to have many assignment operators in one expression. Remember, the associativity for the assignment operator is right to left. In this example, when this line is executed, the program places 0 into *c*, then the value of *c* is placed into *b*, and then the value of *b* is placed into *a*.

```
a = b = c = 0;   //valid assignment setting 0 into c, c into b, b into a
```

Assignments in Declarations   It is valid to assign values to variables in declaration statements. This technique is acceptable for programmers to use.

```
double x, y, z;            // declare variables
x = 3.4;                   // now assign in separate statements
y = 73.8234;
z = 0.0;
```

These statements may be combined into one statement, and the assignments are separated by commas.

```
double x = 3.4, y = 73.8234, z = 0.0;    // declare and assign in one statement
```

Data Types, Assigned Values, and Casting

When values are assigned to Java primitive variables, the type of value must match the variable type. If the value and variable types do not match, Java issues a compile error. What does this mean? Java is very strict when it comes to assigning values into variables. If you are declaring an integer data type, Java expects you to assign an integer to it. For example, in Program 2-8, we declare several types of variables and assign values into them. In this program, the Java compiler is happy and our program runs without error. The program output is shown in Figure 2-14.

```
1   //Program 2-8 Demonstrate Correct Assignments
2   //File:  AssignmentDemo.java
3
4   public class AssignmentDemo
5   {
6      public static void main(String args[])
7      {
8           int n = 7;
9           float f = (float)9.8765;     //cast value into the float
10          double d = 1.23456789123;
11          char letter = 'e';
12          boolean bFlag = true;
13
14          String sInt = "The integer is " + n;
15          String sFloat = "The float is " + f;
16          String sDouble = "The double is " + d;
17          String sChar = "The letter is " + letter;
18          String sBoolean = "The boolean is " + bFlag;
19          System.out.println(sInt);
20          System.out.println(sFloat);
21          System.out.println(sDouble);
22          System.out.println(sChar);
23          System.out.println(sBoolean);
24      }
25  }
```

```
C:\JPT>javac AssignmentDemo.java

C:\JPT>java AssignmentDemo
The integer is 7
The float is 9.8765
The double is 1.23456789123
The letter is e
The boolean is true

C:\JPT>
```

Figure 2-14
The javac and java commands to compile and execute the program contained in the
AssignmentDemo.java file.

When the Java programmer assigns a number into an integer variable, Java expects a whole number in the assignment statement. In the previous code, we see a whole number assigned to an int:

```
int n = 7;        //7 is considered a whole number
                  //It does not have a decimal point.
```

If the programmer assigns a number with decimal precision, that is, the number contains a decimal point, Java views that number as a double variable with fourteen to fifteen digits of decimal precision.

```
//1.2345789123... contains a decimal point, so Java treats this as a double
//This assignment is correct, a double assigned to a double.
      double d = 1.23456789123;
```

If the data type is a float variable and has six to seven digits of decimal precision, the number must be "cast" into the float. In other words, we have to tell Java that the number on the right side of the assignment operator is supposed to be a float. We do this by placing the intended data type in parentheses, like this:

```
//Java considers the value 9.8765 a double because it contains
//a decimal point. If we want to assign it into a float variable,
//we must cast it to a float.

    float f = (float)9.8765;    //double 9.8765 is cast into the float
```

Program 2-9 illustrates problems with value assignments. Figure 2-15 shows the associated compiler errors.

```
1   //Program 2-9 Demonstrate Incorrect Assignments
2   //File:  BadAssignmentDemo.java
3
```

```
 4  public class BadAssignmentDemo
 5  {
 6      public static void main(String args[])
 7      {
 8          //We can't have decimal part for ints.
 9          int n = 7.1;
10
11          //The value 9.8765 is viewed as a double by Java.
12          //We can't assign double into float.
13          float f = 9.8765;
14
15          //The short range is 32767, out of range!
16          short s = 99999;
17      }
18  }
```

Figure 2-15
The javac command and
compiler errors in the
BadAssignmentDemo.java file.

```
C:\JPT>
C:\JPT>javac BadAssignmentDemo.java
BadAssignmentDemo.java:9: possible loss of precision
found    : double
required: int
                int n = 7.1;
                        ^
BadAssignmentDemo.java:13: possible loss of precision
found    : double
required: float
                float f = 9.8765;
                          ^
BadAssignmentDemo.java:16: possible loss of precision
found    : int
required: short
                short s = 99999;
                          ^
3 errors

C:\JPT>_
```

casting or data cast

an operation in which
the value of one type of
data is transformed into
another type of data

Data Casting   Casting a variable or **data cast** is an operation in which the value of one type of data is transformed into another type of data. The general form of a cast is:

`(dataType) expression`

where dataType is the new type of data for that expression. Two examples show data casting:

```
float f = (float) 9.8765;   //9.8765 is a double. Cast it into a float.

int number;
double precNumber = 7.62945214452;
number = (int)precNumber;   //cast the double value into an integer
                            //the decimal portion is truncated
                            //number now contains 7
```

Applying the cast from a double to an integer causes the decimal portion of the double variable to be truncated (lost). The decimal portion of the variable precNumber is ignored, not rounded, and the value 7 is stored in number. The Java compiler issues "possible loss of precision" messages whenever the decimal part of the value is thrown away. If we attempt to assign a value that is out of range, such as assigning 99,999 into a short variable that can only hold up to 32,767, precision is also lost. In order to eliminate the compiler errors in Program 2-9, you need this code:

```
public static void main(String args[])
{
        //cast the double into n, lose the 0.1 precision
        int n = (int) 7.1;

        //cast double into the float
        float f = (float)9.8765;

        //short variable can't hold 99999, use an integer
        int s = 99999;
```

Suffix casts are available for floats (f, F), doubles (d, D), and longs (l, L). A suffix cast uses a letter beside the numeric value to indicate the type of cast instead of the data type enclosed in parentheses. The following code illustrates three different cast operations using suffix casts.

```
public static void main(String args[])
{
        //cast the integer into the double with d
        double x = 15d;

        //could use the suffix f to cast into a float
        float p = 2.345f;

        //cast a value into a long variable
        long bigInt = 2555599999L;
```

Arithmetic Operators

Java provides five arithmetic operators—multiplication (*), division (/), addition (+), subtraction (−), and modulus (%). Addition, subtraction, and multiplication are self-explanatory. The division operator produces different results depending on the type of numbers being divided. Also, the modulus operator is new to many Java programmers.

Division results in Java depend on the data type of the numbers. If the numbers are floating point, the result from the division operation is a floating point

Figure 2-16
Modulus and division operators.

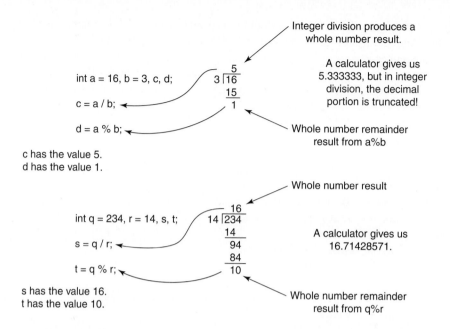

Integer division produces a whole number result.

A calculator gives us 5.333333, but in integer division, the decimal portion is truncated!

```
int a = 16, b = 3, c, d;

c = a / b;

d = a % b;
```

Whole number remainder result from a%b

c has the value 5.
d has the value 1.

Whole number result

```
int q = 234, r = 14, s, t;

s = q / r;

t = q % r;
```

A calculator gives us 16.71428571.

Whole number remainder result from q%r

s has the value 16.
t has the value 10.

value, including the decimal digits. If both of the numbers are integer (whole numbers, including ints, shorts, or longs), the result is only the integer portion of the quotient. If one number is an integer and the other is a double, the integer is promoted to a double, and the result is a double.

The modulus operator (%) must work with integer variables, and it returns the whole number remainder in a division. See Figure 2-16, which illustrates how both the modulus and division operators work in Java. Beginning programmers frequently see no use for the modulus operator; however, it turns out to be a very convenient operator. For example, if you need to know if an integer is odd or even, the number could be mod'ed with 2 and the result checked for 0 (the number is even) or 1 (the number is odd). This scheme is used to determine if a number is evenly divisible by 10 (or any integer). An integer mod'ed with 10 returns 0 if the number is evenly divisible by 10.

The code in Program 2-10 shows the two division/modulus examples seen in Figure 2-16. The output is seen in Figure 2-17.

```
1   //Program 2-10 Division and Modulus Demo
2   //File:  DivideAndModulusDemo.java
3
4   public class DivideAndModulusDemo
5   {
6       public static void main(String args[])
7       {
8           int a = 16, b = 3, c, d;
9           c = a/b;
```

```
10          d  = a%b;
11          String sABDivResult = " 16/3 Division result " + c;
12          String sABModResult = " 16%3 Modulus result " + d;
13          System.out.println(sABDivResult);
14          System.out.println(sABModResult);
15
16          double da = 16.0, db = 3.0, dc;
17          dc = da/db;
18
19          String sDoubleDivResult = " 16.0/3.0 Division result " + dc;
20          System.out.println(sDoubleDivResult);
21
22          int q = 234, r = 14, s, t;
23          s = q/r;
24          t  = q%r;
25          String sQRDivResult = " 234/14 Division result " + s;
26          String sQRModResult = " 234%14 Modulus result " + t;
27          System.out.println(sQRDivResult);
28          System.out.println(sQRModResult);
29      }
30  }
```

```
C:\JPT>
C:\JPT>javac DivideAndModulusDemo.java

C:\JPT>java DivideAndModulusDemo
 16/3 Division result 5
 16%3 Modulus result 1
 16.0/3.0 Division result 5.333333333333333
 234/14 Division result 16
 234%14 Modulus result 10

C:\JPT>
```

Figure 2-17
The javac and java commands and output from the *DivideAndModulusDemo.java* program.

Intermediate Results with Arithmetic Operators   Java has a simple rule for a programmer working with the four arithmetic operators. If the two values on which the operator is working (known as operands) are integers, the result is an integer. If the operands are double, the result is a double. If there is one integer operand and one double operand, the result is a double. If the two operands are different, Java automatically performs a promotion operation and promotes the "smaller" data type to the "larger" data type. The modulus operator only works on and returns integers. Table 2-10 summarizes this rule.

TABLE 2-10

Intermediate results with arithmetic operators.

Operands data types	Result data type	Example	Result
both integer	int	5 * 4	20
		16/3	5
		7 + 8	15
		8 − 2	6
		17 % 5	2
int float	float	5 * 4.0 f	20.000000
int double	double	5 * 4.0	20.0000000000000
float float	float	5.0 f * 4.0 f	20.000000
float double	double	5.0 f * 4.0	20.0000000000000
double double	double	5.0 * 4.0	20.0000000000000

The beginning Java programmer may encounter a problem in his or her program when two integers are divided and an integer result is generated. This result from integer division is an integer. It does not matter into what type of variable the division is being assigned. If the programmer entered the values 4/3 or 5/8 in his or her program, the fractions are integers according to Java, and the results are 1 and 0, respectively, not 1.3333333333 and 0.625 as expected. Examine Program 2-11 and its output in Figure 2-18, which demonstrates

```
C:\JPT>
C:\JPT>javac IntAndDoubleDivision.java

C:\JPT>java IntAndDoubleDivision

Let's do division in Java

Int division 16/3 put results in an int 5
Double division 16.0/3.0 put results in a double 5.333333333333333
Double division 16.0/3.0 put results into an int 5
Int division 16/3 put results into a double 5.0

WOW!

C:\JPT>
```

Figure 2-18

The javac and java commands and output from the *IntAndDoubleDivision.java* program.

how the division and storage results vary according to the data type of the
variables.

```
1    //Program 2-11 Demonstrate Integer and Double Division
2    //File:  IntAndDoubleDivsion.java
3
4    public class IntAndDoubleDivision
5    {
6        public static void main(String args[])
7        {
8            System.out.println("\n Let's do division in Java \n");
9            String sQuot;
10           int a = 16, b = 3, intQuot;
11
12           //Integer division truncates decimal portion of quotient.
13           intQuot = a/b;
14           sQuot = "Int division 16/3 put results in an int " + intQuot;
15           System.out.println(sQuot);
16
17           //Double division produces correct result.
18           double x = 16.0, y = 3.0, dQuot;
19           dQuot = x/y;
20           sQuot = "Double division 16.0/3.0 put results in a double " + dQuot;
21           System.out.println(sQuot);
22
23           //Double division result is cast into an int, losing the
24           //decimal part of the quotient.
25           intQuot = (int)(x/y);
26           sQuot = "Double division 16.0/3.0 put results into an int " + intQuot;
27           System.out.println(sQuot);
28
29           //Integer division produces the value of 5, which is then
30           //stored as a double.
31           dQuot = a/b;
32           sQuot = "Int division 16/3 put results into a double " + dQuot;
33           System.out.println(sQuot);
34
35           System.out.println("\n WOW! ");
36       }
37   }
```

Troubleshooting Using Fractions! (Trouble with Temperature and Volume Calculations) The intermediate results rule can cause programmers an incredible amount of grief when working with fractional calculations. If a number in an expression is entered without a decimal point, it is treated as an integer. Programmers forget this is the case and write code using algebraic expressions.

Suppose we need to code the Celsius to Fahrenheit conversion equation. This conversion is:

$$\text{Fahrenheit} = \frac{9}{5}\text{Celsius} + 32$$

The correct way to write this in Java is so that the fractional part is written as 9.0/5.0, so that this division result is 1.8. Initially, assigning the value 100.0 to the Celsius temperature, the complete code is:

```
double fTemp, cTemp;
cTemp = 100.0;


//be sure to code 9.0/5.0 to have correct division!
fTemp = 9.0/5.0 * cTemp + 32.0;
```

If the fractional portion of this expression is incorrectly written as "9/5" the integer division results in 1, NOT in 1.8, which is what our calculator gives us. This value, 1, is then multiplied by cTemp and 32 is added to it. The result is fTemp = 132.0, not the correct value of 212.0. This is incorrectly written:

```
double fTemp, cTemp;
cTemp = 100.0;

//ACCCKK!    9/5 produces 1, not 1.80
fTemp = 9/5 * cTemp + 32;
```

Converting Fahrenheit to Celsius temperature presents a similar coding problem. The algebraic formula for this conversion is:

$$\text{Celsius} = \frac{5}{9}(\text{Fahrenheit} - 32)$$

The Java code must have 5.0/9.0 to produce 0.5555555555. The division of 5/9 produces a zero result.

```
double fTemp, cTemp;
fTemp = 100.0;


//be sure to code 5.0/9.0 to have correct division!
cTemp = 5.0/9.0 * (fTemp - 32.0);
```

The following code produces incorrect results:

```
double fTemp, cTemp;
fTemp = 100.0;

//cTemp would be zero in all cases!
cTemp = 5/9 * (fTemp - 32);
```

Consider another example where integer division can yield an incorrect numeric result. The volume of a sphere is:

$$Vol = \frac{4}{3}\pi * r^3$$

The fraction 4/3 must be coded as 4.0/3.0 to ensure correct spherical volume results.

Increment and Decrement Operators

The increment (++) and decrement (−−) operators are useful because they provide a quick way to add or subtract one (1) from a variable. Table 2-11 illustrates how these operators are used:

Beginning Java programmers often ask about the placement of the operator, and if there is a difference between these two statements:

```
++i;
i++;
```

The answer is no. When the increment or decrement operator is used with a variable as shown above, there is no difference. However, there is a difference when the operators are used in an assignment statement. The pre-fix operator (the operator placed on the left side of the operand) will increment/decrement and then assign;

TABLE 2-11
Increment and decrement operators.

Operator	Job	Format	Equivalent to
Increment ++	Add 1 to operand	++i; i++;	i = i + 1;
Decrement −−	Subtract 1 from operand	--i; i--;	i = i - 1;

TABLE 2-12
Pre-fix and post-fix increment and decrement operators.

Operator	Job	Format	Equivalent to (see Note)
Pre-fix increment	Add 1 to *i* and then assign *i* into *m*.	`m = ++i;`	`i = i + 1;` `m = i;`
Post-fix increment	Assign *i* into *m* and then add 1 to *i*.	`m = i++;`	`m = i;` `i = i + 1;`
Pre-fix decrement	Subtract 1 from *i* and then assign into *m*.	`m = --i;`	`i = i - 1;` `m = i;`
Post-fix decrement	Assign *i* into *m* and then subtract 1 from *i*.	`m = i--;`	`m = i;` `i = i - 1;`

Note: The *Equivalent to* column shows the sequence of statements equivalent to the statement found in the *Format* column.

whereas, the post-fix operator (the operator placed on the right side of the operand) will assign and then increment/decrement. See Table 2-12. Pre-fix and post-fix operators should be used with caution! Very nasty bugs will result if the operators are used incorrectly.

Accumulation Operators

The accumulation operators (+=, −=, *=, etc.) provide a quick way to write assignment expressions when it is necessary to accumulate values. For example, there are two ways to add a value to a variable and two ways to multiply a value to a variable:

```
sum = sum + x;      //simply add sum + x together, assign into sum
sum += x;           //use the += operator does the same action
number = number * 10;      //multiply a number by 10
number *= 10;              //the *= operator performs the same thing
```

Table 2-13 summarizes these operators. Programmers who are just beginning to write programs may want to use the longer assign/operation statement instead of the accumulation operator because the accumulation operator is a bit more cryptic to read. As we progress through the text, we use the accumulation operators in later chapters because they are commonly used by Java programmers. See Table 2-8 for a complete list of Java's accumulation operators.

TABLE 2-13
Accumulation operators (partial list).

Operator	Use format	Equivalent to
+=	sum += x;	sum = sum + x;
-=	bal -= withd;	bal = bal - withd;
*=	q *= r;	q = q * r;
/=	m /= n;	m = m / n;

Note: The += operator can also be used to concatenate Strings.

2.6
An Introduction to Using Java Libraries

One of the greatest features of the Java language is the vast number of existing software tools that the Java programmer can use in his or her programs. Chances are very good that if you need an item that is common in programming, Java has one ready for you to use! Need to find the square root of a number, read in a certain type of file format, or incorporate a dialog box into your program? Java has these and thousands of other tools built and ready to go. The Sun Microsystems website, java.sun.com is a wonderful resource for locating Java software components.

It is time now to get away from the boring and cumbersome System.out. println() statement that we have been using for our program output. If you are thinking that there must be a message box tool out there to use, you are correct! Let's learn how to incorporate prewritten Java code into our programs by using the JOptionPane class for dialog box based program input and output.

Java Classes and Packages

The fundamental component of Java is the **class**. A class is a data type that consists of program pieces that perform certain actions or tasks (methods) and the data that is necessary for the class to perform its tasks. As described earlier in the chapter, a class can be thought of as a job description. For example, we can have a class called AirplanePilot and a class called Nurse. What properties should an airplane pilot and a nurse possess? We want our pilots to have good eyesight. We want our nurses to be compassionate and to like working with patients. What are the tasks or actions performed by pilot? By a nurse? What data do pilots and nurses need to know in order to perform their unique jobs? The pilot flies the plane and talks to the air traffic control tower. The nurse gives shots and takes blood pressure measurement. These tasks or actions are part of the job description and are the class methods. Our AirplanePilot class has flyThePlane() and talkToTheTower() methods, while our Nurse class contains giveShots() and takeBloodPressure() methods.

class
a program component that combines data and methods into a single, logical unit

JOptionPane

a class in javax.swing that provides easy to use, pop up dialog boxes

Math

a Java class that has methods to perform basic numeric operations such as the elementary exponential, logarithm, square root, and trigonometric functions

Java package

a group of classes that are related in a logical manner and that have been packaged or bundled together

There is a class in Java called **JOptionPane**, which provides the programmer with easy to use, pop up dialog boxes so that the program can show information to the user or get information from the user. Two important methods that we will use are showMessageDialog() and showInputDialog(). Also, there is a Java class called **Math** that has methods to perform basic numeric operations such as the elementary exponential, logarithm, square root, and trigonometric functions. One method we are going to use is the square root method, Math.sqrt(), to find the square root of a value.

Due to the vast number of Java classes, the language must group or "package" the classes together in libraries. A **Java package** is a group of classes that are related in a logical manner and have been "packaged" or bundled together. There are many, many Java packages found in the Sun Microsystems J2SDK SE. Table 2-14 shows six of the J2SDK SE packages. Visit the site: http://java.sun.com/j2se/1.4.1/docs/api/index.html to find a complete package listing.

Packages are named using words (in lower case letters) and dots. In Java, a package name implies a directory or folder hierarchy. This means that the classes found in the package "java.awt.font" are found in a folder named "font," which is contained in a folder named "awt." The awt folder is located in a "java" folder. Packages are set up and named in this manner to avoid name conflicts. For example, there are at least two different Date classes in Java. One Date is located in the java.util package, and one in java.sql. Advanced Topics, Chapter 13, *Packages, Classpaths, and JARs* presents a detailed discussion of packages. For now, do not worry about package hierarchy, just recognize that packages group similar classes together, and we will use packages in our programs.

JOptionPane Class The class JOptionPane is contained in the package javax.swing. If we look at the documentation for this class, we see there are many

TABLE 2-14
Six of Java 2 SDK SE packages.

Package name	Use
java.lang	(Java Language) Provides the classes that are fundamental for designing and building Java programs.
java.io	(Input/Output) Contains classes that perform system input and output through data streams, serialization, and the file system.
java.awt	(Abstract Windowing Toolkit) Contains classes that enable a programmer to build user interfaces and for painting graphics and images.
java.awt.font	Contains the classes for working with fonts.
java.util	(Utility) Contains the classes for working with calendar and time facilities, internationalization, and miscellaneous utility classes.
javax.swing	A package that was initially available as an extension to the Java language, hence "javax." The Swing package provides a set of "lightweight" (all-Java language) components that are designed to work the same on all computer platforms.

methods. Remember, methods are the tasks or actions the class can perform. We will use the showInputDialog() method to obtain data from our user and showMessage-Dialog() method to show data in a dialog box. Program 2-12 illustrates a simple example. The input and output dialog boxes are shown in Figure 2-19a and Figure 2-19b, respectively.

```
1   //Program 2-12 Use JOptionPane to say Hello to our user.
2   //File:  HelloInABox.java
3
4       //Import the JOptionPane class since we are using it in this program.
5       import javax.swing.JOptionPane;
6
7       public class HelloInABox
8       {
9           public static void main(String args[])
10          {
11              String sName, sSayHello;
12
13              //Ask the user to enter his or her name.
14              sName = JOptionPane.showInputDialog("Please enter your name.");
15
16              sSayHello = "Hi there " + sName + "! How do you like Java?";
17
18              //Say hello to our user!
19              JOptionPane.showMessageDialog(null, sSayHello,
20                  "Our First JOptionPane Program", 1);
21
22              //Whenever we use GUI components, we need to call
23              //System.exit to terminate the program.
24              System.exit(0);
25          }
26      }
```

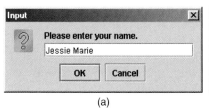

(a)

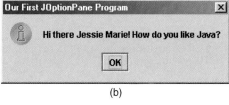

(b)

Figure 2-19
The (a) input and (b) output dialog boxes produced by JOptionPane in the program *HelloInABox.java.*

import Statement   There is a new line of code in our program.

```
import javax.swing.JOptionPane;
```

This **import statement** tells the Java compiler that the program is going to use the class specified in this statement and to load this class to ensure we use it correctly. The import statement helps the compiler find the class—in our case JOptionPane—which is contained in the javax.swing package. The import line is located before the class definition line, and is composed of two parts: the package name and class name. It is possible to use an * symbol, which indicates all classes in the package. This means that we could write this statement:

```
import javax.swing.*;
```

which says to import all of the classes in javax.swing package. When the Java source code is compiled, any superfluous import statements are neither used nor written into the class file.

It is incorrect to write the import statement like this:

```
import javax.*;
```

because the * symbol refers to classes, not packages. This import statement says to import the classes found in javax, and not the packages inside javax.

There are two schools of thought on import etiquette. One school says to specify exactly what classes your program needs to give the reader a clear indication of what the program requires. The second school of thought is to import all the classes using the package name.* in order to simplify your source code.

To complicate matters, you do not need the import statement at all if you use the package name with the class inside your class. In the code sample that follows, no import statement is given, but the full package and class name is used with JOptionPane methods.

```
//No import statement is needed, but full package.ClassName is..
        sName = javax.swing.JOptionPane.showInputDialog("Please enter your name.");

    sSayHello = "Hi there " + sName + "! How do you like Java?";
    javax.swing.JOptionPane.showMessageDialog(null, sSayHello,
            "Our First JOptionPane Program", 1);
```

Initially, we always provide the import statement using the package.ClassName in our code examples to specify exactly what classes we are using. We encourage you to do the same in your code. Once we become "pros" at importing classes, we will use the * convention.

JOptionPane Methods and Reading the Java Documentation We now turn to the details of learning to read Java documentation and how to use the classes and their methods in our program. Usually, each class has many methods. In other words, in each job description, there are many tasks that the class can perform. The trick here is to read the method description and make the correct **call to the method** (or **method call**) so that the Java compiler is happy and the method performs its task. When the program invokes a particular method of a class, this is referred to as "calling the method." For us to call a method, we need to determine the correct syntax in our Java code. If we call the method correctly, the method will then perform its task when the program executes.

Refer to the documentation website at Sun Microsystems to view the complete J2SDK SE documentation: http://java.sun.com/j2se/1.4.1/docs/api/index.html. Investigate the various packages, classes, and their methods. Or better yet, download the J2SDK documentation from the site and install it on your computer. Figure 2-20 shows the first page of the Java 2 Platform, SE, Version 1.4. It shows the classes and package descriptions.

call to the method or method call

when a program invokes a particular method of a class, it is referred to as "calling the method"

2

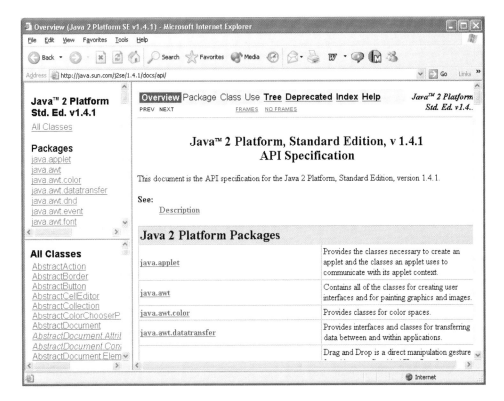

Figure 2-20
The main page of Sun's Java documentation for the Java 2 Platform Standard Edition. Copyright by Sun Microsystems, Inc. Reprinted with permission.

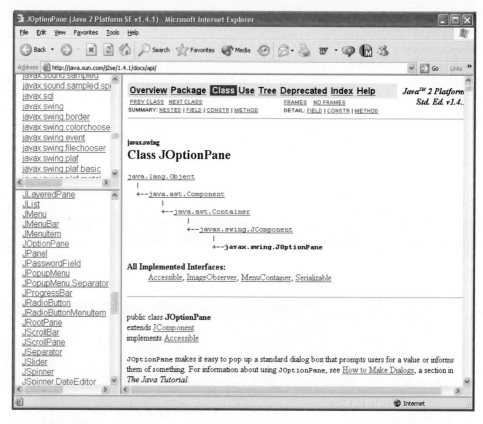

Figure 2-21
The JOptionPane class documentation has an overview of the class, parameter, field, constructor, and methods summaries. Copyright by Sun Microsystems, Inc. Reprinted with permission.

Figure 2-21 shows the documentation for Swing's JOptionPane class. Notice how we have selected the javax.swing package and JOptionPane class. The documentation presents an overview of the class and includes links to demonstration code. Scroll down the page and discover that there are sections describing the class parameters, examples, a field summary section, a constructor summary section, and a method summary section.

Java methods are composed of three parts: the **return type**, the **method name**, and the **input parameters**. The return type is the type of data sent back to whatever portion of the Java program that called the method. The method name is the identifier that we use to call the method, and the input parameters are the data that must be passed to the method.

For our programs in Chapters 2, 3, and 4, we make use of the JOptionPane class to interact with the user. Table 2-15 shows the description and two of the usage examples for JOptionPane's showMessageDialog() method. This method

return type
the type of data sent back to whoever called the method

method name
identifier that is used to call the method

input parameters
data that must be passed to the method

TABLE 2-15
Java's javax.swing.JOptionPane's showMessageDialog method. There are three
different forms of this static method.

Static status and return type	Method and example
static void	**showMessageDialog(Component parentComponent, Object message)** Shows an information-message dialog titled "Message" and displays the message. `JOptionPane.showMessageDialog( null, "Hello from Java");`

static void	**showMessageDialog(Component parentComponent, Object message, String title, int messageType)**
	
	Shows a dialog that displays a message using an icon determined by the messageType. The title of the dialog box is contained in the String title.
	
	`JOptionPane.showMessageDialog(null, "Do you love Java?", "Java`
	`Programming Today", JOptionPane.QUESTION_MESSAGE);`
	
	See Table 2-16 for the JOptionPane messageTypes.

static void	**showMessageDialog(Component parentComponent, Object message, String title, int messageType, Icon icon)** Show a dialog displaying a message, with programmer-specified title, messageType and icon.

2

shows information to the user in a dialog box. The input parameter requirements for showMessageDialog() are inside the parentheses. The first method in the table requires window information and the message that we want displayed to the user (in a String). These methods do not return anything to the caller because the return type is void. We discuss that static term in the next section. Here are the three different versions of this method.

Table 2-16 shows the five different message dialog types. The message type may be used or its associated integer constant. (See example in Program 2-12 and 2-17.)

Let's examine three of the six showInputDialog() methods contained in the JOptionPane class. The showInputDialog() allows the user to type in information in a dialog box. These three methods all have a return type of String, meaning that they return the user input into a String variable. These methods are shown in Table 2-17.

Each of these three different forms of the showInputDialog() method has a unique **method signature**. The method signature refers to the input parameter list. Java allows classes to have methods with identical names as long as the method signatures are different. We cover this in more detail in Chapter 6 when we begin writing our own classes and methods.

Program 2-13 is another example showing how to use JOptionPane's methods for obtaining information from the user. The input message box is Figure 2-22a and the output message box is Figure 22b.

method signature
refers to the return type, method name, and input parameter list

TABLE 2-16
Message dialog types.

Message dialog type	Description and intended use
JOptionPane.ERROR_MESSAGE	Shows a stop sign, and is used to display an error message to the user. (integer constant 0)
JOptionPane.INFORMATION_MESSAGE	Shows an "i" and is used to display information to the user. (integer constant 1)
JOptionPane.PLAIN_MESSAGE	No icon, is used to display a message to the user. (-1)
JOptionPane.QUESTION_MESSAGE	Shows a "?" and is used to ask the user a question. (3)
JOptionPane.WARNING_MESSAGE	Shows an "!" and is used to issue a warning to the user. (2)

TABLE 2-17

Java's javax.swing.JOptionPane's showInputDialog method (3 of 6). These showInputDialog methods are static methods.

Static status and return type	Method and example

static String	**showInputDialog(Object message)**
	
	Shows a dialog displaying a question message, requesting data from the user. The user's input is returned into a String variable.
	
	`String sHowOld;`
	`sHowOld = JOptionPane.showInputDialog( "How old are you?" );`

static String	**showInputDialog(Component parentComponent, Object message)**
	
	Shows a question message dialog that displays the message and returns the user's input into a String variable.
	
	`String sName;`
	`sName = JOptionPane.showInputDialog( null, "Please enter your name" );`

static String	**showInputDialog(Component parentComponent, Object message, String title, int messageType)**
	
	Shows a dialog that displays a message using an icon determined by the messageType. The title of the dialog box is contained in the String title. This method returns the user's input into a String variable.
	
	`String sAnswer;`
	`sAnswer = JOptionPane.showInputDialog(null, "Do you love Java?",`
	`"Java Programming Today", JOptionPane.QUESTION_MESSAGE);`
	
	See Table 2-16 for the JOptionPane messageTypes.

```
1   //Program 2-13 Use JOptionPane to obtain our user's pet's name
2   //File:  PetsName.java
3   //Import the JOptionPane class since we are using it in this program.
4   import javax.swing.JOptionPane;
5
6   public class PetsName
7   {
8       public static void main(String args[])
9       {
10          String sPetName;
11
12          //Ask the user to enter his or her pet's name.
13          sPetName = JOptionPane.showInputDialog(null,
14          "Please enter your pet's name.", "Love Our Animals",
15          JOptionPane.QUESTION_MESSAGE);
16
17          //write out the name
18          JOptionPane.showMessageDialog(null,
19          sPetName + " is your pet's name.", "Love Our Animals",
20          JOptionPane.INFORMATION_MESSAGE);
21
22          //Call System.exit to terminate the program.
23          System.exit(0);
24      }
25  }
```

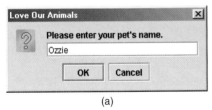
(a)

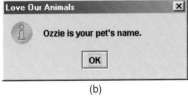
(b)

Figure 2-22
The (a) input and (b) output
dialog boxes produced by
JOptionPane in the program
PetsName.java.

Using Static Methods and Fields

The JOptionPane showMessageDialog() and showInputDialog() are static methods.
If you examine Java documentation, you will see the term "static" beside the return
type. (Refer to Tables 2-15 and 2-17.) A **static method** in Java allows the
programmer to use the class name to call the static method directly, as opposed to
making an object and calling the method by using the object. (We cover using
objects to call methods later in this chapter.) Java classes may contain **static fields**,
which are constant values associated with the class. To access a static field value,
use the ClassName.FieldName syntax.

static method
a method that can be
used with the form
ClassName.static-
Method()

The Java libraries that we use regularly contain many static methods and fields. This makes our Java programming life easier, as the static class members are ready to go—no fuss no muss. For example, the Math class in the java.lang package has a static PI field. (PI is the value that represents the ratio of a circle's circumference to its diameter.) Need the value of PI for a circle calculation? Easy, just use Math.PI. Want to pop up a message box to the user? Simply use JOptionPane.showMessageDialog() method. Need the color red for a drawing? The field Color.red is waiting for you. (Color is a class contained in the java.awt package.) Figure 2-23 summarizes the use of static methods.

> **Note:** There are other properties associated with the keyword static and we discuss them later in the text. (See Chapter 7.)

Package: java.lang   import package & class   → import java.lang.Math;
Class: Math   (not necessary
                           for java. lang since

Field Summary   imported automatically)   double radius = 5.0;
                                             double side1 = 10.0, side2 = 5.0;
                                             double area, hyp;

static double	PI value of pi

Method Summary

static double	sqrt(double a) returns $\sqrt{a}$
static double	pow(double a, double b) returns a^b

area = Math.PI * Math.pow (radius, 2);
hyp = Math.sqrt (Math.pow (side1, 2) + Math.pow (side2, 2));

Figure 2-23
Static methods can be called with the ClassName.staticMethodName. Here, we use the static methods, Math.pow(), and Math.sqrt() and static field from Math.PI in the java.lang.Math class.

Java Imports the java.lang Package Automatically

java.lang

Java package that contains basic classes fundamental to Java

The **java.lang** package contains the basic language support classes that are fundamental to designing Java programs. Because these classes are crucial to the Java language, the compiler loads this class automatically whenever a Java program is compiled. If we look at our very first Java program, we do not see any import statements. How does the compiler know what the System class is?

```
//Program 2-1   Getting Started with Java.
//This is our first program.
//File:  JLove.java


public class JLove
{
        public static void main(String args[] )
        {
                System.out.println("I love Java!!! ");
        }
}
```

As it turns out, the System class is contained in the java.lang package. Therefore, the Java compiler knows what the System class is. We could write this program in the following manner, but the import statement is assumed, not required.

```
//Program 2-1   Getting Started with Java.
//This is our first program.
//File:  JLove.java


import java.lang.System;


public class JLove
{
        public static void main(String args[] )
        {
                System.out.println("I love Java!!! ");
        }
}
```

A partial list of the classes in the java.lang package is shown in Table 2-18. The entire list can be found in J2SDK documentation.

The java.lang package classes are available to the Java programmer without importing the package, because Java always imports it for you. The Math class gives us the tools to take square roots and perform other mathematical operations. String methods make working with character and text data easy. Wrapper classes provide the tools so that the primitive values can be "wrapped" into an object and manipulated as needed. One important task that the wrapper classes give us is a way to convert primitive values to Strings and Strings to primitive values. Table 2-19 shows two of the Double methods. All the wrapper classes have these methods. Note that these methods are static.

Circle Calculation Example Using Static Methods and Fields Let's do an example that ties static methods and fields and wrapper classes together. Program 2-14 is boring on the outside, but exciting on the inside! We ask the user to

TABLE 2-18

A partial listing of the classes contained in Java's java.lang package. The *Note* contains information on wrapper classes.

Class name	Purpose
Boolean	A wrapper class that wraps the value of a primitive type boolean into an object.
Byte	A wrapper class that wraps the value of a primitive type byte into an object.
Double	A wrapper class that wraps the value of a primitive type double into an object.
Float	A wrapper class that wraps the value of a primitive type float into an object.
Integer	A wrapper class that wraps the value of a primitive type integer into an object.
Long	A wrapper class that wraps the value of a primitive type long into an object.
Math	A class that contains methods to do basic numeric operations such as exponentiation, logarithm, square root, and trigonometric functions.
Object	This class, Object, is the root of the Java class hierarchy. Every Java class has Object as a superclass.
Short	A wrapper class that wraps the value of a primitive type double into an object.
String	The class that contains the methods for working with character (textual) data.
System	This class contains several class fields and methods for accessing standard input, output, and error output streams, access to loading files, and libraries and other utility methods. All methods and fields are static.

Note: A wrapper class is a class that "wraps" the value of the primitive type into an object. Useful methods include converting the object value to a String and a String to an object. For example, the Integer class contains the methods for converting a integer to a String and a String to an integer.

TABLE 2-19

Two methods in the java.lang.Double class that convert Strings to numbers and numbers to Strings.

Return type	Method and purpose
static double	**parseDouble(String s)**
	Returns a double value represented by the value specified String.
| | ```
String sNumber = "15.35453";  //number contained in a string
double number;
number = Double.parseDouble(sNumber);  //15.35435 is now a double
``` |
| **static String** | **toString(double d)** |
| | Returns a string representation of the double argument. |
| | ```
double number = 1.234567;  //primitive double data type
String sNumber;
sNumber = Double.toString(number);  //changes number to a String
``` |

enter a circle's radius value, and we calculate the surface area and circumference values. Recall that the circle formulas incorporate the value of PI (π = 3.14159265 ...).

$$\text{Circumference} = 2.0 \cdot \pi \cdot \text{Radius}$$

and

$$\text{SurfaceArea} = \pi \cdot \text{Radius}^2$$

The program code is given below, and the input and output message boxes are seen in Figure 2-24a and Figure 2-24b, respectively.

```
1   //Program 2-14 Static Methods and Fields
2   //File:  CircleCalcs.java
3
4   //java.lang.* package imported automatically
5   //we can use Math, String, System, and Double classes
6
7   import javax.swing.JOptionPane;          //for dialog boxes
8
9   public class CircleCalcs
10  {
11    public static void main(String args[])
12    {
13          String sRadius, sResults;
14          double radius, circumf, area;
15
16          //Ask the user to enter the radius value
17          sRadius = JOptionPane.showInputDialog(null,
18          "Please enter the circle's radius.", "Circle Calcs Program",
19          JOptionPane.QUESTION_MESSAGE);
20
21          //turn the radius String into a double primitive
22          radius = Double.parseDouble(sRadius);
23
24          //perform the calculations, use static Math.PI field
25          //and static power function
26          circumf = 2.0 * Math.PI*radius;
27          area = Math.PI*Math.pow(radius,2);
28
29          //write out the results
30          sResults = " Radius = " + sRadius + "\n Area = " + area +
31          "\n Circumference = " + circumf + "\n\n Wasn't that fun?";
```

```
32
33          JOptionPane.showMessageDialog(null,
34          sResults, "Calculation Results",JOptionPane.INFORMATION_MESSAGE);
35
36          //Call System.exit to terminate the program.
37          System.exit(0);
38      }
39  }
```

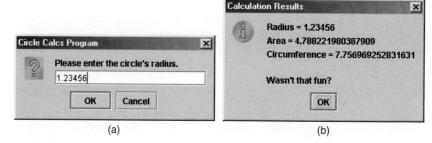

Figure 2-24
The (a) input and (b) output information produced in the program *CircleCalcs.java*.
We use static methods and Math.PI's static value for the calculations.

Using Java Classes and Methods that Aren't Static: An Introduction to Objects

The static methods and fields found in Java classes are handy tools for the Java programmer. Simply import the package and class, and then call the method with the
syntax:

ClassName.methodName(inputs)

However, most Java classes contain methods that are not static. To use these classes,
the programmer must create an object that is used to call the method. What does this
mean? Remember our Plumber example from earlier in this chapter? We had a terrible
problem in our kitchen and we used the yellow pages to look up a plumber. The term
"Plumber" describes the type of worker we needed. We called Don and Donna's
Plumbing Service, and Donna, a Plumber object, came to our house and stopped our
leak. In order for us to stop our leak, we needed a Plumber object to perform that task!

To use a Java class and its methods that are not static, the Java programmer
must create an instance of the class, known as an *object*. This creation process is

known as **instantiation**. When an object is created, memory is allocated for it, and methods and fields (behaviors and data) are associated with the object. Recall our earlier discussion regarding the classes (job descriptions for) AirplanePilot and Nurse. If mike is an AirplanePilot object, you can think of mike as an instance of an AirplanePilot. mike knows how to flyThePlane() and talkToTheTower(). If connie is a Nurse object, connie is an instance of a Nurse. The connie object knows how to giveShots() and takeBloodPressure().

instantiation
the process of creating an instance of an object

The new Keyword and Class Constructors   When a Java programmer needs an instance of a class (such as an instance of an AirlinePilot, a Nurse, or a Plumber), he or she must use the **new** keyword with the class name. The general form for the new keyword and constructor is:

new
a keyword that is used with a class name to create an object

```
ClassName    objectName = new ClassName( );
```

such as:

```
//Note that we name the object variables with lower case
//letters and that the class names begin with a capital letter.
Plumber donna = new Plumber( );
AirplanePilot mike = new AirplanePilot( );
Nurse connie = new Nurse( );
```

When the new keyword is executed in a Java statement, the class's **constructor method** is run automatically. The constructor method is a special type of method that is written as part of the class and has the same name as the class. Java will execute whatever code is inside the constructor method when the object is created. Its job is to initialize the object's data to desired values. It does not have a return type. You can think of the class constructor as performing the necessary tasks in order for the object to get ready to do its job. For example, when connie, our Nurse object, arrives at work, she must wash her hands and get her stethoscope out of its case before she is ready to see patients.

constructor method
method with the same name as the class, it is run automatically when the object is created

The constructor methods have the same name as the class. For our three examples, the constructors are Plumber( ), AirplanePilot( ), and Nurse( ). The objects are used to call the class's methods by the use of the dot operator, such as:

```
donna.stopTheLeak( );
donna.fixTheFaucet( );
mike.flyThePlane( );
mike.talkToTheTower( );
connie.giveShots( );
connie.takeBloodPressure( );
```

Redo The CircleCalcs Program and Say Hi to The DecimalFormat Class

Let's see how the new keyword and constructor methods work by using a Java class that improves the output display of our CircleCalcs program. Notice how the output in Figure 2-24b shows the circle's area and circumference values with fifteen decimal digits (too many). There must be a way to limit the output to a more reasonable number of decimal places, such as three or four. Right you are! Java provides the DecimalFormat class that comes equipped with the methods to format numbers in a variety of ways.

First we should look at the documentation for the java.text.DecimalFormat class. (Can you tell what package contains the DecimalFormat class? It is contained in the java.text package.) The constructor summary in the documentation shows three methods seen in Table 2-20. This means that there are three different ways we can create and initialize our DecimalFormat object.

> **Note:** Constructor methods do not have return types. Table 2-21 is a partial list of the methods of the DecimalFormat class. None of the methods shown are static.

TABLE 2-20

Constructor summary for java.text.DecimalFormat. Constructor methods do not have a return type and have the same name as the class.

DecimalFormat constructors	Explanation
DecimalFormat( )	Creates a DecimalFormat with a default pattern and symbols for the default locale.
DecimalFormat(String pattern)	Creates a DecimalFormat with the given pattern and the symbols for the default locale.
DecimalFormat(String pattern, DecimalFormatSymbols symbols)	Creates a DecimalFormat using the given pattern and symbols. Use this constructor when you need to customize the behavior of the format.

In Program 2-15, we create a DecimalFormat object to help us format our numbers. We need to create this object because none of the DecimalFormat methods are static. Because we want to format our numbers, we create the DecimalFormat object using the constructor that allows us to set the format or pattern when the object is created. We set the pattern to four decimal places by passing "0.0000" into

Chapter 2 ▌ Getting Started with Java Applications

TABLE 2-21
A partial listing of the methods in the java.text.DecimalFormat class.

Return type	Method and purpose
void	**applyPattern(String pattern)**
	Apply the given pattern to this DecimalFormat object.
String	**format(double d)**
	Returns a String representation with the DecimalFormat pattern of the double value. See *Note*.
String	**format(long n)**
	Returns a String representation with the DecimalFormat pattern of the long value. See *Note*.
void	**setMaximumFractionDigits(int newValue)**
	Sets the maximum number of digits allowed in the fraction portion of a number.
void	**setMaximumIntegerDigits(int newValue)**
	Sets the maximum number of digits allowed in the integer portion of a number.

Note: The format methods are inherited from the class java.text.NumberFormat.

the constructor. When the program executes, we enter the value of 1.23456 for our radius, and the formatted results are seen in Figure 2-25. You can see that the results are rounded to four decimal places.

```
1   //Program 2-15 Reworked CircleCalcs program making our numbers pretty.
2   //File:  RedoCircleCalcs.java
3
4   import javax.swing.JOptionPane;      //for dialog boxes
5   import java.text.DecimalFormat;      //to show our numbers to 4 digits
6
7   public class RedoCircleCalcs
8   {
9      public static void main(String args[])
10     {
11           String sRadius, sResults;
12           double radius, circumf, area;
13
14           sRadius = JOptionPane.showInputDialog(null,
15           "Please enter the circle's radius.", "Reworked Circle Calcs Program",
16           JOptionPane.QUESTION_MESSAGE);
```

```
17
18          radius = Double.parseDouble(sRadius);
19          circumf = 2.0 * Math.PI*radius;
20          area = Math.PI*Math.pow(radius,2);
21
22          //Now create a DecimalFormat object to help.
23          DecimalFormat formatter = new DecimalFormat("0.0000");
24
25          //write out the results formatting our doubles as we go
26          sResults = " Radius = " + formatter.format(radius)
27          + "\n Area = " + formatter.format(area)
28          + "\n Circumference = " + formatter.format(circumf)
29          + "\n\n Ohhh what pretty numbers!";
30
31          JOptionPane.showMessageDialog(null,
32          sResults, "Calculation Results (4 Decimal Places)",
33          JOptionPane.INFORMATION_MESSAGE);
34
35          System.exit(0);
36      }
37  }
```

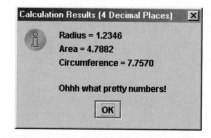

Figure 2-25
The output information produced in the program RedoCircleCalcs.java program. The input value for the radius was 1.23456.

default constructor
the constructor that has no input values and sets default values into the object's data when created

Program 2-16 is a DecimalFormat demonstration in which we create the DecimalFormat object by using the default constructor. We will write out a number to see the default pattern and then call a method that sets the desired pattern. Program 2-16 uses the **default constructor** (that is, the constructor with no input values, that sets default values into the object's data) when we create our formatter object. We then use this object to change the pattern by setting the number of digits that the formatter uses. Figures 2-26a and 2-26b show the default output and formatted output numbers, respectively.

```
1    //Program 2-16 DecimalFormat Demostration
2    //File:  FormatterDemo.java
3
4    import javax.swing.JOptionPane;
5    import java.text.DecimalFormat;
6
7    public class FormatterDemo
8    {
9       public static void main(String args[])
10      {
11            //initialize the number
12            double dNumber = 1.23456789;
13            String sFormattedNumber;
14
15            //Now create a DecimalFormat object using the default format.
16            DecimalFormat formatter = new DecimalFormat();
17
18            //format the double, place it into the String
19            sFormattedNumber = formatter.format(dNumber);
20
21            JOptionPane.showMessageDialog(null,
22            sFormattedNumber, "Default Pattern",JOptionPane.INFORMATION_MESSAGE);
23
24            //now set the formatter to 6 digits and format the number
25            formatter.setMaximumFractionDigits(6);
26            sFormattedNumber = formatter.format(dNumber);
27
28            JOptionPane.showMessageDialog(null,
29            sFormattedNumber, "Set the pattern to 6 digits",
30            JOptionPane.INFORMATION_MESSAGE);
31
32            System.exit(0);
33      }
34   }
```

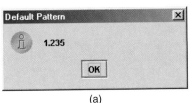

(a)

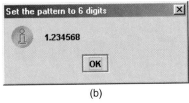

(b)

Figure 2-26
The output dialog boxes showing the formatted double values:
(a) shows the default pattern
with 3 places; (b) shows the
value with our requested
6 places.

Algebra and Java Frequently, algebraic expressions need to be written in Java code. Java code looks similar to algebra in that Java has parentheses ( ) and dot operators. The parentheses and dots have different meanings in Java and should not be confused with ways to represent multiplication. Also, keep in mind that division with integers produces an integer result, which can produce an incorrect result. Table 2-22 illustrates common mistakes made by beginning programmers who write algebraic expressions in Java.

TABLE 2-22
Algebraic equations and Java expressions.

Algebra	Java the right way	Java the wrong way
$v = (a + b)(c - d)$	`double v,a,b,c,d;` `v = (a + b) * (c - d);`	`double v,a,b,c,d;` `v = (a + b)(c - d); //Note 1`

$SA = \pi \cdot \text{radius}^2$	`double surfArea, rad;`
	`surfArea = Math.PI * rad*rad;`
	`//OR`
	`surfArea = Math.PI *`
	`Math.pow(rad,2);`
		`double surfArea, rad;`
		`surfArea =`
		`(Math.PI)(rad)(rad);//Note 1`
		`//OR`
		`surfArea = pi * rad **2;`
		`//See Note 2`
		`//OR`
		`surfArea = Math.PI * rad^2;`

$a = \dfrac{c + b}{x - y}$	`double a, b, c, x, y;` `a = (c+b)/(x-y);`	`double a, b, c, x, y;` `a = c + b/x - y;   //Note 3`
$m = \dfrac{\sqrt{x \cdot 3y}}{w}$	`m = Math.sqrt(x * 3 * y)/w;`	`m = Math.sqrt(x.3y)/w;` `//Note 4 and 5`

$\text{VolSphere} = \dfrac{4}{3}\pi r^3$	`double volSph, rad;`
	`volSph = 4.0/3.0 * Math.PI *`
	`Math.pow(rad,3);`
		`double volSph, rad;`
		`volSph = 4/3 * Math.PI *`
		`Math.pow(rad,3);`
		`//See Note 6`

Note 1: To perform multiplication, the * operator must be used. The expression ( )( ) does not mean multiplication in Java.

Note 2: The rad^2 and rad**2 are not valid ways to do exponentiation in Java.

Note 3: Division has higher priority; b/x would be done first.

Note 4: The dot operator is not a multiplication operator in Java.

Note 5: The term 3y is not a valid way to perform multiplication in Java.

Note 6: The term 4/3 produces an integer result of 1, not 1.33333. The wrong code produces a wrong answer.

2.7
Summary

This chapter introduces the new Java programmer to a variety of software concepts including programming terminology, software construction fundamentals, and the idea of designing software by developing a step by step approach. The step by step approach is known as an algorithm.

We present several simple examples illustrating the concept of classes, objects, and methods. A class can be thought of as a job description, such as a Plumber. An object is the individual who performs the class job, such as Donna, our Plumber. Methods are the various jobs described by the class, such as stopTheLeak() and fixTheFaucet().

Data types can be thought of as a programming container that holds program data. There are many types of containers in the Java language including data types for integers (whole numbers), float and double types (for decimal values), characters, and boolean (true/false) data. Many short program examples show the Java source code along with the Java compiler, javac, and Java interpreter, java, commands as well as errors from the Java compiler. If there are syntax errors in the source code, the compiler issues a description of the errors.

Java keywords are words that are reserved by the language and have special meaning. A few of the Java keywords seen in this chapter are used for declaring variables (int, float, double), defining classes (public class), and making variable values constant (final). We learn new keywords in every chapter of this text. There are many operators, which are character symbols that provide instructions in a Java program. Operators include the arithmetic symbols $*$, $/$, $+$, $-$, and $\%$. We learn about performing arithmetic in Java programs and illustrate the correct and incorrect ways of coding arithmetic and algebraic expressions in Java. We shall see several more operators and how they are used in Chapter 4.

We introduce a brief discussion of Java documentation along with the packages that are in the Java 2 Platform SE from Sun. We see how the java.lang package is imported automatically by our Java programs. The chapter programs demonstrate how to use String, System, Math and primitive wrapper classes. There are many packages in Java. These packages contain a broad range of useful classes. We see how to use classes that have static methods and create Java objects via the new keyword and class constructors.

2.8
Practice!

Modulus and Feet and Inches

The usefulness of integer division and the modulus operator is demonstrated in this short program. We ask the user to enter a whole number of inches (such as 80) and the program converts this distance into feet and inches (6 feet, 8 inches). By dividing 80 by 12, we determine the whole number of feet (6) and the modulus operator 80%12 gives us the inches, which is the whole number remainder, 8. The results from this program are seen in Figure 2-27.

```java
1   //Program 2-17 Demonstrate Usefulness of Integer Division and Modulus
2   //Convert Total Inches to Feet & Inches.
3   //File: FeetAndInches.java
4
5   import javax.swing.JOptionPane;
6
7   public class FeetAndInches
8   {
9       public static void main(String args[] )
10      {
11          int userInches,in, ft;
12          String sUserInches, result, titleOut;
13          sUserInches = JOptionPane.showInputDialog(null,
14                  "Enter Total Inches (a whole number)",
15                  "Feet and Inches", JOptionPane.QUESTION_MESSAGE);
16
17          userInches = Integer.parseInt(sUserInches);
18
19          ft = userInches/12;             //integer division gives us feet
20          in = userInches%12;   //modulus give us remainder, inches
21
22          result = "Result:" + ft + " ft and " + in  + "inches.";
23          titleOut = "You entered " + userInches + " inches.";
24          JOptionPane.showMessageDialog(null,result, titleOut, 1);
25
26          System.exit(0);
27      }
28  }
```

Figure 2-27
Output dialog box showing the feet and inches results.

Primitive Static MAX and MIN Values

The primitive wrapper classes provide static field values for the minimum and maximum values. The programmer can obtain the values from these static fields by ClassName.fieldName. Program 2-18 accesses these values, assigns them to primitive values, and displays them. The maximum and minimum double and float values are shown in Figure 2-28. Just for fun, compare the values from this program with the specifications found in Table 2-5 on page 50.

2

```java
1    //Program 2-18 Primitive Min and Max Values
2    //File: PrimitiveMinMax.java
3    //This class displays the minimum and maximum values
4    //for some primitive data types.
5    import javax.swing.JOptionPane;
6
7    public class PrimitiveMinMax
8    {
9        public static void main(String args [])
10       {
11           /* MAX_VALUE and MIN_VALUE
12                   These are static members contained within
13                   each of the primitive wrapper classes. */
14
15           double maxDouble = Double.MAX_VALUE;
16           double minDouble = Double.MIN_VALUE;
17           String doubleMax = "\nLargest double: " + maxDouble;
18           String doubleMin = "\nSmallest double: " + minDouble;
19
20           float maxFloat = Float.MAX_VALUE;
21           float minFloat = Float.MIN_VALUE;
22           String floatMax = "\nLargest float: " + maxFloat;
23           String floatMin = "\nSmallest float: " + minFloat;
24
25           String result = doubleMax + doubleMin + floatMax + floatMin;
26
27           JOptionPane.showMessageDialog(null,result,"Mins and Max's",1);
28
29           System.exit(0);
30       }
31   }
```

The Movie Starts in Ten Minutes

This next practice program, Program 2-19, illustrates Java's ability to access the computer's date and time features. The Movie Starts in Ten Minutes program creates a Calendar object by making a new GregorianCalendar. We then ask the

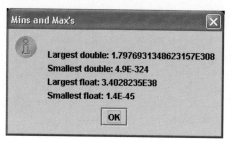

Figure 2-28
Min and max values from the Double and Float wrapper classes.

calendar to get the time and convert it to a String to display it. We then add ten minutes to the current time and display that. This program uses System.out.println() and print() statements, as well as short and float variables for practice. Figure 2-29a illustrates the user's input value for the number of tickets (3), and Figure 2-29b shows the output as seen in the MS-DOS Prompt window.

> **Note:** This conversion to a String illustrates the intention of java.lang.Object's toString() method. Whenever you make your own class, or when Java designers made a class, the toString() method is customized for that class so that it returns a string (textual) representation of the object.

```
1   //Program 2-19 Practice with dates and times.
2   //File: MovieStartsInTen.java
3
4   import java.util.Date;
5   import java.util.Calendar;
6   import java.util.GregorianCalendar;
7   import javax.swing.JOptionPane;
8
9   public class MovieStartsInTen
10  {
11      public static void main(String[] args)
12      {
13      // Get the user's input for later display.
14          String userinput = JOptionPane.showInputDialog(null,
15              "How many tickets for the show?",
16              "Now showing, \"Java, The Movie\" $12.25",1);
17
18      // Parse user's input into a short.
19          short tickets = Short.parseShort(userinput);
20
```

```
21      /* Calculate the total cost of tickets.
22          The trailing f must be used to insure float status by the compiler. */
23              float total = tickets * 12.25f;
24
25      // Using the Float wrapper class to convert total to String.
26              System.out.println("Your total ticket price is $" +
27                          Float.toString(total));
28              System.out.println("Here are " + Short.toString(tickets) +
29                          " ticket(s) for the show. ");
30      // Create a calendar object to access the current time.
31              Calendar calendar = new GregorianCalendar();
32
33      //The getTime() returns a Date object. This is another way to
34      //form an object besides using the new operator.
35              Date timeRightNow = calendar.getTime();
36              System.out.print("Current time and date: ");
37              System.out.println(timeRightNow.toString() );
38
39      //Add ten minutes to the current system time for show time!
40              calendar.add(Calendar.MINUTE, 10);
41              Date movieTime = calendar.getTime();
42              System.out.print("The movie starts in 10 minutes at: ");
43              System.out.println(movieTime.toString() );
44
45              System.exit(0);
46      }
47  }
```

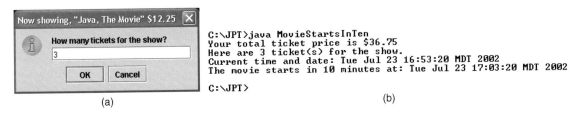

(a)   (b)

Figure 2-29
The (a) input message box and (b) output screen from the program,
MovieStartsInTen.java.

Memory and the Java Garbage Collector

Here is a program that illustrates Java's memory management and garbage
collection in action. The Runtime class is found in the java.lang package, and it is
able to access memory information in the JVM. However, an application cannot
create its own instance of this class (using the new operator). We must declare a
Runtime object and use the getRuntime() method instead of the new operator.

Figure 2-30

The output screen reporting the total and free memory values in the JVM from the program, *SystemInfo.java.*

```
C:\JPT>
C:\JPT>java SystemInfo
1984 Kb of total memory in the JVM.
1737 Kb of available JVM memory.
1849 Kb of free memory after initial garbage collection.
1067 Kb free after reserving memory for 100,000 doubles.
1067 Kb of free memory after 2nd garbage collection.

C:\JPT>
```

In Program 2-20, we ask the Runtime object to show us the total memory in the JVM and the free memory. Referring to Figure 2-30, we see that on this machine, there is 1984 Kb of total memory and 1735 Kb of available memory. We then call the garbage collection method, which attempts to free all unused memory. The Java garbage collection method makes a suggestion to the JVM to recycle all discarded objects to free memory for use. Garbage collection may not be performed by the JVM, depending on other tasks that it is currently doing. Here, the gc() method frees 114 Kb, and we now have 1849 Kb of available memory. We then declare 100,000 doubles, which, at 8 bytes each, reserved 800,000 bytes. (Dividing 800,000 by 1024 gives us 782 kilobytes.) Once again, we ask how much free memory exists, and we see 1067, a difference of 782 Kb!

```
1    //Program 2-20
2    //Demonstrate memory management and garbage collection in Java.
3    //File:  SystemInfo.java
4
5    public class SystemInfo
6    {
7        public static void main(String[] args)
8        {
9            //Runtime is a class in java.lang package.
10            //Runtime shows system information.
11            //We'll use it to see memory usage and garbage collection in action.
12
13            //First, get a Runtime object that is associated with this application.
14            //We can't create a Runtime object with the new operator.
15            //We must use the getRuntime() method.
16            Runtime r = Runtime.getRuntime();
17
18            //The totalMemory() returns total number of bytes in the JVM.
19            //Divide by 1024 to convert bytes into Kilobytes.
20            long total = r.totalMemory() / 1024;
21            System.out.println(total + " Kb of total memory in the JVM.");
22
23            //freeMemory returns number of available bytes in the JVM.
24            long free = r.freeMemory() / 1024;
25            System.out.println(free + " Kb of available JVM memory.");
```

```
26
27          //Call the garbage collector. It suggests to the JVM to
28          //recycle all discarded objects to free memory for use.
29          r.gc();
30          free = r.freeMemory() / 1024;
31          System.out.println(free +
32                  " Kb of free memory after initial garbage collection.");
33
34          //Now grab enough memory for 100,000 doubles (800,000 bytes total)
35          double [] d = new double[100000];
36          free = r.freeMemory() / 1024;
37          System.out.println(free +
38                  " Kb free after reserving memory for 100,000 doubles.");
39
40          //Run the garbage collection again.
41          r.gc();
42
43          free = r.freeMemory() / 1024;
44          System.out.println(free +
45                  " Kb of free memory after 2nd garbage collection.");
46
47          System.exit(0);
48      }
49  }
```

The CoconutEstimator Program

Our last program in this chapter assists you candy lovers in determining your
chances of selecting a piece of candy that contains coconut. Imagine that you love
chocolate with coconut filling, and you wish to know the odds of being happy with
your choice. Program 2-21 uses a series of JOptionPane message boxes to acquire
the candy information, and then performs the division and shows the output in
Figure 2-31.

```
1   //Program 2-21 Practice with Math
2   //File:  JCoconutEstimator.java
3
4   import javax.swing.JOptionPane;
5
6   public class CoconutEstimator
7   {
8       public static void main(String args[])
9       {
```

```
10          int total = 0,              //total number of pieces in box
11                coconuts = 0;         //how many pieces with coconut
12          double chance = 0.0;        //Chance of getting a coconut piece
13          int last=0;                 //percentage amount
14
15          String strTotal,            //user input for total
16                strNuts;              //user input for coconut amount
17
18          String question = "\nWhat are your chances of getting a "
19                    + "\ncoconut filled chocolate in a candy box?";
20
21          String explanation = "\nThis program will show you what your "
22                    + "\nchances are of getting/avoiding the coconut piece.";
23
24          String title = "Coconut Estimator Program";
25          JOptionPane.showMessageDialog(null, question, title,
26                      JOptionPane.QUESTION_MESSAGE);
27          JOptionPane.showMessageDialog(null, explanation, title,
28                      JOptionPane.INFORMATION_MESSAGE);
29
30          //Read user's answers for total in box as string.
31          strTotal = JOptionPane.showInputDialog("Enter number of pieces in box.");
32
33          //Read user's answers for number of coconut pieces as string.
34          strNuts = JOptionPane.showInputDialog(
35                "Enter number of coconut pieces in box");
36
37          //convert answers to Integers
38          total = Integer.parseInt(strTotal);
39          coconuts = Integer.parseInt(strNuts);
40
41          //cast the integers into doubles to perform accurate division
42          chance = (double)coconuts/(double)total;
43          chance = chance * 100;                //get percentage amount
44                                                //could have used chance *= 100;
45
46          String strChance = "Your chance of getting a piece of coconut candy is "
47                    + chance + "%";
48          JOptionPane.showMessageDialog(null,strChance, title,
49                          JOptionPane.INFORMATION_MESSAGE);
50          System.exit(1);
51      }
52  }
```

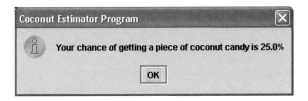

Figure 2-31
The results from the CoconutEstimator program with 12 pieces of candy in the box,
3 of which are coconut.

REVIEW QUESTIONS AND PROBLEMS

Short Answer

1. Describe what you can do to obtain a compiler error.

2. Name five keywords in Java.

3. What is the difference between a data type and a variable?

4. What is meant by *precedence of operations*?

5. What is the purpose of an import statement?

6. Where might you use a newline escape sequence?

7. What package contains the square root method?

8. What is the purpose of a primitive wrapper class?

9. What are the three types of comment styles in Java?

10. What is the range of values of a byte?

11. What are two differences between JOptionPane's showMessageDialog() and showInputDialog() methods?

12. Is javax.swing a package or a class?

13. How do static methods and fields in a class make a Java programmer's life easier?

14. Is it possible to create a DecimalFormat object so that it writes numbers with four digits ("0.0000") and then change that object so that it writes six digits? (Hint, look at the various methods in the class, DecimalFormat.)

15. Describe a business where there are at least three different job titles. For each job, list at least three separate tasks performed by a person with that job title. Finally, describe the relationship between the jobs and job titles with classes, objects, methods, and packages.

16. Imagine a small computer repair business that provides services for personal computers and laptops. Describe how you might model this business using classes.

17. Describe three different classes (job descriptions) that you might find at a package shipping business. Identify the class properties, data, and methods for each of the three types of workers.

18. The following shows names of classes. Identify which names are legal (valid) class names and which of the valid names adhere to the Java naming convention. State why the invalid names are illegal and what makes the nonconventional names not conventional.

dogs_and_cats   DogsAndCats   New England   _MoneyTalks   9Lives
bird brain $4School   1Building   CaseOfWine   sleepingKids

19. The following shows names of methods. Identify which names are legal (valid) method names and which of the valid names adhere to the Java naming convention. State why the invalid names are illegal and what makes the nonconventional names not conventional.

SeeSpotRun()   getThePaper()   sunny Day()   money_4_me()   goFishing()
flyingPigs()   7LuckyGuy()   #studyJava()   ManageParts()   run To Work()

20. The following shows names of variables. Identify which names are legal (valid) variable names and which of the valid names adhere to the Java naming convention. State why the invalid names are illegal and what makes the nonconventional names not conventional.

x   X   convertToPDS   _moneyTalks   9Lives
bird brain $4nothing   1ForYou   U_4_1   sleepingDogs

Debugging Problems

In the following source code examples (Questions 21–25), identify the compiler errors and state what is needed to eliminate the error(s).

21.

```
//File:  saved as Test.class
public class Test
{
      public static void Main( String args[] )
      {
            float x;
            y = x + 8.0;
      }
}
```

22.

```java
//File:  saved as WaitingForSomething.java
import JOptionPane;
public class WaitingForSomething
{
      public static void main( String args[] )
      {
            int whatsNext;
            String something;
            something = showInputDialog("What's next?");
      }
}
```

23.

```java
//File:  saved as mod.java
// This is a little program
that calculates a modulus answer.
public class MOD
{
public static void main()
{
      double x = 26.0,y = 4;
      int modAnswer;
      modAnswer = x%y;
      JOptionPane.showMessage(" answer =" + modAnswer);
}
}
```

24.

```java
//File:  Case.java

public class TestCase
{
      public static void main(string args[] )
      {
      double last = 0.09, final = 6.2;
      int number = 2;
      float sum;
      sum = last + final + number;
      JOptionPane.showMessage(" sum =" + sum);
}
```

25.

```
//File: Bucket.class
public class Bucket
{
        public static void main(String args[] )
        {
                double height = 10.0, radius = 3.5;
                double volume;
                vol = PI * rad *rad * height;

                System.out.println("Bucket volume =" + volume);
                System.exit(0);
        }
}
```

Programming Problems

For problems 26–31, write complete Java programs.

26. The area of a regular octagon is:

$$\text{Area of an octagon} = 4.828a^2$$

where a is the length of the side. Write a complete Java program that asks the user to enter the size of the octagon (side) and calculate and print the area showing three decimal places of accuracy. Use the JOptionPane class for data input and output. Place the length of the side in the title of the output window.

27. The volume of a four-sided pyramid is:

$$\text{pyramid volume} = \frac{A * h}{3}$$

where A is the area of the base and h is the height. Write a complete Java program that asks the user to enter the necessary information about the pyramid (base length, base width, and height) and calculate the volume. Print the results (to two decimal places), as well as all dimensional information. Use the JOptionPane class for input and output.

28. Expand the memory and Java garbage collector program (Program 2-20) so that you reserve enough memory for 10,000 integers, shorts, longs, and doubles. Estimate (using pencil and paper) the required number of bytes and kilobytes for these variables. Show the total memory, request garbage collection, then show free memory. Next, declare the variables and show free memory. Do the pencil and paper results match the results from your program?

29. Expand the CoconutEstimator program so that it calculates the probability of getting a piece of candy with nuts and a piece of candy with caramel filling (as well as the coconut). Add a DecimalFormat object so that the percentages are shown to three decimal places.

30. The volume of a cylinder is:

$$\text{cylinder volume} = \pi r^2 h$$

where r is the radius, h is the height, and π is the mathematical constant. Write a complete Java program that asks the user to enter the necessary information for a cylinder (radius and height), and calculate the volume and surface area of the cylinder. Refer to the *Algorithm Design* section of this chapter and Figure 2-2. Ask the user to enter his or her name, as well as the name of the cylinder, such as "A Tasty Beverage." Show these names along with the volume and surface area values in the JOptionPane output message box. Print the calculation results to two decimal places. Use the JOptionPane class for input and output.

31. Expand the memory and Java garbage collector program (Program 2-20) so that you reserve enough memory for 50,000 integers and 50,000 doubles. Estimate (using pencil and paper) the required number of bytes and kilobytes for these variables. Show the total memory, request garbage collection, then show free memory. Next, declare the variables and show free memory. Do the pencil and paper results match the results from your program?

3

Class Hierarchy in Java

KEY TERMS AND CONCEPTS

applets
applet methods
applet sandbox
appletviewer
AWT and Swing Components
bytecode verifier in JVM for applets
child class
class relationships "is a" and "uses a"
"extends" keyword
Graphics object
HyperText Markup Language
   (HTML)
inheritance hierarchy
java.lang.Object
java.awt.Graphics class
paint() method
root class
security rules for applets
subclass
superclass

CHAPTER OBJECTIVES

Introduce the basic concept of class hierarchy in Java and see how classes inherit data and methods from other classes.

Explain the "extends" keyword and show how it relates to inheritance.

Demonstrate the necessary code to build and run a Java applet program.

Show javac compiler and appletviewer commands.

Have fun with applets by visiting a website that has professionally built applets.

See how Java applets and web browsers interact.

Discuss how the JVM provides security by checking Java applet code from the Internet through the use of the bytecode verifier.

Show the inheritance trees for JApplet and JFrame, and show how these superclasses contribute to the windowing activities.

Develop basic applet and application programs so that we are able to paint graphics and images in this chapter's programs.

Introduce the concept of writing methods for the applet methods and simple class constructors.

Parents and Children

The Oxford Dictionary of Current English defines *inherit* as "(1) receive property, rank, title, etc., by legal succession. (2) derive (a characteristic) from one's ancestors."[1] *Webster's Ninth New Collegiate Dictionary* defines *inheritance* as "1 a: the act of inheriting property; b: the reception of genetic qualities by transmission from parent to offspring; c: the acquisition of a possession, condition or trait from past generations."[2]

What do these definitions have to do with Java? Inheritance and the resulting class hierarchy structure in Java or in any object-oriented language is one of the key capabilities of the language. Java allows the programmer to create a new class known as a subclass, from an existing class known as a superclass. These two classes are related as child and parent. The child inherits the data variables and methods from the parent and has additional data variables and methods of its own. Inheritance is the notion that you acquire traits and behaviors from past generations. Just as a "kid" looks like his or her parents a Java subclass also resembles its parent class.

3.1
java.lang.Object, the Root of all Java Classes

You may be able to trace your family tree for many generations, identifying parents, grandparents, and great-grandparents. Your brown eyes came from your mother while your curly hair came from your father, and you have a sense of humor just like your mother's father. In Java, all classes except one have a parent class. Every class in Java gets characteristics (data and methods) from its parent and grandparent classes. Unlike people, who cannot trace their family trees to the first generation, the family tree for all Java classes eventually stops at the class Object. So Java's ultimate parent class is Object. The Object class is the root of Java's hierarchical tree contained in the java.lang package.

---

[1] The Oxford Dictionary of Current English, s. v. "inherit."

[2] Webster's New Collegiate Dictionary, 9th ed., s. v. "inheritance."

How do we know that all Java classes have inherited things from Object? Let's look at a Java application similar to ones we wrote in Chapter 2. In Program 3-1, we use the JOptionPane's dialog box methods to obtain the user's name, then write a greeting to our user. The output is shown in Figure 3-1.

```
1    //Program 3-1
2    //File:  HelloFromJava.java
3    //No need to import java.lang.*; since Java does that for us.
4
5    import javax.swing.JOptionPane;               //for dialog boxes
6
7    public class HelloFromJava
8    {
9       public static void main(String args[])
10      {
11             //ask for the user's name
12             String sName;
13
14             sName = JOptionPane.showInputDialog(null,
15             "What is your name?","Greetings",
16             JOptionPane.QUESTION_MESSAGE);
17
18             //write a greeting
19             JOptionPane.showMessageDialog(null,
20             "Hello From Java,  " + sName + "!", "Greetings",
21             JOptionPane.INFORMATION_MESSAGE);
22
23             System.exit(0);      //terminate the program
24                                  //0 indicates no error
25      }
26   }
```

Figure 3-1
(a) The message dialog box where the user enters his or her name and (b) the greeting to our user from the HelloFromJava program.

(a)   (b)

The source code for this program requires an import statement for the JOptionPane class used in our program, but we do not need to import the java.lang package because Java imports this package automatically. In our program, we use the System.exit(0) method to terminate the program and a String variable to hold the user's name. The exit(0) indicates no errors occurred in the program. We use exit(1) if the program terminates due to an error. Because Java imports the java.lang package with all its classes, including System and String, we are able to use both of these classes with no import statement. Our program is able to use any of the classes in the java.lang package.

The class definition line requires our attention.

```
public class HelloFromJava
```

Just as we do not need to import the java.lang package, Java makes another assumption regarding our code. If we write our class definition line as shown, Java assumes that our HelloFromJava class's superclass (parent) is Object. A complete way to write the class definition line uses the "extends" keyword, like this:

```
public class HelloFromJava extends Object
```

Program 3-2 generates the same output seen in Figure 3-1, but we import the java.lang package and use the extends Object phrase.

```
1    //Program 3-2  Completely described Java application
2    //File:  HelloFromJava2.java
3
4    import java.lang.*;            //for Object, String, and System
5    import javax.swing.JOptionPane;           //for MessageDialog
6
7    public class HelloFromJava2 extends Object
8    {
9        public static void main(String args[])
10       {
11              //ask for the user's name
12              String sName;
13
14              sName = JOptionPane.showInputDialog(null,
15              "What is your name?","Greetings",
16              JOptionPane.QUESTION_MESSAGE);
17
18              //write a greeting
19              JOptionPane.showMessageDialog(null,
20              "Hello From Java,  " + sName + "!", "Greetings",
21              JOptionPane.INFORMATION_MESSAGE);
22
23              System.exit(0);
24       }
25   }
```

extends Keyword

extends

Java keyword used to make a new class that inherits the content of an existing class

The **extends** keyword in Java allows the programmer to make a new class that inherits the contents of an existing class and all[3] of its parent's content (all the way back to Object). As a rule,

```
public class NewClass extends ExistingClass
```

is the general format. In Program 3-2, we extend Object:

```
public class HelloFromJava extends Object
```

The existing class acts as the superclass, and its data variables and fields and methods are inherited by (passed on to) the new class, which is the subclass or child. The subclass should add special features that the superclass does not have. Our HelloFromJava class inherits all the characteristics of a Java object, and HelloFromJava has custom characteristics that Object does not have. Our subclass obtains the user's name and writes a greeting on the screen. The Object class (its parent) does not do this. Do not assume that the superclass has more features in it than the subclass. The superclass is named so because it is higher on the hierarchical tree.

"is a" and "uses a" Relationships   One skill we acquire as we become object-oriented programmers is the skill to examine how classes and objects relate to each other. Understanding these relationships helps us correctly design and write Java code. Let's look at Program 3-1 again. The relationship between our HelloFromJava class and Java's Object class is that HelloFromJava *is a* Java Object. In our HelloFromJava class, we use a JOptionPane class method to write our message. The relationship between HelloFromJava and JOptionPane is that our HelloFromJava class *uses a* JOptionPane class.

Whenever you start to design and write Java programs, you should always ask yourself how classes relate to each other. Does one class use another class? Is one class a special case of another class? In our programs in Chapter 2, we used String, Math, JOptionPane, DecimalFormat, Runtime, and Calendar classes to help us. We did not perform any special inheritance operations. Although we did not write "extends Object," Java automatically uses Object as the class superclass if no other extended class is present. The "extends Object" was assumed when we wrote our class definition lines.

Inheritance Example: Employees, Airplane Pilots, and CCU Nurses

The concept of inheritance is difficult to grasp at first for most beginning programmers, so let's concentrate on an example we can all understand. Let's write a class definition (job description) for an Employee. Remember, a job description is similar to a class definition in that we identify the data that a person with that job must know and the actions or tasks they perform.

---

[3] Chapter 9 presents details of exactly what is inherited by the subclass. Private class members are not inherited by the subclass.

```
class Employee
- has a name and social security number
- getsAPaycheck( )
- works( )
```

Figure 3-2
Two data and method items for any employee, as described in the class Employee.

First, the data—what data is associated with any employee? Let's restrict ourselves to employees legally working in the United States. Any employee, no matter what type of job he or she performs, has a name and a tax identification number. What actions do all employees perform? You may think this is impossible to describe, because we need to know the specifics of the job. In this top-level description, we keep it very general. All employees work and all employees get a paycheck. The actions of "working" are different for all employees, but whether you work at home, or commute 30 miles to your job, all employees work. Figure 3-2 illustrates the class Employee.

The next step in this example is to build a hierarchical tree of employees. Let's look at employees who work for an airline and employees who work for a hospital and build AirlineEmployee and HospitalEmployee classes. How do these two groups differ? Airline employees work in the travel and transportation industry, whereas the hospital employees work in the health care industry. Figure 3-3 illustrates some basic differences between these two types of employees.

We get more specific as we build our tree of Employee classes. Airline and hospital employees can now be grouped into types of jobs they perform. One group of airline employees is the flight crew, and nurses are a group of hospital employees. Of course, there are other groups of employees in both industries. Airlines have jet mechanics and reservations agents. Hospitals have doctors and insurance specialists. Back to our example, what does the flight crew know and

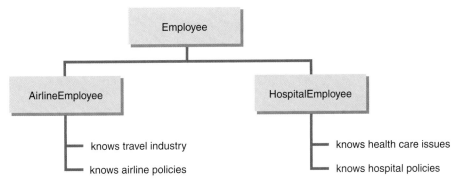

Figure 3-3
The airline and hospital employee hierarchy.

what tasks they should perform? What knowledge data and task skills do all nurses possess? As our examination gets more detailed, the job descriptions become more specialized. Figure 3-4 illustrates a tree of Employee classes showing yet another level in the hierarchy; the subclasses Pilot and CCUNurse (coronary care unit nurse).

Let's make a list of all the data and behaviors contained in a job description for the CCUNurse class. We name the obvious ones first: a CCUNurse knows heart medicines and can operate the heart monitoring equipment. What else? A CCUNurse is a Nurse and knows about patient care, such as how to give a patient a shot and how to take a blood pressure reading. A CCUNurse is a Nurse which is a HospitalEmployee and knows health care issues and hospital policies and procedures. Lastly, a CCUNurse is a Nurse, which is a

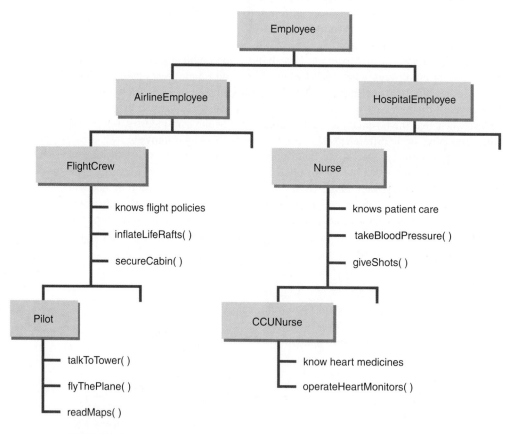

Figure 3-4
The Employee to Pilot and Employee to Nurse hierarchy. Pilots and Nurses are both members of the Employee class.

Chapter 3 ▐ Class Hierarchy in Java

HospitalEmployee, which is an Employee who has a name and SSN, and who works and gets a paycheck. By looking at our Employee description tree, we can trace all the data and behaviors up the tree, all the way to the root job description: Employee.

A Pilot is able to talk to the tower, fly the plane, and read the maps. A Pilot is a FlightCrew member and he or she knows flight policies and safety procedures. A Pilot is a FlightCrew member, which is an AirlineEmployee, and he or she knows travel and transportation issues and Airline policies. A Pilot is a FlightCrew member, which is an AirlineEmployee, which is an Employee, and he or she has a name and SSN, and he or she goes to work and gets a paycheck.

Job characteristics and tasks in the parent class are passed down to the new class. The subclass inherits characteristics from the superclass. We can write these Class descriptions in Java with the "extends" keyword. We have left out the program construction detail concerning code, files, and packages, etc. The important thing to see here is how the Employee hierarchy is built, as seen in Figure 3-5.

3

Note: Java allows only one extends on a class definition line.

```
public class Employee
{
    - has name and SSN
    - works( )
    - getAPaycheck( )
}

public class AirlineEmployee extends Employee
{
    - knows travel industry &
      airline policies
}

public class FlightCrew extends AirlineEmployee
{
    - knows flight policies
    - inflateLifeRafts( )
    - secureCabin( )
}

public class Pilot extends FlightCrew
{
    - talkToTower( )
    - flyThePlane( )
    - readMaps( )
}
```

The AirlinePilot object can fly the plane, secure the cabin, knows travel industry, and gets a paycheck.

Figure 3-5
The Employee hierarchy showing the extends relationship for a Pilot.

Revisit the DecimalFormat Class

Recall in Chapter 2 that we rewrote the CircleCalcs program using the java.text. DecimalFormat class to help us format our numbers. If we examine the Java documentation for the DecimalFormat class, we can now see the pedigree of this class. For all Java classes, we see the package and the inheritance tree. Figure 3-6 shows this.

You can see that the DecimalFormat class is a part of the java.text package. Its parent class is the NumberFormat class, and the parent of the NumberFormat class is the Format class. Object is the parent of the Format class. What do you think the main "job" of the NumberFormat and Format classes are? Table 3-1 summarizes the abilities of these classes.

The Format class is designed to format dates, messages, and numbers. The NumberFormat class has methods for formatting numbers. The DecimalFormat class contains methods that are specific for decimal precision numbers. Notice how the subclasses become more specialized as we go down the hierarchical tree. (Very important!) The DecimalFormat class inherits methods from the NumberFormat class, which inherited methods from the Format class, which inherited methods from the Object class. Whew! This is just like the Pilot, FlightCrew, AirlineEmployee, and Employee example.

When a Java programmer examines the Java documentation for any Java class, such as the DecimalFormat class, it is important that the programmer look at the Constructors and the Method Summary. It is equally important for the programmer to examine the "Methods inherited from" section, which shows the methods that the subclass obtains from the superclasses. By examining these portions of the documentation, the programmer sees all of the available methods in the class. In Programs 2-15 and 2-16, we used the format() method of the DecimalFormat class. This method originates in the NumberFormat class and is inherited by the

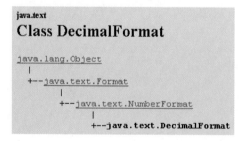

Figure 3-6
The DecimalFormat documentation showing the package and its inheritance tree.
Copyright 1993–2003. Sun MicroSystems, Inc. Reprinted with permission.

TABLE 3-1
Class hierarchy summary of the Object to DecimalFormat classes.

Class	Purpose
Object	Root object for all Java classes.
Format	An abstract class from the java.text package, designed for formatting dates, message, and numbers (see *Note*).
NumberFormat	An abstract class from the java.text package, designed to provide the necessary methods for formatting all numbers (see *Note*). Methods include formatting designations for integer, and currency.
DecimalFormat	A class designed to provide the methods to format decimal numbers (such as doubles and floats), including specifying number of digits of precision, scientific notation and exponentiation patterns, and positive and negative designations.

3

Note: Abstract classes are classes that are designed to be superclasses (parent classes) and expect to have specialized methods implemented in their subclasses. Abstract classes usually provide partial implementation of the methods. Abstract classes cannot be instantiated. See Chapter 9.

DecimalFormat class. Figure 3-7 shows which methods are inherited by the DecimalFormat class.

Refer once again to our airline Pilot class, and the jobs that a Pilot can perform. The Pilot class defines the flyThePlane() and talkToTower() tasks. The fact that the Pilot is a FlightCrew member means that the Pilot can secureCabinDoors() and inflateLifeRafts(). In the Java view of this situation, the Pilot inherited the ability to secureCabin() and inflateLifeRafts() from the FlightCrew class. The Pilot inherited the goToWork() and getAPayCheck() from the Employee class. Java classes inherit the tasks from their superclasses, so it is important to examine the "inherited from" methods when viewing the Java documentation.

Methods inherited from class java.text.NumberFormat

format, format, format, getAvailableLocales, getCurrencyInstance, getCurrencyInstance, getInstance, getInstance, getIntegerInstance, getIntegerInstance, getMaximumFractionDigits, getMaximumIntegerDigits, getMinimumFractionDigits, getMinimumIntegerDigits, getNumberInstance, getNumberInstance, getPercentInstance, getPercentInstance, isGroupingUsed, isParseIntegerOnly, parse, parseObject, setGroupingUsed, setParseIntegerOnly

Methods inherited from class java.text.Format

format, parseObject

Methods inherited from class java.lang.Object

finalize, getClass, notify, notifyAll, toString, wait, wait, wait

---

Figure 3-7
The methods inherited by the DecimalFormat class.
Copyright 1993–2003. Sun MicroSystems, Inc. Reprinted with permission.

Java's Object Class

All Java classes have a parent class, except for the root class: Object. If you write your own class, such as HelloFromJava in Program 3-1, or use a class such as DecimalFormat, the root superclass is Object. Both HelloFromJava and Decimal-Format inherit methods from Object.

Examining Java's documentation of the java.lang.Object class, we see one constructor and eleven methods. It is important to scan through the methods and not worry about them too much now. Several of these methods have been placed in Object, assuming that when you build your own classes, you will write customized versions of these methods as it makes sense for your object. Customizing an inherited method is called overriding. We will write our own classes and methods later in the text and implement some of these Object methods where appropriate. The Object methods are summarized in Table 3-2.

TABLE 3-2
Method Summary for the java.lang.Object class.

Return type	Method name and purpose
protected Object	clone() Creates and returns a copy (clone) of this object.
boolean	equals(Object obj) Compares objects to determine if they are the same.
protected void	finalize() The Java garbage collector calls this method to perform tasks before the object is removed from memory. If there are no more references to this object, garbage collection removes it from memory.
Class	getClass() Returns the runtime representation of the class of this object. When a program runs, the class types have an object that represents them. This method returns information regarding that class.
int	hashCode() Returns this object's hash code value. A hash code value identifies the object uniquely.
String	toString() A convenient method that returns a textual message describing this object.
All five methods return type is void	notify(), notifyAll(), wait(), wait(long timeout), wait(long timeout, int nanoseconds) Used in operating system synchronization protocol. Works with the wait/notify cycles so program components that interact can be timed correctly to wait and notify each other when certain tasks are performed/being performed.

3.2
Java Applets

Java **applets** are Java programs that run in a web browser. For a program to be an applet, java.applet.Applet must be a superclass somewhere in the program's inheritance tree. Applets work in a similar manner to web pages. A web page is placed on a **web server**, which is a computer with shared resources and is attached to the web with a specific web address. There are many types of servers. Web servers, print servers, and disk servers are a few examples of servers. A person using a computer with a **web browser**, such as Netscape[4] or Internet Explorer[5], can download the web page and view it on his or her computer. The user is referred to as a **client**. A client uses the resources provided by the server.

With Java applets, you write and compile the Java applet program and place a HyperText Markup Language (**HTML**) reference to the applet class file in a web page. In other words, the HTML file contains the name of the applet class file. When a user accesses that web page, the Java applet class is downloaded, along with the web page's text and graphics. The web browser contains a JVM, which then executes the applet on the user's computer. The appletviewer program uses the JVM that comes with the J2SDK.

Java applets offer the programmer wonderful opportunities and features. A Java applet can be placed in a web page so anyone anywhere can browse to the page, download that program, and run it without installing anything, as long as the user's browser is Java configured. Applet programs are also easy to run. There are no size restrictions to applets (although applets were once considered little applications).

In the early stages of the WWW, the web only allowed read-only interfaces. This means you could browse a web site and it served you pages containing only text and graphics. Now that web pages can cause a program to run, the browser is rapidly becoming a universal interface for computers.

applet
Java program that runs in a web browser

web server
a computer with shared resources, that is attached to the web, and that has a specific web address

web browser
a program that can view HTML pages on the web

client
a user that downloads and uses information from a server

HTML
HyperText Markup Language that is used to create web pages read by web browsers

3

A Brief Overview of Web Browsers

Web browsers read HTML files and take their orders from the HTML "tags" that are written into the HTML file. These tags give the browser commands, such as put this image here, or make this text bold. In the HTML file, we tell the browser to "go run this Java applet that you can find in this class file." The HTML tags are enclosed within the < > brackets. The following is a short HTML file that we used to run our first applet in Appendix A. This short file contains the applet tag that references the *JLoveApplet.class* file. The width and height dimensions set the size of the applet window.

---

[4] Netscape, a web browser developed by Netscape Corporation.

[5] Internet Explorer, a web browser developed by Microsoft Corporation.

```
<html>
<applet code = "JLoveApplet.class"   width = 300   height = 100 >
</applet>
</html>
```

Figure 3-8 illustrates the relationship between *.java*, *.class*, and *.html* files and web browsers.

Fun with Java Applets

Play before work! Soon enough, we will get into the nuts and bolts of writing applets and applications. It might be fun to spend a few minutes looking at real applets. Carl Ginnow's company, Microprizes, has a website that demonstrates some first-rate applets. These applets are fun to drive, and they illustrate many of the powerful features available in Java.

Refer to www.microprizes.com and test drive several of the applets. While you are at it, make a list of the various types of graphical user interface components you find. Are there any sliders? Are there any buttons? Can you find an applet that performs a certain action when the mouse is clicked or when the mouse button is pressed? Any text fields? Aside from the control items, do

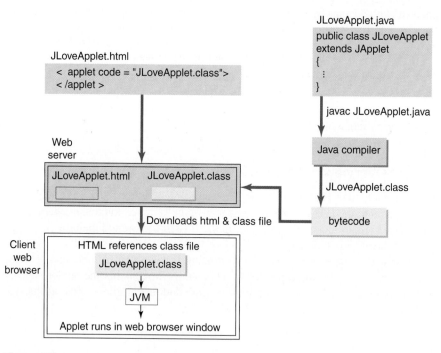

Figure 3-8
How a web browser and *.java, *.class, and *.html files are related.

Welcome to the

Microprizes County Fair

Figure 3-9
The map showing the fairgrounds of the Microprizes County Fair from
www.Microprizes.com. This site contains many Java applets that illustrate powerful
programming features of the Java language.

any of these applets have animations running while you play a game? Can you
hear any sound effects? Visit the Microprizes website (Figure 3-9) and make
your list!

Applets, Inheritance, and Java's JApplet Class

What do applets have to do with inheritance? A simple question with a simple
answer. We are going to write our own applet classes, and our classes inherit all
the characteristics they need to be an applet. We use Java's JApplet class contained
in the javax.swing package as our superclass. JApplet provides us with the necessary methods required to interact with web browsers, display a window, paint
graphics, and play sound clips and animations. Generally speaking, by having
JApplet as the parent class, the subclass is "born" with everything that it needs to
be an applet. Applets are computer programs that run in a web browser's window.
They can have all sorts of user interface components, but we do not have to be
experts in programming windows! The JApplet class has what we need, and we
simply inherit and use it.

Let's briefly examine the JApplet class inheritance hierarchy (seen on following page). The root of our Java inheritance tree is the Object class. What are all the
other classes in the JApplet "family tree?" There is a Component, a Container, a
Panel, and an Applet. The JApplet is contained in the javax.swing package.

```
java.lang.Object
        |
        +-java.awt.Component
                |
                +-java.awt.Container
                        |
                        +-java.awt.Panel
                                |
                                +-java.applet.Applet
                                        |
                                        +-javax.swing.JApplet
```

Each of these classes contains characteristics (attributes) and methods that the JApplet class inherits. After spending a few minutes (or hours) at the Microprizes website, remember that Applets are window-based programs. As a user interacting with these applets, you saw graphics and drawings, pushed buttons, moved slider bars, clicked the mouse, heard music, and watched animations. On the flip side, as a Java programmer, you must have the ability to place graphical controls into windows, listen for these controls to be used (such as knowing when the mouse is moved or a button is clicked), play animations and sounds, update the drawing in the window, and have your program correctly interact with the web browser. That is a large list of capabilities! Where do applets get the ability to do these things?

Examining the inheritance tree, we see the java.awt.Component class. A Component is a graphical object that can be displayed on the screen and provides the ability to interact with the user. A few Components are buttons, scroll bars, and text fields. The java.awt.Container class is a Component that can hold other components. A java.awt.Panel is a Container that provides a place where a Java program can attach components. The java.awt.Applet class has the necessary features so that a program (applet) can be embedded and run within another application, such as a web browser. The applet provides the standard interface needed for the program to interact with the web browser and its environment. We'll cover Swing in the next section.

This all sounds complicated. Components, Containers, Panels, Applets, and to top it all off—Swing! But do not worry. Keep in mind that the important concept is that JApplet comes equipped with all the necessary items so that we can make a window, add graphical controls, draw graphics and art, play music, and interact with the web browser. When we use the JApplet class as a superclass, our new class inherits these capabilities.

Looking ahead to the next program, let's examine the class definition line for the HelloApplet in Program 3-3:

```
import javax.swing.JApplet;
```

```
//Program 3-3
        public class HelloApplet extends JApplet
```

The HelloApplet extends JApplet statement means that JApplet is the superclass (parent) of HelloApplet. HelloApplet is a subclass of JApplet. For us to extend JApplet, we need to import its package, javax.swing. What do we know about subclasses and superclasses? A subclass is a superclass. HelloApplet is a JApplet. By extending the JApplet class, we make our HelloApplet class a JApplet class.

The ability to make a new class from an existing class is a powerful feature of the Java language! Recall our Pilot and CCUNurse example from the previous section. We can make a new type of pilot too—a BiPlanePilot—by having it inherit properties from Pilot. Assuming our Pilot class is ready to go, we create our new type of pilot by simply doing this:

```
public class BiPlanePilot extends Pilot
```

Our new BiPlanePilot inherits all of the Pilot, Flight Crew, Airline Employee, and Employee characteristics and methods, including flyThePlane(), secureCabin(), and goToWork(). Our BiPlanePilot class implements a new ability called flyUpSide-Down().

Writing and Running a Java Applet

The construction of Java applets and Java applications are very similar. Java syntax rules apply whether you are writing an application or an applet. The applet programmer writes the Java source code in a *ClassName.java* file, and compiles it with the Java compiler. However, the applet is run in a web browser instead of from the command line as we did in Chapter 2. The steps to writing and running a Java applet are shown here. Steps 2 and 3 can be interchanged.

Step 1: Write the Java applet code and save it in a *.java* file (*ClassName. java*).

Step 2: Compile the *.java* file using the Java compiler. It produces the *.class* file containing Java bytecode (*ClassName.class*).

Step 3: Write an HTML file that references the *.class* file. The HTML file does not have to be named with the class name, but for our examples we name the associated HTML file *ClassName.html*.

Step 4: Use a web browser to read the HTML file. The browser contains a JVM, which loads and runs the applet program. You may use Java's appletviewer, or a browser of your choice.

Program 3-3 is a simple Java applet that pops up a greeting in JOptionPane's message box. We name our first applet HelloApplet. HelloApplet is an applet, and we must extend the JApplet class.

```
1    //Program 3-3   A Java Applet that says Hello
2    //File:  HelloApplet.java
3
4    import javax.swing.JOptionPane;              //for MessageDialog
5    import javax.swing.JApplet;         //for JApplet class
6
7    public class HelloApplet extends JApplet
8    {
9       public void start()
10      {
11           //write a greeting
12           JOptionPane.showMessageDialog(null,
13           "Hello from a Java Applet!", "New Greeting",
14           JOptionPane.INFORMATION_MESSAGE);
15      }
16   }
```

The associated HTML file for this program is shown here:

```
<!-- HelloApplet.html for Program 3-3 -->
<!-- PS This is how you write a comment in an html file. -->
<html>
<applet     code = "HelloApplet.class"   width = 300   height = 100 >
</applet>
</html>
```

appletviewer

J2SDK's program that executes applets

This program is compiled using the javac compiler. We use the J2SDK's **appletviewer** program. The command line steps for these actions are shown in Figure 3-10. When the appletviewer begins to run, we see an Applet Viewer window pop up on our screen (Figure 3-11a). The size of the Applet Viewer window is dictated by the width and height values in the HTML file. When the applet program runs, we see the message box come up, showing our greeting (Figure 3-11b).

```
C:\JPT>
C:\JPT>javac HelloApplet.java

C:\JPT>appletviewer HelloApplet.html
```

Figure 3-10
The javac and appletviewer commands for the HelloApplet program.

Applet Methods

Applets have a different start-up procedure than Java applications. Recall that all of our Chapter 2 program classes had a main() method. The Java interpreter looks for the main() method and executes it first. Applets are run from web browsers. The

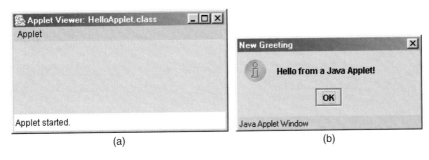

(a)   (b)

Figure 3-11
(a) The AppletViewer window sized to 300 × 100, and (b) the associated
JOptionPane message box showing our greeting.

browser automatically instantiates an object of your applet subclass, and then calls
methods to get the applet running. The first method it calls is the init() method.
Other methods are called in order, including start(), paint(), stop(), and destroy().

Table 3-3 lists the applet methods and purposes that are called automatically
by the web browser or the operating system. Four of the five methods are originally

TABLE 3-3
Summary of Applet methods that are called automatically.

Method	Purpose
public void init( )	The init() method is called by the appletviewer (or the web browser) when the applet is first loaded into memory. It is called only once. It should perform one-time initialization routines for the applet.
public void start( )	The start() method is called by the appletviewer (or the web browser) after the init method has finished its initialization tasks and whenever the user returns to the HTML page containing this applet. The start method should be used to perform any tasks when the applet is loaded or reloaded, such as starting an animation.
public void paint(Graphics g)	The paint() method is called by the window system after init() and start() methods have been called. Paint draws graphics information onto the window. It is called when the browser window needs to be refreshed (repainted). The paint() method is passed a Graphics object that it uses for drawing purposes.
public void stop( )	The stop() method is called when the applet should stop executing, which (typically) is when the user leaves the page containing the applet or minimizes the browser window.
public void destroy( )	The destroy() method is called when the applet is being released from memory, such as when the user closes the browser. It destroys any resources that have been allocated to the applet.

TABLE 3-4
JApplet methods are inherited from superclasses.

JApplet Methods	Inherited from (package.Class)
public void init( )	java.applet.Applet
public void start( )	java.applet.Applet
public void paint(Graphics g)	java.awt.Container
public void stop( )	java.applet.Applet
public void destroy( )	java.applet.Applet

defined in java.awt.Applet. The paint() method is originally defined in the java.awt.Container class. Table 3-4 indicates the classes where these methods originate.

JAppletLifeCycle Demonstration Program   When we write our own Java applets, we may define our own versions of the applet methods shown in Table 3-3. That is, if we wish to have our applet code perform a task once and only once, that task should be placed in our own init() method. If we wish to have our variable values initialized every time the applet is loaded or reloaded, we should place that code inside our own start() method. Any painting in the window is performed in paint(). If we wish to paint in the window, we need our own paint() method. When you write an applet, you do not need to have each of the five methods. For example, the majority of our applets will not have stop() or destroy() methods. If we do not write our own method, Java will call the superclass's version of that method.

For demonstration purposes, Program 3-4 has all five applet methods. The method definition lines must be written as shown. As this applet program executes, the web browser automatically calls these methods. In each of these methods, the applet displays a message in the status bar of appletviewer or a web browser. The status bar is the bottom portion of the window frame.

```
1   //Program 3-4
2   //File: JAppletLifeCycle.java
3
4   /* We use marcsPause() method (written by and named after Marc Benstein)
5    * to pause the applet so that you see the order in which the methods are called.
6    */
7   import java.awt.Graphics;      //for Graphics object in paint()
8   import javax.swing.JApplet;
```

```java
 9
10   public class JAppletLifeCycle extends JApplet
11   {
12     public void init()
13     {
14           marcsPause(1000); // stop the applet for 1000 milliseconds
15
16           // displays a message in the status bar
17           showStatus("JApplet says, \"I'm in init!\"");
18           marcsPause(1000);
19     }
20
21     public void start()
22     {
23           showStatus("JApplet says, \"I'm in start!\"");
24           marcsPause(1000);
25     }
26
27     public void stop()
28     {
29           showStatus("JApplet says, \"I'm in stop!\"");
30           marcsPause(1000);
31     }
32
33     public void destroy()
34     {
35           showStatus("JApplet says, \"I'm in destroy!\"");
36           marcsPause(1000);
37     }
38
39     public void paint(Graphics g)
40     {
41           showStatus("JApplet says, \"I'm in paint!\"");
42           marcsPause(1000);
43     }
44
45     //Marc's Pause method will pause the program by the number of milliseconds (ms).
46     void marcsPause(int ms)
47     {
48           try
49           {
50                 Thread.sleep(ms);
51           }
```

```
52          catch(InterruptedException e)
53          {
54          }
55      }
56  }
```

This program introduces the "marcsPause()" method, written and named after Marc Benstein, an extraordinary Java programming and computer science student. Marc was asked to design a simple way to pause a Java program for a certain amount of time so that *Java Programming Today* readers could better see how these programs behave. Do not worry about what his routine is doing, as we will eventually get to Java's keywords try and catch, as well as Threads. We simply put the statement:

```
marcsPause(1000);   //pause the program for 1000 milliseconds
```

where we wish to pause the program. The method body must also be placed in the class.

```
//Marc's Pause method will pause the program by the number of milliseconds (ms).
    void marcsPause(int ms)
    {
        try
        {
            Thread.sleep(ms);
        }
        catch(InterruptedException e)
        {
        }
    }
```

The best way to understand this program is to type it into the computer (or copy it from the text's CD) and run it! View this applet with appletviewer. Please use the menu from appletviewer to stop, restart, start, and close this applet. This menu can be seen in Figure 3-12. Play with the window by minimizing it, restoring it, or covering it with another window, then watch the status messages.

The associated HTML file for Program 3-4 is shown here:

```
<!-- JAppletLifeCycle.html for Program 3-4 -->
<html>
<applet code = " JAppletLifeCycle.class"   width = 400   height = 100 >
</applet>
</html>
```

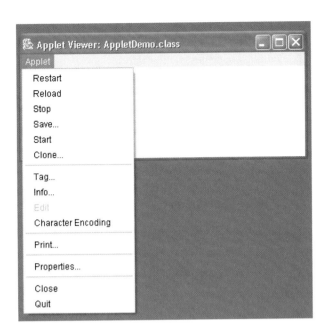

Figure 3-12
The applet window menu provides various applet controls for the applet window.

3

When you run this applet, the status message tells you which methods are called and when they are called. When the web browser first loads the applet, you'll see an "Applet loaded" message in the lower portion of the window frame, and "JApplet says, I'm in init." The applet's start() method is called next and you'll see the message "JApplet says, I'm in start." The message then shows that the paint() method has been called. Pressing the "X" (close) button (or selecting Close or Exit from the Applet window menu) causes the web browser to call the applet's stop() and destroy() methods. Take a few minutes to review the method descriptions in Table 3-3, and then perform the various operations to see how the various applet methods are invoked.

Java Applets Play in The Sandbox

Applets were designed with security in mind. Applets are invoked through the use of a web browser and usually are executed on a client's machine. Java designers did not want people to be able to write destructive applets that other folks could download with terrible results. These designers developed the Java language to have built-in security features with applets.

There is a difference between an applet loaded from the Internet and an applet loaded from the local machine. Where an applet comes from dictates what that applet is allowed to do. If you are loading a local applet, it is assumed to be "trusted." Because you are not sure of the origin of an applet coming in from the web, it *is not* trusted and *is* subject to all of Java's security restrictions.

bytecode verifier

in the JVM, it checks
that the applet
bytecode conforms to
Java language
specifications

A **bytecode verifier** resides within the JVM. This verifier checks that the bytecode conforms to Java language specifications, and checks to see if there are any violations of language. It examines each instruction and makes sure that the bytecode does not perform any illegal operations. Illegal operations include stack overflow or underflow, illegal accesses, or invalid paths. By default, an applet downloaded from the web cannot read or write files, open a socket connection, start up a program on the machine, or call non-Java code.

Applets that are loaded locally from the client's machine are loaded by the file system loader and are not passed through the bytecode verifier. In contrast, applets downloaded from a server via the Internet are loaded by the applet class loader, run through the bytecode verifier, and are subject to the restrictions of the applet security manager. These "untrusted" or "unsigned" applets are encased by a "firewall" in the web browser. The applet executes within this "sandbox," and cannot access system resources. Figure 3-13 illustrates the sandbox concept.

It is possible for an applet to be "signed," meaning that it is tamper resistant and its origin is known. Signing applet code is similar to placing your signature on a legal document such as a bank check. A signed applet allows the browser the chance to identify who wrote the applet. In theory, a signed applet can be trusted and given more privileges. *Java Programming Today* does not describe how to sign an applet, as that is an advanced topic. It is important for the beginning Java student to recognize how applets work and understand restrictions placed upon them.

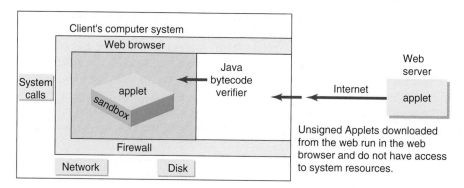

Figure 3-13
An "untrusted" applet downloaded from the web is verified and restricted by the security manager. It cannot get out of the sandbox.

3.3
Java's java.awt.Graphics class

Now let's investigate how we draw and paint items in an applet window. The paint() method is passed a Graphics object, and this object is what we use to draw in our applet window. Imagine that the paint() method's job is to act as a painter and the

Graphics object is the paintbrush. The Graphics object "knows" all about where it is going to draw. It knows the size of the canvas, the font, the color, and the painting operation. Look at the method definition line for paint():

```
public void paint(Graphics g)
```

The "Graphics g" inside the parentheses represents the input data to this method. The Graphics object can be named anything as long as we use valid Java naming rules. For example, we could name the Graphics object drawObject or fred, and the method definition lines are written as:

```
public void paint(Graphics drawObject)
```

or

```
public void paint(Graphics fred)
```

The Graphics class contains many useful methods for drawing into a window. It provides the means for us to draw a rectangle, an arc, a circle, or an oval, filled or outlined objects, as well as place images and strings of text in our window. We can also set the color. Table 3-5 (on page 128) lists a few of the Graphics class methods that we are able to use for drawing.

Note: Many Java references show the first line in a paint() method to be:

```
public void paint (Graphics g)
{
        super.paint(g);
        // rest of paint
}
```

The line super.paint(g) is calling the paint() method of the superclass, which performs certain initialization steps required for more complex drawing and GUI components. It is not required in our simple programs–but it does not hurt to have this statement. In our more complicated painting routines we include it as necessary.

DrawABoxApplet Program Program 3-5 shows a simple applet that asks the user to enter the length and width for a rectangle. In this program, we place the length and width variables after the class definition line and before the init() method definition line. Primitives or objects declared in this location are referred to as **class or instance variables**. Class or instance variables are "seen" by all of the methods inside the class and can be used by any of the class's methods. In this program we ask the user to enter the variable values in start(), and then use them when we draw our rectangle in paint(). We discuss class variables in detail in Chapter 6. Also notice that in this program, the paint() method's definition line shows the

class or instance variables

declared after the class definition line and before any methods. They can be used by all methods inside the class

A partial list of the java.awt.Graphics class's methods. Several methods provide the capability to draw either an outline of or filled items. Note: the *x* and *y* coordinates start at the top left corner of the output window.

Method	Purpose and Example using paint(Graphics g)

abstract void drawArc(int x, int y, int width, int height, int startAngle, int arcAngle)
 	
abstract void fillArc(int x, int y, int width, int height, int startAngle, int arcAngle)
	Draws an outline or filled arc based on a rectangle of size width and height, whose center is located at (*x,y*). Angles are based on 360 degrees. Zero degrees lies along the positive *x* axis, and the angular measurement is in the counter clockwise direction.
	
	`g.drawArc(100, 100, 50, 75, 0, 90);`
	`g.fillArc(100, 100, 50, 75, 0, 90);`

abstract void drawRect(int x, int y, int width, int height)
 	
abstract void fillRect(int x, int y, int width, int height)
	Paints a highlighted or filled rectangle that is drawn or filled with the current color. The *x* and *y* values are starting pixel locations in the window, the width and height are dimensions of the rectangle.
	
	`g.fillRect( 0, 0, 200, 150);`
	`g.drawRect(0, 0, 200, 150);`

abstract bool drawImage(Image i, int x, int y, int width, int height, ImageObserver obs);	Draws as much of the image starting at the *x,y* location that will fit in the width and height specified. In this example, we use the Toolkit to help us read the image.
	
	`Toolkit toolkit =`
	`Toolkit.getDefaultToolkit();`
	`Image myImage =`
	`toolkit.getImage("filename.jpg");`
	`g.drawImage(myImage, 100, 100, 150, 100,`
	`this);`
	`//need to import java.awt.Toolkit and Image`

abstract void drawString(String s, int x, int y)	Draws the string of text at the location *x,y*.
	
	`g.drawString( "This is a string of`
	`information.", 100, 50);`

abstract void setColor(Color c)	Sets the current color to the specific color.
	
	`g.setColor(Color.black);`
	`//need to import java.awt.Color;`

Note: The Graphics class is an abstract class, and so are its methods, as seen by the word "abstract" in the method definitions. We cover abstract classes in detail in Chapter 9. Briefly put, abstract classes are incomplete classes and require further specialization. The methods in the Graphics class will have different implementations depending on which type of platform the program is executing. We do not need to worry about this, as Java has implemented the methods for each platform.

drawObject Graphics object. If we enter 125 for the width and 75 for the length, we
see the rectangle in the applet window in Figure 3-14.

```
1    //Program 3-5
2    //File:  DrawABoxApplet.java
3
4    import javax.swing.JApplet;
5    import javax.swing.JOptionPane;
6    import java.awt.*;       //for Graphics object in paint
7
8
9    public class DrawABoxApplet extends JApplet
10   {
11       //use class variables for box length and width
12       //class variables can be seen by all the methods
13       int boxLength, boxWidth;
14
15       public void init()
16       {
17            JOptionPane.showMessageDialog(null,
18            "Let's Draw a Box!",         "Box Applet ",
19            JOptionPane.INFORMATION_MESSAGE);
20        }
21
22       public void start()
23       {
24            String sWidth = JOptionPane.showInputDialog(null,
25                 "What is the width of your box (limit 175)? ",
26                 "Box Applet",JOptionPane.QUESTION_MESSAGE);
27
28            boxWidth = Integer.parseInt(sWidth);
29
30            String sLength = JOptionPane.showInputDialog(null,
31                 "What is the length of your box (limit 175)? ",
32                 "Box Applet",JOptionPane.QUESTION_MESSAGE);
33
34            boxLength = Integer.parseInt(sLength);
35        }
36
37       public void paint(Graphics drawObject)
38       {
39            //draw a box that begins at 25,25 from upper left corner
40            drawObject.drawRect(25,25,boxWidth,boxLength);
41        }
42   }
```

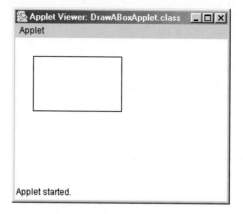

Figure 3-14
The applet window with a 125 × 75 (width × length) rectangle.

The associated HTML file:

```
<!-- DrawABoxApplet.html for Program 3-5 -->
<html>
<applet code = "DrawABoxApplet.class"   width = 300   height = 200 >
</applet>
</html>
```

DrawShapesApplet Example   The Graphics methods presented in Table 3-5 are illustrated in Program 3-6. The reader may reference the Java documentation to see the entire list of useful graphics methods available to the Java programmer. In this applet, we draw an arc, a filled rectangle, and an oval, and place an image in the window. Because we are running this applet in appletviewer, on our own machine, our applet can open and read the image file. If you try to run this in another web browser program, the image file may or may not be presented, depending on the configuration of the browser. Java provides many ways to place an image in a window. We show several different ways in our various program examples. Refer to Figure 3-15 to view the results of this program.

> **Note:**   Java can read JPEG (.jpg) or GIF (.gif) image files. It does not read bitmap (.bmp) files.

```
1    //Program 3-6
2    //File: DrawShapeApplets.java
3
4    import javax.swing.JApplet;
```

```
5    import java.awt.Graphics;
6    import java.awt.Color;
7    import java.awt.Image;
8    import java.awt.Toolkit;
9
10   public class DrawShapesApplet extends JApplet
11   {
12     public void paint (Graphics g)
13     {
14           // set background color of the window
15           // this is inherited from java.awt.Component
16           setBackground(Color.white);
17
18           // draw Arc
19           g.setColor(Color.cyan);
20           g.drawString("Cyan Arc", 20, 40);
21           g.drawRect(50,50,180,120);
22           g.drawArc(0,60,180,100,-60,160);
23
24           // draw oval
25           g.setColor(Color.magenta);
26           g.drawString("Magenta Oval ", 260, 40);
27           g.drawRect(290,50,180,120);
28           g.fillOval(305,65,150,90);
29
30           // draw rectangle
31           g.setColor(Color.green);
32           g.drawString("Green Rectangle ", 20,200);
33           g.drawRect(50,210,180,120);
34           g.fillRect(70, 220, 140, 100);
35
36           // draw image
37           g.setColor(Color.black);
38           g.drawString("Gray Rocks", 260, 200) ;
39           g.drawRect(290,210,180,120);
40
41           // load image
42           Toolkit toolkit = Toolkit.getDefaultToolkit();
43           Image myImage = toolkit.getImage("rocks.jpg");
44
45           // display image
46           g.drawImage(myImage, 300, 220, 150, 100, this);
47     }
48   }
```

Figure 3-15
The applet window showing an arc, a rectangle, an oval, and an image. These graphical items were drawn by methods found in the java.awt.Graphics class.

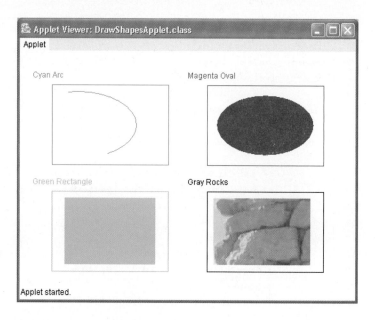

The associated HTML file for the DrawShapesApplet:

```
<!-- DrawShapesApplet.html for Program 3-6    -->
<html>
<applet code="DrawShapesApplet.class" width=520 height=350>
</applet>
</html>
```

PrimitiveDisplay Program   The primitive wrapper classes provide static fields containing the minimum and maximum values for the different data types. In Chapter 2, the PrimitiveMinMax program obtained values for doubles and floats. In Program 3-7, we obtain minimum and maximum values for many of the primitive data types, and write these values in the applet window. Compare the results of this program in Figure 3-16 with the values shown in Table 2-5.

```
1   //Program 3-7
2   //File: PrimitiveDisplay.java
3
4   /* This class displays the minimum and maximum values for some primitive
5     data types. We use java.awt.Color to set the color of the background
6     and to set the color of the strings drawn in the JApplet.
7   */
```

```
8    import java.awt.Color;
9    import java.awt.Graphics;
10
11   import javax.swing.JApplet;
12
13   public class PrimitiveDisplay extends JApplet
14   {
15     public void init()
16     {
17           setBackground(Color.white);
18     }
19
20     public void paint(Graphics g)
21     {
22           int yPos = 5; // the y position of the string to be drawn
23
24           double maxDouble = Double.MAX_VALUE;
25           double minDouble = Double.MIN_VALUE;
26           g.setColor(Color.magenta);
27           g.drawString("Largest double: " + maxDouble, 10, yPos += 15);
28           g.drawString("Smallest double: " + minDouble, 10, yPos += 15);
29
30           float maxFloat = Float.MAX_VALUE;
31           float minFloat = Float.MIN_VALUE;
32           g.setColor(Color.black);
33           g.drawString("Largest float: " + maxFloat, 10, yPos += 15);
34           g.drawString("Smallest float: " + minFloat, 10, yPos += 15);
35
36           long maxLong = Long.MAX_VALUE;
37           long minLong = Long.MIN_VALUE;
38           g.setColor(Color.cyan);
39           g.drawString("Largest long: " + maxLong, 10, yPos += 15);
40           g.drawString("Smallest long: " + minLong, 10, yPos += 15);
41
42           int maxInt = Integer.MAX_VALUE;
43           int minInt = Integer.MIN_VALUE;
44           g.setColor(Color.blue);
45           g.drawString("Largest int: " + maxInt, 10, yPos += 15);
46           g.drawString("Smallest int: " + minInt, 10, yPos += 15);
47
48           short maxShort = Short.MAX_VALUE;
49           short minShort = Short.MIN_VALUE;
50           g.setColor(Color.darkGray);
```

```
51          g.drawString("Largest short: " + maxShort, 10, yPos += 15);
52          g.drawString("Smallest short: " + minShort, 10, yPos += 15);
53
54          byte maxByte = Byte.MAX_VALUE;
55          byte minByte = Byte.MIN_VALUE;
56          g.setColor(Color.red);
57          g.drawString("Largest byte: " + maxByte, 10, yPos += 15);
58          g.drawString("Smallest byte: " + minByte, 10, yPos += 15);
59      }
60  }
```

Figure 3-16
The minimum and maximum values for Java primitive data types.

3.4
Java Applications and the JFrame Class

Java applets inherit their ability to "be an applet" from JApplet. Applets are able to interact with web browsers and draw graphics into a window. Now, how can we have a Java application draw in a window? Java applications are stand-alone programs and do not interact with web browsers, so we know we do not need the JApplet class. If you are thinking that there must be a class or a set of classes that enable drawing to be performed in applications, you are correct!

To draw into a window from a Java application, there are two things we must have: a window and a "painter." The class we need to use is the JFrame class. If you are writing an application, your program must have at least one class that is a subclass of JFrame. This new class is where the drawing occurs.

JFrame Class

The JFrame class is contained in the javax.swing package. Let's look at JFrame's inheritance tree:

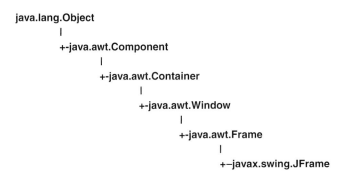

```
java.lang.Object
       |
       +-java.awt.Component
               |
               +-java.awt.Container
                       |
                       +-java.awt.Window
                               |
                               +-java.awt.Frame
                                       |
                                       +–javax.swing.JFrame
```

We see three of the same classes that we saw in the JApplet class—Object, Component, and Container. Components are graphic user interface items such as buttons, sliders, text fields, and combo boxes. Recall that the java.awt.Container class is a component that can hold other components. What do we inherit from Container? Are you thinking that the paint() method comes from Container? Good! (See Table 3-4 on page 122.) The paint() method is a member of the Container class. Examining the rest of the tree, we see java.awt.Window, java.awt.Frame, and javax.swing.JFrame.

The java.awt.Window class contains a borderless window that must have a Frame as its owner. This Window class provides the ability to listen for and handle window events such as window opening and closing or gaining and losing focus. The Frame class is a top-level window that has a window frame (border) and a title bar. The JFrame is extended from Frame, and is in the swing package.

HelloFrame Example and A New Way to Write Our Applications
TheJFrame class comes equipped with the window parts and pieces we need, as well as the ability to perform drawing in the window. In this example, let's create our own application class by extending JFrame. By doing this, our new class comes equipped with the ability to draw graphics inside a window. (Isn't inheritance great?)

The HelloFrame source code is shown in Program 3-8. Our programs are now going to take on a new form. The Java interpreter begins running the application at the main() method. Up to now we have had all of our code inside the main() method. The main() method is a static method that has certain restrictions. We learn about static methods in Chapter 7. Now that we are writing more complicated programs, we do not want to have all of our code within the main() method.

```
1    //Program 3-8 A JFrame that says hello.
2    //File: HelloFrame.java
3
4    import java.awt.Color;
5    import java.awt.Graphics;
6    import javax.swing.JFrame;
7
8    public class HelloFrame extends JFrame
9    {
10      public static void main( String[] args )
11      {
12
13   //We must create a HelloFrame object by using the new keyword.
14   //The new keyword calls the class constructor method below.
15         HelloFrame isaJFrame = new HelloFrame();
16
17   // EXIT_ON_CLOSE is an integer defined in JFrame.
18   // We are telling the program that if the frame is closed, exit the program.
19         isaJFrame.setDefaultCloseOperation( EXIT_ON_CLOSE );
20      }
21
22      public HelloFrame()              //class constructor method
23      {
24
25   //Set the size and title for the window.
26         setSize( 300, 100 );
27         setTitle("Hello Frame Program");
28
29         show();        //force a call to paint
30      }
31
32      /*
33        Here is our paint() method that gets called every time
34        the frame needs refreshing or first appears.
35        We inherit this method from java.awt.Container.
36      */
37
38      public void paint( Graphics g )
39      {
40            g.setColor( Color.magenta );
41            g.drawString( "Hello from javax.swing.JFrame!", 25, 60 );
42      }
43   }
```

For our new program format, we create an object of the class HelloFrame by using the new keyword in the main() method. When we use the new keyword, Java calls that class's constructor method. What our program is doing is making an object reference of the HelloFrame class. When it creates this object, we call the HelloFrame() constructor method, which then calls the various window setup methods for the frame in the constructor. The show() method forces a call to paint(), which performs drawing in the window. This process differs from the applet programs, because the web browser automatically creates an instance of the applet class, and calls the init(), start(), paint(), stop(), and destroy() methods.

Figure 3-17 illustrates the program flow for the HelloFrame program. The output frame is seen in Figure 3-18.

① Java interpreter starts
    with main( ).
② The main( ) method
    creates a HelloFrame
    object.
③ The HelloFrame constructor
    method is called.
④ The constructor sets the size
    and title of window.
⑤ The call to the show( ) method
    forces a call to the paint( )
    method.
⑥ The paint( ) method writes
    magenta colored phrase
    using a Graphics object, g.

```
public class HelloFrame
{
    public static void main (String args [ ])
    {                          ②
        HelloFrame isaFrame = new HelloFrame( );
    }                                    ③
    public HelloFrame( )
    {
④      setSize (300, 100);
        setTitle ("Hello Frame Program");
        show( );
    }              ⑤
    public void paint (Graphics g)
    {
⑥      g.setColor (Color.magenta);
        g.drawString ("Hello from javax.swing.JFrame!");
    }
}
```

Figure 3-17
The main() method creates a HelloFrame object, which forces a call to the HelloFrame constructor. The window is set up and show() forces a call to the paint() method.

Figure 3-18
The output frame from the HelloFrame program.

In the code in Program 3-8, we see the class constructor method. Class constructor methods were introduced in Chapter 2 when we discussed making new objects. Recall that the constructor method is a special type of method that is written as part of the class. The constructor has the same name as the class, and its job is to initialize the object's data to desired values. What actions does our constructor perform?

```java
public HelloFrame()              //class constructor method
{
        //Set the size and title for the window.
        setSize( 300, 100 );
        setTitle("Hello Frame Program");

        show();        //force a call to paint
}
```

Recall that the java interpreter program executes the main() method first. Notice that our main() method contains two lines only (plus several comment lines) and that the layout of this code is different from how we wrote the programs in Chapter 2. Examine the main() method.

```java
public static void main( String[] args )
{


//We must create a HelloFrame object by using the new keyword.
//The new keyword calls the class constructor method below.
        HelloFrame isaJFrame = new HelloFrame();

// EXIT_ON_CLOSE is an integer defined in JFrame.
// We are telling the program that if the frame is closed, exit the program.
        isaJFrame.setDefaultCloseOperation( EXIT_ON_CLOSE );
}
```

We are creating a HelloFrame object that we name "isaJFrame" by using the new operator. You can think of the new operator as the mechanism that calls the constructor method. In this HelloFrame class, the main() method is calling the class's constructor and creating an object of the HelloFrame class. The second line of code in main() has our HelloFrame object, isaJFrame, call the JFrame method, setDefaultCloseOperation(). This method is being passed the EXIT_ON_CLOSE field. This tells the JFrame class to exit the program when the window is closed. See Figure 3-17 again to review the application program flow.

DrawShapesApp Example   In this DrawShapesApp application program, Program 3-9, we borrow the paint() method from the DrawShapesApplet program. We write this program using a JFrame superclass instead of a JApplet superclass. Do we obtain the same results as in the DrawShapesApplet program? (See Figure 3-19.) We lay out the program code following the new format seen in the HelloFrame program. Because this program is an application, not an applet, we must have a main() method. In main() we create a DrawShapesApp object, and this instantiation process calls the class constructor. One more thing to note, the order or layout of the methods in this program are paint(), the constructor, and the main(), which is different from the order in HelloFrame. The Java programmer can place the methods in any order in the class. The DrawShapesApp source code is shown in Program 3-9.

```
1    //Program 3-9
2    //File: DrawShapesApp.java
3
4    import javax.swing.JFrame;
5    import java.awt.Graphics;
6    import java.awt.Color;
7    import java.awt.Image;
8    import java.awt.Toolkit;
9
10   public class DrawShapesApp extends JFrame
11   {
12      //We have borrowed this paint() method from DrawShapesApplet.
13      public void paint (Graphics g)
14      {
15              // set background color of the window
16              // this is inherited from java.awt.Component
17              setBackground(Color.white);
18
19              // draw Arc
20              g.setColor(Color.blue);
21              g.drawString("Blue Arc", 20, 40);
22              g.drawRect(50,50,180,120);
23              g.drawArc(0,60,180,100,-60,160);
24
25              // draw oval
26              g.setColor(Color.magenta);
27              g.drawString("Magenta Oval ", 260, 40);
28              g.drawRect(290,50,180,120);
29              g.fillOval(305,65,150,90);
30
31              // draw rectangle
32              g.setColor(Color.green);
33              g.drawString("Green Rectangle ", 20,200);
34              g.drawRect(50,210,180,120);
35              g.fillRect(70, 220, 140, 100);
36
37              // draw image
38              g.setColor(Color.black);
39              g.drawString("Gray Rocks", 260, 200) ;
40              g.drawRect(290,210,180,120);
41              // load image
42              Toolkit toolkit = Toolkit.getDefaultToolkit();
43              Image myImage = toolkit.getImage("rocks.jpg");
```

```
44              // display image
45              g.drawImage(myImage, 300, 220, 150, 100, this);
46          }
47
48      //Class Constructor Method. It has the same name as the class.
49      //In this method we set the window title, size, and show the window.
50      //Showing the window calls the paint() method.
51      public DrawShapesApp()
52      {
53              //set the title of the window
54              setTitle("DrawShapesApp");
55
56              setSize(520,350);
57
58              //show the window, this forces a call to paint
59              show();
60      }
61      public static void main(String args[] )
62      {
63              //In main, we make a new DrawShapesApp object called theApp.
64              //This causes the class constructor method to be called
65              DrawShapesApp theApp = new DrawShapesApp();
66
67              //Main now waits for the JFrame window to be closed.
68              //When we close the window, theApp terminates the program.
69              theApp.setDefaultCloseOperation(JFrame.EXIT_ON_CLOSE);
70      }
71  }
```

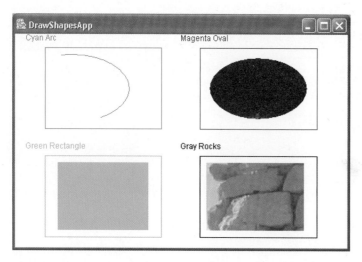

Figure 3-19
The application window showing an arc, a rectangle, an oval, and an image. This application uses the paint() method from the applet code in Program 3-6.

Write Your Name Frame   In the last program of this chapter (Program 3-10), we ask the user to enter his or her name, and we then write the name in the frame at a random location. In Program 3-10 we use the Math.random() method to provide us with the *x* and *y* positions for the drawString() method. In this example, the frame size is set to 250 × 150. To ensure that the user's name is always seen within the frame, we generate the *x* and *y* positions within a subset of the frame. This program uses the classic, nonscientific approach to calculate this subset, known as a wild guess. In a more scientific approach we would obtain the length of the string, obtain the size of the system fonts (or set the fonts), obtain the size of the font, and do a precise calculation. Refer to the Java Affirmations program in Chapter 4 if you'd like to approach this problem in a more scientific fashion. Our output is shown in Figure 3-20.

The Math.random() method returns a random value between 0.0 and 1.0. How do we generate a value between 0 and 200? If you multiply the value from this method by 200, and cast it into an integer, you will obtain a number between 0 and 200. To generate a number between 50 and 300 requires two steps. First, you generate a number between 0 and 250 (the range between 50 and 300 is 250), and then add the 50 to this value. Another way to look at it is, if you obtain a number from Math.random(), it will be between 0.0 and 1.0. Multiply that number by 250, and the result is a number between 0 and 250. Add 50 to this number, and the result is a number between 50 and 300. One last question. What do you expect to see if you minimize and restore the window?

```
1    //Program 3-10 A Frame that writes your name in a random location.
2    //File: WriteYourNameFrame.java
3
4    import java.awt.Color;
5    import java.awt.Graphics;
6    import javax.swing.JFrame;
7
8    import javax.swing.JOptionPane;
9
10   public class WriteYourNameFrame extends JFrame
11   {
12     //use a class variable for your name
13     String name;
14
15     public static void main( String[] args )
16     {
17           WriteYourNameFrame nameFrame = new WriteYourNameFrame();
18           nameFrame.setDefaultCloseOperation( EXIT_ON_CLOSE );
19     }
20
21     public WriteYourNameFrame()            //class constructor method
22     {
23           name = JOptionPane.showInputDialog(null,"What is your name?",
24               "Name Frame Program", 1);
```

```
25
26          setBackground(Color.cyan);
27          setSize( 250, 150 );
28          setTitle("Name Frame Program");
29
30          show();
31    }
32
33    public void paint( Graphics g )
34    {
35          int xPos, yPos;
36
37    //The window width is 250, we'll scale to 200 so the name isn't cut off.
38          xPos = (int)(Math.random()*(200));
39
40    //The window height is 150, the top border takes about 40 pixels.
41    //Generate yPos between 40-150 by scaling to 110 and add 40.
42          yPos = (int)(Math.random()*110.0) + 40;
43
44          g.setColor( Color.magenta );
45          g.drawString( name,xPos,yPos );
46    }
47 }
```

Figure 3-20
The Write Your Name Frame program showing a user name: "Madison."

3.5
Abstract Window Toolkit (AWT) and Swing

By now you are probably wondering what the javax.swing package is. We have seen and used Swing's JApplet and JFrame classes. Before we discuss Swing, we must talk about Java's Abstract Window Toolkit. In the early days of Java (Java 1.0) the Abstract Window Toolkit package provided the basic set of classes for creating graphical user interfaces, painting graphics, and displaying images. Buttons, sliders, and check boxes are all components, and their root or superclass is the java.awt.Component class.

peer components

components that are native to the target machine's operating system

    The Java AWT components are based on **peer components**. Peer components are known as native components. That is, when a Java program needs a button, the

AWT button component code simply draws and uses the operating system's native button. This means that if the Java program is running on a Windows machine, the program draws a Windows button. If the program is running on a Sun machine, a Solaris button is used. Unfortunately, there are many problems with the AWT components due to inconsistencies across platforms.

The Swing package does not use peer or native components. Instead, Swing components are drawn by the Java code onto the screen. In other words, all of the Swing components know how to draw themselves, and they come with the "know-how" to perform their jobs. They do not rely on the target system having the specific native component.

The Swing components have the parent class of JComponent. JComponent keeps track of the information that all on-screen controls need to have, such as size, tooltips, mouse, and keyboard control. Each of the Swing components knows how to interact with the user and the system in the appropriate manner. These Swing components include JButton, JComboBox, JSlider, JLabel, JColorChooser, JFrame, JApplet, and JPanel.

The Swing package, javax.swing, was first introduced as an unbundled extension to Java in version 1.1. Java 1.2 contained the core Swing package, and that's when people began referring to Java 2. Now, the Swing components are intended to completely replace the corresponding AWT peer components, as they are better (less buggy) and simpler to use. We still use the AWT package for all of the noncomponent features and services it provides.

Heavyweight and Lightweight Components and House Guests   The

AWT components are referred to as **heavyweight components**, and Swing components are referred to as **lightweight components**. AWT components are peer components and rely on the native components on the system. These heavyweight components depend on the target system having what they need to do their jobs. Swing components come equipped with everything they need to perform their job and do not rely on system components. (You may think that we have these two terms, heavyweight and lightweight backwards.)

heavyweight components
AWT components

lightweight components
Swing components

One way to keep the heavyweight and lightweight components straight is to imagine two different types of houseguests. You can think of the AWT component as a heavyweight houseguest who comes to visit your home wearing no clothes and bringing nothing. You have to provide it with clothing, shoes, a toothbrush, food, a bed to sleep in, and furniture on which to sit. A Swing component is a lightweight houseguest. It comes to visit your home fully clothed, bringing its own food, its own microwave, refrigerator, stove for cooking, a bed, and a chair. The Swing "houseguest" brings everything it needs, and you (the host or hostess) do not have to provide it with anything.

As a Java programmer, you should always use Swing components to ensure maximum portability and consistent behavior.

How did Swing get its name?   Sun Microsystems began a project to develop

new components, and the term "Swing" was the code name for this project. The nickname was unofficial, but it stuck, especially since the package name Swing is javax.swing.

3.6
Summary

In Chapter 3, we introduced the basic concept of class hierarchy in Java and saw how classes inherit data and methods from other classes. By using the extends keyword in our class definition line, we are able to have our new class inherit the data and methods from the existing class. This very powerful feature of Java allows us to have our class (referred to as the subclass) inherit the superclass abilities. The program examples shown in this chapter have our new classes extend either JApplet or JFrame. Both JApplet and JFrame provide the windowing capabilities and paint() method so that we can draw graphical items within our programs.

Java applets are programs that run in web browsers. The J2SDK provides the appletviewer program, allowing us to run applet programs. Applets make use of the web browser window and it provides our programs with a place in which to paint graphics and text. Java applets automatically call five different methods. The web browser and applet program interact, and the web browser calls the various methods. Each method has an intended purpose. The methods are called in this order: init(), start(), paint(), stop(), and destroy(). The JVM provides security, by checking Java applet code that a user downloads from the Internet, by running the code through the bytecode verifier. Applets are restricted to run within the web browser and do not have access to the user's computer hard disk and other components. Web browsers may be configured to allow trusted (signed) applets certain access to the computer's resources.

We saw how to write a class constructor method and use the new operator to instantiate an object of our class. The new operator calls the class constructor method. The constructor has the same name as the class. In Chapter 6, we study constructors in depth and will see that its primary job is to perform object initialization tasks. In this chapter, we write some of the program code in the constructor. This technique is adequate for the beginning Java programmer, but there are better techniques—and we will learn them in Chapter 6.

We begin declaring class or instance variables in Chapter 3 programs. Class variables are declared after the class definition line and above any methods. These variables are seen and used by all of the methods in the class. We also introduce the marcsPause() method. This method allows us to pause our program by passing it the number of milliseconds.

Lastly, we see that Java has two types of graphical user interface component packages, the Abstrast Windowing Toolkit (AWT) and Swing. The AWT components are part of the original Java language, and these components rely on the platform's native graphical controls. This reliance proved troublesome, as not all operating systems had every control with exact implementation. The Swing package contains user interface controls that are complete and know how to interact with the user correctly. Java programmers should use Swing components for all of their user interface controls.

REVIEW QUESTIONS AND PROBLEMS

Short Answer

1. What class is the root of all Java classes?

2. What is the difference between System.exit(0) and System.exit(1)?

3. Why do we have to import javax.swing.JOptionPane but we do not have to import java.lang.Object?

4. If you wish to use a String object in your program, what package do you have to import?

5. Is it possible to import an entire package? If it is possible, how do you write the import statement?

6. Can we extend two different classes at the same time in our own class, such as public class MyClass extends Class1 extends Class2?

7. Why is it necessary do make a DecimalFormat object in order to have its help in writing formatted output?

8. Why is it important for the programmer to examine the "Methods inherited from" section for a class in the Java documentation?

9. What are two major differences between Java applets and Java applications?

10. Name five methods that are in applets. What is the order in which they are called?

11. Is it necessary for the Java programmer to include all five applet methods in his or her program? Explain.

12. What is the relationship between the *.class* file, the *.html* file, and the appletviewer program?

13. Why are applets considered safe to download from the Internet? Why do web browsers make applets play in the sandbox?

14. Which is a better user interface component to use in your program, a heavy-weight component or lightweight component?

15. Applets have the paint() method. How is it possible that classes that are extended from JFrame have paint() too?

16. When a paint() method is passed a Graphics object, what does that object "know?"

17. Does the HTML file have to be named the same as the class file it is referencing? Explain.

18. How is the class hierarchy the same for JFrame and JApplet? How is it different?

19. Describe how the execution of a Java applet begins. Describe the execution startup for a Java application.

20. Is it possible to have a main() method in a Java applet (i.e., the class extends JApplet) and run it using the java command?

21. Is it possible to have a start() and init() method in a class that extends Object (not JApplet) and runs it using the appletviewer program?

22. What is the purpose of using the setDefaultCloseOperation() method? Where do we call this method?

23. What is the purpose of the setSize() method?

24. In Java applications that extend Jframe, we use the method show(). What does this method accomplish for us?

25. In the WriteYourNameFrame program (Program 3-10) what do we see if we minimize and restore the window? Why do we see this activity?

Debugging Problems—Compiler Errors

Problems 26–30: Identify the compiler errors and state what is wrong with the code.

26.

```
//File: TheApplet.java
import javax.*;
import java.awt.Graphics;

public class TheApplet extends JApplet
{
      public paint(Graphics g)
      {
            theObject.drawString("Hi there", 25,25);
      }
}
```

27.

```
//File: GreenBox.java
import javax.swing.JApplet;
import javax.awt.*;

public class GreenBox extends Japplet
{
      int width,height;
      public start()
      {
            width = 10;
            height = 20;
      }
      public paint()
      {
            g.drawRect(0,0,w,h);
      }
}
```

28.

```java
//File: ThreeOvals.java
import java.awt.Color;
import java.swing.JFrame;

public class ThreeOvals extends JFrame
{
      public void ThreeOvals()
      {
            setSize(500);
            show();
      }
      public show(Graphics g)
      {
            g.drawOval(0,0,width,height);
      }
      public static void main(String args[] )
      {
            ThreeOvals 3ovals = new ThreeOvals();
            3ovals.setDefaultCloseOperation();
      }
}
```

29.

```java
//File:  BlueBox.java

public class BlueBox extends JFrame
{
      public static void main( String args[] )
      {
            BlueBox bb = new BlueBox();
            SystemExit(0)
      }
      public BlueBox()
      {
            setSize(250,250);
            show();
      }
      public void paint(Graphics g)
      {
            g.setColor(BLUE);
            g.drawRect(0,0,50,100);
      }
}
```

30.

```
//File: ThreeBears.html
import java.awt.graphics;
import javax.swing.JApplet;

public class BirdApplet extends JApplet
{
        String birdsong;

        public void start()
        {
                birdsong = "Chirp chirp";
        }

        public void paint(Graphics bird)
        {
                bird.drawString(birdsong, 20,20);
                bird.drawImage("sparrows.jpg", 40,40, 256, 256, this);
        }
}
```

Job Hierarchy Problems

31. Describe an inheritance tree (to four levels), beginning with Employee and ending with HandSurgeon (a doctor specializing in hand surgery). Each level of the tree should have at least one data characteristic (something that individual must know) and two job tasks.

32. Describe an inheritance tree (to four levels) beginning with an Animal and trace to a specific animal. One example is Animal, Reptile, Snake, Diamondback Rattlesnake. Each level should include one characteristic and two behaviors.

33. Write two data items and two actions performed by a Student. Now consider two types of Students—Community College Programming Student and a University Medical Student. Write two more data items and two actions performed by a Community College Programming Student. Write a third set of data items and actions for a University Medical Student.

34. Describe an inheritance tree beginning with a Mechanic (someone who works on engines). Extend it three levels, ending with a very specialized type of mechanic. For example, Mechanic, Airplane Engine Mechanic, Jet Engine Mechanic, and Space Shuttle Main Engine Mechanic.

Programming Problems

35. Write a Java applet that draws three different graphics items in an applet window. Select various items from the Graphics class. Each item should be a different color and have a label below it. Show your name in the status bar of the Applet window.

36. Write a Java applet that writes the system time and date into the window in four different locations, in four different colors. (Hint: see the MovieStartsInTen program in Chapter 2.) Your program should wait one second between each write. Use the marcsPause() method to pause your program.

37. Rewrite the program described in Problem 36 as an application. Design your program in a similar manner to HelloFrame and DrawShapesApp, so that it has a main(), constructor, and paint() method as well as marcsPause(). Place a title in the window's title bar.

38. Write an applet that asks the user to enter his or her name in the init() method. In the paint() method, write the user's name in lower case letters in the top half of the window and upper case letters in the lower half of the window. Investigate the methods in JApplet and determine the width and height of the applet window. Use these numbers to center your user's name in the top and bottom halves of the window. You may guess the approximate length of the name by using the number of characters in the name. Although you know the initial size of your applet window by setting it in the HTML file, the user's name should be centered correctly if the applet window is resized. Hint: there are getWidth(), getHeight(), and setSize() methods inherited from the Component class.

39. Revisit the SystemInfo program in Chapter 2 (Program 2-20). Build an application that extends JFrame, and perform the same steps in your constructor method as we did in Program 2-20 on page 96. Do you see any differences in the available memory when we use a window as opposed to simply writing information to the MS-DOS Prompt window?

40. Revisit the CoconutEstimator program in Chapter 2, Problem 28. Build either an applet or an application that asks the user to enter the total number of pieces of candy, the number with nuts, with coconut, and with caramel filling. In the paint() method, draw a pie chart using different colors to indicate candy piece percentages. Include color coded labels showing the candy type with percentages written to one decimal place.

3

4

Control Statements and Loops

KEY TERMS AND CONCEPTS

associativity
binary operator
branch
conditional statement
evaluate a condition
logical operator
loop
loop altering statement
loop index
nested statements
operand
precedence of operations
relational operator
ternary operator
unary operator

KEYWORDS AND OPERATORS

break, case, continue, default, do
  else, for, if, switch, while
logical operators && || !
relational operators >= > <= <
relational operators ==   !=
conditional operator ? :

CHAPTER OBJECTIVES

Present the concept of program control and logic statements.

Illustrate relational and logical operators in Java.

Demonstrate conditional branching statements using *if* and *switch* statements.

Compare similarities between *if* and *switch* statements.

Describe the three loop controls: the *for*, *while*, and *do while* statements.

Present many common errors that programmers make while coding control statements, and show the associated compiler errors, if possible.

Show the correct and incorrect way to perform numeric and string comparisons.

Present several sample programs illustrating program control and logic and incorporating drawing graphics in applet and frame windows.

Decisions, Decisions!

Any computer programming language must provide methods for checking conditions and making decisions in the program. We need the tools to know if A is greater than B, N is the same as P, Q is equal to R, or S is equal to T. We need the ability to perform statements if certain conditions are met. For example, if the program asks the user to select a menu item, one through five, we need to be able to determine which item was selected and to perform the correct statements. We also need our program to rerun portions of the program. Rerunning portions of a program requires the code to loop back to a statement and repeat certain lines of code. The Java language provides efficient tools for performing these tasks. A summary of Java evaluation and loop tools is shown in Table 4-1.

TABLE 4-1
Summary of Java Evaluation and Loop Tools

Task	Example	Tool
Evaluating a condition	Is A less than B? Is N greater than O and Q the same as P?	relational and logical operators
Branch to correct statements	Pick a menu item and execute the correct statements associated with that menu option.	if statements switch statements
Repeat or loop	Write out "hello world" ten times.	while loop for loop do while loop

4.1
Relational and Logical Operators

In Java, **relational** and **logical operators** are used to evaluate conditional statements. A **conditional statement** is used to determine the state (or states) of a variable (or variables). The result of the evaluation is true or false. Relational operators are shown in Table 4-2; logical operators are shown in Table 4-3. Relational and two logical operators (AND, &&, and OR, ||) are binary; a **binary operator** expects two values or **operands**. The NOT operator (!) is a unary operator; a **unary operator** requires only a single operand. See Figure 4-1.

Evaluating Expressions and Precedence of Operators

It is possible to write conditional statements using both relational and logical operators. Table 4-4 illustrates several combinations of these type of statements. When a programmer writes relational and logical statements in Java (as in arithmetic operations), the precedence and associativity of operators dictate the order of the operations. Table 4-5 presents the precedence and associativity for several operators. (Refer to the section in Chapter 2 that introduces precedence of operations.) The math operator precedence is higher than that for relational operators, and the relational operator precedence is higher than that for logical operators. These facts are important when writing conditional statements.

When relational and logical operators are used in an expression, the end result is either true or false. Figure 4-2 presents two examples using both relational

▌ **TABLE 4-2**

Relational Operators in Java

Relational Operator	Tests For	Example
>	greater than	A > B Is A greater than B?
>=	greater than or equal to	A >= B Is A greater than or equal to B?
<	less than	A < B Is A less than B?
<=	less than or equal to	A <= B Is A less than or equal to B?
==	same as	A == B Is A same as B?
!=	not the same as	A != B Is A not the same as B?

TABLE 4-3

Logical Operators in Java. Logical operators must have boolean operands.
You can not use a Java logical operator on an integer value.

Logical operators	Tests For	Example
&&	AND	Condition A && Condition B Return true if both Condition A and Condition B are true, otherwise return false.
||	OR	Condition A || Condition B Return true if either Condition A or Condition B is true or if both Condition A and Condition B are true.
!	NOT	!A If Condition A is true, the result of this operation is false. If Condition A is false, the result of this operation is true.

4

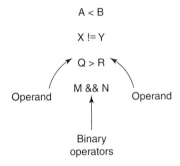

Figure 4-1
Binary and unary operator examples in Java.

The NOT operator is unary and requires one operand.

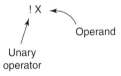

Testing For	Example
Is A greater than B and C greater than D?	(A > B && C > D)
Is E greater than H or E greater than D?	(E > H || E > D)
Is A the same as M or the same as Q?	(A == M || A == Q)
Is B greater than C and C less than E?	(B > C && C < E)

TABLE 4-4
Examples of Relational and Logical Statements.

TABLE 4-5

Java Operators with Arithmetic (Priority 12, 11), Relational (9, 8), and Logical Operators (14, 4, 3).

Priority	Symbol	Purpose	Associativity
16	( ) [ ] .	parentheses, array subscript, and member selection	left to right
16	var++ var−−	post-fix increment/decrement	right to left
15	++ var −−var	pre-fix increment/decrement	left to right
14	~	flip the bits of an integer	right to left
14	**!**	**logical NOT (reverse a boolean)**	**right to left**
14	−var +var	arithmetic plus, negation (These are not addition, subtraction.)	right to left
13	(type name)	creation or casting operator	right to left
12	*** / %**	**multiply, divide, modulus**	**left to right**
11	**+ −**	**addition, subtraction**	**left to right**
10	<< >> >>>	left and right bitwise shift	left to right
9	instanceof < <= > >=	relational operators	left to right
8	== !=	same as, not the same as	left to right
7	&	bitwise AND	left to right
6	^	bitwise exclusive or	left to right
5	|	bitwise inclusive or	left to right
4	**&&**	**conditional AND**	**left to right**
3	**||**	**conditional OR**	**left to right**
2	**? :**	**ternary conditional operator**	**right to left**
1	= *= /= %= += −= <<= >>= >>>= &= ^= |=	assignment operators	right to left

and logical operators. It shows the manner in which Java comes to a resultant value. Remember that Java evaluates only one operator at a time.

Java's relational and logical operators return a boolean data type with a value of either true or false. This differs from other languages that evaluate to an integer-based scheme, 1 or 0. Figure 4-2 presents two examples using both relational and logical operators. It shows the manner in which Java comes to a resultant value. Remember, Java evaluates only one operator at a time.

Example 1

$$5 + 8 < 14 - 2 \;||\; 6 > 3$$

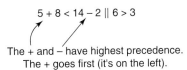

The + and − have highest precedence.
The + goes first (it's on the left).

$$13 < 14 - 2 \;||\; 6 > 3$$

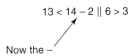

Now the −

$$13 < 12 \;||\; 6 > 3$$

Next the <

$$\text{false} \;||\; 6 > 3$$

Now the >

$$\text{false} \;||\; \text{true}$$

Last, the OR operator

$$\text{true}$$

Example 2

$$6 + 7 >= 12 \;\&\&\; (3+4) > 2 * 4$$

The ( ) is primary and will be performed first. 3 and 4 are added.

$$6 + 7 >= 12 \;\&\&\; 7 > 2 * 4$$

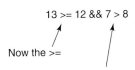

Multiplication now has the highest precedence.

$$6 + 7 >= 12 \;\&\&\; 7 > 8$$

The addition is performed next.

$$13 >= 12 \;\&\&\; 7 > 8$$

Now the >=

And then the >

$$\text{true} \;\&\&\; \text{false}$$

Last, but not least, the AND

$$\text{false}$$

4

Figure 4-2
Examples using relational and logical operators in Java.

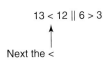

▌4.2
if Statements

Java provides a flexible **if statement** structure allowing the programmer to build almost any series of conditional statements. The if statement is typically based on a relational and/or logical expression that evaluates to a boolean value of true or false. The general form of the if statement is as follows:

if statement
performs statements if the condition is true

```
if(Condition)
{
      //These statements are executed if Condition is true and
      //skipped if Condition is false.
}
```

If the condition is true, the statements within the braces are executed. If the condition is false, the statements are skipped. For example, in the code below, if *a* is greater than *b* then the condition is true and the phrase "Hello from Java" is written to the command window. See Figure 4-3 for an illustration.

```
int a, b;
//obtain values for a and b
if(a > b)
{
        System.out.println("Hello from Java");
}
```

The braces do not have to be on new lines. The following format is also correct.

```
if(Condition){
        //statements are executed if Condition is true
}
```

If there is only one statement to be executed, the braces are not required. The previous sample of code can be written like this:

```
int a, b;
//obtain values for a and b
if(a > b)System.out.println("Hello from Java");
```

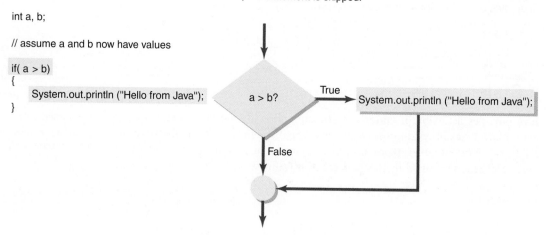

The condition is evaluated and if it is true, the println( ) statement is executed.
If it is false, the statement is skipped.

```
int a, b;

// assume a and b now have values

if( a > b)
{
    System.out.println ("Hello from Java");
}
```

a > b?   True   System.out.println ("Hello from Java");

False

Figure 4-3
if statement

Chapter 4 ▮ Control Statements and Loops

or like this:

```
int a, b;
//obtain values for a and b
if(a > b)
        System.out.println("Hello from Java");
```

The { } braces are needed if more than one statement is to be executed, such as:

```
int a, b;
//obtain values for a and b
if(a > b)
{
        System.out.println("Hello from Java");
        System.out.println("I love the Java language!");
}
```

The next lines of code show an if statement where the angle is checked to see if it is between 0 and 90 degrees. If the angle is within this range, we convert the angle to radians. If the angle is outside this range, the equation is skipped.

```
double angle, radians;
//obtain a value for angle
if(angle >= 0.0 && angle <= 90.0)
{
        radians = angle * Math.PI/180.0;
}
```

if else Statements

For situations where something must be done if the condition is true and something else if the condition is false, Java provides **if else statements**. Here is the general format:

if else statements
performs one set of statements if the condition is true, but performs a second set of statements if the statement is false

```
if(Condition)
{
        //these statements done if Condition is true
}
else
{
        //these statements done if Condition is false
}
```

Once again, the { } braces are needed if more than one statement is to be executed. If only one statement is executed, the braces are not needed, as shown here:

```
if(Condition)   System.out.println("The condition is true.");
else   System.out.println("The condition is false.");
```

Another example is:

```java
int age;
boolean bAdult;
//obtain a value for the age, and set adult status

if(age >= 18) bAdult = true;
else bAdult = false;
```

The statement line can be on the next line, like this:

```java
int age;
boolean bAdult;
//obtain a value for the age, and set adult status

if(age >= 18)
        bAdult = true;
else
        bAdult = false;
```

In this next example, we are checking whether a number is positive or not positive (zero or negative). We only need to check to see if the number is positive, because any values that are zero or negative will fall into the else statement. Figure 4-4 shows the flow of the program statements.

```java
int number;
//obtain a value for number
if(number > 0)
{
        System.out.println("The number is positive!");
}
else
{
        System.out.println("The number is zero or negative!");
}
```

Because we are executing only one statement for each condition, this code can also be written as:

```java
if(number > 0)
        System.out.println("The number is positive!");
else
        System.out.println("The number is zero or negative!");
```

It is recommended strongly that Java programmers always use braces to enclose statements in his or her if else statements. It is permissible not to use the braces in the case where an if statement has a single statement. For any compound if else or if else if format, always use the braces!

The condition is evaluated and if it is true, the first statements are executed.
If it is false, the second statements are executed.

int number;

// assume number now has a value

if(number > 0)
{
    // first set
    System.out.println ("The number is positive.");
}
else
{
    // second set
    System.out.println ("The number is zero or negative.");
}

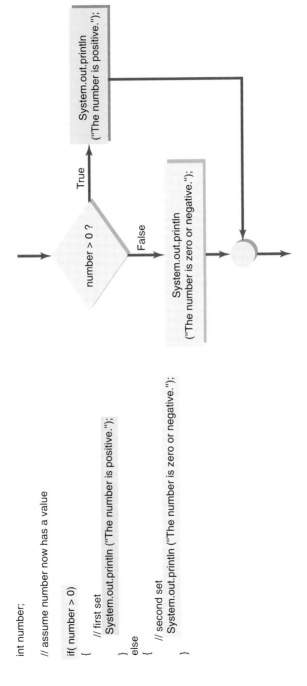

Figure 4-4
if else statements.

4

Troubleshooting: Use Braces with if Statements

A veteran programmer tells the story of spending more than a day trying to find a bug in his optical design code. The error was due to missing braces in an if else statement, which had multiple lines in the else portion. The code in his program had been written like this:

```
//Actual manner in which the code was written.
//program obtains a value for the integer opticsFlag;
if(opticsFlag == 1)
        some_optics_statement;              //Line 1
else
        a_different_optics_statement;  //Line 2
        a_third_optics_statement;      //Line 3
```

In this code, if the opticsFlag is set to 1, he wants Line 1 to be performed. If the opticsFlag is anything else, he wants to skip Line 1 and execute Lines 2 and 3. Best intentions, but in fact, this is how Java interprets the code:

```
// How it is executed in Java
if(opticsFlag == 1)
        some_optics_statement;              //Line 1
else
        a_different_optics_statement;  //Line 2

a_third_optics_statement;        //Line 3
```

This code worked well when the opticsFlag was not 1, because Line 1 was skipped and Lines 2 and 3 were executed as planned. The problem occurred when the opticsFlag was 1. Here, Line 1 was executed, then the else and Line 2 were skipped, but Line 3 was executed. (Remember, when no braces are used, Java is built to assume that just the single statement is associated with the if else statements.) By accidentally executing Line 3 when the flag was true, his program was fouled up. He had unhappy users and it cost him a day to track down the bug! The code should have been written like this:

```
if(opticsFlag == 1)
{
        some_optics_statement;   //Line 1
}
else
{
        a_different_optics_statement;  //Line 2
        a_second_optics_statement;     //Line 3
}
```

if, else if, else Statements

The Java programmer can cascade a series of condition-checking if statements by incorporating the else if structure. The basic format of the **if else if statements** are:

```
if(Condition1)
{
        //Condition 1 statements
}
else if(Condition2)
{
        //Condition 2 statements
}
else
{
        // else statements
}
// Rest of Program statements
```

When executed, the program checks the first condition and, if it is true, executes the Condition1 statements that follow the if statement. Once these statements are completed, program control jumps to the Rest of Program statements. If Condition1 is false, then Condition2 is checked. If Condition2 is true, Condition2 statements are performed and then the control jumps to the Rest of Program statements. Once the program has found one true condition and executes the statements for that condition, program control jumps to the statement at the end of the if block. If none of the conditions are true, the statements in the else are performed. The programmer may cascade many if else series of checks as shown in Figure 4-5 on page 162.

Note the following about the else statement: 1) It is not necessary to have an else statement; you may have an if statement, an if else if set of statements, or series of if, else if, else if statements. 2) You may only have one else statement in an if block.

In this sample code, we check to see if a number is positive, zero, or negative. If the number is not positive and it is not zero, it has to be negative.

```
if(number > 0)
{
        System.out.println("It is positive!");
}
else if(number == 0)
{
        System.out.println("It is zero!");
}
else
{
        System.out.println("It is negative!");
}
```

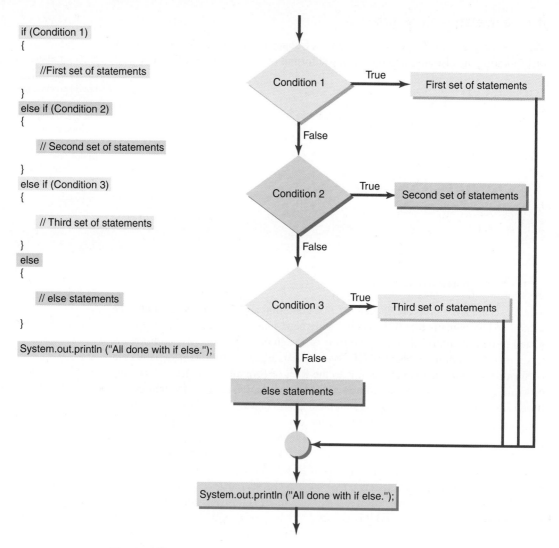

```
if (Condition 1)
{

    //First set of statements

}
else if (Condition 2)
{

    // Second set of statements

}
else if (Condition 3)
{

    // Third set of statements

}
else
{

    // else statements

}

System.out.println ("All done with if else.");
```

Figure 4-5
Cascading if else statement.

Inefficient Programming Techniques

Beginning programmers sometimes forget that the program control falls into the else statements if none of the conditions are true. He or she makes extra work by either checking all the possible cases or checking each case individually. The following two examples have the same programmatic results, but incorporate unnecessary checking.

```
//Example: check if a number is positive, zero or negative.
//This uses an extra (unnecessary) else if statement.
if(number > 0)
{
     System.out.println("It is positive!");
}
else if(number == 0)
{
     System.out.println("It is zero!");
}
else if (number < 0)       //This else if check is not necessary.
{          //We can just use else since only time we get here is
           //if the number is negative.
     System.out.println("It is negative!");
}
```

A second example uses three independent if statements. It is the most inefficient way to write software, because it guarantees that the program executes all three if statements. If the number is positive, there is no need to perform the zero or negative checks!

```
//Example:  check if a number is positive, zero or negative.
//Uses three separate if's when a set of if-else's will do the trick!
if(number > 0)
{
     System.out.println("It is positive!");
}
if(number == 0)
{
     System.out.println("It is zero!");
}
if (number < 0)
{
     System.out.println("It is negative!");
}
```

if else Example, This Old Man Program

We can use this children's rhyme and Java together to illustrate how a program can use a set of if else statements efficiently and perform error checking as well. We see the first four verses of the famous "This Old Man" nursery rhyme. In case you have forgotten it, here it is again:

This old man, he played one, he played knick-knack with his thumb.*
This old man, he played two, he played knick-knack with my shoe.*
This old man, he played three, he played knick-knack on my knee.*
This old man, he played four, he played knick-knack at my door.*
*Chorus: With a knick-knack, paddy whack, give the dog a bone; this old man
    came rolling home.

Program 4-1 asks the user to enter an integer. If it is between one and four, we write out the appropriate knick-knack information. If the user enters any other number, we write an error message. Using an if, else if, else block of statements allows invalid entries to be "caught" or "trapped" in the else condition. If we code this with a series of individual if statements, we need to do separate checking for any values less than one and greater than four. By using the if, else if, else format, error trapping is easy. Figure 4-6 illustrates this program's message boxes.

```java
1    //Program 4-1 Knick-Knack Example Program with if else
2    //File:  KnickKnack.java
3
4    import javax.swing.JOptionPane;
5
6    public class KnickKnack
7    {
8        public static void main(String args[])
9        {
10            int number = 0;
11            String input, saying, start = "\nHe played knick-knack";
12            String titleIn = "Welcome to the Knick Knack Program";
13            String titleOut = "You picked the number ";
14            input = JOptionPane.showInputDialog(null,
15            "\nPlease enter an integer for knick-knacking.",
16            titleIn, JOptionPane.QUESTION_MESSAGE);
17
18            //convert input to Integer
19            number = Integer.parseInt(input);
20
21            if(number == 1) //write out knick-knack information
22            {
23                saying = start + " with his thumb.";
24            }
25            else if(number == 2)
26            {
27                saying = start + " with my shoe. ";
28            }
```

```
29              else if(number == 3)
30              {
31                      saying = start + " on my knee. ";
32              }
33              else if(number == 4)
34              {
35                      saying = start + " at my door. ";
36              }
37              else            //error check, any other number is not valid
38              {
39                      saying = start + "\nWhoa! He doesn't play knick-knack there!";
40              }
41
42              titleOut = titleOut + number;
43              JOptionPane.showMessageDialog(null, saying, titleOut,
44                      JOptionPane.INFORMATION_MESSAGE);
45
46              System.exit(0);
47      }
48  }
```

(a)   (b)

Figure 4-6
a and b) Message boxes from the Knick Knack program.

Nested if else statements

It is possible to **nest** if statements within if statements. "Nested if statements" simply means to have an if statement as part of the code inside the portions of an if statement. Confused? Here is what we mean:

nested statements
one set of statements located inside another set of statements

```
if( Condition)                 // first condition
{
    if( Another Condition )    // this is the nested if statement
    {
        //  statements
    }
    // more statements
}
```

In Java, it is possible to nest most types of statements. The code portion below shows the statements to determine if a number is positive. If the number is positive, we report the value of the number. If the number is not positive (that is, zero or negative) we report that as well.

```java
int number;
//obtain a value for number

if(number > 0)                      //positive number
{
        System.out.println("The number is positive");
        if(number <= 10)
        {
                System.out.println(" and it is between 1 and 10.");
        }
        else
        {
                System.out.println(" and it is greater than 10.");
        }
}
else
{
        System.out.println("The number is zero or negative.");
}
```

The ? : Operator Set

ternary conditional operator

an operator that requires three operands and that works similarly to an if else block of code

The Java language has a ? : operator called a **ternary conditional operator**. A ternary conditional operator requires three operands. This ? : operator set has similar functionality to the if, else statement with some restrictions. Let's review an if, else example:

```java
int moon, star;
//obtain a value for stars

if(star > 100)
        moon = 200;      //if star is greater than 100, assign 200 to moon
else
        moon = 0;        //if star is not greater than 100, assign 0 to moon
```

In this example, the value of star is checked to see if it is greater than 100. If it is greater than 100, moon is assigned the value of 200, or else moon is assigned a value of 0. The ? : operator set works in a similar manner. The format of the ? : operator is this:

```java
Expression1 ? Expression2 : Expression3;
```

Expression1 is evaluated. If it is true Expression2 is assigned in Expression1. If Expression1 is false, Expression3 is assigned. The following statements are equivalent to the if, else statements shown previously.

```
int moon, star;

//obtain a value for star
moon = star > 100 ? 200  : 0;
```

A second example with the ? : operator illustrates a quick way to set a value to either true or false. First, let's show the code in an if, else format. If the value for lightFound is true, we set the value lightsOn to true. In other words, if we found a light, turn it on.

```
boolean lightsOn, lightFound;
//obtain a value for lightFound

if(lightFound == true)
        lightsOn = true;
else
        lightsOn = false;
```

The ternary operator provides a means to perform this check and assignment in one line.

```
boolean lightsOn, lightFound;
//obtain a value for lightFound

lightsOn = lightFound ? true : false;
```

One last example of how this operator works illustrates how String assignments can be performed. First, we examine the code using if, else statements.

```
String emotion;
int testScore;
//obtain your score for your first Java test

if(testScore >= 90)
        emotion = "I am very happy!";
else
        emotion = "I must study harder!";
```

The ternary operator provides a means to perform this check and assignment in one line.

```
String emotion;
int testScore;
//obtain your score for your first Java test
emotion = testScore >= 90 ? "I am very happy" : "I must study harder!";
```

The ? : operator set allows the programmer to write an if, else condition and assignment statements in a single line of code; however, it does not lend itself to producing code that is easily read and understood, nor does it allow for a more complicated if, else if, else if, type of coding. The beginning Java student may find it easier to write conditional statements using the standard if, else coding technique.

4.3
switch Statement

switch statement

evaluates an expression or variable and performs the statements that correspond to the specific case statement. Performs the default statement if none of the cases match the variable or expression value

The **switch statement** provides another way for performing a series of condition checks and statement executions. It is ideally suited for checking conditions where the value of an integer or character dictates which statements are to be performed. The basic form of the switch:

```
switch(variable)
{
        case value1:
                //statements 1
                break;
        case value2:
                //statements 2
                break;
        default:
                //statement n
}
```

In a switch statement, the value of the variable is examined. If the value is one of the values in the case statements, the associated statements are performed. The break statement causes the program to then jump to the close brace. If none of the case values are found, the statements in the default statement are performed. It is also possible to evaluate an expression instead of placing a variable in the switch statement.

Switch Examples

Knick Knack Program   The Knick-knack program can be rewritten, using a switch statement instead of the if statements. Refer to Program 4-2 to see the switch block of code. Figure 4-7 shows the message boxes from this program. We entered a value of 7, which is not a valid Knick-knack number. Program control falls to the default case and builds the "no-play" message.

```
1    //Program 4-2 Knick-Knack Example Program with Switch
2    //File:  KnickSwitch.java
3
4    import javax.swing.JOptionPane;
5
6    public class KnickSwitch
7    {
8          public static void main(String args[])
9          {
10               int number = 0;
11
12               String input, saying, start = "\nHe played knick-knack";
13               String titleIn = "Welcome to the Switch Knick Knack Program";
14               String titleOut = "You picked the number ";
15               input = JOptionPane.showInputDialog(null,
16               "\nPlease enter an integer for knick-knacking.",
17               titleIn, JOptionPane.QUESTION_MESSAGE);
18
19          //convert input to Integer
20               number = Integer.parseInt(input);
21
22               switch(number) //write out knick-knack information
23               {
24               case 1:
25                     saying = start + " with his thumb.";
26                     break;
27               case 2:
28                     saying = start + " with my shoe. ";
29                     break;
30               case 3:
31                     saying = start + " on my knee. ";
32                     break;
33               case 4:
34                     saying = start + " at my door. ";
35                     break;
36               default:  // error check, any other number is not valid
37                     saying = start + "\nWhoa! He doesn't play knick-knack there!";
38               }
39
40               titleOut = titleOut + number;
41               JOptionPane.showMessageDialog(null, saying, titleOut,
42                     JOptionPane.INFORMATION_MESSAGE);
43
44               System.exit(0);
45          }
46   }
```

4

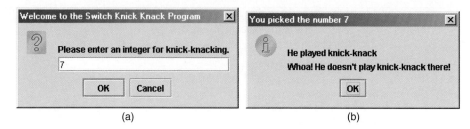

(a)   (b)

Figure 4-7
a and b) Message boxes from the Switch Knick Knack program. The user entered a value of 7, which falls into the default block of code.

Famous Year Program   Beginning programmers often think that the case blocks in a switch statement must begin with the number 1 and proceed in numeric order. This is not true. The case statement may be any integer value. Program 4-3 asks the user to enter a year and the FamousYear program checks to see if any famous events occurred in that year. The resulting information is written into a message box. See Figure 4-8.

```
1    //Program 4-3 Famous Year Program with Switch
2    //File:  FamousYear.java
3
4    import javax.swing.JOptionPane;
5    public class FamousYear
6    {
7         public static void main(String args[])
8         {
9              int year = 0;
10
11             String input, answer, detail;
12             String titleIn = "Welcome to the Famous Year Program";
13             String titleOut = "Famous Year Results ";
14
15             input = JOptionPane.showInputDialog(null,
16             "\nPlease enter your favorite year.",
17             titleIn, JOptionPane.QUESTION_MESSAGE);
18
19      //convert input to Integer
20             year = Integer.parseInt(input);
21
22             switch(year)          //check for a famous year
23             {
```

                            Chapter 4 ▌ Control Statements and Loops

```
24          case 1492:
25                  detail = "\n Columbus sailing the ocean blue!";
26                  break;
27          case 1776:
28                  detail = "\n a convention in Philadelphia!";
29                  break;
30          case 1969:
31                  detail = "\n Neil walking on the moon!";
32                  break;
33          default:
34                  detail = "\n...nothing famous"
35                  +" happened in that year.";
36          }
37
38          answer = "\nYour favorite year is " + year
39                  + " and is famous for " + detail;
40          JOptionPane.showMessageDialog(null, answer, titleOut,
41                  JOptionPane.INFORMATION_MESSAGE);
42          System.exit(0);
43
44      }
45  }
```

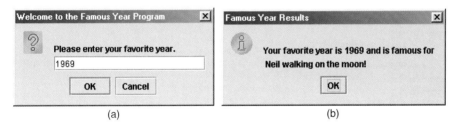

(a)   (b)

Figure 4-8
a and b) Message boxes from the Famous Year program. This program incorporates
a switch for its control statements.

Names and Fruit Program Switch blocks have the ability to use individual
characters, such as letters of the alphabet, in their case statements. But switches are
not able to use String variables, nor are they able to perform complicated logic.
Program 4-4 is a silly program that demonstrates a switch that uses individual letters in the case statements. In this program, the user is asked to enter his or her first
name. The first letter of the name is obtained by using String's charAt() method,
and is then used in the case statements to select a fruit that begins with this letter.
Figure 4-9 illustrates the program's results.

```
1    //Program 4-4 Characters and Switch Statements
2    //File:  NamesAndFruit.java
3
4    import javax.swing.JOptionPane;
5
6    public class NamesAndFruit
7    {
8          public static void main(String args[])
9          {
10               String inputName, fruitType ;
11               String titleIn = "Names and Fruit Program";
12               String titleOut = "The switch checked the letter: ";
13
14               inputName = JOptionPane.showInputDialog(null,
15               "\nPlease enter your first name.",
16               titleIn, JOptionPane.QUESTION_MESSAGE);
17
18               char inputLetter = inputName.charAt(0);
19
20               switch(inputLetter)
21               {
22               case 'b':
23               case 'B':
24                     fruitType = "Bananas";
25                     break;
26               case 'a':
27               case 'A':
28                     fruitType = "Apples";
29                     break;
30               case 'm':
31               case 'M':
32                     fruitType = "Mangos";
33                     break;
34               default:
35                     fruitType = "???";
36               }
37
38               //Here we use the += operator instead of
39               //titleOut = titleOut + inputLetter;
40
41               titleOut += inputLetter;
42
43               fruitType += " begins with your first letter,   "
44                     + inputName;
45               JOptionPane.showMessageDialog(null, fruitType, titleOut,
```

```
46                    JOptionPane.INFORMATION_MESSAGE);
47               System.exit(0);
48          }
49    }
```

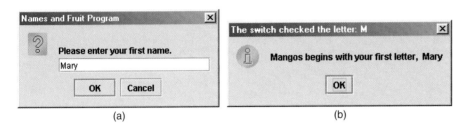

(a)   (b)

Figure 4-9
a and b) Message boxes from the Names and Fruit program. This program uses a
switch statement that checks the first letter of the user's name to determine which
case statements to perform.

Troubleshooting: Don't Forget to break your switch!

Do not forget to include the break statement in the case block—a common beginner's mistake! If the programmer forgets the break statements, the program
continues executing the case statements without breaking out of the switch. For
example, we slightly modify Program 4-2 by using a single string to accumulate the
knick-knack information. (In Program 4-2 we use two strings for this purpose.)
Here, we forget the break statements and the user entered a 2. How does this code
execute? What will we see in the "saying" string? Figure 4-10 shows the results.

```
int number;
//assume the user entered a 2
String saying, "\nHe played knick-knack";

switch(number) //write out knick-knack information
{
      case 1:
            saying = saying + " with his thumb.";
      case 2:
            saying = saying + " with my shoe ";
      case 3:
            saying = saying + " on my knee. ";
      case 4:
            saying = saying + " at my door. ";
      default:  // error check, any other number is not valid
            saying = saying + "\nWhoa! He doesn't play knick-knack there!";
}
```

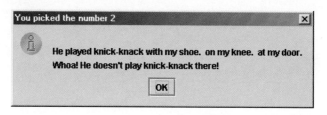

Figure 4-10
The results of a switch statement without breaks. Forgetting the break statement in the switch block results in all the statements from case 2 to the default being executed.

4.4
Loops In General

loop

series of Java statements that enable the program to repeat line(s) of code until a certain condition is met

A **loop** is a fundamental tool for all programming languages. It involves the ability to have the program repeat or "loop-over" statements. This iterative process may be set up so that the loop is executed a predetermined number of times or until a certain condition is met. For example, a program that calculates yearly totals for utilities performs calculations for the twelve months of the year, whereas a program that sets a thermostat needs to continue checking a temperature until a certain temperature is met and the system is turned on or off.

The Java language provides three techniques to perform loops: the *for* loop, the *while* loop, and the *do while* loop. All loops in Java have either a loop index, counter variable, or stopping variable, and the following steps must be taken:

initial assignment

sets the loop counter or stopping variable to a known value

1. An **initial assignment** is made for the loop counter or stopping variable,

2. A **loop condition** is stated so that when it is true, it will cause the loop to be executed, and when it is false, it will cause the program to quit performing the loop.

loop condition

when true loop executes again, false, the loop stops

3. A **loop altering statement** to adjust the counter or stopping variable.

loop altering statement

statement that adjusts the counter or stopping variable

To Brace or Not to Brace?

All three loop formats in Java require open and close braces if the loop is to execute more than one statement. No braces are required if the for and while loops execute only one statement. In fact, the brace requirement is exactly the same as that for the if statements. In this text, we use braces for our loops and encourage our readers to do the same. Using braces with loops and ifs, and indenting code within the braces, makes the code easier to read and aids the programmer in debugging the program.

You Can't Get Out of an Infinite Loop

An infinite loop occurs when a loop starts, but the counter limit or stopping condition is never met. The loop never stops executing. A program starts running, then seems to hang or pause forever when the loop is actually executing. This often requires the programmer to halt the program by pressing the control c combination (Ctrl-c) or closing the window to stop the program execution.

> **Recommendation!** Always be sure that the loop conditions are reasonable, and that once the loop gets started, it will be able to stop.

4.5
for Loop

The **for loop** is a convenient Java statement for use when the programmer knows exactly how many times the statements must be repeated. This loop structure has this format:

```
for(initial condition; condition; increment)
{
      //statements are executed if condition is true
}
```

Here is an example of writing Hello from Java to the command window 10 times:

```
//write Hello from Java 10 times
int i;
for(i = 0; i < 10; ++i)
{
      System.out.println("Hello from Java");
}
```

The for loop, illustrated in Figure 4-11, first executes the initial condition, which is usually an assignment statement. Here, the "i" integer acts as the loop counter or loop index and is assigned a value of zero. The condition is then checked. Is i less than 10? Yes, so the statement(s) within the braces is/are performed. At the end of the statements, the program performs the increment operation (it adds 1 to i) and checks the condition again. If the condition is true, the statements within the braces are executed again. If the condition is false, program control then goes to the statement after the close brace.

for loop
Java loop in the form
for (initial assignment;
condition; increment)
such as
for (i=0; i≤10; ++i)

4

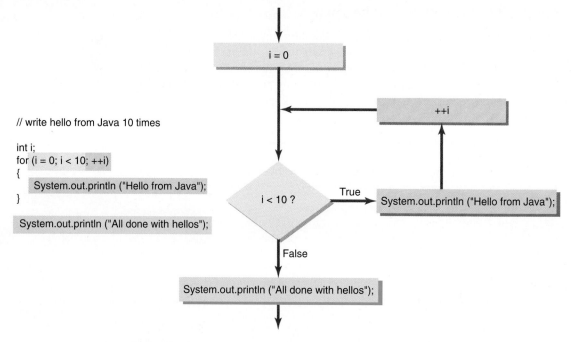

```
// write hello from Java 10 times

int i;
for (i = 0; i < 10; ++i)
{
    System.out.println ("Hello from Java");
}

System.out.println ("All done with hellos");
```

Figure 4-11
for Loop.

It is possible to use the decrement operator to vary the loop variable instead of the increment operator. This loop writes the numbers 15 to 1 to the screen.

```
//write numbers 15 to 1
int ctr;
String sCounter;
for(ctr = 15; ctr > 0; --ctr)
{
        sCounter = Integer.toString(ctr);
        System.out.println(sCounter);
}
```

In for loops, the assignment statement is performed and the condition is checked. If the condition is false, the loop does not execute, as seen here:

```
int t;
for(t = 0; t < 0; ++t)       //this loop will not execute
{
        //loop statements
}
```

The previous examples are by far the most commonly used form of the for loop, but the programmer can use a variety of forms and more complicated logic. The control for the for loop can be based on the value of two or more variables. The example below illustrates this situation:

```
int x,y;
for(x = 0, y = 100; x != 50 && y > 30; ++x, --y)
{
        //statements are executed if condition is true
}
```

The comma can be used to string together the initialization and increment/decrement statements. The condition may use logical operators for complicated conditional checks, but beginning programmers should avoid using this type of programming logic.

Do Not Alter the Loop Index

Programmers should not tinker with the loop counter inside the for loop. This loop structure is built to initialize and to check the condition and increment if the loop statements have been performed. It is poor practice to use creative logic in a for loop. In this example the "*k*" index is altered inside the loop. This results in an infinite loop because *k* never reaches the value of ten.

```
int k;
for(k = 1; k < 10; ++k)        //an infinite loop   BAD EXAMPLE!
{
        //loop statements
        k--;
}
```

for Loop Examples

HowManyHellos   The HowManyHellos program in Program 4-5 asks the user to enter the number of "Hello from Java" phrases he or she wishes to see. The program has a variable for the user's value, as well as a counter for the for loop, which keeps track of the number of times the loop has executed. Figure 4-12 shows the results when the user requested six hellos.

```
1   //Program 4-5 Say Hello with help from a for Loop.
2   //File:  HowManyHellos.java
3
4   import javax.swing.JOptionPane;
```

```
5    public class HowManyHellos
6    {
7         public static void main(String args[])
8         {
9              int counter, howmany = 0;
10             String input, answer= "", hi="\nHello from Java";
11             String title = "How Many Hellos and for Loops";
12                  input = JOptionPane.showInputDialog(null,
13                  "\nHow many hellos would you like to see?",
14                  title,JOptionPane.QUESTION_MESSAGE);
15        //convert input to Integer
16             howmany = Integer.parseInt(input);
17             String titleOut = "You entered :" + input;
18             for(counter = 0; counter < howmany; ++counter)
19             {
20                  answer += hi; // Add hi to whatever answer currently is
21             }
22
23             answer += "\n\nThat's a lot of hellos!";
24
25             JOptionPane.showMessageDialog(null, answer, titleOut,
26             JOptionPane.INFORMATION_MESSAGE);
27             System.exit(0);
28        }
29   }
```

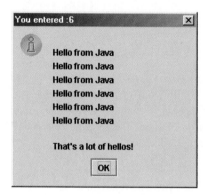

Figure 4-12
The resultant message box for the How Many Hellos program that illustrates the use of a for loop

Writing the Alphabet　In Program 4-6 we write the capital letters of the alphabet on four rows, so that the output looks like this:

```
A    B    C    D    E    F    G
H    I    J    K    L    M    N
O    P    Q    R    S    T    U
V    W    X    Y    Z
```

We can use a for loop and the ASCII character codes to access the letters in a direct way. For example, the letter *A* is stored as a 65, *B* is stored as a 66, etc. In order to write an *A*, we cast a 65 into a character when we assign it to a String variable called *letters*. To write the alphabet on four lines, we use a counter to keep track of how many characters we have written into letters. Once we have written seven characters, we write a newline character into letters and reset the counter. Figure 4-13 shows a message box showing the resultant letters string.

> **Note:**　Java has adopted the Unicode™ Standard for character display, which incorporates the ASCII character set. You may refer to Appendix C: *Bits, Bytes, Hexadecimal Notation, and Unicode™* to see the Unicode and ASCII character sets.

```java
1   //Program 4-6 Write alphabet using for loop
2   //File:  Alphabet.java
3
4   import javax.swing.JOptionPane;
5   public class Alphabet
6   {
7        public static void main(String args[])
8        {
9             int letter_ctr = 0, i;
10            String title = " We're going to write our ABC's!";
11            String letters = "";
12            for(i = 65; i < 91; ++i)    //A = 65, Z = 90
13            {
14                 letters += " " + (char)i;  //add a letter to the string
15                 letter_ctr++;          // incr letter counter
16                 if(letter_ctr == 7) // newline if we've written 7
17                 {
18                      letters += "\n";
19                      letter_ctr = 0;
20                 }
21            }
22
23            letters += "\n Now I've said my ABC's.";
24            letters += "\n Won't you sing along with me?";
```

```
25
26          JOptionPane.showMessageDialog(null, letters, title,
27          JOptionPane.INFORMATION_MESSAGE);
28          System.exit(0);
29      }
30  }
```

Figure 4-13
The alphabet is shown in the message box, a result of using a for loop to build a string of letters.

4.6
while Loop

The **while loop** is needed when the programmer does not know how many times a loop is to be executed. The while loop can also be used to perform a loop an exact number of times. The format of the while loop is shown in the following code and is illustrated in Figure 4-14.

```
//set an initial condition
while(condition)
{
        //these statements executed if condition is true
}
```

The while loop checks the condition, and if it is true, the loop statements are performed. If the condition is false, the statements are skipped.

To avoid becoming stuck in an infinite loop, a more complete form for this loop includes an initialization statement and a loop altering statement, as seen when we write Hello from Java 10 times.

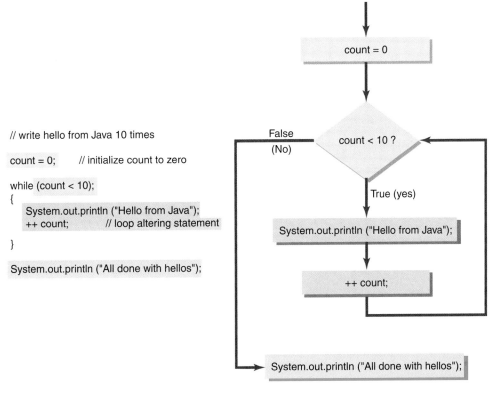

```
// write hello from Java 10 times

count = 0;          // initialize count to zero

while (count < 10);
{
    System.out.println ("Hello from Java");
    ++ count;              // loop altering statement

}

System.out.println ("All done with hellos");
```

Figure 4-14
while Loop

```
int count = 0;              //important to set up initial condition
while(count < 10)           //condition check
{
     System.out.println("Hello from Java");
     count++;               //loop altering statement, incr the counter

}
```

while Loop Examples

In the following examples, we must remember to set up an initial condition for the loop counter. If we forget to assign the initial condition, Java will stop us with a compiler error. Also note that there must be a loop altering statement inside the while loop. If there is not, we find ourselves in an infinite loop.

A Lovely Poem Consider a program that illustrates how the while loop runs until the correct stopping condition is found. Remember, as long as the condition is true, the loop executes. In Program 4-7, we show a poem in a message box

(See Figure 4-15). The user may see the message box again by entering the number 1 in the edit field. As long as the user wants to see it, we keep showing it.

Note that we initialize the answer to the number 1 so that the loop runs the first time. When we show our lovely poem in the message box, the user may enter a 1 to see the box again. Once the user has entered his or her answer, the program then checks the condition in the while statement. As long as the condition is true, the loop executes.

```
1   //Program 4-7 Practice using while loop by writing poem to screen
2   //File:  PoetryWhile.java
3   import javax.swing.JOptionPane;
4   public class PoetryWhile
5   {
6       public static void main(String args[])
7       {
8           int answer = 1;                      //preset answer to start loop
9           String input, title = "While Loops and Poetry";
10          String poem = "Roses are red \nViolets are blue"
11                  "\nI love Java \nHow about you?"
12                  "\n\nDo you want to see my poem again?"
13                  "\n   Enter 1 for yes";
14          while(answer == 1)
15          {
16              input = JOptionPane.showInputDialog(null, poem,
17              title, JOptionPane.INFORMATION_MESSAGE);
18
19          //convert input to Integer
20              answer = Integer.parseInt(input);
21          }
22          System.exit(0);
23      }
24  }
```

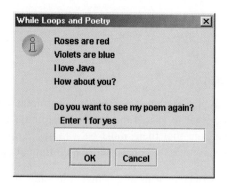

Figure 4-15
The poem message box from the Poetry program. A while loop is used to repeatedly show the poem.

Chapter 4 ▌ Control Statements and Loops

HowManyHellos   Program 4-8 illustrates how an expression with variables can be used in the conditional portion of a while loop. The HowManyHellos program is rewritten incorporating a while loop. The program concatenates the hello message into the answer String variable, as well as the value of the counter. Note how the loop counter begins at 1 and the condition remain valid for less than or equal to the user's requested value. Take a moment to review the for loop version of this program on page 178. Note that the counter here must be initialized and incremented in separate lines of code, as opposed to the for loop where these statements are all performed on one line. Figure 4-16 shows the hellos and counter value for five hellos.

```
1    //Program 4-8 Hellos and While Loop
2    //File:  HellosWithWhile.java
3
4    import javax.swing.JOptionPane;
5    public class HellosWithWhile
6    {
7         public static void main(String args[])
8         {
9              int counter=1, howMany = 0;
10             String input, answer= "", hi = "\n Hello from Java";
11             String title = "Hellos with a While Loop";
12             input = JOptionPane.showInputDialog(null,
13                  "\nHow many hellos would you like to see?",
14                  title, JOptionPane.QUESTION_MESSAGE);
15
16             //convert input to Integer
17             howMany = Integer.parseInt(input);
18             String titleOut = "You requested " + input + " hellos.";
19
20             while(counter <= howMany) //loop executes howMany times
21             {
22                  answer += hi + "    (counter = " + counter + ")";
23                  ++counter;
24             }
25
26             answer += "\n\nThat's a lot of hellos!";
27
28             JOptionPane.showMessageDialog(null, answer, titleOut,
29             JOptionPane.INFORMATION_MESSAGE);
30             System.exit(0);
31         }
32    }
```

Figure 4-16
The hello message and counter values from the HellosWithWhile program.

4.7
do while Loop

do while loop

Java loop in the form
do{
}while (condition);

The third type of loop structure in Java is the **do while loop**. It is very similar to the while loop, except that the condition check is performed at the end of the loop. The loop statements are always performed at least once—unlike the for and while loops, where the condition must be true before the loop is executed. Refer to Figure 4-17.

```
do
{
        //loop statements
}while(condition);
```

The program executes the loop statements and then checks the condition. If the condition is true, the program control returns to the do statement and executes the loop statements again. As in the while and for loops, be sure to initialize your counter or stopping condition, and have loop altering statements. We can write Hello from Java 10 times using a do while loop.

```
int count = 0;
do
{
        System.out.println("Hello from Java");
        count++;
} while(count < 10);
```

do while Example

Counting to 100   In Program 4-9, we write the numbers 0 through 100 to a String variable, and then display the variable in a message box. We place ten numbers

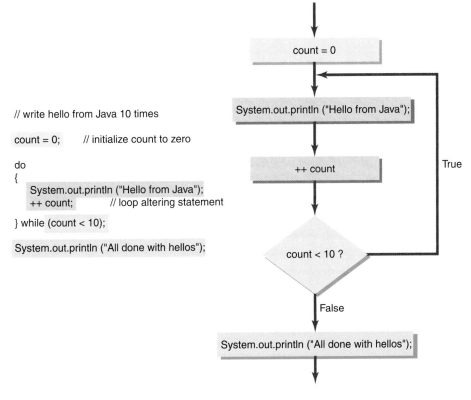

// write hello from Java 10 times

count = 0;   // initialize count to zero

do
{
    System.out.println ("Hello from Java");
    ++ count;   // loop altering statement
} while (count < 10);

System.out.println ("All done with hellos");

Figure 4-17
do while Loop

into the string, and after the tenth, we write a newline escape sequence. The modulus operator helps us to determine if the number is evenly divisible by 10. A do while loop controls this program's looping sequence. The program results are seen in Figure 4-18.

```
1   //Program 4-9 Write the alphabet using a do while loop.
2   //File:  CountTo100.java
3   import javax.swing.JOptionPane;
4
5   public class CountTo100
6   {
7        public static void main(String args[])
8        {
```

```
9          int counter = 1;
10         String title = " We're going to count to 100.";
11         String rowsOfNumbers = "\n";
12         do
13         {
14             rowsOfNumbers += " " + counter;   //add a number to the string
15
16
17             if(counter %10 == 0) //newline if counter is divisble by 10
18             {
19                 rowsOfNumbers += "\n";
20             }
21             ++counter;
22         }while(counter < 101);    //keep looping until we reach 100
23     JOptionPane.showMessageDialog(null, rowsOfNumbers, title,
24     JOptionPane.INFORMATION_MESSAGE);
25     System.exit(0);
26     }
27 }
```

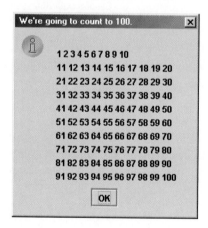

Figure 4-18
Resultant message box from the CountTo100 program. This program loop is performed by a do while loop

breaks and continues in Loops

break

control jumps out of the loop, stopping the loop execution

Two keywords in Java, **break** and **continue**, may also be used in loops. The beginning programmer should concentrate on writing his or her loops in the basic manner that is presented in earlier in this chapter. However, as the programmer gains expertise, he or she may find situations where the use of either the break or continue statement is prudent.

continue

control jumps to the beginning of the loop, skipping remaining statements

Ideally, a stopping condition is used to stop a loop's execution. But the break statement can be used to break out of a loop and cease its execution. The break causes control to jump out of the loop from that break statement. For example, in the following code, we run a loop up to 100 times, asking the user for two numbers. We break out of the while loop if the sum of the user's two input values is 75.

```
int startAt = 0, stopAt = 100;
int x, y, sum;
String sX, sY;

while( startAt < stopAt)
{
        sx = JOptionPane.showInputDialog(this, "Enter an int for X");
        sy = JOptionPane.showInputDialog(this, "Enter an int for Y");
        x = Integer.parseInt(sX);
        y = Integer.parseInt(sY);
        sum = x + y;

        if(sum == 75)
                break;          //We are OUTTA here! See you later alligator!
        ++startAt;
}
```

The continue keyword is a mechanism to skip over statements in a loop and begin the next iteration of that loop. It is usually used in for loops, because the for loop automatically increments the loop index at the start of each loop cycle. For use in a while or do while loop, the program will need to be sure the loop index is incremented correctly. In the code below, we have a for loop that is executing 1000 times. We obtain a random number from Math's random(). Recall that the random() method returns a number between 0.0 and 1.0. The code checks to see if this number is between (but not including) 0.25 and 0.50. If the number is not within this range, we can skip the remainder of the loop and continue—causing a new iteration of the loop.

```
int i;
double x;

for(i = 0; i < 1000; ++i)
{
        x = Math.random();          //get a number from 0.0 to 1.0

        //We check to see if x is between 0.25 and 0.50
        //We want to perform all of the loop if x is within this range.
```

```
//If x is out of range, skip the rest of the loop statements
//and start the next loop cycle.
if(x < 0.25 || x > 0.5)
        continue;

//Here is the rest of the loop.
//We execute these lines if x is within 0.25 - 0.50
//etc.
}
```

4.8
Comparing Numbers, Comparing Strings

Java programmers are constantly tasked with the job of comparing two values in order to determine if they are the same or if one value is greater or less than the other value. Learning a new computer language has many challenges, but performing the simple act of comparing two values shouldn't be a difficult task.

Most computer programmers realize that the computer uses memory to hold values. This memory stores information as bytes, which are composed of bits: 1s and 0s. The computer is able to store whole numbers, such as integers, shorts, and longs, accurately as long as the value is within their designated range. However, the floating point numbers (doubles, and floats), are stored to the best of the computer's ability, but there are limitations to the accuracy of the number. Floating point numbers are approximations of the "real" numbers, and the computer's version of a number may contain a very small amount of inaccuracy. Before we demonstrate comparison techniques, let's examine two examples that show how inaccurate values can be generated in Java.

Illustrating Calculation Accuracy

In an algebraic expression, or on a sheet of paper, if you add the value 0.1 ten times, you obtain the value of 1.0. When a computer program is performing calculations, however, the accuracy of that result may be very, very close, but may not exactly match the pencil and paper result. The accuracy of Java's calculations can be illustrated in a Program 4-10, and the results of this addition are seen in Figure 4-19.

```
1   //Program 4-10 Demonstrate Java's Accuracy
2   //File:  AccuracyDemo.java
3
```

```
4    import javax.swing.JOptionPane;
5    public class AccuracyDemo
6    {
7         public AccuracyDemo()
8         {
9              String output = "Adding 0.1 10 times \n\n";
10             int i;
11             double sum = 0.0;
12             for(i = 0; i < 10; ++i)
13             {
14                  sum = sum + 0.1;
15             }
16
17             output += "Sum = " + Double.toString(sum);
18             if(sum == 1.0)
19                  output += "\n\nSum is the same as 1.0";
20             else
21                  output += "\n\nSum is not the same as 1.0";
22
23             JOptionPane.showMessageDialog(null,output, "Accuracy",1);
24        }
25
26        public static void main(String args [] )
27        {
28             AccuracyDemo theApp = new AccuracyDemo();
29             System.exit(0);
30        }
31   }
```

4

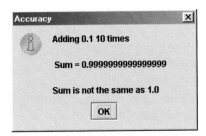

Figure 4-19
Resultant message box from the Accuracy program. This program illustrates that
when adding 0.1 ten times, Java's answer is not exactly 1.0.

This second example shows the limits of Java's accuracy involving the number of digits that may be accurately stored in a variable. In algebra (and on paper), we do not have a problem keeping track of our digits and the associated accuracy. But in a Java program, if we take a very big integer value (a long) and assign it into a decimal variable (float), then reassign back into the long, there is a loss of accuracy. Recall that Java's long variables can have up to 18 digits of precision and floats have 6–7 digits of precision. Program 4-11 performs these assignments, and the results are shown in Figure 4-20.

```java
//Program 4-11 Demonstrate Java's Accuracy
//File:  LosePrecisionDemo.java

import javax.swing.JOptionPane;
public class LosePrecisionDemo
{
        public LosePrecisionDemo()
        {
                String output;
                output = "Place a long value into a float variable" +
                "\n and copy the value back into the long variable. ";

                long bigLong= 100000000000000000L;   //(17 zeros)
                float bigFloat;                //can hold up to 7 digits of precision

                output += "\n\n The Big Long is " + Long.toString(bigLong);

                //assign the long into the float
                bigFloat = (float)bigLong;
                output += "\n The Big Float is " + Float.toString(bigFloat);

                //now copy the value back to the long
                bigLong = (long)bigFloat;

                output += "\n The Big Long from float is " + Long.toString(bigLong);

                JOptionPane.showMessageDialog(null,output, "Loss of Precision",1);
        }
        public static void main(String args [] )
        {
                LosePrecisionDemo theApp = new LosePrecisionDemo();
                System.exit(0);
        }
}
```

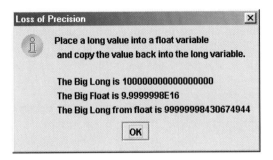

Figure 4-20
This message box shows the results from casting a long value into a float variable, and then recasting the value to the long. We can see the loss of precision in the long value. Programmers must keep in mind the range limitations of the data types when they are working with various types of numbers.

Number Comparisons

When the Java programmer is working with numbers, he or she has several comparison tools available. The Java operators shown in Table 4-5 are primitive operators and are built to evaluate Java primitive variables such as integers, longs, or doubles. These operators compare like values. This means that the operators can compare an integer to an integer. If there are two different numeric types in the comparison statement, Java promotes the "lesser" of the values to the next "bigger" data type, if possible, to perform comparisons. This means that if you try to compare a float to a double, the float is promoted to a double so that the data types are the same. If the programmer attempts to compare nonlike type values, the compiler issues an error. If, by chance, the compiler allows code that contained two different data types to be executed, the operator always returns a false value. There may be inherent inaccuracies in your program. These comparison techniques do not make any assumptions about "what you have" and "what you meant."

Comparing two whole number values in Java is easy. Integers, longs, and shorts evaluate exactly as you would expect. In the following code, we compare two integer values.

```
int x; y;
//obtain values for x and y


if( x == y )         //this checks for same as,  no problem here because
                     //x and y are whole numbers

or

int m, n;
//obtain values for m and n


if( m < n )          //this checks for less than, no problem here
```

If you are trying to determine if two double values are the same, you may run into accuracy problems if your program performed calculations with the variables. There may be small discrepancies in the decimal precision portion of the values.

```
double a, b;
//Obtain values for a and b, by performing calculations with them.
//Now check, do the values contain the same value?

if( a == b )          //there may be problems with this comparison due
                      //to inherent floating point inaccuracies
```

A better approach for comparing two floating point (doubles or floats) to see if they are the same involves taking the difference of the numbers and seeing if that value is a very small number. Let's examine a situation where two doubles can be considered the same if they are identical to four decimal places (0.0000). Here are two doubles, $a = 0.00007$ and $b = 0.00009$. Our program should determine that these two values are "close enough" to be considered the same. If we performed the following statement, we obtain a false result.

```
double a = 0.00007, b = 0.00009;

//We want our program to consider a and b the same
//since they are identical to 0.0000 four decimal places.
//This comparison generates a false result.
if(a == b)
{
        System.out.println("They are the same.");
}
else
{
        System.out.println("They are not the same.");
}
```

But if we examine the absolute value of their difference (described algebraically as $|a - b|$) that value is 0.00002, which is a small enough difference that the two values can be considered the same. When a programmer is working with floating point variables, this approach is a better, safer evaluation for sameness. The code below illustrates this technique.

```
double a, b;
//obtain values for a and b, such as a = 0.00007 and b = 0.00009

//In this example, a and b can be considered "the same" if
//they are the same value to 4 decimal places.
```

```
//We take the difference and examine that value.
//Use Math.abs() method to obtain the absolute value of the difference.

double diff = Math.abs(a-b);      //diff = 0.00002

if( diff < 0.00009 )        //YES 0.00002 is less than 0.00009
{
     System.out.println("a and b are \"the same\"");
}
else
{
     System.out.println("a and b are not the same");
}
```

We must use the absolute value, that is, the positive difference, because depending on the order of subtraction, we might obtain a large negative difference. The following code illustrates that without the absolute value, we do obtain an incorrect "same" result:

```
double a, b;
//obtain values for a and b, such as a = 1.2 and b = 4.3

//Now take the difference
// diff = a - b = 1.2 - 4.3 = -3.1

double diff = a - b;       //the value in diff is -3.1

if( diff < 0.00009 )        //YES! -3.1 is less than 0.00009
{
     System.out.println("a and b are \"the same\"");
}
else
{
     System.out.println("a and b are not the same");
}
```

There are other approaches that the programmer can take when comparing numbers by using Java wrapper classes for primitive data types. Recall that the wrapper classes, Double, Float, and Integer, contain useful methods for working with numbers. Program 4-12 shows the use of the compare() and equals() methods for comparing two doubles. The compare() method returns an integer value of 0 if the values are the same, a value less than 0 if $d1$ is numerically less than $d2$, a value greater than 0 if $d1$ is numerically greater than $d2$. The equals() method is not static, and we must create a Double object, in order to use equals. It returns a boolean value. Figure 4-21 illustrates the comparison results when the value 1.2345678901234567 was entered for both doubles.

```
1    //Program 4-12 Double Comparison Techniques
2    //File:  DoubleComparesApp.java
3
4    import javax.swing.JOptionPane;
5    public class DoubleComparesApp
6    {
7         double d1, d2;
8         String sD1, sD2;
9
10        public DoubleComparesApp()
11        {
12             sD1 = JOptionPane.showInputDialog(null,"Enter a double");
13             sD2 = JOptionPane.showInputDialog(null,"Enter a double");
14             d1 = Double.parseDouble(sD1);
15             d2 = Double.parseDouble(sD2);
16
17             String output = "d1 = " + sD1 + "   d2 = " + sD2;
18
19             //use operator to compare for sameness
20             if(d1 == d2)
21                  output += "\n\n  d1 == d2";
22             else
23                  output += "\n\n  d1 not the same as d2";
24
25             //use static compare, it returns an int
26             int compareResult = Double.compare(d1,d2);
27             if( compareResult == 0)
28                  output += "\n\n  compareResult is 0";
29           else if(compareResult < 1)
30                  output += "\n\n  compareResult is < 1    d1 < d2";
31             else
32                  output += "\n\n  compareResult is > 1     d1 > d2";
33             //use Double objects for comparison, equals returns a bool
34             Double d1Object = new Double(d1);
35             Double d2Object = new Double(d2);
36             if(d1Object.equals(d2Object) )
37                  output += "\n\n  d1Object equals d2Object";
38             else
39                  output += "\n\n  d1Object does not equal d2Object";
40
41             JOptionPane.showMessageDialog(null,output, "Comparing Doubles",1);
42        }
43
```

```
44        public static void main(String args [] )
45        {
46              DoubleComparesApp theApp = new DoubleComparesApp();
47              System.exit(0);
48        }
49   }
```

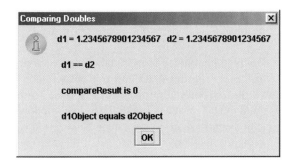

Figure 4-21
The DoubleCompareApp program demonstrates three ways to compare two double values. Other wrapper classes can be used for other primitive data types.

String Comparisons

String comparisons may be performed by using several different techniques, which are shown in the sample program that follows. Before we jump into comparison details, let's review what we know about Strings. The String class is contained in the java.lang package, and is used to hold textual information. The String object can be instantiated in an abbreviated fashion without the use of the new operator. It is a special case in Java. For example, we can create a String object in this manner:

```
String stringObject = "I want to take a vacation.";
```

Or using the new operator, the code is as follows:

```
String stringObject = new String("I want to take a vacation.");
```

Recall that when you create a string variable, you are creating an object reference which actually holds a memory address. A String variable is an object that has many methods. We examine two of these comparison methods, as well as the same as operator (==)

There are two ways to perform string comparisons: (1) by using the equals() method, or (2) by using the compareTo() method. The equals() method returns a boolean value (true or false), whereas the compareTo() returns an integer value. The equals() method is useful if you just wish to determine whether or not the contents of the strings are identical. The compareTo() and compareToIgnoreCase() methods can be used for not only determining "sameness," but also for alphabetizing purposes. The return value is zero if the strings are the same, an integer less than or greater than zero, depending on the alphabetical order of the strings.

The same as operator (==) does not work when comparing strings, unless both String objects are contained at the same address. When the programmer creates a String object, what is stored in the object name is the address in memory where the contents are stored for that object. If you create two separate Strings, each has its own address to separate memory locations. The same as operator, applied to two string objects, compares the addresses instead of the contents of the two Strings.

We study exactly how Java stores objects and primitive variables in Chapters 5 and 6. For now, examine Program 4-13 and the output seen in Figure 4-22. Figure 4-22a shows the output is the program response to the user entering "Woof" for the dog and the cat. You can see in the output window that the equals() and compareTo() methods perform correctly, (steps 1 and 2). In step 3, we see that the same as (==) operator fails when we test to see if the dog says "Woof." Step 4 is using the same as (==) operator to compare the dog and cat strings. It fails because it is actually comparing the two addresses—not the contents. The comparison works in the fifth case because we assigned the address of the sCat object into the sDog object. The operator returns true, because they both contain the same address. Figure 4-22b shows the results with the cat saying "Meow" and dog saying "Woof." Study the results. Can you explain why steps 1 and 2 results are accurate and steps 3, 4, and 5 are not?

```
1    //Program 4-13 String Comparison Techniques
2    //File:   StrCompareApplet.java
3
4    import java.awt.Graphics;
5
6    import javax.swing.JApplet;
7    import javax.swing.JOptionPane;
8
9    public class StrCompareApplet extends JApplet
10   {
11      String sCat, sDog;
12
13      public void start()
14      {
15
16          sCat = JOptionPane.showInputDialog(null,
17          "\nWhat does your cat say? (Enter Woof)  ", "A Dog-like Kitty",
18          JOptionPane.QUESTION_MESSAGE);
19
```

```
20          sDog = JOptionPane.showInputDialog(null,
21          "\nWhat does your dog say? (Enter Woof)  ", "Dog says...",
22          JOptionPane.QUESTION_MESSAGE);
23      }
24      public void paint(Graphics g)
25      {
26          String dogOutput = "The Dog says " + sDog;
27          String catOutput = "The Cat says " + sCat;
28          g.drawString(dogOutput, 10,10);
29          g.drawString(catOutput, 10, 25);
30
31          g.drawString("Now doing comparisons", 10, 50);
32
33
34      //Use equals() to compare against text. THIS WORKS!
35          g.drawString("1. sDog.equals(\"Woof\")", 10, 65);
36          if(sDog.equals("Woof"))
37          g.drawString("1. True--Dog says Woof!",10,80 );
38      else
39          g.drawString("1. False--Dog doesn't say Woof.",10,80);
40
41      //Use compareTo() and check the contents of the String objects.
42      //This always produces accurate compares.
43          g.drawString("2.  sDog.compareTo(sCat)", 10, 105);
44          int compareResult = sDog.compareTo(sCat);
45
46          if(compareResult == 0)
47              g.drawString("2. True--Dogs and Cats say same thing.",
48                  10, 120);
49          else
50              g.drawString("2. False—They don't say the same thing" ,
51                  10, 120);
52
53      //Do not use == to compare to a string of text. THIS DOESN'T WORK!
54          g.drawString("3.  sDog. == \"Woof\"", 10, 145);
55          if(sDog == "Woof")   //Don't compare strings like this!
56              g.drawString("3. True--your dog says Woof! ",10,160);
57          else
58          g.drawString("3. False--your dog doesn't say Woof!", 10,160);
59
60
61      //The String object names hold the addresses in memory where the
62      //contents are stored. The == operator in this case is comparing
63      //the addresses--which are different!
64          g.drawString("4. sDog. == sCat", 10, 185);
65          if(sDog == sCat)   //This compares addresses not contents.
66              g.drawString("4. True--Dogs and cats say the same thing.",
67                      10, 200);
```

```
68          else
69                  g.drawString("4. False--They don't say the same thing.",
70                          10,200);
71
72      //Now we assign the address that's in sPuppySays to sDogSays.
73      //Both of these object names are referencing the same memory location.
74          sDog = sCat;
75
76      //Now we get a true because they both hold the same address.
77          g.drawString("5. sDog = sCat; then do sDog. == sCat", 10, 225);
78          if(sDog == sCat)
79                  g.drawString("5. True--Dogs and cats say the same thing.",
80                          10, 240);
81          else
82                  g.drawString("5. False--They don't say the same thing.",
83                          10, 240);
84
85          //Assign "" in case the applet runs again.
86          sDog = "";
87          sCat = "";
88
89      }
90  }
```

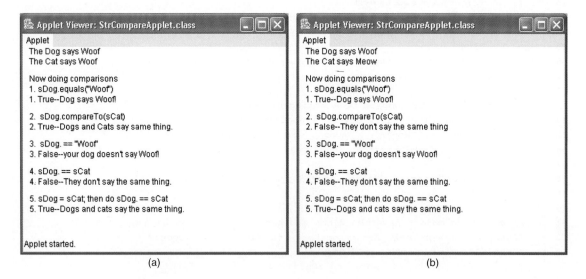

(a)   (b)

Figure 4-22
The StrCompareApplet results show both correct and incorrect results found when
the programmer attempts to perform string comparisons.

4.9
Troubleshooting

Five Common Mistakes

Programmers often write complicated conditional statements. Relational and logical operators can be tricky! Java has strict syntactical rules for writing these statements. Beginning programmers tend to make these common mistakes:

First Mistake: $x > y$ && z   Suppose a programmer needs to check if x is greater than both y and z. (That is, check to see if x is greater than y and x is greater than z.) Each phrase of a conditional statement must be written completely. The correct way to write this statement is:

```
int x, y, z;
//assume they are assigned values


//correct way to write this condition statement
// "Is x greater than y and x greater than z?"
if(x > y  &&  x > z)
```

The following statement shows a common mistake when writing this check:

```
int x, y, z;
//assume they are assigned values


//incorrect way to write this
// "Is x greater than y and z?"
if(x > y && z)
```

The Java compiler stops and presents an error on this statement. The error is:

```
C:\JPT\\>javac IfDemo.java
IfDemo.java:16: operator && cannot be applied to boolean,int
        if(x > z && y )
             ^
```

Recall from Table 4-3 that logical operators in Java only work on boolean values. When the code is compiled, the Java compiler knows that the $x > y$ operation will yield a boolean true or false, because relational operators always return a true or false. The problem is with the AND operator and the y. The y variable is an integer and is not valid for this operator.

Second Mistake: $A = B$ is not $A == B$ The relational operator $==$ evaluates the two operands to see if they have the same value. The assignment operator $=$ assigns the value on the right side of the operator to the variable on the left. Programmers either forget this or mistype the statement in if statements or while loops. This simple error can cause a huge amount of programming grief!

If the Java programmer needs to know if two variables are "the same," the code must be written like this:

```
//This is testing to see if a and b are "the same."
if(a == b)

//OR

while(a == b)
```

The error many programmers make is that he or she writes the code like this:

```
//This is incorrect!
if(a = b)            //assign b into a

while(a = b)         // assign b into a
```

Let's examine how Java reports this coding error. The Java compiler expects to have a boolean (true or false) result when the language is performing a condition checking statement—such as in an if or while statement. The relational operators provide a true or false result. If the programmer codes the statement with an assign operator, the results depend on what type of data is found in the parentheses. Integer data types in these conditional statements result in a compiler error.

```
int x, y;
//obtain values for x and y

if(x = y)            // These two statements do not compile.
                     // The Java compiler issues an error for these statements.
while(x = y)         // The compiler expects a boolean, but see the int types.
```

```
C:\JPT\ >javac CompareDemo.java
CompareDemo.java:17: incompatible types
found   : int
required: boolean
        if(x = y )
             ^
CompareDemo.java:21: incompatible types
found   : int
required: boolean
        while(x = y)
              ^
2 errors
```

However, if the variables are boolean, the conditional statements compile without error.

```
boolean b1, b2;
//obtain values for b1 and b2

if(b1 = b2)        //These two statements compile, but will not execute as desired.
                   //The compiler does not issue an error.
                   //Java assigns the value of b2 into b1
while(b1 = b2)     //The compiler expects a boolean, and sees the boolean types.
```

In both the if and while statements, the value of *b2* is assigned into *b1*. Because *b1* is a boolean, the if and while statements' boolean condition criteria is met, and the program executes. Of course, funny results may occur when the program executes.

4

> **Recommendation!!**   Programmers should get into the habit of calling the == operator the "same as" operator and the = operator the "assign" operator. Too often, students use the word "equals" for both concepts and inadvertently use the = operator when they mean to use the == operator.

Third Mistake: *A* ‖ *B* && *C* ‖ *D* **is really** *A* ‖ *(B* && *C* *)* ‖ *D*   The AND && operator has a higher precedence of operation than the OR ‖ operator. If a conditional statement is using both && and ‖, it is necessary to use a set of parentheses to ensure that the conditions are evaluated in the correct order. For example, if the programmer needs to check if condition *A* or *B* is true and if condition *C* or *D* is true, then the correct way to write it is:

```
if( (A || B) &&  (C || D) ) //written correctly.
                            //to check condition A or B and C or D
```

In the above statement, the parentheses will be evaluated first, and results for the *A*, *B* and *C*, *D* conditions will be rendered. Then the AND condition will be evaluated. Below is a common mistake:

```
if( A || B && C || D)  //incorrectly written
                       //for check A or B and C or D
```

The *B* && *C* condition is evaluated first, then compared with *A*, and lastly compared with *D*. This is not the intended sequence. A more complex example using the

Parentheses must be used to ensure correct evaluation. Three examples follow.

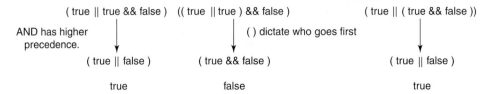

Figure 4-23
AND and OR have different precedence of operations.

relational operators is shown in Figure 4-23. Notice that without the parentheses, the evaluation steps occur in the wrong sequence and results are different.

Fourth Mistake: Semicolons in the wrong place   One of the nastiest little bugs that can strike a program is caused when the programmer accidentally puts a semicolon after the parentheses, such as this:

```
if(x > 5) ;              //This is the offending semicolon.
{
      //if statements
}
```

or

```
while(count < 6 );             //This ; can cause big trouble.
{
      //while statements
}
```

Remember that Java allows you to write an if statement or while loop without the braces if there is only one statement that needs to be performed. This if statement is legal and works correctly:

```
if(x == 3 )
      System.out.println("The value of x is 3");
```

Examine the two portions of the code following this paragraph. If you happen to mistype statements, trouble lies ahead. The Java compiler doesn't issue an error for the if or while statement. In both cases, the compiler believes there is only one statement to be executed, because it sees the semicolon after each set of parentheses. Even though the statement after the ( ) is nothing but a semicolon, Java considered them complete, albeit "empty" statements. The code after the if statement (inside the braces) is then executed because the "empty" statement is executed only if the condition is true. In the case of the while loop, the program gets stuck in an infinite loop, because the empty statement is executed until the condition is false—which never happens. Remember that it is legal in Java to have a single statement that is executed if the condition is true after a conditional expression. Always take a few minutes to look at your conditional statements, to be sure the loop or if statement is in the desired format.

```
if(x == 3 ) ;        //there is an empty statement, only a ;
{
       //These statements are always performed!
       //Statements should be performed only if x == 3.
}
int count = 0;

//Beware! Infinite loop ahead!
//Java thinks the entire loop is on the next line.
while( count < 6) ;        //<<-- bad semi-colon!
{
       //Loop statements
       ++count;

       //We never get into the loop.
       //These statements are never performed!
       //The count is never adjusted.
}
```

Fifth Mistake: Make sure your opening brace {has a partner} *Style is important when programming ifs, switches, and loops!* Beginning programmers often view the requirement of aligning the open and close braces and indenting code as an "after the fact" task. If the program has complicated logic, there will be many pairs of braces in the source code. You will not be able to see all of the braces on the screen while editing. It is good practice to develop a style where the braces are aligned and code within the braces is indented.

The most common mistake programmers make is not having complete sets of braces when using if, else, switch, or loop statements. The compiler does its best to match up the open and close braces, and it will attempt to report the location where it suspects the missing brace should be placed. But compilers are not perfect! If you use the Java editor, jEdit, it has a handy technique for checking brace alignment. Review Appendix B, *jEdit, A Java Source Code Editor*.

To gain a feel for the different types of compiler messages you receive when braces are missing, take any one of the sample programs from this chapter and comment out one or two braces. Compile the code, and examine the messages from the Java compiler. These messages range from "expecting }," to being confused in an if or switch block of code. Playing with the braces in a known situation will aid you in debugging your own programs.

Summary of Control and Loop Formats

Tables 4-6 and 4-7 summarize the basic formats for the if, switch, for, while, and do while statements. These tables can be used as guides for selecting the most appropriate statement(s) for a given task.

if, if else, if else if else, switch summary.

Decision type	When to use	Basic format
if	If a condition is true, perform statements; if the condition is false, skip statements.	```if (condition)` `{` ` //statement` `}```
if else	If a condition is true, perform certain statements; if condition is false, perform different statements.	```if (condition)` `{` ` //true condition statements` `}` `else` `{` ` //false condition statements` `}```
if else if else	If the first condition is true, perform statements and jump to end. If the first condition is false, check next condition. If it is true, perform statements and jump to end. Continue to check until a condition is true. If no condition is true, perform else statements. Can use complicated logic. Note: else is not required.	```if (condition1)` `{` ` //true condition1 statements` `}` `else if (condition2)` `{` ` //true condition2 statements` `}` `else` `{` ` //neither condition is true` `}```
switch	If the value for which you are checking is simple numeric (i.e., 1, 2, 3, etc.) or character (i.e., 'a', 'b', 'c', etc.) Switch will evaluate expression for a value and performs the case that matches the value. Default statements correspond to else statement in an if else structure. Note: default is not required.	```switch(expression)` `{` ` case value1:` ` //statements for value 1` ` break;` ` case value2:` ` // statements for value 2` ` break;` ` default:` ` // no case matches` `}```

TABLE 4-7
for, while, and do while loop summary.

Loop type	When to use	Basic format for performing a loop 10 times

for	Use the for loop if you know exactly how many times the loop should execute.
	
	Condition must be true for it to run.
		```int i;```
		```for (i = 1; i <=10; ++i)```
		```{```
		``` //statements```
		```}```

while	Use the while loop when a loop must continue to run until a condition has been met.
	
	Condition must be true for it to run.
		```int i = 1;```
		```while (i <= 10)```
		```{```
		``` //statements```
		``` ++i;```
		```}```

do while	Use the do while loop when the loop statements must run at least once. The condition will be checked after the first pass, and the loop will continue as long as the condition is true.	```int i = 1;```
		```do```
		```{```
		``` //statements```
		``` ++i;```
		```} while (i <= 10);```

4.10
Summary

Chapter 4 presents the important concepts of program control and logic statements. A beginning programmer possesses a logical sense, and has no trouble grasping the intent of Java's relational and logical operators. However, it is common for him or her to have problems transferring the logic into program statements so that the code performs the programmer's desired actions. This is a normal and sometimes steep part of the Java learning curve. The best way for a new programmer to climb that curve is to practice writing and running short programs, including the ones found in the *Practice* section of this chapter!

Let's review the program control information from the beginning. Relational operators in Java, such as greater than or less than, compare two primitive data items and return either a true or false answer. Logical operators allow us to chain together several relational operations and test for conditions such as "Is x greater than y AND z less than w?" These operators follow precedence of operations rules just as the arithmetic operators do. You should examine the operator table again, Table 4-5.

Control statements such as ifs, switches, and loops are based on testing for a certain condition and jumping (or branching) to another part of the code. The jumping or branching literally means that the program control changes to different lines of code depending on the result of the condition. The various if statement configurations provide a flexible tool for constructing different types of branching patterns. The switch statement provides an easy way to code and replaces a series of if, else if statements.

Java provides three different loop statements, the for, while, and do while statements. The loop control for all three is based on testing a condition. If the condition is true, the loop executes again. If the condition is false, control jumps to the statement after the loop. When the programmer writes a loop, he or she must ensure that the loop condition is met to begin the loop, and something occurs in the code to cause the condition to be false and stop the loop execution. The syntax for the for loop is complete with an initialization, a condition, and increment portion. The while and do while loops provide the programmer with a more flexible manner in which to code the loop.

Another important topic presented in this chapter shows correct and incorrect ways to perform numeric and String comparisons. For example, floating point numbers cannot be tested accurately for an exact decimal portion, and different String objects cannot be compared by using the same as (==) operator.

Lastly, the new programmer should study the common mistakes section of this chapter. These errors are easy to make and difficult to find. A programmer can look over the accidental assign operator (=) inside an if statement or right past the errant semicolon at the end of an if or while statement. By being aware of these errors, the programmer is more likely to be on the lookout for these errors and spot them quickly when they occur.

4.11
Practice!

Let's examine several applications and applets that use a variety of conditional and loop statements. As you begin to write your own programs, remember these three rules for programmers: 1) Fully understand the problem that you are solving and how the final, working program will behave. 2) Make a blueprint of the logic you plan to use on a piece of paper, away from the computer. 3) Write small portions of the code and run and test it to ensure that it behaves correctly before continuing with the program.

Random Lines Applet

This first sample practice program uses Java's random number generator to obtain the starting and ending positions for 15 lines. We generate two pairs of points for each line, (x1,y1) and (x2,y2), then draw the line. We incorporate an if, else if block of code (for alternating line color), as well as a for loop. Our random lines are drawn using the Graphics drawLine() method. This method must be called via a Graphics object. A Graphics object is automatically passed into the paint() method of an applet and the drawLine() method is called in this manner:

```
public void paint(Graphics g)
{
        //g is a Graphics object. We ask it to draw a line for us.

        g.drawLine(x1, y1, x2, y2);
}
```

The $x1$, $y1$ is the starting point of the line, and $x2$, $y2$ is the end point of the line. The values for the xs and ys are window pixels, and the top left corner of the window is the point (0,0). Our HTML file sets the window size to 400 pixels wide by 200 pixels tall. Because the window is 400 by 200, the applet program generates integer values between 0 and 400 for the values of $x1$ and $x2$, as well as values between 0 and 200 for $y1$ and $y2$. The Math.random() function returns a random number between 0.0 and 1.0. We scale this value by multiplying it by 400 (for the xs), by 200 (for the ys), and adding one to the result. Thus we generate a value within the desired range.

We alternate our colors between magenta, black, and green. To alternate the colors, we use the modulus operator in an if block of code. Recall that the modulus gives us the remainder of an integer division. That is, if we divide the number 17 by 4, the quotient is 4 and the whole number remainder is 1. For this program, we set a for loop to run from 0 to 14, and mod the loop index by 3. When any integer is divided by 3, there are three possible remainders—0, 1, and 2. If the remainder is 0, we set the color to magenta. If the remainder is 1, we set the color to black. The only other remainder we might get is 2, and here we set the color to green. The applet writes a status message from its init(), start(), and paint() methods. Lastly, we borrow the marcsPause() method from Chapter 3 so that we can watch our lines being drawn as the applet runs. See Figure 4-24.

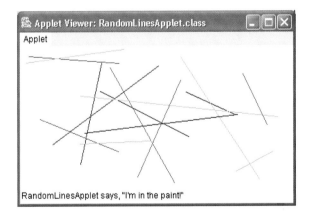

Figure 4-24
The RandomLinesApplet program draws 15 lines where the starting and ending points are selected with the use of Java's random number generator.

Program 4-14 is boring to read about but fun to run! Enter the code yourself (or obtain it from the text's CD) and play with the applet. Minimize the window and restore it, and see for yourself that the applet calls start(), and paint()—which repaints a new set of lines. Cover a portion of the window with another window, and then uncover the applet. What happens? Can you explain what you see?

```java
1   //Program 4-14  Practice with ifs, mods, and for loops.
2   //File:  RandomLinesApplet.java
3   import javax.swing.JApplet;
4   import java.awt.Graphics;
5   import java.awt.Color;
6
7   public class RandomLinesApplet extends JApplet
8   {
9       int x1, y1, x2, y2;
10      public void init()
11      {
12          showStatus("RandomLinesApplet says, \"I'm in init!\"");
13          marcsPause(1000);        //pause for 1000 milliseconds (1 sec)
14      }
15
16      public void start()
17      {
18          showStatus("RandomLinesApplet says, \"I'm in start!\"");
19          marcsPause(1000);
20      }
21      public void paint(Graphics g)
22      {
23          int i;
24          for(i = 0; i < 15; ++i)
25          {
26              if(i%3 == 0)    //mod the loop index to alternate the colors
27              {
28                  g.setColor(Color.magenta);
29              }
30              else if( i%3 == 1)
31              {
32                  g.setColor(Color.black);
33              }
34              else
35              {
36                  g.setColor(Color.green);
37              }
38
```

```
39                  //obtain the four points for our line
40                  x1 = (int)(Math.random()*400 + 1);
41                  y1 = (int)(Math.random()*200 + 1);
42                  x2 = (int)(Math.random()*400 + 1);
43                  y2 = (int)(Math.random()*200 + 1);
44                  g.drawLine(x1, y1, x2, y2);
45
46                  marcsPause(333);    //pause 1/3 of a sec between lines
47
48                  showStatus("RandomLinesApplet says, \"I'm in the paint!\"");
49            }
50      }
51      void marcsPause(int ms)
52      {
53            try
54            {
55                  Thread.sleep(ms);
56            }
57            catch(InterruptedException e){ }
58      }
59 }
```

4

The associated HTML file is:

```
<!-- RandomLinesApplet.html for Program 4-14 -->
<html>
<applet code = "RandomLinesApplet.class"   width = 400   height = 200 >
</applet>
</html>
```

Multiplication Tables and Nested for Loops

This example is another fun to run program! Program 4-15 uses a nested for loop to produce a multiplication table. Figure 4-25 shows the results of this program.

The values in the top row and the left column are the two numbers being multiplied, and their product is written in the intersection of the row and column. For example, if you find the 8 in the left hand column, and scan across that row, you see 16, 24, 32, etc. The value at the top of each column is the number that is multiplying 8. That is, as you examine the row that begins with 8, the next value you see is 16, and there is a 2 at the top of that column. The value 24 is next, and there is a 3 at the top of that column. So if you wish to find the product of 9 time 8, you can find 9 along the top row, 8 along the left column, and scan across to where that row and column intersect. (Of course, you could find the 8 in the top row, the 9 in the left column, and that intersection is also the answer.)

```
1    //Program 4-15 Multiplication Tables in an Applet
2    //File:  Multiplication.java
3
4    import java.awt.Graphics;
5    import javax.swing.JApplet;
6
7    public class Multiplication extends JApplet
8    {
9        String status;
10       int product;
11       final int MAX_PRODUCT = 12;      //we don't want this to change
12       int x = 0, y = 10;
13
14
15       public void paint(Graphics g)
16       {
17           for(int row = 1;  row <= MAX_PRODUCT; row++)
18           {
19               status = "Now working on row " + row;
20               showStatus(status);
21               for(int col = 1; col <= MAX_PRODUCT; col++)
22               {
23                   product = row * col;
24                   x = x + 25;
25                   g.drawString(String.valueOf(product), x, y);
26                   marcsPause(150);
27               }
28               y = y + 15;    //could say y += 15;
29               x = 0;
30           }
31           showStatus("All done multiplying numbers!");
32       }
33       void marcsPause(int ms)
34       {
35           try
36           {
37               Thread.sleep(ms);
38           }
39           catch(InterruptedException e){ }
40       }
41   }
42   }
```

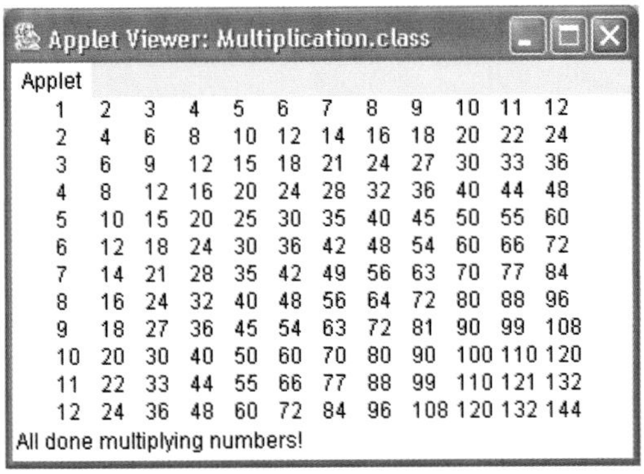

Figure 4-25
A completed multiplication table showing all combinations of multiplication for the numbers 1 through 12, as well as the "All done" status message.

Nested for loops are a confusing topic for most beginning (and some advanced) programmers. In this program, we wish to multiply 1 by 1, 1 by 2, 1 by 3, 1 by 4, and so forth. Once we have multiplied 1 by 12, we start over by multiplying 2 by 1, 2 by 2, 2 by 3, etc. We set up two loops, the outer loop index represents the row values, and the inner loop index represents the columns. Here is basic framework of the nested loops (less a few lines of code):

```
for(int row = 1;  row <= MAX_PRODUCT; row++)   //MAX_PRODUCT is 12
{
        for(int col = 1; col <= MAX_PRODUCT; col++)
        {
                product = row * col;
                //write the product in the window at the correct location
        }
}
```

The drawString() method (in Graphics class) is used to write the product to the screen. The drawString() method takes three inputs: the string to be written, and the horizontal (x) and vertical(y) locations:

```
g.drawString(String.valueOf(product), x, y);
```

We use the String class's static method, String.valueOf() to convert our integer product into a string. The x and y values are incremented so that the values are written in tabular format. (Remember that a static method can be called by using the ClassName.staticMethod format.) Once again, we make use of the marcsPause() method to slow down the painting process. Figure 4-26 shows the window during the painting process.

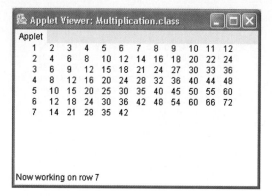

Figure 4-26
A snapshot of the multiplication program as it works on row 7.

Java Affirmations

It is nice to be appreciated. The next practice applet, seen in Program 4-16, writes complimentary messages about your programming skills into the applet window. This silly program asks you for your name, then uses a variety of the Graphic's class fonts and colors. The HTML file sets the window size to 400 × 250. We draw a yellow rectangle of size 400 × 250 using the fillRect() method. We could have simply called g.setBackground(Color.yellow), but using the fillRect() gives us practice with that method. We then set the font, obtain its size and height, and use these values to increment the position of the output line. If the user enters the name *Pooky*, our program produces these Java affirmations (Figure 4-27) regarding Pooky's skill as a programmer.

```
1   //Program 4-16 Write affirming statements about a programmer.
2   //File:  AffirmationApplet.java
3
4   import javax.swing.JApplet;
5   import javax.swing.JOptionPane;
6   import java.awt.*;       //for the Fonts, Color, and Graphics
7
8   public class AffirmationApplet extends JApplet
9   {
10       String name;
11       public void start()
12       {
13       //Obtain the Java Programmer's name.
14           name = JOptionPane.showInputDialog(null,
15           "What is your name? ","The Affirmation Applet",
16           JOptionPane.QUESTION_MESSAGE);
17   }
```

```
18
19          public void paint(Graphics g)
20          {
21                  int x = 30, y = 30;
22
23          //Draw a filled rectangle so the window background is yellow.
24          //Could have said this.setBackground(Color.yellow);
25                  g.setColor(Color.yellow);
26                  g.fillRect(0,0,400,250);
27
28          //First we set the font to bold serif and write the name.
29          //We pass in a "new" Font. We don't have a font object here.
30                  g.setFont(new Font("Ariel", Font.BOLD, 30));
31                  g.setColor(Color.black);
32                  g.drawString( name,x,y);
33
34                  //Now we set the font to a new font.
35                  g.setFont(new Font("Monospaced", Font.ITALIC, 14));
36                  g.setColor(Color.blue);
37
38          //Next, find the font height and use it to increment the y position
39          //of the drawString method. Space the lines equally.
40          //We ask the Graphics object to tell us the font size.
41                  FontMetrics size = g.getFontMetrics();
42                  int h = size.getHeight();
43                  y = 60;
44                  while(y < 150)
45                  {
46                          g.drawString( "You are a wonderful programmer!", x, y);
47                          y = y + h;
48                  }
49
50                  //Change the compliment and set a new font.
51                  String last = name + " builds MARVELOUS code!!!!";
52
53                  g.setFont(new Font("Serif", Font.PLAIN, 20));
54                  g.setColor(Color.red);
55                  size = g.getFontMetrics();
56                  h = size.getHeight();
57
58                  while(y < 225)
59                  {
60                          g.drawString( last, x, y);
61                          y = y + h;
62                  }
63          }
64  }
```

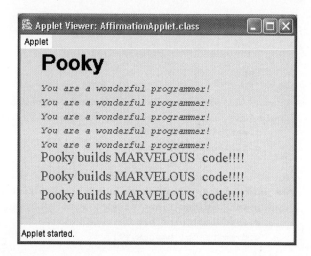

Figure 4-27
Complimentary statements for a programmer named *Pooky*. Many of the Graphics class methods are used in this program.

Output Patterns

No beginning Java text is complete without a few "draw the pattern" problems. We start with an easy pattern that we show in a JOptionPane, and move on to a more complicated pattern in a Frame. In working on these patterns, the new programmer finds that the for loop and nested for loops are a programmer's best friends.

Write a program that prints the pattern shown as follows into a JOptionPane message box. Your program should ask the user to enter the character he or she wishes to use in the pattern and ask the number of lines. (Limit the lines to 20.) Here is a sample output using the + character and five lines:

```
+
++
+++
++++
+++++
```

The trick with any of these pattern problems is to write the pattern on a piece of paper and take note of the process as the pattern develops. For the above pattern, you draw one symbol on the first line, two symbols on the second line, and three symbols on the third line. The number of symbols on the line depends which row is being drawn. For the pattern in Program 4-17, we set up a nested for loop. The outer loop is set for the number of rows. Each row is drawn by the inner loop. The number of times the inner loop executes is set by the current value of the outer loop index. Figure 4-28 shows the JOptionPane message box, where we have written seven rows with the letter *E*.

```
1    //Program 4-17 Practice drawing a simple pattern using for loops
2    //File:  SimplePattern.java
3
4    import javax.swing.JOptionPane;
5    public class SimplePattern
6    {
7            public static void main(String args[])
8            {
9                    int r, c, rows;
10                   String symbol, line_number, output = "";
11           //Read user's answers for character as string.
12                   symbol = JOptionPane.showInputDialog(null,
13                           "What kind of character would you like to use?",
14                           "Character Request", JOptionPane.QUESTION_MESSAGE);
15
16           //Read user's answers for total lines as string.
17                   line_number = JOptionPane.showInputDialog(null,
18                           "Enter number of rows in pattern.",
19                           "Line Number Request", JOptionPane.QUESTION_MESSAGE);
20                   rows = Integer.parseInt(line_number);
21
22                   if (rows > 0 && rows < 21)
23                   {
24                           for (r = 0; r < rows; ++r)    //outer loop counts the rows
25                           {
26                                   output += "\n";
27                                   for (c = 0; c <= r; ++c) // writes row# of symbols
28                                   {
29                                           output += symbol;
30                                   }
31                           }
32                   }
33                   else //number is out of range
34                   {
35                                   output = "Your number is out of range.";
36                   }
37                   String title = "Draw a pattern with '" + symbol + "' and "
38                           + rows + " rows.";
39                   JOptionPane.showMessageDialog(null,output,title, 1);
40
41                   System.exit(0);
42           }
43   }
```

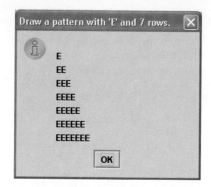

Figure 4-28
The simple pattern generated by using nested for loops.

Some patterns require nested loops to write each row of symbols. The pattern below writes *X*s and *O*s. The pattern below contains six rows. The first row contains six *X*s, the second row has four *X*s and one *O*. The third row contains three *X*s and two *O*s, and so forth until the sixth row contains five *O*s. Here is the pattern:

```
XXXXX
XXXXO
XXXOO
XXOOO
XOOOO
OOOOO
```

A four-row pattern with this same *X* and *O* pattern is:

```
XXX
XXO
XOO
OOO
```

To draw patterns like these, the number of characters on each row is one less than the number of rows. The first row contains the column-number of *X*s. The second row contains the column minus one (col − 1) number of *X*s and one *O*. The third row contains column minus two (col − 2) number of *X*s and two *O*s.

The following code shows how to write this pattern. There is a new inner for loop that writes out the first characters for each row, and the second loop writes the set of second characters. Because the outer loop index (*r*) is the number of rows and

rows minus one (rows − 1) is the total characters on a line, rows minus *r* minus one
is the number of *X*s required for each line.

```
for(r = 0; r < rows; ++r)       //outer loop counts the rows
{
      output += "\n";
      for(c = 0; c < (rows - r - 1); ++c)
      {
            output += "X";
      }
      for(c = 0; c < r; ++c) //inner loop writes row# of O's
      {
            output += "O";
      }
}
```

Concentric Circles in a Frame

This application program uses a for loop to alter the dimensions of circles and
rectangles being drawn in a window by a paint() method. Program 4-18,
ConcentricCircles.java, has a main() method which instantiates an object of the
ConcentricCircle class. That is, the main() method creates an object, which calls
the ConcentricCircle constructor. In the constructor method, we set the window
size, title, and background color. A call to the show() method forces a call to
paint.

The paint() method contains two for loops. The first for loops draw a series of
magenta circles and cyan rectangles with the dimensions adjusted in the loop. The
circles and rectangles are drawn from the outside to the inner part of the frame,
incorporating a call to marcsPause() to slow down the drawing. The second loop
then erases the circles and rectangles by drawing black circles and rectangle in the
same concentric pattern travelling from the center of the frame to the outer edge.
Figure 4-29 illustrates the program window as the items are being drawn to the
center of the frame.

```
1  //Program 4-18
2  //Concentric Circles and Rectangles with the help of two for loops.
3
4  import java.awt.Color;
5  import java.awt.Graphics;
6
7  import javax.swing.JFrame;
```

```
8
9    public class ConcentricCircles extends JFrame
10   {
11          // height and width need to be class variables
12          // They must be accessed in both the constructor and paint() methods.
13          int height;
14          int width;
15
16          public static void main(String[] args)
17          {
18                 ConcentricCircles theApp = new ConcentricCircles();
19                 theApp.setDefaultCloseOperation(EXIT_ON_CLOSE);
20          }
21
22          // set up the JFrame
23          public ConcentricCircles()
24          {
25                 height = 300;
26                 width = 300;
27                 setBackground(Color.BLACK);
28                 setSize(height, width);
29                 setTitle("Concentric Circles");
30                 show();
31          }
32
33          public void paint(Graphics g)
34          {
35                 int x = 0;
36                 int y = 0;
37                 int w = width;
38                 int h = height;
39                 // paint from the outside in
40                 // We subtract 10 from the initial width, since we want
41                 // the circles/rects inside the frame.
42                 for(w = width -10 ; w >= 0; w = w - 10)
43                 {
44                        h = w;  //set the height to the width
45                        x += 5;
46                        y += 5;
47                        g.setColor(Color.CYAN);
48                        g.drawRect(x, y, w, h);
49                        g.setColor(Color.MAGENTA);
```

```
50              g.drawOval(x, y, w, h);
51              marcsPause(200);
52          }
53
54          g.setColor(Color.BLACK);
55          // erase w/ black from the inside outward
56          for(w = 10; w < width; w = w + 10)
57          {
58              h = w;
59              x -= 5;
60              y -= 5;
61              g.drawOval(x, y, w, h);
62              g.drawRect(x, y, w, h);
63              marcsPause(200);
64          }
65      }
66      void marcsPause(long ms)
67      {
68          try
69          {
70              Thread.sleep(ms);
71          }
72          catch(InterruptedException e) {}
73      }
74  }
```

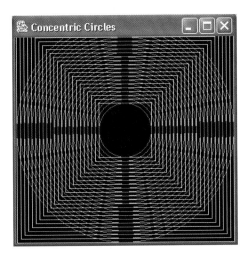

Figure 4-29
Concentric circles and rectangles being painted into a window.

UFO Applet

Alien spaceships and strange spooky lights in the night sky? It must be New Mexico. The last program of the chapter is a fun applet! David Talley, a photographer and Java programming student at TVI, wrote this program (Program 4-19) and we adapted it for our purposes. His applet uses an image of the Albuquerque night sky with a full moon. Incorporating the various graphics methods, we are able to create the illusion of a space ship and random lights. Figure 4-30 shows two views of the window as the applet executes with the spaceship traveling overhead. Run this applet yourself and see that the ship disappears over the mountains.

The animation is accomplished by painting the image into the window. Then, using a while loop in the paint() method, we repeatedly draw the flashing lights as small filled ovals and the ship as a set of ovals. For the last step in the loop, we paint the image again. This "erases" the lights and ship. As the loop code executes, we paint new lights, adjusting the position and size of the ship. After the while loop runs, we set the ranOnce variable to true (saying we have run the animation) and call repaint(). This calls paint() again, which just paints the image into the window, leaving the night sky scene in the window. Note that in the start() method we set the ranOnce to false so that if we restart the applet, the animation is shown again. The marcsPause() method allows our applet to pause for a fraction of a second so our ship travels across the scene at a desired pace. (If we comment out the call to marcsPause() and run this applet, you see nothing but a gray smear across the window.)

(a)   (b)

Figure 4-30
By using the Graphics methods and marcsPause(), we are able to create an animation showing a spaceship traveling across the Albuquerque night sky.
UFO applet and Albuquerque At Night image by David Talley.

There are "better" ways to design and perform this type of animation in Java, which require more tools than are currently in our Java tool belt. We can use arrays, separate methods, and Threads.

```java
1   //Program 4-19
2   //File: UfoApplet.java
3
4   //Written by David Talley and Marc Benstein.
5
6   import java.awt.Graphics;
7   import java.awt.Color;
8   import java.awt.Image;
9   import java.awt.Container;
10
11  import javax.swing.JApplet;
12
13  public class UfoApplet extends JApplet
14  {
15      Image pic;
16      Container canvas;
17
18      boolean ranOnce;
19
20      public void init()
21      {
22          canvas = getContentPane();
23          pic = getImage(getDocumentBase(), "AlbuquerqueAtNight.jpg");
24
25      }
26      public void start()
27      {
28          ranOnce = false;
29      }
30
31      public void paint(Graphics g)
32      {
33          g.drawImage(pic, 0, 0, canvas);              //put up the image
34          //We must allow the spaceship loop to fully execute once to
35          //have consistent behavior. The ranOnce is set true at the
36          //end of this section. Then we paint the image one last time.
37          if(!ranOnce)
38          {
```

```
39          int xp = 0;                    //x position
40          int yp = 175;          //y position
41          int wid = 150;                 //saucer width
42          int high = 75;                 //saucer height
43          int dhigh = 0;                 //dome size
44          int x = 0;                     //random x location
45          int y = 0;                     //random y location
46          final Color c1 = Color.CYAN;
47          final Color c2 = Color.GRAY;
48          final Color c3 = Color.RED;
49
50  //Loop for drawing the ship flying across the sky and blinking lights.
51  // getWidth() tells us the width of the applet.
52          while (xp < getWidth())                 {
53                  //x position for loop
54                  if ((xp % 6) == 0)
55                  {
56                          wid -= 2;      //decrease saucer width
57                          high--;                //decrease saucer height
58                          yp++;          //Increase(lower) y position
59                  }
60                  g.setColor(c2);
61                  g.fillOval(xp, yp, wid, high);
62
63
64                  //Strange flashing lights
65                  x = (int) (Math.random() * 520);
66                  y = (int) (Math.random() * 200);
67                  g.setColor(c1);
68                  g.fillOval(x, y, 8, 8);
69
70                  //Strange flashing lights
71                  x = (int) (Math.random() * 520);
72                  y = (int) (Math.random() * 200);
73                  g.setColor(c1);
74                  g.fillOval(x, y, 8, 8);
75
76                  //saucer dome
77                  if (high > 7)
78
79                  {
80                          //adjust saucer dome to size and center of oval
81                          dhigh = (int) high / 3;
```

```
82                             g.setColor(c3);
83                             g.fillOval(xp + wid / 2 - (dhigh / 2),
84                                          yp + high / 2 - (dhigh / 2),
85                                          dhigh, dhigh);
86                   }
87               xp += 2;
88               marcsPause(50);
89               g.drawImage(pic, 0, 0, canvas);
90             }
91          ranOnce = true;
92          repaint();              //Forces a new call to paint().
93        }
94     }
95
96     void marcsPause(int ms)
97     {
98         try
99         {
100            Thread.sleep(ms);
101        }
102        catch (InterruptedException e)
103        {
104        }
105     }
106 }
```

■ REVIEW QUESTIONS AND PROBLEMS

Short Answer

1. What is the purpose of an *if* statement?

2. A relational operator always returns a value of which data type?

3. Is it possible to have two *else* statements with a single *if* statement? Explain.

4. Describe the precedence of operations for relational and logical operators.

5. What is the difference between a unary and a binary operator?

6. What is the best technique to use for checking whether a floating point value is the same as zero?

7. When are { } braces required in an *if* statement?

8. Is it possible to nest a switch statement inside an *if* statement?

9. Is it possible to have a *while* loop inside another *while* loop? Explain your answer.

10. What are the three different methods for performing a loop in Java?

11. Why is a loop altering statement necessary in a *while* loop?

12. What type of loop always performs loop statements at least once?

13. What is/are the consequence(s) if you forget to break your switch?

14. Name the four keywords associated with a *switch* statement.

15. Explain the different loop actions when a loop encounters a *continue* statement versus a *break* statement.

16. What is the purpose of calling the repaint() method inside paint()?

17. In Figure 4-22B, Program 4-13 (page 198), the user enters "Woof" for the dog and "Meow" for the cat. For each of the five comparisons explain if the result (true or false) is accurate. For example, step 4 should be false because the dog and cat do not say the same thing—but is this really comparing what they are saying?

18. Why is it considered more efficient programming to use an if, else if, series instead of a series of if statements? When is it appropriate to use the if, else if statements versus the single if statements?

19. If the programmer accidentally places a semicolon after the parentheses in a while statement, such as while(x < 100); how does the compiler handle this? If the program can run with this error, how does the program behave?

20. If you see the error "expecting }", what type of coding mistake has the programmer made in his or her code?

Debugging Problems — Compiler Errors

Problems 21–25: Identify the compiler errors and state what is wrong with the code.

21.

```
//File: Test.Java
public class Test
{
        public static void main( String args[] )
        {
                int a = 7, b = 9, c = 2;
                If(a =< b)
                {
                        c == b;
                }
        }
}
```

22.

```
//File: Check.java
public class Check
{
     public static void main()
     {
          int 3ForMe = 3;
          String answer;
          switch(3ForMe)
          {
               case 3: answer = "3";
               Case 7: answer = "hello"; break;
               case 8: answer = "goodbye"; break;
          }
     }
}
```

23.

```
File: ThreePigs.html
public class ThreePigs
{
     public void ThreePigs()
     {
          float inventory, case;
          inventory = 8.0;
          if(inventory = 3)
          {
               case = inventory;
               inventory = 0;
          }
     }
     public static void main(String args[] )
     {
          ThreePigs p = ThreePigs;
     }
}
```

24.

```
//File:  BuyTime.java
public class BuyTime
{
     public static void main( String args[] )
     {
          BuyTime bt = new BuyTime();
          SystemExit(0)
     }
```

```
                public BuyTime()
                {
                        bool bHurryUp = true, bTimesUp = false;
                        while (bHurryUp == true)
                        {
                                if(bTimesUp = false)
                                {
                                        bHurryUp = false;
                                }
                        }
                }
        }
```

25.

```
        File: //ThreeBears.html
        public class ThreeBearsApplet extends JApplet
        {
                int soupTemp;
                string goldi;
                public void start()
                {
                        soupTemp == 99;
                }
                public void paint(Graphics gggggg)
                {
                        if(soupTemp < 60)
                        {
                                goldi = too cold;
                        }
                        else
                        {
                                goldi = just right";
                        }
                        else if(soupTemp > 100 )
                        {
                                goldi = too hot;
                        }
                        g.drawString(goldi, 25,25);
                }
        }
```

Debugging Problems—Run-Time Errors

26–28: Each of the following portions of Java code compiles but does not do what the specification states. What is the incorrect action, and why does it occur?

26. Specification: Write out Hello From Java 25 times, each phrase on a new line.

```
int i = 1;
while(i < 25)
   System.out.println("Hello From Java");
   ++i;
```

27. Specification: Check to see if the user's input is a 0 or a 1. If it is, write out Hello.

```
int userInput;
String sInput;
sInput = JOptionPane.showInputDialog(this "Enter an integer.");
userInput = Integer.parseInt(sInput);
if (userInput == 0 || userInput == 1);
      System.out.println("Hello");
```

28. Specification: Check to see if the user's input is between 1 and 3. Write out the numeric word (such as "ONE") if it is within range; otherwise write "OUT OF RANGE."

```
int userInput;
String sInput;
sInput = JOptionPane.showInputDialog(this "Enter an integer.");
userInput = Integer.parseInt(sInput);
switch(userInput)
{
      case 1:
            System.out.println("ONE");
      case 2:
            System.out.println("TWO");
      case 3:
            System.out.println("THREE");
      default:
            System.out.println("OUT OF RANGE");
}
```

Programming Problems

29–37: Write complete Java programs. For all applications, design your program so that the main() method creates an object of your class—as in Programs 4-12 and 4-18. If you have explored Chapter 12, *JAR Files*, create a *JAR* file for your program.

29. Write a complete Java application program that asks the user for a number between 1 and 100 (0 and 100 are out of range). If the number is between 1 and 9, write out the words "ONE DIGIT BIG!" If it is between 10 and 99 write out the words "TWO DIGITS BIG!". Your program should state if the user's number is outside of the requested range. If it is, write out the phrase "OUT OF RANGE."

30. Rewrite the *Multiplication Tables* practice program so that it fills the table by writing column by column instead of row by row. Include calls to the marcsPause() method so that you can verify that your loops are working correctly, and provide status information by calling the showStatus() method. Expand the program so that it produces the multiplication tables up to 20.

31. Write a complete Java program that asks the user for a calendar date, such as 11/22/2002. The user should enter the month, the day, and the year using the JOptionPane input message boxes. The purpose of this program is to check to ensure that the date is valid. (For example, 1/34/2002 and 4/31/1999 are not a valid dates.) The GregorianCalendar class has an isLeap() method that can help you in determining whether or not the year is a leap year. You will need to construct a series of if, else if, or switch statement blocks for checking the months and days. Present a valid or invalid message to the user, and then ask if the user wishes to enter another date. (You may use this rhyme for assistance in this task: 30 days hath September, April, June, and November. All the rest have 31, except in February alone, and that has twenty-eight days clear, and twenty-nine in each leap year.[1])

32. Write a complete Java program that converts distance values. The program should give the user three options: 1) Convert a whole number of inches to feet and inches. 2) Convert feet and inches to decimal feet. 3) Exit. For example, 80 inches is 6 feet, 8 inches, and 5 feet, 6 inches is 5.5 feet. Write the decimal feet to three decimal places.

33. Write a complete Java applet that prints out one of the following output patterns in a Frame window (not a JOptionPane). Ask the user for the character and number of lines. Remember, your HTML file can set the window size. Limit your user on total lines selected. If the user restarts the applet, ask for another symbol and number of lines. Note: it is important to use a fixed-sized font, such as Courier, to ensure consistently spaced characters. Hint: one way to build this is to write symbols and spaces in a string and then call drawstring().

Possible output patterns:

```
+
++
+++
++++
+++++
+++++
++++
+++
++
+
```

---

[1] A common saying, perhaps dating back to *Holinshed's Chronicle of England*. There have been many modifications since 1577.

```
      +
     +++
    +++++
   +++++++
  +++++++++

  +       +
   +     +
    +   +
     +
```

34. Write a Java applet program that asks the user to enter his or her name and birthday. Write a personalized greeting to the user in the applet window, and show the current time and date. The program then calculates how many days until the user's next birthday or since the most recent birthday. Be creative! Use a variety of colors and fonts. One way to approach this problem has the programmer converting the two dates into days of the year, such as January 31 is the 31st day. February 1st is the 32nd day. Taking the difference shows the days from or to the birthday. (Hints: A GregorianCalendar object can tell you the day of the year for a given date and if a year is a leap year. Also, if you obtain a Date object and set it into a GeorgianCalendar object, that will give you today's date in a useful form. Don't forget the case of today being the user's birthday!)

35. Write a Java applet that draws a pattern of rectangles in a concentric pattern centered in your window. Your rectangles should have the same aspect ratio as the applet window. That is, if your window is square, your rectangles are square. If the width is twice the height, your rectangles' width should be twice their height. Report the window's width and height in the status bar. Write a number on the top of each rectangle, such as Rectangle 1, Rectangle 2, etc. Your program should draw at least ten of the rectangles. Vary the colors. If the user resizes the window, the new rectangles should be drawn to match the new window's aspect ratio.

36. Using the UfoApplet program as a guide, find an image of scenery you like, and use it as a backdrop for your own animation. You can use other images instead of drawing graphics from the Graphics class.

37. Melissa Macpherson, a TVI Java programming student, wrote a fun Java applet that shows a caterpillar moving down a set of stairs. She first draws the stairs and then, with the aid of marcsPause(), she has her slimy insect slink down the steps. Figure 4-31 shows her caterpillar in action. Melissa's applet class has a method called drawWorm() which she calls from paint() and passes the Graphics object, and four pairs of points that represent the window position of her four-segmented caterpillar body. By designing the drawWorm() method in this manner, it allows for an efficient way to draw the bug. Passing the drawWorm() method the Graphic's object, she is able to call fillOval() and setColor() methods.

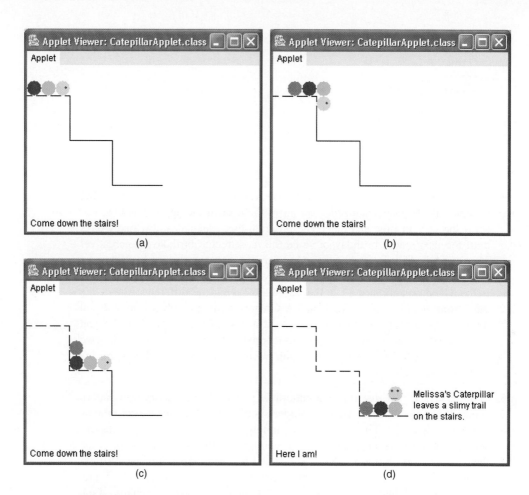

Figure 4-31

A slimy caterpillar slinks down the steps in this animation by TVI programming student, Melissa Macpherson. The bug is drawn by a drawWorm() method that is called from paint() and passed the coordinates and Graphics object. Printed here with Ms. Macpherson's permission.

The code shown here illustrates the basic idea—we draw a red oval moving across the window.

```
public void paint(Graphics g)
{
    for(int x = 0; x < 400; x = x + 50)
    {
        drawMyOval( g, x );
        marcsPause(100);
    }
}
```

```
public void drawMyOval(Graphics g, int x)
{
        //The radius of the circle is 10.
        //We'll set y at 100.
        //Call to drawOval is x1, y1, width, height

        g.setColor(Color.RED);
        g.drawOval(x, 100, 10, 10);
}
```

For Problem 37, can you draw a slinky caterpillar (or perhaps another bug or critter) across your window? Incorporate an efficient draw() method in which you pass the critter's screen location and the Graphics object.

Note: If you attempt to draw a line with drawLine() and then pause with marcsPause(), it seems that marcsPause() does not work correctly. You will see that the program pauses for the total length of time and then draws all the lines at once. Java has optimized the drawLine() (and drawRect() method too) because it gathers all of the lines or rectangles and draws them in one pass. You can force each line to be drawn by calling a drawString() or drawOval() in between the calls to drawLine().

4

5

Arrays in Java

CHAPTER OBJECTIVES

Introduce the concept of an array.

Demonstrate how arrays in Java are zero indexed.

Present several programs that use arrays.

Explore the two array creation techniques: the array creation process and the array initialization statement.

Show how Java automatically initializes arrays.

Describe how Java automatically checks array subscripts at runtime.

Illustrate how for loops are used extensively with arrays.

Describe how to use the arrayName.length field for determining the array size and use this field as the limit in for loops.

Briefly introduce the concept of collections.

Run Faster! Jump Higher!

One goal in writing software is to design the data variables to accurately represent the situation that the program models. The software may be a computer game, an accounting program, an engineering data analysis package, or drivers for a hardware device. Whatever the application, it is important to spend time during the program design phase thinking about what data variables are needed.

In the previous chapters, we declared single primitive variables and created single objects. We had an integer variable for a loop counter and four different integers, $x1$, $y1$, $x2$, and $y2$ for coordinates of our random lines. A single String object was used for a programmer's name, and we created one DecimalFormat object to help us make our numeric output pretty.

In this chapter, we will expand our Java skills and learn how to declare an array that actually contains a list or group of primitive data values or objects of the same type. The data contained in your array should be grouped logically; that is, they should naturally relate to each other. For example, you may declare a single array that is actually a list of phone bills for a year. This phone bill array contains 12 values, one for each monthly bill. Or we may create an array or list of names that represent the players on a baseball team. It's time for us to run faster and jump higher! We're going to take our Java skills to the next level.

5.1
Life Using Single Data Variables

Let's start with a programming problem that shows how being able to create a single variable containing a list of values can simplify life. Suppose that you need to write a program to average the phone bills for a year, starting with January and ending with December. You need twelve variables—one for each month in the year—and you need to ask the user to enter those twelve values. Your program calculates and reports the average value. (Eventually, it would be nice to have the program read the numbers in from a data file instead of entering the data by hand. We present how to read data files in Chapter 11.)

First, we must name our twelve primitive variables. How about using abbreviations as variable names to keep track of the twelve months? Then we ask for the numbers and calculate the average monthly cost.

```java
//Program 5-Incomplete program for finding the average phone costs for a year.
import javax.swing.JOptionPane;
public class AveCost
{
    // Declare variables
    float jan, feb, mar, apr, may, jun, jul, aug, sept, oct, nov, dec;
    float ave;
    String sBill, sResult;

    public AveCost()        //constructor ask for the data
    {
        // Obtain monthly billing information
        sBill = JOptionPane.showInputDialog(
            "Please enter your bill for January");
        jan = Float.parseFloat(sBill);
        sBill = JOptionPane.showInputDialog(
            "Please enter your bill for February");
        feb = Float.parseFloat(sBill);
        sBill = JOptionPane.showInputDialog(
            "Please enter your bill for March");
        mar = Float.parseFloat(sBill);

//The program needs to ask for values for Apr - Dec here.
//I am too lazy to type in the code, but you get the idea—right?
        // Now average
        ave = (jan+feb+mar+apr+may+jun+jul+aug+oct+nov+dec)/ 12.0F;
        sResult = "The monthly average is $" + Float.toString(ave) ;
        JOptionPane.showMessageDialog(null, sResult);
    }

    public static void main(String args[] )
    {
        AveCost a = new AveCost();
        System.exit(0);
    }
}
```

Writing this program could be enough to drive you crazy. It will need twelve input statements, and then the average calculation takes at least two lines. There must be a better way to do this. We will use an array because this data represents a logical group of data items.

5.2
Array Fundamentals

Java allows the programmer to create an **array**. An array is a group of variables, of the same data type (primitives and object references), which is referenced with a single name. When the programmer creates the array, he or she must indicate the size of the array. Java arrays are static in that the array size cannot change once declared. Each of the **array variables** or **elements** is accessed using an **array index** or **subscript** within square brackets [ ]. An array index or subscript is an integer value. As well as the int data type, Java allows the subscript to be an integer-based data type including shorts, bytes, or chars. Programmers usually use the int data type for array subscripts. In Java, arrays are objects, not primitives. When the programmer creates an array, the array name is actually a reference to an object which is an array.

There are two ways that an array can be created in Java. The programmer may use the array creation expression, which requires him or her to first make a reference for the array and then use the new keyword so that memory is allocated for it. (It is a similar action to what we did when we created objects, except in arrays there are no constructor methods.)

The array creation process can be performed in two steps or combined into one. For example:

```
dataType arrayName[];           //This sets up a reference variable for us.
arrayName = new dataType[size];   //This creates the array using new and allocates
                                  //memory for size number of data_type values.
```

where dataType is the data type such as float, int, double, or String, the arrayName is the reference name for the array, and size is an integer that represents how many variables are in this array. For the phone bills program, we declare an array of twelve floating point values. This two-step action first creates the array reference and then allocates memory for twelve floating point values:

```
float phoneBills[];           //The phoneBills is an array reference.
phoneBills = new float[12];   //Now we allocate memory for 12 floats.
```

This process can be accomplished in one step, like this:

```
float phoneBills[] = new float[12];
```

The size often is referred to as the **array dimension**. When a programmer creates a list using one dimension (size) value, as we did with phoneBills, it is referred to as a **single-dimensioned array** or a **one-dimensional array**, and can be thought of as a single list or as a row of values. These values are stored contiguously in memory. Once an array has been created with a given size, the array size cannot be changed.

array
a group of variables of the same data type (primitives and object references) that is referenced with a single name

array variables or elements
members of an array

array index or subscript
an integer value that references one element

5

array dimension
the size of the array

single-dimensioned array or one-dimensional array
an array that represents a single list or column of values or objects

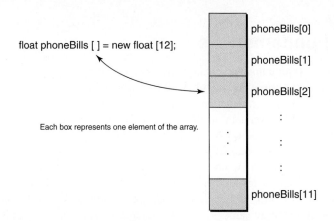

float phoneBills [ ] = new float [12];

phoneBills[0]

phoneBills[1]

phoneBills[2]

Each box represents one element of the array.

phoneBills[11]

Figure 5-1
Single dimension array.

Figure 5-1 illustrates the phoneBills array. It is useful to visualize an array as a group of boxes. Each box represents a separate variable location and each box has its own name.

The array index or subscript is used to access the individual elements in the array, the first element is numbered zero (0), and the last element is numbered one less than the size (size -1). For example:

```
phoneBills[0] = 58.61;          //First element is January's bill
phoneBills[4] = 34.65;          //Fifth element is May
phoneBills[7] = 83.66;          //Eighth element is August
phoneBills[11] = 29.73;         //Twelfth element is December
```

shows how the individual values in the phoneBills array are assigned values.

More array declarations are shown here. Please notice that we are showing both the two-step and one-step approach. You do not use both for one array:

```
//Set up an array of 1000 integers.
//You can do it in two steps like this:
int numbers[];
numbers = new int [1000];


//or in one step like this
int numbers[] = new int [1000];



//We need an array of Sailboats (this assumes we have a class Sailboat)
//One step approach.
Sailboat boats[] = new Sailboats[5];     //array of 5 boats
```

```
//or use the two step approach
Sailboat boats[];
boats = new Sailboat[5];
```

Arrays in Java cannot be declared in this manner:

```
//This is not legal in Java!!!

int numbers[100];          //this won't work!
Sailboat boats[5];         //nope, nope
```

Arrays in Java Are Zero Indexed

Java arrays are referred to as **zero-indexed**, which means that the array element subscripts are numbered starting at zero, *not one*! Look again at the array elements in Figure 5-1. The name of the first element of this array has zero as the first index, phoneBills[0], and the last element's name is phoneBills[11], or phoneBills[size –1].

    Some programming languages, such as FORTRAN and Visual Basic, allow the programmer to specify the starting and ending array indices. Java, like C++, does not allow this. This zero-indexing scheme is a carry over from the C language. In C, an array index is used as an offset from a base memory address. Some beginning Java programmers might have trouble with this, and may try to add an additional array element to the declaration and then ignore the first (index of zero) array element. This technique is normally not recommended. However, advanced programmers using arrays with databases do throw out the zeroth (0th) array element when they are working with SQL database columns, because these columns begin with a subscript of one (1). For now, beginning Java programmers should remember that all arrays in Java have the first index value of zero and the last element index is one less than the size.

    Here are a few more examples showing how arrays are created and how values are assigned to their elements.

```
double speed[] = new double [7];

speed[0] = 1.294352;        //The first element in the array is [0]
speed[6] = 2.3483423;       //The last element is [6]


//Set up an array of three Strings.
String names[];
names = new String [3];
```

zero indexed
the first array element subscript is numbered starting at zero, not one

5

Names can then be assigned into the names array, like this

```
names[0] = "Janet";
names[1] = "Ryan";
names[2] = "Jason";
```

Arrays in Java Are Initialized to "Zero"

The Java language automatically assigns a zero value into each numeric primitive array element. That is, if you declare an array of type double, float, int, short, or long, Java places a number zero into each element. A boolean array is filled with false values, and reference array (non-primitive) elements are assigned null.

Array Creation/Initialization in Java

A second way to create an array in Java uses the array initialization statement. The following are two examples of arrays being set up and initialized in one statement. This differs from the previous examples because we are assigning values directly into the array when we first make it.

```
//Set up an array of integers.
//You can declare and initialize at the same time.
//Java counts how many values within the { } and uses that for the size.
//This array is sized to hold 6 integers.
int numbers[] = { 8, 25, 1, 9, 7, 19 };

//Declare and initialize an array with 3 names in it.
String names [] = {"Janet", "Ryan", "Jason" };
```

When a program creates an array in this manner, the new operator is not needed, nor is the size of the array, because Java counts the number of values in the list and sets the array to that size. This is a handy technique for Java programmers! The array can only be initialized in this manner when it is declared, and you cannot change the size of the array once it is created. Of course, you can change the values in any of the array elements, like this:

```
//Declare and initialize an array with 5 birds in it.
String birdTypes [] = {"robin", "sparrow", "scrub jay", "nuthatch", "finch" };

//Now birdTypes[3] contains "nuthatch"
//If we want to change what is in this element we do it like this:

birdTypes[3] = "chickadee";
```

Note that you cannot assign values like this:

```
//Declare an array for 3 names
String names [] = new String [3];
names = {"Janet", "Ryan", "Jason" };          //Nope, Nope!!!

//This is illegal too.
String names[];
names = {"Janet", "Ryan", "Jason" };      //No Can Do.
```

for Loops and Arrays

When writing software with arrays, the for loop is the programmer's best friend. The for loop provides an efficient way to go through or traverse an array. The index of the loop not only is a counter for the loop, but it can also be used as the subscript value for the array. If you are not comfortable writing for loops, go back to Chapter 4 and reread the for loop section and look at the sample programs in the *Practice* section.

Always Use arrayName.length When Looping Through an Array   Arrays in Java are equipped with an easy way for the programmer to determine their size: by using the arrayName.length field. This value is set for you when the array is created, and can be used whenever the size of the array is needed. It is always available with the array. (In other languages, the programmer must keep the size of the array in a separate variable and pass it along with the array whenever the data must be used in another method.) For example, in our next program, we loop through the twelve months of the year and obtain phone costs. The for loop should be set up as follows:

```
//Use the arrayName.length for looping through an array.
//The month's array is filled with the month names: January, February, etc.
//The phoneBills array is sized to 12. We will use phoneBills.length.
     float phoneBills [] = new float[12];

//The phoneBill.length is 12. Use it for the loop limit.
     for(i = 0; i < phoneBill.length; ++i)
     {
          sBill = JOptionPane.showInputDialog(null,
               "Enter Monthly Amount: ", months[i],1);
               phoneBills[i] = Float.parseFloat(sBill);
     }
```

Java will let you use an integer value in the for loop, but why risk trying to remember the size of the array and causing a program crash? This approach works, but the previous approach is best!

```
float phoneBills [] = new float[12];
```

```
//The programmer must remember the size is 12.
for(i = 0; i < 12; ++i)
{
        sBill = JOptionPane.showInputDialog(null,
                "Enter Monthly Amount: ", months[i],1);
                phoneBills[i] = Float.parseFloat(sBill);
}
```

Phone Bills Program   Program 5-1 is a complete program illustrating how we can obtain the phone cost information for twelve months, average the cost, and display it. We use two arrays in this program, one for the monthly phone costs and the second to hold the names of the twelve months. We use a for loop that executes twelve times, asking the user to enter phone costs. The loop index is used as the array subscript for the phoneBills array. While the for loop is running, we also access the name of the month from the months array and show it in the title of the JOptionPane message box. Figure 5-2 illustrates how the for loop index variable is used to access the array elements, and the for loop limit is set by phoneBills. length. Figure 5-3 illustrates how this index is then used again when calculating the sum. Figure 5-4 shows the input message boxes for the first two months.

```
1    //Program 5-1 The phone bills program using for loops.
2    //File: PhoneBills.java
3
4    import javax.swing.JOptionPane;
5    public class PhoneBills
6    {
7       public PhoneBills()      //constructor ask for the data
8       {
9            // Declare two arrays
10           float phoneBills [] = new float[12];
11           float ave, sum = 0.0f;
12           String months[] = {"January", "February", "March", "April", "May",
13                   "June", "July", "August", "September", "October",
14                   "November", "December"};
15           String sBill, sResult;
16
17           //Use a for loop to obtain monthly billing information
18           int i;
19           for(i = 0; i < phoneBills.length; ++i)
20           {
21                sBill = JOptionPane.showInputDialog(null,
22                    "Enter Monthly Amount: ", months[i],1);
```

```
23                         phoneBills[i] = Float.parseFloat(sBill);
24                 }
25
26                 // Now average
27                 for(i = 0; i < phoneBills.length; ++i)
28                 {
29                         //Use the accumulation operator instead of the more cumbersome
30                         //sum = sum + phoneBills[i];
31                         sum += phoneBills[i];
32                 }
33                 ave = sum / 12.0f;
34                 sResult = "The monthly average is $" + Float.toString(ave) ;
35                 JOptionPane.showMessageDialog(null,sResult);
36         }
37     public static void main(String args[] )
38     {
39                 //A reference variable to the PhoneBills object is not needed
40                 //since we won't ever use it. We can just call the constructor
41                 //like this --> new PhoneBills(); instead of
42                 //PhoneBills b = new PhoneBills();
43
44                 new PhoneBills();
45                 System.exit(0);
46     }
47 }
```

5

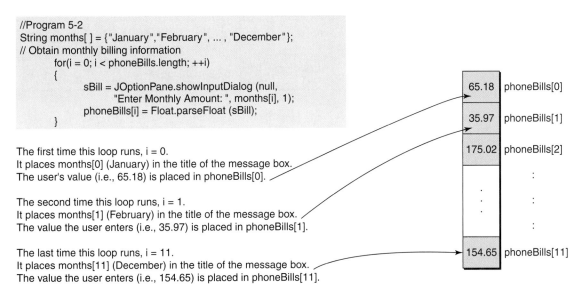

The first time this loop runs, i = 0.
It places months[0] (January) in the title of the message box.
The user's value (i.e., 65.18) is placed in phoneBills[0].

The second time this loop runs, i = 1.
It places months[1] (February) in the title of the message box.
The value the user enters (i.e., 35.97) is placed in phoneBills[1].

The last time this loop runs, i = 11.
It places months[11] (December) in the title of the message box.
The value the user enters (i.e., 154.65) is placed in phoneBills[11].

Figure 5-2
For loop index and array elements.

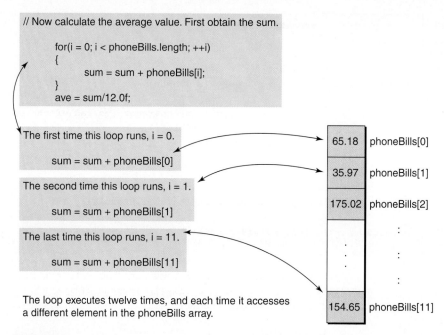

```
// Now calculate the average value. First obtain the sum.

    for(i = 0; i < phoneBills.length; ++i)
    {
        sum = sum + phoneBills[i];
    }
    ave = sum/12.0f;
```

The first time this loop runs, i = 0.

sum = sum + phoneBills[0]

The second time this loop runs, i = 1.

sum = sum + phoneBills[1]

The last time this loop runs, i = 11.

sum = sum + phoneBills[11]

The loop executes twelve times, and each time it accesses a different element in the phoneBills array.

65.18	phoneBills[0]
35.97	phoneBills[1]
175.02	phoneBills[2]
154.65	phoneBills[11]

Figure 5-3
Phone bills program sum calculation

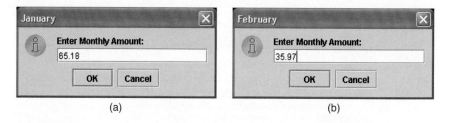

(a)   (b)

Figure 5-4
The a) January and b) February input message boxes for the Phone Bills program.

Polygons and Arrays   Let's run a simple applet to see arrays in action. We use the array initialization expression to set up four different arrays in Program 5-2. Using the drawPolygon() and fillPolygon() methods in the Graphics class, we draw one of each of these polygons. The input list for both the drawPolygon() and fillPolygon() methods are integer array for the *x*-coordinates, an integer array for the *y*-coordinates, and an integer value that is the number of points in the polygon. Figure 5-5a illustrates the relationship between the values in the arrays and the points drawn for the lined polygon. The output showing both the lined and filled polygons from this program is seen in Figure 5-5b.

```
1   //Program 5-2
2   //File: PolygonDemo.java
3
4   import javax.swing.JApplet;
5   import java.awt.Graphics;
6   import java.awt.Color;
7
8   public class PolygonDemo extends JApplet
9   {
10      //initialize four arrays that are polygons' x and y coordinates
11      int xPointsLines[] = { 25, 50, 75, 40, 10 };
12      int yPointsLines[] = { 50, 50, 100, 120, 100 };
13
14      int xPointsFill[] = { 175, 200, 225, 190, 160 };
15      int yPointsFill[] = { 50, 50, 100, 120, 100 };
16
17      public void paint (Graphics g)
18      {
19          // set background color of the window
20          setBackground(Color.white);
21
22          g.setColor(Color.black);
23          g.drawString("Black Lined Polygon", 10, 40);
24
25          //Draws a sequence of connected lines defined by arrays of x and y coords
26          g.drawPolygon(xPointsLines, yPointsLines, 5);
27
28          g.setColor(Color.magenta);
29          g.drawString("Magenta Filled Polygon", 150, 140);
30
31          //Fills a closed polygon defined by arrays of x and y coordinates.
32          g.fillPolygon(xPointsFill, yPointsFill, 5);
33
34      }
35   }
36
```

```
int xPointsLines[ ] = {25, 50, 75, 40, 10};        int xPointsFill[ ] = {175, 200, 225, 190, 160};

int yPointsLines[ ] = {50, 50, 100, 120, 100};     int yPointsFill[ ] = {50, 50, 100, 120, 100};
```

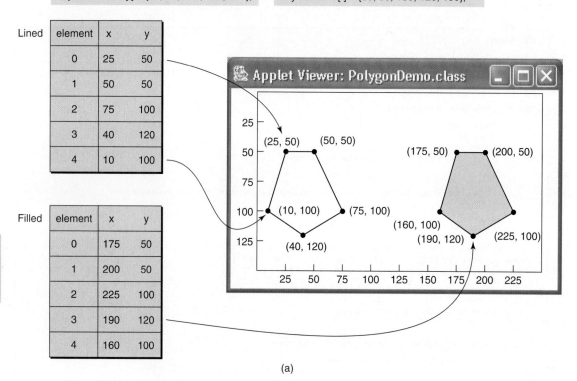

Lined

element	x	y
0	25	50
1	50	50
2	75	100
3	40	120
4	10	100

Filled

element	x	y
0	175	50
1	200	50
2	225	100
3	190	120
4	160	100

(a)

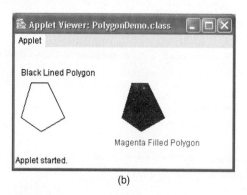

(b)

Figure 5-5

a) The elements in the xPointsLines and yPointsLines form coordinate pairs of points that represent the corners of the five-sided polygon. The xPointsFill and yPointsFill arrays are used to define the corners of a filled polygon. b) The two polygons are drawn in this applet using integer arrays as inputs for the Graphic class's drawPolygon() and fillPolygon() methods.

AveMinMax Program Common requirements when working with numeric arrays are to find the minimum and maximum values and to calculate the average value of the array. Java provides wonderful utility classes known as Collections that work with Lists. These utility classes contain methods that perform many common tasks, such as sorting and finding minimum and maximum values. We will cover these classes later in the text. For now, let's practice using arrays and find the min, max, and average of an array.

Let's set up an array to hold 1000 double values and fill the array with random numbers between 0.0 and 1.0. We will then add the values and divide by 1000 to obtain the average. To find the maximum and minimum value, we set max and min variables to the first element and then traverse the array, comparing each element. If we find a value that is larger than the current max, we reset the current max to that value. We use the same procedure for the min. The code appears in Program 5-3 and the output is seen in Figure 5-6.

```
1    //Program 5-3
2    //File: AveMinMaxFrame.java
3
4    import java.awt.Color;
5    import java.awt.Graphics;
6    import javax.swing.JFrame;
7    import java.text.DecimalFormat;
8
9    public class AveMinMaxFrame extends JFrame
10   {
11      double max, min, ave;     //need to see these in both methods
12
13      public static void main( String[] args )
14      {
15          //Here we make an AveMinMaxFrame object called aveFrame.
16          //We use aveFrame to call the close method.
17
18          AveMinMaxFrame aveFrame = new AveMinMaxFrame();
19          aveFrame.setDefaultCloseOperation( EXIT_ON_CLOSE );
20      }
21
22      public AveMinMaxFrame()              //class constructor method
23      {
24          double numbers[];
25          numbers = new double[1000];
26          int i;
27          for(i = 0; i < numbers.length; ++i)     //fill the array
28          {
29              numbers[i] = Math.random();
30          }
31
```

```
32          max = min = numbers[0];      //set to first element for comparison
33          double sum = 0.0;
34          for(i = 0; i < numbers.length; ++i)
35          {
36                  //Use the += operator instead of sum = sum + numbers[i];
37                  sum += numbers[i];
38
39                  if(numbers[i] > max) max = numbers[i];
40                  if(numbers[i] < min) min = numbers[i];
41          }
42          ave = sum/1000.0;
43
44          setSize( 400, 170 );         //set the window size
45          setTitle("Practice with Arrays The AveMinMax Program");
46
47          show();          //forces a call to paint()
48      }
49
50    public void paint( Graphics g )
51    {
52          DecimalFormat df = new DecimalFormat("0.00000");
53
54          g.setColor( Color.magenta );
55          g.drawString( "Results for our array of 1000 random numbers", 25, 60 );
56
57          String output;
58          output = "The average value is " + df.format(ave);
59          g.drawString(output,25,100);
60
61          output = "The min value is " + df.format(min) + " and the max is " +
62                              df.format(max);
63          g.drawString(output,25,140);
64      }
65  }
```

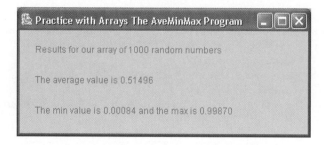

Figure 5-6
The average, minimum, and maximum values of 1000 doubles.

CoffeeLotto Program   Do you have a favorite lottery game? There are many different lottery games across the United States, and they all work in a similar manner. If you play the game, you pay one dollar, and guess a series of numbers within a given range. The actual game numbers are chosen with a technique that randomly selects individually numbered ping-pong balls. These balls are contained in some sort of enclosure. The winning numbers are selected randomly, usually by having the balls jumbled about, allowing a certain number of balls to roll out of the container.

The CoffeeLotto game is *Java Programming Today's* lottery game. In our game, there are ten cream colored "balls," numbered between 1 and 10, inclusive, and twenty coffee colored "balls," numbered between 1 and 20, inclusive. The user plays for free and guesses four unique numbers between, and including, one and ten (representing the cream colored balls), and one number between, and including, one and twenty (for coffee colored balls). Our CoffeeLotto program then randomly generates four cream colored balls and one coffee colored ball. If the user's cream and coffee colored numbers match the program's numbers, the user wins!

This program models a portion of the game. It asks the user to enter his or her guesses, then randomly generates the game numbers. The user's numbers and game numbers are then written to the applet window. Two one-dimensional arrays are used to store the cream colored ball values. Because these balls must be unique, we must check each number to be sure that it isn't a duplicate. For both the user and the computer, we keep the first ball, and then each time we obtain or select another number, we check it against all the other chosen balls. For the game numbers, if there is a duplicate, we throw it away and select another. The code for CoffeeLotto is shown in Program 5-4. The Applet Viewer window results are in Figure 5-7.

A few things to note concerning Java arrays: Arrays in Java are automatically initialized, so we do not need to set initial values in our arrays. However, because an applet may be restarted, we need to initialize the bBallChoice array in the start() method. If the applet is restarted, this array must be reset to contain false values. Also, in this version of the CoffeeLotto program, we do not check to see if the user's value is within the designated range, nor do we have the logic to determine if we have a winner. We will implement those checks in a version of this program in Chapter 6.

```
1   //Program 5-4
2   //File: CoffeeLottoApplet.java
3
4   /* This JApplet models a portion of the game CoffeeLotto.
5   The user guesses four cream colored "balls" numbered between 1-10,
6   and one coffee-colored "ball" numbered between 1-20.
7   The game randomly picks numbers as well.
8   If their numbers match, the players win!!
```

```
9
10    This program only models the portion of asking the user to
11    enter his or her numbers and generating the game numbers.
12    Both sets of cream colored "balls" are checked to ensure
13    the numbers are unique.
14
15    Everytime the applet window is minimized, we generate new numbers.
16
17    We use marcsPause method to pause the applet so that we
18    can see the balls   */
19
20
21    import java.awt.Graphics;
22    import javax.swing.JApplet;
23    import javax.swing.JOptionPane;
24
25    public class CoffeeLottoApplet extends JApplet
26    {
27         //Variables need to be seen by all the methods.
28         int userCreamBalls[] = new int[4];
29         int userCoffeeBall;
30         int gameCreamBalls[] = new int[4];
31         int gameCoffeeBall;
32
33    //For the user's guesses, we have an array of booleans that represent
34    //each of the balls. The user picks 4 numbers between 1-10, inclusive.
35    //We size the array to 11, elements 0 - 10. Once the user guesses a number,
36    //we place a true in that element signaling that the number has been selected.
37
38      boolean bBallChoices[] = new boolean[11];
39
40      public void start()
41      {
42           //Because the applet can be restarted, we need to
43           //set our boolean array to false here.
44           for(int i = 0; i < bBallChoices.length; ++i)
45                bBallChoices[i] = false;
46
47
48           int count = 0, i, newball;
49
```

```
50          String sTitle = "User\'s Coffee Ball";
51          String sCream;
52          String sCoffee = JOptionPane.showInputDialog(null,
53                  "Enter a number between 1-20", sTitle,
54                  JOptionPane.QUESTION_MESSAGE);
55
56          userCoffeeBall = Integer.parseInt(sCoffee);
57
58          sTitle = "Cream Ball Guess # " + Integer.toString(count + 1);
59
60          sCream = JOptionPane.showInputDialog(null, "Enter a number between 1-10",
61                          sTitle, JOptionPane.QUESTION_MESSAGE);
62
63          //A while loop is used to ask the user to enter the white balls.
64
65          while(count < 4)            //First we ask the user for the numbers.
66          {
67              if( count == 0)      //guess is a keeper
68              {
69                      newball = Integer.parseInt(sCream);
70                      userCreamBalls[count] = newball;
71                      bBallChoices[newball] = true;
72                      ++count;
73              }
74              else
75              {
76                      sTitle = "Cream Ball Guess # " + Integer.toString(count+1);
77
78                      sCream = JOptionPane.showInputDialog(null,
79                          "Enter a number between 1-10", sTitle,
80                          JOptionPane.QUESTION_MESSAGE);
81
82                      newball = Integer.parseInt(sCream);
83                      if(bBallChoices[newball] == false)
84                      {
85                              userCreamBalls[count] = newball;  //keep it!
86                              bBallChoices[newball] = true;
87                              ++count;
88                      }
89                      else
90                      {
```

```
91                         JOptionPane.showMessageDialog(null,
92                         "Sorry, you have already guessed " + sCream,
93                         "Duplicate Guess!" , JOptionPane.WARNING_MESSAGE);
94              } //close if
95         } //close if
96    } //close while
97
98
99    //Now generating the game numbers.
100   boolean gotADup;
101   count = 0;                     //Reset the counter for the game numbers.
102   while(count < 4)
103   {
104        if( count == 0)      //first ball, its a keeper
105        {
106             gameCreamBalls[count] = (int)(Math.random() *10 + 1);
107             count++;
108        }
109        else   //not the first ball, have to check it.
110        {
111             newball = (int)(Math.random()*10 + 1);  //get a new ball
112
113   //check it against previous balls to see if we have a duplicate
114             gotADup = false;
115             for(i = 0; i < count; ++ i)
116             {
117
118                  //already have this number
119                  if(newball == gameCreamBalls[i] )
120                  {
121                       gotADup = true;
122   //break out of the for loop, no need to keep checking
123                       break;
124                  }
125             }
126             if(gotADup == false)    //no dups, keep it, incr count
127             {
128                  gameCreamBalls[count] = newball;
129                  ++count;
130             }
131        } //close if
132   } //close while
```

```
133        //now get a Coffee Ball, pick a random number between 1-20
134        gameCoffeeBall = (int)(Math.random()*20 + 1);
135
136        showStatus("Generating new numbers!");
137        marcsPause(1000);
138   }
139
140
141   public void paint(Graphics g)
142   {
143        g.drawString("Welcome to CoffeeLotto!", 25,25);
144        showStatus("Here are the winning numbers! ");
145
146        g.drawString("Game's Cream Balls ", 25, 50);
147        g.drawString("User's Cream Balls ", 250, 50);
148        String output;
149        for(int i = 0; i < gameCreamBalls.length; ++i)
150        {
151             marcsPause(500);
152             output = Integer.toString(gameCreamBalls[i]);
153             g.drawString(output,50+30*i, 75);
154
155             output = Integer.toString(userCreamBalls[i]);
156             g.drawString(output,270+30*i, 75);
157        }
158        output = "Game's Coffee Ball is " + Integer.toString(gameCoffeeBall);
159        g.drawString(output, 25, 100);
160
161        output = "User's Coffee Ball is " + Integer.toString(userCoffeeBall);
162        g.drawString(output, 250, 100);
163
164   }
165
166   //Marc's Pause method will pause the program by the number of milliseconds (ms).
167   void marcsPause(int ms)
168   {
169        try
170        {
171             Thread.sleep(ms);
172        }
173        catch(InterruptedException e){ }
174   }
175   }
```

5

Figure 5-7
The results from the CoffeeLotto program.

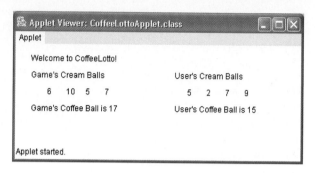

Sorting Arrays

Java programmers often find that they need to sort their arrays in some manner. It is common to sort numeric arrays in either ascending or descending order. Arrays of names are sorted in alphabetical order. The various techniques and actual mechanics of how to sort the array can and do fill college textbooks.

There are many sort routines available to the Java programmer. A visit to the National Institute of Standards and Technology's website (//www.nist.gov), and searching for "sort," generates a reference to http://www.nist.gov/dads/HTML/sort.html. This website provides specific algorithms for more than fifteen different sort routines, including the quicksort, heapsort, shell sort, bucket sort, insertion sort, merge sort, and bubble sort. Following the link for the quicksort routine (or any of the sort routines) takes you to a link that provides the Java code, and an animation showing how the sort routine works. (Under implementation, click on the "animation of code" link.) This animation is an applet provided at the java.sun.com website, http://java.sun.com/applets/jdk/1.0/demo/SortDemo/example1.html. From this site, run the bubble sort example and the quicksort. Notice how slow the bubble sort routine is and how much faster the quicksort example runs.

ShowASortApplet Program We are going to use a bubble sort method to sort numeric arrays, and use an applet to draw a graphical representation of the unsorted and sorted array, similar to what is found at the NIST web site. Refer to Figure 5-8 on page 254. The bubble sort is a simple sort to understand. It receives an array and uses nested for loops to perform the sort. In the sort routine, two adjacent values are compared, and if they are out of order, we swap the values. We travel through the array, checking each adjacent pair, and swap if necessary. We must make one less than the size of the array trips through the elements, and we are essentially sorting the array one element at a time with each pass. Very inefficient, but easy to understand!

In Program 5-5, the class ShowASortApplet contains a bubblesort() method. This method is a class member and it can see the class variable array. Typically though, sort methods are in their own class, and must be passed the array to be sorted. We will see this in an example in Chapter 6.

In this ShowASortApplet program, we fill an array with 100 random numbers between 0 and 200. We use the value in each array element to represent the length of the line that we draw using Graphics' drawLine() method. In other words, if the number in the array element [0] is 125, the 0th (first) line we draw is 125 pixels long. We loop through, drawing all 100 lines. Then we call the bubblesort() method, which sorts the array from low to high, and we draw the 100 lines again. Figure 5-8 shows the two sets of lines.

```
1    //Program 5-5 Bubblesort in Action!
2    //File: ShowASortApplet.java
3
4    import java.awt.Graphics;
5    import javax.swing.JApplet;
6    import java.awt.Color;
7
8    public class ShowASortApplet extends JApplet
9    {
10       int numbers[] = new int [100];
11
12       public void start()
13       {
14           int count = 0;
15           while(count < numbers.length)          //fill the array
16           {
17               numbers[count] = (int)(Math.random()*201);
18               count++;
19           }
20       }
21
22       public void paint(Graphics g)
23       {
24           int i,j;
25
26           g.setColor(Color.magenta);
27
28           //drawLine input is (x1,y1,x2,y2)
29           //x2 is the length of the line we get from the numbers array
30           //the y values are spaced down based on the loop index
31           for(j = 0; j < numbers.length; ++j)
32           {
33               g.drawLine(10, 10+2*j, 10 + numbers[j], 10+2*j);
34           }
35
36           g.drawString("The original array", 10, 225);
37
38           bubblesort( );
39
40           for(j = 0; j < numbers.length; ++j)
41           {
```

```
42              g.drawLine(225, 10+2*j, 225 + numbers[j], 10+2*j);
43          }
44          g.drawString("The sorted array", 225,225);
45
46      }
47
48  //this bubble sort routine sorts integers from low to high
49      public void bubblesort( )
50      {
51          //we can obtain the size of a Java array like this:
52          int size = numbers.length;
53          int x, y, temp;
54
55          for(x = 1; x < size; ++x)
56          {
57              for( y = 0; y < size - 1; ++y)
58              {
59                  if(numbers[y] > numbers[y +1] )
60                  {
61                      temp = numbers[y];
62                      numbers[y] = numbers[y+1];
63                      numbers[y+1] = temp;
64                  }
65              }
66          }
67      }
68  }
```

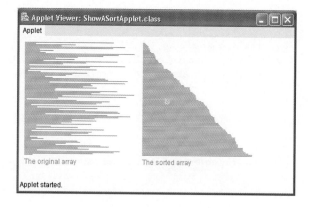

Figure 5-8
The unsorted lines on the left represent the random integer values in a 100-element array. The lines on the right represent array values after it has been sorted.

A Few More Details Concerning Arrays

We need to address a few more details, concerning arrays in Java, before we venture further. The beginning Java programmer should understand how arrays work within the language.

Array Subscripts Are All Checked at Runtime   Java is very careful when it comes to working with arrays and their subscripts. The language checks the subscripts to be sure that they are within the legally declared limits of the array. The language will keep a programmer from accessing an out of bounds array element as follows:

```
//we set up an array for 100 doubles
double numbers [] = new double [100];

//try to go out of bounds
for(int i = 0; i < 500; ++ i)      //STOP! array has 100 elements
{

//At i = 100 we get an error and Java stops running the program!
     numbers[i] = Math.random();

}
```

In this code, there are only 100 elements in the array, numbers[0] to numbers[99], but the loop index will range from 0 to 499. As soon as the value of *i* is 100 and it attempts to place a random number in numbers[100], the program has an error (ArrayIndexOutOfBoundsException) and stops executing. This Java feature is a lifesaver! It stops the program from overwriting some other parts of memory. Other languages do not trap for this error, and an error like this can wreak havoc on a program. This type of error can cause bizarre program behavior, and waste countless programmer hours while he or she tracks down this bug.

That is why it is important that the Java programmer always use the array-Name.length when his or her code is traversing an array. The loop index will never attempt to access an out of bounds array element.

An Array of Objects Must Be Filled Before They Are Used   Let's back up and examine our first examples of array declarations. We declared an array of integers, Sailboats, and Strings.

```
numbers = new int [1000];
Sailboat boats[] = new Sailboats[5];
String names[] = new String [3];
```

When a Java program creates an array of primitives, such as the numbers array, the memory is set up and the programmer can then access any element of the array without problem:

```
numbers[17] = 1955;
numbers[85] = 4928;
numbers[283] = 2945;
```

The second declarations set up an array of Sailboat objects. In Java, when the programmer declares an array of object references, Java requires that the array elements be filled before you use them. Java makes a reference for an array of Sailboats, but we still need to create the Sailboats that will be stored in the array. In other words, you must be sure that each reference element points to an object before you try to access individual object methods!

```
//Create an array of Sailboat references.
Sailboat boats[] = new Sailboats[5];


//Fill all of the Sailboats by calling the Sailboat constructor.
//This allocates memory for each boat.

int i;
for(i = 0; i < boats.length; ++ i)
{
        boats[i] = new Sailboat();              //this is good
}


//Now you can sail your boats!

for(i = 0; i < boats.length; ++ i)
{
        boats[i].setSail();
}
```

If you attempt to create an array of Sailboat objects and forget to set up a boat in each element of the array, the program issues a NullPointerException error and stops execution. The following code does not work in Java!

```
//Set up an array of Sailboats.
Sailboat boats[] = new Sailboats[5];


//Now try to access the third boat in the array

boats[2].setSail();          //STOP! Must create a boat before you sail it!
```

collection classes
a term describing the Java-provided classes, including ArrayList, Vector, List, and Map, that can grow or shrink in size and can be manipulated, searched, or sorted by the collection class

Arrays Are Fixed-Length Collection Structures   The arrays that we are studying in this chapter are nothing more than one way that a programmer may "collect" like data items into a single unit. These arrays are fixed in length, meaning that once we create an array, we can not make it any larger. We must access each array element using the array operator [].

Java provides the programmer with several **collection classes**, including ArrayList, Vector, List, and Map. In using these collection classes, the Java programmer instantiates an object of the collection class and uses methods to add, delete, or manipulate items in the object. These object-based collections are flexible, in that they have no predetermined size, and they can grow or shrink dynamically as the program runs. Java also provides the Collection class, which can work on these different types of collection objects. The Collection class provides static methods for sorting, searching, shuffling, finding the max and min, reversing, and swapping items contained in the various objects. We illustrate these classes later in the text (See Programs 7-6 on page 397 and 11-6 on page 690).

5.3
Array of Arrays

It is possible to declare an **array of arrays**[1] in Java that is composed of two subscripts. Often, but not always, it is used to represent a table of items. You can visualize the table organized in a row and column format. The elements in these multisubscripted arrays are referenced with two numbers, the first representing the row number and the second the column.

> **array of arrays**
> an array composed of two subscripts, which is often —but not always—used to represent a table of items

There are several ways to create and fill a multisubscripted array in Java. The array creation expression is straightforward, as in the single-dimensional array. A reference is declared and then the new keyword is used to allocate the necessary memory. Here, we create a two-dimensional array of integers that consists of 2 rows with 5 columns. Figure 5-9 illustrates how this array is zero indexed. Both the row and column subscripts must be used to access any element in the array.

```
int table [][];          //2 set of [] [] are needed
table = new int [2][5];  //table array is 2 rows and 5 columns

//assign values using both row and column subscript
//here we fill the table with various numbers
table[0][0] = 0;
table[0][1] = 17;
table[0][2] = 18;
table[0][3] = 23;
table[0][4] = 57;
table[1][0] = 84;
table[1][1] = 42;
table[1][2] = 83;
table[1][3] = 2;
table[1][4] = 74;
```

The array initialization expression can be used with multisubscripted arrays. Once again, we set up the table array by providing the initial values when we declare the

---

[1] *Multidimensional array* refers to an array that has more than one set of indices. The ANSI C language calls array of arrays multidimensional arrays. The Ada language has both and they are different. Java has only array of arrays, and only calls them array of arrays.

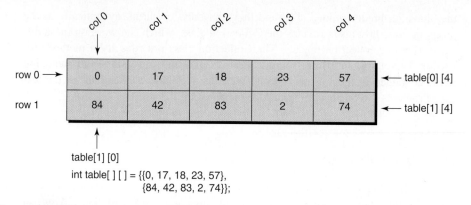

Figure 5-9
A multisubscripted array in Java that contains two rows and five columns.

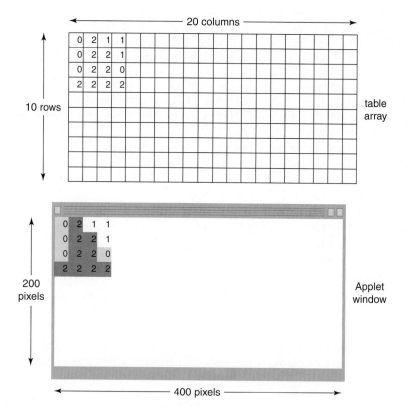

Figure 5-10
The table array is filled with 0s, 1s, and 2s. Colored squares are drawn in the window corresponding to the numbers in the array.

array. The format here shows that each row of values is contained within braces and separated by a comma.

```
int table [][] = {  {0, 17, 18, 23, 57},        //first row
                    {84, 42, 83, 2, 74}  };     //second row
```

Three Colors 2D Applet   The best way to understand two-dimensional arrays in Java is to see an example! As you may suspect, nested for loops will be a very handy tool when working with multisubscripted arrays, because one loop index can be used for the row and one loop index for the column. In this example, we create a two-dimensional array that is 10 rows by 20 columns. We will have a corresponding applet window with a height of 200 pixels and a width of 400 pixels. We fill the array with random numbers: 0s, 1s, and 2s. If the array element has a 0 in it, we paint a cyan colored square. An element containing a 1 paints a white square. Magenta is painted for 2s. Figure 5-10 illustrates this concept. We place the value of the array element in the painted square. The code is seen in Program 5-6, and an example window is shown in Figure 5-11. Restart the applet and watch the pattern change!

```
1    //Program 5-6 Multi-subscripted array in an Applet
2    //File:   ThreeColor2DApplet.java
3
4    import java.awt.Graphics;
5    import javax.swing.JApplet;
6    import java.awt.Color;
7
8    import javax.swing.JOptionPane;
9    public class ThreeColor2DApplet extends JApplet
10   {
11       int table[][] = new int[10][20];    //10 rows by 20 columns
12
13       int ROWSIZE = table.length;
14       int COLSIZE = table[0].length;
15
16       public void start()
17       {
18           //First lets verify that we have 10 rows by 20 columns.
19           String output = "There are "+ ROWSIZE + " rows and   " +
20               COLSIZE + " columns";
21           JOptionPane.showMessageDialog(null,output);
22
23           //fill the table with numbers from 0, 1, or 2
24           for(int row = 0; row < ROWSIZE; ++row)
25           {
```

```
26              for(int col = 0; col < COLSIZE; ++col)
27              {
28                      table[row][col] = (int)(Math.random()*3 );
29              }
30          }
31      }

33      public void paint(Graphics g)
34      {
35          //Each array element corresponds to a 20x20 pixels in the window.
36          //We can use the row and col value *20 to get the window coords.
37          int x1, y1;
38          for(int col = 0; col < COLSIZE; col++)
39          {
40              for(int row = 0;  row < ROWSIZE; row++)
41              {
42                  //first set the color
43                  switch(table[row][col] )
44                  {
45                      case 0:
46                              g.setColor(Color.cyan);    break;
47                      case 1:
48                              g.setColor(Color.white);    break;
49                      case 2:
50                              g.setColor(Color.magenta);    break;
51                  }

53                  //draw the rect, the x value is represented by the col
54                  //the y value is represented by the row
55                  y1 = row*20;
56              x1 = col*20;
57              g.fillRect(x1, y1, 20, 20);

59                  //write the value in the array
60                  g.setColor(Color.black);
61                  g.drawString(Integer.toString(table[row][col]),
62                      x1+12,  y1+12);
63              }
64          }
65          showStatus("Wow, that's a beautiful pattern!");
66      }
67  }
```

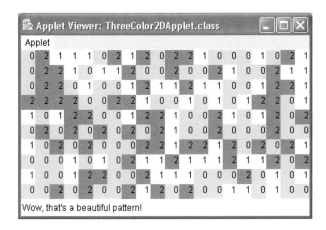

Figure 5-11
An Appletviewer window showing the 10 by 20 grid of colored squares and the array element value for each square. Two-dimensional arrays in Java are often used to represent grids or tables of data.

Nonuniform Array Sizes

The individual arrays that are part of an array of arrays in Java can vary in size, and do not have to be a uniform size as in a grid or table. One way to visualize this is that we can create an array in Java where the rows have varying lengths. The code shown here creates an array that has two elements in the first row, five in the second row, and seven in the third row:

```
int table [][] = new int [3][];
table [0] = new int [2];
table [1] = new int [5];
table [2] = new int [7];
```

If we wanted to place the value 0 in each element, we can use nested for loops and then use the arrayName.length to ask each array for its length:

```
for(int i = 0; i < table.length; ++i)          //table.length is 3
{
       for(int j = 0; j < table[i].length; ++j)  //each row returns a diff length
       {
             table[i][j] = 0;
       }
}
```

Another way to create and initialize this same table array in one expression is:

```
int table [][] = new int [][] {
             new int[] { 0,0 },    //first row has 2 elements
             new int[] { 0, 0, 0, 0, 0},  //second row has 5 elements
             new int[] { 0, 0, 0, 0, 0, 0, 0}   }; //third row has 7
```

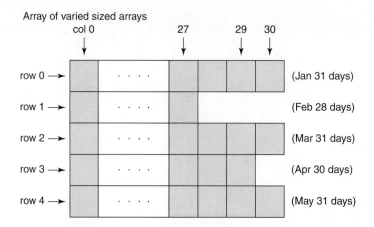

Array of varied sized arrays

col 0   27   29 30

row 0 →   · · · ·   (Jan 31 days)

row 1 →   · · · ·   (Feb 28 days)

row 2 →   · · · ·   (Mar 31 days)

row 3 →   · · · ·   (Apr 30 days)

row 4 →   · · · ·   (May 31 days)

Figure 5-12
Each row in this array is a different length. The length corresponds to the number of days in the first five months of the year.

Days in the Year Applet   In this example, we need to create an array of arrays that accurately represents the first five months of a non-leap year calendar. In this array of arrays, we need 31 days in the first row for January, 28 days in the second for February, 31 in the third for March, 30 in the fourth for April, and 31 in the fifth for May. Figure 5-12 illustrates this concept.

To create an array with varied array sizes, we can use several different array creation expressions. This first example sets all the arrays within the { }:

```
int daysInTheYear[][] = new int[][] {
                                new int[31],
                                new int[28],
                                new int[31],
                                new int[30],
                                new int[31] }
```

Another way to write it is:

```
int daysInTheYear[][];           //create an array reference

daysInTheYear = new int[5][];        //allocate rows
daysInTheYear[0] = new int[31];      //January
daysInTheYear[1] = new int[28];      //February (non-leap year)
daysInTheYear[2] = new int[31];      //March
daysInTheYear[3] = new int[30];      //April
daysInTheYear[4] = new int[31];      //May
```

The beginning programmer might worry that he or she is tasked with needing to remember what the number of columns (length of the rows) are, because they vary from row to row. But that is not a problem because we have the ability to ask the array for its length. Remember, we can use the following expression:

```
arrayName.length
```

to obtain the length of the array. For an array within an array, we must designate which row we want by providing the index, like this:

```
daysInTheYear.length            //returns 5, since the array has 5 rows

daysInTheYear[1].length         //returns 28, since this is referencing the 2nd row
```

Let's rework the ThreeColor2D Applet program so that we incorporate the daysInTheYear array. In Program 5-7, we will use this array and fill each row with the day number of the month. Row 0 represents January, and the elements are filled with 1 through 31. In order to determine the color, we use the modulus operator on the element value and generate a 0, 1, or 2. Notice that we use the arrayName.length expression to assist us. Figure 5-13 shows the output from this program.

```
1    //Program 5-7 Varied-sized arrays in an Array
2    //File:  DaysInTheYearApplet.java
3
4    import java.awt.Graphics;
5    import javax.swing.JApplet;
6    import java.awt.Color;
7
8    public class DaysInTheYearApplet extends JApplet
9    {
10       int   daysInTheYear[][];           //create an array reference
11
12       public void start()
13       {
14            daysInTheYear = new int[5][];       //allocate 5 rows
15            daysInTheYear[0] = new int[31];     //January
16            daysInTheYear[1] = new int[28];     //February
17            daysInTheYear[2] = new int[31];     //March
18            daysInTheYear[3] = new int[30];     //April
19            daysInTheYear[4] = new int[31];   //May
20
21            //fill the array with days in each month
22            for(int row = 0; row < daysInTheYear.length; ++row)
23            {
24                 for(int col = 0; col < daysInTheYear[row].length; ++col)
25                 {
```

```java
26                          daysInTheYear[row][col] = col + 1;
27                  }
28              }
29      }

31      public void paint(Graphics g)
32      {
33              //each array element corresponds to a 20x20 portion of the window
34              //we can use the row and col value *20 to get the window coords.
35              int x1, y1;
36              for(int row = 0;  row < daysInTheYear.length; row++)
37              {
38                      for(int col = 0; col < daysInTheYear[row].length; col++)
39                      {
40                              //mod the day (date) with 3 to set the color
41                              switch(daysInTheYear[row][col] %3 )
42                              {
43                                      case 0:
44                                              g.setColor(Color.cyan);    break;
45                                      case 1:
46                                              g.setColor(Color.white);    break;
47                                      case 2:
48                                              g.setColor(Color.magenta);    break;
49                              }

51                              //draw the rect, the x value is represented by the col
52                              //the y value is represented by the row
53                              y1 = row*20;
54                              x1 = col*20;
55                              g.fillRect(x1, y1, 20, 20);

57                              //write the value in the array
58                              g.setColor(Color.black);
59                              g.drawString(Integer.toString (daysInTheYear[row][col]),
60                                      x1+5,   y1+12);
61                      }
62              }

64              showStatus("The days of the first five months of the year."+
65                  " Top row = Jan, Last row = May");
66      }
67  }
```

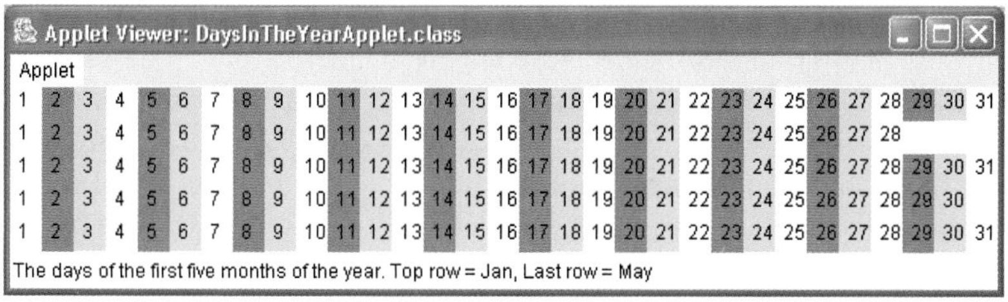

Figure 5-13
The output showing the colored grid pattern of an array with various size arrays.

5.4
Summary

This chapter introduces the concept of an array. An array represents a group of values that are all of the same data type (primitives or objects), and this group is referred to with one name. The size of the array is established when the array is declared, and that size cannot be changed. Each member of the array must be accessed by using the array [] and integer subscript. The first element of the array is numbered zero. The last element in the array is an array and can be declared and filled with values one though ten, as follows:

```
//declare an array of integers
int numbers[] = new int [10];      //this array can hold 10 values

//There are ten numbers, numbers[0] through numbers[9].

//fill the array with 1 - 10
for(i = 0; i < numbers.length; ++i)   //the index i is used to access the array element
{
      numbers[i] = i+1;         //add 1 to i
}
```

or the array can be created and initialized at the same time, like this:

```
//Create and initialize an array of integers in one step.
int numbers[] = { 0, 1, 2, 3, 4, 5, 6, 7, 8, 9 };

//The size is not needed because Java counts the number of
//initial values and sets the size.
```

Arrays in Java are automatically initialized to "zero" values. If you declare a numeric array, that is an array of type double, float, int, short, or long, Java places a number zero into each element. A boolean array is filled with false values, and reference array (non-primitive) elements are assigned null.

The Java programmer should always use the arrayName.length when traversing an array. Java arrays keep track of their length, and the programmer can use arrayName.length instead of needing to remember the actual length, or refer back to the declaration statement. Java also checks the array subscripts at runtime to ensure that the program does not attempt to access an illegal array element.

When the programmer creates an array of objects, Java automatically assigns the null value to each array element. You must be sure to allocate the objects (using the new operator) before you attempt to use any of the objects. This is illustrated in the following code with FootballPlayer objects.

```
//Create an array of 25 FootballPlayer references.
FootballPlayer team[] = new FootballPlayer[25];


//Fill all of the FootballPlayer objects by calling the FootballPlayer constructor.
//This allocates memory for each player in the team array.


//Use arrayName.length, that is, team.length instead of remembering
//that this array is sized to 25.


int i;
for(i = 0; i < team.length; ++i)
{
        team[i] = new FootballPlayer();
}
//Your team of FootballPlayers is now ready to go!
```

Java allows the programmer to create an array of arrays, also known as a multisubscript array. The array of arrays is composed of two subscripts. The array can be used to represent a tabular or grid format:

```
int grid [][];          //2 set of [] [] are needed
grid = new int [3][6];    //the grid array is 3 rows and 6 columns
```

The array initialization expression can be used with multisubscripted arrays. Once again, we set up the grid array by providing the initial values when we declare the array. The format here shows that each row of values is contained within braces and separated by a comma.

```
int grid [][] = {  {0, 17, 18, 23, 52, 57},    //first row
                   {84, 42, 83, 2, 74, 69},    //second row
                   {36, 13, 83, 1, 8, 93} };   //third row
```

The individual arrays that are part of an array of arrays in Java can vary in size, and do not have to be a uniform size as in a grid or table. One way to visualize this is that we can create an array in Java, where the rows have varying lengths. The code shown here creates an array that consists of four arrays of varying sizes:

```
double chart[][] = new double [4][];
chart[0] = new double [3];
chart[1] = new double [6];
chart[2] = new double [7];
chart[3] = new double [9];
```

If we wanted to place a random number valued between 0.0 and 1.0 in each element of the chart array, we can use nested for loops and the arrayName.length to ask each array for its length:

```
for(int i = 0; i < chart.length; ++i)          //chart.length is 4
{
        for(int j = 0; j < chart[i].length; ++j)  //each row returns a diff length
        {
                chart[i][j] = Math.random();
        }
}
```

5

This chapter describes the array fundamentals for the classic or traditional array found in many computer languages. These arrays are of fixed length, and the individual elements are accessed by using the array name, array operator [] and an integer subscript. Java has several classes that can be used to "collect" data, including ArrayList, Vector, List, and Map. These classes offer a more flexible object-based item, to which data can be added at will. The Collection class has many static methods that provide sorting, searching, and shuffling, of these class-based "collectors."

The beginning Java programmer should become proficient in working with the traditional fixed-length array described in this chapter, as arrays are found in most all computer languages. Java offers more powerful utility classes, and it could be argued that these supersede the traditional array. However, it is crucial that the Java programmer understand traditional arrays in order to use collection type classes properly.

5.5
Practice!

Practice makes perfect, and we all want to have our programs work perfectly! In this practice section, we build four different programs that use arrays.

Dice Tossing Program

In this program, we simulate throwing two dice 1000 times. For each toss, we add the two face values together. For any given toss, assuming both dice have an equal chance of rolling a one through six, we get a summed value of two through twelve. We want to keep track of the summed value for all 1000 tosses. In order to do this, we set up an array of "bins" where the index of the array element represents the sum of the dice. Figure 5-14 illustrates this concept.

A common practice in array programming involves having a calculation or program occurrence determine an array subscript instead of being set by a for loop variable. In Program 5-8, we use the random number generator to simulate the die tossing event. The die values are summed, and the sum determines which element is incremented. The bin array keeps track of the frequency (total count) for each of the possible sums. One last thing in this program to note: we use a DecimalFormat object to print the bin number and the bin element to three places padded with zeros. Figure 5-15 illustrates the output for 1000 tosses.

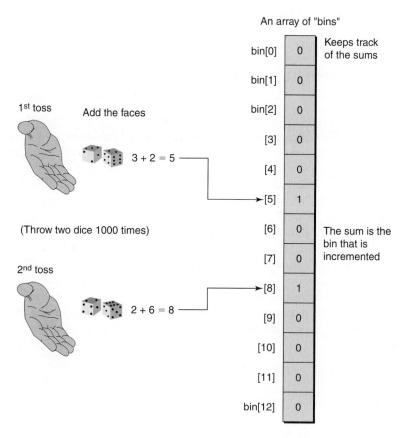

Figure 5-14
Each toss of the dice determines which bin element is incremented.

```
1    //Program 5-8  Obtain toss information for 2 dice.
2    //File: DieTossFrame.java
3
4    import java.awt.Graphics;
5    import javax.swing.JFrame;
6    import javax.swing.JOptionPane;
7    import java.text.DecimalFormat;
8
9    public class DieTossFrame extends JFrame
10   {
11       //We make an array to hold the sum of the dice.
12       //Possible sums from 2 die are 2 - 12
13       //We make the array elements 0 - 12, don't use 0,1
14       int bins [] = new int [13];
15       int total;
16       String sTotal;
17
18       public static void main( String[] args )
19       {
20               DieTossFrame testDice = new DieTossFrame();
21               testDice.setDefaultCloseOperation( EXIT_ON_CLOSE );
22       }
23
24       public DieTossFrame()              //class constructor method
25       {
26               sTotal = JOptionPane.showInputDialog("How many tosses?");
27               total = Integer.parseInt(sTotal);
28
29               int i, die1, die2, sum;
30
31               //Java has initialized our bin array to zero, but let's
32               //write it here for practice working with arrays.
33               //Since the bins hold the toss sums, they all need to
34               //be initialized to zero!
35               for(i = 0; i < bins.length; ++i)
36               {
37                       bins[i] = 0;
38               }
39
40               //fill the array with sum of the dice
41               for(i = 0; i < total; ++i)
42               {
43                       //obtain a number between 1-6 for each dice
44                       die1 = (int)(1 + Math.random()*6 );
45                       die2 = (int)(1 + Math.random()*6 );
46                       sum = die1 + die2;
```

```
47
48          //The sum of the dice is used to designate which bin we increment.
49                    bins[sum]++;
50          }
51
52          setSize( 250, 300 );          //set the window size
53          setTitle("Dice Tossing Program");
54          show();
55      }
56
57      public void paint( Graphics g )
58      {
59          String output = "Result for " + sTotal + " tosses.";
60          g.drawString( output, 25, 60 );
61          output = "Sum of 2 Dice      Frequency";
62          g.drawString( output, 25, 90 );
63          DecimalFormat df = new DecimalFormat("000");    //format # w/ 3 zeros
64
65          //data contained in bins 2 through 12
66          for(int i = 2; i < 13; ++i)
67          {
68                  output = "    " + df.format(i) +
69                  "                    " + df.format(bins[i]);
70                  g.drawString(output,25, 90+15*i);
71          }
72      }
73  }
```

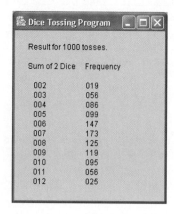

Figure 5-15
The results showing the summed value of two dice tossed 1000 times.

Seven Dwarfs and String Array

This short program (Program 5-9) illustrates using the array initialization expression with a one-dimensional array of Strings. We do not need to use a size value of seven to indicate the length of the array. No, Java doesn't know automatically that there are seven dwarfs, but it does count the number of strings we have in the initialization expression. We can then use the dwarfs.length to determine the number in the array. Because we have seen how to sort numbers, let's borrow the bubble-sort() method from the previous program and sort the dwarf names into alphabetical order. We must modify the method slightly, and use the String's compareTo() method to determine if a String "is greater than" or "less than," lexicographically speaking. This just means that "A" is before "B" in the alphabet; therefore, "A" is less than "B." Refer to Figure 5-16 for the program output.

```java
1    //Program 5-9  Use an array initialization expression for Strings
2    //File: SevenDwarfsFrame.java
3
4    import java.awt.Graphics;
5    import javax.swing.JFrame;
6
7    public class SevenDwarfsFrame extends JFrame
8    {
9       String dwarfs[] = { "Doc", "Sleepy", "Dopey", "Grumpy", "Sneezy",
10                              "Bashful", "Happy" };
11
12      public static void main( String[] args )
13      {
14            SevenDwarfsFrame hiho = new SevenDwarfsFrame();
15            hiho.setDefaultCloseOperation( EXIT_ON_CLOSE );
16      }
17
18      public SevenDwarfsFrame()          //class constructor method
19      {
20            bubblesort();        //sort the names into alphabetical order
21
22            setSize( 250, 175 );       //set the window size
23            setTitle("Seven Dwarfs Program");
24            show();
25      }
26
27      public void paint( Graphics g )
28      {
29            for(int i = 0; i < dwarfs.length; ++i)
30            {
```

```
31              g.drawString(dwarfs[i],25, 60+15*i);
32          }
33      }
34
35      //this bubble sort routine sorts Strings in alphabetical order
36      public void bubblesort()
37      {
38          //we can obtain the size of a Java array like this:
39          int size = dwarfs.length;
40          int x, y;
41          String temp;
42
43          for(x = 1; x < size; ++x)
44          {
45              for( y = 0; y < size - 1; ++y)
46              {
47                  //String's compareTo returns an int
48                  //0 if the Strings hold the same value
49                  // < 0 for "A" < "B" situation
50                  // > 0 for "B" > "A" situation
51                  if( (dwarfs[y].compareTo( dwarfs[y +1])) > 0)
52                  {
53                      temp = dwarfs[y];
54                      dwarfs[y] = dwarfs[y+1];
55                      dwarfs[y+1] = temp;
56                  }
57              } //close for
58          } //close for
59      } //close bubblesort
60  } //close class
```

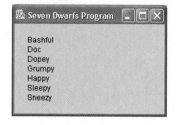

Figure 5-16
The output from our program that uses an array of Strings to store the names of the
seven dwarfs and a bubblesort() method to place the names in alphabetical order.

Chapter 5 ▌ Arrays in Java

Pond Pictures

In Program 5-10, we really flex our Java array muscles and use a two-dimensional array of Images and Strings. We use the Toolkit tools provided in the java.awt package to get our images, and the Graphics class drawImage() method to show them in our frame. Figure 5-17 shows four pond pictures. The important thing to notice here is how we use nested for loops to traverse the arrays. We use the loops to get the images, to draw the images, and to write the titles of the pictures. Study the program. Better yet, practice building a frame of your favorite pictures!

```
1    //Program 5-10  Use 2D Arrays for Images and Strings.
2    //File: PondPicsFrame.java
3
4    import java.awt.Graphics;
5    import javax.swing.JFrame;
6    import java.awt.Toolkit;
7    import java.awt.Image;
8
9    public class PondPicsFrame extends JFrame
10   {
11       Image pictures[][] = new Image [2][2];
12
13       int ROWSIZE = pictures.length;
14       int COLSIZE = pictures[0].length;
15
16       String filenames[][] =
17           {      {"YellowLilly2Small.jpg", "PinkLilly2Small.jpg"},
18                  {"HungryFishSmall.jpg","TwoGoldenOrfesSmall.jpg"} };
19
20       String picTitles[][] =
21           {      {"A yellow lilly", "A pink lilly"},
22                  {"Feed us!", "Two Golden Orfes" } };
23
24       public static void main( String[] args )
25       {
26              PondPicsFrame sb = new PondPicsFrame();
27              sb.setDefaultCloseOperation( EXIT_ON_CLOSE );
28       }
29
30       public PondPicsFrame()          //class constructor method
31       {
32              for(int i = 0; i < ROWSIZE; ++i)
33              {
34                     for(int j = 0; j < COLSIZE; ++j)
35                     {
36                            pictures[i][j] =
37                            Toolkit.getDefaultToolkit().getImage (filenames[i][j]);
38                     }
39              }
```

```
40              setSize( 450, 460 );        //set the window size
41              setTitle("Pond Pictures Program");
42              show();
43      }
44
45      public void paint( Graphics g )
46      {
47              int x = 0, y = 0;
48              for(int i = 0; i < ROWSIZE; ++i)
49              {
50                      for(int j = 0; COLSIZE < 2; ++j)
51                      {
52                              x = i * 210 + 20;      //offset to the right
53                              y = j * 210 + 40;      //offset the y due to title bar
54                              g.drawImage(pictures[i][j], x, y, this);
55                              g.drawString(picTitles[i][j], x+10, y + 200);
56
57                      }
58              }
59      }
60  }
```

Figure 5-17
The pond pictures in a JFrame, the result of a program that uses two-dimensional arrays for Images and Strings.

JOptionPaneDemo Program

Now that we are familiar with arrays in Java, we are able to expand how we use the JOptionPane methods. The showInputDialog() method allows us to pass an array of Objects, as well as an Icon so that we can customize our message boxes. When we pass an array of Objects to the showInputDialog() method, our user can select his or her choice from a drop-down list. In this last program, we ask the user to pick his or her favorite color. We have passed an array of Objects, which contain Strings, into the showInputDialog() along with an icon of a star. We acknowledge the color and ask the user if he or she wishes to change the color. See Program 5-11. Figure 5-18 shows the JOptionPane windows.

Do not be intimidated when you see a method requiring the Object data type. Remember that Object is the root of all Java classes, and all Java classes have it as a superclass.

```
1   //Program 5-11
2   //JOptionPaneDemo.java
3
4   //This program demonstrates using arrays and icons in JOptionPane
5   //input and message boxes.
6
7   import javax.swing.JOptionPane;
8   import javax.swing.Icon;
9   import javax.swing.ImageIcon;
10
11  public class JOptionPaneDemo
12  {
13
14      Object[] possibleColors = {"Red","Blue","Green", "Other"};
15      Object[] possibleChoices = {"Yes", "No", "Maybe"};
16      Icon starIcon;
17
18      public static void main(String args[])
19      {
20              JOptionPaneDemo app = new JOptionPaneDemo();
21              System.exit(0);
22      }
23
24        public JOptionPaneDemo()
25        {
26              starIcon = new ImageIcon( "star.png" );
27              Object doAgain = "Yes";
28              String response;
29
```

```
30              //Loop while the user wants to continue picking a color.
31              while (doAgain.equals("Yes") || doAgain.equals("Maybe") )
32              {
33                      //choose the color
34                      Object selectedColor = JOptionPane.showInputDialog(null,
35                              "What is your favorite color?", "Color Choice",
36                      JOptionPane.INFORMATION_MESSAGE, starIcon,
37                      possibleColors, possibleColors[0]);
38
39                      if(selectedColor.equals("Red") )
40                      {
41                              JOptionPane.showMessageDialog(null,"Red Red Wine!",
42                              "Color Choice", JOptionPane.INFORMATION_MESSAGE, starIcon);
43                      }
44                      else if(selectedColor.equals("Blue") )
45                      {
46                              JOptionPane.showMessageDialog(null,"Deep Blue Sea!",
47                              "Color Choice", JOptionPane.INFORMATION_MESSAGE, starIcon);
48                      }
49                      else if(selectedColor.equals("Green") )
50                      {
51                              JOptionPane.showMessageDialog (null,"Green With Envy!",
52                              "Color Choice", JOptionPane.INFORMATION_MESSAGE, starIcon);
53                      }
54                      else if(selectedColor.equals("Other") )
55                      {
56                              JOptionPane.showMessageDialog(null,
57                              "Hmmmmm, not Red, Blue, or Green",
58                              "Color Choice",
59                              JOptionPane.INFORMATION_MESSAGE, starIcon);
60                      }
61
62                      //Ask the user if he or she wants to change the color
63                      doAgain = JOptionPane.showInputDialog(null,
64                      "Do you want to change your mind?","Pick another color?",
65                      JOptionPane.INFORMATION_MESSAGE,starIcon,
66                      possibleChoices, possibleChoices[0]);
67
68              } //close while
69      } //close constructor
70 } //close class
```

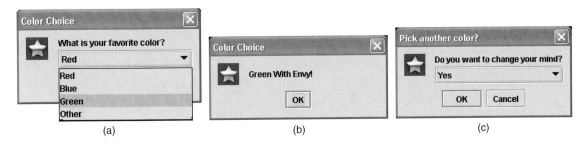

(a)   (b)   (c)

Figure 5-18
The array of color choices and array of response choices are passed into the
JOptionPane showInputDialog() method. An icon is also passed in. a) The input dialog
window with the color choices in a drop-down selection list. b) The program's response
to the color green. c) The "Pick another color" dialog window, in its initial state.

▉ REVIEW QUESTIONS AND PROBLEMS

Short Answer

5

1. What data type must be used as an array index (or array subscript)?

2. How can you visualize a single dimensional array?

3. What is the index value for the first element in a one-dimensional array?

4. Does Java allow the programmer to designate the starting and ending index values for an array?

5. Why is a for loop a convenient tool for the programmer to use when he or she is working with arrays?

6. Is it possible for a Java program to contain an array that is sized to 100, and then change the size of the array to 500?

7. Describe the two ways in which a Java programmer can create an integer array of size ten, and have the value 5 stored in each of the ten elements.

8. Why is it important that the Java programmmer write his or her for loops that traverse arrays with arrayName.length as the loop limit, instead of simply writing the integer value for the size?

9. Where is a source of array sorting routines on the WWW?

10. The Java language checks the array subscripts at runtime. What does this mean?

11. Would it be possible for a Java programmer to declare an array of 1000 integers, and then go ahead and store 2000 integers in the array?

12. Suppose we had a class Airplane and we declare an array reference for 500 Airplane objects, like this:

```
Airplane planes [] = new Airplanes[500];
```

What must we do before we attempt to use or call any of our new objects?

13. What does it mean when we say that Java is zero-indexed?

14. How does a Java program react if the programmer attempts to access an element out of bound of the array?

15. Is it possible to declare an array in a Java applet?

16. How would a Java programmer need to write the code that declares an array of floats that represents a fifty by seventy-five grid of numbers?

17. If you create an array of arrays in Java, how many subscripts are required to access any element?

18. Describe which set of braces are used to designate an array in Java.

19. What sort of array could be used to hold the hourly temperature data for a 24-hour period if you had a digital thermometer outside your window. How would you declare this array?

20. What is the difference between these two array initialization statements?

```
int numbers[] = { 5, 2, 1, 8, 6,   4 };
int numbers[][] = { {5, 2, 1}, {8, 6,   4 }};
```

Debugging Problems — Compiler Errors

For Questions 21–25, identify the compile errors in the code.

21.

```
int list[25];
float i;
for(i = 0, i<25; +i)
{
        list[i] = 0.0;
}
```

22.

```
float x[] = new x [10];
String names [];
names = {"Bob", "Tom", "Bill", "Rick" };
```

23.

```
float address[] = new String [100];
int i;
for(i = 0; i <= 100; ++i)
{
        address[i] = Math.random();
}
```

24.

```
double case[] = new double[3];
case[0] = 1.234;
case[1] = 9.5234;
case[2] = 5.8423;
```

25.

```
double values = {3.52, 6.234, 9.332, 7.123 };
values.length = 5;
values[4] = 7.2334;
```

Debugging Problems—Run-Time Errors

26–30: Each of the following programs compiles but does not do what the specification states. What is the incorrect action, and why does it occur?

26. Specification: Fill a 100-element floating point array with the values 0.01, 0.02, ... 0.99, 1.0.

```
public class Problem26
{
        public static void main(String args[])
        {
                float x[] = new float[100];
                int i;
                for(i = 1; i <= 100;++i)
                {
                        x[i] = i/100;
                }
        }
}
```

27. Specification: Generate two numbers, using the random number generator, and place the smaller value in the first element and the larger number in the second element.

```
public class Problem27
{
        public static void main(String args[])
        {
                double num [] = new double [2];
                int i;
                for(i = 0; i < num.length; ++i)
                        num[i] = Math.random();

                if(num[1] < num[0])
                        num[0] = num[1];
                        num[1] = num[0];
        }
}
```

28. Specification: Fill a 15-element array with random integers between 10 and 90. Search the array and place the highest value in the "largest" variable.

```
public class Problem28
{
        public static void main(String args[])
        {
                int n[] = new int [15];
                int i;
                for(i = 0; i < n.length; ++i)
                        n[i] = (int)(Math.random() % 90 + 10);

                int largest;
                for(i = 0; i < n.length; ++i)
                {
                        if(n[0] < n[i])
                                largest = n[i];
                }
        }
}
```

29. Specification: Fill a fifty-element integer array with randomly selected odd numbers. The numbers should be between the value 1 and 99 (i.e. 1,3,5, ... 97, 99). In order to determine if a number is odd, perform the mod 2 operation on the number. That is, number%2 is zero if even and one if odd. Hint: be sure that you are able to obtain the full range of odd numbers, including 1 and 99.

```
public class Problem29
{
        public static void main(String args[])
        {
                int oddNumbers[] = new int [50];
                int i;
                for(i = 0; i < oddNumbers.length; ++i)
                        oddNumbers[i] = (int)(Math.random() * 100);

                for(i = 0; i < oddNumbers.length; ++i)
                {
                    if(oddNumbers[i]%2 == 0)
                            oddNumbers[i]--;
                }
        }
}
```

30. Specification: Assume that a String array is filled with names. Search the array for the name "Bob" and replace that with the name "Bobby."

```
public class Problem30
{
        public static void main(String arg[] )
        {
                String name[] = new String[100];
                //assume the name array is filled with 100 names

                for(int i = 0; i <= 100; ++i)
                {
                        if(name[i] == "Bob");
                                name[i] = "Bobby";
                }
        }
}
```

Programming Problems

31–40: Write complete Java programs. If you have covered Chapter 12, bundle your class file into a JAR and execute the program by double-clicking it.

31. Write a complete Java applet that draws a stop sign centered in the applet window. Include a red colored polygon that contains the words STOP written in white.

32. Write a Java application that draws a five-pointed gold star. Write your name underneath the star. Incorporate the marcsPause() method so that your name flashes on and off.

33. Write a Java program (either an applet or an application) that draws a yellow, triangular, YIELD sign.

34. Expand the Days in the Year applet to include all 365 days in a non-leap year year. The array of arrays should have the twelve months. Build a String array that contains the names of the twelve months. Create and fill a Color array with four unique colors. Color code the four "Java seasons" of the year. Our Java seasons are a few days off the actual season, but it simplifies the problem. (Java seasons are Winter, December 20–March 19; Spring, March 20–June 19; Summer, is June 20–September 19; and Fall, September 20–December 19). Label each month and also draw the day number. Attempt to build you code using arrays to assist you instead of brute forcing the code. This program is similar to the Days In The Year Applet, except that we color code the Java seasons instead of the days.

35. Modify the ShowASort applet program so that it mimics the behavior of the applets that we see on the NIST.gov website. Your program should draw the original array, pause, and redraw the array during each pass of the bubblesort() method. You will need to modify the bubblesort() method so that it only makes one pass through the data each time the method is called.

36. a) Create six of your favorite images and size them to 100 × 100 pixels. Save them as JPG images. Arrange the six images in a pyramid pattern and write a brief label underneath each image. Use the Pond Pictures program as a guide for your program. b) If you have covered Chapter 11, place your picture file-names and picture labels in a data file and read this information into your program. The labels and filenames should be separated by a comma, like this:

A yellow lilly., yellowlilly.jpg
Feed us!, hungryfish.jpg

37. a) Use three String arrays, each sized to ten, and create three separate lists of words. One list contains the names of colors, one list has adjectives, and one list has nouns. Sort each list into alphabetical order and write each set of same-indexed array elements in your frame. You will need to modify your bubble-sort() routine and use it for sorting. You may have it sort all three arrays, one at a time. For example, if your arrays were sized to three, and the colors were red, blue, and green; the nouns were antelope, pig and horse; and and the adjectives were and happy, hairy, and slow; your frame would contain these three lines:

blue hairy antelope

green happy horse

red slow pig

b) If you have covered Chapter 11, place your three lists for your arrays in three different data files and read them into your program. Place each word on its own line in the files. If you are JAR'ing this program, the data files are not included in the JAR. They must be located in the same folder as the JAR file.

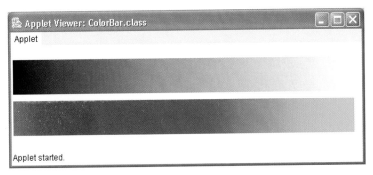

Figure 5-19
The applet window showing two color bars.

38. Figure 5-19 shows an applet window that contains two color bars.

The top color bar consists of 256 filled rectangles, ranging from entirely black to entirely white. (RGB values from 0, 0, 0 to 255, 255, 255). The lower color bar is a spectrum that is created from the following code. Each pass through this loop generates three values between 0 and 255 that represents the pertinent value for the red, green, and blue component of the color band:

```
//generate a spectrum of colors
for (i=0; i<256; i++)
{
    j = 2 * i;
    if (i > 127) j = 511 - (2 * i);
    r = 255 - i - i;
    if (r < 0) r = 0;
    b = -255 + i + i;
    if (b < 0) b = 0;
    //note, the r is red, j is green, and b is blue
}
```

Write an applet program that generates these two color bars. You may vary the size of the bars. You will need two arrays for the Colors, one for the gray color band and one for the red, blue, and green color band. Study the Color class documentation to determine how to instantiate a color with any given color. Fill the two band arrays in the init() method, and perform the actual drawing in the paint() method. Your paint() method should be tidy, following the example code here:

```
//declare and initialize your x, y, width, height variables
//grayBand and rainbowBand are the Color arrays

    for(int i = 0; i < grayBand.length; ++ i)
    {
        g.setColor(grayBand[i] );
        g.fillRect(x, y, width, height);
```

```
            //adjust drawing code

            g.setColor(rainbowBand[i] );
            g.fillRect(x, y, width, height);

            //adjust x and y values
        }
```

39. Figure 5-20 shows a frame window that contains the plot of the line
$y = 0.5x + 20$ for the range $x = -50$ to $x = 50$.
Tick marks are spaced every 10 units.

In this problem, the Java programmer should reproduce this line plot in a
frame window following these specifications. The program should have an
array of integers (could be doubles if you like) that has 101 rows by 2
columns. Each row in the array represents a pair of points that satisfy this
equation. The first column is the x value and the second column is the y value.
The x values should range from -50 to 50. In the constructor, fill the array
with the 101 pairs of points. For example, the first row of the array should be
$(-50, -5)$. If you plug -50 into x, y is calculated to be -5. In the paint()
method you should draw the x- and y-axes in different colors and draw tick
marks every 10 units. Plot the points using the Graphic's fillOval() method.
Your window should show the line ranging from $x = -50$ to $x = 50$ (101
points total). Research the translate() method in the Graphics class to help
make your drawing easier. (Hint: remember that the window's (0,0) location is
normally in the upper left corner.)

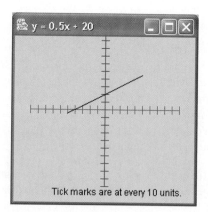

Figure 5-20
A graph of the line $y = 0.5x + 20$. The frame window shows the x-axis in red and
y-axis in blue. Tick marks are spaced at every 10 units. The y-intercept is found
when $x = 0$ at (0,20) and the x-intercept is found when $y = 0$ at $(-40, 0)$.

Chapter 5 ▮ Arrays in Java

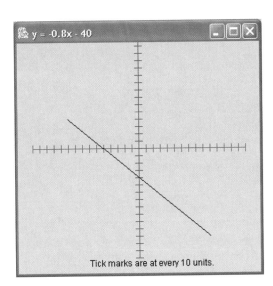

y = -0.8x - 40

Tick marks are at every 10 units.

Figure 5-21
A graph of the line $y = -0.8x - 40$. The frame window shows the x-axis in red and y-axis in blue. Tick marks are spaced at every 10 units. The y-intercept is $(0, -40)$ and the x-intercept is at $(-50, 0)$.

40. Figure 5-21 shows a frame window that contains the plot of the line

$y = -0.8x - 40$ for the range $x = -100$ to $x = 100$.

This problem is similar to Question 39, except the line plot is for

$y = -0.8x - 40$ and the x values range from -100 to 100.

This program should have an array of integers (could be doubles if you like) that has 201 rows by 2 columns. Each row in the array represents a pair of points that satisfy this equation. The first column is the x value and the second column is the y value. In the constructor, fill the array with the 201 pairs of points. For example, the first row of the array should be $(-100, 40)$. If you plug -100 into x, y is calculated to be 40. In the paint() method, you should draw the x- and y-axes in different colors and draw tick marks every 10 units. Plot the points using the Graphic's fillOval() method. Your window should show the line ranging from $x = -100$ to $x = 100$ (201 points total). Research the translate() method in the Graphics class to help make your drawing easier. (Hint: remember that the window's (0,0) location is the upper left corner.)

6

Writing and Using Our Own Java Classes

KEY TERMS AND CONCEPTS

abstraction
abstract classes
access specifiers
array reference
block of code
block scope
class scope
constructor
early binding
encapsulation
finalize() method
garbage collection
heap
inheritance
late binding
method overloading
method overriding
object and array references
object-oriented principles
overloaded constructor
overloaded methods
package access
polymorphism
private
public
push and pop
return statement
scope
stack

CHAPTER OBJECTIVES

Introduce the four main principles of any object-oriented programming language.

Review what we have learned about classes in the first five chapters.

Explain how access specifiers control whether class members are visible to or hidden from other classes.

Rewrite several of our previous programs so that they are in separate classes.

Illustrate how constructors are written and called.

Review the method signature term.

Present a formal discussion of primitive and reference variables.

Introduce the stack and the heap and explain how they relate to variable, object, and array storage.

Describe the details for writing methods and show how primitive, array, and object references are passed to and from methods.

Time to Get Down to Business!

We worked hard in the previous chapters to learn Java fundamentals, including data types, primitives, control statements, for loops, while loops, and arrays. We used inheritance to extend our classes—creating either JFrame or JApplet classes. We instantiated and used objects of classes that Java provides for us. That's quite a list of accomplishments! But there is no time for relaxing as we still have many topics to master.

It is time to undertake one of the most important topics in Java: learning to write and to use our own Java classes that contain our own methods. What makes up a class? Classes contain member variables and methods. It is true that we have been writing our own classes since Chapter 2. Our programs have all been one-class programs. However, in the real world, Java programs consist of many classes. We have classes for our user interface, classes for the nuts and bolts of our program, and classes to provide specialized assistance. We may have to organize our classes into a package, and import and use them in another Java class. If our program is an application, we must have one class that contains the main() method. If our program is an applet, we need a JApplet class that has our init(), start(), and paint() methods. Before we get into the details of writing classes, let's review what we know about them.

6.1
What Do We Know About Classes?

A class can be thought of as a job description. Recall our Pilot class from Chapter 3. What data are associated with the pilot? The pilot has a name, and a social security number. The pilot also has a pilot license with certain types of certifications for the types of planes he or she can fly. What are the actions that a pilot performs? The pilot goes to work, gets a paycheck, flies the plane, reads maps, and talks to the air traffic control tower. The job description for an airline pilot encapsulates the required data pilots must know and tasks that a pilot must perform. Our pals Mike and Rick are

Pilot objects. They both have a name, a SS number, a pilot's license, and a variety of certifications. Both are able to perform all the duties described by the Pilot class.

Java classes also contain data and methods. We have used Java classes that provide a variety of services, such as popping up message boxes, formatting our numbers, or obtaining a square root value. In most cases, when we make an object in our program, we must import the package containing the desired class so that the Java compiler knows which class we need. We create or instantiate an object of a class by using the new operator. When we use the new keyword, the class constructor method is called. To call a method, we must use the object and dot operator, objectName.methodName(). The following portion of code illustrates these concepts, using Java's DecimalFormat class.

```
import java.text.DecimalFormat;            //import the class

public class Demo
{
        public Demo()
        {
                //Create the formatter object by using the new operator.
                //The new keyword calls the constructor
                //DecimalFormat(String pattern)
                //We select the constructor and pass in the desired pattern.
                DecimalFormat fred = new DecimalFormat("0.00000");

                double x = 1.2345678901234;

                //We use the objectName.methodName to invoke one of
                //the object's format() methods.
                String output = "The value of X is" + fred.format(x);
```

The classes are job descriptions and the methods perform the required tasks. We must instantiate an object of the class and the object invokes the method. In the code just illustrated, the DecimalFormat object is named "fred," and we ask fred to perform the formatting task for us. We write "fred.format(x)" which calls the DecimalFormatter format() method, passing it the double value stored in *x*. The DecimalFormat object then produces a string of our double value showing five decimal places of precision. We set the five decimal places by passing in the "0.00000" pattern to the constructor. We can accomplish the same thing in a slightly different manner with this code:

```
import java.text.DecimalFormat;            //import the class

public class Demo
{
```

```
public Demo()
{
        //Create the formatter object by using a different constructor
        //than above. In this constructor DecimalFormat() there are no
        //input values, so it uses its default pattern.
        DecimalFormat fred = new DecimalFormat();

        //now set the pattern via the applyPattern() method
        fred.applyPattern("0.00000");
        double x = 1.23456789;

        //we use the object.methodName to have the object work for us
        String output = "The value of X is" + fred.format(x);
```

While this is review for you, note how the class provided us a way to set the pattern via the constructor or by using the applyPattern() method. A well written class provides flexibility and utility.

Where else have we seen and used classes? If you are thinking of the JOptionPane and Math classes, good for you! We have used static methods from these two classes. Remember that a static method does not require us to instantiate an object of the class. Instead, we use the ClassName.staticMethodName() format. Program 6-1 is a short program to review:

```
1   //Program 6-1 Review classes and objects.
2   //File: SqrtDemo.java
3
4   import javax.swing.JOptionPane;          //import the class
5
6   public class SqrtDemo
7   {
8      public SqrtDemo()
9      {
10          String sNumber;
11
12          //use the static method to show an input dialog box
13          sNumber = JOptionPane.showInputDialog("Enter a number");
14
15          double number, sqrootNumber;
16
17          //static parseDouble converts our string to a double
18          number = Double.parseDouble(sNumber);
19
20          //static sqrt calculates and returns a square root
```

```
21          sqrootNumber = Math.sqrt(number);

22

23          //static toString converts the number back to a string

24          String sAnswer = Double.toString(sqrootNumber);

25

26          //now we use another static method to show the answer

27          JOptionPane.showMessageDialog(null, sAnswer);

28

29      }

30

31      public static void main(String args[])

32      {

33          new SqrtDemo();        //No reference is required since we never

34          System.exit(0);        //use it.

35      }

36  }
```

In the code just illustrated, we use the static methods from JOptionPane to obtain and show the number. The Double class provides two static methods for converting from and to a String. Classes that provide static methods really spoil the Java programmer. We do not need to instantiate any objects to perform these tasks because static methods are available. A subtle point sometimes lost to the new Java programmer—we can call static methods via an object. The code in Program 6-2 performs the same task as that in Program 6-1, but here we create JOptionPane and Double objects in our code.

```
1   //Program 6-2
2   //File SqrtDemo
3
4   import javax.swing.JOptionPane;
5
6   public class SqrtDemo
7   {
8      public SqrtDemo()
9      {
10          String sNumber;
11
12
13          //Make a JOptionPane object named jop
14          JOptionPane jop  = new JOptionPane();
```

```
15
16              //use the jop object to show an input box
17              sNumber = jop.showInputDialog("Enter a number");
18
19              double number, sqrootNumber;
20
21              //make a Double object
22              Double doubleObject = new Double(0.00);
23
24              //use the Double object to convert the string to a double
25              number = doubleObject.parseDouble(sNumber);
26
27              //Java doesn't let us make a Math object. Must use static method.
28              sqrootNumber = Math.sqrt(number);
29
30              //use the double object to convert the answer to a String
31              String sAnswer = doubleObject.toString(sqrootNumber);
32
33              //the jop object shows us the answer
34              jop.showMessageDialog(null, sAnswer);
35      }
36
37      public static void main(String args[])
38      {
39              new SqrtDemo();          //We do not need a class reference here.
40                                       //We just use the new operator to call this
41                                       //class constructor.
42              System.exit(0);
43      }
44  }
```

Lastly, let's review how we wrote our programs in previous chapters. The SevenDwarfsFrame program from Chapter 5 is a perfect one for us to look at. Here is the code:

```
1   //Review the Seven Dwarfs Program
2   //File: SevenDwarfsFrame.java
3
4   import java.awt.Graphics;
5   import javax.swing.JFrame;
6
```

```
 7    public class SevenDwarfsFrame extends JFrame
 8    {
 9        String dwarfs[] = { "Doc", "Sleepy", "Dopey", "Grumpy", "Sneezy",
10                                     "Bashful", "Happy" };
11
12        public static void main( String[] args )
13        {
14            SevenDwarfsFrame hiho = new SevenDwarfsFrame();
15            hiho.setDefaultCloseOperation( EXIT_ON_CLOSE );
16        }
17
18        public SevenDwarfsFrame()          //class constructor method
19        {
20            bubblesort();        //sort the names into alphabetical order
21
22            setSize( 250, 175 );         //set the window size
23            setTitle("Seven Dwarfs Program");
24            show();
25        }
26
27        public void paint( Graphics g )
28        {
29            for(int i = 0; i < dwarfs.length; ++i)
30            {
31                g.drawString(dwarfs[i],25, 60+15*i);
32            }
33        }
34
35        //this bubble sort routine sorts Strings in alphabetical order
36        public void bubblesort()
37        {
38            //we can obtain the size of a Java array like this:
39            int size = dwarfs.length;
40            int x, y;
41            String temp;
42
43            for(x = 1; x < size; ++x)
44            {
45                for( y = 0; y < size - 1; ++y)
46                {
47                    if( (dwarfs[y].compareTo( dwarfs[y +1] ) ) ) > 0 )
48                    {
49                        temp = dwarfs[y];
```

```
50                              dwarfs[y] = dwarfs[y+1];
51                              dwarfs[y+1] = temp;
52                      }
53              } //close for
54          } //close for
55      } //close sort
56  } //close class
```

Refer to Figure 6-1. In the class definition line, we use the extends keyword and extend the JFrame class. This means that our class SevenDrawfsFrame is a JFrame class. We inherit methods from the JFrame hierarchy tree, including a paint() method. The paint() method is passed a Graphics object that we use to draw information into the window.

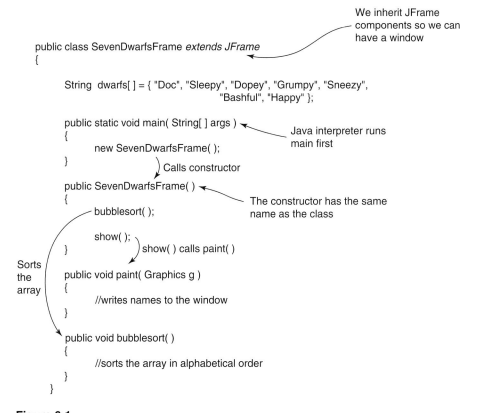

Figure 6-1
Summary of the various parts of the SevenDwarfsFrame class, including the class variable and constructor and paint() methods.

The dwarves array initialization expression is located after the class definition line and before any method definitions. Declaring a variable here makes it visible to all of the methods in the class. This means that the constructor, bubblesort(), and paint() methods can see and use the variables. The main() method is executed first, when the Java interpreter runs the program. The class constructor is called because we use the new keyword. The constructor calls the set up methods for the window. It also calls the bubblesort() method, which sorts our array in alphabetical order. The constructor then calls the show() method, which in turn calls the paint() method and passes it a Graphics object that we can use to paint or draw information to the window.

6.2
Object-Oriented Principles

Java is an object-oriented language, and to fully understand it you must understand object-oriented programming concepts. For a computer language to be object-oriented, it must support the following four key principles: abstraction, encapsulation, inheritance, and polymorphism. These principles sound complicated but they are actually simple ideas.

Abstraction

abstraction

the process of selecting pertinent data describing an item

Remember, we are thinking of classes as job descriptions. To model a real-world item or situation in a computer program, we must identify the essential characteristics of that item or situation and the operations (methods) for that data. **Abstraction** is the process of selecting pertinent data describing the item we wish to model. An object-oriented language provides a disciplined way to bundle this information together.

Consider the real world situation of flying a glider. A glider is an airplane that does not have an engine. They usually seat one or two people, and are made of light-weight fiberglass with a clear canopy. To become airborne, a tow plane tows the glider a few thousand feet above the ground. When he or she is ready, the glider pilot releases the tow hook, setting the glider free. You may search on the web and locate the many sites dedicated to gliders and soaring, including www.ssa.org. Now, imagine that you are a glider pilot. We ask you to identify the essential glider components with which you interact in order to fly this type of plane. You describe four parts: the stick, rudder pedals, the landing gear lever, and the radio. Gliders are composed of hundreds of parts, but these are a few items that the pilot uses to fly the plane.

encapsulation

the process of bundling the data and the associated operations (methods) together and treating them as a single unit

Encapsulation

Encapsulation is the process by which we bundle the data and the associated operations (methods) together and treat them as a single unit. When we write a class in Java, we bundle the data and operations together. Encapsulation also provides a wrapper that protects the code and data from being arbitrarily accessed or misused by outside sources. Now that we have some characteristics or parts that describe the pertinent data for flying a glider, it is equally important to describe the operations that can be performed on them, and the results of our actions.

To relate the encapsulation concept to our glider example, let's briefly examine the control stick. The stick controls the plane's pitch and roll. If the pilot pushes the stick forward, the resulting action pitches the nose downward, causing the glider to go faster. Pulling the stick back pulls the nose up, which slows the glider. Pushing the stick to the left rolls the body to the left. The stick must be pushed to the right to stop the roll. There are control surfaces built into the plane's body and wings that are activated as the pilot moves the stick, causing the various movements of the plane. The pilot does not have to worry about those controls because the stick movement encapsulates them. This means that the complex inner workings of the glider are hidden from our pilot, and he or she has well defined means for interacting with the glider. In object-oriented programming, the goal of the encapsulation process is to provide a well defined interface to the data and to prevent misuse or arbitrary access to the various systems.

In Java, the class provides the encapsulation for data and methods. It is important that we begin to follow the encapsulation rules by hiding our data and providing well defined interfaces to it. Why? Because we don't want any surprises when our programs run. As we write our classes, we will have class data and methods. There are keywords in Java, known as access specifiers, which are used to control whether our data and methods are hidden or visible to other classes. We'll see this shortly.

6

Inheritance

Inheritance is the ability to create a new class from an existing class. The new class is referred to as a subclass, while the existing class is known as a superclass. The subclass inherits characteristics and methods from the superclass, and has new, customized features not found in the superclass. For example, a SportsCar could be created from a Car class and could inherit all the necessary Car characteristics and features. The SportsCar also has customized features that the Car class does not, such as specialized suspension. Inheritance represents an "is a" class relationship, the subclass is a superclass—the SportsCar is a Car. We discussed inheritance concepts in Chapter 3 and have seen inheritance in action with the extends keyword. Inheritance provides us the ability to easily create JApplets or JFrames. Soon we will create our own hierarchy of superclasses and subclasses.

inheritance
the ability to create a new class from an existing class

Polymorphism

Polymorphism means many shapes or many forms. In object-oriented programming languages, it refers to one interface and many methods. Simply put, polymorphism is the ability to use the same name to refer to methods that perform different tasks. One

polymorphism
one interface, many methods, including the ability to use the same name to refer to methods that perform different tasks

type of polymorphism is **method overloading**. Overloading occurs when a class has several methods with the same name. For example, in the DecimalFormat class, there are several different methods named format. The format() methods all format data in different ways. In the JOptionPane class, we used at least two versions of the showMessageDialog() and showInputDialog() methods. In all of these cases, each of these methods has different input values. The compiler reads the source code and determines which method is intended by examining the input data. There is no mystery as to which method is to be used, because the compiler matches the input list to the intended method.

A more complicated form of polymorphism is known as **method overriding**. Method overriding is seen when a superclass and a subclass have the same named method with the identical method inputs. It is said that the method in the subclass overrides the method in the superclass. When a Java program is compiled, the compiler cannot determine which of the methods will be called, because they are identical. However, when the code is executed, the program examines which object is invoking the method, therefore it executes the correct one. This resolution occurs at runtime. In programming jargon, the ability of the compiler to determine which method to call is known as **early binding**, and the ability to choose the correct method during execution is called **late binding**.

A Brief Aside Concerning Abstract Classes

Abstract classes, covered in detail in Chapter 9, embody the concept of abstraction and make use of the basic principles of an object-oriented language. Briefly, a Java programmer can design an abstract class that is a generalized "idea" or "blueprint" for a class of objects and is intended to be a superclass. The abstract superclass is then extended by subclasses, and the abstract methods are overridden in these subclasses. The subclasses are complete classes that may be instantiated, and are referred to as concrete classes.

For example, using our glider discussion, we can develop an abstract class called Airplane. In this class, we can describe a general set of methods and data that are needed for any airplane, including takeOff(), landing(), flightParameters(), fuelType(), and controlStick(). If we then write a class for a glider, a commercial passenger jet, and a six-seater single engine personal aircraft, they all need to include these methods. The controlStick() method for a glider, a jet, and a personal aircraft perform essentially the same tasks, but their implementations are very different. Abstract classes provide a powerful programming technique using the concept of polymorphism to its maximum. We see several examples of abstract classes in Chapter 9.

Object-Oriented Languages Must …

In summary, any object-oriented language must provide a way to abstract and encapsulate data and methods. Java provides the class to accomplish this. You must be able to create new classes by inheriting properties and methods from existing classes. In Java, we use the extends keyword for this operation. Lastly there must be polymorphic capabilities. Java allows you to overload and override methods.

If these four object-oriented principles seem a bit obscure, don't worry. As we continue through this chapter, we will abstract and encapsulate our classes. We will overload methods and see polymorphism in action. In Chapter 9, we explore inheritance and method overriding. These four principles work together nicely! They support a programming environment that produces robust code that is easily reused, maintained, and expanded.

6.3
Where Are We Going?

As we dig deeper into object-oriented principles and learn how to write and use our own classes, keep the big picture in mind. Our goal in this chapter is to learn how to write classes and have the classes interact with each other in a program. Recall the fast-food restaurant example from Chapter 2. Visiting the restaurant, we can see different types of workers, including cooks, order takers, bus people, and managers. If we write a program modeling the restaurant, we need a class for each type of worker, as well as one for the restaurant. Each of these workers has well defined ways to interact with the world and with each other. Worker objects (instances of the classes) call methods to perform their tasks. The CounterWorker object greets the customers, takes the order, and receives payment. This object then asks the cook to prepare the food. The cook prepares the food and packages it for the customer.

The encapsulation principle dictates that we hide our data and provide a well defined interface to the class members. What does it mean to hide the data? First, what data is associated with a manager? Data associated with a manager includes cost of materials and salary of employees. Customers probably should not see the cost of materials because they would think these costs are the same as what they should pay. We hide the information, making it private. When we write a class containing data and methods (tasks), we make the data private (hide it), meaning that the world and other classes cannot see it. We also make the methods that interact with the world public (or visible). There are keywords in Java, known as access specifiers, that provide this visibility/invisibility control for us.

access specifiers or access modifiers

dictate the visibility and accessibility of class members

Access Specifiers

Java has three keywords that dictate the visibility and accessibility of class members and classes. These keywords are used with data, methods, and classes, and are referred to as **access specifiers** or **access modifiers**. The three keywords are private, protected, and public. Java provides a default specification if you forget, either intentionally or not, to provide one of the three modifiers. The term **public**

public

access specifier used to make data or methods visible to all of the other classes

TABLE 6-1
Access specifiers used in Java classes.

Keyword	Definition
private	The private members are not accessible outside of the class. Private members can be seen, used, assigned and/or changed only by other members of the class.
public	Public members are accessible anywhere the class is accessible. This means the public members may be seen, used, assigned, and/or changed by all parts of the program, providing that these other program parts can find the class object.
protected	The protected members are accessible in the subclasses of this class. More on protected specifier in Chapter 9.
none (no specifier is provided) known as package access	Class members that do not have an access specifier are said to have package access, meaning that the members are accessible from classes in the same package. See Chapter 13 for a discussion of packages.

private

access specifier used
to hide data or
methods from all other
classes

6

is used to make data or methods visible to all of the other classes. The term **private** is used if it is to be hidden or invisible to all classes. Table 6-1 summarizes these modifiers.

A rule of thumb: Java programmers should ask for guidance concerning the appropriate usage for access specifiers. Generally speaking, private is used for class data so that we hide the class data from the world. This requires the programmer to provide set() and get() methods for any class data that may be accessible by other classes. However, there are circumstances where methods are private and data are public. For example, we could have a class that computes the retail price of an item. The computeRetailPrice() could be private and the resultant retailPrice variable public. Private class members are not accessible by other classes.

The protected access specifier should be used for superclass data and methods that are intended to be inherited by a subclass. Any class member that has a protected or public access specifier is inherited by subclasses. Private members are not inherited by subclasses. We cover protected access specifiers in Chapter 9.

First Example: Circle Class and CircleApplet

As we progress through this chapter, we will learn many new things concerning Java classes. Before we jump into the new details, let's look at a program to gain a general feel for how the classes and objects interact. Program 6-3 asks the user to enter a value for the radius of a circle. The program calculates the circle's area and circumference (distance around the circle), and we draw a circle in the applet window. We also show the radius, area, and circumference values for the circle. See Figure 6-2, which shows these two windows.

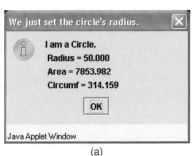

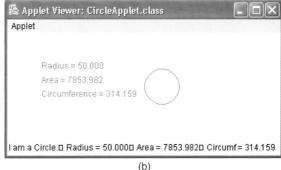

(a)   (b)

Figure 6-2
a) The Circle object's description is shown in the JOptionPane dialog box, and b) the resultant Applet Window shows the Circle object's data as well as draws a circle. Notice that the newline characters are displayed as small rectangles in the window's status bar. This information is obtained from the Circle's toString() method, but drawString() cannot work with newline characters, therefore they are drawn as rectangles.

This program can be written easily in one applet class. But we need to learn how to break our Java programs into separate classes. As we do this, we must also separate the "jobs" of the classes into a logical grouping. In Program 6-3, we build a Circle class and a CircleApplet class. The important thing to notice is that our Circle class takes care of the business of calculating the area and circumference for our circle once it is given the radius. We instantiate a Circle object in the CircleApplet class. The applet's job is to interact with the user. It asks for the radius and then passes that information into a Circle object, which calculates our circle values. The applet then asks the Circle object for the data and reports it to the user. You might think that the Circle class should also draw the circle, but it cannot because it does not have access to the window. The CircleApplet extends JApplet, and it has a paint() method that has the ability to draw a circle using the Graphics object.

```
1   //Program 6-3
2   //File: Circle.java
3
4   //This Circle class performs the Circle calculations.
5   //When the user sets the radius, we automatically
6   //calculate the area and circumference by calling the
7   //calcAreaAndCircumference() method.
8
9   //The resultant values can be obtained by calling the
10  //various get() methods.
11
12  import java.text.DecimalFormat;
```

```
13
14    public class Circle
15    {
16      double radius, area, circumference;
17
18      //Constructor, performs initialization tasks.
19      //Sets the radius to 1 and calls the method to
20      //calculate the area and circumference of the circle.
21      public Circle()
22      {
23            radius = 1.0;
24            calcAreaAndCircumference();
25
26      }
27
28      //Constructor, sets the radius to the input value
29      //and calls method to calc the area and circumf.
30      public Circle(double r)
31      {
32            radius = r;
33            calcAreaAndCircumference();
34      }
35
36      //setRadius is passed a radius value.
37      public void setRadius(double r)
38      {
39            radius = r;
40            calcAreaAndCircumference();
41      }
42
43      //Calculates the area and circumference of the
44      //circle based on the radius value.
45      private void calcAreaAndCircumference()
46      {
47            area = Math.PI*Math.pow(radius,2);
48            circumference = 2.0*Math.PI*radius;
49      }
50
51      //The get methods return the specified variable.
52      public double getRadius(){ return radius; }
53      public double getArea(){ return area; }
54      public double getCircumference(){ return circumference; }
55
56      //We write the toString() method that returns a String
57      //describing the object. We use a DecimalFormat object
58      //to write the values to 3 decimal places.
59      public String toString()
60      {
```

```
61          DecimalFormat df = new DecimalFormat("0.000");
62
63          String desc;
64          desc = "I am a Circle.\n Radius = " + df.format(radius) +
65                  "\n Area = " + df.format(area) + "\n Circumf = " +
66                  df.format(circumference);
67
68          return desc;
69      }
70 }
```

There are new things in this code that we have not seen yet. Do not worry about this, because we plan to present all the new material in this chapter. Please notice, however, that we instantiate a Circle object in the applet class and call the Circle methods with the object name and dot operator. Another new thing to note is that each of the classes are contained in their own *.java* file, all the *.java* files are located in the same directory or folder, and each must be compiled separately. These steps are shown in Figure 6-3. It is possible to compile all the *.java* files using the javac *.java command.

The applet class's HTML file is loaded by the appletviewer. Review Figure 6-2 which shows the results from this program. Once the user has entered a radius, the applet calls ball.toString() and shows how the Circle's toString() method describes the object. This is shown in a JOptionPane message box (Figure 6-2a). The appletviewer window is seen in Figure 6-2b. The ball.toString()'s description is written in the applet's status bar. The square characters in the status bar represent the newline characters in the description string.

The CircleApplet class instantiates a Circle object. The CircleApplet class is seen here:

```
1  //Program 6-3
2  //File: CircleApplet.java
3
4  //The CircleApplet has a Circle object named ball.
5  //In start() we ask the user for the radius value and set
6  //it into the ball object. (The ball object then calculates
7  //the area and circumference for us.)
8
9  //In paint() we get the circle values from the ball object
10 //and draw a circle in the window.
11
12 import java.awt.Graphics;
13 import javax.swing.JApplet;
14 import java.awt.Color;
15 import javax.swing.JOptionPane;
16 import java.text.DecimalFormat;
```

```
17
18    public class CircleApplet extends JApplet
19    {
20       //Here we create a Circle object named ball.
21       //Our applet class uses this object to perform
22       //Circle calculation tasks.
23
24       Circle ball = new Circle();
25
26       public void start()
27       {
28            String sRadius;
29            sRadius = JOptionPane.showInputDialog("Enter the circle's radius. ");
30
31            //We set the radius value of the circle object by passing in a double
32            //value we parse from the sRadius String.
33            ball.setRadius( Double.parseDouble(sRadius) );
34
35            //Just for fun, let's call the ball's toString() method and
36            //see how it describes itself.
37            JOptionPane.showMessageDialog( null, ball.toString(),
38            "We just set the circle's radius.", JOptionPane.INFORMATION_MESSAGE);
39       }
40
41       public void paint(Graphics g)
42       {
43            //Write the ball's information in the applet's status bar.
44            showStatus( ball.toString() );
45
46            g.setColor(Color.magenta);
47
48            //drawOval() input is (xUpperLeft, yUpperLeft,width, height)
49            int r = (int) ball.getRadius();
50            g.drawOval(200,50, r, r);
51
52
53            //We will get the actual radius, area, and circumference values
54            //from the circle object and format them here. Notice that
55            //we combine the ball.get() method in the format() methods.
56            DecimalFormat df = new DecimalFormat("0.000");
57
58            String sRad = "Radius = " + df.format( ball.getRadius() );
59            String sArea = "Area = " + df.format( ball.getArea() );
60            String sCircum = "Circumference = " +
61            df.format( ball.getCircumference() );
62
```

6

```
63          g.drawString(sRad, 50, 50);
64          g.drawString(sArea, 50, 70);
65          g.drawString(sCircum, 50, 90);
66      }
67  }
```

```
C:\JPT>
C:\JPT>javac Circle.java

C:\JPT>javac CircleApplet.java

C:\JPT>appletviewer CircleApplet.html
```

Figure 6-3
The *Circle.java* and *CircleApplet.java* files are located in the same directory or folder, and must be compiled separately. It is possible to use the javac *.java command instead of individual javac commands. The *CircleApplet.html* file references the *CircleApplet.class* file. The appletviewer command reads the HTML file and loads *CircleApplet.class*.

Second Example: Dice Tossing with Die Objects

The dice tossing program from Chapter 5 is a perfect program to use to practice writing our own classes and methods. In this example, we present a complete program and top level diagrams to illustrate how the classes interact. Concentrate on the general idea and program organization. In the next section, we present the details and rules for writing and using methods.

In Program 5-8, we simulated throwing two dice 1000 times and incremented the elements in a bin array where each element represented the possible sum of the two dice. Review Program 5-8 on page 268. Notice that it consists of one class located in the *DieTossFrame.java* file. We perform nearly all of the work in the constructor. We initialize our bin array and simulate the dice tossing by generating two integers between one and six. We do not have dice in the program, but our integers variables hold the two generated values. Using a for loop, we generate 1000 pairs of numbers and keep track of the sums. We then call the show() method, which forces a call to paint(). In paint(), we write the results of our dice tossing in the window.

We build the same program here, but instead of having one class do everything, we build a Die class and then use two Die objects in the Frame class. We split the program into two classes and separate the work into individual methods. Figure 6-4 illustrates the skeletal framework and shows how we separate the parts of our program. The class variables for the frame class include the bin array and two die objects, which we declare as private. The DieTossFrame2 has the main() method, and it calls the DieTossFrame2 constructor just as we have written it in previous programs. The constructor method now performs the initialization tasks as a constructor should. But instead of performing the program tasks itself, the constructor calls a separate method to throw the die. In throwTheDice(), a for loop is used, the

```
// File: DieTossFrame2.java
public class DieTossFrame2 extends JFrame          Class variables are
{                                                  hidden by using the
        private Die die1 = new Die( );             private keyword
        private Die die2 = new Die( );
        private int bins [ ]  =  new int [13];

        public static void main (String args[ ])  ◄──── (1) Java interpreter starts at main( )
        {
                DieTossFrame2 testDice = new DieTossFrame2( );

        }                                  (2) constructor is called
        public DieTossFrame2( )
        {
                //initialize bins, ask for total
                //call throwTheDice( );
                throwTheDice( );
                                            (3)

        }

        public void throwTheDice ( )
        {

                //throws the dice, keeps track by filling the bin array
                show( );
        }                                (4) show( ) calls paint( )
        public void paint ( Graphics g )
        {

                //show the results

        }

}
```

Instantiate
two Die
objects

```
//File: Die.java
public class Die                          Separate
{                                         Java
        //has data and methods for a single die
}
```

Figure 6-4
Summary of the program flow for the reworked dice tossing program. The program
has two class files and the work of the program has been separated into methods
within the classes.

two dice are tossed, and their sum is recorded in the bin array. After the dice throwing is finished, it calls the show() method, forcing a call to paint().

Program 6-4 consists of two *.java* files, *DieTossFrame2.java* and *Die.java*. Both files are located in the same directory and both must be compiled successfully so that their associated class files are created. To run this program we use the java command with the DieTossFrame2 class because it contains the main() method.

Figure 6-5 illustrates the command line steps that are required and resulting window.

The following is the *DieTossFrame2.java* code. Compare it to the program diagram in Figure 6-4.

```
1    //Program 6-4  Rework of Program 5-8 using a Die class.
2    //File: DieTossFrame2.java
3
4    import java.awt.Graphics;
5    import javax.swing.JFrame;
6    import javax.swing.JOptionPane;
7    import java.text.DecimalFormat;
8
9    public class DieTossFrame2 extends JFrame
10   {
11      //We instantiate 2 die objects for our program.
12      private Die die1 = new Die();
13      private Die die2 = new Die();
14
15      //We make the bin array elements 0 - 12, don't use 0,1
16      private int bins [] = new int [13];
17      private int total;
18      private String sTotal;
19
20      public static void main( String[] args )
21      {
22            DieTossFrame2 testDice = new DieTossFrame2();
23            testDice.setDefaultCloseOperation( EXIT_ON_CLOSE );
24      }
25
26      //class constructor initializes values and calls throw the dice
27      public DieTossFrame2()
28      {
29            setSize( 250, 300 );     //set the window size
30            setTitle("Dice Tossing Program");
31
32            sTotal = JOptionPane.showInputDialog("How many tosses?");
33            total = Integer.parseInt(sTotal);
34
35            //first we zero all the values in the bin array
36            for(int i = 0; i < bins.length; ++i)
37            {
```

```
38                    bins[i] = 0;
39                }

40

41            //now call throwTheDice method that throws the dice
42            throwTheDice();

43

44    }

45

46

47    public void throwTheDice() //this method performs the dice throwing
48    {
49            int sum;
50            //fill the array with sum of the dice
51            for(int i = 0; i < total; ++i)
52            {
53                    die1.tossDie();        //calls the Die's tossDie method
54                    die2.tossDie();
55                    sum = die1.getFaceValue() + die2.getFaceValue();

56

57                    bins[sum]++;
58            }

59

60            //finished tossing the dice, now call show() to paint results
61            show();
62    }
63    public void paint( Graphics g )
64    {
65            String output = "Result for " + sTotal + " tosses.";
66            g.drawString( output, 25, 60 );
67            output = "Sum of 2 Dice      Frequency";
68            g.drawString( output, 25, 90 );
69            DecimalFormat df = new DecimalFormat("000");

70

71            //data contained in bins 2 through 12
72            for(int i = 2; i < bins.length; ++i)
73            {
74                    output = "    " + df.format(i) + "                              " +
75                    df.format(bins[i]);
76                    g.drawString(output,25, 90+15*i);
77            }
78    }
79 }
```

```
C:\JPT>
C:\JPT>javac Die.java

C:\JPT>javac DieTossFrame2.java

C:\JPT>java DieTossFrame2
```
(a)

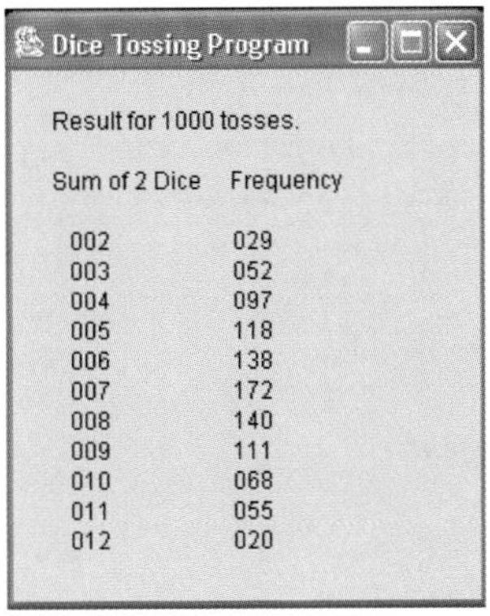

Dice Tossing Program

Result for 1000 tosses.

Sum of 2 Dice	Frequency
002	029
003	052
004	097
005	118
006	138
007	172
008	140
009	111
010	068
011	055
012	020

(b)

Figure 6-5
a) The commands required to compile and run the TossDiceFrame2 program. Both classes are compiled. (We could have used javac *.java command.) The DieTossFrame2 class that contains the main() method is loaded by the java interpreter. b) The Dice Tossing Program window.

The Die class is contained in a file named *Die.java*. Figure 6-6 shows a top-level diagram of this class, which is not complicated. It has only one data member, an integer, representing the face value of the die. We declare the data private because we want to hide it from other classes. There is one constructor method which sets the face value to one. The job of the tossDie() method is to use the random number generator to obtain a number between one and six and assign it to the class variable faceValue(). There are getFaceValue() and toString() methods that return die information. The actual program code is shown in Program 6-4.

```
1    //Program 6-4 The Die class represents one dice cube.
2    //File: Die.java
3
4    public class Die
5    {
6        private int faceValue;
7
8        public Die() //the constructor sets the face to 1
9        {
10               faceValue = 1;
11       }
12
```

```
13    public void tossDie()
14    {
15            //obtain a number between 1-6 for the face value of the die
16            faceValue = (int)(1 + Math.random()*6 );
17    }
18
19    public int getFaceValue()
20    {
21            return faceValue;
22    }
23
24    public String toString()
25    {
26            String definition = "I am a die. My face value is " + faceValue;
27            return definition;
28    }
29
30 }
```

//File: Die.java

public class Die
{
    private int faceValue; ← Class variable is private and hidden from the world

    public Die( )
    {
        faceValue = 1; ← Class constructor sets faceValue to 1
    }

    public void tossDie( )   Random number generator produces a value for faceValue
    {
        faceValue = a # from 1 to 6
    }

    public int getFaceValue( ) ← Public method is the class interface to the private faceValue variable
    {
        return faceValue;
    }

    public String toString( ) ← Provides a string description of the object
    {
        String definition = "I am a die...";
        return definition;
    }
}

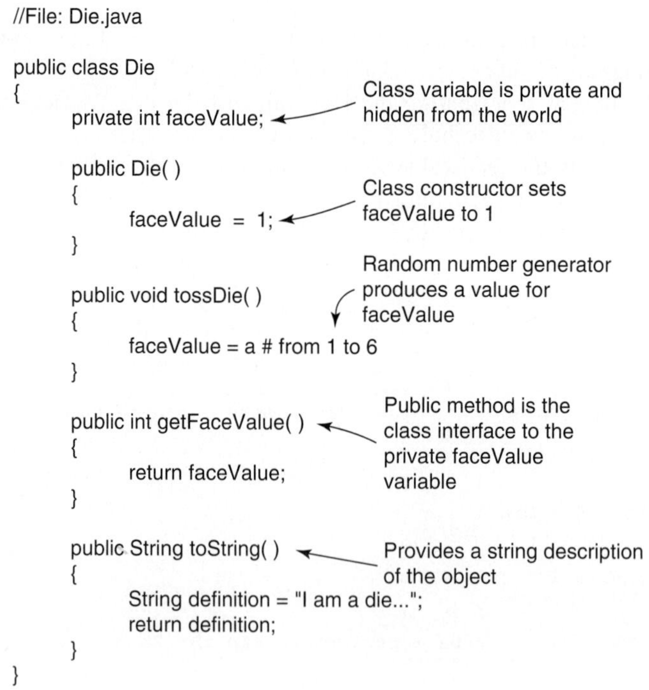

Figure 6-6
Summary of the Die class. Because the faceValue data is private (hidden from the world), we need a getFaceValue() method in order to obtain the value.

Remember, in our object-oriented programs, we want strict control over who has access to the class data. By making the data private, only the class members have access to it. You are probably thinking, what good is the data if I can't get my hands on it? Excellent question. In Java programs, we strive to make the data private, but for data values that will be needed by other classes, you must provide public methods, typically named getDataName() such as getFaceValue(), that pass the data out of the class.

The Die class provides a public method named getFaceValue(). We also provide a toString() method, which passes back a String description of the Die object, including its face value. (We have not called the Die's toString() method in this program because we are tossing many pairs of dice. The toString() method is available to us if we ever want to watch the individual tosses.) Class members can access the private data directly but the get methods must be used by other classes. Figure 6-7 illustrates how the Die class hides the private data and does not allow other classes to access it except through public methods.

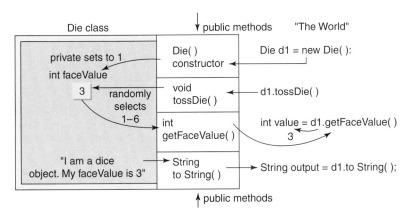

Figure 6-7
Private data in the Die class can be accessed by the class methods directly. The data can be accessed by other classes through public methods.

Revisit RandomLines Applet

In Chapter 4, we wrote an applet that used Java's random number generator to compute the x and y coordinates that were used to draw random lines. In the Chapter 4 program, we had the code for generating the x and y pairs for our lines, alternating the colors, and drawing the lines in the paint() method. Refer to Program 4-14 on page 206.

In this program, we are going to rewrite this applet so that we use a class called LineGenerator to generate the line coordinates and alternate the colors for us.

Our applet class instantiates a generator object and calls its methods to obtain the line information. The applet will draw the lines. It is important to remember that a class is like a job description, and we are separating the tasks of this program into two appropriate classes. You can think of this program as having two different workers working together instead of one worker doing all the tasks. Figure 6-8 illustrates the relationship between the RandomLinesApplet2 and the LineGenerator class. The two classes are contained in their respective *.java* files. In order to run this program, you must compile each of the java files separately. Figure 6-9 illustrates the javac and appletviewer commands and the resultant Applet Viewer window with fifteen random lines. The source code for the RandomLinesApplet2 program is shown in Program 6-5.

```
//File: RandomLinesApplet2.java
public class RandomLinesApplet2 extends JApplet
{
    LineGenerator line = new LineGenerator( ) ;          ⟵  Data includes a
                                                             LineGenerator object
    public void init( )
    {
        line.setWidthRange (400);      ⟵   Set ranges for the generator
        line.setHeightRange (200);          in init( )
    }

    public void paint (Graphics g)
    {
        int coords[ ] = new int [4];       Ask generator for the color, line coordinates
        for(int i = 0; i < 15; ++i) ⟵──── and draw line in for loop that executes 15 times
        {
            g.setColor( line.getColor( ) );
            coords = line.getCoords( );
            g.drawLine(coords[0], coords[1], coords[2], coords[3] );
        }
    }
}
```

```
//File: LineGenerator.java
public class LineGenerator
{                                                          Separate
    //Has all data and methods for generating line   ⟵   Java file
    //coordinates and alternating colors.
}
```

Figure 6-8
The RandomLinesApplet2 class has a LineGenerator object, which produces the information for the applet's random lines.

```
C:\JPT>
C:\JPT>javac LineGenerator.java

C:\JPT>javac RandomLinesApplet2.java

C:\JPT>appletviewer RandomLinesApplet2.html
```
(a)

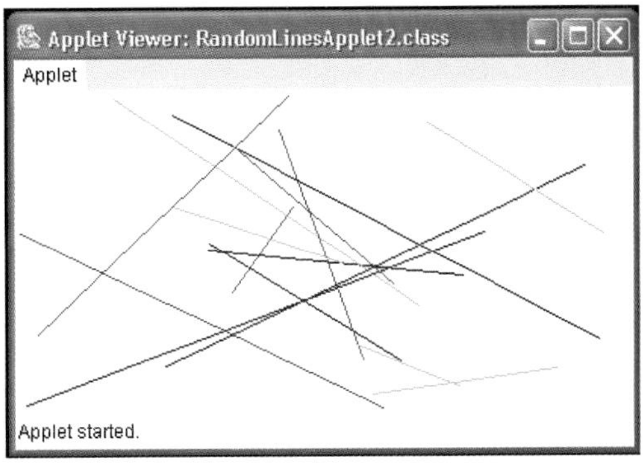

(b)

Figure 6-9
a) The *RandomLinesApplet2.java* and *LineGenerator.java* must be compiled separately. The applet class file is loaded by appletviewer. b) The fifteen random lines are seen in the Applet Viewer window.

```
1    //Program 6-5  Use a LineGenerator to produce random
2    //coordinates for use in drawLine(x1, y1, x2, y2) and
3    //alternating color pattern.
4
5    //This applet obtains the line info and draws the lines
6    //in paint. .
7
8    //File:  RandomLinesApplet2.java
9
10   import javax.swing.JApplet;
11   import java.awt.Graphics;
12   import java.awt.Color;
13
14   public class RandomLinesApplet2 extends JApplet
15   {
16     LineGenerator line = new LineGenerator();
17
18     public void init()
19     {
20          //First we must tell the line generator object the
21          //range for our lines. For this, we use the window
22          //size set in the html file, 400 wide x 200 tall
23
24          line.setWidthRange(400);   //could have called line.setRanges() too
25          line.setHeightRange(200);
26     }
27
28     public void paint(Graphics g)
29     {
30          int coords[] = new int [4];  //x1 y1 x2 y2 order
31
```

```
32          for(int i = 0; i < 15; ++i)
33          {
34              //Call the generator to obtain the color.
35              //We do not need a Color variable here, since we only
36              //pass it on to the setColor() method.
37
38              g.setColor( line.getColor() );
39
40              //obtain the line coords from the generator
41              coords = line.getCoords();
42
43              //draw our line
44              g.drawLine(coords[0], coords[1], coords[2], coords[3] );
45
46              marcsPause(333);    //pause 1/3 of a sec between lines
47
48          }
49      }
50  void marcsPause(int ms)
51  {
52          try
53          {
54              Thread.sleep(ms);
55          }
56          catch(InterruptedException e){ }
57      }
58  }
59
```

6

Figure 6-10
The LineGenerator class has a getCoords() method for calculating and returning the coordinates for our random lines. The getColor() method alternately returns a black, green, or magenta color.

```
//File: LineGenerator.java

public class LineGenerator
{
    private int lineCoords[ ] = new int [4];  ◄──── Private data includes
    private int heightRange, widthRange;            coordinate array, range and
    private int colorCounter;                       color counter

    public LineGenerator( )  ◄──────── Class constructor
    {
        //initialize range and counter
    }
    public Color getColor( )              Returns the color for the
    {                                     line
        //Alternates the colors and returns either
        //black, green, or magenta.
    }                                  Generates the
    public int[ ] getCoords( )  ◄──── x1, y1, x2, y2 points for our line
    {
        //Generates random numbers and fills the array of
        //of coords, then returns it.
    }
}
```

The LineGenerator class is contained in the file *LineGenerator.java*. Figure 6-10 shows the framework for this class. The private data includes an integer array for the line coordinates, range values that are used to calculate numbers within certain values, and a color counter variable that helps us correctly alternate the colors. There are methods for setting the range values, and the getCoords() and getColor() methods generate and return the line and color information. The source code for this class is as follows, also labeled Program 6-5. Please note that this class does not have any applet methods such as start() or paint(), nor does it contain a main() method. An object of this class, is instantiated in the applet class, and its methods help the applet.

```
1   //Program 6-5
2   //Generates random coordinates that are used for drawLine(x1,y1,x2,y2)
3   //Constructor assumes 300 x 300, unless set by calling method.
4   //Also cycles through colors in the black, green, magenta order
5   //First time it is called, it returns black, next time, green, then magenta.
6
7   //File:  LineGenerator.java
8
9
10  import java.awt.Graphics;
11  import java.awt.Color;
12
13  public class LineGenerator
14  {
15     private int lineCoords[] =  new int [4]; //order x1, y1, x2, y2;
16
17     private int heightRange, widthRange;     //ranges of the values
18                                              //always assumes > 0
19
20     private int colorCounter;  //Counts number of times it has returned a color.
21                        //The count value allows us to cycle through the colors.
22
23     public LineGenerator()
24     {
25           heightRange = 300;
26           widthRange = 300;
27
28           //Set the colorCounter to -1 since we incr it when we first
29           //step into the getColor().
30           colorCounter = -1;
31     }
```

```
32
33      public void setRanges(int w, int h)
34      {
35          heightRange = h;
36          widthRange = w;
37      }
38
39      public void setWidthRange(int w)
40      {
41          widthRange = w;
42      }
43
44      public void setHeightRange(int h)
45      {
46          heightRange = h;
47      }
48
49      public Color getColor()
50      {
51          colorCounter++;
52
53          //mod the color counter to alternate the colors
54          if(colorCounter %3 == 0)
55              return Color.black;
56          else if( colorCounter%3 == 1)
57              return Color.green;
58          else
59              return Color.magenta;
60      }
61
62      public int[] getCoords()
63      {
64          //obtain the four random number for the coords
65          lineCoords[0] = (int)(Math.random()*widthRange + 1);   //x1
66          lineCoords[1] = (int)(Math.random()*heightRange + 1);   //y1
67          lineCoords[2] = (int)(Math.random()*widthRange + 1);   //x2
68          lineCoords[3] = (int)(Math.random()*heightRange + 1);   //y2
69
70          return lineCoords;
71
72      }
73  }
```

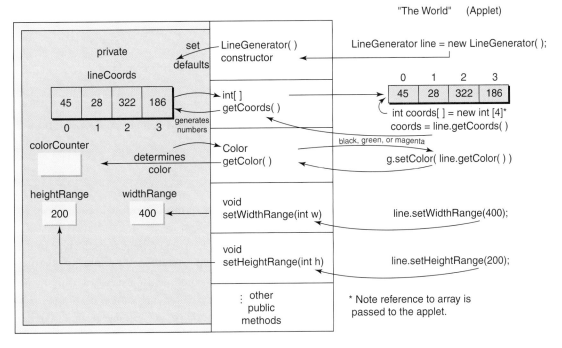

"The World"   (Applet)

LineGenerator line = new LineGenerator( );

```
0    1    2    3
45   28   322  186
```

int coords[ ] = new int [4]*
coords = line.getCoords( )

black, green, or magenta

g.setColor(line.getColor( ))

line.setWidthRange(400);

line.setHeightRange(200);

* Note reference to array is
  passed to the applet.

Figure 6-11
Private data in the LineGenerator object can be accessed by the class methods
directly. The private data can be accessed by other classes through the public
methods via a LineGenerator object.
*Note: Reference to the array is passed to the applet.

6

Let's review once again how the private data in a class is accessed. Figure 6-11
illustrates the data and methods in the LineGenerator class. The class methods can
all access the data directly. In the source code just presented, the constructor method
sets the range and counter values, and the getCoords() method fills and returns the
lineCoords array. However, the other classes in our program (such as our applet
class) cannot see the LineGenerator data. The applet has to call the setRange(),
getCoords() and getColor() methods by the use of a LineGenerator object.

6.4
Writing Class Methods

The term method is the object-oriented name for a function or subroutine. If Java is
your first programming language, then the terms *function* and *subroutine* are new to
you, too. A **method** is a discrete block of code that exists inside a class and
performs a task or tasks for the class. The first line is referred to as the method definition line. It must contain a return type, the name of the method, and list of input
parameters, if any. An access specifier is optional. The method's job is to perform a

method
a discrete block of code
that exists inside a
class and performs a
task or tasks for the
class

task for the class. The general form for a method is:

```
//File: SomeClass.java

public class SomeClass              //class definition line
{

      //method definition line
      accessSpecifier returnType  methodName( input parameter list)
      {
            //code for the method
      }
}
```

- Where the accessSpecifer is either public, protected, private, or not given, and therefore has package or default access.
- The returnType is any valid data type in Java, and it represents the type of data that is passed out of the method. If nothing is returned, the returnType is void.
- The methodName is the name of the method, and must be a legally named identifier.
- The input parameter list contains the data type and variable name of the data that is passed into the method. Both the data type and variable name are required in the list. If there is more than one datum being passed into the method, the data items are separated by commas. The variables in the input parameter list are considered variable declaration statements. That is, the variables are declared (and memory is allocated for them) when a method is called. These variables in the input list are local variables in the method. If nothing is passed to the method, the parentheses are empty ( ).

Let's examine examples of methods and how they are called:

```
public class LineGenerator
{
      private int lineCoords[] =  new int [4];
      private int heightRange, widthRange;
      private int colorCounter;

      public void setWidthRange(int w)
      {
            widthRange = w;
      }
      public void setHeightRange(int h)
      {
            heightRange = h;
      }
      public Color getColor()
      {
            colorCounter++;
```

```
//mod the color counter to alternate the colors
    if(colorCounter %3 == 0)
        return Color.black;
    else if( colorCounter%3 == 1)
        return Color.green;
    else
        return Color.magenta;
}
public int[] getCoords()
{
    //obtain the four random number for the coords
    lineCoords[0] = (int)(Math.random()*widthRange + 1);   //x1
    lineCoords[1] = (int)(Math.random()*heightRange + 1);   //y1
    lineCoords[2] = (int)(Math.random()*widthRange + 1);   //x2
    lineCoords[3] = (int)(Math.random()*heightRange + 1);   //y2

    return lineCoords;

}

}
```

The two get methods (getColor() and getCoords()) have no inputs. The getColor() returns a Color, and the getCoords() returns an integer array reference. These methods are called like this:

```
for(int i = 0; i < 15; ++i)
{
    g.setColor( line.getColor() );

    //obtain the line coords from the generator
    coords = line.getCoords();

    //draw the line
}
```

The getColor() method returns a Color. We could write the code using an intermediate Color variable, like this:

```
//get the color for the line
Color temp;
temp = line.getColor()

//set the color for the graphics object
g.setColor( temp );
```

Instead of making a temporary Color object, filling it, and then passing the temporary object into the Graphics' setColor() method, we take a short cut in our program. We place the call to the line's getColor() method inside the parentheses for the setColor() method.

```
g.setColor( line.getColor() );
```

Because getColor() returns a Color, and setColor() requires a Color, we know that the data types match. Therefore, the Java compiler will allow us to write the code in this manner. This is a common tactic in Java.

The return statement is used in a method to pass one data item from the class. The one data item can be a single variable, an object, or an array. We are limited to one and only one item as seen previously. It is illegal to try and return more than one thing, as in the following example:

```
//File:  LineGenerator.java
public class LineGenerator
{
        public Color, int[] getColorAndCoords( )
        {
                //NO NO, can't return more than 1 thing
                return Color.magenta, lineCoords;
        }
```

Notice that there are two ways to set the range limits in our generator class. We may either call the individual set methods, as we do in the program, or we could call the setRanges() method, which has two input values.

```
//In the LineGenerator class

        public void setRanges(int w, int h)
        {
                heightRange = h;
                widthRange = w;
        }
```

The call to the setRanges() method in the RandomLinesApplet2 class would be like this:

```
public class RandomLinesApplet2 extends JApplet
{
        LineGenerator line = new LineGenerator();

        public void init()
        {
                line.setRanges(400,200);
        }
```

Although we have not written many methods that have several input values, we have used many methods that do. The JOptionPane's showMessageDialog, that we have used many times, has four inputs:

```
//javax.swing.JoptionPane
//shows a message box
//Here is the method signature:
//void showMessageDialog(Component parentComponent, Object message,
          String title, int messageType);

//Here is an example of how we use it:
JOptionPane.showMessageDialog(null, "Hi from Java.", "Hi Box",
          JOptionPane.INFORMATION_MESSAGE);
```

The method max() located in the java.lang.Math class takes two input values. The max() method returns the larger of the two values that are passed to it. The max() method signature that works with doubles is:

```
//java.lang.Math

//returns the larger value of x and y
//Here is the method signature:
//double max( double x, double y);

//Here is how we can call it

double one = 4.251, two = 8.5235, bigger;
bigger = Math.max(one,two);
//bigger receives the value 8.5235 from max().
```

Recommendation! Beginning Java programmers sometimes confuse the method definition line with the call to the method. Programmers should remember that the method definition line contains the input parameter list with *the data type and name*. The method is called by passing the variables to it by using the variable name or constant values. (There are no data types in the call statement unless you are performing a data cast.)

Let's use the call to the LineGenerator's setRanges() to illustrate what we mean. First, we examine the method definition line for the setRanges() method. Notice that the int data type and variable names are included:

```
//File: LineGenerator.java

public class LineGenerator
{
      //The setRanges() method definition line contains data types
```

```
//and variables.
public void setRanges(int w, int h)
{
        heightRange = h;
        widthRange = w;
}
```

Here are legal calls to the setRanges() method in Java:

```
//These examples are all valid calls.
int w = 400, h = 200;
line.setRanges( w, h);


//OR


line.setRanges(400, 200);


//OR use a cast with float values
float w = 400.0, h = 200.0;
line.setRanges( (int)w, (int)h );
```

The following are illegal in Java:

```
//These examples are NOT VALID!.
//Do not put data types in call statements.

int w = 400, h = 200;
line.setRanges( int w, int h);


//OR


line.setRanges(int w = 400, int h = 200);
```

Program Flow, Methods, and Return Statements

Java programs are executed one statement at a time. The Java programmer should be aware of how the program flows and the general order of program execution. For example, we know that when we start a program using the java interpreter program, it looks for the main() method and begins executing statements there.

When a program calls a method, program control steps into the method and executes the method statements. Control remains in the method until it encounters a **return statement** or the end of the method. A return statement forces control of the program to exit the method and return to the calling statement. Return statements can be placed anywhere in a method. In the LineGenerator getColor() method, we have three return values, each one within a branch of the if block.

return statement
forces control of the program to exit the method and return to the calling statement

```
public Color getColor()
{
      colorCounter++;

      if(colorCounter %3 == 0)      //mod the color counter to alternate the colors
            return Color.black;
      else if( colorCounter%3 == 1)
            return Color.green;
      else
            return Color.magenta;

}
```

The getColor() could have been written using a local color variable that has its value set in the if block of code and has one return statement. This requires Java to create the local variable, and the programmer must set and return it. Either approach is acceptable, but if a method can be coded in a simple fashion, that is usually the better technique.

```
public Color getColor()
{
      colorCounter++;

      Color whichOne;

      if(colorCounter %3 == 0)      //mod the color counter to alternate the colors
            whichOne = Color.black;
      else if( colorCounter%3 == 1)
            whichOne = Color.green;
      else
            whichOne = Color.magenta;

      return whichOne;

}
```

Another example showing many return statements is seen in the TeachersHelper class's calculateGrade() method. This method determines and returns the letter grade based on the input parameter gradeAverage. During execution, the program control leaves the method the first time a return statement is encountered.

```
public class TeachersHelper
{
      public char calculateGrade(float gradeAverage)
      {
            if(gradeAverage >= 90.0) return 'A';
            else if(gradeAverage >= 80.0) return 'B';
```

```
            else if(gradeAverage >= 70.0) return 'C';
            else if(gradeAverage >= 60.0) return 'D';
            else return 'F';
    }
}
```

The calculateGrade method could be written with one return statement, like this:

```
public class TeachersHelper
{
        public char calculateGrade(float gradeAverage)
        {
            char grade;
            if(gradeAverage >= 90.0) grade = 'A';
            else if(gradeAverage >= 80.0) grade = 'B';
            else if(gradeAverage >= 70.0) grade = 'C';
            else if(gradeAverage >= 60.0) grade = 'D';
            else grade = 'F';

            return grade;
        }
}
```

In the TeachersHelper class, there are two ways to write calculateGrade(). Beginning Java programmers ask, "What is the correct way to write this method?" Ah, we encounter the classic programming tradeoff of efficiency versus readability. In a method as short as calculateGrade(), either approach is good. The methods are often longer and more complicated though. You should always expect that another programmer is going to read your code, so it is important to write it so that someone else can understand the logic. Speed of execution is always an issue. Do not have your code linger in a method any longer than is absolutely necessary. The key to a happy balance is to name your methods and variables well, and to document your logic.

Return statements can be used in methods that do not pass data back to the calling statement. A programmer may choose to return from a method if a certain condition is encountered. This silly example illustrates this technique of bailing out of the writeGreeting method as soon as the desired greeting has been shown.

```
public class SillyExample
{

//This method doesn't return any data, but return statements are
//used to exit from the method when appropriate.
```

```
public void writeGreeting(String name)
{
    if(name.equals("Thomas Jefferson") )
    {
        JOptionPane.showMessageDialog(null,"Hello Mr. President.");
        return;
    }

    if(name.equals("Madeline Kahn") )
    {
        JOptionPane.showMessageDialog(null,"Hello.Good Day. Come in.");
        return;
    }
    JOptionPane.showMessageDialog(null,"Hi there!" );
}
}
```

Using return statements in methods often simplifies the control statements. For example, the code below shows an incomeRating() method in the MatchMaker class. It is possible to simply return the rating number (as we did in the getColor() method) instead of using a variable.

```
public class MatchMaker
{
    //This method rates potential mates based on their income.
    public int incomeRating( int yearlyIncome)
    {
        if(yearlyIncome > 1000000)      //yes! A millionaire!
            return 10;
        else if(yearlyIncome > 100000)  //100K+ a year OK!
            return 7;
        else if(yearlyIncome > 0)
            return 5;
        else
            return 3;
    }
}
```

Overloaded Methods

Overloaded methods are methods that have the same name and different input parameter lists. Before we study overloaded methods, we should review term, **method signature**. The method signature refers to a method's return type, method name, and input parameter list:

```
returnType methodName( input list);     //method signature
```

For example, the method signature for the LineGenerator's setRanges() method is:

```
void setRanges(int w, int h);     //method signature
```

and the method signature for getCoords() is

```
public int[] getCoords();
```

Overloaded methods have the same name but different method signatures—that is, the key to overloaded methods is that the input lists must differ. It is not adequate for overloaded methods to be different in return type only. The two methods from previous pages, showMessageDialog() and max() actually have several different signatures, meaning that they have different input lists. Examine the various overloaded versions of the methods that follow. JOptionPane's showMessageDialog() has three different methods:

```
//javax.swing.JOptionPane class
//These three methods all show a message box.

void showMessageDialog(Component parentComponent, Object message);

void showMessageDialog(Component parentComponent, Object message, String title,
                       int messageType);

void showMessageDialog(Component parentComponent, Object message, String title,
                       int messageType, Icon icon);
```

There are four max() methods in Java's java.lang.Math class.

```
//java.lang.Math class
//These four methods all return the larger value of x and y.

double max( double x, double y);
float max( float x, float y);
int max( int x, int y);
long max( long x, long y);
```

The following attempt to overload a method is illegal because the signatures differ only in the returnType.

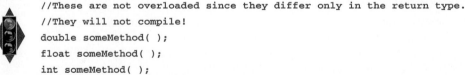

```
//These are not overloaded since they differ only in the return type.
//They will not compile!
double someMethod( );
float someMethod( );
int someMethod( );
```

Review Calling Methods

Methods in classes can be called or accessed in two ways, either from within the class by another class method or constructor, or from outside the class through the use of an object. It never hurts to study these two techniques when you are learning Java. Let's do a silly example to illustrate the two ways to call a method.

The TellMeAJoke class constructor sets the joke's question and answer. The class has askTheQuestion() and tellPunchLine() methods. Notice that the constructor calls the two methods. This means that when a TellMeAJoke object is created, it asks and tells the joke. The code is seen in Program 6-6.

```
1   //Program 6-6
2   //File: TellMeAJoke.java
3
4   import javax.swing.JOptionPane;
5
6   public class TellMeAJoke
7   {
8       private String question, answer;
9
10      public TellMeAJoke()
11      {
12          question = "Why did the chicken cross the road?";
13          answer = "To go where no chicken has gone before. ";
14
15          askTheQuestion();            //call the class methods
16          tellThePunchLine();
17
18      }
19      public void askTheQuestion()
20      {
21          JOptionPane.showMessageDialog(null,question,"Tell Me A Joke",3);
22      }
23
24      public void tellThePunchLine()
25      {
26          JOptionPane.showMessageDialog(null,answer,"Tell Me A Joke",1);
27      }
28  }
```

In the Jokes class, we create a TellMeAJoke object named monty. In order to invoke the joke telling methods in this Jokes class, we must use monty to call the methods. When you execute this program, how many times will you see the joke?

```
1    //Program 6-6 A silly program that illustrates calling methods
2    //File Jokes.java
3
4    public class Jokes
5    {
6          //Creates a TellMeAJoke object named monty.
7
8          //This statement calls the TellMeAJoke constructor.
9          TellMeAJoke monty = new TellMeAJoke();
10
11         public Jokes()
12         {
13               monty.askTheQuestion();    //We call the methods using
14               monty.tellThePunchLine(); //monty, the TellMeAJoke object.
15
16         }
17
18         public static void main( String args[] )
19         {
20               new Jokes();      //we don't need a Jokes object, but use
21               System.exit(0);   //new to call the constructor.
22         }
23   }
```

Constructors

constructor

used only to create and
initialize a new object,
has the same name as
the class

A **constructor** is a special method in Java that is used only to create and initialize a new object. The constructor has the exact same name as the class, including capitalization. Perhaps a better name for a constructor would be a memory allocator and initializer, because that describes the job of the constructor. When declaring an object variable, we use the new keyword. The new keyword says that we are calling the constructor of the class like this:

```
LineGenerator line = new LineGenerator();
```

The job of the constructor is to initialize the class data to known states or values before we use the object. In the LineGenerator constructor, we assigned the value 300 to the range variables and a minus one (−1) to the colorCounter.

```
public class LineGenerator
{
        private int lineCoords[] =  new int [4];
        private int heightRange, widthRange;
        private int colorCounter;
```

6

```
    public LineGenerator()            //constructor method
    {
            heightRange = 300;
            widthRange = 300;
            colorCounter = -1;
    }
```

It is possible to write more than one constructor by providing different input parameter lists of data types and variable names. Our LineGenerator class could have an overloaded constructor in which we passed in the range value. Having a constructor like this allows us to create and set the range values in one step. The constructor would look like this:

```
public class LineGenerator
{
    private int lineCoords[] = new int [4];
    private int heightRange, widthRange;
    private int colorCounter;

    public LineGenerator( int w, int h)      //overloaded constructor method
    {
            heightRange = h;
            widthRange = w;
            colorCounter = -1;
    }
```

To call this overloaded constructor, we need to create and pass in the range values like this:

```
public class RandomLinesApplet2 extends JApplet
{
    private LineGenerator line = new LineGenerator(400, 200);
```

The TellMeAJoke class can have an overloaded constructor where we pass the question and answer to the object when we create it. Program 6-7, TellMeAJoke2, has two constructors: a default (no inputs), and a constructor with two inputs. In the Jokes2 class, we create the joke object by calling the overloaded TellMeAJoke2 constructor. The source code for both classes are contained in the *TellMeAJoke2.java* and *Jokes2.java* files.

```
1   //Program 6-7
2   //File: TellMeAJoke2.java
3
4   import javax.swing.JOptionPane;
5
```

```
6    public class TellMeAJoke2
7    {
8        private String question, answer;
9
10       public TellMeAJoke2()    //default, no argument constructor
11       {
12            question = "Why did the chicken cross the road?";
13            answer = "To go where no chicken has gone before. ";
14
15            askTheQuestion();                        //call the class methods
16            tellThePunchLine();
17
18       }
19
20       public TellMeAJoke2(String q, String a)    //overloaded constructor
21       {
22            question = q; //we pass the joke question and answer to the object
23            answer = a;
24
25            askTheQuestion();                        //call the class methods
26            tellThePunchLine();
27
28       }
29       public void askTheQuestion()
30       {
31            JOptionPane.showMessageDialog(null,question,"Tell Me A Joke",3);
32
33       }
34
35       public void tellThePunchLine()
36       {
37            JOptionPane.showMessageDialog(null,answer,"Tell Me A Joke",1);
38       }
39
40   }
```

```
1    //Program 6-7 We've modified the silly joke program.
2    //We call the overloaded TellMeAJoke2 constructor.
3    //File Jokes2.java
4
5    public class Jokes2
6    {
```

```
7        TellMeAJoke2 monty;      //make a TellMeAJoke2 reference
8
9        public Jokes2()
10       {
11               String quest = "Why doesn't an elephant have a glove compartment?";
12               String answ = "Because it has a trunk.";
13
14
15               //Call the TellMeAJoke2 constructor and pass in our own joke.
16               monty = new TellMeAJoke2(quest,answ);
17
18               monty.askTheQuestion();
19               monty.tellThePunchLine();
20
21       }
22
23       public static void main( String args[] )
24       {
25               new Jokes2();
26               System.exit(0);
27       }
28  }
```

6

Other Constructor Rules   The constructor cannot be called by the programmer, except when he or she creates the object. Beginning programmers see the constructor as a way to initialize data (true) but they mistakenly believe that the constructor can be used to reset the data back to initial values. Wrong! If you expect that the data will need to be reset, then provide a reset() method in the class.

The constructor does not have a return type, as do other class methods. Do not attempt to place a return statement or attempt to pass anything out of a constructor. If there is no constructor in your class, Java assumes that there is a default, no argument constructor that does nothing. It is best for you to provide at least one constructor. Better yet, provide several constructors for your classes because even though you think you'll only need one type of constructor, you never know when various forms of the constructor might come in handy for another programming application.

6.5
Scope

When a Java programmer declares a variable, what is the length of time that the variable exists when the program is running? Does it only exist for a short time and then go away, or is it available at all times while the program is executing? Also, what parts of the program can see and use the variable? The answers to these questions depend on the variable's scope.

scope

the lifetime and visibility of variables, determined by where the variable is declared

Scope is a programming term that describes the lifetime and visibility of variables. The scope of a variable is determined by where the variable is declared. Some variables exist for brief periods of time while others exist for the duration of the program. The scope of a variable determines where the variable can be referenced in the program.

block of code

code that is enclosed in braces

There are three types of scope in Java: block scope, class scope, and package scope. We discuss package scope in later chapters. For block scope and class scope, we first need to define a block of code. A **block of code** is code that is enclosed in braces { }. If you are thinking that we see blocks of code everywhere in Java, you are right! Braces enclose classes, methods, if statements, switches, and loops. The rule is that any variable declared within a block of code has **block scope** and is only visible and accessible to code inside that block. This localizes such variables and in a sense, provides another layer of encapsulation.

block scope

any variable declared within a block of code has block scope, and is only visible and accessible to code inside that block

Let's examine the code in this example and see the block scope.

```java
public void theMethod()
{                                       //this starts method scope

    int count = 100;            //count is declared inside theMethod
                                //count can be used by all code inside theMethod

    System.out.println("Count =" + count );

    if( count == 100)
    {                                   //this if statement is a new block

        int z = 200;            //z is declared inside the if
                                //it is only in scope in this if block

        count = z + z;          //this is OK, both z and count are in scope
    }

    //z is now out of scope, and not available any longer
    System.out.println("Count =" + count);         //count is still in scope here
}
```

Another example shows the scope of a method's input parameter list. Data types and variables that occur in a method definition line actually are being declared. When the method is called, the input parameters come into scope.

```java
public void anotherMethod(int n, String input, double sum)
{                                       //this starts method scope
```

```
        //variables n, input, and sum are now in scope for this, anotherMethod

        int birdbrain = 3;          //birdbrain is in scope for this method

        System.out.println("Birdbrain =" + birdbrain );                //OK!

        if( n == 5)
        {                                //this if statement is a new block

                System.out.println("input =" + input); //OK, input is in scope

                double x= 3.2, y = 6.5;    //declare x and y in the if block
                                          //these are in scope only in this if block

                sum = x + y;       //this is OK, all three are in scope

                birdbrain++;       //birdbrain is in scope throughout the method
        }
        //x and y are now out of scope, and no long exist
        System.out.println("sum =" + sum);              //sum is still in scope here
}
```

Frequently, programmers write loop indices in the manner shown in the code that follows. Notice that the index *i* must be declared twice because the variable comes in and out of scope with each for loop.

```
public void aThirdMethod( )
{                                      //this starts method scope
    for(int i = 0; i < 10; ++ i)
    {                              //i is in scope for this block
        System.out.println("hello");
    }

    //The loop index i is now out of scope.
    //If we need i again, must declare it.

    for(int i = 0; i < 10; ++ i)
    {                              //i is now in scope in this block
        System.out.println("hello again");
    }

    //i is now out of scope
}
```

If we wish to declare *i* to have block scope within the method, we must write the code like this:

```java
public void aThirdMethod( )
{
        int i;                 //i now in scope for the entire method

        for(i = 0; i < 10; ++ i)
        {
                System.out.println("hello");
        }

        for(i = 0; i < 10; ++ i)
        {
                System.out.println("hello again");
        }
}
```

class scope

any variables that are declared within the class { } and outside of any method or block of code are in class scope and are visible to the entire class

Class scope is the same idea as block scope. Basically, any variables that are declared within the class { } and outside of any method or block of code are in class scope and are visible to the entire class. We have seen this many times in our example programs and are now defining it in a formal manner. The code sample that follows summarizes class scope.

```java
public class ScopeExample()
{
        private int fruit, nuts;         //have class scope

//The fruit and nuts access specifier is private meaning they are
//hidden from the world.
//fruit and nuts have class scope meaning they can be accessed
//by any class method
//fruit and nuts are class or instance variables

        public ScopeExample()         //constructor method can set fruit and nuts
        {
                fruit = 5;
                nuts = 10;
        }

        public void doSomethingMethod(int oranges)
        {
                int apples;
```

```
                //oranges and apples have method scope
                //they can be accessed only in doSomethingMethod()

                apples = oranges * 10;

                //fruit and nuts are in scope in this method too
                fruit++;
                nuts = nuts * 100;

                for(int i = 0; i < 10; ++ i)
                {
                        //i has block scope within this for loop
                        //do some loop thing in here
                }
                //i is out of scope now
        }

        public int getFruit()
        {
                return fruit;                   //fruit can be passed out of the class
        }
}
```

6

6.6
Object and Array References, Primitive Variables, and Memory

In Java, there are two types of variables: primitive data type variables and reference variables. **Primitive data type variables** are variables that are declared using byte, char, int, short, long, float, double, or boolean. It is common to mean primitive variables when one refers to a variable. Primitive variables are ready to be used once they are declared, and they only contain data.

primitive data type variables

variables that are declared using byte, char, int, short, long, float, double, or boolean

```
int x, y, z;            //primitive variables

//x, y, and z are ready to be used
x = 7;
y = 8;
z = x + y;
```

reference variables

variables that refer to objects and arrays, and contain the memory location of an object or an array and not the actual data and methods

Reference variables are variables that refer to objects and arrays, and are commonly called references. References contain the memory location of an object or an array and not the actual data and methods. Arrays and objects must be allocated with the new operator. Objects contain both data and methods.

```
LineGenerator line;          //This is a reference variable that
                             //will hold the address of the object
                             //once it is created.

//We can't call the methods yet because we haven't created an object yet.

   line = new LineGenerator();       //call constructor, make the object
   //NOW we are ready to call the object methods

      line.getCoords();
```

We have been using the two terms variables and reference variables throughout the book, and now it is time to explore how and where they are stored in memory.

The Stack and the Heap

We must venture into the realm of stacks and heaps to fully understand where and how Java stores both types of variables and keeps track of program components. The stack and the heap are two components of the computer's memory. Don't panic! We will just touch on the subject and allow the reader to dig further if he or she is so inclined.

A **stack** is the portion of memory that keeps track of certain information for Java methods. When a Java program calls a method, the address of the calling statement, copies of data that are being passed to the method, and the called method's local variables are **pushed onto the stack**. Pushing and popping are computer science terms related to stacks. Being pushed simply means that we are placing that information into the stack's memory. When the program exits a method, information is **popped off the stack** (removed from the stack). The calling address is read and program control returns to the calling statement. The information that was stored on the stack has been popped off and is lost. This is why local variables in methods are in scope only when the program control is executing that method. It is possible to have a method call a method, which in turn calls another method. For each call, the information is pushed onto the stack in the order of the calls. As we leave each method, data is popped off the stack and we return back to the calling statement. Very clever, don't you think?

The **heap** is another portion of memory used to support your program. The memory for the actual data and methods for all objects and array data is located on the heap, never on the stack. That means that the parts and pieces of objects and array elements are stored on the heap and their references are stored on the stack. Unlike the very orderly placement of method variables in the stack, order is not of

stack

the portion of memory that keeps the address of the calling statement, copies of data that are being passed to the method, and the called method's local variables

pushed on the stack

place a data item into the stack memory

popped off the stack

removed a data item from the stack memory

heap

memory location for the actual data and methods for all objects and array data is allocated on the heap, never on the stack

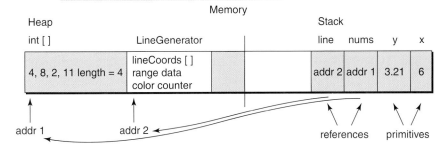

```
public class MemoryDemo
{
    int x = 6
    double y = 3.21;

    int nums [ ] = { 4, 8, 2, 11 };

    LineGenerator line = new LineGenerator ( );
```

Figure 6-12

Primitives and reference variables are stored on the stack. The references contain the address of memory where the object data and methods and array data are located on the heap. Scope rules apply to the variables on the stack, but not heap contents.

importance when discussing how the object information is stored on the heap. The lifetime of an object or array is independent of the scope in which it was allocated. Figure 6-12 illustrates how the primitives and references are stored on the stack and the object and array contents are stored on the heap.

Garbage Collection and the finalize() Method

Local primitive variables are stored on the stack and objects and arrays are located on the heap. The stack works in a very orderly manner. Variables come into scope and are pushed on the stack. Variables go out of scope and are popped off the stack. But what happened to the object data, methods, and arrays that are placed on the heap? How are these objects and arrays destroyed and how is the memory released for future use?

Java accomplishes this clean up task with the use of a garbage collection process. In short, the **garbage collection** process occurs sporadically during program execution. When there are no longer any references to an object or an array on the stack, Java assumes that the object is no longer needed and that the memory is to be released from the heap. This process is known as garbage collection. If the object's class contains a **finalize() method**, this method is called before the memory occupied by that object is released.

garbage collection

when there are no longer any references to an object or an array on the stack, the garbage collector releases the memory for those items from the heap

finalize ( ) method

is called before the memory occupied by that object is released

The finalize() method is one of the methods in the java.lang.Object class, and the programmer can write a finalize() method for any class. However, the finalize() method should be present in a class only if there are special reasons for needing access to an object when garbage collection occurs. The purpose of having a finalize() method is to provide a chance to free resources that we cannot free by some other means. Also, finalize() can be used when the programmer is working with static class members. An example showing a finalize() method is seen in Program 7-2, in the PoliceOfficer class. As a general rule, you have no reason for using finalize(), and you can ignore it most of the time.

Back to our discussion on Java garbage collection—we can explicitly call the garbage collector. The java.lang.System class has a garbage collection method (System.gc( )) that makes a request that garbage collection take place, but there is no guarantee that this process will occur. Different Java runtime environments have different implementations of this method. Programmers can set reference variables to null, which marks the associated object or array for garbage collection.

Let's demonstrate how we can request a call to the garbage collector. In Program 6-8 (modified Program 2-20), we use a Runtime object to query the available memory in the JVM. We allocate an array of 100,000 doubles, checking the free memory. (Once again, we see a difference of 781 Kbytes.) We then set the array reference to null and call the garbage collection method. As it turns out, for this program, Figure 6-13 shows that the garbage collector did indeed release the array memory back to the JVM.

6

```
1   //Program 6-8
2   //Demo how assigning null to a reference aids in garbage collection.
3   //File:  GarbageCollectionDemo.java
4
5   public class GarbageCollectionDemo
6   {
7     public static void main(String[] args)
8     {
9
10        //First, get a Runtime object that is associated with this application.
11        Runtime r = Runtime.getRuntime();
12
13        //Call the garbage collector
14        System.gc();
15
16        //obtain the totalMemory and free memory in the JVM
17        //divide by 1024 to convert bytes into Kilobytes
18        long total = r.totalMemory() / 1024;
19        System.out.println(total + " Kb of total memory in the JVM.");
```

```
20
21              long free = r.freeMemory() / 1024;
22              System.out.println(free + " Kb of available JVM memory.");
23
24              //Now grab enough memory for 100,000 doubles (800,000 bytes total)
25              double [] d = new double[100000];
26
27              //Check the free memory
28              free = r.freeMemory() / 1024;
29              System.out.println(free +
30              " Kb free after reserving memory for 100,000 doubles.");
31
32              //now set the d array to null, marking the array for garbage collection
33              d = null;
34
35              //Run the garbage collection again.
36              System.gc();
37
38              free = r.freeMemory() / 1024;
39              System.out.println(free +
40              " Kb of free memory after d = null, and 2nd garbage collection.");
41
42              System.exit(0);
43      }
44  }
```

```
C:\JPT>javac GarbageCollectionDemo.java

C:\JPT>java  GarbageCollectionDemo
1984 Kb of total memory in the JVM.
1848 Kb of available JVM memory.
1066 Kb free after reserving memory for 100,000 doubles.
1849 Kb of free memory after d = null, and 2nd garbage collection.

C:\JPT>
```

Figure 6-13
Setting an array (or object reference) to null marks it for garbage collection. In this program example, the garbage collector did reclaim the memory that was used for the array. Garbage collection can be requested but there is no guarantee it will occur.

Passing Data To and From Methods

We have one last topic to cover, that will help us to understand methods completely. This topic deals with the mechanics of how data are passed to and from methods. When a program calls a method, what data are placed on the stack? The answer has three parts: 1) the calling statement's address (so the program knows where to return to), 2) copies of the data that are being passed to the method, and 3) the method's local variables.

Passing Data To Methods We are interested in examining how data are passed into methods and what happens to that data in both the calling and called methods. When program information is passed to a method, whether it is a primitive, an object, or an array reference, the value that was on the stack is passed to the method. That means that if we are passing a primitive value to the method, such as an int or a double, the value of the primitive is copied (via the stack) into the local variable of the method. If we are passing an object or array to a method, the reference is passed.

Figure 6-14 illustrates two classes (A and B), the stack, and the heap. Class A has a primitive integer, x, and an array of numbers. We instantiate an object of the B class in A. In A's passEm() method, we call the bObject's give-MeAnInt() method, passing A's x to it. In B's class giveMeAnInt() method, the value of 6 is passed to the method's y variable. The integer y is locally declared. In

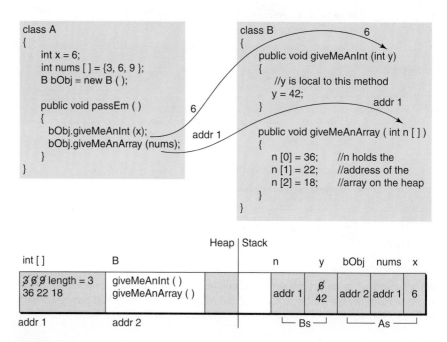

Figure 6-14
In Class A, a copy of the value of x is passed to B's giveMeAnInt() method. If giveMeAnInt() changes its value, it does not change the x in Class A. We pass the array reference to B's giveMeAnArray() method. Any change to the data in this method changes the data stored on the heap, therefore, A's number array is changed.

A's passEm() method, we call bObject's giveMeAnArray() method, passing A's number array to it.

Notice how both methods in the B class assign new values to their variables. Because a copy of the integer is passed to B, when a change occurs to B's *y* variable, no changes are made in the A class. However, because we passed A's array reference, any changes made by the B class are changing the contents on the heap, so A's array is changed. B's giveMeAnArray() method changes the array values to 36, 22, and 18. When control returns to the A class, its numbers array now contains these new values.

Now let's expand this example to include classes. What happens when we pass an object to a class? Object names are also references. Think it works just like arrays? You are right! Figure 6-15 illustrates three classes: A, B, and C. Class A instantiates an object of both B and C classes. Class C's sayHello() method requires an object of Class B as an input value. In A's showGreetings() method, we call C's sayHello() method and pass it the bObject reference. We are passing the sayHello() method the reference (address) of Class A's B object. C's sayHello() method can call B's sayHiFromB() method.

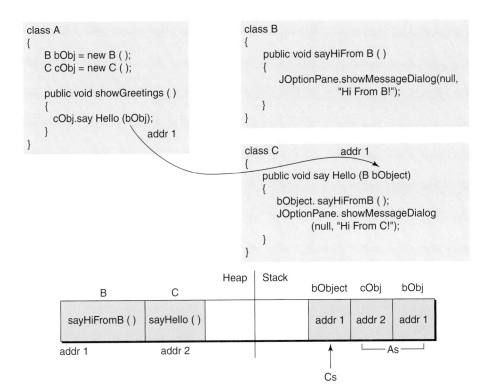

Figure 6-15
Class A has instantiated objects of Class B and Class C. In A's showGreeting() method, we pass the bObject reference to Class C's sayHello() method. The reference contains the location of the bObject that is stored on the heap.

Passing Data From Methods   We need to examine the mechanics of returning data from methods. It is the same idea as passing data to the methods, as the data values are copied onto the stack and returned to the calling statement. Java allows one datum to be returned from a method. That datum can be a primitive or reference value. It is important for the beginning Java programmer to remember to assign the returned value to a variable, or else the value is lost.

First we look at returning a primitive value and an array. Once again, we use the A and B classes. In A's callEm() method, we call B's getAnInt() method, which returns an integer value. We must remember to assign the value into a variable in Class A! We then call B's getAnArray() method. This method creates a new array, referenced as *n*, which is allocated on the heap. The getAnArray() method returns the reference to the array, which is stored in A's num array. In Figure 6-16, we see that the getAnInt() method is returning 42 and the getAnArray() method is returning addr2.

Last but not least, we examine returning an object from a method. Once again, we ask our old friends, Classes A, B, and C to assist with this example. Class A instantiates an object of Class C, but only declares a reference for a Class B object. In A's getMeABObject() method, Class C's makeABObject() method is called. Inside this method, a Class B object is allocated and stored

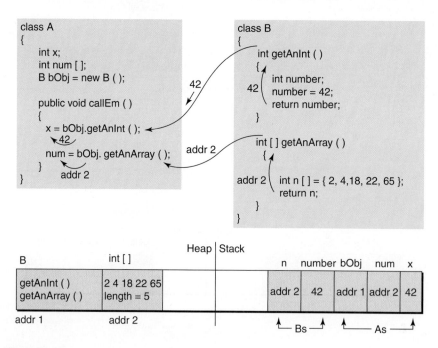

Figure 6-16
Class B's getAnInt() method is returning an integer value to Class A's *x* value and getAnArray() is returning a reference location to the array on the heap. It is important to assign the returned values into like variables.

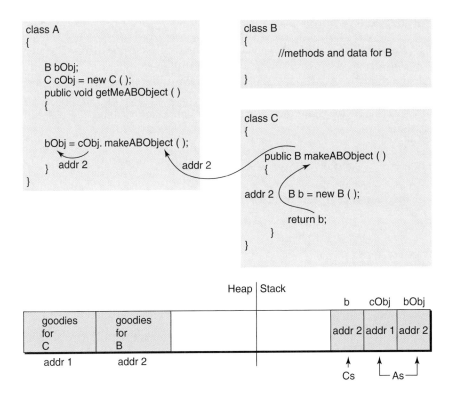

Figure 6-17
The reference containing the address of Class C's B object is passed from Class C's makeABObject() method and is assigned into the A class' bObject variable. The bObject is a reference to a B class.

on the heap. The reference to the B object is then returned to Class A and assigned into its bObject reference. Figure 6-17 illustrates how these three classes interact.

6.7
Practice!

We can talk about classes and methods all day long. You can read the chapters and study the figures into the wee hours of the night. You know what's coming don't you? The only way to really get it is to do it. (As they say in kindergarten, the only way to make mud pies is to get dirty!) In these practice examples, we will mix water with soil and get our hands dirty. Spend time entering the code and running these examples. The problems at the end of the chapter provide more fun!

ShowASort Revisited

Let's examine the ShowASort Applet (Program 5-5, page 252) from Chapter 5. In this program, we filled an array with random numbers and drew lines corresponding to the value of the number. We then called the bubblesort() method located in this class and drew the lines again. The portion of code below shows how the paint method called the bubblesort method and passed the array to it.

```java
public class ShowASortApplet extends JApplet
{
        int numbers[] = new int [100];

        public void start()
        {
                //fill the numbers array with random numbers
        }

        public void paint(Graphics g)
        {
                //draw the unsorted lines

                bubblesort();          //here we call the bubblesort method

                //draw the sorted lines
        }

//this bubble sort routine sorts integers from low to high
        public void bubblesort( )
        {
                //code for sorting the numbers array
        }
}
```

A better way to write this program is to place the sorting method in its own Sort class. By doing this, the Sort class is available to any other classes that require arrays to be sorted instead of being buried in this Applet. In the ShowASortApplet2 program a Sort object is created and its bubblesort() method is called.

In the bubblesort() method, we pass the array reference into it. Why do we not "return" the array? Review Figure 6-14. When we pass the array reference into the method, the bubblesort() method sorts the array data located on the heap. When the method is finished, and control returns to the SortFrame class, the array is sorted! The two classes are shown below in Program 6-9.

6

```
1    //Program 6-9 Pass an array reference to a method.
2    //File: ShowASortApplet2.java
3
4    import java.awt.Graphics;
5    import javax.swing.JApplet;
6    import java.awt.Color;
7    import java.text.DecimalFormat;
8
9    public class ShowASortApplet2 extends JApplet
10   {
11       int numbers[] = new int [100];
12       Sort sorter = new Sort();              //create a Sort object
13
14       public void start()
15       {
16           int count = 0;
17           while(count < 100)          //fill the array
18           {
19               numbers[count] = (int)(Math.random()*201);
20               count++;
21           }
22       }
23
24       public void paint(Graphics g)
25       {
26           g.setColor(Color.magenta);
27
28           for(int j = 0; j < 100; ++j)
29           {
30               g.drawLine(10, 10+2*j, 10 + numbers[j], 10+2*j);
31           }
32
33           g.drawString("The original array", 10, 225);
34
35           sorter.bubblesort(numbers);
36
37           for(int j = 0; j < 100; ++j)
38           {
39               g.drawLine(225, 10+2*j, 225 + numbers[j], 10+2*j);
40           }
41           g.drawString("The sorted array", 225,225);
42
43       }
44   }
```

The Sort class is as follows:

```
1   //Program 6-9
2   //File: Sort.java
3
4   public class Sort
5   {
6
7       public Sort()
8       {
9       }
10
11      //this bubble sort routine sorts integers from low to high
12      public void bubblesort(int numbers[] )
13      {
14          //we can obtain the size of a Java array like this:
15          int size = numbers.length;
16          int x, y, temp;
17
18          for(x = 1; x < size; ++x)
19          {
20              for( y = 0; y < size - 1; ++y)
21              {
22                  if(numbers[y] > numbers[y +1] )
23                  {
24                      temp = numbers[y];
25                      numbers[y] = numbers[y+1];
26                      numbers[y+1] = temp;
27                  }
28              } //close for
29          } //close for
30      } //close sort
31  }  //close class
```

Revisit CoffeeLotto

In our original version of the CoffeeLotto program in Chapter 5 (Program 5-4, page 247) the program simulated a portion of a lottery game where the user guessed a series of numbers and the computer also generated a series. In the CoffeeLotto program, there are four random numbers that represent the values of the cream colored balls, numbered between 1 and 10, and one coffee colored ball numbered between 1 and 20. Program 5-4 is a JApplet class. The numbers are generated in the start method and they are shown in the paint method.

This program can easily be separated into two classes: the CoffeeLottoDriver class and the CoffeeLotto class What do you think are the jobs of the CoffeeLotto class? To generate the four cream colored ball values and one coffee colored ball value is the right answer! In order to determine if we have a winner, the CoffeeLotto class will use a Sort object from the ShowASort program to sort both ball arrays. Once they are sorted, it is easy to compare the user and game balls to determine if they match and if we have a winner. What will the job of the driver class be? This driver class will be an applet, and it has a CoffeeLotto object. In the start() method, we play a round of the game and then show the result in paint(). The code is seen below in Program 6-10. The compilation steps and resultant Applet Viewer window is seen in Figure 6-18.

```
1    //Program 6-10
2    //File: CoffeeLotto.java
3
4    //This class provides the methods for generating the
5    //game balls, asking the user to enter his/her choices,
6    //checking if we have a winner, and returning the ball
7    //values. We use the Sort class to sort our arrays
8    //for us for easy comparison.
9
10   import javax.swing.JOptionPane;
11
12   public class CoffeeLotto
13   {
14      //Variables need to be seen by all the methods.
15      private int userCreamBalls[] = new int[4];
16      private int userCoffeeBall;
17      private int gameCreamBalls[] = new int[4];
18      private int gameCoffeeBall;
19
20      //For the user's guesses, we have an array of booleans
21      //that represent each of the balls. The user picks 4
22      //numbers between 1-10, inclusive. We size the array
23      //to 11, elements 1 - 10. Once the user guesses a number,
24      //we place a true in that element signalling that the
25      //number has been selected.
26
27      private boolean bBallChoices[] = new boolean[11];
28
29      private Sort sorter = new Sort();
30
31      private int count, newball;
32      private String sTitle, sCream, sCoffee;
33
```

```
34        public CoffeeLotto()
35        {
36               reset();      //call reset() to initialize bBallChoices array
37        }
38
39        private void reset()
40        {
41               //Because the applet can be restarted, we need to
42               //set our boolean array to false here.
43               for(int i = 0; i < bBallChoices.length; ++i)
44                     bBallChoices[i] = false;
45        }
46
47
48        public void askUserForChoices()     //asks the user to enter his/her choices
49        {
50               //Call the reset() to make sure bBallChoices contains false values.
51               //Since an applet can be restarted, must make sure this is done
52               //otherwise the array would contain the last play's values.
53               reset();
54
55               count = 0;
56
57               sTitle = "User\'s Coffee Ball";
58               sCoffee = JOptionPane.showInputDialog(null,
59               "Enter a number between 1-20", sTitle, JOptionPane.QUESTION_MESSAGE);
60
61               userCoffeeBall = Integer.parseInt(sCoffee);
62
63               sTitle = "Cream Ball Guess # " + Integer.toString (count + 1);
64
65               sCream = JOptionPane.showInputDialog(null, "Enter a number between 1-10",
66                                 sTitle, JOptionPane.QUESTION_MESSAGE);
67
68               //A while loop is used to ask the user to enter the white balls.
69
70               while(count < 4)              //First we ask the user for the numbers.
71               {
72                      if( count == 0)   //guess is a keeper
73                      {
74                            newball = Integer.parseInt(sCream);
75                            userCreamBalls[count] = newball;
76                            bBallChoices[newball] = true;
77                            ++count;
78                      }
```

```
 79                else
 80                {
 81                        sTitle = "Cream Ball Guess # " + Integer.toString(count+1);
 82
 83                        sCream = JOptionPane.showInputDialog(null,
 84                        "Enter a number between 1-10",sTitle,
 85                        JOptionPane.QUESTION_MESSAGE);
 86
 87                        newball = Integer.parseInt(sCream);
 88                        if(bBallChoices[newball] == false)
 89                        {
 90                                userCreamBalls[count] = newball; //keep it!
 91                                bBallChoices[newball] = true;
 92                                ++count;
 93                        }
 94                        else
 95                        {
 96                                JOptionPane.showMessageDialog(null,
 97                                "Sorry, you have already guessed " + sCream,
 98                                "Duplicate Guess!" , JOptionPane.WARNING_MESSAGE);
 99                        }
100                }
101        }
102
103        sorter.bubblesort(userCreamBalls);
104   }
105
106
107   public void generateGameBalls()     //Now generating the game numbers.
108   {
109
110        boolean gotADup;
111        count = 0;                        //Reset the counter for the game numbers.
112        while(count < 4)
113        {
114             if( count == 0)         //first ball, its a keeper
115             {
116                     gameCreamBalls[count] = (int)(Math.random()*10 + 1);
117                     count++;
118             }
119             else   //not the first ball, have to check it.
120             {
121                     newball = (int)(Math.random()*10 + 1);
122
123   //check it against previous balls to see if we have a duplicate
124                     gotADup = false;
```

```
125                         for(int i = 0; i < count; ++ i)
126                         {
127                                 if(newball == gameCreamBalls[i] )
128                                 {
129                                         gotADup = true;
130                                         break;
131                                 }
132                         }
133                         if(gotADup == false)    //no dup, keep it, incr count
134                         {
135                                 gameCreamBalls[count] = newball;
136                                 ++count;
137                         }
138                 }
139         }
140         //now get a Coffee Ball, pick a random number between 1-20
141         gameCoffeeBall = (int)(Math.random()*20 + 1);
142
143         sorter.bubblesort(gameCreamBalls);
144
145   }
146
147   public boolean doWeHaveAWinner()
148   {
149         //First check the coffee balls.
150         //If they match then check cream ball.
151
152         if(gameCoffeeBall != userCoffeeBall)
153             return false;
154
155         //since the arrays are sorted, can check each element in order
156
157         for(int i = 0; i < gameCreamBalls.length; ++i)
158         {
159             if( gameCreamBalls[i] != userCreamBalls[i] )
160                 return false;
161         }
162
163         //If we make it to here, we have a winner!
164         return true;
165   }
166
167
168   public int getGameCoffeeBall()
169   {
```

```
170            return gameCoffeeBall;
171    }
172    public int[] getGameCreamBalls()
173    {
174            return gameCreamBalls;
175    }
176    public int getUserCoffeeBall()
177    {
178            return userCoffeeBall;
179    }
180    public int[] getUserCreamBalls()
181    {
182            return userCreamBalls;
183    }
184 }
```

```
1   //Program 6-10
2   //File: CoffeeLottoDriver.java
3
4   import java.awt.Graphics;
5   import javax.swing.JApplet;
6
7   public class CoffeeLottoDriver extends JApplet
8   {
9       //Instantiate a CoffeeLotto object. It provides us all the
10      //methods we need to generate/obtain game and user values,
11      //and check if we have a winner.
12
13      //This applet has to write the results to the window.
14      //The CoffeeLotto object doesn't know/care about the window.
15
16      private CoffeeLotto game = new CoffeeLotto();
17
18      public void start()
19      {
20              //We'll play a round of the game in start().
21
22              //First ask the user to select his/her ball values.
23              game.askUserForChoices();
24
25              //Now we generate the game balls.
26              game.generateGameBalls();
27      }
28
```

```java
29    public void paint(Graphics g)
30    {
31          //The majority of the paint is just like in Program 5-4
32          //except that we must ask the game object for the values.
33
34          //We must have local arrays and values for the game values.
35
36          int userCreamBalls[] = new int[4];
37          int userCoffeeBall;
38          int gameCreamBalls[] = new int[4];
39          int gameCoffeeBall;
40
41          g.drawString("Welcome to CoffeeLotto!", 25,25);
42          showStatus("Here are the winning numbers! ");
43
44          g.drawString("Game's Cream Balls ", 25, 50);
45          g.drawString("User's Cream Balls ", 250, 50);
46
47          //Get the values from the object.
48          userCreamBalls = game.getUserCreamBalls();
49          userCoffeeBall = game.getUserCoffeeBall();
50          gameCreamBalls = game.getGameCreamBalls();
51          gameCoffeeBall = game.getGameCoffeeBall();
52
53          String output;
54          for(int i = 0; i < gameCreamBalls.length; ++i)
55          {
56                  marcsPause(500);
57                  output = Integer.toString(gameCreamBalls[i]);
58                  g.drawString(output,50+30*i, 75);
59
60                  output = Integer.toString(userCreamBalls[i]);
61                  g.drawString(output,270+30*i, 75);
62          }
63          output = "Game's Coffee Ball is " + Integer.toString(gameCoffeeBall);
64          g.drawString(output, 25, 100);
65
66          output = "User's Coffee Ball is " + Integer.toString(userCoffeeBall);
67           g.drawString(output, 250, 100);
68
69          //Now let's see if we have a winner.
70          boolean bWinner = game.doWeHaveAWinner();
71
72          if( bWinner )
73                  g.drawString("We have a CoffeeLotto Winner!!" , 25, 125);
```

```
74          else
75               g.drawString("Not a winner. Please play again!" , 25, 125);
76    }
77
78  //Marc's Pause method will pause the program by the number of milliseconds (ms).
79    void marcsPause(int ms)
80    {
81        try
82        {
83            Thread.sleep(ms);
84        }
85        catch(InterruptedException e){ }
86    }
87 }
```

```
C:\JPT>
C:\JPT>javac Sort.java

C:\JPT>javac CoffeeLotto.java

C:\JPT>javac CoffeeLottoDriver.java

C:\JPT>appletviewer CoffeeLottoDriver.html
```
(a)

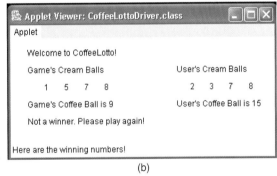

(b)

Figure 6-18
a) The compilation steps for the three classes used in the CoffeeLotto program.
b) One round of results with the balls in sorted order. The CoffeeLotto object performs all the tasks dealing with the game, except for painting results to the window, which is performed by the applet class.

User Login Validation Program

Once the Java programmer becomes comfortable writing and using classes, the next task for him or her is to start thinking in terms of designing classes. When the programmer starts to write a class, he or she must identify the pertinent data and define the associated tasks. This is the abstraction process. The data and methods are encapsulated in the class structure. Data should be hidden with public access to them through the class's methods.

In the User Login Validation program, we write three classes. Instead of presenting the program's big picture up front, let's concentrate on the individual classes and then tie them together in a program. First, we design a ComputerUser class. What data values are needed for a computer user? The user needs a user name, a password, and a code that describes the user's privileges. In this class, we have private Strings for userName and password, and an integer accessCode. We write two constructors, one set method that is passed the three data items, and three get methods. Notice how the three get functions are each written on one line. The code for this class is shown here in Program 6-11.

```java
1   //Program 6-11 A class that describes a computer user.
2   //File: ComputerUser.java
3
4   public class ComputerUser
5   {
6       private      String userName, password;
7       private int accessCode;
8           //0 = standard user, read/write own area, read group drives
9           //1 = write access to group drives
10          //2 = read/write access to entire system
11
12      public ComputerUser()
13      {
14          userName = "";
15          password = "";
16          accessCode = 0;
17      }
18
19      public ComputerUser(String name, String passwd, int code)
20      {
21          userName = name;
22          password = passwd;
23          accessCode = code;
24      }
25
26      public void setUser(String name, String passwd, int code)
27      {
28          userName = name;
29          password = passwd;
30          accessCode = code;
31      }
32
33      public String getUserName() {  return userName;  }
34
35      public String getPassword() {  return password;  }
36
37      public int getAccessCode() {  return accessCode; }
38  }
```

The second class is a Login class. The job of the Login class is to obtain a user name and password (as if someone were logging into a computer system) and validate this name and password. The validateUser() method found in the Login class checks the name and password by searching an array of ComputerUser objects. A boolean true value is returned if the user is in the ComputerUser array and the passwords match. A boolean value of false is returned if there is a problem with the user name and/or password. If there is a problem with the user, the Login class can report the problem if its reportProblem() method is called. The class's toString() method returns the current user and password. Notice how the Login class handles all the details of obtaining and checking the user as well as the means of reporting errors. Study the following code and observe that we use JOptionPane to request the name and password. Java provides a JPasswordField class, in the javax.swing package, that allows the password to be entered and asterisks shown. For now, we will use JOptionPane's message box to help us gather data from the user.

```
1    //Program 6-11 A class that obtains computer user name and logic
2    //and validates the user by checking the infomation in an array
3    //of computer users.
4
5    //File: Login.java
6
7    import javax.swing.JOptionPane;
8
9    public class Login
10   {
11      private String loginName, loginPassword;
12      private String loginDetails;
13
14      public Login()
15      {
16            loginName = "";
17            loginPassword = "";
18            loginDetails = "No user and password has been obtained.";
19      }
20
21      public Login(String n, String p)
22      {
23            loginName = n;
24            loginPassword = p;
25            loginDetails = "No user and password has been obtained.";
26      }
27
```

```java
28      public void askForLoginInfo()
29      {
30              loginName = JOptionPane.showInputDialog("Enter User Name");
31              loginPassword = JOptionPane.showInputDialog ("Enter Password");
32      }
33
34      public boolean validateUser(ComputerUser userArray[])
35      {
36              //Return true if valid, false if not valid.
37              //Login details are written into the details String.
38
39              //search the userArray for the current login name
40              for(int i = 0; i < userArray.length; ++i)
41              {
42                      if(loginName.equals( userArray[i]. getUserName() ) )
43                      {
44                              if(loginPassword.equals( userArray[i].getPassword() ) )
45                              {
46                                      //we have a valid user, write details and return true
47                                      loginDetails = "Valid user and password.";
48                                      return true;
49                              }
50                              else  //valid name but passwords don't match
51                              {
52                                      loginDetails = "Valid user but invalid  password.";
53                                      return false;
54                              }
55                      }
56              }
57
58              //if we get to here, we don't have a valid user,
59              loginDetails = "User name not found in array of ComputerUsers.";
60              return false;
61      }
62
63      public String loginReport() { return loginDetails;    }
64
65      public String toString()
66      {
67              String current = "User: " + loginName + "
68                      (password: " + loginPassword +")";
69              return current;
70      }
71  }
```

The third class will tie the ComputerUser and Login classes together and let us see the results of our work. Unless we want to use the boring System.out.println() method to show the results in the MS-DOS window, we must have a class that inherits the ability to display and write into a window. We will use the JFrame as our super-class for this example. The LoginUsersFrame class extends JFrame.

In the LoginUsersFrame class, we create an array reference for ComputerUser objects. In the constructor, we set the window size and title. *We must fill the array with ComputerUser objects before we use them!* If you do not do this, the program reports an error and stops running. The last thing the constructor does is to call the loginAUser() method.

In the loginAUser method, our Login object, todd, asks for login information and then validates it against the user array. The show() method is called to show our results. The loginDetails() and toString() methods are called in paint() to obtain login information. The code for this class is shown in Program 6-11 and the results for a valid user are shown in Figure 6-19.

```
1    //Program 6-11
2    //File: LoginUsersFrame.java
3
4    import java.awt.Graphics;
5    import javax.swing.JFrame;
6
7    public class LoginUsersFrame extends JFrame
8    {
9       //We instantiate a Login object named todd.
10      private Login todd = new Login();
11
12      //We create an array reference called users.
13      //The array is sized to hold 5 users.
14      //NOTE: this is not ready to use until we allocate objects!
15      private ComputerUser users[] = new ComputerUser[5];
16
17      private String findings;
18      boolean bOK;
19
20      public static void main( String[] args )
21      {
22            LoginUsersFrame hal = new LoginUsersFrame();
23            hal.setDefaultCloseOperation( EXIT_ON_CLOSE );
24      }
25
26      //class constructor initializes values
27      public LoginUsersFrame()
28      {
```

```
29          setSize( 450, 200 );       //set the window size
30          setTitle("Login Users Program");
31
32          //Before we can use the User array, we must fill the array with
33          //ComputerUser objects!!!
34          for(int i = 0; i < users.length; ++i)
35          {
36                  users[i] = new ComputerUser();
37          }
38
39          //Now we set 5 users and their passwords.
40          users[0].setUser("BlueDog", "arfarf", 0);
41          users[1].setUser("KiowaTheWonderDog", "awooooooo", 0);
42          users[2].setUser("Doc","Irun4you",0);
43          users[3].setUser("Maddie","WhenDoWeGo",1);
44          users[4].setUser("HannahBanana","BarkBark",2);
45
46           loginAUser();    //now call LoginAUser
47      }
48
49  public void loginAUser()
50  {
51          //have todd ask for the login information
52          todd.askForLoginInfo();
53
54          //now todd validates the current login by checking it
55          //against the array of users
56          bOK = todd.validateUser(users);
57
58          //bOK would be checked and the user allowed to login if true
59
60          //now that we have a user, show the results
61          show();
62      }
63  public void paint( Graphics g )
64  {
65          String output = "Results ";
66          g.drawString( output, 25, 60 );
67          output = "Login Request for " + todd.toString();
68          g.drawString( output, 25, 90 );
69
70          findings = todd.loginReport();
71          g.drawString( findings, 25, 120);
72      }
73  }
```

Figure 6-19
The valid user results from LoginUsersFrame class, which incorporates an array of
ComputerUser objects and a Login object.

REVIEW QUESTIONS AND PROBLEMS

Short Answer

1. Name the four key principles that a computer language must support in order to be object-oriented.

2. Name the access specifier keywords in Java.

3. Describe how a Java method is related to a Java class.

4. Is it legal in Java to name a method starting with a numeric value, such as 2forMe() or 1onTop()?

5. The method

    ```
    void calculateCosts( float c[] )
    ```

    has a floating point array reference as an input. Write the method definition lines for three other overloaded versions of this method.

6. What is the job of the constructor? How is it called?

7. Can an overloaded method have different return types and the same input parameter list? Explain your answer.

8. Is it possible for a Java programmer to overload a constructor? Explain.

9. Why is it a good idea to provide several different constructors for your classes?

10. Name three types of scope in Java.

11. If a variable is declared inside a class and outside of any method, what part of the class can see and access this variable inside the class? Who can see and access this variable from outside the class?

12. If you declare a variable inside a for loop, can any other for loop see and access this variable? Explain.

13. Describe the difference between a reference variable and a primitive variable.

14. What sort of data is always contained in a reference variable? Do primitive variables always contain the same type of data? Explain.

15. Can the Java programmer designate whether he or she wants the program data stored on the stack or on the heap? Explain your answer.

16. Assume you are working with an Airplane class. If you declare a reference variable for an Airplane object, where is the reference variable stored? Where is the actual Airplane object data stored?

17. What type of data is stored on the stack? When, and by whom, is the data removed from the stack?

18. What type of data is stored on the heap? When, and by whom, is the data removed from the heap?

19. Is it possible for an object reference variable to be out of scope but the object's data still reside on the heap? Explain.

20. Describe when and how a class's finalize() method is called.

21. Can a Java programmer force the garbage collection process to occur as a Java program executes?

22. An integer is declared and initialized in class A's method1(), and it is passed to class B's method2(). Suppose method2() changes the value of the integer. Does it change the value of the integer in class A's method1()? Explain.

23. An integer array is declared and initialized in class A, and the array reference is passed to class B's method1(). Class B's method1() changes the values in the array. Does it change the values of the array in class A? Explain.

24. Why should Java programmers hide their class data? If the data is hidden, how does the outside world gain access to the data?

25. Can a Java programmer write a class that does not contain a class constructor? How does the Java compiler react to this situation?

Abstraction/Encapsulation

Problems 25–35: Select the pertinent data required for each of the following items. Then describe how you can bundle the data with relevant tasks associated with the item. Write the initialization tasks that the constructor should perform. Assuming that the data is hidden, describe the interface you need in order to interact with each item.

For example: Compact Digital Portable AM/FM Alarm Clock
Pertinent data: AM or FM mode, Radio station selected, Volume Control, Power on/off
Tasks: turnOnOff(), setVolume(), setStation(), setAMorFM_Mode()
Constructor: set default mode (AM or FM), set the volume, set the station

26. Gas grill.

27. Motorized lawn mower that you have to push (non-self-propelled).

28. 35 mm film camera (autofocus and automatic settings).

29. Digital watch with alarm.

30. Steam iron for pressing clothing.

31. Refrigerator with freezer compartment.

32. Electric portable heater with thermostat.

33. Soft drink vending machine.

34. Cable TV control box.

Compiler Problems

35–39. Each of the following portions of program code does not compile. Can you identify the incorrect code? What is required to correct it?

35.

```
//File: Problem35.java
public class Program35
{
      DooDad d = new DooDad();

      //other parts of class
}


//File: doodad.java
public class DooDad
{
      private int number;

      public DooDad(int m )
      {
            number = m;
      }
}
```

36.

```java
//File: Problem36.java
public class Program36
{
        int x, y;
        SayHi hi = new SayHi();

        public Program36
        {
                x = 7;
                y = 8;
                hi.greeting();
        }
        //other parts of class
}


//File: SayHi.java
public class SayHi
{
        public SayHi()
        {
                System.out.println("Hello");
        }
}
```

37.

```java
//File: Problem37.java
public class Program37
{
        private int values = { 4,6,1,98,3,34,62 };
        private FindIt  = new FindIt();

        public Program37
        {
                bool gotOne = FindIt.searchForOne(values);
        }
        //other parts of class
}


//File: FindIt.java
public class FindIt
{
        public FindIt()
        {
```

```
                System.out.println("Inside FindIt constructor");
        }
        private boolean search4One(int x[] )
        {
                for(i = 0; i < values.length; ++ i)
                {
                        if(values[i] == 1) return true;
                }
                return false;
        }
}
```

38.

```
//File: Problem38.java
public class Test
{
        public Program38
        {
                String name = "Rex";
                Dog pup = new Dog(String name);

                walkTheDog();
        }
        public void walkTheDog()
        {
                Rex.walk();
                Rex.bark();
        }
        //other parts of class
}
//File: Dog.java
public class Dog
{
        private String name;
        public Dog()
        {
                System.out.println("Dog constructor");
        }
        public Dog(String n)
        {
                name = n;
        }
        public walk( )
        {
                System.out.println("Go for a walk!");
        }
```

```
        public void bark()
        {
                System.out.println("BARK!");
        }
}
```

39.

```
//File: Problem39.java
public class Problem39
{
        Writer scribe = new Writer();
        double x = 84.24;
        int n = 52;
        String name = "Madison";

        public Program39
        {
                writeThingsToTheScreen();
        }
        public void writeThingsToTheScreen();
        {
                scribe.write();
                scribe.write(name);
                scribe.write(x);
                scribe.write(int);
        }
        //other parts of class
}


//File: ScreenWriter.java
public class ScreenWriter
{
        public ScreenWriter()
        {
                System.out.println("Writer constructor");
        }
        public void write()
        {
                System.out.println("Hello");
        }
        public void write(int a, double b)
        {
                System.out.println(a + "and " + b);
        }
```

```
      public void write(String n)
      {
              System.out.println( n );
      }
}
```

Programming Problems

40–48: Write complete Java programs. If you have studied Chapter 12, bundle your program into a JAR file.

40. Write a program that has a Box class and a BoxFrame or BoxApplet class. (This is similar to Program 6-3.) The Box class data include length, width, and height of the box, as well as volume and surface area. The Box class has overloaded constructors. The no-input constructor (default) sets the dimension values to 1.0. The overloaded constructor is passed the length, width, and height. The Box class has set() methods for the three dimension data items, as well as a calcVolAndSA(), getVolume() and getSurfaceArea() methods. When the program executes, the Frame constructor (or Applet start() method) uses JOptionPane message boxes to ask the user for the box dimension data. The data is then passes to a Box object. The box object calculates the volume and the surface area. The Frame calls the box object's get() methods and reports the box dimensions, volume, and surface area as well as draws a line drawing of the box. This drawing should be a simple, to-scale representation of the box data input by the user. (If you have studied Chapter 11, allow the user to input the three values separated by commas, and use a StringTokenizer to parse out these input values in the String returned from JOptionPane.)

41. Write a program that has a Pyramid class and a PyramidFrame or PyramidApplet class. (This is similar to Program 6-3.) The Pyramid class represents a four-sided pyramid and the data include the length and width of the base and height of the pyramid, as well as volume and surface area. The volume of a four-side pyramid can be computed using the following formula:

$$\text{VolPyramid} = \frac{1}{3}(\text{BaseArea})(\text{height})$$

The surface area of the pyramid requires the programmer to determine the surface area of the base and add it to the surface area of each of the four triangular sides. The triangle on each side of the pyramid is *not* guaranteed to be a right triangle—but each side can be constructed using right triangles. Draw many pictures of a pyramid and convince yourself that this is true. Hint: draw a line straight down from the tip of the triangle to the base. What do you know about the two new triangles? The programmer needs to use the area of a right triangle, which can be determined by using the following formula:

$$\text{AreaRightTriangle} = \frac{1}{2}(\text{base})(\text{height})$$

Another formula the programmer will find useful is the Pythagorean theorem:

$$c = \sqrt{a^2 + b^2}, \quad \text{or} \quad c^2 = a^2 + b^2$$

where c is the hypotenuse of a right triangle, and a and b are the sides of a right triangle. The Pythagorean theorem (and pyramid height and base information) will help you determine the length of the face of each side of the pyramid. Draw pictures! You'll figure it out! Hint: if you dropped a rope from the tip of the pyramid into the center of the pyramid, how does this rope-line relate to each face of the pyramid?

The Pyramid class has overloaded constructors. The no-input constructor (default) sets the dimension values to 1.0. The overloaded constructor is passed the base length, width, and pyramid height. The Pyramid class has set() methods for the three dimension data items, as well as a calcVolAndSA(), a getVolume() method, and getSurfaceArea() methods. When the program executes, the Frame constructor (or Applet start() method) uses JOptionPane message boxes to asks the user for the pyramid data. The data is then passed to a Pyramid object. It calculates the volume and the surface area of the Pyramid object. The Frame calls the pyramid get() methods and reports the dimensions, volume, and surface area, as well as draws a simple, to scale line drawing of the pyramid. (If you have studied Chapter 11, allow the user to input the three values separated by commas, and use a StringTokenizer to parse out these input values.)

42. Write a program that is similar to the RandomLines Applet, but instead of random lines, have random triangles. You should write a TriangleGenerator class that creates an array of 3 pairs of integers that represent a triangle. (The triangle does not have to be a right triangle.) The generator class is passed the size of the window (width and height) that represents the limits or range values for the generator. The generator's getTriangle() method is passed two integer array references, one for x and one for y, and it fills these values. Each (x,y) pair represents a corner point on the triangle. There should also be a getColor() method, which randomly selects and returns one of five colors. Your TriangleApplet class should instantiate a TriangleGenerator object. Have a 400 × 400 window, and draw a series of ten randomly produced triangles. Note: If the applet window is covered or minimized, ten new triangles are drawn.

43. In Problem 42, the HTML file sizes the TriangleApplet window to 400 × 400. In this problem, set the initial size of the window to 400 × 400 and allow the user to resize the window. When the user resizes the window, the TriangleGenerator should be passed the new window dimensions, and the generator uses these new dimensions to generate the triangle points. If the applet window is

covered or minimized, ten new triangles are drawn. Hint: applets have a getWidth() and getHeight() method.

44. Write a program that is similar to the RandomLines Applet, but instead of random lines, have random filled ovals. You should write an OvalGenerator class that creates the randomly selected x and y point for the oval. The generator class is passed the size of the window (width and height) that represents the limits or range values for the generator and the desired oval width and height. The generator returns the four values needed for drawing a filled oval. You may design the method or methods for the generator. You may bundle the oval data into an array (document which element represents which part of the oval) or have separate get() methods. There should also be a getColor() method that randomly selects and returns one of five colors. Your OvalApplet class should instantiate an OvalGenerator object. Have a 400 × 400 window and draw a series of ten randomly produced ovals. Number each oval as it is drawn. Two notes for the programmer: 1) Be sure that the oval is drawn completely in the window. 2) If the applet window is covered or minimized, four new ovals are drawn.

45. In Problem 44, the HTML file sizes the OvalApplet window to 400 × 400 and the programmer chose the oval's width and height. In this problem, set the initial size of the window to 400 × 400 and allow the user to resize the window. When the user resizes the window, the OvalGenerator should be passed the new window dimensions. The generator will use these new dimensions to generate new ovals that are sized to $^1/_{10}$ of the window. That is, if the new window is 300 × 400, the ovals are 30 × 40. Report the window size in the status bar. Be sure the ovals are drawn completely in the applet window.

6

46. a. Modify the ComputerUser class so that it contains a private Department number class variable. You will need to modify the class methods to handle this additional data member. Then, modify the Sort class from the ShowASort Applet example to include a new bubblesort() method for ComputerUsers array. Your new sort method should be passed the ComputerUser array and a flag that indicates whether the array is to be sorted by name or department number. Write an application that has an array of ten ComputerUsers. Fill the ten users and assign random department numbers from 100–999. Sort the array by name, write it in the Frame window, re-sort by department number, and also display this.

b. If you have studied Chapter 11, read the user's name, password, department number, and access code status from a data file. Each line of the data file should hold one user's set of information. Each of the data fields in the data file should be separated by a comma. If you JAR this application, do not place the user information file in the JAR but have it in the same directory.

47. In Chapter 5, Problems 39 and 40, we practiced drawing lines that are based on the standard line equation:

$$y = mx + b$$

where m is the slope and b is the y-intercept. In this problem, you are to build a class called LineEqn that is passed the slope and y-intercept values, and includes these three methods; 1) a method that returns a y value given any x, 2) a method that returns the y-intercept, and 3) a method that returns the x-intercept. The LineEqn class default (no-input) constructor sets the m and b values to 1.0. There are set() methods for the slope and y-intercept values. The getY() method is passed a double value that represents x and returns the corresponding y that is calculated, using the m and b values. The getYintercept() method returns the b value. Remember that the y-intercept is the y-location when $x=0$. The getXintercept() method returns the x value where the line crosses the x-axis, and by definition is where $y=0$. The programmer should perform a bit of algebra to be convinced that the x-intercept is found when:

$$x = \frac{-b}{m}$$

For this problem, write an EqnFrame that instantiates a LineEqn object. The frame should be sized to 300×300 pixels. Draw a set of axes centered in the window spanning -100 to $+100$ for both the x- and y-axes. Place tick marks every 10 units. In the frame constructor, use JOptionPane message boxes to obtain the slope and y-intercept value, and pass them into the LineEqn object. Ask the user for the number of points he or she wishes to plot between the values $x = -50$ and $x = 50$. Equally space the requested number of points with the first point drawn at $x = -50$ and the last point drawn at $x = 50$. Unlike the problems in Chapter 5, this problem simply passes the x value into the LineEqn object, receives the y value, and the EquFrame then plots the (x,y) pair. Somewhere in the frame, your program should write the equation of the line, and write the x-intercept and y-intercept values.

48. a. Create a class named SillySayings that contains a class variable that is an array of Strings. This array contains ten silly sayings such as "elephants look funny in petticoats," or "roadrunners wouldn't wear tennis shoes." (Remember, your sayings must be silly!) The getSillySaying() method uses the random number generator to randomly select one of the silly String. The program requires a SillyApplet that instantiates a SillySayings object. Whenever the applet window is painted (due to being created, minimized, or covered), cycle through five random sayings, pausing between each one. Display only one saying at a time. Vary the size of font you use for each saying that your write. The applet takes care of varying the font size, not the SillySaying class.

b. If you have studied Chapter 11, have the SillySaying class read the silly sayings from a file. Each saying should be listed on a separate line in the file.

7

More on Classes and Implementing Interfaces

CHAPTER OBJECTIVES

Introduce the keyword *this*.

Present the concept of "one-only" static data, methods, and classes.

Demonstrate how Java programmers can write and use static class members.

Discuss the various types of nested and inner classes in Java, and refer the reader to Appendix D, which discusses nested classes.

Introduce Java interfaces and show how to implement a Java interface in a class.

Show how user interface components are implemented with the ActionListener interface.

Describe and illustrate how to use anonymous classes.

Develop simple user interfaces that contain Swing components.

Show how Java user interface components and listeners work together in Java programs to provide GUI controls and event handling code.

It's fun to have fun!

Now that we are comfortable with writing our own Java classes, we can begin creating programs that are fun to write and fun to run! This chapter presents a hodge-podge of material that expands upon the concepts in the previous chapter, and that the Java programmer must know. This necessary material completes our basic preparation and includes how to write our own classes with static members. You may have a programming situation where a static method would be a convenient and appropriate tool—just like the JOptionPane static methods we use. We will learn the basics of writing user interface controls, such as buttons and combo boxes, and how to incorporate them into our programs. Once the controls are in our window, we must make our program "listen" and respond to events such as a button press.

We need a firm grounding in writing, instantiating, and using Java classes because it is a fundamental concept for expanding our programming capabilities. Whether we are incorporating user interface components, creating classes with static methods, or writing advanced Java applications by implementing an interface design, understanding Java classes is key. In this chapter we cover many different Java topics, and the discussion may seem disjointed during the first read. Just hold on to your Java hat—remember that we will soon tie the material together. Ready? Let's go.

7.1
The *this* Reference

Here is a question for you to ponder. Suppose we write a class that contains instance variables and methods. For example, in Program 7-1, the HelloYou class has a name member variable that is passed to and set in the constructor, and one other method, sayHello() which writes the name of the person contained in the class variable. By the way, notice that this class does not have a main() method. A main() method is required to run a program, but is not required to write a usable Java class.

```
1    //Program 7-1
2    //File:  HelloYou.java
3
4    import javax.swing.JOptionPane;
5
6    public class HelloYou
7    {
8        String name;
9        public HelloYou(String n)
10       {
11           name = n;
12       }
13
14       public void sayHello()
15       {
16           String output = "Hello " + name + "!";
17           JOptionPane.showMessageDialog(null,output,"HelloYou Program",
18               JOptionPane.INFORMATION_MESSAGE);
19       }
20   }
```

In the HelloForTwo class shown below, we instantiate two HelloYou objects. In the h1 object, we place Marc's name, and we place Gina's name in the h2 object. Question: If we have a class (HelloForTwo) that contains two objects of the same class (HelloYou), and call a method in that class using an object, how does Java know which object is which? Both objects have the same method. Take a look at the code here:

```
1    //Program 7-1 This class instantiates two HelloYou objects .
2    //File HelloForTwo.java
3
4    public class HelloForTwo
5    {
6        //We create two HelloYou objects.
7
8        HelloYou h1 = new HelloYou("Marc");
9        HelloYou h2 = new HelloYou("Gina");
10
11       public static void main(String args[])
12       {
13           new HelloForTwo();
14           System.exit(0);
15       }
```

```
16
17      public HelloForTwo()
18      {
19            //We now call the sayHello() method.
20            //How does Java keep the objects straight?
21
22            h1.sayHello();
23            h2.sayHello();
24      }
25  }
```

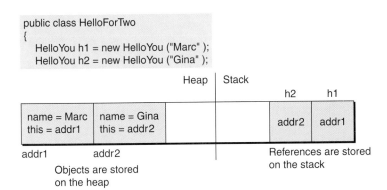

Figure 7-1
The *this* reference contains the reference to object. We create two HelloYou objects in the HelloForTwo class. Each HelloYou object has a *this* reference, which contains its own heap address.

How does Java ensure that the proper object is being referenced?

Java is helping us keep our objects straight because each object has a reference to itself, which is known as the **this** reference. The *this* keyword contains the object's reference or address value. Let's examine how these objects are stored in memory. Figure 7-1 shows the stack where the h1 and h2 object references are stored. Recall that the object reference is the location in the heap where the actual object data is stored. Each object contains a *this* reference, which contains its address on the heap.

When the programmer calls a method with the object reference and dot operator, Java helps by also passing the reference (address) of the object to the method. You can imagine that, behind the scenes, the method call looks like the code shown here:

this
contains the object's reference or address value, which is its address on the heap

```
//This is not real Java code, but illustrates how Java passes the
//object reference to the class's method.

HelloYou.sayHello(h1);    //The HelloYou class has one sayHello() method.
HelloYou.sayHello(h2);    //Java passes the reference to the method
                          //so the method knows which object it is to work with.
```

Whenever an object is created, Java automatically creates a *this* reference as part of the object's data, and the *this* reference is assigned the address of where the object is stored on the heap. (A similar analogy is that you carry your driver's license with you. It contains your address. The driver's license is like your *this* reference.) Just remember, if you create an object using new, you get a *this* reference. (Or the Java shorthand saying: Use new, get *this*.)

The *this* reference can be used inside a method to reference the current object. For example, in previous chapters, we extended JFrame in order to have a window in which to paint our pictures and text. In the programs, we had calls to setSize(), setTitle(), and show() methods.

```
//File: LoginUsersFrame.java

public class LoginUsersFrame extends Jframe
{
        //private data


        //class constructor initializes values
        public LoginUsersFrame()
        {
                setSize( 450, 200 );      //set the window size
                setTitle("Login Users Program");

                //later in the code we had
                show();
```

Another way to write this code would be to use the *this* reference inside the class:

```
//File: LoginUsersFrame.java

public class LoginUsersFrame extends Jframe
{
        //private data


        //class constructor initializes values
        public LoginUsersFrame()
        {
                this.setSize( 450, 200 );   //set the window size
                this.setTitle("Login Users Program");

                //later in the code we had
                this.show();
```

The *this* reference, with these three methods, helps explain to the reader where methods are coming from. By writing this.setSize(450, 200), someone reading the

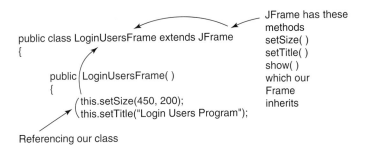

public class LoginUsersFrame extends JFrame
{

    public LoginUsersFrame( )
    {
        this.setSize(450, 200);
        this.setTitle("Login Users Program");

Referencing our class

JFrame has these
methods
setSize( )
setTitle( )
show( )
which our
Frame
inherits

Figure 7-2
The *this* reference always references the current object. By writing this.setSize() and
this.setTitle(), the reader would know that these two methods come from the Frame
class—which inherited them from JFrame.

code knows that setSize() comes from JFrame instead of having that person look at
the code and say, "Hmm, where's setSize coming from?" Figure 7-2 illustrates how
this always references the current object, such as in the JFrame example.

Another situation in which the *this* reference is very handy involves setting
class data or reference variables that are passed into the class. Suppose that we had
a Rectangle class in which the constructor is passed the length and width values.
We could write the code like this:

```
public class Rectangle
{
        private double length, width;      //class variables
        public Rectangle(double l, double w)           //we use l and w
        {
                length = l;
                width = w;
        }
```

Writing the constructor with the *l* and *w* requires the programmer to keep track of
which input values should be assigned to which class variable. (Granted, this is not
a difficult example.) If we use the *this* reference, we are able to name the input
parameters exactly like the class variables, as seen here:

```
public class Rectangle
{
        private double length, width;                  //class variables
//We can name the input variables exactly as the class variable.
        public Rectangle(double length, double width)
        {
                //this.length refers to the class variable
                this.length = length;
                this.width = width;
        }
```

The *this* reference can also be used with object references. The mechanics of using the *this* reference in the Rectangle class (above) and Bird class (below) is the same:

```
public class Bird
{
        private FlightPattern first, second;

        public Bird(FlightPattern first, FlightPattern second)
        {
                this.first = first;
                this.second = second;
        }
}
```

Java has many rules concerning the use of the *this* reference, and many of these rules are beyond the scope of this chapter. We introduce the rules for the keyword *this* as they are relevant to the text material. A complete description for the *this* reference can be found in the *Java Language Specification* found at the java.sun.com site. The previous code examples illustrate the common uses for the *this* reference. Soon we will also see other uses in this chapter when we cover user interface components and ActionListeners. Stay tuned!

7.2
Static Items in Java

Java classes define data and methods. When the programmer instantiates a Java object, each object stores its own data as well as a reference to itself in its *this* reference. The methods access the data and perform the required tasks. Recall that in Chapter 6 we instantiated a LineGenerator object named line in our RandomLinesApplet class. We had to set the number range, and then we used this object to call the getCoords() method, which provided the two sets of random points we used to draw our lines. In another Chapter 6 example, the UserValidation program, it had an array of five ComputerUser objects. Each object contained the user's name, password, and access code and we used the objects to set and get the user data.

There are situations where the programmer may need to have only one copy of a data item that represents information for the entire class, regardless of the number of objects. Or you may need a method to perform class-wide operation, which does not apply to individual objects. In order to set up this "only-one" type of data or method, the Java language provides the keyword **static**. Static items in Java exist on a per-class basis, not a per-instance basis. There are four varieties of static items in Java: data, methods, blocks, and classes, and they are described in Table 7-1.

static

static items in Java exist on a per-class basis, not a per-instance basis

TABLE 7-1
Static "Only One" Items in Java.

Item	Definition
data	Static data belongs to the entire class and not to any individual object. All objects of the class share static data. Static data represents class-wide information. If a static data variable is public, it can be accessed by use of the class name and dot operator, such as Math.PI. A private static data variable is accessed by use of a public static class method.
methods	Static methods are sometimes referred to as class methods, and they perform class-wide operations. Static methods can only access static data. Static methods can be accessed in two ways: 1) By the use of an object of the class and dot operator, or 2) By use of the class name and dot operator, such as JOptionPane.showMessageDialog().
| blocks | A static block of code is code contained within braces and is executed only once. The static block of code must be located inside a class but outside of any methods. Static blocks of code are used for initialization. The code is executed when the class is loaded into the JVM. Static blocks can only access static data.<br><br>```java
static
{
    //block of code, can only access static members
}
``` |
| classes | Static classes are located within another class and can be accessed independently from outside the class.

See Appendix D, Nested Classes for more information. |

Static Data and Methods

Java classes define data and methods, and every object of the class has its own copy of the class members. When a Java program begins to execute, and an object is instantiated, the object reference is placed on the stack and the object members are allocated on the heap. A *this* reference is created for the object. There are situations where the programmer may want one variable to be shared by all objects of the class. This variable can only be declared as static.

Java Police Department Program   Let's work through the concept of static data and methods by using an example. We can design a PoliceOfficer class that represents the data and methods for a police man or woman. What data do you expect in a PoliceOfficer class? Name, rank, and badge number? Yes. In this example, we have other data including boolean flags that indicate whether the officer is on or off duty, and if the officer is available to be sent to a call or is currently busy. Obviously, other methods for police officers could be writeTicket(), directTraffic(), catchCriminals(), or investigateCrimes(), but we will not include these methods in this example.
```

We want to know the total number of police officers we have in a program, and of those, how many are on duty and available for taking a call. In our PoliceOfficer class, we create three static integer variables: totalOfficers, totalOnDuty, and totalAvailable. These counters are incremented or decremented inside the class as we instantiate each officer and track his or her duty status. At any time, we are able to ask the class for the total number of officers and number of officers on duty and available for a call. We make these counters private and provide public static methods to access this data. Program 7-2 shows the PoliceOfficer class here:

```
1   //Program 7-2 Static Class Variables
2   //File: PoliceOfficer.java
3
4   public class PoliceOfficer
5   {
6       private String name, rank;
7       private int badgeNumber;
8       private boolean bOnDuty, bAvailable;
9
10      //These are class-wide variables.
11      private static int totalOfficers, totalOnDuty, totalAvailable;
12
13      public PoliceOfficer()
14      {
15          name = "TBA";
16          rank = "Patrol Officer";
17          badgeNumber = 10000;
18          totalOfficers++;            //Increment the totalOfficers each time
19          bOnDuty = false;            //an officer is created.
20          bAvailable = false;
21
22      }
23      public PoliceOfficer(String n, String r, int b)
24      {
25          name = n;
26          rank = r;
27          badgeNumber = b;
28          totalOfficers++;
29          bOnDuty = false;
30          bAvailable = false;
31
32      }
33      public void setOfficer(String n, String r, int b)
34      {
35          name = n;
36          rank = r;
37          badgeNumber = b;
```

Chapter 7 ▌ More on Classes and Implementing Interfaces

```
38              bOnDuty = false;
39              bAvailable = false;
40
41      }
42      public void setDutyStatus(boolean bOnJob)
43      {
44              //When an officer comes on duty,
45              //we assume he/she is available for a call
46              bOnDuty = bOnJob;
47
48              if(bOnDuty)
49              {
50                      totalOnDuty++;          //increment the class-wide counters
51                      totalAvailable++;
52                      bAvailable = true;
53              }
54              else
55              {
56                      totalOnDuty--;          //off duty, decrement class-wide counters
57                      totalAvailable--;
58                      bAvailable = false;
59              }
60
61      }
62      public void setCallStatus(boolean bAvail)
63      {
64              bAvailable = bAvail;
65              if(bAvailable)          totalAvailable++;  //adjust the count as the
66              else    totalAvailable--;                  //call status changes
67      }
68
69      public static int getTotalOfficers(){ return totalOfficers; }
70
71      public static int getTotalOnDuty(){ return totalOnDuty; }
72
73      public static int getTotalAvailable(){ return totalAvailable; }
74
75      public String toString()
76      {
77              String desc;
78              desc = rank + " " + name + " Badge Number: " + badgeNumber;
79              if(bOnDuty)
80              {
81                      desc += "\n I am on duty ";
82
83                      if(bAvailable)
```

```
84                    desc += "and available for a call.";
85              else
86                    desc += "and not available for a call.";
87          }
88          else
89          {
90              desc += "\n I am not on duty." ;
91          }
92
93          return desc;
94      }
95
96      protected void finalize()
97      {
98          //When a PoliceOfficer object goes out of scope the
99          //garbage collector calls finalize() to clean up the object.
100         //Here is where we decrement the total number of Officers.
101         --totalOfficers;
102     }
103 }
```

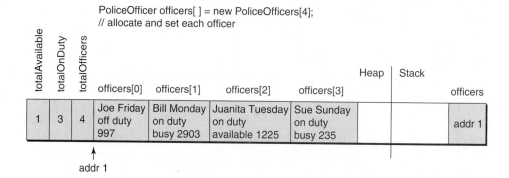

Figure 7-3
The static class variables: totalOfficers, totalOnDuty, and totalAvailable, are data representing all the objects in the class PoliceOfficer.

Our PoliceDeptFrame class contains an array of four PoliceOfficers. In the frame, we instantiate our officers and designate three of them to be on duty, and two are unavailable for calls. The static variables in the PoliceOfficer class are set when the constructor is run and the on duty and available numbers incremented or decremented as the officer status changes in the PoliceDeptFrame class. Figure 7-3 illustrates how the officer objects are stored.

Chapter 7 ▌ More on Classes and Implementing Interfaces

In the PoliceDeptFrame class, the static count variables are accessed in the paint() method by use of the PoliceOfficer.get() methods. Notice that we use the class name to call these static methods instead of an object name. We could have used any of the object references to access this data, but because the counts represent class-wide information, Java's convention says to use the class name. Figure 7-4 shows the results from this program.

```
1    //Program 7-2
2    //File: PoliceDeptFrame.java
3
4    import java.awt.Graphics;
5    import javax.swing.JFrame;
6
7    public class PoliceDeptFrame extends JFrame
8    {
9        //We create an array reference for PoliceOfficers
10       PoliceOfficer officers[] = new PoliceOfficer[4];
11
12       public static void main( String[] args )
13       {
14               PoliceDeptFrame jpd = new PoliceDeptFrame();
15               jpd.setDefaultCloseOperation( EXIT_ON_CLOSE );
16       }
17
18       //class constructor initializes values
19       public PoliceDeptFrame()
20       {
21               this.setSize( 550, 200 ); //set the window size
22               this.setTitle("Java Police Dept");
23
24               //Before we can use the officers array, we must fill the array with
25               //PoliceOfficer objects!!!
26               for(int i = 0; i < officers.length; ++i)
27               {
28                       officers[i] = new PoliceOfficer();
29               }
30
31                //Now we set 4 officers
32                officers[0].setOfficer("Joe Friday", "Detective", 997);
33                officers[1].setOfficer("Bill Monday", "Patrolman", 2903);
34                officers[2].setOfficer("Juanita Tuesday","Sergeant",1225);
35                officers[3].setOfficer("Sue Sunday","Captain",235);
36
```

```
37              //officers are created in the off duty status
38              //assign on duty and availability status
39
40              officers[1].setDutyStatus(true); //these 3 are now on duty
41              officers[2].setDutyStatus(true); //and available
42              officers[3].setDutyStatus(true);
43
44              officers[1].setCallStatus(false); //something has happened
45              officers[3].setCallStatus(false); //these 2 are not available
46
47              this.show();
48      }
49   public void paint( Graphics g )
50   {
51              String output = "Total number of officers on the force: "
52                              + PoliceOfficer.getTotalOfficers();
53         g.drawString( output, 25, 50 );
54
55         output = "Total number of officers on duty: " +
56              PoliceOfficer.getTotalOnDuty();
57         g.drawString( output, 25, 70 );
58
59         output = "Total number of officers on available for a call: "
60                              + PoliceOfficer.getTotalAvailable();
61         g.drawString( output, 25, 90 );
62
63         //show the officers
64         for(int i = 0; i < officers.length; ++i)
65         {
66                 g.drawString( officers[i].toString(), 25, 125 + i*15 );
67         }
68      }
69   }
```

Figure 7-4
The PoliceDeptFrame class writes the
officer information to the frame as well
as the class-wide information regarding total officers, total officers on duty,
and total available to respond to a call.

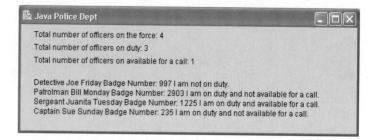

finalize() Method   One last question that you might have is: "How do we decrement the totalOfficers count value"? If our program uses a PoliceOfficer object, and then the reference goes out of scope, we have one less officer in our police department. When and how do we subtract one from the totalOfficers?

Java's java.lang.Object class provides a finalize() method. Because all Java classes have Object as its root class, the finalize() method is inherited in all classes. The **finalize() method** is called automatically by the garbage collector whenever an object goes out of scope. The job of the finalize() method is to perform any clean up activity that is required. For our PoliceOfficer class, we include a finalize() method where we decrement the totalOfficers counter.

finalize() method
called automatically by the garbage collector whenever an object goes out of scope and its job is to perform any clean up activity that is required

Static Methods Can Only Access Static Data

An important aspect of static data and methods is that static methods can only access static data. Notice how the getTotalOfficers() method has the static keyword in its method definition line and it returns the static integer totalOfficers. Nonstatic methods can access static members, as we see in the many of the PoliceOfficer methods. Figure 7-5 illustrates this with the PoliceOfficer's static totalOfficers.

Cooks Helper Program   The idea behind static class members is that these members are available to the program as soon as the class is loaded into memory

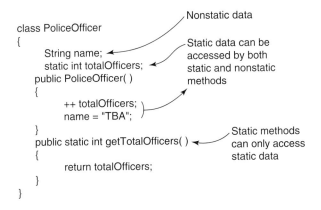

Figure 7-5
The static class method, getTotalOfficers(), can access the static int totalOfficers, but it could not access name. Static class methods can only access static data. Nonstatic methods can access static and nonstatic data.

at execution time. You do not need to have an object instantiated to use the static class members. Because we do not need to use the new operator to create the class, we do not have a *this* reference either. Recall how we import the JOptionPane class and call the show dialog methods by using the ClassName.staticMethod(), such as JOptionPane.showMessageDialog(). The Math class provides Math.PI and Math.sqrt() for us too.

Let's look at another example that shows how static methods can only access static data. Have you ever found yourself in the kitchen trying to remember how many teaspoons are in a tablespoon, or how many cups are in a pint? If you have, you will really like this sample program. We have a class called Cooks-Helper, which contains many public static integers with the common conversion values that cooks require. The class also contains a few static methods that perform conversions from one volume measurement to another. Program 7-3 shows the CooksHelper class.

```
1   //Program 7-3 Static Class Variables
2   //File: CooksHelper.java
3
4   public class CooksHelper
5   {
6
7       //These are class-wide static variables.
8       //Volume measurement equivalents
9
10      public final static int QTS_IN_GALLON = 4, PINTS_IN_QT = 4, CUPS_IN_PINT = 2;
11      public final static int OZ_IN_CUP = 8, TBSP_IN_OZ = 2;
12      public final static int TSP_IN_TBSP = 3, TBSP_IN_CUP = 16;
13
14      //Pass in ounces, return equivalent number of Tablespoons
15      public static float convertOzToTbsp(float ounces)
16      {
17          return ounces*TBSP_IN_OZ;
18      }
19
20      //Pass in cups, return equivalent number of ounces
21      public static float convertCupsToOzs(float cups)
22      {
23          return cups*OZ_IN_CUP;
24      }
25
26  }
```

The class KitchenFrame is boring on the outside but exciting on the inside! The program prints the conversion values for two of the data items in the Cooks-Helper class, and uses two of the static methods to convert cups to ounces and ounces to tablespoons. Notice how the class name and dot operators are used to access the CooksHelper static members, and we do not instantiate a CooksHelper object in this program. The output can be seen in Figure 7-6. Figure 7-7 illustrates how Java loads the class into memory and the static members are available without having an object created. Static methods can only access static data because the nonstatic members are not created until an object is created.

```
1    //Program 7-3 Use static data and methods from CooksHelper class.
2    //File: KitchenFrame.java
3
4    import java.awt.Graphics;
5    import javax.swing.JFrame;
6
7    public class KitchenFrame extends JFrame
8    {
9      public static void main( String[] args )
10     {
11          KitchenFrame baker = new KitchenFrame();
12          baker.setDefaultCloseOperation( EXIT_ON_CLOSE );
13     }
14
15     public KitchenFrame()
16     {
17          this.setSize( 400, 200 );
18          this.setTitle("Cooks Helper");
19
20          this.show();
21     }
22     public void paint( Graphics g )
23     {
24          //CooksHelper static members are accessed using the
25          //class name and dot operator.
26
27          String output =
28          "Kitchen conversions compliments of the CooksHelper class.";
29          g.drawString( output, 25, 50 );
```

```
30
31          output = "There are " +
32          CooksHelper.QTS_IN_GALLON + " quarts in a gallon.";
33           g.drawString( output, 25, 80 );
34
35           output = "There are " +
36          CooksHelper.TBSP_IN_OZ + " tablespoons in an ounce.";
37          g.drawString( output, 25, 100 );
38
39          float cups = (float)4.5;
40           float ozs = (float)12.5;
41
42          output = "There are " + CooksHelper.convertCupsToOzs(cups) +
43                  " ounces in " + cups + " cups.";
44          g.drawString( output, 25, 120 );
45
46          output = "There are " + CooksHelper.convertOzToTbsp(ozs) +
47                  " tablespoons in " + ozs + " ounces.";
48          g.drawString( output, 25, 140 );
49
50
51      }
52  }
```

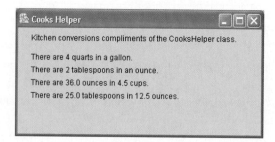

Figure 7-6
The static members of the CooksHelper class are accessed in the KitchenFrame
class by using the class name and dot operator. We did not instantiate a
CooksHelper object to perform these conversions.

```
public class CooksHelper
{
    public final static int TBSP_IN_OZ = 2;

    public static float convert OzToTbsp (float ounces)
    {
        return ounces * TBSP_IN_OZ;
    }

}

Call by using
float tbsp, ounces = 8.0f;
tbsp = CooksHelper.convert OzToTbsp(ounces);
```

        Class name   Static method

Figure 7-7
The static members of the CooksHelper class are loaded into memory and are
available to the program by use of ClassName.staticMethod() calling format, such
as CooksHelper.convertOzToTbsp(). Static methods can only access static data,
because nonstatic data is not created until an object of the class is instantiated. In
the KitchenFrame class, we do not instantiate a CooksHelper object, but we use the
static methods and data directly.

7.3
A Brief Introduction to Java Interfaces

In order to build a program using graphic user interface components, we must
understand how to implement a Java interface. This portion of Chapter 7 presents a
brief introduction to Java interfaces and we see how to implement an interface in a
class. We will revisit them in Chapter 9, where we complete the presentation of
interface material.

A Java interface is a class-like entity, and is used by Java programmers as a
way to design certain types of behavior for a class by providing the final public data
fields and method signatures. An interface typically contains the skeleton of a class,
including a general purpose design for class behavior. This skeleton or blueprint
can be thought of as promised behavior, and the intent is to write the implementation (methods bodies) once the actual type of class is known.

Let's look at a simple example to help clarify the concept of an interface. If we
wish to set up an interface called AnimalBehavior, the methods inside the class may be
breathe(), eat(), and communicate(). We cannot describe how an animal breathes, eats,
or communicates until we know the specific type of animal. For example, classes for a
Person, Shark, and GrassHopper could all be designed with the help of the Animal-
Behavior interface, because this interface describes behaviors for these three animals.

An **interface** is defined by using the interface keyword instead of class, and it
may contain public final fields and method signatures. The interface provides a list

interface
contains public final
fields and method
signatures, and
provides a skeleton for
a class

implements

a Java keyword that is used in the class definition line when implementing interfaces

of method signatures—that is, the method names and input and output values, but no method bodies. When we need to use an interface, we implement it in a class by using the **implements** keyword, and that class contains the completed interface methods. Java allows us to implement one or more interfaces in a class.

Let's review a class in Java and compare it to an interface. A class in Java contains class variables and methods. Typically, our class data is private and the methods provide a way to access the private data. The methods also perform tasks. When we write a class, we must write the code inside the methods in order for our class to be complete. Interfaces are like classes because they describe what a class must do; however, interfaces are different from classes in that they only contain method signatures. The interface does not contain the method code. When the Java programmer implements an interface, it is up to him or her to write the actual method code for the interface method. In other words, the interface tells us the method name, input, and return values, but the programmer must write the code for the interface method.

The AnimalBehavior interface could be described like this:

```
//File:  AnimalBehavior.java
public interface AnimalBehavior
{
        public String eat();
        public String communicate();
        public String breathe();
};
```

The Person, Shark and GrassHopper classes could all be designed by implementing the AnimalBehavior interface. This means that each of the classes would need to define the specifics for eating, communicating and breathing. This interface offers a good starting point for designing the three different types of animals. For example, here are the Person and Shark classes that implement the AnimalBehaviors interface:

```
//File:  Person.java
//We assume that the AnimalBehavior.class is in the same directory.
public class Person implements AnimalBehavior
{
        public String eat()
        {
                return "Three squares a day.";
        }
        public String communicate()
        {
                return "Cell phones, of course." ;
        }
        public String breathe()
        {
                return "Deep breaths using our lungs";
        }
}
```

```
//File:  Shark.java
public class Shark implements AnimalBehavior
{
      public String eat()
      {
           return "Smaller fish whenever I can find them.";
      }
      public String communicate()
      {
           return "We wiggle our tail back and forth. (?)" ;
      }
      public String breathe()
      {
           return "Water moving over our gills is how we breathe.";
      }
}
```

An Overview of Listener Interfaces and Swing Components

In Chapter 3, we discussed the differences between **Abstract Windowing Toolkit (AWT) peer components** and Java's **Swing components**. Recall that **components** refer to user interface controls, such as buttons, radio buttons, text fields, or sliders. The AWT "heavyweight" components rely on the target system's native components. We always use the "lightweight" Swing components in our programs, because they all know how to draw themselves and they come with all the "know how" they need to perform their jobs. They do not rely on the target system having the specific native component. The Swing components belong to the package javax.swing, and include user interface components such as JButton, JCheckBox, JDialogBox, JLabel, JMenu, JOptionPane, JSlider, and JToolBar.

Java package java.awt.event contains many interfaces that are designed for "listening" for events that occur in a program. An event could be a button press or someone entering text into a text field. Slider bar movements are events, as well as selecting an item from a combo box. When an event occurs in a Java program, the event is received and handled by a **Java listener**. The listeners are provided to us as interfaces. The job of the listener interfaces is to "listen for" or be aware when an event occurs, and to provide the necessary program control to perform the required tasks. We write our event handling code in the interface's method. An important concept for the new Java programmer is that the Swing components and listeners work hand in hand in your program.

In this chapter, we present the basic steps that must be taken for obtaining and placing a Swing component in our window, listening for a particular event, and

Abstract Windowing ToolKit (AWT) peer components
"heavyweight" components that rely on the target system's native components

Swing components
"lightweight" components that know how to draw themselves and come equipped with all the "know how" to perform their jobs

components
user interface controls, such as buttons, radio buttons, text fields, or sliders

Java listener
listens for an event that occurs in a Java program and the necessary program control to perform the required tasks

7

Figure 7-8
A window that contains two buttons. When the user presses the Bang button, a JOptionPane is presented with the word "Bang." If the user presses the Pop button, a "Pop" message is shown.

handling the event when it occurs. There are new concepts for us to learn in order to do this, and we use a few Swing components only to illustrate these concepts. In Chapter 8, we review these steps briefly, and present many of the Swing components and various types of listeners.

Basic Steps Required to have a JButton

Let's make sure we understand where we are going with all these new concepts. What we are learning is how to place user interface components in a window and have our program respond to an event that occurs with these components. In this first example, we build a window that contains two buttons, labeled "Bang" and "Pop." If the user presses a button with a mouse click, the program presents a message. Figure 7-8 shows the two-button window and the Bang message.

If you wish to have a button in your program, there are several steps you must take. These steps apply for any Swing component—we use a JButton as an example. (We present the steps here as an overview, and we will review them again shortly.) First, your program must have a window (container) to hold your button. This means that our program class must extend either JFrame or JApplet. (There are also other container classes. We will see these classes in Chapter 8.) You must import the javax.swing package and create your Swing JButton object component using the new keyword. You will need to obtain a Container object. A Container is a Java class that can hold components. We are familiar with JFrame or JApplet, so here we obtain the JFrame's or JApplet's contentPane, which is its Container. The button must be added into the contentPane so that it is drawn in the window. These steps take care of making the button and placing it in the window. If we stopped our work here and ran our program, we would see the button in the window. It would click up and down when we pressed it, but this event is not registered with the program, therefore, nothing happens.

In order to have the program respond when you press the button, the event must be registered with the program. To register the event, the programmer must tell the button the type of event it must listen for—such as being pressed or if the mouse moves over it. All Swing components have the appropriate addSomeKindOfListener()[1]methods. Using our button object, we must call the button's addActionListener() method to register this event. There are many types of listeners, such as ChangeListener, MouseListener, and KeyListener. These listeners are all Java interfaces.

Finally, the programmer must tell the program where it should go when that particular event has occurred and must also provide the necessary event handling code. The event handling code is written in the Listener's method. In the Bang and Pop example, when the Bang button is pressed, program control jumps to the ActionListener's event handling code, which presents a JOptionPane.show-MessageDialog(). We shall see two ways to provide event handling code. 1) by implementing an interface by means of the implements keyword, and 2) by means of an anonymous class.

ActionListener Interface

The **ActionListener interface** provides one method, which processes or handles a component event in a program. (Remember that an interface is a class skeleton, and we cannot write the interface method until we know what the type of component in which we are working.) One such component event we want to listen for and handle is a button press. Of course, there are many other events for which we could listen, and there are other listeners available. The ActionListener interface describes one method, **actionPerformed()**, which is passed an **ActionEvent object**. The ActionEvent object contains the event information. Let's look at the ActionListener's interface:

```
//This interface is contained in java.awt.event package.
//The EventListener is the superclass for all of the
//Event Listener interfaces.

public interface ActionListener extends EventListener
{
        //This method is called with an action occurs.
        public void actionPerformed(ActionEvent ae);
}
```

Java provides this interface to the programmer. The Java programmer must import the java.awt.event package and implement this interface whenever he or she wants to handle certain events, such as a button press.

A Brief Introduction to Containers and Layout Managers

Before we introduce our first program, which uses buttons and listeners, we must discuss the notion of containers and layout managers. In all of our previous programs in Chapters 2 through 6, we made use of the JApplet or JFrame's paint(Graphics g) method to draw into our window. The Graphics object that is passed to our program

ActionListener interface

provides one method, which processes or handles a component event in a program, such as a button press

actionPerformed( )

the only method in the ActionListener interface

actionEvent object

passed into the actionPerformed() method, this contains the event information

7

---

[1] addSomeKindOfListener() is the author's term, not an actual Java method.

knows where the window is located and knows how to draw into it. Now that we are expanding our Java programs to include user interface components, we need to have our hands on our JFrame or JApplet's actual **Container object**. Once we have the container, we are then able to add and arrange our components in our window.

It is very simple to get the Container object for our frame or applet. We must import the Container class and use the getContentPane() method. This method returns the container object and we are then free to add our components to it. The code for this operation typically looks like this:

```
import javax.swing.JFrame;
import java.awt.Container;

public class SomeClass extends JFrame
{
    public SomeClass()
    {
        Container canvas;          //We name our container canvas, since
                //we are going to place our components and paint into it.

                //The Container can be local to the constructor if we
                //do all of our setup in the constructor.

                //The getContentPane() returns the JFrame's container.
        canvas = getContentPane();

                //We are now ready to use our frame's canvas, a Container object.
    }
}
```

Layout managers dictate how the components are arranged in the window. We examine several layout managers in Chapter 8, but for our Chapter 7 programs we will use either a **GridLayout** or a **FlowLayout**. As their names imply, a grid layout is a tabular format based on rows and columns. A flow layout has the component flow into the window in a line. When a GridLayout manager is used, the components are placed in the window in the order that they are added to the container, and the components are all equally spaced in the window.

In order to set a layout type in your program, you obtain the frame or applet's container and then call the Container object's setLayout() method. This method requires us to create a LayoutManager object and pass it into the setLayout() as its input. We can write the code that creates a layout object and passes the object into the setLayout() method:

```
import javax.swing.JFrame;
import java.awt.Container;
import java.awt.GridLayout;

public class SomeClass extends JFrame
{
```

```
        public SomeClass()
        {
                Container canvas = getContentPane();


                //Create a GridLayout object.
                GridLayout grid = new GridLayout(2,1);        //2 rows by 1 col


                //Now set the layout for the canvas.
                canvas.setLayout( grid );
        }
```

Because we will never use the grid object again in our program, there is no need to
create a reference to it. We can write the code in a more efficient manner here:

```
Container canvas = getContentPane();


//We don't need a reference variable to the GridLayout
//since we use it only once. Set the grid to 2 rows by 1 column.


canvas.setLayout( new GridLayout(2,1) );
```

The flow layout is set up in a similar manner. We import the FlowLayout class and
call the Container's setLayout() method, like this:

```
import javax.swing.JFrame;
import java.awt.Container;
import java.awt.FlowLayout;


public class SomeClass extends JFrame
{
        public SomeClass()
        {
                Container canvas = getContentPane();


                //Set the flow layout for the canvas.
                canvas.setLayout( new FlowLayout() );
        }
```

We have examples of both GridLayout and FlowLayout in the following programs.

The BangPopApp Program   Our first few programs that use buttons are
simple on the outside but exciting on the inside. In the BangPopApp program, we
create a Java application that has two buttons. We add the buttons to the frame's
container and implement the ActionListener interface method, actionPerformed(),
to handle our two button presses. When a button is pressed, we must know who
triggered the event. We perform a getSource() query from the ActionEvent object in
the actionPerformed() method. If the bang button is pressed, a JOptionPane dialog

box that contains the word "Bang!" is presented. The pop button gives us a "Pop!" message. Before we examine the code, let's look at the window with its buttons in Figure 7-9. The code is seen in Program 7-4.

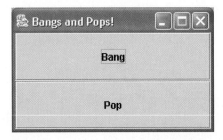

Figure 7-9
The window for the BangPopApp program. The two buttons are arranged in a grid layout, two rows by one column. The interface ActionListener's actionPerformed() method performs the handling code for the button clicks.

```
1    //Program 7-4
2    //BangPopApp.java
3
4    import javax.swing.JFrame;
5    import javax.swing.JButton;
6    import javax.swing.JOptionPane;
7    import java.awt.Container;
8    import java.awt.GridLayout;
9    import java.awt.event.ActionListener;
10   import java.awt.event.ActionEvent;
11
12   public class BangPopApp extends JFrame implements ActionListener
13   {
14      JButton bangButton = new JButton("Bang");
15      JButton popButton = new JButton("Pop");
16
17      //Here are my buttons, need to add them in THIS container
18
19      public BangPopApp()
20      {
21            //call to set the Frame's title
22            this.setTitle("Bangs and Pops!");
23
24            //The getContentPane() returns the JFrame's container.
25            //We are getting this frame's container.
26            Container canvas = getContentPane();   //returns a container
27
```

```
28              //Use a grid layout manager to place the buttons
29              //We don't need a reference variable to the GridLayout
30              //since we use it only once. Set the grid to 2 rows by 1 column.
31              canvas.setLayout( new GridLayout(2,1) );
32
33              //Now add the buttons to the canvas
34              canvas.add(bangButton);
35              canvas.add(popButton);
36
37              //Now need to add the listeners for the buttons
38              //THIS class is implementing actionListener
39              bangButton.addActionListener(this);
40              popButton.addActionListener(this);
41
42              //Set the size of the window and show it.
43              this.setSize(250,150);
44              this.show();   //Show method for this App could say this.show()
45
46      }
47
48      public static void main(String args[] )
49      {
50              BangPopApp theApp = new BangPopApp();
51              theApp.setDefaultCloseOperation(JFrame.EXIT_ON_CLOSE);
52      }
53
54      public void actionPerformed(ActionEvent e)
55      {
56              //Where did this event come from?????
57              if(e.getSource() == bangButton)
58              {
59                      //Here is where have the code for handling the Bang Button event.
60                      JOptionPane.showMessageDialog(this,"Bang!");
61              }
62              else if( e.getSource() == popButton)
63              {
64                      //Here is where have the code for the Pop Button.
65                      JOptionPane.showMessageDialog(this,"Pop!");
66              }
67      }
68 }
```

7

We should look at the code for the button event handling. We create our buttons as
class members by using the new operator. We pass in the labels for the buttons to
the JButton constructor.

```
JButton bangButton = new JButton("Bang");
JButton popButton = new JButton("Pop");
```

We obtain the container object for our frame using the getContentPane() method.

```
Container canvas = getContentPane();
```

The buttons are added to the container. We are using a GridLayout manager and our buttons will be placed automatically in a two-row by one-column format.

```
canvas.setLayout( new GridLayout(2,1) );


//Now add the buttons to the canvas.
canvas.add(bangButton);
canvas.add(popButton);
```

Next, we must add the type of listener we want to use for each button. For a button press, we need the ActionListener. The input argument to the button's addAction-Listener() method is the ActionListener interface object for handling the event. In other words, our Java program needs to be told where to go to handle the button press. In this case, we are using an ActionListener interface, which requires us to write an actionPerformed() method. By placing the *this* reference as the input, we are saying, "Come back to this class and you'll find the actionPerformed() method you are looking for." Figure 7-10 shows this relationship.

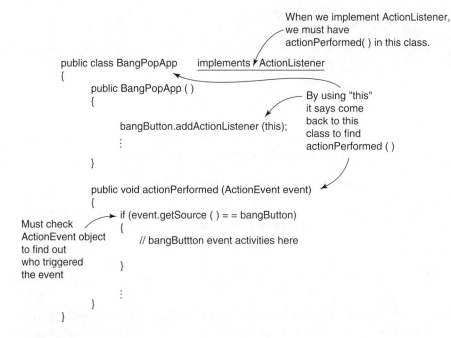

Figure 7-10
The addActionListener(this) tells Java to come back to this class to find the ActionListener's actionPerformed() method. We must check the event object to determine who triggered the event.

Primitive Data Types and Keywords in Java

Type	Data it can hold (and special notes).	Java Keywords
boolean	true/false (cannot be compared to 0 or 1)	boolean, char, byte, int, long, short, double, float, strictfp void
byte	Holds generic 8-bit values. Range: -128 to 127	new, this, super
char	A printable character should hold only character or bit data.	if, else, switch, case, break, default
short	A signed whole number. Range $-32,768$ to $+32,767$	for, continue, do, while
int	A signed whole number. Range $-2,147,483,648$ to $+2,147,483,647$	return, throw, try, catch, finally, assert, synchronized
long	A signed whole number. Range -2^{63} to $+(2^{63} - 1)$	static, abstract, final, private, protected, public
float	A signed number with approximately 6-7 digits of decimal precision. Range: $-3.4E^{38}$ to $+3.4E^{38}$	class, instanceof, throws, native, transient, volatile
double	A signed number with approximately 13-14 digits of precision. Range: $-1.7E^{308}$ to $+1.7E^{308}$	extends, interface, implements, package, import, const, goto

Conditional and Loop Control Statements

Condition	Basic format	Loops	Basic format

if	`if(condition)`
	`{`
	  `//true condition statements`
	`}`
		for	`for(i = 0; i < 10; ++i)`
			`{`
			  `System.out.println("Hi");`
			`}`

if
else if
else
	`if(condition1)`
	`{`
	  `//true condition1 statements`
	`}`
	`else if(condition2)`
	`{`
	  `//true condition2 statements`
	`}`
	`else`
	`{`
	  `//neither condition is true`
	`}`
		while	`int i = 0;`
			`while(i < 10)`
			`{`
			  `System.out.println("Hi");`
			  `++i;`
			`}`

switch	`switch( variable)`
	`{`
	  `case value1:`
	  `//variable is value1 statements`
	    `break;`
	  `case value2:`
	  `//variable is value2 statements`
	    `break;`
	  `default:`
	  `//variable value not in case statements`
	`}`
		do while	`int i = 0;`
			
			`do`
			`{`
			  `System.out.println("Hi");`
			  `++i;`
			`}while(i < 10);`

Array Declaration Examples

Primitives	Objects

`//Set up an array of 5 integers.`
 	
`//You can do it in two steps like this:`
`int numbers[];`
`numbers = new int [5];`
 	
`//Or use a one-step like this`
`int numbers[] = new int [5];`
 	
`//or initialize when you create`
`int numbers[] = { 6,9,12,43,4 };`
	`//Set up an array of Sailboats`
	
	`//Use the two step approach`
	`Sailboat boats[];`
	`boats = new Sailboat[5];`
	
	`//Or use the one-step approach.`
	`Sailboat boats[] = new Sailboats[5];`
	
	`//REMEMBER to create the objects before`
	`//you use them!`
	`for(int i = 0; i < boats.length; ++i)`
	`{`
	`    boats[i] = new Sailboat();`
	`}`

Common Exceptions

Exception	When Thrown
ArithmeticException	If a program performs an illegal arithmetic operation such as a divide by zero.
ArrayIndexOutOfBoundsException	If a program attempts to access an out of bound element in an array
Exception	General catch-all exception which can be used by the programmer to catch any error. Use printStackTrace() method to see exact errors.
FileNotFoundException	If Java cannot find an input file.
NullPointerException	Whenever a Java program tries to use or access an object reference that has not had an object created by the new operator. If you see this, ask yourself if you remembered to perform Class object = new Class();
NumberFormatException	If the parse() method does not find a valid number, such as if Integer.parseInt(s) does not find an integer in the String s.

String to Numeric Conversions

String to Numbers	Numbers to Strings

`String sInput;`
 	
`//Obtain sInput`
 	
`//Convert to an integer:`
`int n = Integer.parseInt(sInput);`
	`int n;    //Obtain numeric value in n.`
	
	`//Two ways to convert to a String`
	`String sNumber;`
	
	`//first way`
	`sNumber = Integer.toString(n);`
	
	`//or use valueOf(), pass it the int`
	`sNumber = String.valueOf(n);`

Two ways to create a JAR file with a manifest:
```
jar  cvfm  MyJar.jar WhereIsMain.txt   *.class
jar  cvmf  WhereIsMain.txt  MyJar.jar   *.class
```
To execute an application in a JAR:
```
java   -jar  MyJar.jar
```
Compile and run a class that imports your package:
```
javac -classpath  %CLASSPATH%;c:\path_to_package     MyClass.java
java   -cp  %CLASSPATH%;c:\path_to_package        MyClass
```

```
//Now need to add the listeners for the buttons.
//THIS class is implementing actionListener
        bangButton.addActionListener(this);
        popButton.addActionListener(this);
```

We place the actionPerformed() method in our BangPopApp class because we are
implementing the ActionListener interface. The actionPerformed() method is passed
an ActionEvent object that "knows" which button was pressed. Our ActionEvent
object's name is event, and we perform the event.getSource() method call so that we
can determine which component triggered the event by comparing the references.

```
public void actionPerformed(ActionEvent event)
{
        //Where did this event come from?????
        if(event.getSource() == bangButton)
        {
//Here is where we have the code for handling the Bang Button event.
                JOptionPane.showMessageDialog(this,"Bang!");
        }
        else if( event.getSource() == popButton)
        {
//Here is where we have the code for handling the Pop Button.
                JOptionPane.showMessageDialog(this,"Pop!");
        }
}
```

Inside the actionPerformed() method, we have the ActionEvent object named event.
We call the ActionEvent's method getSource() to determine which button was pressed.

JBangApplet Example   We can use the same programming scheme from the
BangPopApp application in applets. The JBangApplet class creates three Swing
JButton objects, obtains the applet's container, sets the layout manager to a flow
type, adds the buttons to the container, and implements ActionListener to handle the
button presses. The resultant window is shown in Figure 7-11 and the code is seen
in Program 7-5.

7

Figure 7-11
The Applet Viewer window for the JBangApplet program.
The three buttons are arranged using a flow layout. The
interface ActionListener's actionPerformed() method performs the handling code for the button clicks.

```
1    //Program 7-5
2    //File: JBangApplet.java
3
4    import javax.swing.JApplet;
5    import javax.swing.JButton;
6    import javax.swing.JOptionPane;
7    import java.awt.Container;
8    import java.awt.FlowLayout;
9    import java.awt.event.ActionListener;
10   import java.awt.event.ActionEvent;
11
12   public class JBangApplet extends JApplet implements ActionListener
13   {
14      JButton bangButton = new JButton("Bang");
15      JButton popButton = new JButton("Pop");
16      JButton wowButton = new JButton("Wow");
17
18      public void init()
19      {
20              //We are getting this Applet's container
21              Container canvas = getContentPane();  //returns a Container object
22
23              //Use a flow layout for our applet.
24              canvas.setLayout( new FlowLayout() );
25
26              //Now add the buttons to the canvas.
27              canvas.add(bangButton);
28              canvas.add(popButton);
29              canvas.add(wowButton);
30
31              //Need to add the listeners for the buttons.
32              //THIS class is implementing ActionListener interface.
33              bangButton.addActionListener(this);
34              popButton.addActionListener(this);
35              wowButton.addActionListener(this);
36
37      }
38
39      public void actionPerformed(ActionEvent event)
40      {
41              //where did that event come from?????
42              if(event.getSource() == bangButton)
43              {
44                      JOptionPane.showMessageDialog(this,"Bang!");
45              }
```

```
46              else if( event.getSource() == popButton)
47              {
48                      JOptionPane.showMessageDialog(this,"Pop!");
49              }
50              else if( event.getSource() == wowButton)
51              {
52                      JOptionPane.showMessageDialog(this,"Wow!");
53              }
54      }
55  }
```

Western States Combo Box Program   Did you know that New Mexico is known as the Land of Enchantment, and Arizona is the home of the Arizona Diamondbacks? When you execute our next program, fun facts on western states are yours for the asking. In Program 7-6, we use a JComboBox to allow the user to select a state, then we write a statement into the window by using a JTextField. (See Figure 7-12.)

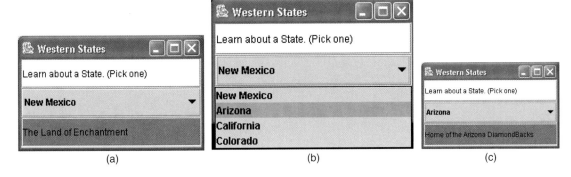

(a)   (b)   (c)

Figure 7-12
a) Our three components, two JTextFields and one JComboBox. We implement ActionListener's actionPerformed() method to change the text concerning the state when a new state is selected. b) The drop-down combo box with the various states. c) Arizona's information.

As we begin using the different Swing components, it is important for you to examine the documentation for that component. Chances are very good that whatever you want to do with your component, there is a method available for you. Want to change the color of your text field? There are methods to do this. Look at the setBackground(Color c) method and setForeground(Color c) in the JTextField documentation. Remember to also examine all of the inherited methods documentation.

Vector class

a helpful, collection-type class which can grow or shrink as the program runs (includes add(), clear(), remove(), get(), indexOf(), and isEmpty() methods)

Just for fun, we use a **Vector class** to hold the name of the states and an array of Strings for state facts. This enables us to compare the difference between an array and a Vector. We know that an array is declared with a certain size and that size cannot change. A Vector is one of the many helpful collection-type classes provided to us in the java.util package. Vectors can be thought of as dynamic arrays that hold objects. When we refer to something as dynamic, it means that the size can grow and shrink as the program runs. In fact, many Java programmers believe we should never make an array of objects, but simply use the Vector class.

Examine the Java documentation for Vector and see the many supporting methods, such as add(), clear(), remove(), get(), indexOf(), and isEmpty(). We instantiate a Vector object and we can use the add() method to place objects into the Vector object. When we create the JComboBox object, we can place the vector object in the constructor to initialize its list of state names. If we were going to read the states from a data file and were not sure how many states were in the file, the Vector object is an ideal choice because it can grow in length as we read and add() each state to it. In this program, we set the state name and facts directly in code. We could have just used JComboBox's addItem() method, placing the String into each of the array elements.

We add an ActionListener on the JComboBox object because we want to change the text field string when the user selects a new state. When the user picks a new state, Java calls the actionPerformed() method. (In Chapter 8 we demonstrate the use of an ItemListener for a JComboBox.) Here we ask the combo object which item was selected using the getSelectedIndex() method. The combo box keeps track of the items via an integer, zero being the first item, one the second, and so on. Once we know which state was picked, we pass the corresponding stateSaying into the JTextField's setText() method to update the field object.

The program code is shown in Program 7-6. Review the output which was shown in Figure 7-12.

```
1    //Program 7-6
2    //File: StatesComboApp.java
3
4    import java.util.Vector;
5    import javax.swing.JFrame;
6    import javax.swing.JComboBox;
7    import javax.swing.JTextField;
8    import java.awt.Color;
9    import java.awt.Container;
10   import java.awt.GridLayout;
11   import java.awt.event.ActionListener;
12   import java.awt.event.ActionEvent;
13
14
```

```
15   public class StatesComboApp extends JFrame implements ActionListener
16   {
17     private Vector stateList = new Vector();
18     private JComboBox combo;
19     private JTextField field;
20     private JTextField title = new JTextField("Learn about a State. (Pick one)");
21     private Container holder;
22
23     private String stateSaying[] = new String [4];
24
25
26     public StatesComboApp()
27     {
28           this.setTitle("Western States");
29           fillStateList();
30
31           this.setSize( 250,150);
32           holder = getContentPane();
33           holder.setLayout( new GridLayout(3,1) );
34           combo = new JComboBox( stateList );
35
36           //the components appear in the window in the order they are added
37           holder.add(title);
38           holder.add(combo);
39           holder.add(field);
40
41           combo.setSelectedIndex(0);        //show the first state in the list
42
43           //Change the field according to which state is picked.
44           combo.addActionListener(this);
45
46   //Set the foreground and background color of the text field.
47           field.setForeground(Color.black);
48           field.setBackground(Color.magenta);
49           this.show();
50     }
51
52     private void fillStateList()
53     {
54           //Here we add a String to the Vector object.
55           stateList.add( "New Mexico");
56
57           //Here we place text in the String array's [0] element.
58           stateSaying[0] = "The Land of Enchantment";    //
```

```
59
60                 stateList.add( "Arizona");
61                 stateSaying[1] = "Home of the Arizona DiamondBacks";
62
63                 stateList.add( "California");
64                 stateSaying[2] = "Wonderful wineries!";
65
66                 stateList.add( "Colorado" );
67                 stateSaying[3] = "Rocky Mountain High";
68
69                 field = new JTextField( stateSaying[0] );
70         }
71
72     public static void main( String[] args)
73     {
74             StatesComboApp app = new StatesComboApp();
75             app.setDefaultCloseOperation( EXIT_ON_CLOSE );
76     }
77
78     public void actionPerformed(ActionEvent event)
79     {
80             //Obtain the selected state from the combo box and
81             //set the text in the field.
82
83             int pick = combo.getSelectedIndex();
84             field.setText(stateSaying[pick] );
85
86     }
87 }
```

7.4
Nested Classes

top-level class

a class whose source code is contained in its own file named with the *.java* extension

nested classes

a class that is defined within the body of another class

In completely object-oriented programs, everything must be contained in a class. Even if you wish to write one general purpose method, that method must be within a class. In the early stages of developing the Java language, every class had to be a **top-level class**, meaning that the class source code is contained in its own file named with the *.java* extension. All of the classes we have written in this text have been top-level classes.

As Java designers improved and expanded the language, Java JDK 1.1 provided **nested classes**. Nested classes are classes that are defined within the body of another class. For example, the following code shown has the Inner class defined inside the Outer class.

```
//File: Outer.java
public class Outer
{
      //data for Outer class
      public Outer()
      {
            //Outer constructor
      }
      public void outerMethod()
      {
            //body of method
      }

      //Here is the inner class. It is defined inside the Outer class.
      public class Inner
      {
            public Inner()
            {
                  //constructor for Inner class
            }
            public void innerMethod()
            {
                  //body of the innerMethod
            }
      }
}
```

When the Java compiler compiles a class contained within a *.java* file, the compiler creates a *.class* file. If the class contains an inner class, the compiler creates a second *.class* file that is named with a "$" separating the outer and inner class name. For example, if we compiled the *Outer.java* file, the Java compiler creates an *Outer.class* file and an *Outer$Inner.class* file too.

There are four types of nested classes in Java. We introduce all of them here, but only cover anonymous classes in detail in this chapter. Students often ask, "Why would a Java programmer write a nested class?" In day-to-day programming, nested classes are not often used. A programmer may choose to write a nested class if the nested class is useful only to the outer class that contains it. The nested class that we study in this chapter and will use often in event handling is the anonymous class. We see them again in Thread programs in Chapter 8. *Java Programming Today* presents details and examples of static nested, inner, and local classes in Appendix D. Java's nested classes are summarized in Table 7-2.

Anonymous Inner Classes

An **anonymous inner class** is a class that is defined inside another class (inner) and is not assigned a reference name (anonymous). Anonymous inner classes are used for writing event handlers. They facilitate and simplify the code that a programmer writes. The best way to see how an anonymous inner class works is to look at an example.

anonymous inner class

a class that is defined inside another class and is not assigned a name. Used for writing event handling code

TABLE 7-2

Nested classes in Java.

Type of class	Definition
Nested static class	A nested static class has the static keyword in its class definition line. A nested static class is defined inside another class and works in the same manner as a top-level class. The name of the enclosing class must be used when a nested class object is instantiated.
Member class or inner class	A member or inner class is a class that is contained inside another class. The inner class can reference any members in its parent class.
Local class	A local class is also an inner class, but it is contained inside a block of code in the top-level class. A local class is usually defined in a method.
Anonymous class	An anonymous class is a special variation of an inner class. The class is declared and instantiated within a single expression.

Let's look at the BangPopApp2 application program, a rework of the Bang-PopApp program, concentrating on how the ActionListener interface is implemented and how it performs the event handling work. Program 7-7 works exactly like the first BangPopApp program seen earlier in the chapter. And don't forget—we must use the ActionListener interface's method, actionPerformed(), for our event handling code. Notice though, that we do not use ActionListener in the class definition line, and the code for addActionListener() is different. We are writing the entire class inside the parentheses in the button's addActionListener() method call.

7

```
1   //Program 7-7
2   //File: BangPopApp2.java
3   //Use anonymous inner classes to perform event handling.
4
5   import javax.swing.*;   //for JButton, JFrame, JOptionPane
6
7   import java.awt.Container;
8   import java.awt.GridLayout;
9   import java.awt.event.ActionListener;
10  import java.awt.event.ActionEvent;
11
12  public class BangPopApp2 extends JFrame
13  {
14      JButton bangButton  = new JButton("Bang");
15      JButton popButton = new JButton("Pop");
16
```

```
17      public BangPopApp2()
18      {
19              this.setTitle("Bangs and Pops");
20              this.setSize(250,150);
21              Container canvas = getContentPane();
22
23              canvas.setLayout( new GridLayout(2,1) );
24
25              canvas.add(bangButton);
26              canvas.add(popButton);
27
28              //Use an anonymous class with the Action Listener.
29              bangButton.addActionListener(  new ActionListener()
30              {
31                      public void actionPerformed(ActionEvent event)
32                      {
33                              JOptionPane.showMessageDialog(null,"Bang!");
34                      }
35              } );
36
37              popButton.addActionListener( new ActionListener()
38              {
39                      public void actionPerformed(ActionEvent event)
40                      {
41                              JOptionPane.showMessageDialog(null,"Pop!");
42                      }
43              } );
44
45              this.show();
46
47      }
48
49      public static void main( String args[]   )
50      {
51              BangPopApp2 theApp = new BangPopApp2();
52              theApp.setDefaultCloseOperation(JFrame.EXIT_ON_CLOSE);
53      }
54  }
```

When the Java compiler successfully compiles this program, the compiler
writes three class files. The *BangPopApp2.class* file is created, and each of the
anonymous classes also have their own class files. There are *BangPopApp2$1.
class* and *BangPopApp2$2.class* files. Recall that when inner classes are
compiled, the compiler writes separate class files for the inner classes, using the

OuterClassName$InnerClassName.class format. Because we are using anonymous classes, the compiler uses a number for the anonymous class name. The anonymous class files are numbered uniquely, beginning at 1.

If you examine the Java documentation for JButton's addActionListener() call, it is:

```
public void addActionListener( ActionListener al)
```

where *al* is an object of the ActionListener class. This says that when we add the ActionListener to the JButton object, we must pass in an ActionListener object. The way we accomplish this task is to instantiate the ActionListener object and write the entire ActionListener class, including its required method actionPerformed(), inside the parentheses of the addActionListener( ) call. We create an object of ActionListener with the new operator. This object is anonymous because it does not have a reference name.

```
addActionListener(  new ActionListener()
{

        //actionPerformed() method here


} );    //we use the } to close the class
        // and ); to close addActionListener method
```

The complete anonymous inner class is shown in the following code. Figure 7-13 illustrates this concept. Compare it to Figure 7-10, which illustrates implementing the ActionListener interface's actionPerformed() method within the class instead of within the method call.

```
//Use an anonymous class with the Action Listener.
        bangButton.addActionListener(  new ActionListener()
        {
                public void actionPerformed(ActionEvent event)
                {
                        JOptionPane.showMessageDialog(null,"Bang!");
                }
        } );
```

Figure 7-13

An anonymous inner class for ActionListener interface is written inside the addActionListener(), including the actionPerformed() method. It is anonymous because there is no object reference created for the ActionListener.

```
public class BangPopApp 2
{
    public BangPopApp 2 ( )
    {
        bangButton.addActionListener (new ActionListener ( )
        {
            public void actionPerformed (ActionEvent event)
            {
                //handle bangButton activities here
            }
        } );
```

Here is the anonymous inner class that handles the bangButton event

Color My Buttons Programs   The Swing package includes a JColorChooser that allows a user to select a color from a grid of colors. In this next program, let's set up three buttons in a window. When the user presses a button, we are able to select a color for the button's background color. We will write this program two ways, one that implements ActionListener and one that uses anonymous inner classes. Program 7-8 shows the event handling code in one actionPerformed() method. Figure 7-14 shows the button window, along with a ColorChooser window. Notice how the ColorChooser is requesting a color for the Left button and is currently displaying the Left button's color.

```java
1    //Program 7-8
2    //ColorButtons.java      This implements ActionListener.
3
4    import javax.swing.*;    //for JFrame, JButton, JColorChooser
5    import java.awt.Container;
6    import java.awt.FlowLayout;
7    import java.awt.event.ActionListener;
8    import java.awt.event.ActionEvent;
9    import java.awt.Color;
10
11   public class ColorButtons extends JFrame implements ActionListener
12   {
13      JButton leftButton = new JButton("Left");
14      JButton centerButton = new JButton("Center");
15      JButton rightButton = new JButton("Right");
16
17      public ColorButtons()
18      {
19           this.setTitle("Color My Buttons!");
20
21           Container canvas = getContentPane();   //returns a container
22
23           //Use a flow layout manager to place the buttons
24           canvas.setLayout( new FlowLayout() );
25
26           //Now add the buttons to the canvas
27           canvas.add(leftButton);
28           canvas.add(centerButton);
29           canvas.add(rightButton);
30
31           //Register the button events with the program.
32           leftButton.addActionListener(this);
33           centerButton.addActionListener(this);
34           rightButton.addActionListener(this);
35
```

```
36          //Set the size of the window and show it.
37          this.setSize(250,100);
38          this.show();
39
40   }
41
42   public static void main(String args[] )
43   {
44          ColorButtons theApp = new ColorButtons();
45          theApp.setDefaultCloseOperation(JFrame.EXIT_ON_CLOSE);
46   }
47
48   public void actionPerformed(ActionEvent ae)
49   {
50          String buttonText;
51          Color current, newColor;
52          JButton whichButton = new JButton();
53
54          //Determine which button triggered the event.
55          if(ae.getSource() == leftButton)
56                 whichButton = leftButton;
57          else if( ae.getSource() == centerButton)
58                 whichButton = centerButton;
59          else if( ae.getSource() == rightButton)
60                 whichButton = rightButton;
61
62          //Get the button's label.
63          buttonText = whichButton.getText();
64
65          //Get the button's current color.
66          current = whichButton.getBackground();
67
68          //Show the ColorChooser with the button's label and
69          //current color.
70          newColor = JColorChooser.showDialog(null,
71                 "Pick a color for "+ buttonText , current);
72
73          //If the user cancels out of the ColorChooser, it returns a null.
74          //We'll change the color if newColor isn't null.
75          if(newColor != null)
76                 whichButton.setBackground(newColor);
77
78   }
79 }
```

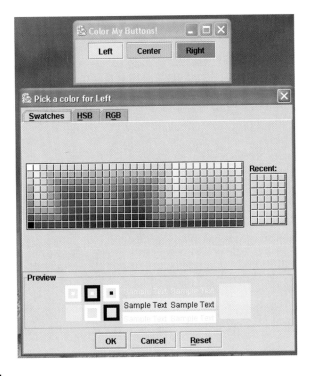

Figure 7-14
The top window shows our three buttons in a flow layout and the ColorChooser window. The ColorChooser is obtaining a new color for the Left button. Notice that we have passed the Left button's current color into the ColorChooser for its preview color.

We now rewrite the ColorButtons program in Program 7-9, using anonymous inner classes to handle the button events. Notice how we duplicate the code in all three actionPerformed() methods, and do not have to ask which button triggered the event. The program output is exactly like the previous program.

```
1   //Program 7-9
2   //ColorButtons2.java      This uses anonymous inner classes.
3
4   import javax.swing.*;      //for JFrame, JButton, JColorChooser
5   import java.awt.Container;
6   import java.awt.FlowLayout;
7   import java.awt.event.ActionListener;
8   import java.awt.event.ActionEvent;
9   import java.awt.Color;
10
```

```
11    public class ColorButtons2 extends JFrame
12    {
13      JButton leftButton = new JButton("Left");
14      JButton centerButton = new JButton("Center");
15      JButton rightButton = new JButton("Right");
16
17      public ColorButtons2()
18      {
19            this.setTitle("Color My Buttons!");
20
21            Container canvas = getContentPane();   //returns a container
22
23            //Use a flow layout manager to place the buttons
24            canvas.setLayout( new FlowLayout() );
25
26            //Now add the buttons to the canvas
27            canvas.add(leftButton);
28            canvas.add(centerButton);
29            canvas.add(rightButton);
30
31            //Register the button events with the program.
32            //Now we use anonymous inner classes to implement
33            //the event handling code.
34
35
36            leftButton.addActionListener(new ActionListener()
37            {
38                  public void actionPerformed(ActionEvent ae)
39                  {
40                        String buttonText = leftButton.getText();
41                        Color current = leftButton.getBackground();
42                        Color newColor = JColorChooser.showDialog(null,
43                              "Pick a color for "+ buttonText , current);
44                        if(newColor != null)
45                              leftButton.setBackground(newColor);
46                  }
47            });
48
49
50            centerButton.addActionListener(new ActionListener()
51            {
52                  public void actionPerformed(ActionEvent ae)
53                  {
```

```
54              String buttonText = centerButton.getText();
55              Color current = centerButton.getBackground();
56              Color newColor = JColorChooser.showDialog(null,
57                   "Pick a color for "+ buttonText , current);
58              if(newColor != null)
59                   centerButton.setBackground(newColor);
60          }
61      });
62
63      rightButton.addActionListener(new ActionListener()
64      {
65          public void actionPerformed(ActionEvent ae)
66          {
67              String buttonText = rightButton.getText();
68              Color current = rightButton.getBackground();
69              Color newColor = JColorChooser.showDialog(null,
70                   "Pick a color for "+ buttonText , current);
71              if(newColor != null)
72                   rightButton.setBackground(newColor);
73          }
74      });
75
76      //Set the size of the window and show it.
77      this.setSize(250,100);
78      this.show();
79  }
80
81  public static void main(String args[] )
82  {
83      ColorButtons2 theApp = new ColorButtons2();
84      theApp.setDefaultCloseOperation(JFrame.EXIT_ON_CLOSE);
85  }
86 }
```

7.5
Summary

This chapter presents several Java topics required to round out the new Java programmer's knowledge of the language. These miscellaneous topics include an
introduction to the *this* keyword. When a Java program instantiates an object,
part of the object's data is a reference to itself. In other words, the object keeps
track of its own address on the heap, and the *this* reference stores that reference

(which is just an address in memory). The *this* reference is used by the Java language to keep track of objects and can be used to clarify source code method calls. For example, the following code, shows the *this* reference with this.setSize(), this.setTitle(), and this.show(). The *this* reference is referring to the LoginUsersFrame class, which inherited the setSize(), setTitle(), and show() methods from JFrame.

```java
//File: LoginUsersFrame.java

public class LoginUsersFrame extends Jframe
{
    //private data


    //class constructor initializes values
    public LoginUsersFrame()
    {
        this.setSize( 450, 200 );  //set the window size
        this.setTitle("Login Users Program");

        //later in the code we had
        this.show();
```

We also show that the *this* keyword is used by the programmer when he or she incorporates user interface components in a window and implements a Java listener interface. The *this* reference is used when the programmer must call the addSomeKindOfListener() method of a component, such as calling a JButton object's addActionListener(this). Placing *this* in the method call tells Java to "come back to this class" to find the actionPerformed() method. Below is a portion of the BangPopApp program showing these relevant lines of code:

```java
//Partial code listing from Program 7-4
public class BangPopApp extends JFrame implements ActionListener
{

    //Here are two user interface components, JButtons.
    JButton bangButton = new JButton("Bang");
    JButton popButton = new JButton("Pop");

    public BangPopApp()
    {
        //The getContentPane() returns the JFrame's container.
        //We are getting this frame's container.
        Container canvas = getContentPane();
```

7

```
        //Now add the buttons to the canvas.
        canvas.add(bangButton);
        canvas.add(popButton);


    //Here is where we tell the buttons what type of event
    //they are "listening." The ActionListener listens for a button press.

    //By using "this" in the method call, Java knows to come back to
    //THIS class to find the ActionListener's actionPerformed() method.

        bangButton.addActionListener(this);
        popButton.addActionListener(this);


    }


    public void actionPerformed(ActionEvent event)
    {
        //Where did this event come from?????
        if(event.getSource() == bangButton)
        {
            JOptionPane.showMessageDialog(this,"Bang!");
        }
        else if( event.getSource() == popButton)
        {
            JOptionPane.showMessageDialog(this,"Pop!");
        }
    }
}
```

7

We study the concept of "one-only" static data and methods. Static classes and other nested classes are covered in Appendix D. A Java programmer can declare a class variable to be static, and no matter how many objects of that class are created, there is only one of the static, class variable. All of the objects can access that one variable. We see how static variables work in the Java PoliceOfficer, Senator, and SoftballPlayer classes in this chapter's sample and practice programs.

Java also provides static methods. When a programmer places the static keyword in a method definition line, that method can access only static data, and that method may be called by using just the ClassName.staticMethodName() format. That is, an object of that class does not need to be created in order to use that class's static methods. The CooksHelper program contains static methods that provide the user with an easy way to perform cooking measurement conversions. In the PoliceOfficer program, we use the PoliceOfficer.getTotalOfficers() format to access the static totalOfficers variable.

After the discussion on static items in Java, we switch gears and begin to explore the required material for incorporating graphical user interface (GUI) components into our programs. The first piece of business in this complex topic is an introduction to Java interfaces. Interfaces can be thought of as class-like items that contain data and method signatures. A programmer must implement the methods. The only listener interface we see in this chapter is the ActionListener. It contains one method: the actionPerformed() method.

GUI components must be created and added to a window's container. We can designate the exact size and position of the component or utilize a layout manager to help us with this task. There are many layout managers but we only see the GridLayout (rows by columns) and FlowLayout in this chapter. (Much more to come on the GUI components and other listeners in Chapter 8!)

Java components, such as JButtons and JComboBoxes work hand in hand with Java listeners. If we want our JButton object to respond to being pressed, we must tell the button object to "listen" for the button event. We register the button event with the program by calling the addActionListener() method. Now that the button knows to listen for being pressed, the Java programmer must provide the code to "handle" the event. When the button event occurs (when the user presses the button with the mouse) the ActionListener's actionPerformed() method is called. The programmer provides the code in this method to perform whatever is desired when the button is pressed. In this case our event handling code popped up a JOptionPane message box.

We see two ways to write the code for a component event in this chapter. One way is to implement the ActionListener interface and then include the actionPerformed() method. Another approach is to write an anonymous inner class. The anonymous inner class is written in the addActionListener( ) method call. The main features of these two programmatic techniques are illustrated here:

```
//Partial code listing from Program 7-4

//We use the "implements ActionListener in the class definition
//line. This requires us to write the actionPerformed() method
//in this class.

public class BangPopApp extends JFrame implements ActionListener
{

        //Here is a JButton.
        JButton bangButton = new JButton("Bang");

        public BangPopApp()
        {
                //The getContentPane() returns the JFrame's container.
                //We are getting this frames's container.
                Container canvas = getContentPane();
```

```
            //Now add the button to the canvas.
            canvas.add(bangButton);

        //We use "this" in the method call and Java knows
        //that THIS class contains the actionPerformed() method.

            bangButton.addActionListener(this);
        }

        public void actionPerformed(ActionEvent event)
        {
            if(event.getSource() == bangButton)
            {
                JOptionPane.showMessageDialog(this,"Bang!");
            }
        }
}
```

Here is a portion of the BangPopApp2 program, which is functionally identical to the previously stated code, except that we instantiate and write an anonymous inner class that performs the event handling activity:

```
//A portion of the BangPopApp2 Program
//Use anonymous inner class to perform event handling.

//We do not need to write "implements ActionListener" because we
//write a complete class in the bangButton.addActionListener( ); line.

public class BangPopApp2 extends JFrame
{
        JButton bangButton = new JButton("Bang");
        public BangPopApp2()
        {
            Container canvas = getContentPane();

            canvas.add(bangButton);

        //Use an anonymous class and write the ActionListener.
            bangButton.addActionListener(  new ActionListener()
            {
                public void actionPerformed(ActionEvent event)
                {
                    JOptionPane.showMessageDialog(null,"Bang!");
                }
            } );
        }
}
```

7.6
Practice!

Our three practice programs present more views of static methods and variables, and code using graphic user interface components and listeners. The first example is a partial program that illustrates static class members. This program shows how static members are handy tools for a Java programmer by writing the code both with and without static members. The second example is another silly applet with JButtons and images. Here, we use Swing's JLabel to show an image in a window. The third program has both static members and GUI components. This program shows a situation where static members can be helpful, and a second version shows how static members cannot be extended for multiple cases. Study the classes carefully, and have fun while you're at it!

Senators, the Senate, and Static Members

Recall that static class variables represent class-wide information, not object-wide data, meaning that when we declare a static variable in a class, there is only one variable—no matter how many objects we have created. In the first version of this program we see Senator and Senate classes. In the United States Senate, there are 100 Senators, two from each state in the nation. There must be a quorum (majority) of senators present on the Senate floor in order for the Senate to conduct business. Refer to www.senate.gov, the official web site of the United States Senate, for a complete guide to the Senate.

In our Senator class, we have a static floorCount variable that is incremented when the senator object "signs in," that is, is present on the floor and is available for Senate business. This floorCount variable is decremented when the senator leaves the chambers and is not available. We also keep track of party affiliations with the use of static counters for Republicans, Democrats, and Independents. Program 7-10 is a partial program and does not run. Examine the two classes and note how clean and easy the Senate class's method calls are, which access the Senator static members. In order to visualize how Java stores the static and non-static data, refer to Figure 7-15, which shows how the senator objects and data are stored on the stack and heap.

```
1   //Program 7-10
2   //File Senator.java
3
4   //This version contains static class members.
5
6   public class Senator
7   {
8       private String name, state, party;
9       private boolean bOnTheFloor;
```

```
10
11          //Have a static floorCount to keep track of total number of
12          //Senators on the Senate floor at a given time.
13          public static int floorCount;
14
15          //Static variables keep track of the number of Senators in
16          //each party. (Eagles are for independents.)
17          public static int donkeyCount, elephantCount, eagleCount;
18
19
20          public Senator()
21          {
22                  name = state = party = "";
23                  bOnTheFloor = false;
24          }
25          public void setSenator(String name, String state, String party)
26          {
27                  this.name = name;
28                  this.state = state;
29                  this.party = party;
30
31                  if(party.equals("Republican"))
32                          ++elephantCount;
33                  else if( party.equals("Democrat"))
34                          ++donkeyCount;
35                  else if( party.equals("Independent"))
36                          ++eagleCount;
37          }
38
39          public void signIn()
40          {
41                  //The senator is now on the floor.
42                  bOnTheFloor = true;
43
44                  //Increment the floor count.
45                  ++floorCount;
46          }
47
48          public void signOut()
49          {
50                  //The senator has now left the senate chambers.
51                  bOnTheFloor = false;
52
53                  //Decrement the floor count.
54                  --floorCount;
55          }
56  }
```

```
1    //Program 7-10
2    //File Senate.java
3
4    //Accesses the static members of the Senate class to determine
5    //if we have a quorum and the party affiliations.
6
7    public class Senate
8    {
9        private Senator senators[] = new Senator[100];
10
11       public Senate()
12       {
13            //Don't forget to allocate objects for each senator.
14            for(int i = 0; i < 100 ; ++i)
15                    senator[i] = new Senator();
16
17           //Open and read a file with the 100 senators.
18           //This is not implemented.
19
20           //We could also take a roll call to determine
21           //who is in attendance on the floor.
22       }
23       public boolean doWeHaveAQuorom()
24       {
25       //Here is where we obtain the floor count.
26           if(Senator.floorCount >= 51)
27                   return true;
28           else
29                   return false;
30       }
31
32       public void senateStats()
33       {
34
35           //Gather the statistics on the three parties.
36
37           int totalRep = Senator.donkeyCount;
38           int totalDems = Senator.elephantCount;
39           int totalIndep = Senator.eagleCount;
40
41           //Other code.
42       }
43   }
```

Each Senator object has a name, state, and party.
There is one floorCount, and three party count variables
   for all the Senators we create.

Class Senator
{
    private String name, state, party;
    private boolean bOnTheFloor;
    public static int floorCount;
    public static int donkeyCount, elephantCount, eagleCount;
    private Senator senators [ ] = new Senators [100];

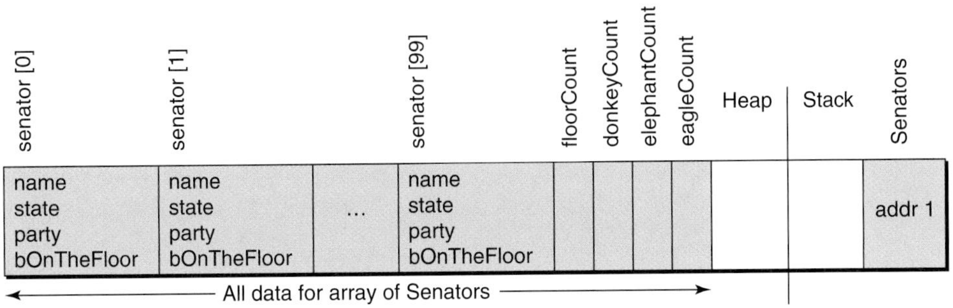

Figure 7-15
The array of Senators have four public static class members, which each object updates directly in the setSenator() and signIn() and signOut() methods. The Senate class can obtain the static floorCount using Senator.floorCount. Static members are useful for class-wide information.

In the second version of the Senators and Senate program, the Senator class does not contain any static variables. Now it is up to the Senate class to query each of the Senators if it wants to know if there is a quorum of Senators or wants to know party statistics. The *SenatorNoStatic.java* and *SenateNoStatic.java* files contain these rewritten classes. The code is shown in Program 7-11. Study these two classes and compare them to the previous versions. Which set of classes would you rather use?

```
1    //Program 7-11
2    //File SenatorNoStatic.java
3
4    //This class contains no static class members.
5
6    public class SenatorNoStatic
7    {
8        private String name, state, party;
9        private boolean bOnTheFloor;
```

```
10
11        public SenatorNoStatic()
12        {
13                name = state = party = "";
14                bOnTheFloor = false;
15        }
16        public void setSenator(String name, String state, String party)
17        {
18                this.name = name;
19                this.state = state;
20                this.party = party;
21
22        }
23
24        public void signIn()
25        {
26                //The senator is now on the floor.
27                bOnTheFloor = true;
28        }
29
30        public void signOut()
31        {
32                //The senator has now left the senate chambers.
33                bOnTheFloor = false;
34        }
35
36        public String getParty(){return party; }
37
38        public boolean amIOnTheFloor(){return bOnTheFloor; }
39 }
```

```
1    //Program 7-11
2    //File SenateNoStatic.java
3
4    //This class must query the Senators and keep its own count
5    //for quorum and party affiliations.
6
7    public class SenateNoStatic
8    {
9        private SenatorNoStatic senators[] = new SenatorNoStatic[100];
10
11       //Have a floorCount to keep track of total number of
12       //senators on the Senate floor at a given time.
13       public int floorCount;
```

```
14
15          //Count variables keep track of the number in
16          //each party. (Eagles are for independents.)
17          public int donkeyCount, elephantCount, eagleCount;
18
19          public SenateNoStatic()
20          {
21                  //Don't forget to allocate objects for each senator.
22                  for(int i = 0; i < 100 ; ++i)
23                          senators[i] = new SenatorNoStatic();
24
25                  //Open and read a file with the 100 senators.
26                  //This is not implemented.
27
28                  //We could also take a roll call to determine
29                  //who is in attendance on the floor.
30          }
31          public boolean doWeHaveAQuorom()
32          {
33                  //We need 51 senators on the floor to have a quorom.
34                  floorCount = 0;
35
36                  //Ask each senator if he/she is on the floor.
37                  for(int i = 0; i < 100; ++i)
38                  {
39                          if(senators[i].amIOnTheFloor() )
40                                  ++floorCount;
41                  }
42                  if(floorCount >= 51)
43                          return true;
44                  else
45                          return false;
46          }
47
48          public void senateStats()
49          {
50                  String p;
51
52                  //Ask each Senator for his/her party affiliation.
53                  for(int i = 0; i < 100; ++i)
54                  {
55                          p = senators[i].getParty();
56                          if(p.equals("Republican"))
57                                  ++elephantCount;
58                          else if( p.equals("Democrat"))
```

```
59                          ++donkeyCount;
60                 else if( p.equals("Independent"))
61                          ++eagleCount;
62            }
63      }
64  }
```

ShowADog Applet

In this short program, we use the Swing package's JLabel component to show an image in an applet window. Using a FlowLayout manager, we place two buttons and two labels that have images associated with them. An ImageIcon object can be passed to a JLabel constructor. Notice how we have added ActionListeners to the JButtons and handle the button events in the actionPerformed() method. Figure 7-16 shows the Applet Viewer window.

```
1   //Program 7-12
2   //File:  ShowADogApplet.java
3
4   //A silly applet that introduces you to two dogs.
5   //We use JButtons and JLabels.
6
7   //import swing for JApplet, JLabel, JButton,ImageIcon,message boxes
8   import javax.swing.*;
9   import java.awt.*;                //for FlowLayout
10  import java.awt.event.*;          //for ActionListener
11
12  public class ShowADogApplet extends JApplet implements ActionListener
13  {
14    //use a label for the Image Icons
15    JLabel dog1PicLabel = new JLabel(new ImageIcon("Shadow.jpg"));
16    JLabel dog2PicLabel = new JLabel(new ImageIcon("Molly.jpg"));
17
18    JButton dog1Button = new JButton( "Who is the first dog?");
19    JButton dog2Button = new JButton("Who is the second dog?");
20
21    public void init()
22    {
23          Container canvas = getContentPane();
24          canvas.setLayout(new FlowLayout());
25
26          dog1Button.addActionListener(this);
27          dog2Button.addActionListener(this);
```

```
28
29          canvas.add(dog1PicLabel);
30          canvas.add(dog1Button);
31          canvas.add(dog2PicLabel);
32          canvas.add(dog2Button);
33     }
34
35     public void actionPerformed (ActionEvent ae)
36     {
37          if(ae.getSource() == dog1Button)
38          {
39               JOptionPane.showMessageDialog(null,
40               "Meet Shadow!",      "Dog Pictures ",
41               JOptionPane.INFORMATION_MESSAGE);
42          }
43          else if(ae.getSource() == dog2Button)
44          {
45               JOptionPane.showMessageDialog(null,
46               "Meet Molly!",       "Dog Pictures ",
47               JOptionPane.INFORMATION_MESSAGE);
48          }
49     }
50 }
```

Figure 7-16
The applet class contains two JLabel objects and two JButton objects. ActionListeners
have been added to both buttons and the button events are handled in the actionPer-
formed() method. We use the implements ActionListener format instead of anonymous
classes. These dogs are owned by Donna Finley, used with permission.

The Softball Program

Have you ever played on a slow pitch, summer softball team? Softball is like baseball only the ball is bigger, and each team may have nine or ten players on the field at a time. The tenth player is usually a fourth outfielder. Many cities around the country offer different levels of league play, ranging from beginner to very serious. There are men's teams, women's teams, and co-ed teams.

In this last program of Chapter 7, we have a SoftballPlayer class that includes the player's name, position (infielder or outfielder), jersey number, and a variable indicating whether or not the player is available to play. Players may not be able to play in a scheduled game due to injuries, travel, or schedule conflicts. The SoftballPlayer class has a boolean variable, bCanPlay, that represents his or her game status. There is a static availablePlayers variable that is incremented based on the player's availability status. The code for this class is shown below in Program 7-13.

```
1    //Program 7-13
2    //File SoftballPlayer.java
3
4    public class SoftballPlayer
5    {
6        private String name, position;
7        private int jerseyNumber;
8        private boolean bCanPlay;   //is available for the game
9
10       //Have a static availablePlayers to keep track of total number of
11       //players available for the game.
12       private static int availablePlayers;
13
14       public SoftballPlayer()
15       {
16           name = position = "";
17           bCanPlay = false;
18       }
19       public void setPlayer(String name, String position, int num, boolean bPlay)
20       {
21           this.name = name;
22           this.position = position;
23           jerseyNumber = num;
24           bCanPlay = bPlay;
25           if(bCanPlay) ++ availablePlayers;
26       }
27
```

```
28        //We use a static method to return the availablePlayers total.
29        public static int getAvailablePlayers()
30        {
31                return availablePlayers;
32        }
33   }
```

The SoftballTeam class has an array of SoftballPlayer objects. Many leagues limit the size of the team to fifteen or eighteen players. We will limit our team to fifteen players. The team constructor asks the user to enter the name of a data file that contains the team name and roster. The constructor reads the file and fills the team name and players array. The SoftballTeam has a doWeHaveEnoughPlayers() method, which queries the SoftballPlayer class. If the team does not have at least nine players that can play, the team must forfeit the scheduled game. The code for the SoftballTeam class is shown below. If you have not yet read Chapter 10, Exception Handling, and Chapter 11, Java I/O, then now is a good time to do so and use this example as another reference for these topics.

```
1    //Program 7-13
2    //File: SoftballTeam.java
3
4    //These import statements are needed for reading the file.
5    import java.io.FileReader;
6    import java.io.BufferedReader;
7    import java.io.IOException;
8    import java.io.FileNotFoundException;
9    import java.util.StringTokenizer;
10
11   import javax.swing.JOptionPane;
12
13   public class SoftballTeam
14   {
15     private SoftballPlayer players[] = new SoftballPlayer[15];
16     private String teamName;
17
18     private int totalPlayers;
19
20     public SoftballTeam(String boxTitle)
21     {
22             //Don't forget to allocate objects for each player.
23             for(int i = 0; i < players.length ; ++i)
24                     players[i] = new SoftballPlayer();
```

```
25
26          String filename = JOptionPane.showInputDialog(null,
27          "Enter the filename for the softball team.", boxTitle ,
28          JOptionPane.QUESTION_MESSAGE);
29
30
31          //Open and read a file with up to 15 players.
32          String name, position, avail;
33          int number, i = 0;
34          try
35          {
36                  //FileNotFoundException thrown if we can't find the file.
37                  BufferedReader bufReader =
38                  new BufferedReader( new FileReader( filename) );
39
40                  //The line holds the line read by BufferedReader
41                  String line;
42
43                  //The string tokenizer helps us separate the data items.
44                  StringTokenizer sepToken;
45
46                  //Both ready() and read() might throw IOException.
47                  if(bufReader.ready())
48                  {
49                          //First we read the teamName.
50                          teamName = bufReader.readLine();
51
52                          //Now we loop while there are still players to read.
53                          while( bufReader.ready() )
54                          {
55                              ++totalPlayers;
56
57                              //Each line is a player, such as:
58                              //Susan,infielder,9,canPlay
59                              line =  bufReader.readLine();
60
61      //Each line is constructed with "," as the element delimiter
62                              sepToken = new StringTokenizer( line, ",");
63
64                              //The first Token is the name.
65                              name = sepToken.nextToken();
66
67                              //Now the position, pull off the space after the ,.
68                              position = sepToken.nextToken();
69
```

```
70                          //Now we get the number
71                          number = Integer.parseInt ( sepToken.nextToken() );
72
73                          //Last, can he/she play in the next game?
74                          avail = sepToken.nextToken();
75
76                          if(avail.equals("canPlay"))
77                          players[i].setPlayer(name,position,number,true);
78                          else
79                          players[i].setPlayer(name,position, number,false);
80
81                          ++i;
82                      }
83                      // close the Buffered Reader
84                      bufReader.close();
85              }
86          }
87          catch(FileNotFoundException fnfe)
88          {
89              JOptionPane.showMessageDialog(null,
90                  "Can't find the file!", filename, 2);
91          }
92          catch(IOException ioe)
93          {
94              JOptionPane.showMessageDialog(null, "Trouble!", filename, 2);
95          }
96
97      }
98
99      public boolean doWeHaveEnoughPlayers()
100     {
101         if(SoftballPlayer.getAvailablePlayers() >= 9)
102             return true;
103         else
104             return false;
105     }
106
107     public String getTeamName(){ return teamName; }
108
109     public int getTotalPlayers(){ return totalPlayers; }
110
111     public int getAvailablePlayers()
112     {
113         return SoftballPlayer.getAvailablePlayers();
114     }
115 }
```

7

In the first version of this program, we build a SoftballTeamFrame that has one SoftballTeam object. The frame instantiates the team object, which then asks the user for a softball team data file. The file is read one line at a time, and the player data is set in the SoftballPlayer objects. The frame has JLabels which show the team name and total players. A JButton can be pressed to report whether or not the team is able to play its game.

We have included two different women's softball team files for this program, *SwitchHitters.txt* (for the Switch Hitters team) and *JavaJays.txt* (for the Java Jays team). The *SwitchHitters.txt* file is shown here. Note that there are twelve players on the roster, and all but one are available for the next game.

Switch Hitters
Brenda,outfielder,34,canPlay
Elizabeth,infielder,28,canPlay
Earnestine,infielder,39,canPlay
Barbara,outfielder,33,canPlay
Cheryl,outfielder,35,canPlay
Cristina,infielder,22,canPlay
Mary Jane,infielder,94,canPlay
Jeanette,outfielder,44,canPlay
Chris,outfielder,52,canPlay
Agnes,outfielder,24,canPlay
Gina,infielder,58,cannotPlay
Mia,infielder,39,canPlay

The source code for the frame class is shown in Program 7-13. Figure 7-17a shows the input message box where the user enters the team file. The program output for the Switch Hitters team is shown in Figure 7-17b.

```
1    //Program 7-13
2    //File: SoftballTeamFrame.java
3
4    import java.awt.Graphics;
5    import javax.swing.*; //for JFrame, JLabel, JButton
6    import java.awt.*;    //for Container, GridLayout
7    import java.awt.event.*;  //for listeners
8
9    public class SoftballTeamFrame extends JFrame
10   {
11
12       SoftballTeam girlsTeam = new SoftballTeam("Women's Softball Team");
13
14       //Make JLabels to show the team name. Just have a reference here.
15       //We set the text when we allocate the JLabels in the constructor.
16       JLabel teamNameLabel;
```

```
17
18      JLabel nameLabel = new JLabel( "TEAM NAME");
19      JLabel totalPlayersLabel, howManyCanPlayLabel;
20      JLabel playLabel = new JLabel();
21
22      JButton playButton = new JButton("Enough For a Game?");
23
24      public static void main( String[] args )
25      {
26            SoftballTeamFrame playBall = new SoftballTeamFrame();
27            playBall.setDefaultCloseOperation( EXIT_ON_CLOSE );
28      }
29
30   public SoftballTeamFrame()
31   {
32
33        //Set the label text by getting the team name from the
34        //SoftballTeam object.
35        teamNameLabel = new JLabel( girlsTeam.getTeamName() );
36
37        int p = girlsTeam.getTotalPlayers();
38        totalPlayersLabel = new JLabel( "Total on Roster: "
39              + Integer.toString(p)  );
40
41        Container canvas = getContentPane();
42        canvas.setLayout( new GridLayout(4,1) );
43
44        //Add labels and button to the frame.
45        canvas.add(nameLabel);
46        canvas.add(teamNameLabel);
47        canvas.add(totalPlayersLabel);
48        canvas.add(playButton);
49
50        playButton.addActionListener( new ActionListener ()
51        {
52              public void actionPerformed( ActionEvent ae)
53              {
54                        int c = girlsTeam.getAvailablePlayers();
55                        String output = "Available: " + Integer.toString(c);
56
57                        if(girlsTeam.doWeHaveEnoughPlayers() )
58                              JOptionPane.showMessageDialog(null,
59                                    "YES! Play Ball!",output,
60                                    JOptionPane.INFORMATION_MESSAGE);
```

```
61                         else
62                              JOptionPane.showMessageDialog(null,
63                                  "No. Have to Forfeit.",   output,
64                                  JOptionPane.ERROR_MESSAGE);
65              }
66        } );
67
68        this.setSize( 200, 200 );  //set the window size
69        this.setTitle("Softball Team!");
70
71         this.show();
72    }
73 }
```

(a)   (b)

Figure 7-17
a) The file containing the team name and roster of players is entered by the user.
The SoftballPlayer class contains a static availablePlayers variable. The
SoftballTeam has an array of players. b) The SoftballTeamFrame shows the results
for the Switch Hitters. The SoftballTeam asks the SoftballPlayer class for the number
of available players when the button is pressed.

You may be thinking that we can use the SoftballPlayer and SoftballTeam
classes to build a SoftballGameFrame. In this new frame class, you can have two
SoftballTeam objects. Each has its own count of available players, and the game
frame could report whether or not we have a game by checking each team's
doWeHaveEnoughPlayers() method. What a wonderful idea! The only problem is
that if we use the static availablePlayers variable in the SoftballPlayer class, then it
is the only variable for all of the players. It does not discern between one array of
players or many arrays of players.

To illustrate this feature of static variables, let's write a SoftballGameFrame and
use the SoftballPlayer and SoftballTeam classes from Program 7-13. We instantiate

the home and visiting team objects. We'll have the Switch Hitters as the home team and Java Jays as the visitors. Our game frame will report only the available players for each team. Here is the *JavaJays.txt* file, showing that only eight players are available for the game.

Java Jays
Susan,infielder,9,canPlay
Martha,infielder,13,cannotPlay
Melissa,outfielder,3,canPlay
Janis,outfielder,24,canPlay
Elizabeth,infielder,18,cannotPlay
Halley,infielder,29,canPlay
Ricki,outfielder,63,cannotPlay
Bonnie,outfielder,36,cannotPlay
Jane,infielder,27,cannotPlay
Liz,infielder,78,cannotPlay
Juanita,outfielder,44,canPlay
Beth,infielder,14,canPlay
Holly,infielder,64,canPlay
Becky,outfielder,2,canPlay

The Switch Hitters have eleven available players and the Java Jays have eight. We expect to see 11 and 8 on the game frame. Examine the code in Program 7-14 and results in Figure 7-18. We see that both teams have 19 players. This program error is due to the fact that the static availablePlayers variable spans both arrays of SoftballPlayer objects.

The use of static class members for the softball game does work. How will we have to change the SoftballPlayer, SoftballTeam, and SoftballGameFrame class so that we can query the teams for an accurate count of available players? That is left as an exercise for you. (See end of chapter problems.)

7

```
1   //Program 7-14
2   //File: SoftballGameFrame.java
3
4   import java.awt.Graphics;
5   import javax.swing.*; //for JFrame, JLabel, JButton
6   import java.awt.*;    //for Container, GridLayout
7   import java.awt.event.*;  //for listeners
8
9   public class SoftballGameFrame extends JFrame
10  {
11
12      SoftballTeam homeTeam = new SoftballTeam("Home Team");
13      SoftballTeam visitors = new SoftballTeam("Visiting Team");
```

```
14
15      JLabel homeTeamLabel, visitorTeamLabel;
16
17      JLabel homeLabel = new JLabel( "Home Team");
18      JLabel visitorLabel = new JLabel( "Visitors");
19      JLabel homePlayers, visitorPlayers;
20      JLabel playLabel = new JLabel();
21
22
23      public static void main( String[] args )
24      {
25              SoftballGameFrame playBall = new SoftballGameFrame();
26              playBall.setDefaultCloseOperation( EXIT_ON_CLOSE );
27      }
28
29      public SoftballGameFrame()
30      {
31
32              homeTeamLabel = new JLabel( homeTeam.getTeamName() );
33              visitorTeamLabel = new JLabel(visitors.getTeamName() );
34
35              int homeAvail = homeTeam.getAvailablePlayers();
36              homePlayers = new JLabel( "Available Players: " +
37                                  Integer.toString(homeAvail)  );
38
39              int visAvail = visitors.getAvailablePlayers();
40              visitorPlayers = new JLabel( "Available Players: " +
41                                  Integer.toString(visAvail)  );
42
43              Container canvas = getContentPane();
44              canvas.setLayout( new GridLayout(3,2) );
45
46              canvas.add(homeLabel);
47              canvas.add(visitorLabel);
48              canvas.add(homeTeamLabel);
49              canvas.add(visitorTeamLabel);
50              canvas.add(homePlayers);
51              canvas.add(visitorPlayers);
52
53              this.setSize( 300, 150 );  //set the window size
54              this.setTitle("Softball Game!");
```

```
55
56            this.show();
57        }
58    }
```

Figure 7-18
The SoftballGameFrame has two SoftballTeam objects. We attempt to see the number of available players for our two teams, but the SoftballPlayer static available-Players variable spans both team arrays, and we see the total number of available players for both teams. The static variable is a class-wide variable spanning all of the objects, whether they are each declared separately or grouped into arrays.

REVIEW QUESTIONS AND PROBLEMS

Short Answer

1. If there are two objects of the same class in a Java program, how are the two objects stored on the stack and the heap?

2. Every time an object is created, what is placed in the object's *this* reference?

3. How does the *this* reference help clarify Java source code for someone who is reading the code?

4. If the Java programmer wants to name the input variables in the method definition line the same names as the associated class variables, how can the *this* reference aid in this programming style?

5. What is meant by the phrase, "if you use new, you get this?"

6. How many types of static items are there in Java? Name them.

7. What do we mean when we say a static class variable is a class-wide variable, not an object-wide variable?

8. Assume you have a class named *XYZ* that contains a private integer named *x* and two private static integers named *y* and *z*. Your program instantiates ten

7

different *XYZ* objects. How many *x* variables do you have? How many *y* and *z* variables? Explain your answer.

9. Static methods can only access static data. What are the data access rules for non-static methods?

10. When a Java programmer uses the static keyword for a variable, is it possible to set that variable to be private too? Explain.

11. Is it possible to declare a static variable inside a class method? Explain your answer.

12. Explain how the finalize() method can be used by a programmer when he or she is working with static variables.

13. Does Java's garbage collector call the finalize() method? If so, when is it called? If not, who calls finalize()?

14. What is the main difference between Java classes and Java interfaces?

15. If we implement an ActionListener interface in a class, what method must be included in the class? What is that method's main job?

16. Why should Java programmers use Swing components in their program interfaces instead of AWT components?

17. Why is it important to register your event with your program? How is the registration process performed?

18. Refer to Java's Swing package documentation and list eight different Swing user interface components.

19. List the steps required for including a JComboBox in your frame window. Remember to include the steps so that the combo box in the window reacts to the user selecting a new item.

20. What is the purpose for using a layout manager in a Java program?

21. If the programmer did not wish to use a layout manager, what would the programmer have to do instead?

22. When should a Java program consider using a Vector object instead of using a fixed array?

23. What is meant by the term *nested class?*

24. Why is an anonymous inner class anonymous? Why is an anonymous inner class an inner class?

25. The Java compiler writes class files that include *$* in the name. What compile situation causes the compiler to write these types of files?

26. There are two approaches for writing event handling code in Java programs. For a button, we must call the addActionListener() method and there must be

7

the method actionPerformed(). Describe the two different approaches for incorporating the actionPerformed() method in a class.

27. If you have a button, and you call its setBackground() method, what are you attempting to do?

28. How does a FlowLayout manager differ from a GridLayout manager?

29. Is it possible to have something other than textual data in a JLabel? If so, explain your answer.

30. Why does a static count for the Senators present on the floor of the Senate work well, yet a static available players count for a softball player class not work for a softball game class? (See the first and third practice programs of this chapter.)

Programming Problems

31–40: Write complete Java programs. If you have studied, Chapter 12, JAR Files, bundle your program into a JAR file.

31. Rewrite the softball team program in the Practice section of this chapter so that the SoftballGameFrame shows both team names, the number of players on the roster, and the number of players available for the game. Incorporate a JButton that reports whether the two teams will play ball or not. Feel free to make up your own team data files. Hint: static variables may not work for this program.

32. Locate four of your favorite JPG images and size them each to 100 × 100 pixels. Set up a FlowLayout manager. Set up a JLabel array to be used with the four images. Using a for loop, place the images into a 450 × 450 pixel box, creating a tiled effect in the window.

33. Create a JFrame class that contains two JButtons. When each button is pressed, generate a random number between 1 and 10, and use the JButton's setText() method to display the number as the button's label. The program should keep track of the two button values. When the values are the same, set that value in the title of the JFrame window. The title should include the number of times that the buttons have had the same value at the same time. Note, the user does not have to press the buttons in any sort of order. One button can be pressed once, and the second button can be pressed ten times.

34. Create a JFrame class that contains a JComboBox and a JTextField. Fill the combo box with the names of five colors. When the user selects a color, change the field background to that color and write the name of the color in the field. Be sure the frame's initial color in the combo box is shown in the field.

35. Create a JFrame class than contains a JComboBox and JLabel. Fill the combo box with five animals, such as cat, dog, turtle, etc. Your program should have a

Vector object that contains the list of animals. When the user selects an animal, the label shows that animal. The last option in the combo box list should be "add new animal." When this last item is selected, a JOptionPane input box is presented, and the user may enter a new animal. This animal should become one of the listed animals in the combo box, next to the last item (before "add new animal").

36. a. Create a JFrame class that contains a JComboBox and JLabel. The combo box should list the names of six images, such as "New Mexico Sky" or "Ocean Scene." When the user selects an image, the image is displayed in the label object. Use a String array for the image filenames.

b. If you have studied Chapter 11, Java I/O, create a data file that lists the image title and filename on each line of the file, separated by a comma, such as:

New Mexico Sky, NMSky.jpg
Ocean Scene, ocean.jpg

37. a. Create a CalculatorFrame that uses a 4 × 2 grid layout manager and performs simple arithmetic tasks. The first row should be two text fields where the user may enter numbers. The next two rows should be JButtons for addition, subtraction, multiplication, and division. The last row should be two JLabels, one showing an equal size and the other label prints results of the operation. (If you are using double, format your output to three decimal places.) The title of the frame should contain the equation, such as 4 + 2 = 6. Initialize your two operands to the number one.

b. If you have studied the Chapter 10, Exception Handling, trap for invalid numeric input and zero division.

38. Create a Picnic class that contains String variables describing at least six picnic food items such as watermelon, potato chips, chicken, or bread. (You make up your own picnic list.) The Picnic class includes a constructor that sets the food items. You must also set associated weight for each food item in ounces. For example, you may have one watermelon weighing ten pounds (160 ounces) and a seven-ounce bag of potato chips. Create a JavaAnts class that represents a colony of our little six-legged noninvited picnic guests. These JavaAnts are of the super-enhanced variety, and each ant object can carry one ounce. The JavaAnts class contains variables for totalJavaAnts that exist and totalAtPicnic. Other variables may be required in the JavaAnts class. You will need to decide what methods are required for the Picnic and JavaAnts classes.

Create a JFrame that contains a JComboBox that shows the food items. There is a JLabel that shows the number of ants currently at your picnic. This label (and ant count) should initially be zero. There is a JButton that, when pressed, creates twenty-five JavaAnt objects. Assume these twenty-five ants are now at your picnic, wishing to carry off your food items. There is a JButton that, when pressed, reports whether there are enough ants to carry

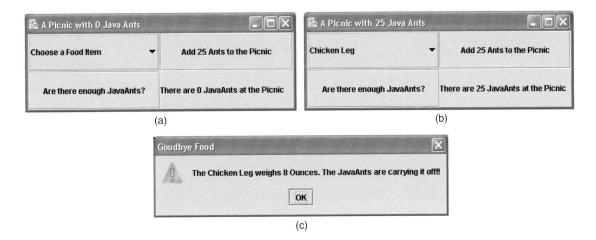

Figure 7-19
a) An initial Picnic frame. b) The frame after adding 25 JavaAnts and selecting a chicken leg. c) What happens when the "enough" button is pressed.

off and eat the selected food item. This report may be in a JLabel or JOption-Pane message box. If there are enough ants to carry off the item, allow them to do so. When a group of ants carry off a food item, they are no longer at your picnic (update the number of ants at your picnic) and the item should be removed from the list in the combo box. The JavaAnts are very efficient and only use the exact number of ants to carry off any item. For example, if the chicken leg weighed three ounces, then only three ants would carry it away. If the selected food item is heavier than the current ants at your picnic, the ants cannot carry the item away. Figure 7-19a shows an example of a Picnic frame. After adding 25 JavaAnts, selecting a chicken leg (Figure 7-19b), and pressing the "enough" button, the Goodbye Food message is displayed. The frame is then updated so that the chicken leg is gone, as well as eight of the ants.

Hint: you will need to build a Vector to contain your food items. You must use the JavaAnts variables to help determine your program's actions. DO NOT keep separate ant counters in your frame.

39. Have you ever played the Rock, Paper, Scissors game? Two (or more) people make a fist, and on the count of three, you make either scissors (two fingers out in a "V"), a rock (closed fist), or paper (open palm down). The rules are that scissors cut paper, paper covers rocks, and rocks break scissors. If two players played a round of the game, and one made scissors and the other made a rock, the rock would win that round.

In this program you are to build a RPS class that generates a Rock, Paper, or Scissors randomly. This class has a play() method that generates a String containing the words Rock, Paper, or Scissors. Use Math's random number generator to randomly determine the result (it'll be Rock, Paper, or Scissors). The play() method returns the result as a String, not an integer! The class should also have an integer for totalPlays. Every time the play() method is called, it is incremented. There is a getTotalPlays() method that returns this value.

Build a Person class. A Person has a name, and a Person has the ability to play the RPS game. That is, a Person class has (contains) an RPS object. The Person also keeps track of how many games he or she has won and lost. The Person class should have setName(), getName(), setWinner(), setLoser(), getWins(), getLosses(), and getTheRPSPlay() methods.

Build an applet that models this game. The applet should require the user to enter the names of two players, and then incorporate a "Play Button." When the user presses the Play button, each Person calls his or her RPS play() method that generates scissors, paper, or rock. The applet shows each person's name, reports what each person did (Rock, Paper, or Scissors), reports who won the round, presents a current tally of wins, ties, and total rounds played.

> **Note:** The logic for who won the game is in the applet class. The applet has the two persons who play the game, and the "winner" logic is in the applet. The applet sets the win/loss information into the two people objects, then asks each person for the stats when it reports the winner and the statistics for the game.

You should use JLabels and JButtons in your applet. You may use the show-Status() applet method to help you report information. You should have a button that, when pressed, displays the rules of the game in a message box. You may use a GridLayout. Your window should be sized to a reasonable dimension. For an extra challenge, use images of Rocks, Paper, or Scissors to show the results of the play. That is, show an image of what each person did and then report who won. Hint: use JLabels and ImageIcons.

Figure 7-20 shows two different applet windows of the Rock, Paper, Scissors program written by TVI Java programming students, Edna Cardenas and Tim Wright. Edna's window, shown in Figure 7-20a, uses the showStatus() method to report her Game Results. The images in her applet were drawn by Blue Soroos and are used here with their permission. Tim's window, seen in Figure 7-20b, uses smiley face images to report the winner and loser, as well as images of Rock, Paper, and Scissors. Tim produced these images and we use them here with his permission.

40. Sally sells seashells in a seaside shack. Create a program that will help her track her sales. You will need to create a Seashell class with type and cost variables along with static variables to keep track of the total number of seashells available to sell, the total value of the current inventory, and total sales for the day. The

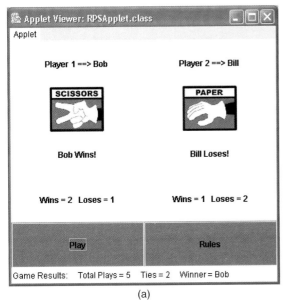

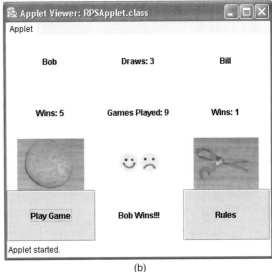

(a)   (b)

Figure 7-20
Two different applet interfaces produced by TVI programming students Edna
Cardenas (a) and Tim Wright (b). Used by permission.

main program will use an array of seashells. Have at least five different types of
shells in your inventory array. Each seashell in the array should be a different
kind of shell, such as clam, mussel, conch, or oyster (search on the web to find
other types of shells). Once the one clam shell (or other variety) has been pur-
chased, a "sold out" message should be displayed if the buyer tries to purchase
another one. Buyers should be able to pick the type of shell they want from a
menu of your design. Figure 7-21 shows one example of a user interface.

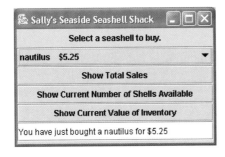

Figure 7-21
A possible design for Sally's shell inventory program.

8

Java Graphical User Interface Construction

CHAPTER OBJECTIVES

Introduce the fundamental steps for constructing a graphical user interface (GUI) for a Java program.

Describe the relationship between the Java Container, Components, Events, and Listeners.

Demonstrate various layout managers and how they control where the components are placed.

Show how Java components require different listener interfaces.

Illustrate many commonly used components.

Present the concept that JPanels should be used to group components and then place JPanel objects into the frame.

Introduce Java's Thread class.

Show how Thread objects are used with GUI components.

Have a drink or prime the pump?

Two Java programmers found themselves on a deserted farm where an old well pump was located in a wooden box. The programmers had just enough water with them for a few more days. The well pump was still operational and directions on the side of the box indicated that if the pump were primed with water, it would be operational and would provide the programmers with all the water they needed for months. The programmers had a dilemma on their hands—to drink their remaining water or risk losing it in their attempt to prime an old, yet reliable well pump.

At this point in our Java life it is now time to study **Graphical User Interface (GUI)** construction. The GUI is the program's front end, which typically consists of buttons, menus, sliders, toolbars, and other controls that react to events such as mouse clicks or key presses. The material we need to cover in this chapter presents a dilemma similar to the one confronting our two programmer friends. Do we spend our time studying a few user interface components in depth, quenching our thirst for complete knowledge for a few components, or do we spend our time understanding construction steps in general and then use any component that Java provides us? We choose the latter approach. Keep in mind that we are priming the pump. Principles we discuss in detail are applicable to many other components. Let's get started!

8.1
Event Handling Overview

The **procedural programs** of the past were constructed so that the program execution flowed from a starting point to an end point. The program events occurred in a sequential, step-by-step manner. For example, a typical procedural program began execution by opening and reading a data file. Routines would be called to sort, manipulate, and process the data. Program results were then reported in some manner such as displaying results, writing summary reports, or writing new data files.

A Java program that presents a GUI is an **asynchronous program**, meaning that events occur in the program at unpredictable times. This program is referred to as an **event-driven program** because the program waits for input from the user

GUI
the program's front end, which includes buttons, menus, sliders, toolbars, etc. It reacts to events such as mouse clicks or key presses

procedural program
program constructed so that execution flows from a start point to an end point.

asynchronous program
an event-driven program where events such as button clicks or mouse movement occur at unpredictable times

event-driven program
waits for input from the user before performing a task

before performing a task. For example, if the program presents two buttons to the user, the designer of the program does not know which (if either) button will be pressed by the user. If the user presses a button, a message is sent from the operating system to the program and it performs a task.

Event-driven programming is now the standard program interface for window-based operating systems. The **event model** is the name we use for the program framework that takes the user's interaction with the GUI control, such as a mouse click, and calls the code to process it. The event model is the design for hooking your code to asynchronous events. Object-oriented languages such as Java fit well with windowing systems and lend themselves to event-driven programming techniques.

The Big GUI Picture

Swing GUI components

"lightweight" components written and implemented so that they have all the "know-how" to perform a job

Java's Swing library provides many GUI components, as well as the supporting software for the basic functionality of the components. Recall from our discussion in Chapters 3 and 7 that the javax.swing package contains the **Swing GUI components**. Swing components are referred to as "lightweight" components. They are written and implemented completely so that each one knows how to draw itself and comes with all the "know-how" to perform its job. Swing controls do not rely on the target platform's peer components.

In general, Java separates the Swing components and the code you want to run when an event happens. Each Swing component can report all the events that might happen to it, and the programmer must decide if he or she is interested in a particular event. For example, a JButton can report two different mouse events: 1) if the mouse passes over it, or 2) if a mouse click occurs on it. If the programmer wants to know that a particular event occurs (such as a mouse click or a button press), he or she must register that event with the program. The way we register our interest in events is to add a Listener to our control object with an addSomeKindOfListener() method. (The name "addSomeKindOfListener()" is a catch-all term used by the author, not a real Java method! We could use addActionListener() or addMouseListener() with our JButton.) The SomeKindOfListener represents a Java interface that we implement. For example, in Chapter 7 we saw that JButtons needed an addActionListener() method to react to being pressed with the mouse. When an event of interest occurs, such as a mouse click on the button, the interface method is called. We write our event handling code inside the method. Recall that in Chapter 7's JButton program examples, we implemented the ActionListener interface and placed our code for our button in the actionPerformed() method. We also wrote ActionListener anonymous classes that contained the actionPerformed() method.

Do not expect that you will fully grasp the "ins and outs" of GUI controls from just reading the previous paragraph. If you have worked through Chapter 7 programs, you should be getting the hang of GUIs. We examine more GUI controls and examples in this chapter—the material and concepts will become clearer as you work through the programs!

To get started, let's go through a more detailed list of programming steps to follow whether you are creating a single text field with a label and a button

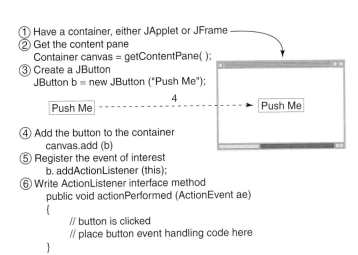

Event : Mouse click on a button

1. Have a container, either JApplet or JFrame
2. Get the content pane
   Container canvas = getContentPane( );
3. Create a JButton
   JButton b = new JButton ("Push Me");

Push Me ----------- 4 ----------→ Push Me

4. Add the button to the container
   canvas.add (b)
5. Register the event of interest
   b. addActionListener (this);
6. Write ActionListener interface method
   public void actionPerformed (ActionEvent ae)
   {
        // button is clicked
        // place button event handling code here
   }

Figure 8-1
The basic steps for setting up a Swing control object and implementing the event handling code.

or a complicated, multicontrol program interface. Figure 8-1 illustrates these steps.

Step 1: You must have a window of some sort for your program. This may be either a JApplet that uses the web browser's window or a JFrame.

Step 2: You must have a Java Container object that will hold your GUI components. The container is what you see on the screen. As it turns out, the Java Container comes to us when we extend JApplet or JFrame. We can also import and extend other types of containers, such as JPanel and JDialog.

Step 3: Create your GUI component objects by instantiating the objects with the new operator. Do not forget to import the appropriate class. A few GUI controls include JButton, JTextField, JLabel, JCheckBox, and JScrollPane.

Note: We will allow Java to assist us in arranging our GUI components by incorporating a layout manager for our container. Layout managers are easy to use because they determine the positions in the container for our controls. Three popular layout managers include FlowLayout, GridLayout, and BorderLayout. If we choose not to use a layout manager then we must specify the exact locations for each of our items.

Step 4: The GUI components are added to the container's content pane, which is a special type of container. The way your controls look on the screen depends on the type of layout manager and the order in which you add your components to the container.

Step 5: Once we have our controls in place in the container, we must register the events by adding listeners to the controls. By calling the object's addSomeKindOfListener() method, we register that event for that control.

Step 6: We must implement the associated Listener interface method (or methods) that will perform tasks when the event of interest occurs. That is, these listener methods handle the control's event. Each of the controls generates a specific type of event. For example, a JButton requires the ActionListener interface for a button click, whereas JCheckBox requires ItemListener.

User Interface Actions and Listener Interfaces

user interface actions
various activities that a user can perform to interact with a program, such as pushing a button or typing textual input

Many of us have spent years working on computers with window-based operating systems. We know how to use the mouse and we understand the purposes for buttons, sliders, radio buttons, and scrollbars. That's good. We now examine the various **user interface actions** and see the corresponding events and Java interfaces with which we will be working. Examine Table 8-1 and scan through the list of actions and events. You do not need to memorize this material. Just realize that Java has separated the various actions taken by the user into different events that are handled by different interfaces.

▌**TABLE 8-1**
User interface actions and corresponding events/interfaces.

User interface action	Corresponding event and interface
Control selections such as a button or menu press	Generates an ActionEvent implemented by the ActionListener interface
Mouse click or release	Generates a MouseEvent implemented by the MouseListener interface
Mouse dragging and moving	Generates a MouseEvent implemented by a MouseMotionListener
Mouse wheel	Mouse wheel event implemented by MouseWheelListener
Key press or key release	Generates a KeyEvent implemented by the KeyListener
Text input	Generates a TextEvent when a new line is entered, and is implemented by TextListener
Selecting an item from a list, check box, combo box, etc.	Generates an ItemEvent implemented by the ItemListener
Scroll bar slider	When the slider is moved, it generates an AdjustmentEvent implemented by AdjustmentListener
Slider thumb move	Generates a ChangeEvent implemented by a ChangeListener
Keyboard focus change caused by tabbing between control	Generates a FocusEvent implemented by FocusListener
Resize, hide, or move a component	Generates a ComponentEvent implemented by ComponentListener
Add a component to, or remove it from, a container	Generates a ContainerEvent implemented by ContainerListener

8

Now let's examine what methods the Listener interfaces provide us. The Listener interfaces and their method signatures are shown in Table 8-2.

TABLE 8-2
A partial listing of Awt and Swing Listener interfaces and their associated methods.

Listener interface	Interface methods
ActionListener[a]	actionPerformed(ActionEvent)
AdjustmentListener[a]	adjustmentValueChanged(AdjustmentEvent)
ComponentListener[a] ComponentAdapter[a]	componentHidden(ComponentEvent) componentShown(ComponentEvent) componentMoved(ComponentEvent) componentResized(ComponentEvent)
ContainerListener[a] ContainerAdapter[a]	componentAdded(ContainerEvent) componentRemoved(ContainerEvent)
FocusListener[a] FocusAdapter[a]	focusGained(FocusEvent) focusLost(FocusEvent)
ItemListener[a]	itemStateChanged(ItemEvent)
KeyListener[a] KeyAdapter[a]	keyPressed(KeyEvent) keyReleased(KeyEvent) keyTyped(KeyEvent)
MouseListener[a] MouseAdapter[a]	mouseClicked(MouseEvent) mouseEntered(MouseEvent) mouseExited(MouseEvent) mousePressed(MouseEvent) mouseReleased(MouseEvent)
MouseMotionListener[a] MouseMotionAdapter[a]	mouseDragged(MouseEvent) mouseMoved(MouseEvent)
WindowListener[a] WindowAdapter[a]	windowOpened(WindowEvent) windowClosing(WindowEvent) windowActivated(WindowEvent) windowDeactivated(WindowEvent) windowIconified(WindowEvent) windowDeiconified(WindowEvent)
ChangeListener[s]	stateChanged(ChangeEvent)
PopupMenuListener[s]	PopupMenuCanceled(PopupMenuEvent e) PopupMenuWill BecomeInvisible(PopupMenuEvent e) PopupMenuBecomeVisible(PopupMenuEvent e)

Note: (a) are found in java.awt.events; (s) are found in javax.swing.events. Refer to these two packages for a complete listing.

an interface for
processing mouse
events that provides us
with five different
mouse handling
methods

> **Note:**   Adapter classes are covered later in this chapter. Some of these methods do not make sense now, but a few of them are obvious. For example, the **MouseListener** provides us five different mouse handling methods, including mouseEntered() and mouseExited(). Each of the methods shown in the table shows the type of Event object that is passed to it. When the Java programmer wishes to use a certain type of listener with his or her control object, he or she registers it with an addSomeKindOfListener() call such as addActionListener() or add KeyListener(). At the time the user performs the action, Java passes a specific event object to the interface method.

Listener Adapters

Recall our discussion of Java interfaces in Chapter 7. We found that when we implement ActionListener, we have to include the actionPerformed() method in our class. Whenever a Java programmer implements any interface, such as KeyListener or MouseListener, all of the interface methods must be defined. This means that if you write a class that implements MouseListener, all five mouse methods must be defined in the class. (Review the AnimalBehaviors interface example in Chapter 7 if you need a refresher on this topic.) If the programmer wishes to use only one of the methods in the interface, Java provides **Listener Adapter classes**. Listener Adapter classes provide default empty methods so that all we need to do is write the method we are interested in using. Several of our examples make use of Listener Adapters because they are handy classes to have when working with GUI controls. We will see these examples soon.

**Listener Adapter
classes**

provide default empty
methods and all we
need to do is write the
interface method we
are interested in using

▌8.2
An Introduction to Swing Components

In this section, we present many of the Java Swing components in short, complete application programs that use JFrame. We also show a variety of supporting methods for the components, such as changing colors, selecting fonts, and adding different types of listeners. Some of the examples are written using the "implements SomeKind-OfListener" format, while others use anonymous classes. Review the comparison examples in Chapter 7 if you need a refresher on these two coding techniques.

control

general programming
term for GUI items

widget

an XWindows term for
a GUI control

component

a Java specific term for
a GUI control item

We should clarify some terminology at this point. We see the terms *control*, *component*, and *widget* when we work with GUI gadgets. The term **control** refers to the group of items that are considered GUI items that a user can press, scroll, select, type into, and draw on. The XWindows environment in the Unix world calls a control a **widget**. Controls and widgets are not specific to Java, but belong to the windowing world in general. However, the term **component** is a Java specific term. In Java's Swing package, all of the controls inherit the methods and data fields of JComponent.

The JComponent class is the superclass for most controls that can appear on the screen. Our on-screen GUI controls need to have the following, general information:

- size (minimum, maximum, and preferred)
- tooltip (pop-up help that is displayed when you "rest" the mouse on the control)
- display features (line thicknesses, colors, and fonts)
- some controls have support for icons
- some controls have support for left-, center-, and right-aligned contents
- support for internationalization and accessibility
- appropriate appearance and behavior
- supporting methods

Tables 8-3, 8-4, and 8-5 present the basic Swing components including controls, displays, and containers. The reader is encouraged to examine the Java documentation for each component. Do not forget to look at the variety of constructor formats and "methods inherited from" section in the Java API documentation. The majority of listeners are inherited by the components. For example, the JButton inherits addActionListener() from the Abstract Button, addPropertyChangeListener() the JComponent, and addContainerListener() from JContainer. We present

TABLE 8-3
Basic Swing controls.

Control types	Swing components
Buttons	JButton
	JCheckBox
	JRadioButton
Combo box	JComboBox
List	JList
Menus	JMenu
	JMenuBar
	JMenuItem
Slider	JSlider
Toolbar	JToolbar
Text fields	JTextField
	JPasswordField
	JTextArea
	JFormattedTextField

TABLE 8-4
Basic Swing displays.

Uneditable	Swing components
Label	JLabel
Tooltip	JToolTip
Progress bar	JProgressBar
Editable	
Table	JTable
Text	JTextPane
	JTextArea
	JEditorPane
Tree	JTree
Color chooser	JColorChooser
File chooser	JFileChooser
Value chooser	JSpinner

8

TABLE 8-5
Swing containers.

Container types	Swing components
Frame	JFrame
Applet	JApplet
Dialog	JDialog
	JOptionPane
Panel	JPanel
Panes	JLayeredPane
	JRootPane
Internal Frame	JInternalFrame

several, but not all of the components in this chapter. The Sun Microsystems web site contains an on-line tutorial for Swing and can be found at http://java.sun.com/docs/books/tutorial/uiswing/index.html

JButton, JLabel, JTooltip

JLabel

a one-line string and image, which cannot have multiple lines of text

JButton

a push-button

JTooltip

presents a string of textual information that is seen when the user rests the mouse on the control

The **JLabel** is the simplest of the Java JComponents, consisting of a one-line string and image. It is not possible to have multiple lines of text in one label. The label contents can be left-, center-, or right-aligned. JLabels are used to help the user work with other controls by providing a place for the programmer to add a description or instructions. JLabel also provides an easy way to get a picture on the screen.

The **JButton** is a push-button and the Java programmer must supply the code for the program to perform when the button is pressed. The **JTooltip** presents a string of textual information that is seen when the user rests the mouse on the control. The tooltip is intended to be a hint or further explanation for the user. Tooltips are easy to use and do not require any event handling, so use them whenever possible.

In Program 8-1 we set up two JLabels and one JButton, all equipped with JTooltips. One JLabel has an image associated with it and the other does not. We have changed the fonts for the button and the text-only label. Notice how we set the foreground and background colors for the various objects with a set() method. Figure 8-2 shows the resultant window and one tooltip.

```
1   //Program 8-1
2   //File: JButtonJLabelFrame.java
3
4   import javax.swing.JFrame;
5   import java.awt.Color;
```

```
6    import java.awt.Font;
7    import java.awt.Container;
8    import java.awt.FlowLayout;
9    import java.awt.event.ActionListener;
10   import java.awt.event.ActionEvent;
11   import javax.swing.JButton;
12   import javax.swing.JLabel;
13   import javax.swing.JOptionPane;
14   import javax.swing.ImageIcon;
15
16   public class JButtonJLabelFrame extends JFrame implements ActionListener
17   {
18      JButton b1 = new JButton("Click Me!");
19      ImageIcon icon = new ImageIcon("rocks.jpg");
20      JLabel rockLabel = new JLabel("See the rocks?", icon, JLabel.LEFT);
21      JLabel textLabel = new JLabel("Ohhhh, a pretty label.");
22
23      public JButtonJLabelFrame()
24      {
25           //set the title and size of the window
26           setTitle("JButtonJLabelFrame Program");
27           setSize(600,150);
28
29           //get the Frame's container and set the background
30           Container canvas = getContentPane();
31           canvas.setBackground(Color.white);
32
33           //change the button's colors and fonts
34           b1.setBackground(Color.cyan);
35           b1.setForeground(Color.white);
36           b1.setFont( new Font("Ariel",Font.BOLD, 22) );
37
38           //add the tooltips
39           b1.setToolTipText("Click the button, see what happens!");
40           rockLabel.setToolTipText("This is a label with an icon.");
41           textLabel.setToolTipText("This is a label in Times Roman font.");
42
43           //set the font for the pretty label
44           textLabel.setFont( new Font("TimesRoman",Font.ITALIC, 26) );
45           textLabel.setForeground(Color.magenta);
46
47           //set a flow layout
48           canvas.setLayout( new FlowLayout() );
49
```

8

```
50          //add the controls to the window
51          canvas.add(b1);
52          canvas.add(rockLabel);
53          canvas.add(textLabel);
54
55          //we want to handle the button click
56          b1.addActionListener(this);
57
58          show();
59      }
60
61   public void actionPerformed(ActionEvent e)
62   {
63          JOptionPane.showMessageDialog(this,"Thank you!");
64   }
65   public static void main(String args[] )
66   {
67          JButtonJLabelFrame theApp = new JButtonJLabelFrame();
68          theApp.setDefaultCloseOperation(JFrame.EXIT_ON_CLOSE);
69   }
70 }
```

Figure 8-2
The JButton and JLabels are
drawn in the window using a
FlowLayout manager. The tooltip
for the button is also shown. We
changed the colors and set the
fonts.

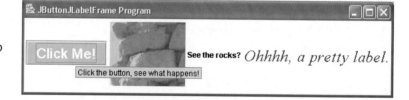

JRadioButton, ButtonGroup, and JCheckBox

JRadioButton

a single button that is
intended to be toggled
on or off (selected or
deselected)

Groups of radio buttons and sets of check boxes are standard fare in windows-based programs. Java has **JRadioButton** and **ButtonGroup** classes that work together to make a group of buttons. Using the **JCheckBox** class creates the check box object. In Program 8-2 we query the user for the sort of ice cream cone and toppings he or she prefers. Because we can have only one type of cone, a group of radio buttons presents the cone selections. Just like car radio controls allow only one selected station at a time, software radio buttons follow suit and should be used when there can only be one selected item. Check boxes allow for multiple selections of items. In our program, we use check boxes to allow the user to pick one or several of the toppings for the ice cream cone.

The program code shows that we instantiate three radio button objects, three check box objects, one button group, and four label objects. Using a grid layout, we add the objects to the container. Grid layouts fill the rows first, so we must alternate the addition of the check boxes and buttons. The radio buttons are added to the button group object, so that the buttons work together as a group. If we did not use a button group, each button would react individually. We also use the setSelected(true) method to set the first item in the button group and set the dessert-Label to Waffle Cone so the program starts up, showing a selected button and item. We want our program to react whenever we select a topping or a cone type, so we add ItemListeners to all the buttons and check boxes. Inside the itemState-Changed() method we ask each object if it is selected and change the dessertLabel text. Notice that we use getText() for each object's textual label. Figure 8-3 shows one user's favorite type of ice cream cone.

button group
if you create a set of buttons and add them to the same button group object, then turning one of those buttons on turns off all other buttons in the group

JCheckBox
a control that allows the user to check an item on or off

```java
1   //Program 8-2     Ice Cream Cone Selections
2   //File: JRadioButtonJCkBox.java
3
4   import javax.swing.*;       //for JFrame, JCheckBox, JLabel, JRadioButton
5   import java.awt.Color;
6   import java.awt.Font;
7   import java.awt.Container;
8   import java.awt.GridLayout;
9   import java.awt.event.ItemListener;
10  import java.awt.event.ItemEvent;
11
12
13  public class JRadioButtonJCkBox extends JFrame implements ItemListener
14  {
15     JCheckBox cbox1 = new JCheckBox("Choc Syrup");
16     JCheckBox cbox2 = new JCheckBox("Nuts");
17     JCheckBox cbox3 = new JCheckBox("Whipped Cream");
18
19     JLabel toppingsLabel = new JLabel("Select the toppings for your ice cream.");
20     JLabel coneLabel = new JLabel("What type of cone?");
21     JLabel dessertLabel = new JLabel("Waffle Cone");
22     JLabel finalChoices = new JLabel("You have selected:   ", JLabel.RIGHT);
23
24     JRadioButton rb1 = new JRadioButton("Waffle Cone");
25     JRadioButton rb2 = new JRadioButton("Sugar Cone");
26     JRadioButton rb3 = new JRadioButton("Cookie Cone");
```

```
27
28      ButtonGroup group = new ButtonGroup();
29
30      public JRadioButtonJCkBox()
31      {
32              //set the title and size of the window
33              setTitle("Radio Buttons and Check Boxes Program");
34              setSize(600,150);
35
36              //get the Frame's container and set the background
37              Container canvas = getContentPane();
38
39              //add the radio buttons into the group
40              group.add(rb1);
41              group.add(rb2);
42              group.add(rb3);
43
44              //set the fonts for the labels
45              toppingsLabel.setFont( new Font("TimesRoman",Font.ITALIC, 16) );
46              coneLabel.setFont( new Font("TimesRoman",Font.ITALIC, 16) );
47
48              //set a grid layout with 5 rows and 2 cols
49              canvas.setLayout( new GridLayout(5,2) ) ;
50
51              //add the controls to the window
52              canvas.add(toppingsLabel);
53              canvas.add(coneLabel);
54              canvas.add(cbox1);
55              canvas.add(rb1);
56              canvas.add(cbox2);
57              canvas.add(rb2);
58              canvas.add(cbox3);
59              canvas.add(rb3);
60              canvas.add(finalChoices);
61              canvas.add(dessertLabel);
62
63              //Select the first radio button so one of the buttons is
64              //pressed when the program begins.
65              rb1.setSelected(true);
66
```

```
67            //add item listener for the check boxes and radio buttons
68            cbox1.addItemListener(this);
69            cbox2.addItemListener(this);
70            cbox3.addItemListener(this);
71            rb1.addItemListener(this);
72            rb2.addItemListener(this);
73            rb3.addItemListener(this);
74            show();
75        }
76
77    public void itemStateChanged(ItemEvent ie)
78        {
79            String output   = "";
80            if(rb1.isSelected() ) output += rb1.getText();
81            if(rb2.isSelected() ) output += rb2.getText();
82            if(rb3.isSelected() ) output += rb3.getText();
83
84            if(cbox1.isSelected()) output += " + " + cbox1.getText();
85            if(cbox2.isSelected()) output += " + " + cbox2.getText();
86            if(cbox3.isSelected()) output += " + " + cbox3.getText();
87
88            dessertLabel.setText(output);
89        }
90    public static void main(String args[] )
91        {
92            JRadioButtonJCkBox theApp = new JRadioButtonJCkBox();
93            theApp.setDefaultCloseOperation(JFrame.EXIT_ON_CLOSE);
94        }
95    }
```

8

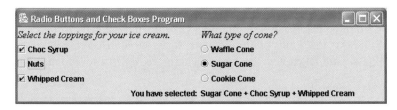

Figure 8-3
The JRadioButtons are grouped together using a ButtonGroup object. The labels,
check boxes, and radio buttons are organized using a grid layout. The bottom right label
has been right justified via the JLabel.RIGHT flag passed into the JLabel constructor.

JComboBox and JList

The combo box and list box each provide the user with the ability to select an item from a list. Java's combo box allows only one item to be selected from the list; whereas Java's list objects can be designed for single or multiple selection. The combo box and list box controls are created using **JComboBox** and **JList**, respectively.

The combo box is a space saving GUI control, showing one item in the list. When the user clicks on the combo box, a drop down list showing all of the items is presented. Java's JComboBox does not allow the user to type in his or her own selection as the Windows combo box does, but Java's list can be expanded via an addItem() method.

The list box differs from the combo box in appearance and functionality. (See Figure 8-4 on page 455.) The list occupies a fixed number of lines on the screen. If the programmer would like to have a scroll bar beside the list, he or she must use a JScrollPane to provide the scrolling capability. We do this in this example. It is possible to have a JList object allow the user to select a single item in the list by using the setSelectionMode() method. There are three possible modes:

ListSelectionModel.SINGLE_SELECTION allows only one item to be selected at a time

ListSelectionModel.SINGLE_INTERVAL_SELECTION allows one contiguous group to be selected

MULTIPLE_INTERVAL_SELECTION allows contiguous or miscellaneous items to be selected.

The user must use the Shift key and/or Control key in conjunction with the mouse clicks for multiple selections. The multiple selection can be obtained by using the getSelectedValue() method that returns an array of Objects.

In Program 8-3 we create a JComboBox and fill it by using a Vector object. We create two JList objects, each filled with an array of Strings. The petList is a single selection list, and the carList is a multiple selection list. We add the appropriate listeners for each and update a label with the current selected item or items.

We also see our first Listener Adapter class. We wish to listen for the window being closed. The **WindowListener** has six methods (review Table 8-2). We only need the windowClosing() method. Therefore, we write an anonymous class using a **WindowAdapter** class and write our own code for the windowClosing() method. Figure 8-4 shows the results of our program. Study the source code and see how the listener classes are set up with the various addSomeKindOfListener() methods.

JComboBox

a component that has a button or editable field and a drop-down list. The user can select an item from the drop-down list

JList

a component that allows the user to select one or more objects from a list

WindowListener

a Java interface used to listen for windowing activities such as opening, closing, and iconification

WindowAdapter

Java Adapter classes allow us to write individual listener methods instead of all methods described in the listener

```
1    //Program 8-3  JComboBox and JList
2    //File:  JComboBoxJList.java
3
4    import java.util.Vector;
5    import java.awt.Container;
6    import java.awt.GridLayout;
```

```
7    import java.awt.event.*; // for WindowEvent, ItemEvent, ActionEvent;
8    import java.awt.event.WindowAdapter;
9    import javax.swing.*;  //for JFrame, JComboBox, JList, JLabel
10   import javax.swing.event.*;
11
12   public class JComboBoxJList extends JFrame
13   {
14     //Create a Vector object, which is a dynamic array that hold objects.
15     private static Vector stateList = new Vector();
16     private JComboBox statesCombo;
17     private String petTypes[] = { "dog", "cat", "bird", "fish", "horse",
18                              "skunk", "pig", "turtle", "donkey" };
19     private String carTypes[] = { "van", "truck", "SUV", "wagon", "sedan",
20                              "sportscar", "limo" };
21     private JList petList, carList;
22
23     private JLabel petLabel = new JLabel("Select a pet");
24     private JLabel stateLabel = new JLabel("Select a state");
25     private JLabel carLabel = new JLabel("Select several vehicles");
26
27     private JLabel whichState = new JLabel("New Mexico");
28     private JLabel whichPet= new JLabel("No Pet Picked" );
29     private JLabel whichCars = new JLabel("No Cars Picked" );
30
31     public JComboBoxJList()
32     {
33           this.setTitle( "JComboBox and JList");
34           this.setSize( 450,300);
35
36           //The pet list is a single selection list.
37           petList = new JList(petTypes);
38           petList.setSelectionMode(ListSelectionModel.SINGLE_SELECTION);
39
40           //The car list is a multiple selection list.
41           carList = new JList(carTypes);
42           carList.setSelectionMode(ListSelectionModel.MULTIPLE_INTERVAL_SELECTION);
43
44           //Fill the vector and make the combo box.
45           fillVector();
46           statesCombo = new JComboBox( stateList);
47
48           Container canvas = getContentPane();
49           canvas.add(stateLabel);
50           canvas.add( petLabel);
51           canvas.add(carLabel);
52
53           canvas.add(statesCombo);
54
```

```
55          //use a JScrollPane to give us a scroll bar for the lists
56          canvas.add( new JScrollPane(petList) );
57          canvas.add( new JScrollPane(carList) );
58
59          canvas.add(whichState);
60          canvas.add(whichPet);
61          canvas.add(whichCars);
62
63          canvas.setLayout(new GridLayout(3,3) );
64
65          //Update the whichPet label when the petList is changed.
66          petList.addListSelectionListener( new ListSelectionListener()
67          {
68                  public void valueChanged( ListSelectionEvent lse)
69                  {
70                          int c = petList.getSelectedIndex();
71                          whichPet.setText( "one " + petTypes[c] );
72                  }
73          } );
74
75          //Update the whichCars label when the cartList is changed.
76          //The list returns all selected items into an Object array.
77          //We then use the toString() method to get the item's text description.
78          carList.addListSelectionListener( new ListSelectionListener()
79          {
80                  public void valueChanged( ListSelectionEvent lse)
81                  {
82                          String carChoices = "";
83                          Object [] items = carList.getSelectedValues();
84                          for(int i=0; i < items.length; ++i)
85                          {
86                                  carChoices += items[i].toString();
87                                  if(i != items.length-1)
88                                          carChoices += ", ";
89                          }
90                          whichCars.setText(carChoices);
91                  }
92          } );
93
94          //ItemListener is used for the JComboBox.
95          //Update the whichState label when the combobox is changed.
96          //The getItemAt returns an Object. We use toString() for the text.
97          statesCombo.addItemListener( new ItemListener()
98          {
99                  public void itemStateChanged( ItemEvent ie)
100                 {
101                         int c = statesCombo.getSelectedIndex();
102                         Object state = statesCombo.getItemAt(c);
103                         whichState.setText(state.toString() );
```

```
104                }
105            } );
106
107        this.show();
108    }
109
110    private void fillVector()
111    {
112            stateList.add("New Mexico");
113            stateList.add("Hawaii");
114            stateList.add("Ohio");
115            stateList.add("Maine");
116            stateList.add("Texas");
117    }
118
119    public static void main( String[] args)
120    {
121            JComboBoxJList app = new JComboBoxJList();
122
123    //Add a window listener that listens for the closing the window.
124            app.addWindowListener( new WindowAdapter()
125            {
126                public void windowClosing( WindowEvent e)
127                {
128                        System.exit( 0);
129                }
130            });
131    }
132 }
```

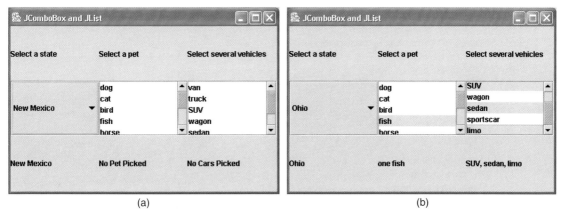

(a)   (b)

Figure 8-4
The combo box and two list boxes are seen in this program output. a) The initial window. As the items are selected, the labels are updated, as seen in b. b) ListSelectionListener and ItemListener are needed for the JList and JComboBox, respectively.

JSlider

JSlider

lets the user select a
value by sliding a
"thumb" within a
bounded interval

A slider enables a user to select an integer value within a set range of integer values. Java's **JSlider** component can be customized by the programmer to include the starting and ending values, major and minor tick marks, and labels for the ticks. The JSlider object is also controllable via the arrow keys on the keyboard. Sliders may be placed in a horizontal position where the left end represents the lower value of the range and the right end represents the higher value. A vertical slider has the low value at the bottom and the high value at the top. The tab that is grabbed and moved with the mouse is referred to as the thumb. The slider's getValue() method returns the value of the thumb's position within the range of values.

Program 8-4 demonstrates how we can place a horizontal and vertical slider in a frame's container as shown in Figure 8-5 on page 458. The horizontal slider format is the JSlider default. We must specifically set the vertical property if desired. We use major and minor ticks for the horizontal slider, and only major ticks for the vertical slider. We did not use a layout manager and therefore had to size and place each component in the window. This activity makes a Java programmer appreciate layout managers or development environments that allow the programmer to design an interface via a control palette.

```
1    //Program 8-4
2    //File: SliderDemo.java
3
4    //Demonstrate a JSlider and how components must be placed
5    //if the LayoutManager is null (i.e., not used).
6
7    import javax.swing.*;
8    import java.awt.*;
9    import javax.swing.event.*;    //needed for changeListener
10
11   public class SliderDemo extends JFrame
12   {
13     String vTxt="", hTxt="";
14     JSlider hSlider, vSlider;
15     JLabel hLabel = new JLabel(hTxt);
16     JLabel vLabel = new JLabel(vTxt);
17     int hValue, vValue;
18
19     public SliderDemo()
20     {
21          Container canvas = getContentPane();
22
23          // Make sure default layout manager is turned off.
24          canvas.setLayout( null);
25          canvas.setBackground(Color.yellow);
26
```

```
27              //Instantiate horizontal slider (it is the default).
28              //Inputs are (low range, high range, start value)
29              hSlider = new JSlider(0, 50, 25);
30              hSlider.setMajorTickSpacing(5);
31              hSlider.setMinorTickSpacing(1);
32              hSlider.setPaintTicks(true);
33              hSlider.setPaintLabels(true);
34
35              //Show the initial slider values in a text string:
36              hValue = hSlider.getValue();
37              hTxt= "The Horizontal Value is " + hValue;
38              hLabel.setText(hTxt);
39
40              //We must use a ChangeListener for a slider.
41              hSlider.addChangeListener( new ChangeListener()
42              {
43                      public void stateChanged( ChangeEvent e)
44                      {
45                              hValue = hSlider.getValue();
46                              hTxt= "The Horizontal Value is " + hValue;
47                              hLabel.setText(hTxt);
48                      }
49              });
50
51              //We must specify if the slider is to be vertical.
52              vSlider = new JSlider(JSlider.VERTICAL, 10, 25, 10);
53              vSlider.setMajorTickSpacing(5);
54              vSlider.setPaintTicks(true);
55              vSlider.setPaintLabels(true);
56
57
58              //Show the initial slider in the window.
59              vValue = vSlider.getValue();
60              vTxt= "The Vertical Value is " + vValue;
61              vLabel.setText(vTxt);
62
63              vSlider.addChangeListener( new ChangeListener()
64              {
65                      public void stateChanged( ChangeEvent e)
66                      {
67                              vValue = vSlider.getValue();
68                              vTxt= "The Vertical Value is " + vValue;
69                              vLabel.setText(vTxt);
70                      }
71              });
72
73              //Set the size and position of components.
74              //Inputs are(x pos, y pos, width, height);
```

8

```
75          hSlider.setBounds(70, 10, 200, 50);
76          vSlider.setBounds(10, 30, 50, 200);
77          hLabel.setBounds(80, 70, 200, 20);
78          vLabel.setBounds(80, 85, 200, 20);
79
80          //Color the components to see the placement.
81          vSlider.setBackground(Color.magenta);
82          hSlider.setBackground(Color.cyan);
83
84          //Add components to canvas.
85          canvas.add(hSlider);
86          canvas.add(vSlider);
87          canvas.add(hLabel);
88          canvas.add(vLabel);
89
90          this.setSize(300,275);
91          this.setTitle("Slider Demonstration Program");
92          this.show();
93      }
94
95   public static void main( String args[] )
96      {
97          SliderDemo app = new SliderDemo();
98          app.setDefaultCloseOperation(JFrame.EXIT_ON_CLOSE);
99      }
100  }
```

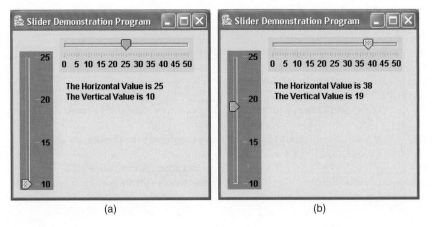

(a)   (b)

Figure 8-5
The two sliders update the text information in the window when the user adjusts the
thumb value with the mouse or via the left/right/up/down arrow keys. Hitting the tab
key alternates the window focus between slider controls.

Layout Managers

As we have seen in the previous program, it can be tedious to place the Java GUI controls "by hand" in a window. It takes time to make the window look professional, and we never know if what looks good on our Microsoft Windows-based machine will look good on a Mac or Sun workstation. Java provides **layout managers**— classes that specify how the components are placed in a container. Every container has a default layout manager. For example, JApplet and JFrame's content pane has a BorderLayout manager, whereas a JPanel has a FlowLayout manager. Some layout managers adjust the size of their components to fit in the container while other managers simply place them without changing their sizes. (We'll soon see an example of this.)

layout managers
classes specify how components are placed in a container

We saw the GridLayout and FlowLayout managers in action in Chapter 7, so we will spend minimal time on them in this chapter. We will also present examples using the BorderLayout, CardLayout, and BoxLayout managers. We forgo both GridBagLayout and SpringLayout. The GridBagLayout is more complicated than what we need right now. SpringLayout is not a practical layout manager to code by hand. SpringLayout is found in Java development environments that generate source code automatically. See Sun Microsystem's website tutorial if you wish to investigate these two layout managers.

Layout managers are beneficial to programmers because the managers provide an automatic resize feature when the container/window is resized. Most Java programmers will not find one layout manager that does everything he or she needs, so we learn to separate our user interfaces into panels with an appropriate layout manager for each panel. Let's work two simple, straightforward examples with GridLayout and BorderLayout managers and then explore the other managers once we have been introduced to panels.

GridLayout Manager

The **GridLayout manager** is a simple manager based on a row-by-column format. The grid layout divides the container equally for each grid element and changes the component size to fit that region. One side effect of grid layout is that it can be annoying to have a gigantic label in one grid element and a squished combo box in another. The grid layout is a good manager for a series of radio buttons or check boxes.

GridLayout manager
places components in a row-by-column format. Components are resized to fit within the grid

8

As with all layout managers, you call the setLayout() method of the container (or panel) and pass in a layout manager object. It is possible to perform this task like this:

```
//Just use new in the method call because we don't need a
//reference to the layout manager.
Container canvas = getContentPane();

canvas.setLayout( new GridLayout(4,2) );
```

or you may create an object and pass the object to setLayout() method.

```
//Create a layout manager object and pass it
//to the setLayout() method.
Container canvas = getContentPane();

GridLayout gridman = new GridLayout(4,2);

canvas.setLayout( gridman );
```

Program 8-5 illustrates how you can change the layout dimensions if necessary and repaint the window. This is accomplished by calling the JFrame's validate() method to layout current components and repaint() calls paint().We fill the frame's container with nine buttons, and eight of the button labels are the name of cities. Only one button is active. When the "Show California Cities" button is pressed, the layout then shows the buttons with California cities. It also has one active button, "Show All Cities." This button toggles back to the three by three view of all the city buttons. Figure 8-6 shows the two windows produced by this program. Notice how the buttons resize equally to fit the width and height of the window.

```
1   //Program 8-5
2   //File:  GridDemo.java
3
4   //This program sets a 3x3 grid layout and then changes it
5   //to a 2x2 layout.
6
7   import javax.swing.*;
8   import java.awt.*;
9   import java.awt.event.*;
10
11  public class GridDemo extends JFrame
12  {
13    //Set up an array of 10 buttons.
14    JButton buttonArray [] = new JButton [10];
15
16    //Set up a String array for the button labels.
17    String buttonText[] =  { "San Diego", "New York","Los Angeles",
18         "San Francisco", "Santa Fe", "Baltimore", "Chicago", "Sarasota",
19    "Show California Cities", "Show All Cities" };
20
21    Container canvas = getContentPane();
22
23    public GridDemo()
24    {
```

```java
25            //Here's where we make our buttons and set their text.
26            for(int i = 0; i<buttonArray.length; ++i)
27                    buttonArray[i] = new JButton( buttonText[i] );
28
29            addAllTheCities();
30            buttonArray[8].setBackground(Color.CYAN);
31            buttonArray[9].setBackground(Color.MAGENTA);
32
33            //Just going to show the California cities.
34            buttonArray[8].addActionListener( new ActionListener()
35            {
36                    public void actionPerformed( ActionEvent ae)
37                    {
38                            addCaliforniaCities();
39
40                            //validate() causes a container to lay out its components
41                            //again after the components it contains have been
42                            //added to or modified.
43                            canvas.validate();
44
45    //repaint() forces a call to paint() so that the window is repainted.
46                            canvas.repaint();
47                    }
48            } );
49
50            //Now show all the cities.
51            buttonArray[9].addActionListener( new ActionListener()
52            {
53                    public void actionPerformed( ActionEvent ae)
54                    {
55                            addAllTheCities();
56                            canvas.validate();
57                            canvas.repaint();
58                    }
59            } );
60
61            this.setSize(500,150);
62            this.setTitle("Grid Layout Demonstration Program ");
63            this.show();
64    }
65
66    //Sets the container's canvas to 3x3 and adds all cities.
67    public void addAllTheCities()
68    {
69            canvas.removeAll();
70            canvas.setLayout(new GridLayout(3, 3));
```

```
71          for(int i = 0; i < 9; ++i)
72          {
73                 canvas.add(buttonArray[i]);
74          }
75    }
76
77    //Sets the container's canvas to 3x2 and adds CA cities.
78    public void addCaliforniaCities()
79    {
80          canvas.removeAll();
81          canvas.setLayout(new GridLayout(2, 2));
82          canvas.add(buttonArray[0]);
83          canvas.add(buttonArray[2]);
84          canvas.add(buttonArray[3]);
85          canvas.add(buttonArray[9]);
86    }
87
88    public static void main( String args[] )
89    {
90          GridDemo app = new GridDemo();
91          app.setDefaultCloseOperation(JFrame.EXIT_ON_CLOSE);
92    }
93 }
```

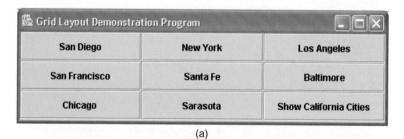

(a)

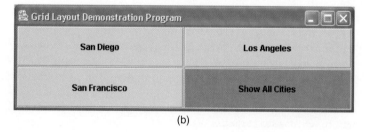

(b)

Figure 8-6

The grid layout can be modified and the window redrawn. The components are sized equally in a grid layout.

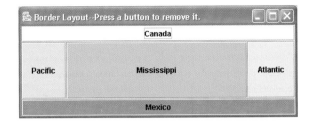

Figure 8-7
The five buttons are placed in this window using a BorderLayout manager.

BorderLayout Manager

BorderLayout allows you to place components on the four borders of the container and a fifth component in the middle. You may place anywhere from one to five components in the container. Figure 8-7 shows a window with five buttons placed using a BorderLayout manager.

Each of the component's positions are specified in the add() method. In Program 8-6, we set up five buttons and place them in the container. Here is a portion of the program that adds each of the buttons to the container by specifying the border section using the directional point of a compass. We also change the color of the button while we are setting up our canvas.

```
public void setUpBorderLayout()
{
        canvas.add(b1, BorderLayout.NORTH);
        b1.setBackground(Color.white);
        canvas.add(b2, BorderLayout.SOUTH);
        b2.setBackground(Color.red);
        canvas.add(b3, BorderLayout.WEST);
        b3.setBackground(Color.cyan);
        canvas.add(b4, BorderLayout.EAST);
        b4.setBackground(Color.blue);
        canvas.add(b5, BorderLayout.CENTER);
        b5.setBackground(Color.green);
}
```

This program illustrates how the BorderLayout components remain in their location even if there are not five components in the container. If you press a button, the program removes it from the container. Here is one of the button handler methods that illustrates removing the button from the container:

```
//Use anonymous classes for each button event.
b1.addActionListener( new ActionListener()
{
        public void actionPerformed( ActionEvent ae)
        {
```

8

```
            //Remove the button from the container.
            canvas.remove(b1);

            //validate() causes a container to lay out its components
            //again after the components it contains have been
            //added to or modified.
            canvas.validate();

            //Forces a call to paint() to repaint the container.
            canvas.repaint();
        }
    } );
```

If we click on the Canada (NORTH) button, Mississippi (CENTER) button, and Atlantic (EAST) button, our program removes the components and the remaining two components are slighty resized, as seen in Figure 8-8. The complete program is as follows.

```
1   //Program 8-6
2   //File: BorderDemo.java
3
4   import javax.swing.*;
5   import java.awt.*;
6   import java.awt.event.*;
7
8   public class BorderDemo extends JFrame
9   {
10    //Create our buttons.
11    JButton b1 = new JButton("Canada");
12    JButton b2 = new JButton("Mexico");
13    JButton b3 = new JButton("Pacific");
14    JButton b4 = new JButton("Atlantic");
15    JButton b5 = new JButton("Mississippi");
16
17    Container canvas = getContentPane();
18
19    public BorderDemo()
20    {
21
22          setUpBorderLayout();
23
24          //Use anonymous classes for each button event.
25          b1.addActionListener( new ActionListener()
26          {
27                public void actionPerformed( ActionEvent ae)
28                {
```

```
29              //Remove the button from the container.
30              canvas.remove(b1);
31
32              //validate causes a container to lay out its components
33                  //again after the components it contains have been
34                  //added to or modified.
35              canvas.validate();
36
37              //Forces a call to paint() to repaint the container.
38              canvas.repaint();
39          }
40      } );
41
42      b2.addActionListener( new ActionListener()
43      {
44          public void actionPerformed( ActionEvent ae)
45          {
46              canvas.remove(b2);
47              canvas.validate();
48              canvas.repaint();
49          }
50      } );
51
52      b3.addActionListener( new ActionListener()
53      {
54          public void actionPerformed( ActionEvent ae)
55          {
56              canvas.remove(b3);
57              canvas.validate();
58              canvas.repaint();
59          }
60      } );
61
62      b4.addActionListener( new ActionListener()
63      {
64          public void actionPerformed( ActionEvent ae)
65          {
66              canvas.remove(b4);
67              canvas.validate();
68              canvas.repaint();
69          }
70      } );
71
72      b5.addActionListener( new ActionListener()
73      {
```

8

```
74                    public void actionPerformed( ActionEvent ae)
75                    {
76                            canvas.remove(b5);
77                            canvas.validate();
78                            canvas.repaint();
79                    }
80            } );
81
82            this.setSize(450,175);
83            this.setTitle("Border Layout--Press a button to remove it.");
84            this.show();
85    }
86    public void setUpBorderLayout()
87    {
88            canvas.add(b1, BorderLayout.NORTH);
89            b1.setBackground(Color.white);
90            canvas.add(b2, BorderLayout.SOUTH);
91            b2.setBackground(Color.magenta);
92            canvas.add(b3, BorderLayout.WEST);
93            b3.setBackground(Color.cyan);
94            canvas.add(b4, BorderLayout.EAST);
95            b4.setBackground(Color.yellow);
96            canvas.add(b5, BorderLayout.CENTER);
97            b5.setBackground(Color.green);
98
99    }
100   public static void main( String args[] )
101   {
102           BorderDemo app = new BorderDemo();
103           app.setDefaultCloseOperation(JFrame.EXIT_ON_CLOSE);
104   }
105 }
```

Figure 8-8
The Canada, Mississippi, and Atlantic buttons have been pressed, thus removing the NORTH, CENTER, and EAST components from the container. The remaining two components are resized but remain in their WEST and SOUTH locations.

JPanels, Panes, and More Layout Managers

The **JPanel** Swing component is a container that provides a screen area used for drawing graphics or receiving user input. A JPanel object can hold other components, such as buttons or labels, and the programmer can set a layout manager for the panel object as well. This is a powerful programming tool! You may separate your user interface into different regions, placing a JPanel object into each region.

JPanel
a container that provides a screen area used for drawing graphics or holding other components. You may set a layout manager for the panel object

A Simple Panel Demonstration

In the next program demonstration, we use two JPanels to help us make our program output look good. Examine Figure 8-9 on page 470, which shows the resultant output window of this program. We divide the basic window into three different regions using a BorderLayout manager. In the WEST portion, we place a panel that has a GridLayout manager containing a radio button group. Then CENTER portion is a panel that has a FlowLayout manager that contains two labels (one with an image icon associated with it). The SOUTH portion has a label that tells who drew the pictures. Figure 8-10 illustrates a sketch of the relationship of the two panels and the container. Program 8-7 shows the complete program.

```
1   //Program 8-7
2   //File:  RadioControlled.java
3
4   //Use two panels to separate groups of components in a GUI.
5
6
7   import java.awt.event.*;
8   import java.awt.GridLayout;
9   import java.awt.FlowLayout;
10  import java.awt.Container;
11  import java.awt.BorderLayout;
12  import java.awt.Dimension;
13  import javax.swing.*; //for Icon, ImageIcon, JFrame, JPanel,
14                        //JRadioButton, ButtonGroup, and JLabel
15
16  public class RadioControlled extends JFrame implements ActionListener
17  {
18    private Icon star;
19    private Icon moon;
20    private Icon heart;
```

```
21
22      private JRadioButton starJRadioButton = new JRadioButton( "star" );
23      private JRadioButton heartJRadioButton = new JRadioButton( "heart" );
24      private JRadioButton moonJRadioButton = new JRadioButton( "moon" );
25
26      private JPanel imageJPanel = new JPanel();
27      private JPanel radioJPanel = new JPanel();
28
29      private JLabel imageJLabel = new JLabel();
30      private JLabel youPickedLabel = new JLabel("You selected a ");
31      private JLabel creditLabel = new JLabel(" Pictures by Marc",
32                                JLabel.CENTER);
33
34      public RadioControlled()
35      {
36              this.setTitle( "RadioButton Controlled" );
37
38              //First we set up the button panel.
39              //We will place the button in a column, use grid 3x1.
40              radioJPanel.setLayout( new GridLayout(3,1) );
41              radioJPanel.add( starJRadioButton );
42              radioJPanel.add( heartJRadioButton );
43              radioJPanel.add( moonJRadioButton );
44
45              //Don't forget the button group.
46              ButtonGroup group = new ButtonGroup();
47              group.add( starJRadioButton );
48              group.add( heartJRadioButton );
49              group.add( moonJRadioButton );
50
51              //For the image, we'll use a FlowLayout
52              imageJPanel.setLayout(new FlowLayout() );
53              imageJPanel.add( youPickedLabel);
54              imageJPanel.add( imageJLabel );
55
56              //Now add the panels and credit label to the frame's container.
57              Container canvas = getContentPane();
58              canvas.setLayout(new BorderLayout() );
59              canvas.add( imageJPanel, BorderLayout.CENTER);
60              canvas.add( radioJPanel, BorderLayout.WEST );
61              canvas.add( creditLabel, BorderLayout.SOUTH);
62
63              //We want to change the picture when a new button
64              //is selected. We add AL's to each button.
```

```
65          starJRadioButton.addActionListener( this );
66          moonJRadioButton.addActionListener( this );
67          heartJRadioButton.addActionListener( this );
68
69          //Assigns an image into an ImageIcon.
70          moon = new ImageIcon( "shape3.png" );
71          star = new ImageIcon( "shape1.png" );
72          heart = new ImageIcon( "shape2.png" );
73
74          //Initialize the star button and show sun image.
75          starJRadioButton.setSelected(true);
76          imageJLabel.setIcon( star );
77          imageJLabel.setText( "star." );
78
79          this.setSize(250,150);
80          show();
81      }
82
83      public static void main( String[] args )
84      {
85          RadioControlled app = new RadioControlled();
86          app.setDefaultCloseOperation( JFrame.EXIT_ON_CLOSE );
87      }
88
89      public void actionPerformed( ActionEvent e )
90      {
91          if( e.getSource() == starJRadioButton )
92          {
93              imageJLabel.setIcon( star );
94              imageJLabel.setText( "star." );
95          }
96          else if( e.getSource() == moonJRadioButton )
97          {
98              imageJLabel.setIcon( moon );
99              imageJLabel.setText( "moon." );
100         }
101         else if( e.getSource() == heartJRadioButton )
102         {
103             imageJLabel.setIcon( heart );
104             imageJLabel.setText( "heart." );
105         }
106     }
107 }
```

Figure 8-9
There are two separate JPanel objects in this frame's container. The container is using a BorderLayout manager. The button group on the WEST is in a JPanel with a grid layout and the image labels in the CENTER are in JPanel with a flow layout. The bottom credits label is placed in the SOUTH position.

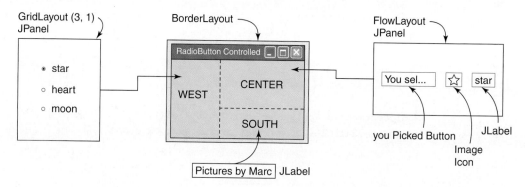

Figure 8-10
A diagram showing the relationships and layout managers for Program 8-7.

If we play with the different layout managers we are able to give our program output many different appearances. For example, if we use a grid layout for the container instead of a border layout, (see Figure 8-11) and place our panels and label in the grid elements, we see squished radio buttons. The output is shown in Figure 8-12. The code below shows how we modified this original program.

```
//Now add the panels and credit label to the frame's container.
Container canvas = getContentPane();
canvas.setLayout(new GridLayout(3,1) );
canvas.add( radioJPanel);
canvas.add( imageJPanel);
canvas.add( creditLabel);
```

But do not take our word for it. Obtain the code from the text's CD and change the layout managers and the assigned positions for each of the controls. Change

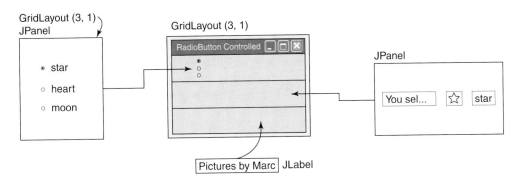

GridLayout (3, 1)
JPanel

GridLayout (3, 1)

RadioButton Controlled

JPanel

You sel...   ☆   star

Pictures by Marc JLabel

Figure 8-11
A diagram showing the relationship of the container and two panels and label for a modified Program 8-7. We change the frame's container so that it uses a 3 by 1 grid layout.

Figure 8-12
Program output from a modified Program 8-7. By using a 3 by 1 grid layout for the frame's container, each of the grid elements are sized to fit in the equally spaced window portions. The radio button panel is placed in the top element and the buttons are squished in order to fit in its share of the window.

the layout managers in the panels as well. Convince yourself how easy it is to alter the look of your program by using various layout managers.

FlowLayout Demonstration using JPanels

The **FlowLayout** class in Java is easy to use. This layout manager adds the components into the container from left to right. If the container is resized, the components are moved. Components might be moved to a new line if there is not enough room, however, components placed in a container with FlowLayout are never resized.

All components have a setPreferredSize() method, which requires a Dimension object as input. The programmer can specify the desired size by calling this method. Some layout managers, such as FlowLayout will honor this request and size the components accordingly. Other managers, such as GridLayout, ignore the request and resize the component's size to the actual dimensions of the container.

FlowLayout

adds components into the container from left to right. If the container is resized, the components are moved. Components are never resized

In Program 8-8, we set up three panels and place three buttons in each panel using different FlowLayout configurations. The frame's container is a GridLayout and the panels are added to it. Notice how the top panel's buttons are sized by the setPreferredSize() method, to the detriment of their appearance. Program 8-8 shows the source code, and comments in the code explain the various configuration of the FlowLayout manager. Figure 8-13a shows the original output from this program, and Figure 8-13b shows the appearance of the window after a resizing operation. Notice how the FlowLayout manager does not resize any buttons. It does move components to the next line and some of the components are not shown at all.

```
1   //Program 8-8
2   //File: FlowDemo.java
3
4   //Demonstrate various ways of using the FlowLayout manager.
5
6   import javax.swing.*;
7   import javax.swing.border.*;
8   import java.awt.*;
9
10  public class FlowDemo extends JFrame
11  {
12      //A TitledBorder implements an arbitrary border with a
13      //title in a specified position and justification.
14      TitledBorder t1, t2, t3;
15
16      JButton b1 = new JButton("Chicago");
17      JButton b2 = new JButton("Portland");
18      JButton b3 = new JButton("New Orleans");
19      JButton b4 = new JButton("Chicago");
20      JButton b5 = new JButton("Portland");
21      JButton b6 = new JButton("New Orleans");
22      JButton b7 = new JButton("Chicago");
23      JButton b8 = new JButton("Portland");
24      JButton b9 = new JButton("New Orleans");
25
26      JPanel sp1 = new JPanel();
27      JPanel sp2 = new JPanel();
28      JPanel sp3 = new JPanel();
29
30      public FlowDemo()
31      {
32          Container canvas = getContentPane();
33
34          //Use GridLayout to position three rows in one column.
35          canvas.setLayout( new GridLayout(3,1) );
36          canvas.add(sp1);
```

```
37              canvas.add(sp2);
38              canvas.add(sp3);
39
40              //Size the first three buttons.
41              b1.setPreferredSize(new Dimension(50,20));
42              b2.setPreferredSize(new Dimension(60,25));
43              b3.setPreferredSize(new Dimension(70,30));
44
45              //First panel
46              sp1.setBackground(Color.red);
47              sp1.setLayout(new FlowLayout());
48
49              //To make a titled border, use the BorderFactory class and then
50              //call the panel's setBorder() method.
51              t1 = BorderFactory.createTitledBorder(
52                              "Default FlowLayout Constructor");
53              sp1.setBorder(t1);
54              sp1.add(b1);
55              sp1.add(b2);
56              sp1.add(b3);
57
58
59              //For the second panel, right justify the components in it.
60              sp2.setLayout(new FlowLayout(FlowLayout.RIGHT));
61              sp2.setBackground(Color.white);
62              t2 = BorderFactory.createTitledBorder(
63                              "FlowLayout with Right Justification");
64              sp2.setBorder(t2);
65              sp2.add(b4);
66              sp2.add(b5);
67              sp2.add(b6);
68
69              //The third panel should have the components centered.
70              //We can specify the horizontal and vertical pixel gap
71              //between the components too.
72              sp3.setBackground(Color.yellow);
73              sp3.setLayout(new FlowLayout(FlowLayout.CENTER, 40, 0));
74              t3 = BorderFactory.createTitledBorder(
75                              "FlowLayout with gap difference changed");
76
77              sp3.setBorder(t3);
78              sp3.add(b7);
79              sp3.add(b8);
80              sp3.add(b9);
81
82              this.setSize(500,200);
83              this.setTitle("Flow Layout Demonstration Program ");
84              this.show();
85      }
```

```
86
87    public static void main( String args[] )
88    {
89          FlowDemo app = new FlowDemo();
90          app.setDefaultCloseOperation(JFrame.EXIT_ON_CLOSE);
91    }
92  }
```

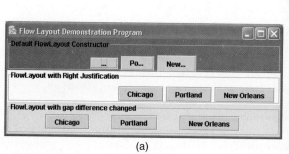
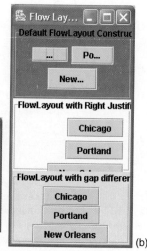

(a)   (b)

Figure 8-13

a) The window for Program 8-8, which has three panels, each with a different varia-
tion of the FlowManager. In the top panel, the button sizes are set by the programmer. The FlowManager does not resize components. b) The window has been
resized. Some components are moved to the next line and some are not visible in
this smaller window.

JPanels as Separate Classes

As you may imagine, if you have a complex user interface, the source code for it
can become large and unwieldy. In the previous examples we designed our user
interface so that groups of components could be placed in separate panels. Now
we will take this concept one step further. Each panel has its code written in its
own class, which is contained in a separate *.java* file. We then must instantiate
an object of each of our panel classes and add them to the frame or applet's
container.

An example is in order here. We will build a silly program that contains several JPanel objects. Examine Figure 8-14 on page 477. This is the output from

Program 8-9. The frame's container has a BorderLayout manager. The NORTH position contains the MoviePanel object. The WEST position contains the Vacation-Panel object. The EAST panel contains the PasswordPanel object. The CENTER position contains one JButton object. The SOUTH position has a SummaryPanel. As the user interacts with the program components, and he or she then presses the Summary button, the pertinent data from each panel is reported in the Summary-Panel—beside the button. Here we have picked an ocean cruise for a vacation, a romantic movie, the password is GoLobos, and the selected color has been used to shade the Summary button.

Let's first examine an individual panel and then see how it is incorporated into the frame's container. We need a class that is a panel, so we use the JPanel as a superclass for our class. The VacationPanel is a JPanel. The *VacationPanel.java* contains the following source code:

```java
1   //Program 8-9
2   //File:  VacationPanel.java
3
4   //This panel obtains the user's vacation preference.
5   //The getVacationChoice() return the user's choice.
6
7
8   import javax.swing.*; //for JRadioButton, JGroupButton,JPanel;
9   import java.awt.*;
10  import java.awt.event.*;
11
12  public class VacationPanel extends JPanel
13  {
14     JRadioButton beachButton = new JRadioButton("The beach");
15     JRadioButton skiButton = new JRadioButton("Mountain resort");
16     JRadioButton shipButton = new JRadioButton("Ocean cruise");
17
18     JLabel vacationLabel = new JLabel("Pick a vacation locale" );
19     JLabel responseLabel = new JLabel("Oh I love the beach.");
20
21     ButtonGroup group = new ButtonGroup();
22
23     String vacationChoice = "The beach";
24
25     public VacationPanel()
26     {
27         group.add(beachButton);
28         group.add(skiButton);
29         group.add(shipButton);
```

```
30
31          setLayout( new GridLayout( 5, 1) );
32
33          add(vacationLabel);
34          add(beachButton);
35          add(skiButton);
36          add(shipButton);
37          add(responseLabel);
38
39          beachButton.setSelected(true);
40
41          beachButton.addActionListener( new ActionListener ()
42          {
43                  public void actionPerformed(ActionEvent ae)
44                  {
45                          responseLabel.setText("Oh I love the beach.");
46                          vacationChoice = "The beach";
47                  }
48          });
49
50          skiButton.addActionListener( new ActionListener ()
51          {
52                  public void actionPerformed(ActionEvent ae)
53                  {
54                          responseLabel.setText("The skiing is great!");
55                          vacationChoice = "Mountains";
56                  }
57          });
58
59          shipButton.addActionListener( new ActionListener ()
60          {
61                  public void actionPerformed(ActionEvent ae)
62                  {
63                          responseLabel.setText("Eat ice cream on the ship.");
64                          vacationChoice = "Cruise ship";
65                  }
66          });
67   }
68
69   public String getVacationChoice() { return vacationChoice; }
70 }
```

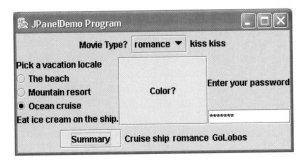

Figure 8-14
The vacation, movie, and password information is handled by separate JPanel classes that we have written. When the user presses the summary button, information is obtained from the three JPanel objects and is presented. A JButton is placed in the CENTER of the window. It brings up the JColorChooser so that the user may select a color.

Notice that we do not obtain a container for this code. This is because the JPanel is a container and it comes with the add() and setLayout() methods. This makes it easy for us to place other controls in this panel.

The *JPanelDemo.java* file contains the source code for the window that we see on the screen. We instantiate vacation, movie, and password panels in this class and add them to the frame's container. This class must call the VacationPanel's getVacationChoice() method in order to learn the user's choice. The panels should be viewed as separate entities and their data must be obtained via get() methods. Figure 8-15 illustrates the relationship between the JPanelDemo and VacationPanel classes. JPanelDemo, MoviePanel, and PasswordPanel are shown below.

```
1   //Program 8-9
2   //A JPanel demonstration that uses three separate JPanel objects.
3   //The JPanel objects are located in separate classes.
4
5   import javax.swing.*; //for JRadioButton, JGroupButton,JPanel;
6   import java.awt.*;
7   import java.awt.event.*;
8
9   public class JPanelDemo extends JFrame
10  {
11      //These three Panels are located in separate .java files.
12      VacationPanel vp = new VacationPanel();
13      MoviePanel mp = new MoviePanel();
14      PasswordPanel pp = new PasswordPanel();
15
16      //We make a separate panel for this container.
17      //It will show a summary of data from the other panels.
18      JPanel summaryPanel = new JPanel();
19      JButton summaryButton = new JButton("Summary");
20
21      //These labels are in the summary panel.
22      JLabel vacationLabel = new JLabel();
```

```
23      JLabel movieLabel = new JLabel();
24      JLabel passwordLabel = new JLabel();
25
26      JButton colorButton = new JButton("Color?");
27      Color buttonsColor = new Color(0.75f, 0.75f, 0.75f);
28
29      public JPanelDemo()
30      {
31              Container canvas = getContentPane();
32              canvas.setLayout( new BorderLayout() );
33
34              //Add the panels and button to the frame's container.
35              canvas.add(vp, BorderLayout.WEST);
36              canvas.add(mp, BorderLayout.NORTH);
37              canvas.add(pp, BorderLayout.EAST);
38
39              canvas.add(colorButton, BorderLayout.CENTER);
40
41              //Heads up! Someone pressed the Color button!
42              colorButton.addActionListener( new ActionListener()
43              {
44                      public void actionPerformed( ActionEvent ae)
45                      {
46                              buttonsColor = JColorChooser.showDialog(null,
47                                      "Pick a color for this button", buttonsColor);
48                              colorButton.setBackground(buttonsColor);
49                      }
50              } );
51
52              fixUpSummaryPanel();
53              canvas.add(summaryPanel, BorderLayout.SOUTH);
54              this.setSize(400,200);
55              this.setTitle("JPanelDemo Program ");
56              this.show();
57      }
58
59      public void fixUpSummaryPanel()
60      {
61              summaryPanel.setLayout( new FlowLayout() );
62              summaryPanel.add(summaryButton);
63              summaryPanel.add(vacationLabel);
64              summaryPanel.add(movieLabel);
65              summaryPanel.add(passwordLabel);
66
67              //Get ready to handle the summary button event!
68              summaryButton.addActionListener( new ActionListener()
69              {
```

```
70              public void actionPerformed( ActionEvent ae)
71              {
72                  vacationLabel.setText(vp.getVacationChoice() );
73                  movieLabel.setText( mp.getMovieChoice() );
74                  passwordLabel.setText( pp.getPassword() );
75                  summaryButton.setBackground(buttonsColor);
76              }
77          } );
78      }
79
80      public static void main( String args[] )
81      {
82          JPanelDemo app = new JPanelDemo();
83          app.setDefaultCloseOperation(JFrame.EXIT_ON_CLOSE);
84      }
85
86  }
```

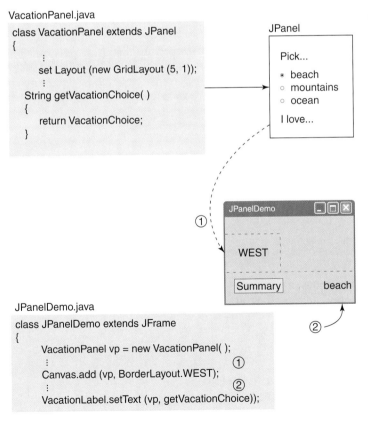

VacationPanel.java

```
class VacationPanel extends JPanel
{
    ⋮
    set Layout (new GridLayout (5, 1));
    ⋮
String getVacationChoice( )
{
    return VacationChoice;
}
```

JPanel

Pick...
- beach
- mountains
- ocean

I love...

JPanelDemo.java

```
class JPanelDemo extends JFrame
{
    VacationPanel vp = new VacationPanel( );      ①
    ⋮
    Canvas.add (vp, BorderLayout.WEST);           ②
    ⋮
VacationLabel.setText (vp, getVacationChoice));
```

JPanelDemo

WEST

Summary   beach

Figure 8-15
VacationPanel handled the layout and user interaction for the vacation information. JPanelDemo has a Vacation-Panel object added to the WEST region of its BorderLayout container. The data in VacationPanel must be obtained by using a get() method.

8

```
1    //Program 8-9
2    //File:  MoviePanel.java
3
4    //This panel obtains the user's choice for type of movie.
5    //The getMovieChoice() return the panel's information.
6
7    import javax.swing.*; //for JRadioButton, JGroupButton,JPanel;
8    import java.awt.*;
9    import java.awt.event.*;
10
11   public class MoviePanel extends JPanel
12   {
13     JComboBox movieBox;
14     String movieTypes[] = {"comedy", "romance", "scary",
15                       "mystery", "sci-fi" };
16     String movieComments[] = {"very funny", "kiss kiss", "Ohhhh!!!",
17                       "who dun it","bold new world"};
18     JLabel pickLabel = new JLabel("Movie Type?" );
19     JLabel responseLabel = new JLabel("very funny");
20
21     int choice;
22
23     public MoviePanel()
24     {
25           setLayout( new FlowLayout() );
26
27           movieBox = new JComboBox(movieTypes);
28
29           add(pickLabel);
30           add(movieBox);
31           add(responseLabel);
32
33           movieBox.addItemListener( new ItemListener()
34           {
35                 public void itemStateChanged( ItemEvent ie)
36                 {
37                       choice = movieBox.getSelectedIndex();
38                       responseLabel.setText(movieComments[choice] );
39                 }
40           } );
41
42     }
43     public String getMovieChoice(){return movieTypes[choice] ; }
44   }
```

```
1    //Program 8-9
2    //File:  PasswordPanel.java
3
4    //This panel obtains the user's password
5    //The getPassword() return the panel's information.
6
7
8    import java.awt.event.*;
9    import javax.swing.*;
10   import java.awt.*;
11
12   public class PasswordPanel extends JPanel
13   {
14     JPasswordField passwordField = new JPasswordField();
15     JLabel label = new JLabel("Enter your password");
16     char password[] = new char[15];
17     String strPassword;
18
19     public PasswordPanel()
20     {
21         setLayout( new BorderLayout() );
22
23         add(label, BorderLayout.CENTER);
24         add(passwordField, BorderLayout.SOUTH);
25
26         passwordField.addActionListener( new ActionListener()
27         {
28             public void actionPerformed( ActionEvent ae)
29             {
30                 password = passwordField.getPassword();
31                 strPassword = String.valueOf(password);
32
33             }
34         } );
35
36     }
37     public String getPassword(){return strPassword ; }
38   }
```

Panels in a Tabbed Pane Layout

Java's **JTabbedPane** class offers the programmer a space saving tool for your screen that can present panels and controls on a one-at-a-time basis. Anyone who has spent much time using a windows based operating system is familiar with the tabbed pane control. Figure 8-16 on page 484 shows a tabbed pane component with

JTabbedPane
allows the user to switch between a group of components by clicking on a tab or icon

the tabbed dividers across the top. Each tab has a label. When the user presses the tab, the page is presented.

The JTabbedPane class default configuration has the tabs located across the top of the folder, as shown in Figure 8-16. This tabbed pane object is created by calling the default constructor:

```
JTabbedPane jtp = new JTabbedPane();
```

The programmer may place the tabs on the left, right, or bottom by passing in a SwingConstant value such as:

```
JTabbedPane jtp = new JTabbedPane(SwingConstants.LEFT);
//The other two constants are
//SwingConstants.RIGHT or SwingConstants.BOTTOM.
```

The JTabbedPane component has several add() and addTab() methods. An icon may be added to each tab as well as the text for a tooltip that is presented when the mouse rests on the tab. (The tooltip for the Vacation tab can be seen in Figure 8-16.) For our program we add the panels we wrote in Program 8-9 to the tabs and place tooltips for the three panel classes. Examine the source code in Program 8-10 and concentrate on the JTabbedPane source lines. Notice that we create a JTabbedPane object, add it to the frame's container, and then add the panels and button to the tabbed pane.

```
1    //Program 8-10
2    //File JTabbedDemo.java
3
4    //Use a JTabbedPane to display our Vacation, Movie, and Password
5    //JPanels. Each of the controls are added as a separate page
6    //in the JTabbedPane.
7
8    import javax.swing.*; //for JRadioButton, JGroupButton,JPanel;
9    import java.awt.*;
10   import java.awt.event.*;
11
12   public class JTabbedDemo extends JFrame
13   {
14      JTabbedPane jtp = new JTabbedPane();
15
16      //Here are our three panel classes.
17      VacationPanel vp = new VacationPanel();
18      MoviePanel mp = new MoviePanel();
19      PasswordPanel pp = new PasswordPanel();
20
21      //We make a separate panel here that is a member of this class.
22      JPanel summaryPanel = new JPanel();
23
```

```
24        JButton summaryButton = new JButton("Summary");
25
26        JLabel vacationLabel = new JLabel();
27        JLabel movieLabel = new JLabel();
28        JLabel passwordLabel = new JLabel();
29
30        JButton colorButton = new JButton("Color?");
31        Color buttonsColor = new Color(0.75f, 0.75f, 0.75f) ;
32        public JTabbedDemo()
33        {
34              Container canvas = getContentPane();
35              canvas.add(jtp);
36
37              //JTabbedPane has several add() and addTab() methods.
38              //Here we pass in the title of the tab, null indicating no icon,
39              //the Component, and the tooltip text.
40
41              jtp.addTab("Vacation", null,  vp, "Vacation locale?");
42              jtp.addTab("Movies",  null, mp, "Movie preference?");
43              jtp.addTab("Password",null, pp, "Tell me your password");
44
45              //For the color and summary we just add the title and component.
46              //No icon, no tooltip.
47              jtp.addTab(" Pick a color",  colorButton);
48
49              fixUpSummaryPanel();
50              jtp.addTab("Summary", summaryPanel);
51
52              colorButton.addActionListener( new ActionListener()
53              {
54                    public void actionPerformed( ActionEvent ae)
55                    {
56                          buttonsColor = JColorChooser.showDialog(null,
57                                "Pick a color for this button", buttonsColor);
58                          colorButton.setBackground(buttonsColor);
59                    }
60              } );
61
62
63              this.setSize(400,200);
64              this.setTitle("JTabbedDemo Program ");
65              this.show();
66        }
67
```

```
68      public void fixUpSummaryPanel()
69      {
70              summaryPanel.setLayout( new FlowLayout() );
71              summaryPanel.add(summaryButton);
72              summaryPanel.add(vacationLabel);
73              summaryPanel.add(movieLabel);
74              summaryPanel.add(passwordLabel);
75
76              summaryButton.addActionListener( new ActionListener()
77              {
78                      public void actionPerformed( ActionEvent ae)
79                      {
80                              vacationLabel.setText(vp.getVacationChoice() );
81                              movieLabel.setText( mp.getMovieChoice() );
82                              passwordLabel.setText( pp.getPassword() );
83                              summaryButton.setBackground(buttonsColor);
84                      }
85              } );
86      }
87
88      public static void main( String args[] )
89      {
90              JTabbedDemo app = new JTabbedDemo();
91              app.setDefaultCloseOperation(JFrame.EXIT_ON_CLOSE);
92      }
93  }
```

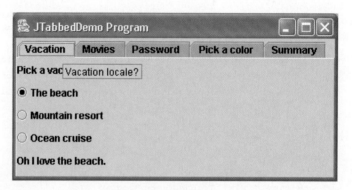

Figure 8-16
The JTabbedPane provides a space saving technique to display and toggle between various panels. Here we show the VacationPanel tab. The tooltip for this tab is displayed as well. We see the tooltips when the mouse rests on the tab.

Panels in a CardLayout

CardLayout is a bit more complicated than the layout managers we have examined previously, but it can be quite useful for managing your screen's real estate. CardLayout is similar to the JTabbedPane in that there is one display area that shows one panel at a time. Instead of using labeled tabs across the top, sides, or bottom area of a region, CardLayout allows you to page through panels as if you were flipping through a deck of cards. There are five ways to display your components that have been added to a CardLayout and they are: first(), last(), next(), previous(), and show().

Figure 8-17 on page 489 shows the CardLayoutDemo program output. We have created six panels and set their background color. We add a CardLayout to the display panel, as well as the six colored panels. There are a series of buttons across the top of the frame that provide the ability to access the first, last, next, and previous panels as well as individual buttons at the lower part of the frame that will display its associated colored panel. Examine the code in Program 8-11. The comments in the program explain the required steps.

> **CardLayout**
> allows you to pass through panels as if you were flipping through a deck of cards, including showing first, last, next, and previous

```
1    //Program 8-11
2    //File CardLayoutDemo.java
3
4    //This program demonstrates how the CardLayout allows the
5    //user to page through a series of panels.
6
7    import javax.swing.*; //for JRadioButton, JGroupButton,JPanel;
8    import java.awt.*;
9    import java.awt.event.*;
10
11   public class CardLayoutDemo extends JFrame
12   {
13
14       JPanel displayPanel = new JPanel();   //holds the CardLayout manager
15       CardLayout displayMgr = new CardLayout();   //holds the six colored panels
16       JPanel positionPanel = new JPanel();   //hold the first, prev, next, last buttons
17       JPanel namePanel = new JPanel();   //holds the six colored buttons
18       JPanel yp = new JPanel();
19       JPanel cp = new JPanel();
20       JPanel wp = new JPanel();
21       JPanel gp = new JPanel();
22       JPanel bp = new JPanel();
23       JPanel rp = new JPanel();
24
25       JButton firstButton = new JButton("First");
26       JButton lastButton = new JButton("Last");
27       JButton nextButton = new JButton("Next");
28       JButton prevButton = new JButton("Prev");
29
```

```
30    JButton yellowButton = new JButton("Yellow Panel #1");
31    JButton cyanButton = new JButton("Cyan Panel #2");
32    JButton whiteButton = new JButton("White Panel #3");
33    JButton greenButton = new JButton("Green Panel #4");
34    JButton blueButton = new JButton("Blue Panel #5");
35    JButton redButton = new JButton("Red Panel #6");
36
37    public CardLayoutDemo()
38    {
39         Container canvas = getContentPane();
40         canvas.setLayout( new BorderLayout());
41
42         setUpNamePanel();
43         setUpPositionPanel();
44
45    //The CardLayout object is set in the panel.
46         displayPanel.setLayout(displayMgr);
47
48    //The various colored panels are added to the display panel.
49    //A name is also added. This name is referenced in the show().
50         yp.setBackground(Color.yellow);
51         displayPanel.add(yp, "Yellow");
52
53         cp.setBackground(Color.cyan);
54         displayPanel.add(cp, "Cyan");
55
56         wp.setBackground(Color.white);
57         displayPanel.add(wp, "White");
58
59         gp.setBackground(Color.green);
60         displayPanel.add(gp, "Green");
61
62         bp.setBackground(Color.blue);
63         displayPanel.add(bp, "Blue");
64
65         rp.setBackground(Color.red);
66         displayPanel.add(rp, "Red");
67
68         canvas.add(positionPanel, BorderLayout.NORTH);
69         canvas.add(namePanel, BorderLayout.SOUTH);
70         canvas.add(displayPanel, BorderLayout.CENTER);
71
72         //The display manager keeps track of which panel is
73         //shown and knows the first, last, prev, and next panels.
74         firstButton.addActionListener(new ActionListener()
75         {
```

```
76                    public void actionPerformed(ActionEvent e)
77                    {
78                         displayMgr.first(displayPanel);
79                    }
80        });
81
82        lastButton.addActionListener(new ActionListener()
83        {
84                    public void actionPerformed(ActionEvent e)
85                    {
86                         displayMgr.last(displayPanel);
87                    }
88        });
89
90        nextButton.addActionListener(new ActionListener()
91        {
92                    public void actionPerformed(ActionEvent e)
93                    {
94                         displayMgr.next(displayPanel);
95                    }
96        });
97
98        prevButton.addActionListener(new ActionListener()
99        {
100                   public void actionPerformed(ActionEvent e)
101                   {
102                        displayMgr.previous(displayPanel);
103                   }
104       });
105
106
107       //The button for each panel can ask the display manager
108       //to show its panel.
109       yellowButton.addActionListener(    new ActionListener()
110       {
111                   public void actionPerformed(ActionEvent e)
112                   {
113                        displayMgr.show(displayPanel, "Yellow");
114                   }
115       });
116
117       cyanButton.addActionListener(new ActionListener()
118       {
119                   public void actionPerformed(ActionEvent e)
120                   {
121                        displayMgr.show(displayPanel, "Cyan");
122                   }
123       });
```

8

```
124
125        whiteButton.addActionListener(    new ActionListener()
126        {
127            public void actionPerformed(ActionEvent e)
128            {
129                displayMgr.show(displayPanel, "White");
130            }
131        });
132
133        greenButton.addActionListener(    new ActionListener()
134        {
135            public void actionPerformed(ActionEvent e)
136            {
137                displayMgr.show(displayPanel, "Green");
138            }
139        });
140
141        blueButton.addActionListener(new ActionListener()
142        {
143            public void actionPerformed(ActionEvent e)
144            {
145                displayMgr.show(displayPanel, "Blue");
146            }
147        });
148
149        redButton.addActionListener(new ActionListener()
150        {
151            public void actionPerformed(ActionEvent e)
152            {
153                displayMgr.show(displayPanel, "Red");
154            }
155        });
156
157        this.setSize(400, 225);
158        this.setTitle("The two uses of CardLayout");
159        this.show();
160   }
161
162   public void setUpPositionPanel()
163   {
164        positionPanel.setLayout( new FlowLayout());
165        positionPanel.add(firstButton);
166        positionPanel.add(prevButton);
167        positionPanel.add(nextButton);
168        positionPanel.add(lastButton);
169   }
```

8

```
170
171    public void setUpNamePanel()
172    {
173            namePanel.setLayout( new GridLayout(2,3));
174
175            cyanButton.setBackground(Color.cyan);
176            whiteButton.setBackground(Color.white);
177            greenButton.setBackground(Color.green);
178            blueButton.setBackground(Color.blue);
179            yellowButton.setBackground(Color.yellow);
180            redButton.setBackground(Color.red);
181
182            namePanel.add(yellowButton);
183            namePanel.add(cyanButton);
184            namePanel.add(whiteButton);
185            namePanel.add(greenButton);
186            namePanel.add(blueButton);
187            namePanel.add(redButton);
188
189    }
190
191    public static void main(String args[])
192    {
193            CardLayoutDemo app = new CardLayoutDemo();
194            app.setDefaultCloseOperation(JFrame.EXIT_ON_CLOSE);
195    }
196    }
```

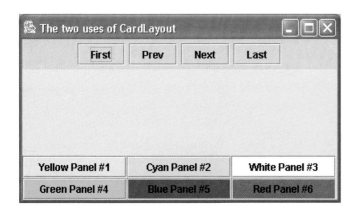

Figure 8-17
CardLayout is similar to the JTabbedPane because it provides a single area of the
screen that can show several different panels. The CardLayout remembers the first,
last, previous, and next components and uses JButtons to toggle between panels.

JSplitPane and JToolbar Demo

JSplitPane

provides a means for
the user to divide two
(and only two)
components, which
then can be resized by
the user

JToolbar

control is useful for
displaying a group of
controls. The JToolbar
can be dragged into a
separate window

The **JSplitPane** class provides a means for the user to divide two (and only two) components, which then can be resized by the user. The **JToolbar** control is useful for displaying a group of controls. The user may drag the toolbar into a separate window as long as the floatable property is set to true. (It is set to true by default.) For JToolbar to work correctly, it should be placed in a border region of a container with a BorderLayout.

In Program 8-12, we place two panels in a split pane object and then provide controls so that the user may choose a color for each of the panels. Figure 8-18 on page 493 illustrates the panels, toolbar, and split pane relationship. Figure 8-19 on page 494 illustrates three variations of the program's window. Grabbing the "bumpy" region located on the left-hand side of the toolbar with the mouse is how the user can move the toolbar. Read the comments in the source code for further explanation.

> **Note:** This program design uses a slightly different technique with the event handling code. Within each anonymous class, we call another method that performs the event tasks. This streamlines the anonymous classes and allows the programmer to organize the program in a different manner. This approach is often seen in code produced in a Java integrated development environment.

```
1    //Program 8-12  JSplitPane and JToolbar Demonstration
2    //File:  ColorFun.java
3
4    //This program adds the controls for the split pane into
5    //a toolbar. The toolbar can be moved and separated into
6    //its own window.
7
8    //We also show a new way of writing the event handling code.
9    //Instead of performing the handling tasks in the
10   //actionPerformed(), we call separate methods.
11
12
13   import java.awt.*;
14   import java.awt.event.*;
15   import javax.swing.*;
16
17
18   public class ColorFun extends JFrame
19   {
20      //Set up the pane and panels.
21      private JSplitPane splitPane = new JSplitPane();
22
23      private JPanel leftPanel = new JPanel();
24      private JPanel rightPanel = new JPanel();
25      private JPanel radioPanel = new JPanel();
26
27      //A toolbar will hold the radio panel and buttons.
28      private JToolBar toolBar = new JToolBar();
```

```
29
30     private JRadioButton rightRadio = new JRadioButton("Right");
31     private JRadioButton leftRadio = new JRadioButton("Left");
32     private ButtonGroup group = new ButtonGroup();
33
34     private JButton colorButton = new JButton("Choose Color");
35     private JButton funButton = new JButton("Fun!");
36     private String activeJSplitPane = JSplitPane.RIGHT;
37     private Color selectedColor;
38
39
40     public ColorFun()
41     {
42         this.setTitle( "Color Fun" );
43         initializeFrame();
44         setSize( new Dimension( 350, 150 ) );
45         show();
46     }
47
48     private void initializeFrame()
49     {
50         Container contentPane = getContentPane();
51
52         //In order to have a toolbar, we must use a BorderLayout.
53         contentPane.setLayout( new BorderLayout() );
54
55         //We put the splitPane in the CENTER and then add the
56         //two color panels to the splitPane.
57         contentPane.add( splitPane, BorderLayout.CENTER );
58         splitPane.add( leftPanel, JSplitPane.LEFT );
59         splitPane.add( rightPanel, JSplitPane.RIGHT );
60
61         //The toolbar is added to the SOUTH region of the container.
62         contentPane.add( toolBar, BorderLayout.SOUTH );
63
64         //Next we group the radio buttons and add to their panel.
65         rightRadio.setSelected( true );
66         group.add( rightRadio );
67         group.add( leftRadio );
68         radioPanel.add( leftRadio );
69         radioPanel.add( rightRadio );
70
71         //We set the layout and add controls to the toolbar.
72         toolBar.setLayout( new FlowLayout() );
73         toolBar.add( radioPanel );
74         toolBar.add( colorButton);
75         toolBar.add(funButton);
76
77         //Lastly we add listeners to the buttons.
78         leftRadio.addActionListener(
79             new ActionListener()
80             {
81                 public void actionPerformed( ActionEvent e )
82                 {
```

```
83                          //Instead of placing the handling code here,
84                          //we call another method to perform the work.
85                          leftRadio_actionPerformed();
86                      }
87              } );
88
89          rightRadio.addActionListener(
90              new ActionListener()
91              {
92                  public void actionPerformed( ActionEvent e )
93                  {
94                          //This method performs the event handling tasks.
95                          rightRadio_actionPerformed();
96                  }
97              } );
98
99          colorButton.addActionListener(
100             new ActionListener()
101             {
102                 public void actionPerformed( ActionEvent e )
103                 {
104                         colorButton_actionPerformed();
105                 }
106             } );
107
108         funButton.addActionListener(
109             new ActionListener()
110             {
111                 public void actionPerformed( ActionEvent e )
112                 {
113                         funButton_actionPerformed();
114                 }
115             } );
116     }
117
118     //Set which button is active when pressed.
119     void leftRadio_actionPerformed()
120     {
121         activeJSplitPane = JSplitPane.LEFT;
122     }
123
124     void rightRadio_actionPerformed()
125     {
126         activeJSplitPane = JSplitPane.RIGHT;
127     }
128
129     //Get a color from the ColorChooser and set the active panel's color.
130     void colorButton_actionPerformed()
131     {
132         selectedColor = JColorChooser.showDialog( null,
133                     "Color Chooser", Color.cyan );
```

```
134            if( activeJSplitPane.equals( JSplitPane.RIGHT ) )
135            {
136                    rightPanel.setBackground( selectedColor );
137            }
138            else if( activeJSplitPane.equals( JSplitPane.LEFT ) )
139            {
140                    leftPanel.setBackground( selectedColor );
141            }
142    }
143
144    //Display a comment for this program!
145    void funButton_actionPerformed()
146    {
147            JOptionPane.showMessageDialog(null,
148                    "Aren't toolbars and split panes fun?");
149
150    }
151    public static void main( String[] args )
152    {
153            ColorFun app = new ColorFun();
154            app.setDefaultCloseOperation( EXIT_ON_CLOSE );
155    }
156 }
```

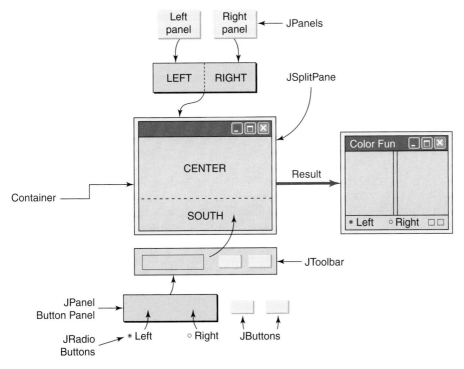

Figure 8-18
Various buttons, panels, and other controls for the ColorFun program.

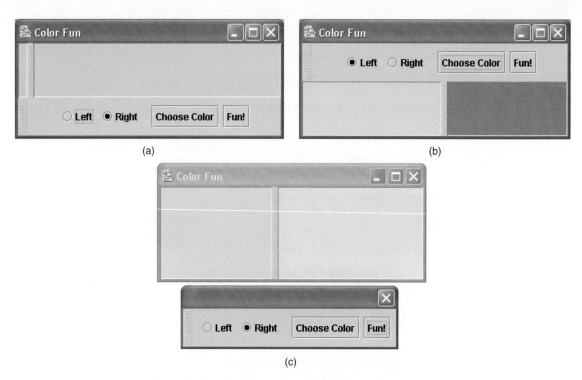

Figure 8-19
a) The original configuration for the ColorFun program shows the two panels and toolbar at the bottom. b) The user has moved the toolbar to the top and changed the panel colors. c) The toolbar can be pulled off as a separate window.

8.5
Mouse Activity

Java provides the programmer MouseListener and MouseMotionListener interfaces as well as MouseAdapter and MouseMotionAdapter classes. Table 8-6 is a portion of Table 8-2 showing just the mouse interfaces. If a programmer chooses to implement an interface, he or she must write all of the methods in the interface. That means if the programmer wants to use MouseListener, he or she must write methods for the Clicked, Entered, Exited, Pressed, and Released methods.

The Adapter classes provide default empty methods. All we need to do is write the method we are interested in using. Therefore, if we are just interested in knowing if the mouse button has been clicked inside a window, we can use a MouseAdapter and write the mouseClicked() method. The following programs use MouseAdapter classes.

TABLE 8-6

Mouse Listeners for user interface actions and corresponding events/interfaces (a more complete listing of all listeners is shown in Table 8-2).

Listener interface	Interface methods
MouseListener MouseAdapter	mouseClicked(MouseEvent) mouseEntered(MouseEvent) mouseExited(MouseEvent) mousePressed(MouseEvent) mouseReleased(MouseEvent)
MouseMotionListener MouseMotionAdapter	mouseDragged(MouseEvent) mouseMoved(MouseEvent)
	see Note

Note: The mouseDragged() method is invoked when the mouse button is pressed on a component and then dragged, whereas a mouseMoved() method is invoked when the mouse is moved onto a component with no mouse buttons pressed.

The I Love JPT Program

The I Love JPT Program is an applet that responds to two mouse activities. The window is seen in Figure 8-20. When the user presses the mouse button and drags the mouse, a string of text "follows" the mouse and it appears that the mouse is dragging the string. The mouse coordinates are reported in the applet's status bar at the bottom of the window. This trick is accomplished by obtaining the mouse

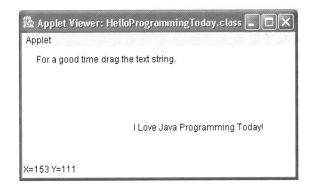

Figure 8-20
The Applet Window shows the two text Strings. "I Love Java Programming Today" follows the mouse when the button is pressed. An audio clip is played when the mouse button is released.

coordinates and passing them into the showStatus() method. Then, in paint(), we clear the window and paint the string. Here is the anonymous class that accomplishes these tasks:

```
//As the mouse is dragged, we get its position and display
//it in the status bar. Call repaint() which calls paint().
this.addMouseMotionListener( new MouseMotionAdapter()
{
        public void mouseDragged( MouseEvent e )
        {
                x = e.getX();
                y = e.getY();
                showStatus("X=" + x + " " + "Y=" + y);
                repaint();              //forces a call to paint()
        }
} );
```

The *this* reference is referring to the applet class and indicates the applet window. Because we are writing a MouseAdapter, we need only to write the method in which we are interested.

We introduce how to play a *.wav* file in an applet program. It is straightforward, as are most things in Java. We obtain an audio file that is written in **.wav* format and place it in our source code folder. *Java Programming Today* does not include any audio files on the text's CD, but wav files are abundant on your Windows machine and can be downloaded from the Internet. If you have a Windows operating system, search for **.wav*. On XP machines, the *C:\Windows\Media* folder contains many audio files.

AudioClip

a class in the java.applet package. It has three methods: loop(), play(), and stop(). It plays *.wav* files

In this program we make a reference for an **AudioClip** object. The AudioClip is a class in the java.applet package, and has three methods, loop(), play(), and stop(). To load the clip call the applet class' getAudioClip() method.

```
//Here is our AudioClip reference, named sound:
private AudioClip sound;

//Then in init() we load the .wav file and set up the
//MouseAdapter to play the sound when the mouse button
//is released.
public void init()
{

        //Load the audio clip.
        sound = getAudioClip( getDocumentBase(), "sound.wav" );

        this.addMouseListener( new MouseAdapter()
        {
```

```
      public void mouseReleased( MouseEvent e )
      {
            sound.play();
      }
  } );
}
```

Examine the source code for Program 8-13 and Figure 8-20 (on page 495) to see the Applet Window. Better yet, obtain the program from the text's CD and run and play with it yourself.

```
1    //Program 8-13 Demonstrate mouse listeners
2    //MouseMotionAdapter and MouseAdapter.
3    //Also show how a program can play an audio clip .wav file.
4
5    //File:  HelloProgrammingToday.java
6
7    import java.awt.*;
8    import java.awt.event.*;
9    import javax.swing.*;
10   import java.applet.*;
11
12   public class HelloProgrammingToday extends JApplet
13   {
14
15     private int x, y;
16     private AudioClip sound;
17     private int winWidth, winHeight;
18
19     public void init()
20     {
21           x = 30;
22           y = 50;
23           this.setBackground( Color.white );
24
25           //Load the audio clip.
26           sound = getAudioClip( getDocumentBase(), "sound.wav" );
27
28           //As the mouse is dragged, we get its position and display
29           //it in the status bar. Call repaint() which calls paint().
30           this.addMouseMotionListener( new MouseMotionAdapter()
31           {
32                 public void mouseDragged( MouseEvent e )
33                 {
```

8

```
34              x = e.getX();
35              y = e.getY();
36              showStatus("X=" + x + " " + "Y=" + y);
37              repaint();
38          }
39      } );
40      //Play the sound when the button is released.
41      this.addMouseListener( new MouseAdapter()
42      {
43          public void mouseReleased( MouseEvent e )
44          {
45              sound.play();
46          }
47      } );
48  }
49
50  //We draw two Strings each time the window is repainted.
51  public void paint( Graphics g )
52  {
53      g.setColor( Color.white );
54      winWidth = this.getWidth();
55      winHeight = this.getHeight();
56      g.fillRect(0,0,winWidth,winHeight);
57
58      g.setColor( Color.black );
59      g.drawString("For a good time drag the text string.", 20,20);
60      g.drawString("I Love Java Programming Today!",x,y);
61  }
62
63  public void stop()
64  {
65      //This stops playing the clip when the applet is closed.
66      sound.stop();
67  }
68 }
```

The Mousey Program

Program 8-14 tracks the mouse when it is in the frame window and draws "on-
the-fly" as the mouse moves. Figure 8-21 on page 501 shows that if the user moves
the mouse into the window, the program draws lines from the corners of the window
to the corners of a rectangle. The rectangle is centered about the current mouse position. We write information in the window that reports the mouse status (in or out), the

current position of the mouse, and the current color. If the mouse is pressed in the window, we change the color of the drawing by adjusting an index that references a color stored in a Color array. We write the MouseAdapter's mouseEntered(), mouse-Exited(), and mouseClicked() methods, as well as the MouseMotionAdapter's mouse-Moved() method. The program drawing is based on the current window size, obtained from the frame's getWidth() and getHeight() methods. Examine Figure 8-21 again to see how the messages change as the position of the mouse changes.

```
1    //Program 8-14
2    //Mousey.java
3
4    //This program illustrates more mouse listeners adapters and
5    //mouse motion listeners
6
7    import java.awt.Graphics;
8    import java.awt.Color;
9    import java.awt.event.*;
10
11   import javax.swing.JFrame;
12
13   public class Mousey extends JFrame
14   {
15      private int x,y, colorCounter = 0;
16
17      //Set up an array of colors that we'll use for drawing.
18      private final Color[] line = {
19                    Color.BLUE,
20                    Color.RED,
21                    Color.MAGENTA,
22                    Color.CYAN,
23                    Color.GREEN   };
24
25      private Color currentColor = line[colorCounter];
26
27      private String mouseStatus = "The mouse is OUT of the window";
28
29      public Mousey()
30      {
31            this.setBackground(Color.WHITE);
32
33            //Handle the event if the mouse goes in/out of the
34            //window or is clicked.
35            this.addMouseListener(new MouseAdapter()
36            {
```

```
37              public void mouseEntered(MouseEvent e)
38              {
39                      mouseStatus = "The mouse is IN the window.";
40              }
41              public void mouseExited(MouseEvent e)
42              {
43                      mouseStatus = "The mouse is OUT of the window.";
44                      repaint();
45              }
46              public void mouseClicked(MouseEvent e)
47              {
48                      //Cycle thru the line colors then repaint the window.
49                      colorCounter++;
50                      if(colorCounter == line.length )colorCounter = 0;
51                      currentColor = line[ colorCounter ];
52                      repaint();
53              }
54          });

56          //If the mouse is moved in the window, get the
57          //window coordinates and repaint the window.
58          this.addMouseMotionListener( new MouseMotionAdapter()
59          {
60              public void mouseMoved(MouseEvent e)
61              {
62                      x = e.getX();
63                      y = e.getY();
64                      repaint();
65              }
66          });

68          this.setSize(400,400);
69          this.setTitle("The Mousey Program");
70          this.show();
71      }

73  //This method paints lines from the corners of the window
74  //to the corners of a rectangle. The rectangle is
75  //centered about the current mouse position.
76  public void paint(Graphics g)
77  {
78      //Clear the window.
79      g.clearRect(0, 0, getWidth(), getHeight());
```

```
80
81          //Set the color.
82          g.setColor(currentColor);
83
84          //Write lines of info to the window.
85          g.drawString(mouseStatus, 15,50);
86          g.drawString("The color is "+currentColor.toString(),  15,90);
87          String position = "X = " + String.valueOf(x) +
88                          " Y = " + String.valueOf(y);
89          g.drawString(position, 15, 70);
90
91          //Draw the lines and box.
92          g.drawLine(0, 0, x - 25, y - 25);
93          g.drawLine(0, getHeight(), x - 25, y + 25);
94          g.drawLine(getWidth(), 0, x + 25, y - 25);
95          g.drawLine(getWidth(), getHeight(), x + 25, y + 25);
96          g.drawRect(x - 25, y - 25, 50, 50);
97      }
98
99  public static void main( String[] args )
100     {
101         Mousey app = new Mousey();
102         app.setDefaultCloseOperation( EXIT_ON_CLOSE );
103     }
104 }
```

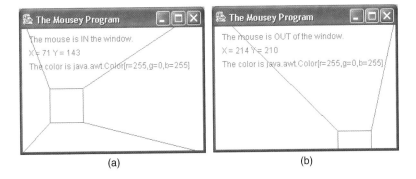

(a)   (b)

Figure 8-21

The mouse is tracked as it enters and exits the window. If the mouse is clicked in the
window, the line color changes. As the mouse moves in the window, the rectangle is
drawn to be centered about the mouse and the mouse position is updated.

The MusicBox Program

Mouse listeners can be placed on many Java components. In this MusicBox program, we build an applet with three JButton objects seen in Figure 8-22 on page 504. Mouse listeners are placed on all three buttons so that each button changes color if the user moves the mouse over the button. If the mouse is pulled off the button, the color changes back to gray. We also listen for a button press and play an audio clip if the mouse is pressed while on the button. Three *.wav* files selected from our *C:\Windows\Media* directory are used in this program, including the sounds of a ding, (*Ding.wav*), a phone ringing (*Ringin.wav*), and the Ta Da! sound (*Tada.wav*). Search your system for **.wav* files and copy and paste three audio clips into your folder so you may see and hear how this program (Program 8-15) works! Figure 8-22 shows the applet window with its three buttons. The mouse is currently over the Ring button.

```java
1   //Program 8-15 Demonstrate Mouse Listeners on JButtons.
2   //File: MusicBox.java
3
4   import java.awt.*;
5   import java.awt.event.*;
6   import java.applet.AudioClip;
7   import javax.swing.*;
8
9   public class MusicBox extends JApplet
10  {
11    private AudioClip soundDing, soundRing, soundTaDa;
12
13    private JButton dingButton = new JButton( "Ding");
14    private JButton ringButton = new JButton( "Ring");
15    private JButton tadaButton = new JButton( "Ta Da!");
16
17    public void init()
18    {
19        // The place to add GUI widgets.
20        Container canvas = getContentPane();
21
22        // We always need a layout.
23        canvas.setLayout( new GridLayout( 1, 3));
24
25        // Load the *.wav clips.
26        soundDing = getAudioClip( getDocumentBase(), "Ding.wav");
27        soundRing = getAudioClip( getDocumentBase(), "Ringin.wav");
28        soundTaDa = getAudioClip( getDocumentBase(), "Tada.wav");
29
30        //Place mouse listeners on the buttons.
31        //Change the button color when the mouse moves over the button.
```

```
32          //If the mouse is pressed, play a sound.
33          ringButton.addMouseListener(new MouseAdapter()
34          {
35                  public void mouseEntered(MouseEvent e)
36                  {
37                          ringButton.setBackground(Color.CYAN);
38                  }
39                  public void mouseExited(MouseEvent e)
40                  {
41                          ringButton.setBackground(Color.lightGray);
42                  }
43                  public void mousePressed(MouseEvent e)
44                  {
45                          soundRing.play();
46                  }
47          });
48
49          tadaButton.addMouseListener(new MouseAdapter()
50          {
51                  public void mouseEntered(MouseEvent e)
52                  {
53                          tadaButton.setBackground(Color.MAGENTA);
54                  }
55                  public void mouseExited(MouseEvent e)
56                  {
57                          tadaButton.setBackground(Color.lightGray);
58                  }
59                  public void mousePressed(MouseEvent e)
60                  {
61                          //Will play on both the mouse pressed down and up event.
62                          soundTaDa.play();
63                  }
64          });
65
66          dingButton.addMouseListener(new MouseAdapter()
67          {
68                  public void mouseEntered(MouseEvent e)
69                  {
70                          dingButton.setBackground(Color.YELLOW);
71                  }
72                  public void mouseExited(MouseEvent e)
73                  {
74                          dingButton.setBackground(Color.lightGray);
75                  }
76                  public void mousePressed(MouseEvent e)
77                  {
```

8

```
78                          soundDing.play();
79                      }
80              });
81
82          // Add the buttons to the contentPane.
83          canvas.add( dingButton);
84          canvas.add( ringButton);
85          canvas.add( tadaButton);
86      }
87
88      // Stop playing any audio if stop is called.
89      public void stop()
90      {
91          soundDing.stop();
92          soundRing.stop();
93          soundTaDa.stop();
94      }
95  }
```

Figure 8-22
The mouse is currently over the Ring button in this applet. Mouse listeners track the mouse's movement in and out of the buttons, changing their color if the mouse enters the button. An audio clip is played if the mouse button is pressed.

JMenuBar

the bar across the top of the frame. Holds JMenus objects

JMenus

pop-up windows that contain JMenuItems and JSeparators

JMenuItems

menu items that have associated actions and perform tasks for the Program

8.6
Java Menus

Implementing menus in Java is not a difficult task if the programmer understands the basic menu layout system and menu terminology. In a nutshell, the programmer creates a **JMenuBar** and adds **JMenus** to the menu bar. **JMenuItems** are added to the JMenus. ActionListeners are used to implement the desired menu events. The menu bar is set into the frame by using a setJMenuBar() method. Java provides hot keys, also known as accelerators, as well as mnemonics, which are the underlined

TABLE 8-7

TABLE 8-7
Menu terminology.

Menu component or part	Description and purpose
JMenuBar	The JMenuBar is the bar across the top of the frame that holds JMenus objects. You must add JMenu objects to the JMenuBar object to construct a menu. The MenuMadness menu bar contains the File and Help JMenu objects.
JMenu	JMenu objects are pop-up windows that contain JMenuItems and JSeparators.
JMenuItem	JMenuItems are menu items that have an associated action. You may think of a JMenuItem object as a button sitting in a list. When the user selects the "button," the action associated with the menu item is performed.
Accelerator	An accelerator is a key event that is associated with a JMenuItem. In the MenuMadness program, File → Save has the Ctrl-S accelerator. If the user presses Ctrl-S, that menu item action is invoked. The user does not need to go through the chain of menu and menu items.
Mnemonic	A mnemonic is a key event that is associated with JMenus or JMenuItems. In the MenuMadness program, the JMenu File has the "F" as a mnemonic. The File → Save has the "S" as a mnemonic. In order to use the mnemonic keys, the user must press Alt-F (for File) and then just S for Save. The Alt key is required for the first menu or menu item in the menu chain.

letters in the menu items that allow the user to use the keys instead of the mouse to activate the menu events.

The MenuMadness Program

In Program 8-16, MenuMadness, we create a frame that has a menu bar. The menu bar has two pull-down menus, one named File, the other named Help. Table 8-7 shows basic menu terminology and Figures 8-23 and 8-24 on page 510 illustrate the MenuMadness menu components. Study these figures and the above table! The mechanics of building the menu structure in this program are much clearer if the reader understands these two items.

In the MenuMadness program, all of the menu items pass a message to a showDialog() method that pops up a JOptionPane dialog box. We use the this.get-ContentPane() for the parent component so that our dialog box pops up within the frame. In regards to menu events, we keep it simple sweetie, so that you may concentrate on how the menu is built.

Read through the source code in Program 8-16 and study Table 8-7 and Figure 8-23 carefully. Notice how we create and add the various menu components. We create a JMenuBar and add JMenu objects to it. We create JMenuItems and add them to the JMenus. For each JMenuItem we have an ActionListener to handle the menu event. Figure 8-24 shows the menus this program creates.

```java
1    //Program 8-16 Demonstrate Menu Features in Java
2    //File:  MenuMadness.java
3
4    import java.awt.Event;
5    import java.awt.event.*;
6    import javax.swing.*;
7
8    public class MenuMadness extends JFrame
9    {
10       private JMenuBar menubar;
11       private Icon saveIcon, saveAllIcon, deleteIcon;
12
13       public MenuMadness()
14       {
15            this.setTitle("Menu Madness");
16            this.setDefaultCloseOperation(EXIT_ON_CLOSE);
17
18            loadIcons();
19            createFileMenu();
20            createHelpMenu();
21
22            //Here is where the menu bar is set into the JFrame.
23            this.setJMenuBar(menubar);
24            this.setSize(350, 200);
25            this.show();
26       }
27
28   //Displays a dialog internally to MenuMadness class.
29   //The various menu handlers pass the message, title,
30   //type of option and JOptionPane icon to this method.
31     public void showDialog(String message, String title,
32                 int option, int icon)
33     {
34            JOptionPane.showInternalConfirmDialog(this.getContentPane(),
35                message, title, option, icon);
36     }
37
```

```
38      //Loads the icons which are displayed in the File Menu.
39       private void loadIcons()
40       {
41              saveIcon = new ImageIcon("Save16.gif");
42              saveAllIcon = new ImageIcon("SaveAll116.gif");
43              deleteIcon = new ImageIcon("Delete16.gif");
44       }
45
46      //Creates the File Menu with all Listeners, Virtual Keys and Icons.
47      //The File menu has Save, Save All, and Delete menu items.
48       private void createFileMenu()
49       {
50              JMenu menu = new JMenu("File");
51              menu.setMnemonic(KeyEvent.VK_F);    //underlined letter F
52
53              //File->Save menu item
54              JMenuItem menuItem = new JMenuItem("Save", saveIcon);
55              menuItem.setMnemonic(KeyEvent.VK_S);
56
57              //Accelerators set up the hotkeys for the menu items.
58              menuItem.setAccelerator(
59                      KeyStroke.getKeyStroke(KeyEvent.VK_S, Event.CTRL_MASK));
60              menuItem.addActionListener(     new ActionListener()
61              {
62                      public void actionPerformed(ActionEvent e)
63                      {
64                              showDialog("Are you sure you want to save?", "Save?",
65                                      JOptionPane.YES_NO_CANCEL_OPTION,
66                                      JOptionPane.QUESTION_MESSAGE);
67                      }
68              });
69
70              menu.add(menuItem);
71
72              //File->Save All menu item
73              menuItem = new JMenuItem("Save All", saveAllIcon);
74              menuItem.setMnemonic(KeyEvent.VK_A);
75              menuItem.addActionListener(     new ActionListener()
76              {
77                      public void actionPerformed(ActionEvent e)
78                      {
79                              showDialog("Are you sure you want to save all?",
80                              "Save All?", JOptionPane.YES_NO_CANCEL_OPTION,
81                              JOptionPane.QUESTION_MESSAGE);
82                      }
83              });
84              menu.add(menuItem);
85
```

8

```
86          menu.addSeparator();
87
88          //File->Delete menu item
89          menuItem = new JMenuItem("Delete", deleteIcon);
90          menuItem.setMnemonic(KeyEvent.VK_D);
91          menuItem.setAccelerator(
92                      KeyStroke.getKeyStroke(KeyEvent.VK_D, Event.CTRL_MASK));
93          menuItem.addActionListener( new ActionListener()
94          {
95                  public void actionPerformed(ActionEvent e)
96                  {
97                          showDialog("Are you sure you want to delete all?",
98                          "Delete?", JOptionPane.YES_NO_CANCEL_OPTION,
99                          JOptionPane.ERROR_MESSAGE);
100                 }
101         });
102         menu.add(menuItem);
103
104         menubar = new JMenuBar();
105         menubar.add(menu);
106     }
107
108  //Creates the Help Menu and adds it to the main Menu of the application.
109  //The Help has Other>  JMenu and About Menu item.
110   private void createHelpMenu()
111   {
112         JMenu menu = new JMenu("Help");
113         menu.setMnemonic(KeyEvent.VK_H);
114
115         //Help->Other JMenu
116         JMenu otherMenu = new JMenu("Other");
117         otherMenu.setMnemonic(KeyEvent.VK_O);
118
119         //Help->Other->Curious menu item.
120         JMenuItem menuItem = new JMenuItem("Curious");
121         menuItem.setMnemonic(KeyEvent.VK_C);
122         menuItem.addActionListener(      new ActionListener()
123         {
124                 public void actionPerformed(ActionEvent e)
125                 {
126                         showDialog("Is your name Barbara?", "Curious?",
127                         JOptionPane.YES_NO_OPTION,
128                         JOptionPane.QUESTION_MESSAGE);
129                 }
```

8

```
130           });
131           otherMenu.add(menuItem);
132
133           //Help->Other->Smart Guy menu item.
134           menuItem = new JMenuItem("Smart Guy");
135           menuItem.setMnemonic(KeyEvent.VK_G);
136           menuItem.addActionListener( new ActionListener()
137           {
138                 public void actionPerformed(ActionEvent e)
139                 {
140                       showDialog("Would you believe I am intelligent?",
141                       "Yes, Marc is a smart guy!",
142                       JOptionPane.YES_OPTION,
143                       JOptionPane.INFORMATION_MESSAGE);
144                 }
145           });
146           otherMenu.add(menuItem);
147           menu.add(otherMenu);
148
149           menu.addSeparator();
150
151           //Help->About menu item
152           menuItem = new JMenuItem("About");
153           menuItem.setMnemonic(KeyEvent.VK_A);
154           menuItem.addActionListener( new ActionListener()
155           {
156                 public void actionPerformed(ActionEvent e)
157                 {
158                       showDialog("Java Programming Today, Menus!",
159                             "Menu Madness About",
160                             JOptionPane.YES_NO_OPTION,
161                             JOptionPane.INFORMATION_MESSAGE);
162                 }
163           });
164           menu.add(menuItem);
165           menubar.add(menu);
166     }
167
168     public static void main(String[] args)
169     {
170           new MenuMadness();
171     }
172 }
```

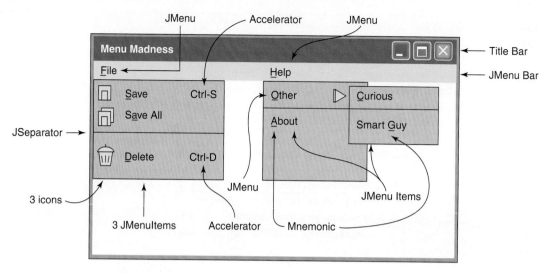

Figure 8-23
The MenuMadness program's menu layout showing the JMenuBar, JMenus, JMenu-Items, and other parts. If a JMenu has a JMenu added to it, such as the Help →
Other, an arrow is automatically drawn indicating another list of menu items.

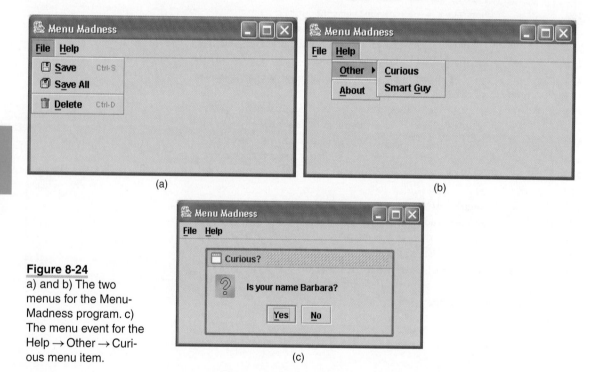

(a)   (b)

Figure 8-24
a) and b) The two menus for the Menu-Madness program. c) The menu event for the Help → Other → Curious menu item.

(c)

Menus, Dots, Lines, and JPanel's paintComponent()

This next program illustrates how we can use menu items and a slider control to supply the drawing parameters for a JPanel object. In Program 8-17 and Figure 8-25, we draw randomly placed colored lines or dots (of different colors) in a window. We control the number of dots and/or lines with the aid of a JSlider that has a selection range from one to twenty-five. We incorporate a JMenu that has a Draw menu with two JCheck-BoxMenuItem objects—one that toggles the lines and one that toggles the dots.

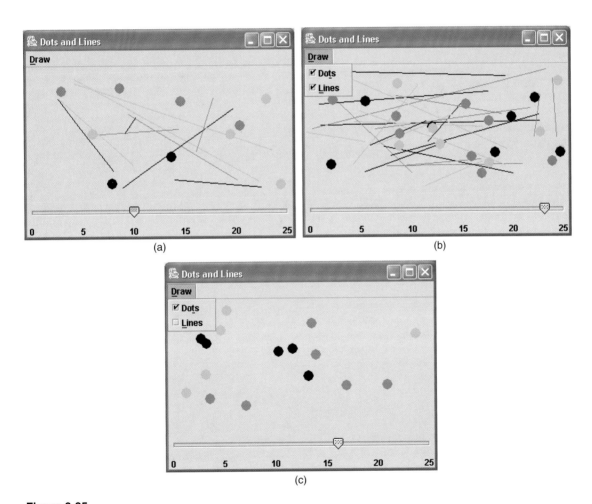

Figure 8-25
The menu items and slider control the drawing in the panel seen in the window.
a) The initial window on program start-up. b) and c) The slider determines the number of lines and/or dots that are displayed.

Examine Figure 8-25a. This shows the initial window when the program begins. We have set the initial slider value to ten, and turned on both the lines and dots. Figure 8-25b shows twenty-three lines and dots as well as the two check menu items. (Two dots are covered by the menu.) Unchecking the lines and running the slider to sixteen produces the window we see in Figure 8-25c. If the random lines portion of this program sounds familiar, you are correct! We wrote a LineGenerator class in Chapter 6, and have used this class in this program to generate the line (and dot) coordinates for us.

```
1    //Program 8-17 Menus and Drawing
2    //File:  MenuDraw.java
3
4    import java.awt.*;
5    import java.awt.event.*;
6    import javax.swing.*;
7    import javax.swing.event.*;
8
9    public class MenuDraw extends JFrame
10   {
11       private JMenuBar menubar;
12       private int numberToDraw;
13       private JSlider slider;
14
15       private DotsLinesPanel myPanel = new DotsLinesPanel();
16
17       //These bools controls the dot and line drawing.
18       //If they they are true, we'll draw the dots and/or lines.
19       boolean bDotsOn, bLinesOn;
20
21       private JCheckBoxMenuItem menuItemD =
22                       new JCheckBoxMenuItem("Dots");
23       private JCheckBoxMenuItem menuItemL =
24                       new JCheckBoxMenuItem("Lines");
25
26       public MenuDraw()
27       {
28           this.setTitle("Dots and Lines");
29
30           menubar = new JMenuBar();      //Set up menu.
31           createDrawMenu();
32           bDotsOn = true;
33           bLinesOn = true;
34
35           //Show the menu items checked.
36           menuItemD.setState(bDotsOn);
37           menuItemL.setState(bLinesOn);
```

```
38
39              //Set the range of the window for the line generator.
40              myPanel.setRanges(375,175);
41
42              createSlider();
43
44              Container canvas = this.getContentPane();
45
46              this.setJMenuBar(menubar);
47              canvas.setLayout( new BorderLayout() );
48              canvas.add(myPanel, BorderLayout.CENTER);
49              canvas.add(slider,BorderLayout.SOUTH);
50              this.setSize(400, 300);
51
52              myPanel.drawMe(bDotsOn,bLinesOn,numberToDraw);
53              this.show();
54      }
55
56      public void createSlider()
57      {
58              //Horizontal slider is default,
59              //just add range, initial position,ticks.
60              slider = new JSlider(0,25,10);
61              slider.setMajorTickSpacing(5);
62              slider.setMinorTickSpacing(1);
63              slider.setPaintTicks(true);
64              slider.setForeground(Color.CYAN);
65              slider.setSnapToTicks(true);
66              slider.setPaintLabels(true);
67
68              //set number to the slider's initial value
69              numberToDraw = slider.getValue();
70
71              //If the slider's thumb is moved, redraw the panel.
72              slider.addChangeListener( new ChangeListener()
73              {
74                      public void stateChanged( ChangeEvent ce)
75                      {
76                              numberToDraw = slider.getValue();
77                              myPanel.drawMe(bDotsOn,bLinesOn,numberToDraw);
78                      }
79              });
80      }
81
82  //Creates the Draw Menu and adds it to the main Menu.
83      private void createDrawMenu()
84      {
85              JMenu menu = new JMenu("Draw");
86              menu.setMnemonic(KeyEvent.VK_D);
```

```
87
88              //Draw->Dots menu item.
89              menuItemD.setMnemonic(KeyEvent.VK_T);
90              menuItemD.addActionListener( new ActionListener()
91              {
92                      public void actionPerformed(ActionEvent e)
93                      {
94                              //Toggle the dot's bool and use it
95                              //to set/unset the menu item check.
96                              bDotsOn = !bDotsOn;
97                              menuItemD.setState(bDotsOn);
98                              myPanel.drawMe(bDotsOn,bLinesOn,numberToDraw);
99                      }
100             });
101             menu.add(menuItemD);
102
103             //Draw->Lines menu item.
104             menuItemL.setMnemonic(KeyEvent.VK_L);
105             menuItemL.addActionListener( new ActionListener()
106             {
107                     public void actionPerformed(ActionEvent e)
108                     {
109                             //Work the lines just like the dots.
110                             bLinesOn = !bLinesOn;
111                             menuItemL.setState(bLinesOn);
112                             myPanel.drawMe(bDotsOn,bLinesOn,numberToDraw);
113                     }
114             });
115
116             menu.add(menuItemL);
117             menubar.add(menu);
118     }
119
120     public static void main(String[] args)
121     {
122             MenuDraw theApp = new MenuDraw();
123             theApp.setDefaultCloseOperation(EXIT_ON_CLOSE);
124     }
125 }
```

The design of this program includes a DrawMenu class that extends JFrame. The menu and slider are set up in this class, and we instantiate a DotsLinesPanel object. We use a BorderLayout in the DrawMenu class and place the slider in the SOUTH region and the panel in the CENTER region. We place ActionListeners on the two menu items and a ChangeListener on the slider. In a nutshell, we allow the panel to draw itself when our program needs to have the panel redrawn. First, study the DrawMenu class and see how we set up the menu and slide, and instantiate the panel.

The DotsLinePanel class extends JPanel. We instantiate a LineGenerator object in this class, and its getCoords() method is called to acquire the random values for the lines and the dots. The DotsLinePanel's drawMe() method is called from the DrawMenu class whenever we wish to draw in the panel. The drawMe() method calls repaint(), which in turn calls the paintComponent() method. The **paintComponent()** method is passed a Graphics object that gives us the capability to draw items such as lines or dots (little circles) on the screen. Remember that in a JFrame or JApplet we write the paint() method. It too is passed a Graphics object. The JPanel uses paintComponent() instead of paint(). A better name for paintComponent() could be howToDrawMyself(). Study the code carefully or better yet, run the program from the text's CD. The LineGenerator class is not shown here. You will find it in Chapter 6, Program 6-5, on page 309.

paintComponent
this method is passed a Graphics object and gives us the capability to draw items for the component, such as for a panel

```
1   //Program 8-17
2   //File:  DotsLinesPanel.java
3
4   //This class uses paintComponent() to draw itself.
5   //We have a drawMe() method that calls paint()
6   //which in turn calls paintComponent().
7
8   //We'll use the LineGenerator from Chapter 6.
9
10  import javax.swing.*;
11  import java.awt.*;
12
13  public class DotsLinesPanel extends JPanel
14  {
15     private boolean bLinesOn, bDotsOn;
16     private int number;
17
18     //Here is our LineGenerator from Chapter 6!
19     private LineGenerator lines = new LineGenerator();
20     private      int coords[] = new int [4];
21
22     public DotsLinesPanel()
23     {
24           //For default, we set line gen. range to 200,200.
25           lines.setRanges(200,200);
26     }
27
28     public void setRanges(int width, int height)
29     {
30           lines.setRanges(width,height);
31     }
```

8

```
32
33     public void drawMe(boolean bDotsOn, boolean bLinesOn, int number)
34     {
35          this.bLinesOn = bLinesOn;
36          this.bDotsOn = bDotsOn;
37          this.number = number;
38
39          repaint();            //calls paintComponent()
40     }
41
42     //The paintComponent() method draws the panel for us.
43     //It replaces the paint() method.
44     public void paintComponent(Graphics g)
45     {
46          //We must call the super method to ensure drawing is correctly done
47          super.paintComponent(g);
48
49          if(bLinesOn)
50          {
51               for(int i = 0; i < number; ++i)
52               {
53                    g.setColor(lines.getColor() );
54
55                    //coords are x1, y1, x2, y2
56                    coords = lines.getCoords();
57                    g.drawLine(coords[0],coords[1], coords[2], coords[3]);
58               }
59          }
60
61          if(bDotsOn)
62          {
63               for(int i = 0; i < number; ++i)
64               {
65                    g.setColor(lines.getColor() );
66
67                    //we'll use x1,y1 for center pt
68                    coords = lines.getCoords();
69                    g.fillOval(coords[0],coords[1], 15,15);
70               }
71          }  //end if
72     } //end paintComponent()
73 } //end class
```

8.7
Threads

At times it seems that computers are able to perform several tasks at once. If you are sitting at your computer and have an Internet news service updating headlines in one window while you are writing your Java program in another, and the controls for your current music selection are in a third window, your computer appears to be performing several tasks at once! Actually, the computer's operating system splits its time between the different processes. This means that the system runs one process for a short time (fractions of a second), switches to the next process and runs it, and so forth. The operating system must remember each program state as it jumps from one process to the next.

In a Java program you may need to perform several tasks at once. The Java Virtual Machine adopts the same timesharing scheme as the operating system in that it works on a portion of the program, switches to the next portion and works on it, etc. Java allows the programmer to use this timesharing operation by incorporating **control threads** into his or her program. Control threads, or threads, are Java's way to allow a program to switch between different functions executing at the same time. Up until now, we have written unthreaded programs—meaning that only one thing occurred at a time.

control thread
Java's way to allow a program to switch between different functions executing at the same time

> **Note:** We present the Thread topic with the GUI components because it is an easy place to visualize how Thread works. The reader should not assume that Threads are a subset of GUI construction nor that Threads are only used with GUI components. Refer to an advanced Java reference (see bibliography) for a complete discussion on Threads.

BadGoStopCounter: An Example That Needs Threads

Let's examine a Java program that produces disasterous results. The idea behind this program is simple. We set up two buttons, a Go button and a Stop button. The Go button starts a loop that prints a counter value (an integer) to the MS-DOS Prompt Window. The counter values increase as the loop runs, i.e., 1, 2, 3, 4, 5, ... When the user presses the Stop button, the program stops the counter. We incorporate a boolean flag in the condition part of a while loop and the two buttons toggle the value of this flag (On or Off).

Program 8-18 (Bad) shows this bad example. If you are brave enough to run this, you will see that when you press the Go button, the loop begins and the program writes the counter value to the window. The trouble begins when you press Stop. Pressing the Stop button is futile because the program is busy performing the loop and never acknowledges the button press. Pressing the X on the title bar is also useless. The program never returns to "listen" for any GUI commands. You may kill

8

this program by pressing Control-c (Ctrl-c) in the MS-DOS Prompt window or using the Task Manager to stop the process.

```
1   //Program 8-18 (Bad)
2   //BadGoStopCounter.java
3
4   //When the user presses the Go button, this BAD
5   //example starts a counter running and the program
6   //becomes non-responsive. The JVM is busy running the loop
7   //and never comes back to us. If you run this, you will have to
8   //stop it by killing the task via the Task Manager. :-(>
9
10  //We would expect that when we press the Stop button, the
11  //go variable is set to false and stops the counter loop.
12  //Ha ha. Nope. It doesn't work that way.
13
14  import javax.swing.*;
15  import java.awt.*;
16  import java.awt.event.ActionListener;
17  import java.awt.event.ActionEvent;
18
19  public class BadGoStopCounter extends JFrame implements ActionListener
20  {
21     JButton goButton = new JButton("Go");
22     JButton stopButton = new JButton("Stop");
23     JLabel goStopLabel = new JLabel("Start and stop the counter",
24                                     JLabel.CENTER);
25     JLabel counterLabel = new JLabel("Look in the System window!",
26                                     JLabel.CENTER);
27
28     int counter;
29     boolean go;
30
31     public BadGoStopCounter()
32     {
33         //We set the counter flag to true so we
34         //start on the button push.
35         go = true;
36         this.setTitle("Bad Go and Stop Counter!");
37
38         Container canvas = getContentPane();
39
40         canvas.setLayout( new GridLayout(4,1) );
41
42         //Add the controls to the container.
```

```
43              canvas.add(goStopLabel);
44              canvas.add(goButton);
45              canvas.add(stopButton);
46              canvas.add(counterLabel);
47
48              //Put listeners on the buttons.
49              goButton.addActionListener(this);
50              stopButton.addActionListener(this);
51
52              //Set the size of the window and show it.
53              this.setSize(275,150);
54              this.show();
55      }
56
57      public static void main(String args[] )
58      {
59              BadGoStopCounter theApp = new BadGoStopCounter();
60              theApp.setDefaultCloseOperation(JFrame.EXIT_ON_CLOSE);
61      }
62
63      public void actionPerformed(ActionEvent e)
64      {
65              System.out.println("button push");
66              if(e.getSource() == goButton)
67              {
68                      //As long as go is true, write the counter value.
69                      while(go)
70                      {
71                              ++counter;
72                              System.out.println("Counter = " +
73                                              Integer.toString(counter);
74
75                              //We'll slow down this loop with marcsPause().
76                              marcsPause(100);
77                      }
78              }
79              else if( e.getSource() == stopButton)
80              {
81                      go = false;          //set to false, stop the loop
82              }
83      }
84
85      void marcsPause(int ms)
86      {
87              try
```

```
88              {
89                      Thread.sleep(ms);
90              }
91              catch(InterruptedException e){ }
92      }
93  }
```

How to use Threads

Java programmers should use threads so that their programs never "go away," as seen in the above example. Programs should be designed so that GUI events have their own threads and are able to respond to and perform their tasks while other threads perform tasks such as file I/O, computations, and sorting large lists. You can think of threads as subprograms within your program.

A **Thread** is a class in the java.lang package. There are three ways to obtain a thread in Java. You may extend the Thread class, write your own class that implements the Runnable interface, or write Threads as inner classes. Writing a Thread class lets the programmer have many threads, whereas a class that implements Runnable gains only one thread. We present three thread examples here that show how threads may be used with GUI components. These are the three ways that threads are commonly used in Java programs.

GoodGoStopCounter implements Runnable   We rewrite our GoStop-Counter example so that we implement the **Runnable interface**. When a programmer uses this approach, he or she must write a run() method and the thread must be started by explicitly calling the thread's start() method. The run() method should contain the portion of our program that runs independently. We will place our counter loop in the run() method.

In the GoodGoStopCounter program, we make a Thread reference named counterThread as a class variable. In the Go button's actionPerformed() method, if we do not have a counterThread object already, we create one using the new

8

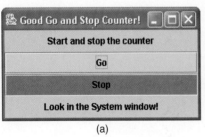

```
C:\JPT\Ch8_JavaCode\GoStopCounters-18>java  GoodGoStopCounter
****Go button push!
Counter = 1
Counter = 2
Counter = 3
Counter = 4
Counter = 5
Counter = 6
====>Stop button push.
****Go button push!
Counter = 7
Counter = 8
Counter = 9
====>Stop button push.
```

(a)   (b)

Figure 8-26
a) The frame with the Go and Stop buttons. b) The MS-DOS Prompt window showing the counter value and go and stop messages.

operator. We must pass in the GoodGoStopCounter class to the thread's constructor. We also start the counterThread by calling its start() method. The start() method calls the thread's run() method. Study Program 8-18 (Good) and Figure 8-26.

```java
//Program 8-18 (Good)
//GoodGoStopCounter.java

//We implementing Runnable with this class.
//We must write a run() method, and start the thread explicitly.
//By implementing Runnable we get one extra thread

//When the user presses the Go button, this GOOD example
//creates a Thread and start() calls run(). A loop begins
//and we print a counter value to the console window.
//If we press Stop, the loop stops. The program
//timeshares between the main program thread and the counterThread.

import javax.swing.*;
import java.awt.*;
import java.awt.event.ActionListener;
import java.awt.event.ActionEvent;

public class GoodGoStopCounter extends JFrame
                implements ActionListener, Runnable
{
    JButton goButton = new JButton("Go");
    JButton stopButton = new JButton("Stop");
    JLabel goStopLabel = new JLabel("Start and stop the counter.",
                    JLabel.CENTER);
    JLabel counterLabel = new JLabel("(Look in the System window!)",
                    JLabel.CENTER);

    //We need a Thread reference.
    Thread counterThread;

    int counter;
    boolean go;

    public GoodGoStopCounter()
    {

        this.setTitle("Good Go and Stop Counter!");

```

```
40              Container canvas = getContentPane();
41              canvas.setLayout( new GridLayout(4,1) );
42
43              //Add the controls to the container.
44              canvas.add(goStopLabel);
45              canvas.add(goButton);
46              canvas.add(stopButton);
47              canvas.add(counterLabel);
48
49              //Put listeners on the buttons.
50              goButton.addActionListener(this);
51              goButton.setBackground(Color.CYAN);
52              stopButton.addActionListener(this);
53              stopButton.setBackground(Color.MAGENTA);
54
55              //Set the size of the window and show it.
56              this.setSize(275,150);
57              this.show();
58        }
59
60     public static void main(String args[] )
61     {
62              GoodGoStopCounter theApp = new GoodGoStopCounter();
63              theApp.setDefaultCloseOperation(JFrame.EXIT_ON_CLOSE);
64     }
65
66     public void actionPerformed(ActionEvent e)
67     {
68              if(e.getSource() == goButton)
69              {
70                   System.out.println("****Go button push!");
71
72                   //If we haven't made a thread, make one and start it.
73                   if(counterThread == null)
74                   {
75                        go = true;
76
77                        //Pass this class in to the Thread so that it
78                        //knows where it belongs.
79                        counterThread = new Thread(GoodGoStopCounter.this);
80
81                        //Now start the thread. This calls run() automatically.
82                        counterThread.start();
83                   }
```

```
 84                    }
 85              else if( e.getSource() == stopButton)
 86              {
 87                      System.out.println("====>Stop button push.");
 88                      go = false;              //set to false, stop the loop
 89
 90                      //Have to set to null if we want to restart.
 91                      counterThread = null;
 92              }
 93      }
 94
 95      //This method must be present when we implement Runnable.
 96      //This is the counterThread's run() method.
 97      public void run()
 98      {
 99              while(go)
100              {
101                      ++counter;
102                      System.out.println("Counter = " + Integer.toString(counter) );
103
104                      //Ah ha! We can ask our counterThread to sleep().
105                      //Thread's sleep() method must be called in a try block.
106                      try
107                      {
108                              counterThread.sleep(100);
109                      }
110                      catch(InterruptedException ie){}
111              }
112      }
113 }
```

UpDownCounters Program, Two Threads and Inner Classes Java programmers find that they often need more than one thread in a program, and that the GoodGoStopCounter example that implements Runnable is not adequate. Why? In our UpDownCounters program we have two counters, one that counts up from zero to one hundred, and one that counts down from one hundred to zero. We wish to start one counter. Once we get it started we want it to keep counting while we start the other one. Do you think we need a thread with each counter? Yes! We will write a complete Thread class for each button's event handling method.

In order to set up a Thread class inside a method we write a local inner class. If you have not yet read Appendix D, *Nested Classes*, now is a good time to read it. In this program we set up two buttons and two labels. When each button is pressed it starts its own thread to perform the counting/displaying task. Figure 8-27 shows this program window.

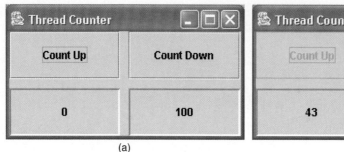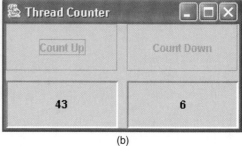

(a)   (b)

Figure 8-27
a) The frame with the Count Up and Count Down buttons. b) The counters in action. Note that the buttons are disabled while the counting tasks are being performed.

Let's examine the most exciting part of the UpDownCounter program here. When the Count Down button is pressed its actionPerformed() method calls the backwardButtonActionPerformed() method. Inside this method we write an inner class (which is a class inside another class or method). This inner class is a thread class. Notice how we make a Thread reference called downThread. We write the entire Thread class inside the backwardButtonActionPerformed() method and call the downThread.start() method at the bottom. Here is a skeleton of the method and class:

```
private void backwardButtonActionPerformed(ActionEvent evt)
{

        //Here is a local inner class. We are writing the Thread
        //class here including the run() method.
        downThread = new Thread()
        {
              //This is where we write the entire class.
              //We must write a run() method.

              public void run()
              {
                    //Performing the counting task here.

              }  //close of run()

        };//close of inner class

        //Now we call downThread's start so that it calls run().
        downThread.start();

}  //close method
```

When the Count Down button is pressed, this method makes its own thread object and starts it running and performing the counting task. The complete program is shown in Program 8-19.

```java
//Program 8-19 Threads and Inner Classes
//File: UpDownCounters.java

//In this program we write local inner classes within
//the actionPerformed() methods.
//This program has a CountUp and CountDown button and
//each button has its own thread.
//We use a more streamlined technique here. Instead of
//obtaining a Container object, we just call getContentPane().

import java.awt.*;
import java.awt.event.*;

import javax.swing.*;
import javax.swing.border.BevelBorder;

public class UpDownCounters extends JFrame implements ActionListener
{

    JButton upButton = new JButton("Count Up");
    JButton downButton = new JButton("Count Down");
    JLabel upLabel = new JLabel("0", JLabel.CENTER);
    JLabel downLabel = new JLabel("100", JLabel.CENTER);

    private Thread upThread;
    private Thread downThread;

    public UpDownCounters()
    {
        //GridLayout inputs( rows, cols, horizGap, vertGap)
        getContentPane().setLayout(new GridLayout(2, 2, 10, 10));
        this.setTitle("Thread Counter");

        initComponents();
        this.setSize(275,150);
        this.show();
    }

```

```
39      private void initComponents()
40      {
41              //Set up the actionListeners and add the
42              //buttons to the content pane.
43
44              upButton.addActionListener(this);
45              getContentPane().add(upButton);
46              downButton.addActionListener(this);
47              getContentPane().add(downButton);
48
49              upLabel.setBorder(new BevelBorder(BevelBorder.LOWERED));
50              getContentPane().add(upLabel);
51
52              downLabel.setBorder(new BevelBorder(BevelBorder.LOWERED));
53              getContentPane().add(downLabel);
54      }
55
56      public void actionPerformed(ActionEvent ae)
57      {
58              if (ae.getSource() == upButton)
59              {
60                      forwardButtonActionPerformed(ae);
61              }
62              else if (ae.getSource() == downButton)
63              {
64                      backwardButtonActionPerformed(ae);
65              }
66      }
67
68      private void backwardButtonActionPerformed(ActionEvent evt)
69      {
70              //Turn off the button so we can't press it again.
71              downButton.setEnabled(false);
72
73              //Here is a local inner class. We are writing the Thread
74              //class here including the run() method.
75              downThread = new Thread()
76              {
77                      public void run()
78                      {
79                              for (int i=100; i > -1; i--)
80                              {
81                                      downLabel.setText(String.valueOf(i));
82                                      try
83                                      {
```

```
84                                   Thread.currentThread().sleep(50);
85                              } catch (InterruptedException e) {}
86                      }
87                      downButton.setEnabled(true);
88              }
89      };    //close of inner class
90
91      //Now we call downThread's start so that it calls run().
92      downThread.start();
93  }
94
95  //The forward button works the same as the backwards button.
96  private void forwardButtonActionPerformed(ActionEvent evt)
97  {
98      upButton.setEnabled(false);
99
100     //The inner class for this Thread.
101     upThread = new Thread()
102     {
103             public void run()
104             {
105                     for (int i=0; i < 101; i++)
106                     {
107                             upLabel.setText(String.valueOf(i));
108                             try
109                             {
110                                     Thread.currentThread().sleep(50);
111                             } catch (InterruptedException e) {}
112                     }
113                     upButton.setEnabled(true);
114             }
115     };
116
117     //Now run the Thread's run() method by calling start().
118     upThread.start();
119 }
120
121 public static void main(String[] args)
122 {
123     UpDownCounters theApp = new UpDownCounters();
124     theApp.setDefaultCloseOperation(EXIT_ON_CLOSE);
125 }
126 }
```

8

StopThreadCounters Program and volatile Threads The next logical question you may ask is, "How do I stop a thread while it is performing its task?" Good question. The answer is shown in the StopThreadCounters program. The trick required for stopping a thread as it runs is to declare the Thread reference as **volatile**. Volatile is a keyword modifier that allows us to change the value of the Thread reference during execution. If we build in a check to ensure that the Thread reference is still current, we have a way to stop the task that is being performed if the Thread reference value changes. It may seem like rocket science at first glance, but in reality (and in this example), we are relying on a for loop condition to fail to make the process stop.

In this StopThreadCounters program we place four buttons and two labels in a frame, as seen in Figure 8-28. We initialize the counter values to zero, and when the buttons are pressed, the program begins counting up or counting down. If left alone, the counters would continue to run until the program reaches the far end of the integer ranges. Figure 8-28B shows the program where the Forward counter was started and a few seconds later the Backward counter started. Figure 8-28C shows how we have stopped the Backwards counter and continue to run the Forward counter.

volatile

a keyword modifier that allows us to change the value of the thread reference during execution. The volatile modifier can also be used for other purposes

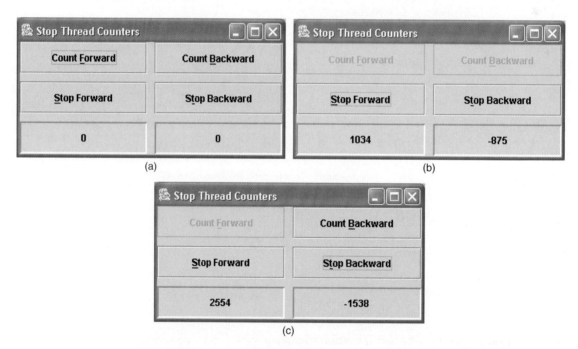

(a)   (b)

(c)

Figure 8-28
a) The frame with the four buttons and two labels. b) Both counters in action. Note that the buttons are disabled while the counting tasks are being performed. c) How it is possible to stop one of the counters while the other counter continues. This functionality is due to the fact that we use volatile Thread objects that allow us to change their values during execution.

Chapter 8 ▌ Java Graphical User Interface Construction

A note concerning Threads. If two or more Threads are accessing the same class data, it is important that the programmer synchronize the Thread objects so that the data values remain consistent and true. Threads make their own local copy of class data and it is possible that each Thread could have different values in "the same" class variable. To avoid a problem with class data, the Thread objects can be synchronized and class data can be locked when a Thread is using it. Thread synchronization is an advanced Java topic and we'll allow you to explore it with your advanced Java instructor (or research it in one of the many fine references listed in the bibliography).

Now, back to examining the StopThreadCounters program, you can see the Thread references are declared volatile on lines 39 and 40 (page 530):

```
private volatile Thread fThread;
private volatile Thread bThread;
```

The ActionListener's actionPerformed() method checks to see which of the four buttons has been pressed. The Count Forward and Count Backward buttons call methods that contain the Thread inner classes that perform the counting activity. The Stop buttons set their respective Thread references to null and re-enable their buttons.

```
//Handles all of the action events.
public void actionPerformed(ActionEvent ae)
{
        if (ae.getSource() == fb)   //Count Forwards
        {
                forwardButtonActionPerformed(ae);
        }
        else if (ae.getSource() == bb)      //Count Backward
        {
                backwardButtonActionPerformed(ae);
        }
        else if (ae.getSource() == bsb)//Stop Backwards
        {
//We set the back Thread to null. This goofs up the for loop ;-).
                bThread = null;
                bb.setEnabled(true);
        }
        else if (ae.getSource() == fsb) //Stop Forwards
        {
//Set the forward Thread to null here.
                fThread = null;
                fb.setEnabled(true);
        }
}
```

We use inner classes again (as we did in the previous program) for writing Threads classes. The counting activity is performed in both of the Thread's run()

methods. Examine the complete program and notice how changing the Thread references causes the for loop condition to fail (see lines 135 and 160 on page 533), thus stopping the loop and the counting task.

```
1    //Program 8-20
2    //File:  StopThreadCounters.java
3
4    //In this program we make the threads volatile.
5    //This allows us to change the value of the thread
6    //during its execution.
7
8    import java.awt.*;
9    import java.awt.event.*;
10
11   import javax.swing.*;
12   import javax.swing.border.BevelBorder;
13
14   public class StopThreadCounters extends JFrame implements ActionListener
15   {
16
17   // Buttons: forward fb, back bb, forward stop fsb, and back stop bsb
18
19       JButton fb = new JButton("Count Forward");
20       JButton bb = new JButton("Count Backward");
21       JButton fsb = new JButton("Stop Forward");
22       JButton bsb = new JButton("Stop Backward");
23
24       // forward stores the current forward counter value.
25       int forward = 0;
26       JLabel fl = new JLabel(String.valueOf(forward),
27                              JLabel.CENTER);
28
29       // backward stores the current backward counter value.
30       int backward = 0;
31       JLabel bl = new JLabel(String.valueOf(backward),
32                              JLabel.CENTER);
33
34       //Using the volatile keyword allows us to change the value of
35       //the thread quickly during mid-execution per the stop request
36       //If we set the volatile Thread to null the for loop quits.
37       //Access to these threads could also be synchronized
38
39       private volatile Thread fThread;
40       private volatile Thread bThread;
```

```
41
42      public StopThreadCounters()
43      {
44            this.setTitle("Stop Thread Counters");
45            initComponents();
46
47            //GridLayout inputs (rows, cols, horizGap, vertGap)
48            getContentPane().setLayout(new GridLayout(3, 2, 10, 10));
49
50            this.setSize(350,175);
51            this.show();
52      }
53
54      //Initialize all the GUI components.
55      private void initComponents()
56      {
57
58      //Set mnemonics for each button to provide keyboard control
59      //of the buttons--i.e. use alt-f for the forward button, etc.
60            fb.setMnemonic('f');
61            fb.addActionListener(this);
62            getContentPane().add(fb);
63
64            bb.setMnemonic('b');
65            bb.addActionListener(this);
66            getContentPane().add(bb);
67
68            fsb.setMnemonic('s');
69            fsb.addActionListener(this);
70            getContentPane().add(fsb);
71
72            bsb.setMnemonic('t');
73            bsb.addActionListener(this);
74            getContentPane().add(bsb);
75
76            fl.setBorder(new BevelBorder(BevelBorder.LOWERED));
77            getContentPane().add(fl);
78
79            bl.setBorder(new BevelBorder(BevelBorder.LOWERED));
80            getContentPane().add(bl);
81      }
82
83      //Handles all of the action events.
84      public void actionPerformed(ActionEvent ae)
85      {
```

```
86              if (ae.getSource() == fb)   //Count Forwards
87              {
88                      forwardButtonActionPerformed(ae);
89              }
90              else if (ae.getSource() == bb)     //Count Backward
91              {
92                      backwardButtonActionPerformed(ae);
93              }
94              else if (ae.getSource() == bsb)     //Stop Backwards
95              {
96
97      //We set the back Thread to null. This goofs up the for loop ;-).
98              bThread = null;
99              bb.setEnabled(true);
100             }
101             else if (ae.getSource() == fsb) //Stop Forwards
102             {
103     //Set the forward Thread to null here.
104             fThread = null;
105             fb.setEnabled(true);
106             }
107     }
108
109     //The member "int backward" holds the current value of the counter
110     //The thread is stopped due to the check "bThread == thisThread"
111     //in the for loop. If bThread is set to "null" it is no longer the
112     //same as "thisThread".
113     //Note that the ActionEvent object is not used
114
115     private void backwardButtonActionPerformed(ActionEvent evt)
116     {
117             bb.setEnabled(false);
118
119             //Here is a local inner class. We are creating the
120             //bThread object and writing Thread class and run() method here.
121
122             bThread = new Thread()
123             {
124                     public void run()
125                     {
126                             //The Thread.currentThread() method returns a
127                             //reference to the currently executing thread object
128                             //As the JVM cycles through the different threads in
129                             //this program, if our threads match, we decrement
```

```
130                         //our counter. If the threads don't match,
131                         //the loop fails and stops executing.
132
133                         Thread thisThread = Thread.currentThread();
134
135                         for(int i = backward; i > Integer.MIN_VALUE
136                                 && bThread == thisThread; i--)
137                         {
138                                 backward = i;
139                                 bl.setText(String.valueOf(i));
140                                 try
141                                 {
142                                         sleep(10);
143                                 } catch (InterruptedException e) {}
144                         }
145                         bb.setEnabled(true);
146                 }
147         };
148         bThread.start();
149 }
150
151 //Same idea as backwardButton code above.
152 private void forwardButtonActionPerformed(ActionEvent evt)
153 {
154         fb.setEnabled(false);
155         fThread = new Thread()
156         {
157                 public void run()
158                 {
159                         Thread thisThread = Thread.currentThread();
160                         for (int i = forward; i < Integer.MAX_VALUE
161                                 && fThread == thisThread; i++)
162                         {
163                                 forward = i;
164                                 fl.setText(String.valueOf(i));
165                                 try
166                                 {
167                                         sleep(10);
168                                 } catch (InterruptedException e) {}
169                         }
170                         fb.setEnabled(true);
171                 }
172         };
173         fThread.start();
174 }
```

8

```
175    public static void main(String[] args)
176
177    {
178            StopThreadCounters theApp = new StopThreadCounters();
179            theApp.setDefaultCloseOperation(EXIT_ON_CLOSE);
180    }
181 }
```

8.8
Summary

In this chapter we introduced the fundamental steps for constructing a GUI for a
Java program. We used the Swing components and set up event handling parts in
our program. No matter what type of component you select, Swing components are
set up in the same manner. A component object can be created by using the new
operator. The object is then placed in a container of some sort, and a listener is
associated with it. When the GUI component receives input from the user, the program runs the appropriate event code.

Layout managers help us arrange our components. In order to have a window
on the screen we must have a class that extends either JFrame or JApplet. We can
then set a layout manager for the frame's container and place individual components such as buttons and sliders, in the container or place JPanel objects that also
have layout managers.

In this chapter we demonstrated many of the commonly used Swing components, including JButtons, JCheckBoxes, JSliders, and JRadioButtons. We showed
how the different layout managers behave, including FlowLayout, GridLayout,
BorderLayout, and CardLayout. JPanels are handy items to group components and
give the programmer flexibility in building their interfaces.

Menus and the relationship between Menus and the JMenuBar, which holds
the JMenus, were described. JMenus are simply lists of JMenuItems. The JMenu-
Item objects have event listeners associated with them so that when a user selects
a menu item from the list, the Java program performs the desired task. Menus in
Java are very flexible, allowing radio buttons, check boxes, and most any Java
control.

Lastly, we presented Threads and how they work hand-in-hand with GUI
components. A Thread allows program portions to run simultaneously because the
JVM performs a timesharing activity that splits its attention between the program
portions. Although we demonstrated Threads with JButtons (for program simplic-
ity) a Thread can be used with many of Java's components or when the program
needs to perform a time-intensive task.

8.9
Practice!

This chapter contains two practice programs, which both present problems commonly encountered by Java GUI builders. The problems involve circumstances where information that is located in JPanels must be "passed up the chain" to the frame or panel that contains it. Or, in a similar situation, JPanels within a frame must interact with each other. The programming solutions shown are straightforward, but advanced object-oriented designers may solve the same problems by using a different, more complicated and elegant design technique. For now, we will (once again) keep it simple, sweetie.

The Mediator Program

A mediator is a person who helps two (or more) people talk to each other. The Mediator Program presents a situation where a JFrame contains three JPanel objects that must interact with each other. For example, Figure 8-29 shows the frame window for this program. This frame has a BorderLayout, and the StudentPanel object has been added in the EAST region of the frame. This panel contains fields for the Java student's name and identification number. The CoursePanel object in the WEST has a combo box for selecting the favorite course. The SummaryPanel in the NORTH has two buttons. When the user presses the Show Summary button, the frame presents a message box with data from both panels. The Reset button clears the student information and resets the favorite course to Java.

   In this chapter's previous panel examples, the frame was able to make requests of the panel by calling a panel's public methods, but the panel was not able

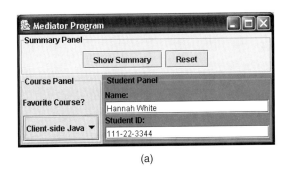
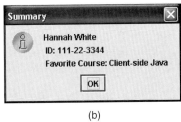

(a)   (b)

Figure 8-29
a) The frame contains three JPanel objects. Student and course data is gathered in two separate panels. b) A request to see a summary message box is made by pressing the button in the top panel. The top panel must communicate to the frame that a button has been pushed. This program shows what must be accomplished in order to have individual panels interact with the JFrame.

to make requests of the frame. Our frames had GUI controls, such as a button. When the button was pressed, the frame gave orders, such as "give me your data," to the panels. But the panels had no way to tell the frame if a button was pressed or to ask the frame to perform a task. Now we have a situation where the panels contain the GUI controls that interact with the user. Our panels must be able to tell the frame when an event has occurred in the panel.

The solution to this problem involves passing a reference to the frame into the panel's constructor. The panel may then use this reference to call the frame's public methods. We place call statements to the frame's methods in the event handling methods of the panels. The frame can then act as a switchboard between the various panels.

Let's look at how we accomplish this task. The MediatorFrame contains the three panel objects. We specify that the panel objects are private data. Remember that any object that has a reference to our MediatorFrame will be able to access the public class members—but not the private ones. By making the panels private, we are not allowing the panels to call methods in other panels.

In order for the SummaryPanel to communicate with the frame, it must have a reference to the frame. We pass it to the panel's constructor:

```
public class MediatorFrame extends JFrame
{
        //These three Panels are located in separate .java files.
        //We make the class data private so that the data is hidden.
        //This means no one outside the class can access the private members.
        private StudentPanel sp = new StudentPanel();
        private CoursePanel cp = new CoursePanel();

        private SummaryPanel sumP = new SummaryPanel(this);
```

The SummaryPanel constructor sets the MediatorFrame reference into its class member, named mrGotPanels.

```
public class SummaryPanel extends JPanel
{
        private JButton showButton = new JButton("Show Summary");
        private JButton resetButton = new JButton("Reset");

        //This is a reference to the JFrame that contains this panel.
        private MediatorFrame mrGotPanels;

        //The constructor receives the reference to the frame.
        public SummaryPanel(MediatorFrame d)
        {
                mrGotPanels = d;
                setUpPanel();
        }
```

8

In the SummaryPanel's actionPerformed() methods we are able to tell the frame about the button press by calling the frame's method.

```
//We call the Frame's public methods from here.
    showButton.addActionListener( new ActionListener ()
    {
        public void actionPerformed(ActionEvent ae)
        {
            mrGotPanels.showSummary();
        }
    });
    resetButton.addActionListener( new ActionListener ()
    {
        public void actionPerformed(ActionEvent ae)
        {
            mrGotPanels.resetPanels();
        }
    });
}
```

We do not allow the individual panels to tell each other what to do because that would tightly bind the panels to one another. That is, if we made a change in one panel, we might then have to make changes in other panels. Therefore, we have the frame act as the switchboard[1] between the panels. In the frame's showSummary() and reset() methods, which are called by the SummaryPanel, the frame calls the appropriate methods in the other two panels:

```
//MediatorFrame methods
    public void showSummary()
    {
            output = sp.getName() + "\n ID: " + sp.getSSN() +
                " \n Favorite Course: " + cp.getFavCourse();

            JOptionPane.showMessageDialog(null,output,"Summary",
                JOptionPane.INFORMATION_MESSAGE);
    }

    public void resetPanels()
    {
            sp.reset();
            cp.reset();
    }
```

---

[1] In "the old days," a telephone switchboard operator would connect one caller to another. A person would pick up his or her phone to connect to the operator who sat in front of a switchboard. The caller would request the person he or she wished to speak with, and the operator would make the connection. The switchboard analogy loosely models what is happening in this program.

The complete program, including all four classes, is shown here in Program 8-21. The MediatorFrame class is shown here:

```
1    //Program 8-21
2    /*In the Mediator program, we have three panels.
3     The StudentPanel gathers info on a student, name and ID.
4     The CoursePanel is used to select your favorite course.
5     The SummaryPanel has two buttons, one for showing the
6     student and course information and one for resetting the
7     panels. We pass the frame's reference to the summary panel.
8     By passing the frame's reference to the summary panel, it
9     can then call the frame's methods.
10
11    This gives us a way to have our panels interact with the
12    frame and therefore with other panels.  */
13
14   import javax.swing.*;
15   import java.awt.*;
16   import java.awt.event.*;
17
18   public class MediatorFrame extends JFrame
19   {
20   //These three Panels are located in separate.java files.
21   //We make the class data private so that the data is hidden.
22   //This means no one outside the class can access the private members.
23
24   private StudentPanel sp = new StudentPanel();
25   private CoursePanel cp = new CoursePanel();
26
27   private SummaryPanel sumP = new SummaryPanel(this);
28
29   String output;
30
31   public MediatorFrame()
32   {
33        Container canvas = getContentPane();
34        canvas.setLayout( new BorderLayout() );
35
36        //Add the panels and button to the frame's container.
37        canvas.add(cp, BorderLayout.WEST);
38        canvas.add(sumP, BorderLayout.NORTH);
39        canvas.add(sp, BorderLayout.CENTER);
40
```

```
41          this.setSize(400,200);
42          this.setTitle("Mediator Program ");
43          this.show();
44     }
45
46     public void showSummary()
47     {
48          output = sp.getName() + "\n ID: " + sp.getSSN() +
49               " \n Favorite Course: " + cp.getFavCourse();
50
51          JOptionPane.showMessageDialog(null,output,"Summary",
52               JOptionPane.INFORMATION_MESSAGE);
53     }
54
55     public void resetPanels()
56     {
57          sp.reset();
58          cp.reset();
59     }
60
61     public static void main( String args[] )
62     {
63          MediatorFrame app = new MediatorFrame();
64          app.setDefaultCloseOperation(JFrame.EXIT_ON_CLOSE);
65     }
66 }
```

The SummaryPanel class receives a reference to the MediatorFrame in its constructor method. (See line 22 on page 540.)

8

```
1   //Program 8-21
2   //File:  SummaryPanel.java
3
4   //This panel is passed the MediatorFrame object reference.
5   //With the MediatorFrame reference, this panel can call
6   //the Frame's resetPanel() and showSummary() methods.
7
8   import javax.swing.*;
9   import java.awt.*;
10  import java.awt.event.*;
11  import javax.swing.border.*;
12
```

```
13   public class SummaryPanel extends JPanel
14   {
15     private JButton showButton = new JButton("Show Summary");
16     private JButton resetButton = new JButton("Reset");
17
18     //This is a reference to the JFrame that contains this panel.
19     private MediatorFrame mrGotPanels;
20
21     //The constructor receives the reference to the frame.
22     public SummaryPanel(MediatorFrame d)
23     {
24          mrGotPanels = d;
25
26          setUpPanel();
27     }
28
29     public void setUpPanel()
30     {
31          //To make a titled border, use the BorderFactory class and then
32          //call the panel's setBorder() method.
33          TitledBorder t1 = BorderFactory.createTitledBorder(
34                          "Summary Panel");
35          setBorder(t1);
36          setLayout( new FlowLayout() );
37          setBackground(Color.CYAN);
38          add(showButton);
39          add(resetButton);
40
41          //We call the Frame's public methods from here.
42          showButton.addActionListener( new ActionListener ()
43          {
44                  public void actionPerformed(ActionEvent  ae)
45                  {
46                          mrGotPanels.showSummary();
47                  }
48          });
49
50          resetButton.addActionListener( new ActionListener ()
51          {
52                  public void actionPerformed(ActionEvent ae)
53                  {
54                          mrGotPanels.resetPanels();
55                  }
56          });
57     }
58   }
```

8

The StudentPanel class has text fields for gathering the student's name and identification number. It does not communicate with the frame. The frame calls its getName() and getSSN() methods.

```
1    //Program 8-21
2    //File: StudentPanel.java
3
4    //This panel obtains the user's name and SSN.
5
6    import javax.swing.*;
7    import java.awt.*;
8    import java.awt.event.*;
9    import javax.swing.border.*;
10
11   public class StudentPanel extends JPanel
12   {
13       private JTextField nameField = new JTextField();
14       private JTextField ssnField = new JTextField();
15       private JLabel nameLabel = new JLabel("Name: " );
16       private JLabel ssnLabel = new JLabel("Student ID: ");
17
18       private String name = "", ssn = "";
19
20       public StudentPanel()
21       {
22           TitledBorder t1 = BorderFactory.createTitledBorder(
23                           "Student Panel");
24           setBorder(t1);
25           setLayout( new GridLayout( 4, 1) );
26
27           setBackground(Color.MAGENTA);
28           add(nameLabel);
29           add(nameField);
30           add(ssnLabel);
31           add(ssnField);
32       }
33
34       public String getName()
35       {
36           name = nameField.getText();
37           return name;
38       }
```

8

```
39
40       public String getSSN()
41       {
42              ssn = ssnField.getText();
43              return ssn;
44       }
45
46       public void reset()
47       {
48              name = ssn = "";
49              nameField.setText("");
50              ssnField.setText("");
51       }
52   }
```

The CoursePanel has a single combo box for favorite course selection. It does not communicate with the frame. The frame calls the panel's getFavCourse() method when it needs to know what the user has selected.

```
1    //Program 8-21
2    //File:  CoursePanel.java
3
4    import java.awt.event.*;
5    import javax.swing.*;
6    import java.awt.*;
7    import javax.swing.border.*;
8
9    public class CoursePanel extends JPanel
10   {
11      private  JComboBox courseBox;
12      private String courseNames[] = {"Java", "Advanced Java",
13           "Client-side Java", "JavaBeans", "Java for All" };
14
15      private JLabel courseLabel = new JLabel("Favorite Course?" );
16      private int choice;
17      private String favCourse = courseNames[0];
18
19      public CoursePanel()
20      {
21
```

```
22              TitledBorder t1 = BorderFactory.createTitledBorder(
23                              "Course Panel");
24          setBorder(t1);
25          setLayout( new GridLayout(2,1) );
26          courseBox = new JComboBox(courseNames);
27
28          add(courseLabel);
29          add(courseBox);
30
31          courseBox.addItemListener( new ItemListener()
32          {
33                  public void itemStateChanged( ItemEvent ie)
34                  {
35                          choice = courseBox.getSelectedIndex();
36                          favCourse = courseNames[choice];
37                  }
38          } );
39      }
40
41      public void reset()
42      {
43              courseBox.setSelectedIndex(0);
44      }
45
46      public String getFavCourse(){return favCourse ; }
47 }
```

Threads and Panels

In the Threads and Panels program (Program 8-22), we have three panels in one frame. This program is similar to the UpDownCounters program found on page 523. By pressing a button in the frame, we start counting up (or down). The counting process occurs within the run() method of a Thread. This enables the program to spend its time performing several tasks instead of just one.

In this program, instead of updating the value of a JLabel, we paint a number in the window in the panel's paintComponent() method by using the Graphic's drawString(). Figure 8-30 shows the frame, panels, and counting process. The font grows larger as we count up, and smaller as we count down. Each panel has its own drawMe() method (called by the frame), which calls repaint(), which issues a call to paintComponent().

In the drawMe() method of each panel there is a Thread. Within the run() method is a for loop that calls repaint(). Repaint() calls paintComponent(). The actual painting process for each panel is simple. We call the superclass's paintComponent()

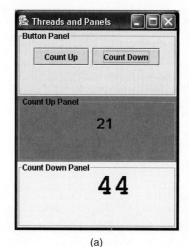 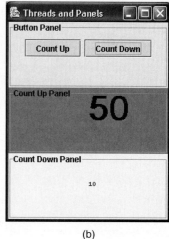

(a)   (b)

Figure 8-30
The Count Up panel counts from 10 to 50 and Count Down panel from 50 to 10.
a) An instant in time as the counting process occurs. b) The frame when each panel
has finished its counting loop.

and then set the color and font before we draw the number into the panel. Here is the
paintComponent() of the DownPanel:

```
public void paintComponent(Graphics g)
{
        super.paintComponent(g);
        g.setColor(Color.BLACK);
        g.setFont( new Font("Courier", Font.BOLD, number) );
        g.drawString(String.valueOf(number), centerW, centerH);
}
```

The drawMe() method determines the center point of the panel and contains an
inner class for the Thread object. Within the loop, we call the sleep() method, to
slow down the painting animation.

```
public void drawMe()
{
        centerW = this.getWidth() / 2;
        centerH = this.getHeight() / 2;

//The thread is here in order to control the call to repaint().
        downThread = new Thread()
        {
            public void run()
            {
```

```
                for (int i = 50; i >= 10; --i)
                {
                        number = i;
                        repaint();
                        try
                        {
                                Thread.currentThread().sleep(100);
                        } catch(InterruptedException e) {}
                }
        }
}; //close of inner class

//Now we call Thread's start so that it calls run()
downThread.start();
}
```

For the buttons in the ButtonPanel to start the panel counting process, our frame will once again act as a mediator or switchboard between the panels. The ButtonPanel is passed a reference to the frame and then calls the frame's methods, which calls the drawMe() methods for the counting panels. Here is the TandPFrame class (Program 8-22):

```
1    //Program 8-22  Threads and Panels Program
2    //File: TandPFrame.java
3
4    //This frame has three panels. The button panel is passed
5    //a reference to this frame, and therefore is able to
6    //call this frame's public methods.
7
8    import javax.swing.*;
9    import java.awt.*;
10   import java.awt.event.*;
11
12   public class TandPFrame extends JFrame
13   {
14      //These three Panels are located in separate .java files.
15      private UpPanel up = new UpPanel();
16      private DownPanel dp = new DownPanel();
17
18      private ButtonPanel bp = new ButtonPanel(this);
19
20      public TandPFrame()
21      {
22              Container canvas = getContentPane();
23              canvas.setLayout( new GridLayout(3,1) );
24
```

```
25              //Add the panels and button to the frame's container.
26              canvas.add(bp);
27              canvas.add(up);
28              canvas.add(dp);
29
30              this.setSize(250,325);
31              this.setTitle("Threads and Panels");
32              this.show();
33      }
34
35      //These methods call the drawMe() methods of the panels.
36      public void drawUp()
37      {
38              up.drawMe();
39      }
40
41      public void drawDown()
42      {
43              dp.drawMe();
44      }
45
46      public static void main( String args[] )
47      {
48              TandPFrame app = new TandPFrame();
49              app.setDefaultCloseOperation(JFrame.EXIT_ON_CLOSE);
50      }
51  }
```

The ButtonPanel is passed the frame reference and calls the frame's drawUp() or
drawDown() method in the button actionPerformed() methods.

```
1   //Program 8-22
2   //File: ButtonPanel.java
3
4   //This panel is passed the TandPFrame object reference.
5   //With this reference, this panel can call the frame's
6   //methods, which calls the panel methods.
7
8
9   import javax.swing.*;
10  import java.awt.*;
11  import java.awt.event.*;
12  import javax.swing.border.*;
```

```
13
14    public class ButtonPanel extends JPanel
15    {
16        private JButton upButton = new JButton("Count Up");
17        private JButton downButton = new JButton("Count Down");
18
19        //This is a reference to the JFrame that contains this panel.
20        private TandPFrame frame;
21
22        //The constructor receives the reference to the frame.
23        public ButtonPanel(TandPFrame f)
24        {
25            frame = f;;
26
27            setUpPanel();
28        }
29
30        public void setUpPanel()
31        {
32            //Make a titled border.
33            TitledBorder t1 = BorderFactory.createTitledBorder(
34                              "Button Panel");
35            setBorder(t1);
36            setLayout( new FlowLayout() );
37            setBackground(Color.CYAN);
38            add(upButton);
39            add(downButton);
40
41    //We are able to call the frame's public methods from here.
42            upButton.addActionListener( new ActionListener ()
43            {
44                public void actionPerformed(ActionEvent ae)
45                {
46                    frame.drawUp();
47                }
48            });
49
50            downButton.addActionListener( new ActionListener ()
51            {
52                public void actionPerformed(ActionEvent ae)
53                {
54                    frame.drawDown();
55                }
56            });
57        }
58    }
```

8

The DownPanel and UpPanel are identical, except for the font type and direction of the for loop. Here is the complete DownPanel class. The UpPanel is not shown here, but the complete program can be found on the text's CD.

```
1   //Program 8-22
2   //File:  DownPanel.java
3
4   //This panel uses a thread to control the painting.
5   //We count down from 50 to 10 and paint the number
6   //in the center of the panel with a varying size font.
7
8   import javax.swing.*;
9   import java.awt.*;
10  import javax.swing.border.*;
11
12  public class DownPanel extends JPanel
13  {
14      private Thread downThread;
15
16      //Number has to exist outside the thread in order to be painted
17      private int number;
18
19      private static int centerH, centerW;
20
21      public DownPanel()
22      {
23      //Make a titled border.
24          TitledBorder t1 = BorderFactory.createTitledBorder(
25                          "Count Down Panel");
26          setBorder(t1);
27
28          setBackground(Color.YELLOW);
29
30      }
31
32      public void drawMe()
33      {
34          centerW = this.getWidth() / 2;
35          centerH = this.getHeight() / 2;
36
37      //The thread is here in order to control the call to repaint().
38          downThread = new Thread()
39              {
```

```
40          public void run()
41          {
42                  for (int i = 50; i >= 10; --i)
43                  {
44                          number = i;
45                          repaint();
46                          try
47                          {
48                                  Thread.currentThread().sleep(100);
49                          } catch(InterruptedException e) {}
50                  }
51          }
52      }; //close of inner class
53
54      //Now we call Thread's start so that it calls run()
55      downThread.start();
56  }
57
58  public void paintComponent(Graphics g)
59  {
60      super.paintComponent(g);
61      g.setColor(Color.BLACK);
62      g.setFont( new Font("Courier", Font.BOLD, number) );
63      g.drawString(String.valueOf(number), centerW, centerH);
64  }
65 }
```

REVIEW QUESTIONS AND PROBLEMS

Short Answer

8

1. What is meant when programmers refer to an event-driven program?

2. How do Listener Interfaces and Listener Adapters differ? How are they alike?

3. What are the possible actions a user can perform with a mouse? What type of events are generated by these actions?

4. If the Java programmer created a Swing component such as a JButton, but forgot to add it to the frame's container, what happens when the program is compiled? What happens when the program is executed, assuming there are no compile errors?

5. What is the difference between a GridLayout and a BorderLayout?

6. Name eight Swing components.

7. What is the best way to implement an event handler in a Java program if the programmer needs to know if the mouse has been moved onto the CENTER region of a frame (with a BorderLayout)? Hint: You may add a component into the CENTER region.

8. What are the necessary method calls to make if you wish to see labels and major tick marks on your JSlider object?

9. Why is it important to have your radio buttons in a button group?

10. If a Java programmer wants the user to see tooltips on his or her buttons, what additional steps must be taken by the programmer?

11. What is the difference between editable and uneditable Swing components? Give an example of each.

12. Explain how JPanels and the GridLayout manager are handy tools for the programmer when he or she is developing radio button or check box groups.

13. What is the difference between ItemListener and ActionListener?

14. What is the main difference between Java's JComboBox and JList box components?

15. If we wanted to have a user interface with a horizontal slider, a vertical slider, and a large drawing area, what would be the best layout manager to use? (Assume you are not using additional JPanels.) Explain your answer. What would be a poor choice?

16. If a Java programmer wishes to set the sizes of his or her components, what is an appropriate layout manager to use? Which manager would be a poor choice?

17. In the program demonstration that uses the MoviePanel, VacationPanel, and PasswordPanel (Program 8-9), would it be possible to have a separate SummaryPanel class (in *SummaryPanel.java*) so that the program still has the same functionality? Explain your answer.

18. How is the label text set on the JTabbedPane tab? Is it possible to change the text on the tab as the program executes? If it is possible, what are the method calls necessary to accomplish this task?

19. List the steps required by a Java programmer so that the JToolBar can be docked in a different position or pulled off as a separate window.

20. Examine the ColorFun program. Is it possible to have four different split pane panels in a Java window? Is it possible to have five split pane panels?

21. Is it possible for a Java program to play an audio clip in response to a radio button press? How would this task be accomplished? List the steps needed for setting up the audio clip as well as the radio button.

22. If a programmer decided to rewrite the Mousey program (Program 8-14) using "implements MouseListener, implements MouseMotionListener" in the class

definition line, what changes to the program must be added in order to maintain the original functionality?

23. Describe a JMenuBar, JMenu, and JMenuItem. Is it possible to place a JMenuItem in a JMenuBar?

24. Can a mnemonic be added to a JButton so that it responds to a keyboard event? If it is possible, explain how this is accomplished and the steps the user must take in order for the keyboard event to activate the button.

25. Can a JMenuItem have both an accelerator and a mnemonic? What is the main difference in how a user interacts with an accelerator and a mnemonic?

26. When should a Java programmer write a paintComponent() method instead of a paint() method? In what Swing component is the paintComponent() most commonly found?

27. If you wanted to have the date and time displayed in the lower right hand corner of your window and have it updated every second, how would you accomplish this task? Explain the steps you would need to take to make this happen.

28. Assume you have several controls in a frame window—each with its own associated event listener. If one event occurs and that component's event handling method is called, does Java automatically listen for the other events? Explain your answer.

29. Is it possible to have a Thread associated with a paintComponent() method on a panel? If so, explain a situation where this would be an appropriate programming technique.

30. Why is it necessary to synchronize Thread objects if they use the same class data?

Programming Problems

In Questions 31–38 write complete Java programs. If you have studied Advanced Topics, Chapter 12, *JAR Files*, bundle your program into a JAR file.

31. Write a Java program that contains the following controls (or control groups) that describe the various options for an automobile. You should have a radio button group that has the vehicle type include sedan, convertible, van, and SUV. There should be a series of check boxes for options, such as sun roof (should be disabled if the convertible button is selected), CD player, all wheel drive, and two others. Incorporate a slider that allows the user to select an estimated price to the nearest $100 (show the price value in a label) and two buttons and two labels for setting and displaying the interior and exterior colors. Include a button that presents a JOptionPane message box that summarizes the user's selections when pressed. Please separate your vehicle type, options, color, and price components into separate JPanels contained in their own .*java* files. Select appropriate layout manager(s) so that all the program components are visible to the user. Be sure that there are initial values set for each of the

components and if the Summary button is selected before any controls are altered, these initial values are displayed in the message box. Hint: The Mediator Program on page 535 might be a useful guide for this program.

32. Follow the guidelines from Problem 31, but rewrite the car program so that the window presents tabbed panes for each group of options. Include a summary tab that always shows the currently selected items. (This replaces the Summary button from Problem 31.)

33. Rewrite Program 8-9 so that there is a SummaryPanel class that is located in its own .java file. Your new program should have the same functionality as the demo program in the text.

34. Rework the ColorFun split pane demonstration program so that there are four color panes instead of two. Each pane should be numbered 1, 2, 3, and 4 (you may use a JLabel if you wish). The pane selection should be controlled by a slider instead of group of radio buttons. The slider must have snap-to-tick enabled so that the slider value represents which pane should have the new color. You may use a toolbar if you wish.

35. Rewrite the Mousey program so that if the window changes size, the program responds by adjusting the lines to be drawn into the corners (as seen in the initial condition in the text example). Adjust the rectangle that is drawn surrounding the mouse so that it has one-tenth the window size and has the same aspect ratio as the window. That is, if the window is resized to 400 × 300, the center rectangle is 40 × 30. Have your initial window size set to 300 × 300 pixels. Keep the color cycling for the lines if you wish.

36. Write a program that has two sliders, one that controls the width of a rectangle and one that controls the height of the rectangle. For example, if the user moves the vertical slider, it changes the height of the rectangle. The horizontal slider changes the width. You will need to have a RectanglePanel with a paintComponent() method.

37. Set up a program so that your favorite image is displayed in the window. (Use a JLabel if you wish). The image should be sized to be no larger than 150 × 150 pixels. Build in the necessary functionality so that if the user rests the mouse on your image, some text that describes the images displayed, such as "My favorite cat." Allow the user to click and drag the image with the mouse. When the user releases the mouse button, leave the image positioned in that location in the window.

38. Remember the game Tic Tac Toe?[2] Set up a TicTacToePanel that uses a GridLayout manager and nine buttons. The TicTacToePanel should be placed in the

---

[2] I assume everyone knows how to play the game Tic Tac Toe. If you are unsure of the rules, search on the WWW for Tic Tac Toe. There are many game sites that not only explain the rules but allow you to play against the computer.

CENTER portion of the frame's container. There should be a right button player and left button player. Allow the user to enter the names of the two players in JTextFields. The game buttons are pressed with either the right or left button. The right button is the "X" and the left button is the "O." As the players "take turns" clicking the buttons, the button labels change to reflect which player clicked it. The game should not allow one of the players to take two turns in a row or to click on a position that has already been played. When one player has three in a row, change the color of the buttons to indicate that the game is over and write a summary as to who won in the SOUTH region of the container. If the players play to a draw, report that it is a draw. Don't forget a New Game button, which clears the game board. Note: There is a TicTacToe game included in the J2SDK folder. Although it is designed differently than the game described here, it is a good reference for the programmer.

39. Using the Mediator Program as a guide, build a Font Control program where the frame has a FontPanel and a TextPanel. The FontPanel contains controls for setting the font (such as Ariel or Courier), size, and style (bold, italic, or bold and italic.) Have a combo box for the font, a slider for the size, and check boxes for the style. The TextPanel has a text field where the user may enter a phrase. As the user types letters into the text field, print the letters in a label below the text field. You will need to place a key listener on the text field and update the label as it is typed. If the user changes the fonts, immediately update the label so that it is written in the desired font.

40. Following the Threads and Panels Program, build a Java program that has an AnimationPanel that performs animation that incorporates a Thread. The animation should be controlled by use of an animation control panel. The ControlPanel must have GUI components that set at least three parameters for the animation, as well as a "Start Animation" button. When the button is pressed, the parameters are used to control the animation. For example, your animation control may set a color by way of popping up a JColorChooser dialog box, set the size of an item with a slider, determine how long the animation runs, or select a type of graphical object.

8

9

Inheritance and Interfaces

CHAPTER OBJECTIVES

Review superclasses and subclasses and the manner in which we have used them.

Review the concept of inheritance in an object-oriented language.

Introduce the *protected* keyword and demonstrate its use in Java.

Show how to write, use, and extend our own superclasses.

Discuss how default and overloaded constructors are written and used in a Java program.

Demonstrate how *super* is used to call superclass members.

Show how subclasses may override superclass methods.

Describe the concept of abstract classes and illustrate their use.

Illustrate how you may assign subclass references into an array of superclass references and use this array to access the correct subclass methods.

Present a complete discussion of Java interfaces and demonstrate their purposes in Java program design and implementation.

Illustrate how using an interface in program design can act as a standard blueprint for a class and program, and promote code reusability and speed development time.

Discuss how abstract classes and interfaces are similar and different, and how and where they should be used in program design.

We're on the home stretch!

Have you ever planned a long trip? It is fun to think about your destination and your activities while you will be there. You need to decide what clothes to take, and you need to go through a checklist of possible items you may need while you're traveling. Once you get underway, it is exciting to see new places and meet new people. As the trip winds down you may long for home or be ready to sleep in your own bed again. But sometimes on your travels, the best part of the journey is at the end!

We began a long trip traveling through the Java material, and it has been exciting to see our programs develop as we learn new programming skills and concepts. We have learned how Java classes are great to work with as we grew and refined our programming talent. Our journey has taken us through data primitives and arithmetic; control statements and methods; importing, writing, and extending classes; implementing interfaces; and setting up and handling GUI components. As we enter the home stretch of learning the basics of the Java language, we must now learn how we can write our own hierarchy of classes and interfaces. We know how to extend Java's classes and implement Java's interfaces. Now we will learn how to write our own classes and interfaces.

▓ 9.1
A Review of Superclasses, Subclasses, and Interfaces

Let's review what we know about superclasses and subclasses. In Chapter 3 we introduced the notion of a hierarchy of classes or job descriptions. We developed our own hierarchy in one example with Employee, AirlineEmployee, FlightCrew, and Pilots. The Employee is the superclass of the AirlineEmployee. The AirlineEmployee is the superclass of the FlightCrew. The FlightCrew is the superclass of the Pilot. Each class contains properties, data, and methods for its particular type of job description. As the job description becomes more specialized, we add the new duties for that job.

As we developed our code writing skills we learned how to extend Java's JApplet or JFrame class with our own class so that our class inherited the ability "to be a JApplet" or "to be a JFrame." By inheriting the JApplet or JFrame class, our class became a JApplet or JFrame and we then had a window and a paint() method in which to draw graphical items. In this short example, the class MyCatFrame inherits all it needs to be a JFrame by using the *extends JFrame*:

```java
//We import the classes we need to use.
//JFrame will be extended by our class.
import javax.swing.JFrame;

//The Graphics class helps us draw into the window.
import java.awt.Graphics;

public class MyCatFrame extends JFrame
{
       String name;
       public void MyCatFrame()
       {
              name = "Chet the Cat";
              setSize(100,100);
              show();
       }

       public void paint(Graphics g)
       {
              String output = "Hello " + name + "!";
              g.drawString(output, 25,25);
       }
}
```

In Chapters 7 and 8 we explored Java interfaces such as ActionListener and MouseListener. The rule we learned with interfaces is that if a class "implements" an interface, we must write all of the methods that are described in the interface. That is, if we implement ActionListener, we must write the actionPerformed() method. If we implement MouseListener, we must write the five methods in the MouseListener interface including mouseClicked(), mouseEntered(), mouseExited(), mouse-Pressed(), and mouseReleased(). We also saw how listener interfaces are used with GUI controls. Here is a short version of the ShowADogApplet from Chapter 7. The interface ActionListener is used with the JButton to handle the button press event.

```java
//Shortened version of Program 7-12
import javax.swing.*;         //for JButton and JFrame
import java.awt.FlowLayout;
import java.awt.event.ActionListener;
```

```
//When our class implements ActionListener we must
//write the actionPerformed() method inside our class!

public class ShowADogApplet extends JApplet implements ActionListener
{
        //use a label for the Image Icons
        JLabel dog1PicLabel = new JLabel(new ImageIcon("Shadow.jpg"));
        JButton dog1Button = new JButton( "Who is the first dog?");

        public void init()
        {
                Container canvas = getContentPane();
                canvas.setLayout(new FlowLayout());

        //We add a listener to the button object so that the program
        //knows to respond to the button press.
                dog1Button.addActionListener(this);

                canvas.add(dog1PicLabel);
                canvas.add(dog1Button);
        }
        //Here is the ActionListener interface method.
        public void actionPerformed (ActionEvent ae)
        {
                if(ae.getSource() == dog1Button)
                {
                        JOptionPane.showMessageDialog(null,
                        "Meet Shadow!",      "Dog Pictures ",
                        JOptionPane.INFORMATION_MESSAGE);
                }
        }
}
```

9.2
Writing Our Own Superclasses in Java

9

The class relationship that models inheritance is the "is a" relationship. The super-class typically is a general-purpose class, while the subclass is a special case or customized version of the superclass. You should ask yourself if the phrase "is a" correctly describes how your superclasses and subclasses are related. The ShowADogApplet is a JApplet. The MyCatFrame is a JFrame. The relationship for both of these examples is not true in the reverse. The JApplet is not a ShowADog-Applet, JFrame is not a MyCatFrame.

When a subclass is created, it inherits data and methods from its superclass. The format for class inheritance is:

```
//File: MySuperClass.java
class MySuperClass
{
        // data and methods of the superclass
}
```

And the subclass is usually located in its own Java file:

```
//File: MySubClass.java
class MySubClass extends MySuperClass
{
        //The subclass inherits members of the superclass
        //which have public or protected access specifiers.
        //The superclass access specifiers determine what is
        //inherited by the subclass.

        //The subclass has new data and/or methods that make it a
        //customized version of the superclass.
}
```

Make Our Own Superclass: The CounterPanel Program

Let's work through an example to see how easy it is to write our own superclasses and subclasses. In Program 9-1 we build a class named CounterPanel, and we will use it as our superclass in the next program. Figure 9-1a on page 562 shows a frame which contains two of these CounterPanel objects. First, we see how this simple class works. It provides the programmer with a panel containing a button, a reset button, and two labels. Each time the user presses the "Press Me" button, the Counter-Panel object adds a value that is stored in an increment variable to the class counter. If the increment value is 1, then each button press adds 1 to the counter. If the increment value is 5, each button press adds 5 to the counter.

The code inside the class includes a setIncrValue() method that sets the increment value. It is possible to assign a name to the CounterPanel objects by calling the setName() method. The value in the counter may be retrieved by calling get-CounterValue().The reset button sets the counter value back to zero. The Counter-Panel class is a JPanel because we have extended JPanel.

The CounterPanel's constructor initializes the data values and sets up the components for the panel. As you study the source code for the class shown in Program 9-1, note that we have placed System.out.println() calls in the constructor, right before we set up the components, and in the actionPerformed() methods. This allows us to track the sequence of method calls as the program executes. Figure 9-1b shows this sequence.

```java
1   //Program 9-1
2   //File:  CounterPanel.java  A panel that has buttons and "counts."
3
4   //This panel class has two buttons. When the "Press Me"
5   //button is pressed, an increment value is added to the
6   //counter. There is a reset button that zeros out the
7   //counter value.
8
9   import javax.swing.*;
10  import java.awt.*;
11  import java.awt.event.*;
12  import javax.swing.border.BevelBorder;
13
14  public class CounterPanel extends JPanel
15  {
16    private int counterValue, incrValue;
17    private String name, output;
18    private JButton pressMeButton = new JButton("Press Me");
19    private JButton resetButton = new JButton("Reset to zero");
20    private JLabel incrLabel = new JLabel("", JLabel.CENTER);
21    private JLabel countLabel = new JLabel("",JLabel.CENTER);
22
23    public CounterPanel()
24    {
25          System.out.println("In CounterPanel's constructor. ");
26          counterValue = 0;
27          incrValue = 1;
28          name = "";
29          output = "";
30
31          System.out.println("Now setting up CounterPanel components.");
32          output = name + " press count = ";
33          countLabel.setText(output + Integer.toString(counterValue));
34
35          setLayout(new GridLayout(4,1));
36          add(pressMeButton);
37          add(countLabel);
38
39          countLabel.setBorder(new BevelBorder(BevelBorder.LOWERED));
40          incrLabel.setBorder(new BevelBorder(BevelBorder.LOWERED));
41
42          add(incrLabel);
43          add(resetButton);
44
45          //Pressing the pressMeButton adds the increment value to
46          //the counter.
```

```
47          pressMeButton.addActionListener(new ActionListener ()
48          {
49                  public void actionPerformed(ActionEvent ae)
50                  {
51                          System.out.println("CounterPanel " + name
52                                          + "Press Me pressed.");
53                          counterValue += incrValue;
54                          countLabel.setText(output +
55                                  Integer.toString(counterValue));
56                  }
57          });

58
59          //Pressing the resetButton zeros the counter.
60          resetButton.addActionListener(new ActionListener ()
61          {
62                  public void actionPerformed(ActionEvent ae)
63                  {
64                          System.out.println("CounterPanel " + name
65                                          + "Reset pressed.");
66                          counterValue = 0;
67                          countLabel.setText(output +
68                                  Integer.toString(counterValue));
69                  }
70          });
71      }

72
73      public void setCounterName(String n)
74      {
75          name = n;
76          output = name + " press count = ";
77          countLabel.setText(output +
78                                  Integer.toString(counterValue));
79          resetButton.setText(name+" Reset");
80      }

81
82      public void setIncrValue(int iv)
83      {
84          incrValue = iv;
85          incrLabel.setText("Incr Value = " +
86                      Integer.toString(incrValue));
87      }

88
89      public int getCountValue(){return counterValue; }
90  }
```

To demonstrate how our CounterPanel class works, we build a CounterFrame class and instantiate two CounterPanel objects. The CounterPanel's constructor also contains a System.out.println() call. We set the increment values and names into the objects and then add them to the frame's container. The source code for the frame is shown below in Program 9-1. Figure 9-1A shows the frame window with our two counters "Left" and "Right." You can see that the "Left" counter has an increment value of 1 and the "Right" counter has an increment value of 5. Figure 9-1B shows the sequence of calls via the various System.out.println() statements. Notice how the panel methods are called before the frame's constructor. This order is required because the class data primitives and objects are created before the actual class constructor is executed. The output from this example shows that the "Right" counter's "Press Me" button was pressed twice and the "Left" counter's button was pressed three times, reset, and then pressed once again.

```
1    //Program 9-1 Counter Frame that hold two CounterPanels
2    //File:  CounterFrame.java
3
4    //This frame contains two CounterPanel objects in a
5    //GridLayout format.
6
7
8    import java.awt.*;
9    import javax.swing.*;
10
11   public class CounterFrame extends JFrame
12   {
13      //We create two counter panel objects.
14      private CounterPanel cp1 = new CounterPanel();
15      private CounterPanel cp2 = new CounterPanel();
16
17      public CounterFrame()
18      {
19            System.out.println("In CounterFrame's constructor. ");
20            this.setTitle("Two Counters");
21            Container canvas = this.getContentPane();
22            canvas.setLayout( new GridLayout(1,2) );
23
24            //Set the names for the two counter panels.
25            cp1.setCounterName("Left ");
26            cp2.setCounterName("Right ");
27
28            //Set the increment value for each counter.
29            cp1.setIncrValue(1);
30            cp2.setIncrValue(5);
```

```
31
32          canvas.add(cp1);
33          canvas.add(cp2);
34
35          this.setSize(350, 150);
36
37          this.show();
38      }
39
40   public static void main(String[] args)
41   {
42          CounterFrame theApp = new CounterFrame();
43          theApp.setDefaultCloseOperation(EXIT_ON_CLOSE);
44      }
45 }
```

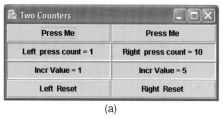

```
C:\JPT\Ch9_JavaCode\CounterPanel-1>java CounterFrame
In CounterPanel's constructor.
Now setting up CounterPanel components.
In CounterPanel's constructor.
Now setting up CounterPanel components.
In CounterFrame's constructor.
CounterPanel Right Press Me pressed.
CounterPanel Right Press Me pressed.
CounterPanel Left Press Me pressed.
CounterPanel Left Press Me pressed.
CounterPanel Left Press Me pressed.
CounterPanel Left Reset pressed.
CounterPanel Left Press Me pressed.
```

(a)   (b)

Figure 9-1
a) The CounterFrame has two CounterPanel objects. The two CounterPanel references are cp1 and cp2. We set the name variables in the CounterPanel objects to "Left" and "Right." b) The sequence of method calls.

Better, Faster, Prettier Software

Our CounterPanel is not very flashy. Functional? Yes. Exciting? No. It is a normal trait for programmers to want to make their software better, faster, and their GUIs prettier. However, there is one important issue to keep in mind. For most organizations, time and money constraints on software projects keep the free wheeling nature of their programmers reined in. There isn't the time or money to pay for a programmer to "twiddle" with the software forever.

Assume that our CounterPanel is fully tested, works well, and is incorporated in programs that are installed on operational systems. Placing a new version of software on a system that is used by many people is an important and critical step for an organization. The software that is installed at your place of business, government facility, or college campus affects many people's jobs and lives. Programmers are not able to go in and make software changes at will. Once software goes through a successful test phase and is turned over to the users, changes cannot be made without involving many people!

Object-oriented programming allows us to take an existing class and create a new class by applying the inheritance principle. Our new subclass will inherit the existing class's methods and data. We may then add the new features to the subclass. Let's do this by using the CounterPanel as a superclass and make a new class that has more capabilities than the CounterPanel.

FancyCounterPanel extends CounterPanel

We now have a CounterPanel that works well, and we wish to add more features. While we're able to make changes, we will make the GUI prettier too. Our list of new features includes the ability to set the button increment value to an integer within the range of 1 up to and including 10. (A JSlider will work nicely for this feature.) We also want to set the color of the buttons. Examine Figure 9-2. It shows a frame that contains a new, fancy counter on the left as well as the plain counter that we built in Program 9-1 on the right.

Instead of starting over and modifying the CounterPanel class, we can use it as our superclass and make a new FancyCounterPanel class. The CounterPanel class works well and is completely built and tested, so we do not need to reinvent the wheel! We can extend the CounterPanel class, inherit its members, and add the desired new features to the FancyCounterPanel. To do this, we must first make minor changes to the CounterPanel class.

Recall that we have used two access specifiers for class members: private and public. **Private class members** are seen by all members within the class and *not seen* by any parts of the program outside the class. Object-oriented principles state that we should hide our data, and this task is accomplished by making the data private. All members within the class, as well as outside of the class, also see public class members. It is now time to introduce the **protected access specifier**.

private class members

seen by all members within the class but not by any parts of the program outside the class. Private members are not inherited by subclasses

protected access specifier

protected class members in a superclass are inherited by the subclass but are not accessible outside the class

![Figure 9-2 screenshot: A frame titled "Fancy and Plain Counters" showing two counter panels. Left panel: "Press Me", "Fancy Left press count = 0", "Incr Value = 5", "Fancy Left Reset", with a slider marked 1 3 5 7 9. Right panel: "Press Me", "Right press count = 0", "Incr Value = 1", "Right Reset".]

Figure 9-2
This frame contains two counter panels. The left panel counter is a subclass of the right panel. The "Fancy Left" counter has more features than the superclass' CounterPanel.

TABLE 9-1
Compare private and protected assess specifiers with a simple Java class.

	Private and Public members	Protected and Public members
| Superclass | ```
public class Count
{
  private int count;
  public Count(){count = 0;}
  public int getCount()
    { return count;}
  public void setCount(int c)
    {   count = c;   }
}
``` | ```
public class Count
{
  protected int count;
  public Count(){count = 0;}
  public int getCount()
    { return count;}
  public void setCount(int c)
    {   count = c;   }
}
``` |
| Subclass | ```
public class NewCount extends Count
{
}
``` | ```
public class NewCount extends Count
{
}
``` |
What does the subclass get?	The public getCount() and setCount() methods but not the private data nor constructor	The protected int count and the public getCount() and setCount() methods but not the constructor
How does the subclass access the count variable?	The subclass must use the get and set method to access count	The subclass has the int count and can access it directly
What can the world see?	Only the public members	Only the public members

As we learn about inheritance, we see that there is a new, protected access specifier. In Java, public and protected class members are inherited from the superclass by the subclass. Private class members in a superclass *are not* inherited by the subclass. Protected class members are visible to class members within the class (just like private and public members), and are inherited in subclasses, but they are private to the world. Table 9-1 summarizes the access specifiers using a simple Java class.

If we wish to use our CounterPanel as a superclass, we must change the access specifiers of the class members that are to be passed down to the Fancy-CounterPanel subclass. Go back to page 559, lines 16–23 and take a quick look at the CounterPanel code in Program 9-1. Notice that the data members are private and the methods and constructor are public. Now examine the code that follows. It is the CounterPanel class and we are going to use it as a superclass. The only difference between this class and the one in Program 9-1 is that we have changed the private data members to protected.

```
//Program 9-2                This class has protected data members.
//File:  CounterPanel.java

//This will be a superclass to the FancyPanelCounter class.

//import statements

public class CounterPanel extends JPanel
{
        //These data members must be protected instead of private
        //in order for them to be inherited (and accessible) by the subclass.
        protected int counterValue, incrValue;
        protected String name, output;
        protected JButton pressMeButton = new JButton("Press Me");
        protected JButton resetButton = new JButton("Reset to zero");
        protected JLabel incrLabel = new JLabel("", JLabel.CENTER);
        protected JLabel countLabel = new JLabel("",JLabel.CENTER);

        public CounterPanel()
        {
                System.out.println("In CounterPanel's constructor. ");
                counterValue = 0;
                incrValue = 1;
                name = "";
                output = "";

                //Rest of constructor.
        }
        //Rest of class. No changes from Program 9-1.
}
```

In the FancyCounterPanel class, we need to inherit all of the CounterPanel data members and methods, as well as write the new custom capabilities. Our fancy counter has a slider that we use to set the increment value. We can make pretty buttons too! The FancyCounterPanel class is shown here in Program 9-2. Study the code and see that we have added the new features for the class.

9

```
1   //Program 9-2
2   //File:  FancyCounterPanel.java
3
4   //This FancyCounterPanel has a JSlider that lets the user select
5   //the increment value for the counter and set the button's color.
6
```

```
7    import javax.swing.*;
8    import java.awt.*;
9    import java.awt.event.*;
10   import javax.swing.event.*;    //For the ChangeListener
11
12   public class FancyCounterPanel extends CounterPanel
13   {
14     //This class has inherited these protected variables from
15     //the CounterPanel class. (We had to change the private members
16     //to protected.) Here are the variables:
17     //counterValue, incrValue,  name,
18     //pressMeButton, resetButton, two labels and output String.
19
20     //Classes do not inherit their superclass constructor.
21
22     //The FancyCounterPanel needs these variables:
23     private Color buttonColor = Color.lightGray;
24     private JSlider slider = new JSlider(1,10,1);
25
26     public FancyCounterPanel()
27     {
28
29           System.out.println("In FancyCounterPanel constructor.");
30
31     //The default CounterPanel() constructor is called automatically.
32
33           //Here is the additional code for this new class.
34           //Change the layout to 5 x 1.
35           setLayout(new GridLayout(5,1));
36
37           //Set up the slider.
38
39           slider.setMajorTickSpacing(2);
40           slider.setMinorTickSpacing(1);
41           slider.setPaintTicks(true);
42           slider.setPaintLabels(true);
43           slider.setSnapToTicks(true);
44           add(slider);
45
46           slider.addChangeListener(new ChangeListener()
47           {
```

```
48              public void stateChanged(ChangeEvent ce)
49              {
50                      System.out.println(
51                              "In the Fancy C's slider stateChanged()");
52                      incrValue = slider.getValue();
53                      incrLabel.setText("Incr Value = " +
54                              Integer.toString(incrValue));
55              }
56          });
57      }
58
59      //We have to set our button colors here.
60      //Notice that we access the buttons here with no problem! :-)))
61      public void setButtonColor(Color c)
62      {
63          System.out.println("In the Fancy C's setButtonColor().");
64          buttonColor = c;
65          pressMeButton.setBackground(buttonColor);
66          resetButton.setBackground(buttonColor);
67      }
68
69      //Since we have a slider involved in our increment business
70      //we need to have a setIncrValue() method in this class.
71      //Here we call the superclass' method and then we set the slider.
72      //We could have set the incrValue directly too.
73
74      public void setIncrValue(int iv)
75      {
76          //Informational message to show when we are in here:
77          System.out.println("In the Fancy C's setIncrValue().");
78
79          //Pass the increment value to the super class's method.
80          super.setIncrValue(iv);
81
82          //Then set the slider to reflect this new value.
83          slider.setValue(incrValue);
84      }
85  }
```

In the FancyCounterPanel we have a setButtonColor() method that sets the pressMeButton and resetButton's color, and the slider's stateChanged() method sets the increment value. We must write a new version of the setIncrValue() method for the FancyPanelCounter class because the increment value is controlled and reported by the slider. As the increment value is set, such as being called in the frame class, we must set the associated slider value as well. We can call the superclass's setIncrValue() method passing the increment value to it, and then set the slider:

```
public void setIncrValue(int iv)
{
        //Informational message to show when we are in here:
        System.out.println("In the Fancy C's setIncrValue().");

        //Pass the increment value to the super class's method.
        //The superclass sets the increment value and label text.
        super.setIncrValue(iv);

        //Then set the slider to reflect this new value.
        slider.setValue(incrValue);
}
```

Or, we can simply set the increment value and label text directly:

```
public void setIncrValue(int iv)
{
        //Informational message to show when we are in here:
        System.out.println("In the Fancy C's setIncrValue().");

        //Assign the increment value to the class variable.
        incrValue = iv;

        //Set the label text.
        incrLabel.setText("Incr Value = " +
                        Integer.toString(incrValue));

        //Then set the slider to reflect this new value.
        slider.setValue(incrValue);
}
```

9

method overriding
when we write a new, customized version of a method in the subclass that is also found in the superclass

In either case, when we write a new, customized version of a method in the subclass that is also found in the superclass, this is known as **method overriding**. We override the superclass's setIncrValue() method because the subclass must provide additional or different coding tasks.

The CounterFrame2 class contains a CounterPanel and FancyCounterPanel object. We must set the names and increment values for each counter, and we must set button colors for the fancy counter. Notice that we have System.out.println() statements describing the object creation and setup activities. Study the program code that follows, and look at Figure 9-3 on page 570, which shows the sequence of steps that occurred as our CounterFrame2 object was built and displayed. It is important to note that whenever a subclass *default* constructor is called, its superclass *default* constructor is automatically executed before the subclass constructor. This makes sense when you think about it—the subclass extends the superclass, therefore we need to take care of the superclass business before we deal with the subclass. This automatic execution is performed for default (no input) constructors only.

```
1    //Program 9-2 Counter Frame that hold one CounterPanel
2    //and one FancyCounterPanel
3    //File:  CounterFrame2.java
4
5    import java.awt.*;
6    import javax.swing.*;
7
8    public class CounterFrame2 extends JFrame
9    {
10     private FancyCounterPanel fcp1;
11     private CounterPanel cp2;
12
13     public CounterFrame2()
14     {
15         System.out.println("\n ***In CounterFrame2's constructor. ");
16         System.out.println("\n ***Now making a FancyCounterPanel object. ");
17         fcp1 = new FancyCounterPanel();
18
19         System.out.println("\n ***Now making a CounterPanel object. ");
20         cp2 = new CounterPanel();
21
22
23         this.setTitle("Fancy and Plain Counters");
24         Container canvas = this.getContentPane();
25         canvas.setLayout( new GridLayout(1,2) );
26
27         //Here we set the fancy counter's name, incr value and color.
28         System.out.println("\n ***Now setting Fancy Counter params.");
29         fcp1.setCounterName("Fancy Left ");
30         fcp1.setIncrValue(5);
31         fcp1.setButtonColor(Color.RED);
32
33         //We need only to set the name and incr value of the
34         //CounterPanel object.
35         System.out.println("\n ***Now setting Counter params.");
36         cp2.setCounterName("Right ");
37         cp2.setIncrValue(1);
38
```

```
39          //Add to the container, set the size and show it!
40          canvas.add(fcp1);
41          canvas.add(cp2);
42          this.setSize(450, 250);
43          this.show();
44      }
45
46      public static void main(String[] args)
47      {
48          CounterFrame2 theApp = new CounterFrame2();
49          theApp.setDefaultCloseOperation(EXIT_ON_CLOSE);
50      }
51  }
```

```
C:\JPT\Ch9_JavaCode\FancyCounterPanel-2>java CounterFrame2

***In CounterFrame2's constructor.

***Now making a FancyCounterPanel object.
In CounterPanel's constructor.
In FancyCounterPanel constructor.

***Now making a CounterPanel object.
In CounterPanel's constructor.

***Now setting Fancy Counter params.
In the CounterPanel's setCounterName().
In the Fancy C's setIncrValue().
In the CounterPanel's setIncrValue().
In the Fancy C's slider stateChanged()
In the Fancy C's setButtonColor().

***Now setting Counter params.
In the CounterPanel's setCounterName().
In the CounterPanel's setIncrValue().
```

Figure 9-3

This figure shows the sequence of calls performed when a FancyCounterPanel and CounterPanel are created in the CounterFrame2 class. Notice that when the FancyCounterPanel is created, its superclass constructor is executed automatically before the FancyCounterPanel constructor is run. Also note that when the frame class sets the subclass parameters, some parameters belong to the superclass and some to the subclass.

Overloaded Constructors in Superclasses and Subclasses

Java automatically executes the superclass default (no input) constructor before it executes the subclass's *default* constructor. We watched this activity in Program 9-2. You are probably thinking, "What about the situation where the constructors are overloaded?" After all, it makes a programmer's life easier to pass initial values to a constructor instead of needing to set each of the values—like we did with the previous counter examples.

Java deals with overloaded constructors differently than it deals with default constructors. If the programmer wishes to use overloaded constructors in his or her class hierarchy, then he or she has a few options on how the class data is initialized. If the programmer passes data into the subclass constructor, the subclass constructor may explicitly call its superclass constructor and pass its data to it. The call to the superclass constructor must be the first line of code in the subclass constructor. We can modify our CounterPanel and FancyCounterPanel constructors to illustrate this rule.

Let's write just the necessary portions of the classes here because the program execution and behavior does not change. The complete program can be found on the text's CD in the Chapter 9 folder named MoreFancy-3. Here is an overloaded constructor for the CounterPanel class:

```
//Program 9-3               This class now has an overloaded constructor.
//File:  CounterPanel.java


//This will be a superclass to the FancyPanelCounter class.
//This version of the code has overloaded constructor.


//import statements

public class CounterPanel extends JPanel
{
        //protected class data is here

        //Here is our overloaded constructor.
        //It is passed the name of the counter and increment value.
        public CounterPanel(String n, int incr)
        {
                System.out.println("In CounterPanel's constructor. ");
                counterValue = 0;
                incrValue = incr;
                name = n;

                //rest of constructor

        }


        //rest of class
}
```

The FancyCounterPanel's overloaded constructor passes the data to the superclass's overloaded constructor shown as follows. Examine the superclass's constructor and see that the subclass passes the data parameters to it in the correct order, just as data values are passed to any method.

```
//Program 9-3
//File:  FancyCounterPanel.java


//This FancyCounterPanel has a JSlider that lets the user select
//the increment value for the counter and set the button's color.
```

```
        //It has an overloaded constructor.

        //import statements

        public class FancyCounterPanel extends CounterPanel
        {
                //The FancyCounterPanel needs these variables:
                private Color buttonColor = Color.lightGray;
                private JSlider slider = new JSlider(1,10,1);

                //Overloaded subclass constructors may pass data
                //to the superclass constructor. with an explicit call.

                public FancyCounterPanel(String n, int incr, Color bc)
                {
                        //The call to the super class' constructor must be
                        //the first line in the subclass constructor.
                        super(n,incr);

                        //Lines of code to set up the slider are here.

                        //Now set the slider value and button color.
                        slider.setValue(incrValue);
                        setButtonColor(bc);
                }
                //rest of class
        }
```

 The programmer could opt to assign superclass variables and perform the necessary superclass setup in the subclass constructor instead of calling the superclass constructor. In this situation, because the superclass constructor is not being called at all, the programmer must remember to initialize all of the data variables. We would also need to perform all of the superclass constructor duties including setting the layout manager, labels, adding the components to the content pane, and writing the actionPerformed() methods.

```
//This subclass sets all of the data instead of calling the superclass constructor.

public class FancyCounterPanel extends CounterPanel
{
        //The FancyCounterPanel needs these variables:
        private Color buttonColor = Color.lightGray;
        private JSlider slider = new JSlider(1,10,1);

        public FancyCounterPanel(String n, int incr, Color bc)
        {
```

```
            counterValue = 0;
            incrValue = incr;
            name = n;

            //Perform all initialization for labels, layout, add components,
            //write the actionPerformed() methods.

            //Lines of code to set up the slider are here.

            //Now set the slider value and button color.
            slider.setValue(incrValue);
            setButtonColor(bc);
        }
        //rest of class
}
```

It is best practice to pass the superclass constructor its data from the subclass constructor when the programmer is using parameter list constructors because the superclass handles whatever setup and initializations it needs to perform. Remember, we know that the superclass works. Our subclass inherits all the good stuff and we should not redo the superclass.

In the CounterFrame3 class, we build two panels (one of each type) and place them in the frame. The initial panel parameters for each of the panel objects are passed into their constructors. Once again, review Figure 9-2 on page 563 to see the results of this program.

```
//Program 9-3 Counter Frame that hold one CounterPanel
//and one FancyCounterPanel
//File:  CounterFrame3.java

//This class passes initial parameter data to the panel
//constructors upon object instantiation.

//import statements

public class CounterFrame3 extends JFrame
{
        private FancyCounterPanel fcp1;
        private CounterPanel cp2;

        public CounterFrame3()
        {
                //We call the overloaded constructors for both counters.

                fcp1 = new FancyCounterPanel("Fancy Left", 5, Color.RED);
```

```
                    cp2 = new CounterPanel("Right", 1);

               //rest of constructor
          }

          //rest of class
     }
```

Another Example: The HousePets Superclass

Do you have a friend who has a house full of pets? Dogs, cats, tropical fish, pond fish, guinea pigs, and birds—what a menagerie! Let's build a Java class hierarchy that models the relationships of a household that has many mouths to feed. We again keep it simple, sweetie, with our focus on default and overloaded constructors and method overriding.

Our superclass for this program will be the HousePet class. House pets typically have a name, an owner, and always have a favorite food. We build a default (no input) and overloaded (pass parameters into) constructor for this class. We also write a toString() method that provides a String description of the object. Recall that toString() is a method in the java.lang.Object class. We are overriding the Object's toString() method here. What is HousePet's superclass?

```
1    //Program 9-4
2    //File:  HousePet.java
3
4    //This class is a superclass for all of the pet classes.
5
6    public class HousePet
7    {
8       protected String name, favoriteFood, owner;
9
10      public HousePet()
11      {
12           //We'll name all of our pets Pooky initially.
13           name = "Pooky";
14
15           //We'll assume Donna owns all of the pets.
16           owner = "Donna";
17
18           //We'll assume all of our pets like cookies.
19           favoriteFood = "cookies";
20      }
21
```

```
22      //Here is our overloaded constructor.
23      public HousePet(String n, String o, String ff)
24      {
25              name = n;
26              favoriteFood = ff;
27              owner = o;
28      }
29
30      public void setName(String n) { name = n; }
31
32      public void setFavoriteFood(String ff) { favoriteFood = ff; }
33
34      public void setOwner(String o) { owner = o; }
35
36      public String toString()
37      {
38              String output = "I am " + name + " a house pet. "
39                          +"\nMy favorite food is " + favoriteFood
40                          +".\nMy owner is " + owner +".";
41              return output;
42      }
43  }
```

Venturing on from the HousePet class, let's write a Dog class. A Dog is a HousePet, and dogs require walks, so we'll include a class variable for the number of walks per day. Remember, the Dog class inherits the protected name, favorite Food, owner and public set() methods, and toString() methods from HousePet. Study the Dog class and see that we do not need to call the superclass constructor in the Dog's default constructor but we do explicitly call the HousePet's overloaded constructor in the Dog's overloaded constructor. In the Dog's toString() method, we call the super class toString() and obtain the HousePet's String description and then expand the text to include the dog information.

```
1   //Program 9-4
2   //File:  Dog.java
3
4   public class Dog extends HousePet
5   {
6     protected int numberOfWalksPerDay;
7
8     public Dog()
9     {
```

9

```
10            //This calls HousePet() automatically.
11            numberOfWalksPerDay = 2;
12      }
13
14      public Dog(String n, String o, String ff, int numWalks)
15      {
16            //We must explicitly call the HousePet() overloaded
17            //constructor, passing it the name, owner, and food info.
18            super(n,o,ff);
19            numberOfWalksPerDay = numWalks;
20      }
21
22      public String toString()
23      {
24            String output = super.toString();
25            output += "\nI am a dog and walk " + numberOfWalksPerDay
26                              + " times a day.";
27            return output;
28      }
29  }
```

Some people have tanks of fish and consider the fish important members of their family. We will now write a Fish class. A Fish is a HousePet, and fish require their water temperature to stay within a certain range. For this program example we will have a water temperature variable in our Fish class. Notice that we write the Fish class constructors and toString() in the same manner as the Dog class.

```
1  //Program 9-4
2  //File:  Fish.java
3
4  public class Fish extends HousePet
5  {
6    protected float waterTemp;
7
8    public Fish()
9    {
10           //This calls HousePet() automatically.
11           waterTemp = 80.0f;
12     }
13
```

```
14      public Fish(String n, String o, String ff, float temp)
15      {
16              super(n,o,ff);
17              waterTemp = temp;
18      }
19
20      public String toString()
21      {
22              String output = super.toString();
23              output += "\nI am a fish and my water temp is "
24                                      + waterTemp + " degrees.";
25              return output;
26      }
27  }
```

We now write a PondFish class that extends the Fish class. Pond fish are fish, and can tolerate a larger range of water temperature than aquarium fish. Most pond fish hibernate during the cold part of the year. With this in mind, we see the Pond-Fish class here and it includes a String that will describe the hibernation time.

```
1   //Program 9-4
2   //File:  PondFish.java
3
4
5   public class PondFish extends Fish
6   {
7     protected String hibernateTime;
8
9     public PondFish()
10    {
11            //This calls Fish() automatically.
12            hibernateTime = "November until March";
13    }
14
15    public PondFish(String n, String o, String ff, float temp,
16                              String hib)
17    {
18            super(n, o, ff, temp);
19            hibernateTime = hib;
20    }
21
```

9

```
22      public String toString()
23      {
24              String output = super.toString();
25              output += "\nI am a pond fish and hibernate from "
26                              + hibernateTime + ".";
27              return output;
28      }
29
30  }
```

To demonstrate these classes in action, we build a frame class that contains three buttons, and we also instantiate Dog, Fish, and PondFish objects. This program is boring on the outside but exciting on the inside! The boring user interface allows the user to press a button and see a JOptionPane message box that displays the object's String description. The exciting part of this program is that we have classes extending classes. Also, the objects' toString() methods generate a detailed description of each object! Examine the PetsFrame class and trace how the constructors and toString() methods are called. Check the frame window and message box output shown in Figure 9-4.

```
1   //Program 9-4
2   //PetsFrame.java
3
4   import javax.swing.*;
5   import java.awt.*;
6   import java.awt.event.ActionListener;
7   import java.awt.event.ActionEvent;
8
9   public class PetsFrame extends JFrame implements ActionListener
10  {
11    Dog doggie;
12    Fish fishie;
13    PondFish goldie;
14
15    JButton dogButton = new JButton("Show Dog Info");
16    JButton fishButton = new JButton("Show Fish Info");
17    JButton pondFishButton = new JButton("Show Pond Fish Info");
18
19    public PetsFrame()
20    {
21
22            //Dogs need their name, owner, fav food, and #walks/day.
23            doggie = new Dog("Norman","Susan", "Cookies", 3);
```

```
24
25          //Let's initially take the default values for our fishie.
26          fishie = new Fish();
27
28          //Fish don't eat cookies. We'll set the appropriate food.
29          fishie.setFavoriteFood("Loachie Tablets");
30
31          //Pond fish need their name, owner, favorite food,
32          //water temperature, and hiberation time.
33          goldie = new PondFish("Zena","Maddie","Pond Tabs", 70.0f,
34                                      "December through March");
35
36          this.setTitle("House Pets!");
37
38          Container canvas = getContentPane();
39          canvas.setLayout( new GridLayout(3,1) );
40
41          //Now we add the buttons to the canvas
42          canvas.add(dogButton);
43          canvas.add(fishButton);
44          canvas.add(pondFishButton);
45
46          //Now need to add the listeners for the buttons
47          dogButton.addActionListener(this);
48          fishButton.addActionListener(this);
49          pondFishButton.addActionListener(this);
50
51          //Set the size of the window and show it.
52          this.setSize(275,150);
53          this.show();
54      }
55
56   public static void main(String args[] )
57   {
58          PetsFrame theApp = new PetsFrame();
59          theApp.setDefaultCloseOperation(JFrame.EXIT_ON_CLOSE);
60   }
61
62   //Each button event show a message box that displays
63   //the object's toString() information.
64   public void actionPerformed(ActionEvent e)
65   {
66          if(e.getSource() == dogButton)
67                  JOptionPane.showMessageDialog(this,doggie.toString(),
68                      "Dog Class", JOptionPane.INFORMATION_MESSAGE);
```

9

```
69          else if( e.getSource() == fishButton)
70              JOptionPane.showMessageDialog(this,fishie.toString(),
71                  "Fish Class", JOptionPane.INFORMATION_MESSAGE);
72          else if( e.getSource() == pondFishButton)
73              JOptionPane.showMessageDialog(this,goldie.toString(),
74                  "Pond Fish Class", JOptionPane.INFORMATION_MESSAGE);
75      }
76  }
```

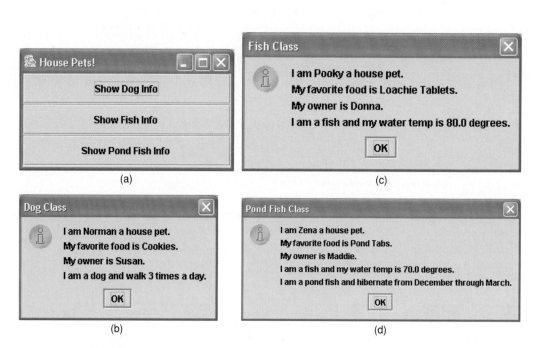

Figure 9-4
a) The PetsFrame output window shows three buttons, each one pops up a message box showing the object's String description. b), c), and d) The Dog, Fish, and PondFish information.

9.3
Abstract Classes

abstract class

an incomplete class that must be extended and its methods must be overridden in its subclasses

The Java language provides a way for programmers to write an **abstract class**. An abstract class can be thought of as an incomplete class with the intention that it will be extended and its methods must be overridden in order for the class to be instantiated. An abstract class is not an actual thing, and it wouldn't make sense as an object. An abstract class is more like an idea or a concept. One analogy is to think of an abstract class as an outline for an essay. You write the outline so that it lists key ideas you want to cover in your paper. The real, working subclass in Java is similar to the completed essay written by using the outline. We are able to create an abstract class by using the term *abstract* in the class declaration line and we are also able to define zero, some, or all of its methods as abstract.

Inheritance and Polymorphism

The four basic principles of an object-oriented language presented in Chapter 6 include abstraction, encapsulation, inheritance, and polymorphism. Any language that is object-oriented provides the programmer with the means to perform or implement these four concepts. Inheritance is the ability to create a new class from an existing class. We first performed the inheritance operation earlier in the text by making our own classes that extended JApplet, JFrame, or JPanel. In the previous examples in this chapter, we created new classes from classes that we wrote; i.e., FancyCounterPanel extended our CounterPanel, and Dog and Fish both extended HousePet.

Polymorphism means many shapes or many forms. In object-oriented programming languages it refers to one interface and many methods. Simply put, polymorphism is the ability to use the same name to refer to methods that perform different tasks. One type of polymorphism is **method overloading**, which simply means a class may have several methods with the same name.

Another form of polymorphism is known as **method overriding**. Method overriding is seen when a superclass and a subclass have the same named method with the identical method inputs. It is said that the method in the subclass overrides the method in the superclass. Abstract classes, being incomplete classes that have abstract methods, require that the Java programmer write these method bodies in the subclasses. As each subclass (that extends the abstract class) is written, the programmer writes (and will call) the overridden methods. This is polymorphism in action!

Abstract HousePets

The best way to understand abstract classes and polymorphism is by seeing several examples. As we built our HousePet class in Program 9-4, we could have included various data and methods for the class, but we could not write some of the methods adequately until we knew the actual type of pet. For instance, if our HousePet class had a method called where_I_Sleep(), we could have placed a vaguely worded statement such as "in the house." Then, once we know what type of pet we have, we are able to state accurately their sleeping locations. Fish sleep in their rock house in the fish tank, dogs sleep on the bed, and birds sleep on their perches.

An abstract class allows us to describe the methods and data that should be in the class—and this includes **abstract methods** that we are unable to write fully in the abstract class. The abstract method describes a behavior or an action for the abstract class, but will not be written until we have extended the abstract class into a real, concrete class. You cannot create an object of an abstract class. You design

method overloading
when the programmer writes two or more methods that have the same name but different input parameters

method overriding
when the programmer writes a method with the same name and input parameter list in a superclass or a subclass. The method in the subclass overrides the method in the superclass

9

abstract methods
a behavior or action for a method in the abstract class. The method is not written in the abstract class but in an extended subclass

and write an abstract class that is intended to be a superclass and will have two or several different subclasses with the same types of behaviors.

In Program 9-5, Abstract HousePets, we add two new abstract methods in our HousePets class: (1) where_I_Sleep() and (2) how_I_Move(). Not all methods must be abstract in an abstract class. We then extend our abstract class and write the methods to make the subclasses complete. The complete program can be found on the text's CD. The following is our abstract HousePet class. Notice that we write the methods for the constructors, set methods, and toString(), but only place the abstract method definition line followed by a semicolon for our abstract methods. See lines 29 and 31.

```
1    //Program 9-5
2    //File:  HousePet.java
3
4    //This abstract class describes methods for house pets.
5    //It is intended to be a superclass of the actual pet classes.
6
7    public abstract class HousePet
8    {
9      protected String name, favoriteFood, owner;
10
11     public HousePet()
12     {
13           //Set initial values.
14           name = "Pooky";
15           owner = "Donna";
16           favoriteFood = "cookies";
17     }
18
19     //Here is our overloaded constructor.
20     public HousePet(String n, String o, String ff)
21     {
22           name = n;
23           favoriteFood = ff;
24           owner = o;
25     }
26
27     //These abstract methods must be overridden in the
28     //subclasses.
29     public abstract String where_I_Sleep();
30
31     public abstract String how_I_Move();
32
33
```

```
34   public void setName(String n) { name = n; }
35   public void setFavoriteFood(String ff) { favoriteFood = ff; }
36   public void setOwner(String o) { owner = o; }
37
38   public String toString()
39   {
40       String output = "I am " + name + " a house pet. "
41                       +"\nMy favorite food is " + favoriteFood
42                       +".\nMy owner is " + owner +".";
43       return output;
44   }
45 }
```

The Dog class is a concrete class, meaning that it is complete and may be instantiated. All its methods are written here, and we are able to create a Dog object. Now
that we have a class that represents a "real" object, we are able to complete the
where_I_Sleep() and how_I_Move() methods. We also expand our toString() so
that it returns a complete description of the Dog object.

```
1  //Program 9-5
2  //File:  Dog.java
3
4  public class Dog extends HousePet
5  {
6    protected int numberOfWalksPerDay;
7
8    public Dog()
9    {
10       //This calls HousePet() automatically.
11       numberOfWalksPerDay = 2;
12   }
13
14   public Dog(String n, String o, String ff, int numWalks)
15   {
16       //We must explicitly call the HousePet() overloaded
17       //constructor, passing it the name, owner, and food info.
18       super(n,o,ff);
19       numberOfWalksPerDay = numWalks;
20   }
21
22   //Here are the two methods that are abstract in the superclass.
23   //We override them here, thus making Dog a complete class.
```

9

```
24      public String where_I_Sleep()
25      {
26             return "I sleep on the bed, of course.";
27      }
28
29      public String how_I_Move()
30      {
31             return "I run on four legs. ";
32      }
33
34
35      public String toString()
36      {
37             String output = super.toString();
38             output += "\nI am a dog and walk " + numberOfWalksPerDay
39                                   + " times a day."
40                                   + "\n" + where_I_Sleep()
41                                   + "\n" + how_I_Move();
42             return output;
43      }
44  }
```

The Fish class is shown here. We have completed this class because we have written all of the inherited methods. We are now able to create an object of the Fish class.

```
1   //Program 9-5
2   //File:  Fish.java
3
4   public class Fish extends HousePet
5   {
6      protected float waterTemp;
7
8      public Fish()
9      {
10             //This calls HousePet() automatically.
11             waterTemp = 80.0f;
12      }
13
14      public Fish(String n, String o, String ff, float temp)
15      {
```

```
16              super(n,o,ff);
17              waterTemp = temp;
18      }
19
20      //Here are the two methods that are abstract in the superclass.
21      //We override them here, thus making Fish a complete class.
22      public String where_I_Sleep()
23      {
24              return "I sleep in the rock house in my tank.";
25      }
26
27      public String how_I_Move()
28      {
29              return "I swim! ";
30      }
31
32      public String toString()
33      {
34              String output = super.toString();
35              output += "\nI am a fish and my water temp is "
36                                  + waterTemp + " degrees."
37                                  + "\n" + where_I_Sleep()
38                                  + "\n" + how_I_Move();
39              return output;
40      }
41 }
```

The PetsFrame2 class will create Dog and Fish objects, and we have modified the button handling code so that it call the objects' where_I_Sleep() method. Figure 9-5a shows the PetsFrame2 window and Figure 9-5b shows the results from pressing the Dog button. The frame source code is as follows:

```
1  //Program 9-5
2  //PetsFrame2.java
3
4  import javax.swing.*;
5  import java.awt.*;
6  import java.awt.event.ActionListener;
7  import java.awt.event.ActionEvent;
8
9  public class PetsFrame2 extends JFrame implements ActionListener
10 {
```

9

```
11        Dog doggie;
12        Fish fishie;
13
14        JButton dogButton = new JButton("Where does the dog sleep?");
15        JButton fishButton = new JButton("Where does the fish sleep?");
16
17        public PetsFrame2()
18        {
19
20                //Create the Dog and Fish objects.
21                doggie = new Dog("Norman","Susan", "Cookies", 3);
22                fishie = new Fish("Barnum", "Maddie", "Loachie Tablets", 1);
23
24                this.setTitle("Sleeping House Pets!");
25
26                Container canvas = getContentPane();
27                canvas.setLayout( new GridLayout(2,1) );
28
29                //Now we add the buttons to the canvas
30                canvas.add(dogButton);
31                canvas.add(fishButton);
32
33                //Now need to add the listeners for the buttons
34                dogButton.addActionListener(this);
35                fishButton.addActionListener(this);
36
37                //Set the size of the window and show it.
38                this.setSize(275,150);
39                this.show();
40        }
41
42        public static void main(String args[] )
43        {
44                PetsFrame2 theApp = new PetsFrame2();
45                theApp.setDefaultCloseOperation(JFrame.EXIT_ON_CLOSE);
46        }
47
48        //Each button event shows a message box that displays
49        //the object's where_I_Sleep() information.
50        public void actionPerformed(ActionEvent e)
51        {
52                String output = "", title = "";
53                if(e.getSource() == dogButton)
54                {
55                        output = doggie.where_I_Sleep();
56                        title = "Dog Class";
57                }
```

9

586   Chapter 9 ▌ Inheritance and Interfaces

```
58          else if( e.getSource() == fishButton)
59          {
60              output = fishie.where_I_Sleep();
61              title = "Fish Class";
62          }
63
64          JOptionPane.showMessageDialog(this,output,title,
65                  JOptionPane.INFORMATION_MESSAGE);
66      }
67 }
```

(a)   (b)

Figure 9-5
a) The PetsFrame2 output window shows two buttons. b) Where the Dog sleeps.

Abstract Employee and Salary Calculation Program

Abstract classes are especially handy when the programmer has a group of related subclasses and he or she needs to perform a task differently, depending on the subclass. Consider the abstract class Employee. All employees have a name and an identification number, and each employee earns a weekly salary. We create an abstract Employee class that contains a protected float for the weekly salary and an abstract method named calcWeeklySalary(). All employees will have their salary calculated—but the actual formulas vary depending on the type of employee. Here is the Employee class, which is part of Program 9-6.

```
1  //Program 9-6
2  //File:  Employee.java
3
4  //The Employee class is abstrast. It is intended to be
5  //extended and each of its subclasses must complete the
6  //calcWeeklySalary() method based of the type of employee.
7
8  public abstract class Employee
9  {
```

```
10      protected String name, SSN;
11      protected float weeklySalary;
12
13      public Employee()
14      {
15            name = "";
16            SSN = "";
17      }
18
19      public Employee(String name, String SSN)
20      {
21            this.name = name;
22            this.SSN = SSN;
23      }
24
25      public String getName(){ return name; }
26
27      public float getWeeklySalary() { return weeklySalary; }
28
29      //The salary calculation method is abstract since we
30      //use a different formula for each type of employee.
31      public abstract void calcWeeklySalary();
32
33   }
```

We use the Employee as our superclass and write three classes that extend Employee, Secretary, SalesPerson, and Manager. Secretaries are paid an hourly rate with time-and-a-half for every hour over forty.

```
1    //Program 9-6
2    //File:  Secretary.java
3
4    //A secretary's weekly salary is based on the number of
5    //hours worked times an hourly rate. Every hour over forty
6    //is paid at time and one-half.
7
8    import java.text.DecimalFormat;
9
10   public class Secretary extends Employee
11   {
```

```
12      protected String dept;
13      private float weeklyHours, payRate;
14
15      public Secretary()
16      {
17              dept = "";
18              weeklyHours = 0.0f;
19              payRate = 15.0f;
20      }
21
22      public Secretary(String name, String SSN, String dept, float hours, float rate)
23      {
24              super(name, SSN);
25              this.dept = dept;
26              weeklyHours = hours;
27              payRate = rate;
28      }
29
30      public void calcWeeklySalary()
31      {
32              weeklySalary = weeklyHours * payRate;
33              if(weeklyHours > 40)
34                      weeklySalary += (weeklyHours - 40)*1.5*payRate;
35      }
36  }
37
```

Sales persons are paid a flat weekly rate plus a commission based on their total sales for the week.

```
1   //Program 9-6
2   //File:  SalesPerson.java
3
4   //A sales person's weekly salary is based on a flat weekly
5   //rate plus a commission from the total sales.
6
7   import java.text.DecimalFormat;
8
9   public class SalesPerson extends Employee
10  {
11    protected String region;
12    private float baseWkPay, totalWkSales, commission;
```

```
13
14     public SalesPerson()
15     {
16          totalWkSales = 0.0f;
17          commission = 0.10f;          //base rate is 10%
18          baseWkPay = 250.0f;          //base pay is $250/week
19     }
20
21     public SalesPerson(String name, String SSN, String reg, float basePay,
22                                   float salesTotal, float comm)
23     {
24          super(name, SSN);
25          region = reg;
26          totalWkSales = salesTotal;
27          commission = comm;
28          baseWkPay = basePay;
29     }
30
31     public void calcWeeklySalary()
32     {
33          weeklySalary = baseWkPay + totalWkSales*commission;
34     }
35
36 }
```

Managers are paid a flat yearly salary. Managers may receive a bonus at the end of the year, but we will ignore that situation here.

```
1   //Program 9-6
2   //File:  Manager.java
3
4   //A manager's weekly salary is 1/52 or his/her yearly salary.
5
6   import java.text.DecimalFormat;
7
8   public class Manager extends Employee
9   {
10    protected String dept;
11    private float yearlySalary;
12
```

```
13      public Manager()
14      {
15            yearlySalary = 60000;
16      }
17
18      public Manager(String name, String SSN, String dept, float yearPay)
19      {
20            super(name, SSN);
21            this.dept = dept;
22            yearlySalary = yearPay;
23      }
24
25      public void calcWeeklySalary()
26      {
27            weeklySalary = (float)(yearlySalary/52.0);
28      }
29
30   }
31
```

We build a JFrame class that instantiates Secretary, SalesPerson, and Manager objects, passing information into the three constructor methods. This program has three buttons. The button event handlers use the appropriate object to get the employee's name, calculate and get the salary, and then shows this information in a JOptionPane message box. Here is the frame source code and Figure 9-6 shows the frame and the sales person's information message box.

```
1    //Program 9-6
2    //ThreeEmployeesFrame.java
3
4    import javax.swing.*;
5    import java.awt.*;
6    import java.awt.event.ActionListener;
7    import java.awt.event.ActionEvent;
8    import java.text.*;
9
10   public class ThreeEmployeesFrame extends JFrame implements ActionListener
11   {
12     JButton secButton = new JButton("Show Secretary Info");
13     JButton salesButton = new JButton("Show SalesPerson Info");
14     JButton bossButton = new JButton("Show Manager Info");
15
```

```
16        //Secretary input is name, SSN, dept, hours worked, hourly pay
17        Secretary sec = new Secretary("Gloria","555-11-2222", "Western States",
18                                                    45.0f, 14.00f);
19
20        //Sales input is name, SSN, region, base wk pay, total sales, comm rate
21        SalesPerson sales = new SalesPerson("Janet","222-33-4444", "Phoenix Area",
22                                                    250.0f, 6000.0f, 0.20f);
23
24        //Manager input is name, SSN, dept, yearly pay
25        Manager boss = new Manager("Paul","333-44-5555",
26                          "Arizona and New Mexico", 65000f);
27
28        public ThreeEmployeesFrame()
29        {
30              this.setTitle("Secretary, SalesPerson, and Boss");
31              Container canvas = getContentPane();
32              canvas.setLayout( new GridLayout(3,1) );
33
34              //Now add the buttons to the canvas
35              canvas.add(secButton);
36              canvas.add(salesButton);
37              canvas.add(bossButton);
38
39              //Now need to add the listeners for the buttons
40              secButton.addActionListener(this);
41              salesButton.addActionListener(this);
42              bossButton.addActionListener(this);
43
44              //Set the size of the window and show it.
45              this.setSize(350,175);
46              this.show();
47        }
48
49        public static void main(String args[] )
50        {
51              ThreeEmployeesFrame theApp = new ThreeEmployeesFrame();
52              theApp.setDefaultCloseOperation(JFrame.EXIT_ON_CLOSE);
53        }
54
55        public void actionPerformed(ActionEvent e)
56        {
57              String output = "", title = "";
58              DecimalFormat df = new DecimalFormat("0.00");
59              float pay ;
60
61              if(e.getSource() == secButton)
62              {
```

9

```
63                    sec.calcWeeklySalary();
64                    title = "Job Title: Secretary ";
65                    output = "Name: "+ sec.getName();
66                    pay = sec.getWeeklySalary();
67                    output += "\nWeekly Pay:  $ " + df.format( pay );
68
69            }
70            else if( e.getSource() == salesButton)
71            {
72                    sales.calcWeeklySalary();
73                    title = "Job Title: Sales Person ";
74                    output = "Name: "+ sales.getName();
75                    pay = sales.getWeeklySalary();
76                    output += "\nWeekly Pay:  $ " + df.format( pay );
77            }
78            else if( e.getSource() == bossButton)
79            {
80                    boss.calcWeeklySalary();
81                    title = "Job Title: Manager";
82                    output = "Name: "+ boss.getName();
83                    pay = boss.getWeeklySalary();
84                    output += "\nWeekly Pay:  $ " + df.format( pay );
85            }
86
87            JOptionPane.showMessageDialog(this,output,
88                    title, JOptionPane.INFORMATION_MESSAGE);
89      }
90  }
```

(a)   (b)

Figure 9-6
The abstract class Employee has an abstract calcWeeklySalary() method. Employee
is extended in the Secretary, SalesPerson, and Manager classes and each of the
different type of employees have a different formula for the weekly salary calculation.
a) The frame window. b) The resultant salary calculation for the SalesPerson object.
(Manager and Secretary message boxes are not shown here.)

The Power of Polymorphism

In the previous two programs we saw how we can write an abstract class and then override the superclass methods. By using the object name, we can call the desired method. The true power of the Java language can be seen in Program 9-7, a modified version of the Three Employees program. If you have a superclass, and then create several subclasses, it is possible to assign the object references into an array of superclass references, and then use the superclass array to access the individual subclass object methods. This sounds confusing, so let's write a few lines of code to illustrate what we mean.

In the previous example, we have an Employee superclass and three subclasses: (1) Secretary, (2) Salesperson, and (3) Boss. Each subclass has a calcWeeklySalary(), getName(), and getWeeklySalary() methods. Look back at the actionPerformed() method in Program 9-6 on page 593 and see that we used the different objects to calculate and show the weekly salaries.

Java allows us to assign a subclass reference into its superclass reference, and then use the superclass to call the subclass's method. First create the subclass objects, as per normal:

```
Secretary sec = new Secretary("Gloria","555-11-2222", "Western States",
                       45.0f, 14.00f);


SalesPerson sales = new SalesPerson("Janet","222-33-4444", "Phoenix Area",
                       250.0f, 6000.0f, 0.20f);


Manager boss = new Manager("Paul","333-44-5555",
                         "Arizona and New Mexico", 65000f);
```

Next, we create a superclass array:

```
//Here is the array of superclass object references.
Employee emp[] = new Employee[3];
```

In the constructor, we assign each subclass object into the Employee array:

```
public ThreeEmployeesFrame2()
{
        //Assign each object reference into the
        //superclass array elements.
        emp[0] = sec;
        emp[1] = sales;
        emp[2] = boss;
```

In the ThreeEmployeesFrame2 class, we have one button that gathers information for all three employees and displays it at once. Then, in the actionPerformed()

method for this one button, we write a for loop that calls the calcWeeklySalary(), getName(), and getWeeklySalary() methods. Java examines the object in the Employee array and then calls the correct method!

```java
public void actionPerformed(ActionEvent e)
{
      //declare variables here
//The emp[] checks the objects and executes the appropriate method.
      for(i = 0; i < emp.length; ++i)
      {
            emp[i].calcWeeklySalary();
            output += "Name:  " + emp[i].getName();
            pay = emp[i].getWeeklySalary();
            output += "\nWeekly Pay:  $ " + df.format( pay );
            output += "\n\n";
      }

      JOptionPane.showMessageDialog(this,output,
            title, JOptionPane.INFORMATION_MESSAGE);
}
```

Program 9-7 shows the ThreeEmployeesFrame2 class. Figure 9-7 shows the frame and resultant JOptionPane message box.

```java
1   //Program 9-7          Illustrates polymorphism in action!
2   //ThreeEmployeesFrame.java
3
4   import javax.swing.*;
5   import java.awt.*;
6   import java.awt.event.*;
7   import java.text.*;
8
9   public class ThreeEmployeesFrame2 extends JFrame implements ActionListener
10  {
11    JButton doItAllButton = new JButton("Show Everyone's Info");
12
13    //Secretary input is name, SSN, dept, hours worked, hourly pay
14    Secretary sec = new Secretary("Gloria","555-11-2222", "Western States",
15                           45.0f, 14.00f);
16
17    //Sales input is name, SSN, region, base wk pay, total sales, comm rate
18    SalesPerson sales = new SalesPerson("Janet","222-33-4444", "Phoenix Area",
19                           250.0f, 6000.0f, 0.20f);
20
```

```
21    //Manager input is name, SSN, dept, yearly pay
22    Manager boss = new Manager("Paul","333-44-5555",
23                               "Arizona and New Mexico", 65000f);
24
25    //Here is the array of superclass object references.
26    Employee emp[] = new Employee[3];
27
28
29    public ThreeEmployeesFrame2()
30    {
31          //Assign the each object reference into the
32          //superclass array elements.
33          emp[0] = sec;
34          emp[1] = sales;
35          emp[2] = boss;
36
37          this.setTitle("Secretary, SalesPerson, and Boss");
38          Container canvas = getContentPane();
39          canvas.setLayout( new GridLayout(1,1) );
40
41          //Now add the buttons to the canvas
42          canvas.add(doItAllButton);
43
44          //Now need to add the listeners for the buttons
45          doItAllButton.addActionListener(this);
46
47          //Set the size of the window and show it.
48          this.setSize(350,175);
49          this.show();
50    }
51
52    public static void main(String args[] )
53    {
54          ThreeEmployeesFrame2 theApp = new ThreeEmployeesFrame2();
55          theApp.setDefaultCloseOperation(JFrame.EXIT_ON_CLOSE);
56    }
57
58    public void actionPerformed(ActionEvent e)
59    {
60          int i;
61          String output = "", title = "Three Employees' Weekly Salary";
62          DecimalFormat df = new DecimalFormat("0.00");
63          float pay;
64
```

```
65
66              //The emp array holds a Secretary, Salesperson, and
67              //Boss reference.
68              //Java looks at the object reference and is able to call
69              //the appropriate objects' methods.
70
71              for(i = 0; i < emp.length; ++i)
72              {
73                      emp[i].calcWeeklySalary();
74                      output += "Name:  " + emp[i].getName();
75                      pay = emp[i].getWeeklySalary();
76                      output += "\nWeekly Pay:  $ " + df.format( pay );
77                      output += "\n\n";
78              }
79
80              JOptionPane.showMessageDialog(this,output,
81                              title, JOptionPane.INFORMATION_MESSAGE);
82
83      }
84 }
```

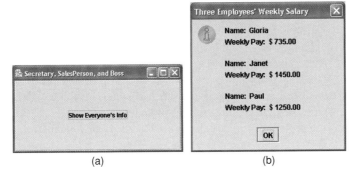

(a)   (b)

Figure 9-7
The ThreeEmployeesFrame2 class has an array of Employee objects that contain
the subclasses Manager, SalesPerson, and Secretary. The array can be used to
access the appropriate subclass method. a) The one-button frame. b) The resultant
message box showing all three employee salaries.

You may understand this Java example but still may ask the question, "Why
is this useful?" Imagine that you are writing a flight simulator game that includes
several different types of airplanes. The abstract class Airplane contains the
abstract methods takeOff(), fly(), landing(), and a drawMyself() method. The
superclass has a boolean flag, bOnScreen, which denotes the status of the plane on

the screen. That is, if bOnScreen is true, then the plane is currently seen "on-screen," at the screen locations in (*x,y*) pixel coordinates. Your abstract class may look like this:

```
public abstract class Airplane
{
        protected name;
        protected int xPos, yPos;
        protected boolean bOnScreen;

        public amIOnScreen(){return bOnScreen; }
        public getXPosition() { return xPos; }
        public getYPosition() { return yPos; }

        public abstract void takeOff();
        public abstract void fly();
        public abstract void landing();

        public abstract void drawMyself();

        //rest of class
}
```

Your simulator game has many types of airplanes, including gliders; single-engine, six-passenger, personal aircraft; Boeing 737s; and F-16 jets. Each of these airplane classes is completely written and includes the necessary code for taking off, flying, and landing, and each class knows how to draw itself on the screen. In the class that controls the game, you may have several airplanes "in the air" at once. If you have assigned the different plane objects into an Airplane object array, the individual planes can be tracked by using the array element number. The flying, landing, take-off, and drawing portion of code can be written in a very tidy manner:

```
//Assume each airplane subclass object is assigned into the planes array.

int n;        //number of planes in the game

//Create all of the various plane objects. Assume there are n of them.
Boeing737 boe737 = new Boeing737();
Boeing737 boe737a = new Boeing737();
F16 jet = new F16();
//etc.

Airplanes planes[] = new Airplanes[n];

//Assign each plane's reference into the planes array.
```

```
planes[0] = boe737;
planes[1] = boe737a;
planes[2] = jet;
//etc.

//Drawing and flying portion of the Airplane Simulation Game.
for(i = 0; i < planes.length; ++i)
{
        if(planes[i].amIOnScreen() )
        {
                planes[i].fly();
                planes[i].drawMyself();
        }
}
```

Each plane in the game can quickly be referenced by the superclass planes array. The programmer should neither keep track of the individual plane nor call each object's methods directly. This is a powerful feature of object-oriented programming language.

final Classes

An abstract class can be thought of as an incomplete class, requiring the programmer to extend it to a subclass and then write the abstract methods. The opposite of an abstract class is a **final class**. When the final modifier is used in the class declaration line, it tells the compiler that this class is complete and is not to be extended, changed, or overridden. You may think of a final class as the last node on an inheritance tree. We have seen final used with class data, meaning the data is not to be changed. The final modifier may also be used with methods. A final method cannot be overridden in a class that inherits it.

final class
a complete class that should not be extended, changed, or overridden

9.4
Writing Java Interfaces

In Chapter 7, we learned that a **Java interface** is a class-like entity that is used by Java programmers as a way to design certain behaviors for a class by providing the final public data fields and public method signatures. An interface typically contains the skeleton of a class, including a list of class behaviors. This skeleton or blueprint can be thought of as promised behavior and the intent is to write the implementation, i.e., bodies of methods, once the actual type of class is known. For example, we implemented the ActionListener and MouseListener interfaces in program examples in Chapters 7 and 8 when we wanted our program to react to button presses and mouse movement.

Java interface
A class-like entity that can be thought of as a blueprint of class behavior. Used to design behaviors for a class by providing final public data fields and public method signatures.

9

Another way to visualize an interface is that it provides a way for unrelated items to interact with each other. For example, you can use a remote control device to interact with your television. The remote control unit allows you to turn on the TV, change channels, and adjust the volume. You may think of the TV remote as a way for you to interface with your television. For military personnel, there are certain rules of behavior or protocol that describe how troops interact with each other. These rules dictate how a Sargent (enlisted person) interacts with a Major (officer). And if you hear a siren behind you as you are driving your car, there is a set of behaviors you are required to perform—slow down, pull over to the right, and stop your car until the emergency vehicles have passed. In Java, interfaces provide an agreed upon set of methods, and an interface is a means for unrelated objects to interact with each other.

Let's see an example to illustrate this concept. What behaviors are needed to play baseball? You must be able to hit the ball, throw the ball, catch the ball, and run. We can define these baseball skills in an interface:

```
//A Java interface defining baseball behavior.
//File:  Baseball.java

public interface BaseballSkills
{
        public void hitTheBall();
        public void catchTheBall();
        public void throwTheBall();
        public void run();
}
```

Recall our SoftballPlayer example in Chapter 7. It makes sense to have our SoftballPlayer class implement the BaseballSkills interface, as these are required skills for all those who play the game of softball. Java requires that we write the methods defined by the interface in the classes that implement the interface. In other words, it is up to the programmer to provide the correct implementation for these interface methods. We write the SoftballPlayer class like this:

```
//A SoftballPlayer acquires the skills to play baseball by
//implementing the BaseballSkills interface.

//File: SoftballPlayer.java

public class SoftballPlayer implements BaseballSkills
{
        private String name, position;
        private int jerseyNumber;
        private boolean bCanPlay;   //is available for the game

        //etc.
```

```
//We must write the methods of BaseballSkills in this class.

public void hitTheBall()
{
        //How does the SoftballPlayer hit the ball?
}
public void catchTheBall()
{
        //How does the SoftballPlayer catch the ball?
}
public void throwTheBall()
{
        //How does the SoftballPlayer throw the ball?
}
public void run()
{
        //How does the SoftballPlayer throw the ball?
}
}
```

Now, if we want our Fish objects to play baseball, we have a Java interface ready to go! Our BaseballSkills interface describes the necessary behavior of a baseball player. Fish don't play baseball, you say? Ha! If we want our Fish to have baseball skills, we implement the BaseballSkills interface in the Fish class—it is up to the programmer to figure out how Fish objects throw and catch baseballs. The Fish class code looks like this:

```
//For a Fish to play baseball, we use the BaseballSkills interface.
//File:  Fish.java

public class Fish extends HousePet implements BaseballSkills
{
        protected float waterTemp;

        public Fish()
        {
                //This calls HousePet() automatically.
                waterTemp = 80.0f;
        }

        public Fish(String n, String o, String ff, float temp)
        {
                super(n,o,ff);
                waterTemp = temp;
        }
```

9

```java
public String toString()
{
        String output = super.toString();
        output += "\nI am a fish and my water temp is "
                            + waterTemp + " degrees.";
        return output;
}


//Here are the BaseballSkills methods. The programmer has to
//determine how Fish perform these tasks.
public void hitTheBall()
{
        //How does a Fish hit the ball?
}
public void catchTheBall()
{
        //How does a Fish catch the ball?
}
public void throwTheBall()
{
        //How does a Fish throw the ball?
}
public void run()
{
        //How does a Fish run the bases?
}
}
```

You may think that interfaces and abstract classes are alike, and in a sense they are, because each provides a framework of methods for a class. But interfaces and abstract classes differ in several ways! The abstract class is a superclass and hence the "is a" class relationship should be true in order to maintain the integrity of the object-oriented design philosophy. A Fish *is a* HousePet. A SoftballPlayer IS NOT a BaseballSkills. Abstract classes and their subclasses should always have the "is a" relationship.

A class may implement many interfaces whereas a class may extend only one superclass. An interface specifies a set of behaviors for a class. For a programmer to implement many interfaces in a class, he or she must write the methods dictated by the interfaces. When the program extends an abstract class, the programmer may or may not write the methods. If the methods are not written, the extended subclass must also be declared abstract.

As a Java programmer you will use interfaces more often than abstract classes. You may design a tree of Java classes with the root of the tree being abstract. As your subclasses branch out from the abstract root, you fill in the methods for the subclasses as we did with HousePets and Employees. You will use an interface for event handling, and you will design interfaces to provide the framework for desired behaviors in your classes.

Interface Example: The GameRules Program

An interface helps us design and write our programs by providing the public, final, static data fields and method signatures. An interface typically contains the general-purpose design for class behavior that can be implemented specifically where appropriate. Let's examine an interface that contains the method definitions for the rules of any game. Program 9-8 shows the source code for an interface named GameRules. It is contained in the file *GameRules.java* and is compiled in the usual manner by the Java compiler, that is, *javac GameRules.java*.

```
1   //Program 9-8
2   //File: GameRules.java
3
4   //A Java interface describing the rules for a game.
5
6   public interface GameRules
7   {
8       public String legalPlays();
9       public String playBoundries();
10      public String winningDefinition();
11      public String whoGoesNext();
12      public String timingRules();
13  }
```

We do not write the rule methods in this interface because methods are not defined in interfaces and we do not know what game we are referring to at this time. An interface designs the method signatures. In this case, all of the game rules will be returned as Strings.

Now let's implement the GameRules interface in two Game example classes. We describe a portion of JavaDarts (a dart game) and War, a card game. Notice how each of the class definition lines below implements GameRules. And also note how each of the five GameRules methods describes the specific rule for the JavaDarts and War classes.

```
1   //Program 9-8
2   //File:  JavaDarts.java
3
4   //A partial program which illustrates how we implement
5   //the GameRules interface.
6
```

```
7    public class JavaDarts implements GameRules
8    {
9      //Dart class data
10
11     // defining the interface methods
12     public String legalPlays()
13     {
14            return  "The player must stand at the designated throw line." +
15                    "\nThe player throws one dart at a time." +
16                    "\nThe dart must hit the dart board to score any points." ;
17     }
18
19     public String playBoundries()
20     {
21            return  "If the dart hits the border of two section" +
22            " the higher point will be given." +
23            "If the dart does not hit the board, no points are scored.";
24     }
25
26     public String winningDefinition()
27     {
28            return "The player with the most points wins. ";
29     }
30
31     public String whoGoesNext()
32     {
33            return  "Each player will throw 3 darts in a row.";
34     }
35
36     public String timingRules()
37     {
38            return "The game must be finished in an agreed upon time.";
39     }
40
41     //There are many other methods for the actual dart game too.
42     public void play()
43     {
44            //Dart play is implemented here.
45     }
46   }
```

Here is the source code for War, the card game:

```
1    //Program 9-8
2    //File:  War.java
3
4    //A partial listing of the source code for the War card game class.
5
6    public class War implements GameRules
7    {
8      //Data specific to the War card game
9
10     public void play()
11     {
12         //Method that performs the actual play for the game.
13     }
14
15     public String legalPlays()
16     {
17         return "Each player turns over the top card on your deck.";
18     }
19
20     public String playBoundries()
21     {
22         return "Play must occur on the card table.";
23     }
24
25     public String winningDefinition()
26     {
27         return "Winner of round is person with highest ranked card."+
28             "\nWinner takes both players' cards. " +
29             "\nGame winner is person with most cards.";
30     }
31
32     public String whoGoesNext()
33     {
34         return "Winner of previous round takes his or her card first.";
35     }
36
37     public String timingRules()
38     {
39         return "Game goes until players agree to quit.";
40     }
41   }
```

The Power of the Interface

Proper uses of interfaces can speed Java code development because the interface dictates the design of the class. Time can be saved later if changes must occur within these classes, but their interface to other classes does not change. Once an interface is designed and implemented in a class, other classes that use the class have a clear and exact set of methods for the class. Sounds confusing, doesn't it? Examine the AddressBook example and you'll see what we mean.

AddressBook Interface   Imagine that we are writing an address book class that contains the name, address, and phone number of our acquaintances. The address book methods are described in the AddressBook interface shown here in Program 9-9:

```
1   //Program 9-9
2   //File: AddressBook.java
3
4   //A Java interface describing the methods for an Address Book.
5
6   public interface AddressBook
7   {
8      //All methods return true if successful
9      //and false if unable to complete the task.
10
11     //Add a new person to the book.
12     public boolean addPerson(Person p);
13
14     //Search for a person in the book.
15     public boolean findPerson(Person p);
16
17     //Edit a person's entry in the book.
18     public boolean editPerson(Person p);
19
20     //Delete a person from the book.
21     public boolean deletePerson(Person p);
22  }
```

In our Java class, JPTAddressBook, we implement these AddressBook methods. Because we are high-tech, we use the make believe database program "ABC" to contain our data. The class JPTAddressBook implements AddressBook using the ABC specific database calls. Note that the class methods in our program are the methods from the AddressBook interface, but we have to use the ABC methods to perform the actual database tasks.

```
1   //Program 9-9
2   //File: JPTAddressBook.java
3
4   //A Java class that implements the AddressBook interface.
5   //This means we must have the AddressBook methods
6   //defined in here. However the actual work is being performed
7   //by the make-believe ABC database
8   //You database experts, please forgive my lack of database savvy.
9
10  public class JPTAddressBook implements AddressBook
11  {
12     //Create a database object.
13     ABC abc = new ABC();
14
15     boolean result;
16
17     public JPTAddressBook()
18     {
19          //Class constructor connects to the abc database and
20          //performs other initialization tasks.
21          abc.setConnection( /*pass connection & driver info for DB*/ );
22     }
23
24     public boolean addPerson(Person p)
25     {
26          //Adds a person using the ABC specific call.
27          result = abc.putEmInThere(p);
28          return result;
29     }
30
31     public boolean findPerson(Person p)
32     {
33          //Searches for a person in the book.
34          result = abc.areYouInThere(p);
35          return result;
36     }
37
38     public boolean editPerson(Person p)
39     {
40          //Edits a person in the book.
41          result = abc.gottaChangeEm(p);
42          return result;
43     }
44
```

```
45      public boolean deletePerson(Person p)
46      {
47            //Deletes a person from the book.
48            result = abc.seeYouLaterAlligator(p);
49            return result;
50      }
51   }
```

If we were to use JPTAddressBook, we would create an object and call the methods in the manner shown below. We do not call the ABC methods, we call the JPTAddressBook methods dictated by the AddressBook interface.

```
1    //Program 9-9
2    //File: ILoveTheJPTAddressBook.java
3
4    //Here we make a JPTAddressBook object and use it.
5    //We don't know which database is used by the JPTAddressBook class.
6
7    //Partial program.
8
9    public class ILoveJPTAddressBook extends JFrame
10   {
11     //Create an address book object.
12
13     JPTAddressBook book = new JPTAddressBook();
14
15     Person p = new Person();
16
17     public ILoveJPTAddressBook()
18     {
19            //Class constructor does constructor business.
20     }
21
22
23     //The authors of the JPTAddressBook may change the underlying
24     //source code in their class, but by implementing AddressBook,
25     //these method calls will always be the same.
26     public void accessBook()
27     {
28            boolean result;
29            //Obtain the user's choice and Person information.
```

```
30          switch(choice)
31          {
32                  case 1:               //add a person
33                          result = book.addPerson(p);
34                          break;
35                  case 2:               //find a person
36                          result = book.findPerson(p);
37                          break;
38                  case 3:               //edit a person
39                          result = book.editPerson(p);
40                          break;
41                  case 4:               //delete a person
42                          result = book.deletePerson(p);
43                          break;
44          }
45      }
46  }
```

Now let's assume that JPTAddressBook is a favorite class for many Java programmers and that thousands of people are using it. But there is a new database called XYZDeluxe that is better, faster, and cheaper than ABC and we want to use it instead. Because we implemented our program with the AddressBook interface, we can go into our JPTAddressBook code and make the necessary changes for calling the database, but our users will not see any difference in the method calls. See how the database code changes here within the JPTAddressBook class methods. But the code above in ILoveJPTAddressBook would not change.

```
1   //Program 9-9
2   //File on the disk for reference is: NewJPTAddressBook.java
3   //File for Java's use: JPTAddressBook.java
4
5   //This Java class that implements the AddressBook interface.
6   //The class was originally written using the make-believe ABC database.
7
8   //Now the NEW (and improved ;-) class uses the make-believe
9   //XYZDeluxe database. Because we have implemented the AddressBook,
10   //the users of our address book don't have to make different calls.
11
12  public class JPTAddressBook implements AddressBook
13  {
14    //create a database object
15    //ABC abc = new ABC();
```

```
16
17          //Now use the XYZDeluxe database.
18          XYZDeluxe xyz = new XYZDeluxe();
19
20          boolean result;
21
22          public TheBestAddressBook()
23          {
24                  //Class constructor connects to the xyz database
25                  //instead of the abc database. It also
26                  //performs other initialization tasks.
27
28                  //abc.setConnection( /*pass connection & driver info for DB*/ );
29
30                  xyz.setConnection( /*pass connection & driver info for DB*/ );
31          }
32
33
34          public boolean addPerson(Person p)
35          {
36                  //Adds a person using the ABC specific call.
37                  //result = abc.putEmInThere(p);
38
39                  result = xyz.insertPerson(p);
40                  return result;
41          }
42
43          public boolean findPerson(Person p)
44          {
45                  //Searches for a person in the book.
46                  //result = abc.areYouInThere(p);
47
48                  result = xyz.allPointsBulletin(p);
49                  return result;
50          }
51
52          public boolean editPerson(Person p)
53          {
54                  //Edits a person in the book.
55                  //result = abc.gottaChangeEm(p);
56
57                  result = xyz.changeIdentity(p);
58                  return result;
59          }
60
```

9

Chapter 9 ▌ Inheritance and Interfaces

```
61       public boolean deletePerson(Person p)
62       {
63               //Deletes a person from the book.
64               //result = seeYouLaterAlligator(p);
65
66               result = xyz.youAreOuttaHere(p);
67               return result;
68       }
69   }
```

> **Note:** You might question the need for the use of an interface in the JPTAd-
> dress Book class because the internal database changes did not affect the
> code in the ILoveJPTAddressBook class. Why use an interface?
>   Interfaces provide a standard template that Java programmers can follow
> during code development. Imagine that you are one programmer, working at a
> large research facility that has many types of sensors and cameras.
>   Your development team could design a DataCollection interface with meth-
> ods pertaining to the sensors, including bandwidth, frame rate, frame size, and
> data storage techniques. As the programs for various sensors are written, all
> of the programmers are familiar with and are following the DataCollection
> interface. The resulting programs have consistent methods calls across the
> various sensors and standard method calls. This will speed development time
> and make the code easier to maintain.

Using Interfaces for Constant Values

The interface is a handy way to establish a group of constant values that are related
in some manner. As we have seen, Java permits us to extend only one class but we
may implement many interfaces. Let's use the GameRules interface with a Foot-
ballGame class and to implement a FootballScoring interface. This interface contains constant values for scoring.

```
//File: FootballScoring.java
//A Java interface containing constant values for Football.

public interface FootballScoring
{
        public static final int FIELDGOAL = 3;
        public static final int TOUCHDOWN = 6;
        public static final int POINTAFTER = 1;
        public static final int SAFETY = 2;
        public static final int TWOPOINTCONVERSION = 2;
}
```

9

The FootballApplet class definition line illustrates how we extend JApplet, and implement the GameRules and FootballScoring interfaces.

```
File: FootballApplet.java

public class FootballApplet entends JApplet
       implements GameRules, FootballScoring
{
       private int score;
       private String playType;

       public void play()
       {
               if( playType.equals("Touchdown") )
                       score += TOUCHDOWN;
       }

       //Must write all of the methods for all of the GameRules.
       //Here's one of them.

       public String timingRules()
       {
               return "Game is played in 4-15 minute quarters.";
       }
}
```

One last note on interfaces. If we implement a Java interface in a class but do not complete the interface method(s), that is, we do not write the method body, we must declare the interface method(s) and the class to be abstract. This is a legal programming technique often used in Java. Anytime you have a method definition line in a Java class and do not write the method, that method, as well as the class, must be declared as abstract. We see this technique in the Practice section's Boxes and Stars program.

9.5
Summary

In this chapter we reviewed how we have used Java superclasses such as JApplet, JFrame, and JPanel. When we extend a superclass, we inherit that class's public and protected data and methods. Private data and methods are not inherited by the subclasses. The protected class members are accessible to all methods within the class (as all class members are), but are not accessible to the world.

We presented how to write, use, and extend our own superclasses and how default and overloaded constructors work in a Java program. If the programmer instantiates a subclass by calling the default (no input) constructor, the superclass's default constructor is automatically called by Java. If the programmer chooses to pass data into a subclass constructor, the programmer can write the constructor so that it either passes data on to the superclass's overloaded constructor or the programmer must perform all the superclass initialization steps in the subclass. Passing data on to the superclass constructor is the preferred approach.

An abstract class is an incomplete class that must be used as a superclass. An abstract class usually contains abstract methods that describe intended behaviors or tasks for the subclass. If the same named method is found in both the superclass and subclass, the subclass method overrides the superclass method.

Polymorphism is an object-oriented concept that means one interface, many implementations. We have seen that method overloading, that is, when methods have the same name but different input parameters, is known as early-binding polymorphism because the Java compiler can discern the exact method to execute at runtime. Method overriding demonstrates late-binding polymorphism. Overridden methods are methods that are the same (including input lists) and are found in a superclass and its subclasses. We demonstrated that we are able to assign subclass references into an array of superclass references and then access the correct subclass method by using the superclass array elements. When methods are overriden, the Java compiler does not know which overridden method to execute until the program is running.

The concept of Java interfaces was presented and we demonstrated their purpose in program design. Interfaces are class-like entities that are intended to describe class behaviors or tasks. The methods are defined in the interface, but not written. A programmer may implement the interface in his or her class by writing the method bodies described by the interface. Interfaces can also be used to define constant values.

9.6
Practice!

Our only practice program presents an example illustrating the concepts presented in this chapter. We use an abstract class and interface to help us build a fun to run graphical program. Because it is our last program in *Java Programming Today*'s core chapters, we throw in MouseListeners, Vectors, Enumerations, and some advanced code involving double buffering for smooth, on-screen drawing.

Boxes and Stars!

In Program 9-10, the BoxStarFrame program, we create five randomly placed, randomly colored boxes, and five white stars in a JPanel object that is added and shown in a JFrame. We add MouseListeners to the panel to listen if the mouse is pressed on one of our boxes or stars. If the mouse is pressed and then dragged

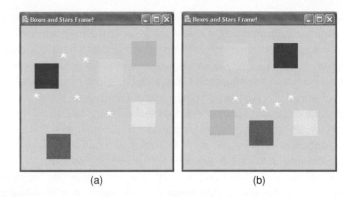

Figure 9-8
a) The BoxStarFrame, which has five boxes and stars that are randomly placed in the frame. b) The resultant frame after clicking and dragging the items with the mouse.

while over one of our boxes or stars, the box or star is also dragged by the mouse. Figure 9-8a on page 614 shows the BoxStar frame in its initial state, the boxes and stars randomly placed thanks to the use of the random number generator. Figure 9-8b shows the same frame after the boxes and stars have been rearranged by dragging them with the mouse.

We now turn to examining the code. We will look at each piece of source code soon, but for now, let's get the big picture of how this program is constructed. Figure 9-9 shows a diagram of the classes and interface relationship. The BoxStarFrame class is easy. It contains a PaintingPanel—which is a JPanel. This panel

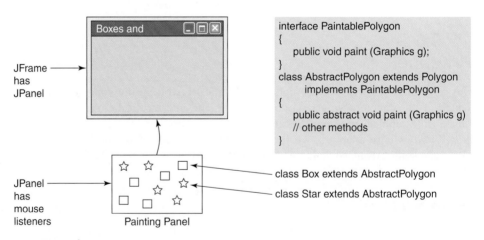

Figure 9-9
The BoxStarFrame program class and interface relationships. The frame has the panel, the panel has the five boxes and stars.

contains the five boxes and stars and implements the MouseListener methods that we need.

There is a PaintablePolygon interface that contains a paint() method. This interface is saying, "If your class implements me, you must tell the program how to paint the class's object." We build an AbstractPolygon class that extends Polygon and implements the PaintablePolygon interface. What this means is that we are making a polygon class that includes a paint() method for each polygon object. In other words, each polygon will know how to paint itself if it is given a Graphics object. Our Box and Star classes extends the AbstractPolygon. The Box and Star classes are polygons that know how to paint themselves.

Let's look at the PaintablePolygon interface code (Program 9-10). It is short and sweet.

```
1    //Program 9-10
2    //File:  PaintablePolygon.java
3
4    //This interface requires a paint() method.
5
6    import java.awt.Graphics;
7
8    public interface PaintablePolygon
9    {
10     public void paint(Graphics g);
11   }
```

Next, we see the AbstractPolygon class. By extending Polygon, it inherits all it needs to be a polygon. We pass two arrays and the number of sides into the AbstractPolygon Constructor. These arrays will contain the actual (x,y) positions for each point on the polygon. We are adding the ability to paint itself—but we declare the paint() method abstract because we do not know exactly how the polygon needs to be painted until we have an actual polygonal class.

```
1    //Program 9-10
2    //File:  AbstractPolygon.java
3
4    //The AbstractPolygon is a Polygon, and has a paint()
5    //method as well.
6
7    import java.awt.*;
8
```

```
9    public abstract class AbstractPolygon extends Polygon
10                          implements PaintablePolygon
11   {
12
13      protected String name;
14
15      public AbstractPolygon(int xpoints[], int ypoints[], int sides)
16      {
17            super(xpoints, ypoints, sides);
18      }
19
20      public abstract void paint(Graphics g);
21
22      public String toString()
23      {
24            return name;
25      }
26   }
```

The Box and Star classes extend AbstractPolygon. These classes are passed the array of point coordinates (*x,y*), which are then passed to the AbstractPolygon Constructor. Remember, the Box and Star are polygons that are able to paint themselves. Here is the Box class:

```
1    //Program 9-10
2    //File:  Box.java
3
4    //This class makes a box. The program sets the color.
5
6    import java.awt.Graphics;
7    import java.awt.Color;
8
9    public class Box extends AbstractPolygon
10   {
11      private Color color;
12
13        public Box(int[] xpoints, int[] ypoints, Color color)
14        {
15            super(xpoints, ypoints, 4);
16            this.color = color;
17            name = "box";
18        }
```

```
19
20        public void paint(Graphics g)
21        {
22                g.setColor(color);
23                g.fillPolygon(this);
24        }
25    }
```

The Star class sets the color to white in its paint() method.

```
1    //Program 9-10
2    //File:  Star.java
3
4    //This class makes white stars.
5    import java.awt.*;
6
7    public class Star extends AbstractPolygon
8    {
9      public Star(int xpoints[], int ypoints[])
10     {
11            super(xpoints, ypoints, 10);
12            name = "Star";
13       }
14
15     public void paint(Graphics g)
16     {
17            g.setColor(Color.white);
18            g.fillPolygon(this);
19       }
20   }
```

The BoxStarFrame class is another short piece of source code. We create a PaintingPanel object and add it to the frame's Container object and show the frame.

```
1    //Program 9-10
2    //File: BoxStarFrame.java
3
4    //This frame hold the PaintingPanel that contains
5    //boxes and stars.
6
```

```
7
8     import javax.swing.*;
9     import java.awt.*;
10
11    public class BoxStarFrame extends JFrame
12    {
13      PaintingPanel pp = new PaintingPanel();
14
15      public static void main( String[] args )
16      {
17            BoxStarFrame frame = new BoxStarFrame();
18            frame.setDefaultCloseOperation( EXIT_ON_CLOSE );
19      }
20
21      public BoxStarFrame()
22      {
23            Container canvas = getContentPane();
24            canvas.add(pp);
25
26            this.setSize( 350, 350 );   //set the window size
27            this.setTitle("Boxes and Stars Frame!");
28
29            this.show();
30      }
31    }
```

We have saved the best for last. The PaintingPanel class is a large piece of source code (shown in its entirety). The reader should examine the class and keep the following items in mind. In the code, we create a Vector object called components to hold each of the boxes and star objects. We make each box and star and randomly translate their vertices. The Polygon's translate() method just moves the corners of the polygon. Once the star and box are made, they are added to the components array.

When the mouse is pressed, we pass the mouse point to the hitTest() method. This method determines if the mouse has been clicked on one of our polygons by looping through the components vector. For each polygon, we call the Polygon's contains() method. It tells us if that point is contained within the polygon. If the mouse has been clicked on one of our boxes or stars, we set it into the lastHitComponent reference. If the mouse has been clicked off of the box or the star, the lastHitComponent is set to null.

If the user drags the mouse, the mouseDragged() method is called. In this method, if the lastHitComponent is not null, the mouse position is used to translate coordinates of the lastHitComponent polygon. The repaint() method is called, which in turn calls the panel's paint() method.

The magic of this code is in the panel's paint() method. We use double buffering in this paint() method, which results in smooth drawing. That is, there are no jagged lines or screen flickering. **Double buffering** is a technique used in many graphics programs. The idea is simple. In the createBackBuffer() method, we create a Graphics object called "background" that is the same size as our currently displayed Graphics object. In paint(), we construct our scene in this object. We fill a rectangle with the background color, and have each of the stars and boxes paint themselves into the background object. We then swap this background Graphics object with the currently displayed Graphics object. Essentially, we perform our drawing off-screen into the Graphics object, and then swap it on screen. The result is smooth, flicker-free drawing!

```
1   //Program 9-10
2   //PaintingPanel.java
3
4   import javax.swing.*;
5   import java.awt.*;
6   import java.awt.event.*;
7   import java.util.*;
8
9   public class PaintingPanel extends JPanel implements
10                     MouseMotionListener, MouseListener
11  {
12    Vector components = new Vector();
13    AbstractPolygon lastHitComponent;
14    private Image backBuffer;
15    private Graphics background;
16    Color c[] = new Color []
17         {Color.red, Color.blue, Color.green, Color.CYAN,Color.YELLOW};
18
19    public PaintingPanel()
20    {
21         this.addMouseListener(this);
22         this.addMouseMotionListener(this);
23
24         initStars();
25         initBoxes();
26    }
27
28    //Create five randomly placed stars.
29    private void initStars()
30    {
```

```
31          int xp[] = {7, 9, 15, 10, 15, 7, 0, 5, 0, 6};
32          int yp[] = {0, 5, 5, 7, 15, 9, 15, 7, 5, 5};
33
34          Star s = null;
35          for(int i = 0; i<5; ++i)
36          {
37                  s = new Star(xp, yp);
38                  s.translate( randPt(),randPt() );
39                  components.add(s);
40          }
41    }
42
43    //Create five randomly placed boxes.
44    private void initBoxes()
45    {
46          int xp[] = {20, 75, 75, 20};
47          int yp[] = {20, 20, 75, 75};
48
49          Box b = null;
50          for(int i = 0; i < 5; ++i)
51          {
52                  b = new Box(xp, yp, c[i]);
53                  b.translate( randPt(), randPt());
54                  components.add(b);
55          }
56    }
57
58    //Generate a random number between 0 and 250.
59    //Used for translating our components.
60    private int randPt()
61    {
62          return (int)(Math.random()*250);
63    }
64
65    //This method is passed a mouse point, and cycles through our
66    //Vector of polygons to determine if we are inside one of them.
67    public AbstractPolygon hitTest(Point p)
68    {
69          AbstractPolygon hit, ret = null;
70
71          //We use an Enumeration object to loop through the vector.
72          for (Enumeration e = components.elements(); e.hasMoreElements(); )
73          {
74                  //We cast the vector element into an AbstractPolygon.
75                  hit = (AbstractPolygon) e.nextElement();
```

```
76
77              //The Polygon contains() method tests if the Point is
78              //inside this polygon.
79              if (hit.contains(p))
80              {
81                   ret = hit;
82              }
83         }
84      return ret;
85   }
86
87   public void paint(Graphics g)
88   {
89      //We do our painting "off-screen" and when we're finished,
90      //we swap our buffer on to the screen.
91      if (backBuffer == null)
92      {
93              createBackBuffer();
94              if (backBuffer == null)
95                    return;
96      }
97
98      //Set the color and then let each polygon draw itself.
99      background.setColor(this.getBackground());
100     background.fillRect(this.getX(), this.getY(), this.getWidth(),
101                                     this.getHeight());
102     background.setColor(new Color(42, 0, 150));
103
104     for (Enumeration e = components.elements(); e.hasMoreElements(); )
105     {
106             ((AbstractPolygon) e.nextElement()).paint(background);
107     }
108
109     // Swap the backbuffer.
110     g.drawImage(backBuffer, 0, 0, this);
111  }
112
113  private void createBackBuffer()
114  {
115     Dimension screenSize = Toolkit.getDefaultToolkit().getScreenSize();
116     backBuffer = this.createImage(screenSize.width, screenSize.height);
117
118       if (backBuffer == null)
119             return;
120
121       background = backBuffer.getGraphics();
122  }
```

```
123
124         //This is called when the mouse is moved while a mouse button
125         //is pressed down. This method takes care of moving the polygon.
126         public void mouseDragged(MouseEvent mouseEvent)
127         {
128                 AbstractPolygon h = lastHitComponent;
129
130                 if (lastHitComponent != null)
131                 {
132                         int x = mouseEvent.getX() - h.xpoints[0];
133                         int y = mouseEvent.getY() - h.ypoints[0];
134
135                         h.translate(x, y);
136                         repaint();
137                 }
138         }
139
140         //When the mouse is pressed, determine if we are in any
141         //of our polygons. Set the lastHitComponent to null
142         //to ensure we don't get random movement from previous hits.
143         public void mousePressed(MouseEvent mouseEvent)
144         {
145                 lastHitComponent = null;
146                 AbstractPolygon ap = hitTest(mouseEvent.getPoint());
147
148                 if (ap != null)
149                         lastHitComponent = ap;
150         }
151
152         public void mouseReleased(MouseEvent mouseEvent)
153         {
154                 lastHitComponent = null;
155         }
156
157         //Remaining mouse methods that must be included in the class
158         //since we are implementing MouseListener
159
160         //mouseMoved() is called whenever the mouse is moved.
161         //We don't perform any tasks here!
162         public void mouseMoved(MouseEvent e) { }
163         public void mouseClicked(MouseEvent mouseEvent) {   }
164         public void mouseEntered(MouseEvent mouseEvent) {   }
165         public void mouseExited(MouseEvent mouseEvent) { }
166 }
```

9

REVIEW QUESTIONS AND PROBLEMS

Short Answer

1. What is the difference between a superclass and a subclass? Can a superclass be a subclass? Can a subclass be a superclass?

2. Why is it necessary to make some or all of the data in a superclass protected instead of leaving it private?

3. How does a Java programmer decide if private data and methods in a superclass should be changed to protected?

4. If data is protected in a superclass, is it accessible to the methods inside that class? Is the data accessible to its subclasses? Is the data accessible to any parts of the program outside of either the superclasses or subclasses? Explain your answers.

5. If data is private in a superclass, is it accessible to the methods inside that class? Is the data accessible to its subclasses? Is the data accessible to any parts of the program outside of either the superclasses or subclasses? Explain your answers.

6. If you create an object of a subclass using the default (no input) constructor, does the subclass constructor need to explicitly call the default constructor of the superclass? Explain.

7. If you create an object of a subclass using an overloaded constructor (i.e., pass data values into the constructor), does the subclass constructor need to explicitly call the overloaded constructor of the superclass? Explain.

8. When a Java programmer declares a class to be abstract, how many of the methods must be declared abstract as well?

9. What do we mean when we say an abstract class is an incomplete class?

10. Is it possible to "implement" an abstract class like we "implement" interfaces? Explain.

11. Come up with two different topics or items that would make sense as an abstract class. (The two can be unrelated items.) For each of the two, identify two concrete subclasses that should extend the abstract class. For example, a Drug class would be abstract because it is difficult to write a precise "Drug," and two concrete classes could be Aspirin and Antacid.

12. Expand your two abstract classes from Problem 11 so that each one has an intermediate abstract class. For example PainKiller and Antibiotic could also be abstract classes. From these, we could have Aspirin, Morphine, Penicillin, and Erythomyocin.

13. Taking your abstract and concrete classes from Problem 11 and 12, can you write two abstract methods for each level of in the abstract classes? For

example, Drug could have calcDose(), and timesPerDay(), PainKiller could have typeOfPain(), isAddictive(), and Antibiotic could have typeOfGermItKills(), and isSunSensitive().

14. Is it possible to declare an abstract method inside a concrete class? Explain your answer.

15. What are the four principles that must be supported in any object-oriented language?

16. What is the difference between method overloading and method overridding?

17. How are Java abstract classes and Java interfaces alike?

18. What are three differences between Java abstract classes and Java interfaces?

19. If we implement a Java interface in a class, but do not complete the interface method(s), what must we do in order for the class to compile? Will the class be abstract or concrete? Will the incomplete interface methods be abstract?

20. Is it possible for a Java interface to be used to contain mathematical constants? Is it possible for your Java class to change the constant values in a Java interface? Explain your answer.

21. The JPTAddressBook program illustrates how interfaces may be used for consistent coding and speedy development. What would happen if the JPTAddressBook did not use the AddressBook interface and simply used the ABC database method calls and then had to switch to XYZ method calls? How would the class that uses JPTAddressBook have to change when the database changed?

22. In the ThreeEmployeesFrame2 program, we calculate employees' salary based on different formulas. We create an array of Employee objects and assign the three different employees into each array element. Explain the three pieces of "Java magic" that were used to build this program so that we can use a for loop to loop through the Employee objects quickly and easily.

23. If you wanted your Dog object to be able to play baseball, play football, and be a HousePet, what would you need to do?

24. The Boxes and Stars program uses an AbstractPolygon class as the superclass for the Box and Star classes. Why is it that the Box class and Star classes have a paint() method? How is it that Box and Star objects can check a mouse point (x,y) to know if that point is contained within it?

25. If a Java programmer did not want to use interfaces, could he or she write a Java class that extends more than one class? Explain your answer.

Programming Problems

In Questions 26–33, write complete Java programs. If you have studied Advanced Topics, Chapter 12, *JAR Files*, bundle your program into a JAR file.

26. Using the HousePets program as a guide, write a superclass and then three subclasses for a topic of your choosing. Your superclass should be abstract and should have at least two data items as well as a default and overloaded constructor and two abstract methods. Your subclasses should all extend the superclass and should have at least one additional data item. Build a frame and create an object of each of your subclasses. The frame should have three buttons, one for each object, which pop up message boxes showing the data for each object.

27. Use the calculate salary example in this chapter as a guide, and expand Problem 26 by adding one more button, "Show All Info," which pops up a message box displaying the data for all three objects. In your program, create an array of superclass references, assign the object references into the array, and then loop through this array to acquire the information to display.

28. Create an abstract superclass called Vehicle. In this class, include a String for manufacturer and fuel type. Include the abstract methods how_I_Move(), and calcFuelRating(). Using this superclass, create three subclasses and include at least one data item and one custom method for that vehicle. Use your imagination! There are many types of vehicles—cars, planes, trains, boats, motorcycles, skateboards, snow skis, bicycles, buses, and dogsleds. The how_I_Move() method describes the vehicle's propulsion system. For example, a car has a gasoline engine and a skateboard uses foot-power. The calcFuelRating() describes an accurate measure of distance per fuel volume. A car is rated by miles per gallon, and a skateboard is rated in candy bars per city block. Build a frame that shows your three vehicles. Be creative! Show us a picture of your vehicles.

29. Expand Problem 28 so that you implement a RulesOfTheRoad interface with each of your vehicles. Rules of the road describe the general rules governing the behavior of vehicles in certain situations. Rules of the road typically address speed, right of way, passing, signaling, and turning. For example, sailboats have the right of way over motorized boats. Aircraft on runways have the right of way over aircraft on taxiways. Your RulesOfTheRoad interface should have three methods—each of which is implemented in your three vehicles. Show your rules information along with the vehicles in your frame.

30. Remember the AnimalBehaviors interface we introduced in Chapter 7? (Refer to page 385.) This interface included the breathe(), eat(), and communicate() methods. Let's modify this interface so that we now have these three methods: (1) favoriteFoodToEat(), (2) napActivity(), and (3) talkTalkTalk(). These three methods describe the animal's favorite food, all napping activity and location information, and how the animal communicates. Write an abstract superclass for FarmAnimal. It includes data for the farm's name, the animal's species (i.e., pig, cow, etc.), and abstract methods for jobOnTheFarm(), and howMany-HowOften(). This latter method describes the farm animal's reproductive productivity. Write three subclasses. Each subclass should have one additional

9

method specific to it. Build a frame that instantiates three different farm animal objects. The frame should have the capability to display information for its three farm animals.

31. Did you ever play hide and seek? You and a group of friends pick one pal to be the "seeker" and you must have a "home base." Standing at the home base, the seeker hides his or her eyes and counts to ten while the others go and hide. After the count, the seeker tries to find the pals who are hiding. In the mean-time, the folks who are hiding want to sneak into home base before the seeker sees them. If the seeker finds someone, he or she must run to the home base and yell out the hider's name before the hider reaches the base.

With all this in mind, write an interface called HideAndSeek. Include at least three methods that describe the behaviors of the hide and seek game. For example, there must be a count() method and bestHidingPlace() method. Once you have built your interface, implement it in your FarmAnimals program in Problem 30. (What? You didn't know that farm animals play hide and seek?) For example, the count() must describe how the animal hides their eyes and counts. A horse would bow its head and stamp its foot ten times. A goat could never be the seeker because goats are so curious they would never be able to keep their eyes shut to count to ten!

Write a HideAndSeekFrame that contains your three farm animal objects. Set up radio buttons so that we can select the seeker. Supply buttons and other con-trols so that the user can play rounds of hide and seek with your three animals. Incorporate marcsPause() to simulate the counting, and use the random number generator to randomly determine whether the animal makes it back to home base before the seeker finds them. This GUI may be simple or complex. You may need to incorporate individual panels in the frame so that your GUI behaves as you imagine it should.

32. Write an abstract superclass called Boat that contains the boat's name and dimension data including the length, beam (width), and draught (depth of water needed to float a boat). The superclass should have at least two Strings that hold the names of two image files, an abstract method for getImageFilename(), and get and set methods for the data. Write a Sailboat class to extend the Boat class. It has number of sails as a data item. Write another class called SkiBoat to model a boat that pulls water skiers. A ski boat typically has an inboard engine in the center of the boat, has fins on the bottom of its hull for a straight pull, and produces a very small wake when it zooms through the water. A ski boat can pull skiers on a professional slalom course. A boat with an outboard motor (mounted on the rear of the boat) can pull water skiers for fun. (Investi-gate http://usawaterski.org for more information.) Have default and overloaded constructors for all classes.

The Sailboat and SkiBoat classes should have at least two images associated with them. The getImageFilename() method in the boat objects should return the name of the appropriate image file according to how the data is set. For example, if the ski boat is for professional skiers (has inboard motor), show an image of a pro ski boat. For sailboats, you would show pictures of boats with different numbers of sails.

Create a BoatPanel class that has the necessary components to set the boat's name, length, beam, and draught as well as a label that will display an image. The BoatPanel should have a Show Boat Data button that presents a summary of the boat information. It should call the toString() method of its boat object. Using the BoatPanel as a superclass, create a SailboatPanel that has the necessary components for a Sailboat object and a SkiBoatPanel that has additional components for the ski boat. Refer to the CounterPanel and FancyCounterPanel example in this chapter for reference. The SailboatPanel should have a Sailboat object and the SkiBoatPanel should have a SkiBoat object. The panels should pass initial data into the boat objects.

The program should be designed so that it has a frame that contains both boat panels. When the program begins, the frame should show the two panels. Each panel should have its components set to the initial data and show the appropriate picture of each boat. If the user makes changes to the boat data the appropriate picture is displayed. By pressing the Show Data button, the data in the GUI components is shown in the message box.

For example, when the program starts you may show a ski boat and a sailboat with three sails. If you change the sails to two (with a radiobutton), the image changes to a sailboat with two sails.

33. Expand the Boxes and Stars program in this chapter so that there are two more items in the window: (1) ovals and (2) a new type of polygon, such as an octagon or a triangle. You may design your own, new polygon type. Place the necessary GUI controls so that the user may change the color of the boxes, ovals, and octagons. The stars remain white. You can model your interface after Program 8-12 on page 490 so that the radio buttons allow the user to select the item. Add the necessary code to the panel so that if the mouse is dragged over the item, the color of that item changes to a different color. When the mouse exits the item, the color is changed back to its basic color.

9

10

Advanced Topic: Exception Handling

KEY TERMS AND CONCEPTS

ArithmeticException
ArrayIndexOutOfBoundsException
catch
catch(Exception e)
Error
Exception
finally
NullPointerException
NumberFormatException
OutOfMemoryError
printStackTrace()
run-time error
Runtime Exception
Throwable
throw new
throws
try

CHAPTER OBJECTIVES

Introduce Java's Exception handling classes.

Show how Java throws an Exception object when it encounters a run-time error.

Illustrate the relationship between the try and catch statements.

Discuss the finally block.

Present how a Java programmer can write and throw his or her own exceptions by using the Exception superclass.

Demonstrate how to use the throws keyword in a method definition line to indicate the type of Exception object that the method might throw.

Show how when an exception is thrown—not caught in the method—the exception is passed up the chain of calling methods in search of a try and catch statement.

Illustrate how methods can be called within a try block.

Got Bugs?

Programmers and software engineers write their code using best intentions for flawless execution. Unfortunately, unexpected things can occur. The program may have violated a language rule, the user might enter something the programmer never thought of, or the programmer could made a mistake in his or her logic. Ask a professional programmer to tell you about his or her "favorite" programming bug. It is common that the programmer can tell you the problem and the root of its cause. Sometimes a software problem can take days to track down. Perhaps it caused the programmer (and employer) embarrassment or had dire consequences. Writing software is tricky business!

The Java compiler catches language syntax errors, but a host of problems can occur when the program runs. These problems are referred to as run-time errors or exceptions. What do we mean by a **run-time error**? Have you ever tried to divide by zero? You learned in elementary school that you cannot use zero as a divisor. Try this in a program on a computer—in any language—and it won't let you divide by zero either. What if your program cannot open a file, runs out of memory, tries to go out of the legal boundary of an array, or reads in the wrong type of data? How the program reacts to these operations depends on how the language reacts to the problem and the programmer's skill in anticipating and handling problems.

run-time error
an error that occurs while the program is running

Java provides the programmer with the necessary tools so that he or she can catch or trap run-time errors. Java has two major categories of "errors'" (1) errors and (2) exceptions. The majority of problems that we anticipate are actually classified as exceptions and the technique for catching or trapping and dealing with these problems is referred to as **exception handling**. Predefined exceptions and predefined errors can be generated by the Java run-time system, or a programmer-defined exception can be generated by your code. The purpose for exception handling in Java is to change the flow of the program when an error has occurred so that the program can either alert the user to the problem for a possible fix or shut down gracefully. Changing the flow of the program literally means that when the program has a problem or an error, the execution jumps to a different portion of the code and runs the code to handle the error.

exception handling
techniques for catching problems that occur during program execution

10.1
What is an Exception? Why Write Exception Handling Code?

exception

a run-time error

An **exception** is a run-time error. Java programmer should build exception handling code into his or her programs for several reasons. First, exception handling code provides a distinct path for dealing with errors. This path provides the means for the programmer to organize the error handling code and avoid having it scattered throughout the program. Second, the Java programmer should provide his or her users with an understandable error message if the program fails. The program may be beyond repair, but at least a graceful exit is possible. Exception handling does not reduce the amount of work a programmer must do—it usually increases the work. The benefits of having a location in the program to deal with errors and provide useful information to the user is well worth the time it takes to write the handling code.

There are several new terms we must introduce and define, and then we will learn how exception handling is performed in Java. Table 10-1 presents these new terms, along with brief definitions.

▌ TABLE 10-1

Java Exception handling terms.

Term	Definition
bug	A general purpose term for an error in a program.
exception	An error that occurs while the program is executing. Also known as a run-time error.
throw	When an error occurs, the program "throws" an error or exception.
try	The Java keyword that is used to begin a block of code in which an error may be generated.
catch	The Java keyword, that is used in a block of code to specify the type of exception it can catch. After an error has been thrown, the error is captured or caught and the error handling statements are executed. The program attempts to resolve the error by executing statements in the catch block of code.
stack trace	A list of method calls that show the events leading up to where the exception occurred.
crash	When a program halts execution in an ungraceful manner.
booby trap (Note 1)	A disguised, explosive devise triggered by the unknowing victim. (Note 2)

Note 1: The author's term for describing potential error-producing problems in Java programs.
Note 2: *The Oxford Dictionary of Current English, 8th Edition,* S.V. "booby trap."

In Java, there is an **Exception class**. When an error occurs, an Exception object is "thrown." Exceptions are objects of classes that are all derived from the superclass called Exception. The inheritance tree for this superclass is:

java.lang.Object
    |
      + java.lang.Throwable
           |
              + java.lang.Exception

Exception class
an Exception object is thrown when an error occurs

Java's **Throwable** class is the superclass for all exceptions, and only objects of this class (or its subclasses) are able to be thrown by either the Java run-time system or by using the throw statement. We see how to throw our own exceptions later in this chapter. The Exception class is used when an application is on the lookout for a predictable error that the program should catch and handle. Java's other error class, Error, also is derived from Throwable. The Error class is used for major errors that may be caught but are so serious that they are not expected to be resolved. For example, if the program attempts to allocate more memory than what is available, an Error object is thrown and if caught, we are able to tell the user "out of memory" instead of having the program crash.

Throwable
the superclass for all Java exceptions

Table 10-2 shows a partial listing of the various exception classes in Java. The names of the classes suggest the sort of error condition that the exception classes trap. Table 10-3 shows a partial listing of the subclasses of **RuntimeException**. Many of these classes are of interest to us.

We will examine several types of exceptions that are generated by Java's run-time system and will see how to catch and handle them. We will define our own custom errors that use Exception (or a subclass of Exception) as their superclass. Table 10-4 lists the predefined exceptions we will examine in this chapter.

RuntimeException
the superclass for many commonly-thrown exceptions

TABLE 10-2
A partial listing of predefined Java Exception classes.

Exception classes	General purpose
ClassNotFoundException	Thrown when an application tries to load a class but its definition is not found.
DataFormatException	Thrown when a data format error has occurred.
IllegalAccessException	Thrown when an application tries to create an instance, access a field, or call a method but the current method does not have access to the specified class.
NoSuchMethodException	Thrown when an application attempts to call a method that cannot be found.
RuntimeException	The superclass of the exceptions that the JVM can throw during normal program operations.

10

TABLE 10-3

A partial listing of predefined Java Exception classes.

Exception classes	Subclasses

RuntimeException	IllegalArgumentException
	    subclass: NumberFormatException
	IndexOutOfBoundsException
	    subclass: ArrayIndexOutOfBoundsException
	    subclass: StringIndexOutOfBoundsException
	ArithmeticException
	ArrayStoreException
	NullPointerException
	SecurityException

TABLE 10-4

Java Exception Examples in this Chapter.

Exception	Definition
ArithmeticException	Occurs during an illegal arithmetic condition or operation.
ArrayIndexOutOfBoundsException	Occurs if the program attempts to access an array element that is out of bounds.
Exception	General catch-all exception that can be used by the programmer to catch any error.
NumberFormatException	Occurs when an illegal attempt is made to convert a String to a numeric data type.
NullPointerException	Occurs when a program attempts to use a reference variable that contains a null value instead of a valid object reference.
OutOfMemoryError	Occurs when the program attempts to allocate more memory than what is available.

Crashing a Java Program

Let's play with a short program and enter data that causes it to crash. The program, TwoCrashDemo, compiles with no errors. This means that the syntax of our program is correct and that we have followed the rules for writing Java code. TwoCrashDemo asks the user to enter two integers and then it performs division. If the user enters two valid integers, the program executes without error and provides the integer division results in the message box. There are two booby traps in this program. First, if we enter zero as the divisor, the program attempts to divide by zero. The program crashes when this line is executed! Second, when you enter data in the JOptionPane.showInputDialog() message box, the data comes into the program as a String. When we attempt to parse an integer from the input String, an error occurs if the parseInt() does not obtain a valid integer value. This also causes the program to crash. For example, if the user enters the phrase "I Love Java!" in our input dialog box, a **NumberFormatException** will be thrown from the parse-Int() method. Figure 10-1 shows the incorrect input and resultant NumberFormat-Exception messages (stack trace) in the command window.

The *TwoCrashDemo.java* file contains the code in Program 10-1.

NumberFormat-Exception

thrown from the parse() method if it does not have a valid number

```
1   //Program 10-1
2   //File: TwoCrashDemo.java
3
4   import javax.swing.JOptionPane;
5
6   public class TwoCrashDemo
7   {
8       String sNum, sDenom, sQuot;
9       String title = "No Exception Handling Demo";
10      int num, denom, quot;
11
12      public TwoCrashDemo()
13      {
14          sNum = JOptionPane.showInputDialog(null,
15              "Enter the numerator (int).",
16              title, JOptionPane.QUESTION_MESSAGE);
17
18          sDenom = JOptionPane.showInputDialog(null,
19              "Enter the denominator (int).",
20              title, JOptionPane.QUESTION_MESSAGE);
21
22      //parseInt throws a NumberFormatException if it doesn't get a valid int
23          num = Integer.parseInt(sNum);
24          denom = Integer.parseInt(sDenom);
25
26      //an ArithmeticException is thrown if the denom. is a zero
27          quot = num/denom;
28          sQuot = Integer.toString(quot);
29
30          JOptionPane.showMessageDialog(null,
31              "Integer division result: " + sQuot,
32              title, JOptionPane.INFORMATION_MESSAGE);
33      }
34
35      public static void main(String args[] )
36      {
37          TwoCrashDemo theApp = new TwoCrashDemo();
38          System.exit(0);
39      }
40  }
```

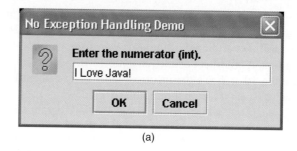

(a)

```
C:\JPT>
C:\JPT>javac TwoCrashDemo.java

C:\JPT>java TwoCrashDemo
Exception in thread "main" java.lang.NumberFormatException: I Love Java!
        at java.lang.Integer.parseInt(Integer.java:426)
        at java.lang.Integer.parseInt(Integer.java:476)
        at TwoCrashDemo.<init>(TwoCrashDemo.java:23)
        at TwoCrashDemo.main(TwoCrashDemo.java:37)
```

(b)

Figure 10-1

The invalid input for the numerator results in a NumberFormatException thrown from the parseInt() method at line 23. The call to the method that threw the exception occurs at line 37, in main(). Java reports the chain of method calls if an exception is thrown and not caught. The first line in the command window shows the invalid input.

ArithmeticException

thrown when an arithmetic error, such as an integer division by zero, occurs

This same code can throw an **ArithmeticException** if it attempts to perform division by zero. Figure 10-2a shows that we enter a zero for the denominator and Figure 10-2b shows the resulting messages from Java.

Figure 10-2

A zero denominator input and subsequent integer division operation causes an ArithmeticException to be thrown at line 27. The call to the method that threw the exception occurs at line 37, in main(). The first line in the command window shows the divide by zero (/ by zero) message.

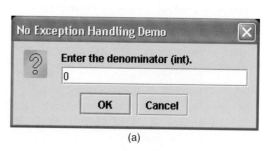

(a)

```
C:\JPT>
C:\JPT>
C:\JPT>java TwoCrashDemo
Exception in thread "main" java.lang.ArithmeticException: / by zero
        at TwoCrashDemo.<init>(TwoCrashDemo.java:27)
        at TwoCrashDemo.main(TwoCrashDemo.java:37)
```

(b)

10.2
try and catch Blocks

Java has several keywords designated for exception handling. Table 10-5 introduces the terms. These terms assist us in writing programs that handle errors gracefully. The basic idea is this: we place any code that we know may generate an exception inside a **try block**. The try statement instructs the program to try the statements and see if there are any errors. There must be at least one **catch** statement following the try block. The catch statement instructs the program to handle exceptions that match its type. All execution is halted thereafter within the try block. There may be many catch statements, with different types of exception. Java automatically throws exceptions, as we have seen in the TwoCrashDemo program. (We use the **throw** statement if we need to throw our own exception object.) If an exception occurs within a try block, program control exits the try block and

try block
code that may throw an exception should be placed in a try block

catch
the statement that follows the try block. The catch block handles exceptions

throw
statement used when we need to throw our own exception object

▌ **TABLE 10-5**
Java Exception handling keyword.

Keyword	Definition
try	Used to begin a block of code that may generate an exception. If an exception occurs, program control jumps to the appropriate catch block and executes that code.
catch	Used to begin a block of code that specifies the type of exception it can catch. The catch statement and block of code are located after the try block.
throw throw new (Note)	Statement that is used to indicate an error has occurred. When we throw an Exception object, Java automatically throws certain exceptions. We use the throw new statement when we throw our own specialized exception object.
finally	Used to begin a block of code that is always executed, regardless of whether any exceptions have occurred. The finally block is located after all the catch blocks.

throws	Used in a method definition line indicating the type of exception the method throws. Several exceptions can be listed in a comma-separated list. A method showing one type of potential exception is:
	
	`public void doCalculations( ) throws ArithmeticException`
	`{`
	`   //method code that might generate an`
	`   //ArithmeticException`
	`}`

Note: Because we throw an exception object, we must use the new operator in the throw statement, such as throw(new MyOwnException( )) or throw new MyOwnException( ).

jumps to the corresponding catch statement, executing the code within the catch block. If there are no errors, catch statements are skipped. If a finally block is present, control jumps to it. Java guarantees that a finally block is executed whether or not an exception has occurred.

Integer Division Example

Let's rewrite the TwoCrashDemo program so that we use try and catch statements to handle the errors and prevent a crash. The IntegerDivisionExcDemo below illustrates the best way to write this code. The parseInt() and division statements are placed inside the try block. There are two catch statements following the try block. Because this program can throw either a NumberFormatException or an ArithmeticException, we trap for both types of exceptions. If an error occurs, control jumps immediately to the catch statement and does not return to the try block. Figure 10-3 illustrates the possible program flow for the IntegerDivisionExcDemo, Program 10-2.

```
1    //Program 10-2   Use a try with two catches.
2    //File: IntegerDivisionExcDemo.java
3
4    import javax.swing.JOptionPane;
5
6    public class IntegerDivisionExcDemo
7    {
8        String sNum, sDenom, sQuot;
9        String title = "Exception Handling";
10       int num, denom, quot;
11
12       public IntegerDivisionExcDemo()
13       {
14           try
15           {
16               sNum = JOptionPane.showInputDialog(null,
17               "Enter the numerator (int).",
18               title, JOptionPane.QUESTION_MESSAGE);
```

```java
19
20                   sDenom = JOptionPane.showInputDialog(null,
21                       "Enter the denominator (int).",
22                       title, JOptionPane.QUESTION_MESSAGE);
23
24       //parseInt throws a NumberFormatException if it doesn't get a valid int
25                   num = Integer.parseInt(sNum);
26                   denom = Integer.parseInt(sDenom);
27
28       //an ArithmeticException is thrown if the denom. is a zero
29                   quot = num/denom;
30                   sQuot = Integer.toString(quot);
31
32                   JOptionPane.showMessageDialog(null,
33                       "Integer division result: " + sQuot,
34                       title, JOptionPane.INFORMATION_MESSAGE);
35           }
36           catch(NumberFormatException nfe)
37           {
38                   JOptionPane.showMessageDialog(null,
39                       "Must enter valid integers!",
40                       title, JOptionPane.INFORMATION_MESSAGE);
41           }
42           catch(ArithmeticException ae)
43           {
44                   JOptionPane.showMessageDialog(null,
45                       "Divide by zero not allowed!",
46                       title, JOptionPane.INFORMATION_MESSAGE);
47           }
48       }
49
50       public static void main(String args[] )
51       {
52           IntegerDivisionExcDemo theApp = new IntegerDivisionExcDemo();
53           System.exit(1);
54       }
55   }
```

10

```
public class IntegerDivisionExcDemo
{
        int num, denom, quot;

        public IntegerDivisionExcDemo( )
        {
                try
                {
                        sNum = ...

                        sDenom = ...

                //parseInt throws a NumberFormatException if it doesn't get a valid int
                        num = Integer.parseInt (sNum);
                        denom = Integer.parseInt (sDenom);          error?

                //an ArithmeticException is thrown if the denom. is a zero
                        {
                                quot = num/denom;                          Control
      error here?                                                          jumps
                        //No Errors! Show result here.                     to
      Control         //Control jumps over catch statements.
      jumps
      to here             }
                        catch (NumberFormatException nfe)
                        {
                                //tell parse error here
                        }
                        catch (ArithmeticException ae)
                        {
                                //tell zero divide error here
                        }
                }
        }
}
```

Figure 10-3
Possible program flow for the IntegerDivisionExcDemo program. The catch statements are skipped if no exceptions occur.

catch(Exception e)

There are numerous Java exception classes that encompass any errors that the language has anticipated. But how does the Java programmer know which Exception class to use? Review Tables 10-2 and 10-3 for a partial list, or consult the Java Exception documentation for a complete list. But if your program is crashing, and you aren't sure of the cause, a sure way to discover the exact type of Exception that was thrown is to place your code in a try block and use the superclass Exception in the catch statement. It will catch any and all of Java's exceptions! We then use the Exception object's **printStackTrace()** method to show us what we caught.

10

printStackTrace( )
a method in the
Exception class that
reports all exception
information to the
command window

Out of Bound Array and catch (Exception e) Example In Program 10-3, ArrayExceptionDemo, we have a five-element array that we intend to fill with random numbers. The program asks the user to enter the number of entries he or she wishes to make into the array. Five is the limit, but our user may ask the program to exceed the legal boundaries of the array, thus generating some sort of exception. If the user enters an integer value between one and five, the program runs without a problem. If the user enters an invalid entry, or exceeds the array limit, exceptions are thrown. Our program pops up JOptionPane message boxes in the try and catch statements so that we may follow the program flow as the program executes.

```java
//Program 10-3
//File: ArrayExceptionDemo.java

//We set up an array of 5 random numbers. We ask the user to enter
//how many numbers they wish to place in the array (more than 5 numbers,
//Java throws an exception.

//Use the printStackTrace() to see exactly what Exception was thrown.

import javax.swing.JOptionPane;

public class ArrayExceptionDemo
{
   double numbers [] = new double[5];

   int howManyNumbers;
   String sHowMany;
   String title = "Array Exceptions Demo";

   public ArrayExceptionDemo()
   {
        fillArray();
   }

   public void fillArray()
   {
        sHowMany = JOptionPane.showInputDialog(null,
        "How many random numbers do you wish to place in the array (5 max).",
        title, JOptionPane.QUESTION_MESSAGE);

//Now we put the code that might generate an error inside a try block
        try
        {
```

```
34      //The parseInt will throw an exception if it doesn't get a valid int.
35                      howManyNumbers = Integer.parseInt(sHowMany);
36
37      //If we try to go beyond our array bounds we will get an exception!
38      //(This is a good example why we should use numbers.length
39      //in for loops that traverse arrays.)
40                      for(int i = 0; i < howManyNumbers; ++i)
41                      {
42                              numbers[i] = Math.random();
43                              System.out.println( numbers[i] );
44                      }
45           }
46
47      //We use the superclass Exception to catch everything!
48           catch(Exception e)
49           {
50                      JOptionPane.showMessageDialog(null,"Error happened ",
51                      "In the catch", 2);
52
53      //printStackTrace prints the exception to the command window.
54                      e.printStackTrace();
55           }
56      }
57
58      public static void main(String args[] )
59      {
60           ArrayExceptionDemo theApp = new ArrayExceptionDemo();
61           System.exit(0);
62      }
63 }
```

Figure 10-4 illustrates the input value (Isn't Java cool?) and resultant stack trace in the command window. A NumberFormatException is thrown by parseInt(). Figure 10-5 shows the input value (25) that will cause our program to attempt to access an out of bounds element. A System.out.println() statement in the for loop writes the random numbers to the screen. As you can see in Figure 10-5B, there are five numbers. The exception was thrown when the program attempted to access numbers[5]. The stack trace shows the **ArrayIndexOutOfBoundsException**. Java does not allow the program to access an array element beyond the legally declared array length. Java throws an ArrayIndexOutOfBoundsException if this occurs.

ArrayIndexOutOf-BoundsException

thrown if the program attempts to access an array element beyond the legally declared array length

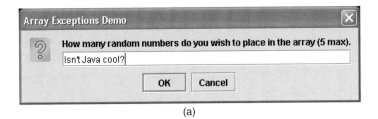

(a)

```
C:\JPT>
C:\JPT>java ArrayExceptionDemo
java.lang.NumberFormatException: Isn't Java cool?
        at java.lang.Integer.parseInt(Integer.java:426)
        at java.lang.Integer.parseInt(Integer.java:476)
        at ArrayExceptionDemo.fillArray(ArrayExceptionDemo.java:35)
        at ArrayExceptionDemo.<init>(ArrayExceptionDemo.java:22)
        at ArrayExceptionDemo.main(ArrayExceptionDemo.java:60)

C:\JPT>_
```

(b)

Figure 10-4
a) A NumberFormatException is thrown at line 35 when the user enters a noninteger
input. The catch statement will catch any Exception. The printStackTrace() method
shows which exception was thrown. b) The chain of method calls (lines 22 and 60)
can be seen in the output window.

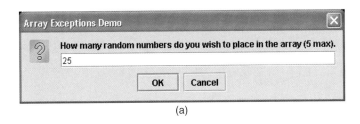

(a)

```
C:\JPT>java ArrayExceptionDemo
0.659394339900346
0.41758073981760857
0.35500384691693276
0.5747626914293895
0.5492611736082738
java.lang.ArrayIndexOutOfBoundsException
        at ArrayExceptionDemo.fillArray(ArrayExceptionDemo.java:42)
        at ArrayExceptionDemo.<init>(ArrayExceptionDemo.java:22)
        at ArrayExceptionDemo.main(ArrayExceptionDemo.java:60)

C:\JPT>_
```

(b)

Figure 10-5
An ArrayIndexOutOfBoundsException is thrown at line 42 when the program
attempts to exceed the array limit. We entered 25, but the program threw and caught
the error when it attempted to access the 6th element.

10

Now that we know the exact exceptions, we can rewrite this program with catch blocks that relay the problem to the user. In Program 10-4, ArrayExceptions-Demo2, we have two separate try and catch blocks. Please notice that if the Integer.parseInt() method encounters invalid data, it assigns zero to the numeric value and throws the exception. In this situation, invalid data will cause the catch to issue an error. Then the second try block is executed. Because the value of how-ManyNumbers is zero, the for loop is not executed and does no harm. Programmers should be careful, when they are writing several try and catch blocks, to be sure that an earlier error will not cause unexpected problems later in the code.

Please note that this program is reworked twice at the end of this chapter to illustrate more complete exception handling techniques. (See Programs 10-11 and 10-12.)

```
1    //Program 10-4
2    //File: ArrayExceptionDemo2.java
3
4    //We set up an array of 5 random numbers. We ask the user to enter
5    //how many numbers they wish to place in the array (more than 5 numbers,
6    //Java throws an exception.
7
8    //Trap for the exact exceptions.
9
10   import javax.swing.JOptionPane;
11
12   public class ArrayExceptionDemo2
13   {
14     double numbers [] = new double[5];
15
16     int howManyNumbers;
17     String sHowMany;
18     String title = "Array Exceptions Demo, 2nd Version";
19
20     public ArrayExceptionDemo2()
21     {
22          fillArray();
23     }
24
25     public void fillArray()
26     {
27          sHowMany = JOptionPane.showInputDialog(null,
28          "How many random numbers do you wish to place in the array (5 max).",
29          title, JOptionPane.QUESTION_MESSAGE);
30
```

```
31              try
32              {
33                      howManyNumbers = Integer.parseInt(sHowMany);
34              }
35              catch(NumberFormatException nfe)
36              {
37                      JOptionPane.showMessageDialog(null,"Must enter integers! ",
38                      "Error in parseInt ", 2);
39                      System.out.println(howManyNumbers);
40              }
41
42              try
43              {
44                      for(int i = 0; i < howManyNumbers; ++i)
45                      {
46                              numbers[i] = Math.random();
47                              System.out.println( Double.toString(numbers[i]) );
48                      }
49              }
50              catch(ArrayIndexOutOfBoundsException e)
51              {
52                      JOptionPane.showMessageDialog(null,
53                      "You have exceeded the array boundries!",
54                      "Array Out Of Bounds Error! ", 2);
55              }
56      }
57
58      public static void main(String args[] )
59      {
60              ArrayExceptionDemo2 theApp = new ArrayExceptionDemo2();
61              System.exit(0);
62      }
63 }
```

Null Pointer Exception Example   When we introduced the concept of an array of objects, we cautioned that it was very important to allocate an object with the new operator before you attempt to use it, or else the infamous **NullPointerException** is thrown. Most of us dutifully nod our heads and promise to always allocate before we use. Well, most of us need an example to see why it is important. The User Login Validation program from Chapter 6 is a perfect example for us.

Review Program 6-11 on page 351. We created an array of ComputerUser objects and then used a Login object to obtain a user's login and password,

NullPointerException
thrown if you attempt to use an object before the object has been created with the new operator

10

validating it in a Login method. Program 10-5 is an abbreviated version of the LoginUserFrame class. In the LoginUserFrameCrash program we leave out the majority of the code. We create an array of users on Line 12, then we neglect to allocate the ComputerUser objects before we use them on lines 31–35. Figure 10-6 shows the results of our program crash.

```
1    //Program 10-5 A modified LoginUsersFrame program.
2    //We do not allocate our objects before we use them.
3    //File: LoginUsersFrameCrash.java
4
5    import java.awt.Graphics;
6    import javax.swing.JFrame;
7
8    public class LoginUsersFrameCrash extends JFrame
9    {
10     //We create an array reference called users.
11
12     private ComputerUser users[] = new ComputerUser[5];
13
14     public static void main( String[] args )
15     {
16           LoginUsersFrameCrash hal = new LoginUsersFrameCrash();
17           hal.setDefaultCloseOperation( EXIT_ON_CLOSE );
18     }
19
20     //class constructor initializes values
21     public LoginUsersFrameCrash()
22     {
23           setSize( 450, 200 );       //set the window size
24           setTitle("Login Users Program");
25
26           //We attempt to fill the User array but we don't have objects yet!
27
28           //Hold onto your hat, we're about to crash.
29
30           //Now we set 5 users and their passwords.
31           users[0].setUser("BlueDog", "arfarf", 0);
32           users[1].setUser("KiowaTheWonderDog", "awoooooooo", 0);
33           users[2].setUser("Doc","Irun4you",0);
34           users[3].setUser("Maddie","WhenDoWeGo",1);
35           users[4].setUser("HannahBanana","BarkBark",2);
36
37     }
38
39  }
```

10

```
C:\JPT>javac LoginUsersFrameCrash.java

C:\JPT>java LoginUsersFrameCrash
Exception in thread "main" java.lang.NullPointerException
        at LoginUsersFrameCrash.<init>(LoginUsersFrameCrash.java:31)
        at LoginUsersFrameCrash.main(LoginUsersFrameCrash.java:16)

C:\JPT>
```

Figure 10-6
A NullPointerException is thrown at line 31 when the program attempts to set data
into the first ComputerUser object. We create an array reference but have not allocated the objects for the array. The values in the array are all null.

We can trap this error by putting the calls to ComputerUser's setUser() method in a
try block and catching the exception. This prevents the crash, but we are basically
out of business in this program because we do not have the ComputerUser objects
in place. The try and catch sequence is shown here:

```
try
{
        //Now we set 5 users and their passwords.
        users[0].setUser("BlueDog", "arfarf", 0);
        users[1].setUser("KiowaTheWonderDog", "awooooooo", 0);
        users[2].setUser("Doc","Irun4you",0);
        users[3].setUser("Maddie","WhenDoWeGo",1);
        users[4].setUser("HannahBanana","BarkBark",2);
}
catch( NullPointerException npe)
{
        JOptionPane.showMessageDialog(null, "Whoops!");
}
```

Ideally, when the programmer sees the NullPointerException, he or she goes back
and allocates the array objects:

```
//Before we can use the User array, we must fill the array with
//ComputerUser objects.
        for(int i = 0; i < users.length; ++i)
        {
                users[i] = new ComputerUser();
        }
```

```
        //Now we set 5 users and their passwords.
        users[0].setUser("BlueDog", "arfarf", 0);
        users[1].setUser("KiowaTheWonderDog", "awooooooo", 0);
        users[2].setUser("Doc","Irun4you",0);
        users[3].setUser("Maddie","WhenDoWeGo",1);
        users[4].setUser("HannahBanana","BarkBark",2);
```

10

10.3
The finally Block

finally

a block of code
following the last catch
statement. The finally
block is always
executed

When a Java program encounters an exception, program execution jumps to the appropriate catch statement, often skipping other code statements in the method. It is possible that there is an early return from a method due to the error condition, but there may be unfinished business that must be performed before control leaves the method. The **finally** keyword designates a block of code, which is associated with a try block, that is performed whether or not an exception is thrown. There is only one finally block for each try (there may be many catch statements for each try), and the finally block is placed after the last catch statement. When the code executes, if no errors occurred in the try block, the catch blocks are skipped and the finally block is executed. The finally block is also executed if any errors occur and a catch statement is executed.

The finally block can be used for cleaning up and releasing resources. For example, if a file was opened in a method, and the file should be closed when control leaves the method, the file could be closed in the finally block whether there was an error in reading the file or not.

Product and Quotient Example

In Program 10-6 we ask the user to enter two integers and then perform multiplication and division with the numbers. We build the output message as we step through the various portions of the code. If there is an error with the values entered by the user or an attempt to divide by zero, the message is constructed in the different catch statements. We show the program results in the finally block. Figure 10-7a illustrates an error-free program result. Figure 10-7b shows the results when a zero divide error is caught.

```
1   //Program 10-6
2   //File: FinallyDemo.java
3
4   import javax.swing.JOptionPane;
5
6   public class FinallyDemo
7   {
8      String sNum1, sNum2;
9      String title = "finally Demo";
10     String output = "Program Results ";
11     int num1, num2, product, quot;
12
13     //We declare an integer and assign the appropriate
14     //icon for the JOptionPane dialog boxes.
```

```
15        //We'll change the icon as needed.
16        int jopIcon = JOptionPane.QUESTION_MESSAGE;
17
18        public FinallyDemo()
19        {
20             sNum1 = JOptionPane.showInputDialog(null,
21                   "Enter the first number (int).",
22                   title, jopIcon);
23
24             sNum2 = JOptionPane.showInputDialog(null,
25                   "Enter the second (int).",
26                   title, jopIcon);
27             try
28             {
29
30             //Java throws NumberFormatException if not integer
31                   num1 = Integer.parseInt(sNum1);
32                   num2 = Integer.parseInt(sNum2);
33
34                   output += "\n\nNumber 1 = " + sNum1 + "       Number 2 = " + sNum2;
35                   product = num1 * num2;
36                   output += "\n\nProduct:  " + Integer.toString(product);
37
38             //Java throws ArithmeticException if zero divide.
39                   quot = num1/num2;
40
41             //No errors so we write the quotient into the output String.
42                   output += "\n\nQuotient:  " + Integer.toString(quot);
43                   jopIcon = JOptionPane.INFORMATION_MESSAGE;
44             }
45
46             catch(NumberFormatException nfe)
47             {
48                   output += "\n\nInput error:  must enter valid integers!";
49                   jopIcon = JOptionPane.ERROR_MESSAGE;
50             }
51             catch(ArithmeticException ae)
52             {
53                   output +=
54                   "\n\nQuotient:  not performed due to zero divide error!";
55                   jopIcon = JOptionPane.ERROR_MESSAGE;
56             }
57             finally
58             {
59                   JOptionPane.showMessageDialog(null,output,
60                   title, jopIcon);
61             }
62        }
```

```
63
64      public static void main(String args[] )
65      {
66              FinallyDemo theApp = new FinallyDemo();
67              System.exit(0);
68      }
69   }
```

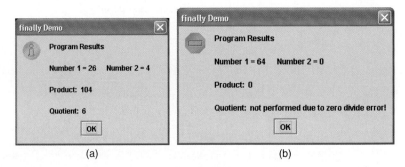

(a)   (b)

Figure 10-7
The finally block is always executed when present in exception handling code.
a) The output when no error occurred. b) The results when the catch statement writes
the error into the output String. The message box is presented in the finally block.

Out of Memory Error

Error

serious programming
problems that typically
are unrecoverable

OutOfMemoryError

thrown if the program
cannot allocate
memory

This next example illustrates a Java Error (not an Exception). **Errors** are considered serious problems in a program that usually cannot be resolved. At best, we alert the user of the error and exit the program gracefully. In Program 10-7 we ask the user to enter the number of double values and the number of Strings that he or she wishes to allocate in two arrays. This program shows how the size of an array can be a variable. We have the allocation statements in a try block and are on the lookout for an **OutOfMemoryError**. Once again, we use the finally block to report the program success or failure. Figure 10-8 illustrates an out of memory condition.

```
1   //Program 10-7
2   //File: OutOfMemoryDemo.java
3
4   import javax.swing.JOptionPane;
5
6   public class OutOfMemoryDemo
7   {
```

```
8      String aBunchOfStrings[];
9      double aBunchOfNumbers[];
10     String sNums, sStrings;
11     String title = "Did We Run Out of Memory?";
12     String output = "Program Results ";
13     int numberOfStrings, numberOfNumbers;
14     int iconResult;
15
16     public OutOfMemoryDemo()
17     {
18         sNums = JOptionPane.showInputDialog(null,
19             "Enter the number of numbers (int).",
20             title, JOptionPane.QUESTION_MESSAGE);
21
22         sStrings = JOptionPane.showInputDialog(null,
23             "Enter the number of Strings (int).",
24             title, JOptionPane.QUESTION_MESSAGE);
25     try
26     {
27
28     //Java throws NumberFormatException if not integer
29         numberOfNumbers = Integer.parseInt(sNums);
30         numberOfStrings = Integer.parseInt(sStrings);
31
32         output += "\n The number of numbers is " + sNums;
33         output += "\n The number of Strings is " + sStrings;
34
35     //OutOfMemoryError is thrown if we don't have enough memory.
36         aBunchOfNumbers = new double [numberOfNumbers];
37         aBunchOfStrings = new String [numberOfStrings];
38
39     //If we make it here, we didn't throw an error or exception!
40
41         title += " NO!";
42         iconResult = 1;             // put an i icon
43     }
44
45     catch(OutOfMemoryError oome)
46     {
47         output += "\n\nWhoa Baby! Out of memory! ";
48         title += " YES!  ";
49         iconResult = 2;             // put an ! icon
50     }
```

```
51          catch(NumberFormatException nfe)
52          {
53                  output += "\n\nSilly User. You must enter integers.";
54                  title += " ?? ";
55                  iconResult = 3;                 // put a ? icon
56          }
57          finally
58          {
59                  JOptionPane.showMessageDialog(null,output,
60                  title, iconResult);
61          }
62      }
63
64   public static void main(String args[] )
65   {
66          OutOfMemoryDemo theApp = new OutOfMemoryDemo();
67          System.exit(0);
68      }
69 }
```

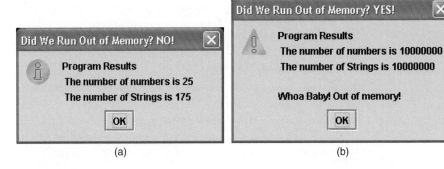

(a)   (b)

Figure 10-8
The user enters the number of doubles and Strings to be allocated. The program
traps for the OutOfMemoryError. The title String and JOptionPane icon value is modified depending on the results of the allocation. a) The output when no error
occurred. b) The results when we have exceeded the memory. The message box is
presented in the finally block.

▨ 10.4
Writing Our Own Exceptions

Consider the situation where a certain condition unique to your Java program may
occur. That is, there are situations that constitute error conditions that must be dealt
with in a program. For example, if you are writing a method to calculate the length

of someone's shadow, you should throw an exception if the program tries to do this at night when the sun is down and there is no other light in the area!

The Java programmer can create his or her own exception class by extending java.lang's Exception class. The programmer can throw this new type of exception in a method. The thrown exception may also be caught and handled in the method, or declared part of the method signature. By using the Exception as the superclass, we inherit all we need to make our own specialized error catching mechanism.

NoCockroaches!

The MakeOurOwnException program asks the user what type of insect (bug) they have. The String containing the user's bug is checked to see if it is a cockroach. If it is a cockroach, we throw a NoCockroachesException object. This exception is caught and a message is displayed on the screen. Program 10-8 shows the try, throw, and catch statements. Figure 10-9 shows the program input and output.

```
1    //Program 10-8
2    //File: MakeOurOwnException.java
3
4    //We create our own exception, called NoCockroachesException
5    //If the type of bug is a cockroach, we throw an exception!
6
7    import javax.swing.JOptionPane;
8
9    public class MakeOurOwnException
10   {
11      String sBugType;
12      String title = "Make Our Own Exception Demo";
13
14      public MakeOurOwnException()
15      {
16          getBugType();
17      }
18
19      public void getBugType()
20      {
21          sBugType = JOptionPane.showInputDialog(null,
22          "Enter the type of bug that you have.",
23          title, JOptionPane.QUESTION_MESSAGE);
24
25          try
26          {
27
```

```
28          //Our code must check the bug type.
29                  if(sBugType.equalsIgnoreCase("cockroach"))
30                  {
31
32          //We throw a NoCockroachException object.
33          //We use the new operator to create a NoCockroachException.
34                      throw (new NoCockroachesException() );
35                  }
36
37          //If we made it to here, we have an acceptable insect.
38                  JOptionPane.showMessageDialog(null,"Oh, we can live with a "
39                  + sBugType, title, JOptionPane.INFORMATION_MESSAGE);
40          }
41
42          catch(NoCockroachesException nce)
43          {
44                  String excMessage = nce.getMessage();
45
46                  JOptionPane.showMessageDialog(null,"Yeeckkk a "
47                  + sBugType + excMessage, "Caught the exception.",
48                  JOptionPane.WARNING_MESSAGE);
49          }
50      }
51
52  public static void main(String args[] )
53  {
54          MakeOurOwnException theApp = new MakeOurOwnException();
55          System.exit(0);
56  }
57 }
```

(a)   (b)

Figure 10-9
The method getBugType() throws an object of NoCockroachesException if the user enters a cockroach. We use the equalsIgnoreCase() method to compare the strings.

10

Examine the try and catch block below. We see that we need to catch a NoCock-roachesException object. In the throw statement we make a new NoCockroaches-Exception object without an object name because we only need to throw this object here and will never use it again. This is perfectly acceptable Java code.

```
try
{
    //Our code must check the bug type.
    if(sBugType.equalsIgnoreCase("cockroach"))
    {
            //create an exception object without an object reference
            //we only need it here and use it once
//Calls the no argument constructor of NoCockroachException class.
            throw (new NoCockroachesException() );
    }

    //If we made it to here, we have an acceptable insect.
            JOptionPane.showMessageDialog(null,"Oh, we can live with a "
            + sBugType, title, JOptionPane.INFORMATION_MESSAGE);
}
catch(NoCockroachesException nce)
{
    String excMessage = nce.getMessage();

    JOptionPane.showMessageDialog(null,"Yeeckkk a "
            + sBugType + excMessage, "Caught the exception.",
            JOptionPane.WARNING_MESSAGE);
}
```

Another way to write this code is to create an object reference and then throw it:

```
NoCockroachesException bug = new NoCockroachesException();
throw ( bug );
```

A second thing to notice is that in the catch statement we use a method with the exception object to obtain a message that was passed to the constructor.

```
catch(NoCockroachesException nce)
{
    String excMessage = nce.getMessage();

    JOptionPane.showMessageDialog(null,"Yeeckkk a "
            + sBugType + excMessage, "Caught the exception.",
            JOptionPane.WARNING_MESSAGE);
}
```

10

Examining Figure 10-9B, we see that the exception message is

NO COCKROACHES ALLOWED
STOMP ON IT!!!

How does that message get set? Let's look at the NoCockroachesException class itself.

```
1   //Program 10-8 Make Our Own Exception Demo
2   //File: NoCockroachesException.java
3
4   //Associate the message with the exception.
5
6   import java.lang.Exception;
7
8   public class NoCockroachesException extends Exception
9   {
10    public NoCockroachesException()
11    {
12        super("\n NO COCKROACHES ALLOWED \n STOMP ON IT!!!");
13    }
14
15    public NoCockroachesException(String msg)
16    {
17        super(msg);
18    }
19  }
```

The message gets set in the constructor. The call to super() passes the message to the superclass constructor, which has a message member variable. In our exception we have two constructors, the no argument constructor sets the message and the second constructor is passed the message when the exception is created (typically in the throw statement).

No Mosquitoes Either

The NoCockroachesException shows us how to write one type of exception. We write an exception class for each type of bug for which we are interested using the Exception class as the superclass. This technique requires us to write individual catch statements for each type of bug in our program.

What if our program had to trap for several types of insects? Writing an Exception class for each insect could be inefficient. Let's see how we can write a group of related exceptions. This approach involves writing a class of related exceptions by using a superclass that extends Exception, then our individual bug

classes extend our superclass. Modifying the insect example, let's say we are looking for ants, mosquitoes, and tomato worms. The inheritance relationship for these
related errors looks like this:

```
NoBugsException extends Exception        //this is our superclass
NoAntsException extends NoBugsException
NoMosquitoesException extends NoBugsException
NoTomatoWormsException extends NoBugsException
```

Using this approach simplifies the catch statement as it catches any NoBugsException object. In the catch block we then examine the object to determine which type
of exception it is. Examine lines 47, 52, and 57, and note that we use the **instanceof**
operator. This operator is checking the Exception e object against the various
Exception classes. In Program 10-9 we are on the lookout for ants, tomato worms,
and mosquitoes. Our code checks for any of these three insects and throws the
appropriate exception object. We write a message to the user in the catch statement.
Notice that instead of passing a message into the exception classes, we incorporate
a toString() method into each. The toString() method returns a String description of
the exception. Program 10-9 shows the MakeOurOwnExceptions2 code and the
exception classes. Figure 10-10 shows the compilation steps for all of these classes
as well as the java interpreter command for this program. Figure 10-11 shows the
results if the user has a tomato worm.

instanceof operator
compares an object to
a class and returns true
if the object is of that
class or a subclass

```
1   //Program 10-9
2   //File: MakeOurOwnExceptions2.java
3
4   //We create a group of exceptions.
5   //If the type of bug is an ant, mosquito, or tomato worm we throw an exception!
6
7   //We use one catch statement, using the superclass NoBugsException.
8
9   import javax.swing.JOptionPane;
10
11  public class MakeOurOwnExceptions2
12  {
13    String sBugType;
14    String title = "Make Our Own Exceptions 2 Demo";
15
16    public MakeOurOwnExceptions2()
17    {
18        getBugType();
19    }
20
21    public void getBugType()
22    {
```

```
23            sBugType = JOptionPane.showInputDialog(null,
24            "Enter the type of bug that you have.",
25            title, JOptionPane.QUESTION_MESSAGE);
26
27            try
28            {
29                    if(sBugType.equalsIgnoreCase("ant") )
30                    {
31                            throw (new NoAntsException() );
32                    }
33                    else if( sBugType.equalsIgnoreCase("mosquito") )
34                    {
35                            throw (new NoMosquitoesException() );
36                    }
37                    else if( sBugType.equalsIgnoreCase("tomato worm") )
38                    {
39                            throw (new NoTomatoWormsException() );
40                    }
41
42                    JOptionPane.showMessageDialog(null,"Oh, we can live with a "
43                    + sBugType, title, JOptionPane.INFORMATION_MESSAGE);
44            }
45            catch(NoBugsException e)
46            {
47                    if(e instanceof NoAntsException)
48                    {
49                            JOptionPane.showMessageDialog(null, e.toString(),
50                            "Ants Ants", JOptionPane.WARNING_MESSAGE);
51                    }
52                    if(e instanceof NoMosquitoesException)
53                    {
54                            JOptionPane.showMessageDialog(null, e.toString(),
55                            "Buzzzzzzzz", JOptionPane.WARNING_MESSAGE);
56                    }
57                    if(e instanceof NoTomatoWormsException)
58                    {
59                            JOptionPane.showMessageDialog(null, e.toString(),
60                            "Big Green Worms", JOptionPane.WARNING_MESSAGE);
61                    }
62            }
63    }
64
65    public static void main(String args[] )
66    {
67        MakeOurOwnExceptions2 theApp = new MakeOurOwnExceptions2();
68        System.exit(0);
69    }
70 }
```

```
C:\JPT>javac NoBugsException.java

C:\JPT>javac NoAntsException.java

C:\JPT>javac NoMosquitoesException.java

C:\JPT>javac NoTomatoWormsException.java

C:\JPT>javac MakeOurOwnExceptions2.java

C:\JPT>java  MakeOurOwnExceptions2
```

Figure 10-10
The exception classes are all compiled separately and the java command is used
with the *MakeOurOwnException2.class* file. Note that we could have compiled all of
the *.java* files using javac *.java.

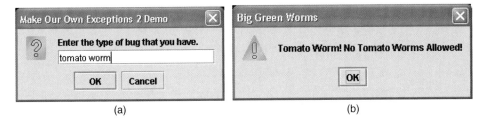

(a)   (b)

Figure 10-11
The method getBugType() throws an object of whatever type of bug is found, but we
catch the superclass, NoBugsException object.

The NoBugsException class is shown here, followed by the NoTomatoWormEx-
ception class. Notice how we need only to import the java.lang.Exception for our
superclass. The complete Java source code for this program is on the CD that
accompanies this text.

```
1   //Program 10-9 Create our own superclass of Exceptions.
2   //File: NoBugsException.java
3
4   import java.lang.Exception;
5
6   public class NoBugsException extends Exception
7   {
8       public NoBugsException()
9       {
10      }
11
```

```
12        public NoBugsException(String msg)
13        {
14                super(msg);
15        }
16    }
```

```
1     //Program 10-9
2     //File: NoTomatoWormsException.java
3
4     public class NoTomatoWormsException extends NoBugsException
5     {
6       public NoTomatoWormsException()
7       {
8       }
9
10      public String toString()
11      {
12              return "Tomato Worm! No Tomato Worms Allowed!";
13      }
14    }
```

▓▓▓10.5
throws Interface and
Propagating Exceptions

In Java, if an exception is thrown in a method, and the exception is not caught and handled in that method, the exception is passed up the chain of calling methods in search of a try and catch statement. If the exception is not caught by the time it is passed out of the "top" of the program, execution stops. Figure 10-12 illustrates this concept with a zero division attempt.

The examples shown in this chapter have had the try and catch blocks in the same method. This approach is tidy, but may not be the best way to build a program. You may be writing a Java program and may not want to have the try and catch statements in the method where the exception occurs. Or you may plan to use another class where there is a method that might throw an exception. It is possible to place a call to a method that throws an exception inside the try block and place the associated catch statement(s) after the try.

Program 10-10, the ThrowsDemo program, illustrates how we place the call to the doDivision() method inside a try block in the doMath() method. There are two possible exceptions that could be thrown in the doDivision() method, and we

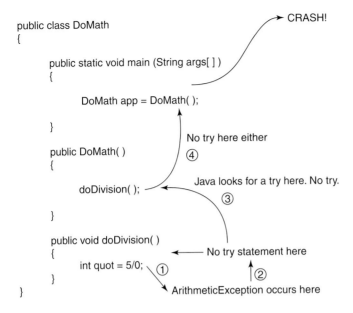

public class DoMath
{

    public static void main (String args[ ])   → CRASH!
    {

        DoMath app = DoMath( );

    }
    public DoMath( )   No try here either
    {   ④

        doDivision( );   Java looks for a try here. No try.
                    ③

    }
    public void doDivision( )
    {   ← No try statement here
      int quot = 5/0; ①
    }   ②
}   ArithmeticException occurs here

Figure 10-12
If an exception is thrown in a method and not caught, the exception is propagated
back through the calling methods in search of a try and catch. If the exception is
never caught and handled, the program crashes.

catch them in the doMath() method. Notice how the method definition line includes
the throws keyword and lists the exceptions. This tells anyone who may want to use
this method what the possible exceptions are and to guard against problems by
placing the call to the method inside a try. Associated catches can then handle any
problems that arise.

```
1    //Program 10-10
2    //File: ThrowsExcDemo.java
3
4    //If an exception is thrown in a method, with no try/catch,
5    //the exception is propagated up through the calling methods.
6
7    import javax.swing.JOptionPane;
8
9    public class ThrowsExcDemo
10   {
11      String title = "Methods that throw Exception Demo";
12      String input;
13
```

10

```
14      public ThrowsExcDemo()
15      {
16              doMath();
17      }
18
19      public void doMath()
20      {
21              int quotient = 0;
22
23              try
24              {
25                      //doDivision might throw Exceptions
26                      //Guard against problems by calling in a try and
27                      //have a catches just in case.
28                      quotient = doDivision();
29              }
30
31              catch(ArithmeticException ae)
32              {
33                      JOptionPane.showMessageDialog(null,"Can't divide by zero!",
34                       "ArithmeticException.",
35                      JOptionPane.WARNING_MESSAGE);
36                      return;
37              }
38              catch(NumberFormatException nfe)
39              {
40                      JOptionPane.showMessageDialog(null,"Enter an integer! ",
41                       "NumberFormatException.",
42                      JOptionPane.WARNING_MESSAGE);
43                      return;
44              }
45
46              JOptionPane.showMessageDialog(null,"7 / " +input + " = "
47                      + Integer.toString(quotient),
48                      "No problem here.",JOptionPane.INFORMATION_MESSAGE);
49      }
50
51      public int doDivision() throws ArithmeticException, NumberFormatException
52      {
53              int num = 7,denom, quot;
54              input = JOptionPane.showInputDialog(null,
55                      "Enter an integer value for the denominator.",
56                      "Divide 7/?", JOptionPane.QUESTION_MESSAGE);
57
58              //ohhhh could be a problem
59              denom = Integer.parseInt(input);
60
```

```
61              //look out, here's an exception waiting to happen!
62              quot = num/denom;
63
64              return quot;
65      }
66
67      public static void main(String args[] )
68      {
69              ThrowsExcDemo theApp = new ThrowsExcDemo();
70              System.exit(0);
71      }
72 }
```

Java requires that the exceptions be listed in the method definition line unless they
are RuntimeException or Errors, or any of their subclasses. However, it is a good
idea to always list the exceptions in a method definition line that may be thrown
and not handled in that method.

Revisit Array Out of Bounds Example

A well written program provides the user clear error messages when the program
(or programmer) has committed an error. Additionally, it is important to provide the
user a path back to a place where he or she can reinsert good data in case of an
error. One of the strengths of Java's exception handling is that it provides the programmer the necessary framework to route the user back to a place that he or she
can correct the input error(s).

We rework Program 10-4 in two ways in this final section. The first way has
the fillArray() method contain a try-catch block of code. In the try block we call the
askHowManyNumbersAndFillIt() method. This long-named method might throw
the two exceptions we've been watching in this example. Notice that we incorporate a while statement around the try-catch block, which keeps us in this loop as
long as the user wishes. Examine the code in Program 10-11 or obtain the program
from the text's CD and run it yourself!

```
1  //Program 10-11
2  //File: ArrayExceptionDemo3.java
3
4  //We place the method that throws exceptions in a try block.
5
6
7  import javax.swing.JOptionPane;
8  import java.text.DecimalFormat;
9
```

10

```
10   public class ArrayExceptionDemo3
11   {
12     double numbers [] = new double[5];
13
14     int howManyNumbers;
15     String sHowMany;
16     String title = "Array Exceptions Demo, 3rd Version";
17
18
19     public ArrayExceptionDemo3()
20     {
21           fillArray();
22     }
23
24     public void fillArray()
25     {
26           //ok is set to true when user enters valid input.
27           boolean bKeepAsking = true;
28
29           while(bKeepAsking)
30           {
31                   try
32                   {
33                           askHowManyNumbersAndFillIt();
34                           showTheNumbers();
35
36                   }
37                   catch(NumberFormatException nfe)
38                   {
39                           JOptionPane.showMessageDialog(null,"Must enter integers! ",
40                           "Error in Input ", 2);
41                   }
42                   catch(ArrayIndexOutOfBoundsException e)
43                   {
44                           JOptionPane.showMessageDialog(null,
45                           "You have exceeded the array boundries!",
46                           "Array Out Of Bounds Error! ", 2);
47                   }
48                   finally
49                   {
50                           String answer = JOptionPane.showInputDialog(null,
51                               "Would you like to enter more numbers? yes or no",
52                           "yes or no ??? ", 3);
```

```
53
54                            if(answer.equals("no") )bKeepAsking = false;
55              }
56          }
57      }
58
59
60      //This method might throw exceptions, which are sent back
61      //to the calling method and handled there.
62      public void askHowManyNumbersAndFillIt()
63              throws ArrayIndexOutOfBoundsException, NumberFormatException
64      {
65          sHowMany = JOptionPane.showInputDialog(null,
66          "How many random numbers do you wish to place in the array (5 max).",
67              title, JOptionPane.QUESTION_MESSAGE);
68
69          //parseInt() throws NumberFormatException if it doesn't get an int.
70          howManyNumbers = Integer.parseInt(sHowMany);
71
72          //If we attempt to go beyond 5 elements, Java throws
73          //an ArrayIndexOutOfBoundsException.
74          for(int i = 0; i < howManyNumbers; ++i)
75          {
76              numbers[i] = Math.random();
77          }
78      }
79
80      //Show the user his or her numbers!
81      public void showTheNumbers()
82      {
83          String output = "The numbers are: ";
84          String temp;
85
86          DecimalFormat df = new DecimalFormat("0.000");
87
88          for(int i = 0; i < howManyNumbers; ++i)
89          {
90              temp = df.format(numbers[i]);
91              output += temp + "   ";
92          }
93
94          JOptionPane.showMessageDialog(null,output, "Here are your numbers!",
95              JOptionPane.INFORMATION_MESSAGE);
96      }
```

```
97
98       public static void main(String args[] )
99       {
100              ArrayExceptionDemo3 theApp = new ArrayExceptionDemo3();
101              System.exit(0);
102      }
103  }
```

Exception Handling with Java GUI Components

Event-driven programs

wait for the user to issue a command, usually with a GUI control

Event-driven programs are programs that wait for the user to issue a command of some sort, such as a button-click, selection of a menu item, or activation of a variety of other controls. Programs that have GUIs are event-driven programs. Event-driven programs, by their nature, make exception handling easier because we have an event handling method in place.

In Program 10-12, we place a GUI front end on our array program. The user enters the number of random numbers in the text field. When the show button is pressed, if it is valid, the numbers are shown. Figure 10-13 on page 667 illustrates the results when the user enters "5".

In this program, we use an anonymous class to handle the button press event. In the actionPerformed() method, we call the fillArray() method. If the boolean ok flag is set to true, it means we did not have any errors and we have valid random numbers to show the user. The fillArray() has a similar structure as the previous program in that we call the askHowManyNumbersAndFillIt() method in a try block. We do not need to have the while loop. Because this is an event-driven program, the program waits for the user to press the show button again after we report the error message. Figure 10-14 on page 668 shows how the program pops up an error message if the user enters invalid input.

```
1    //Program 10-12
2    //File: ArrayExceptionDemo4.java
3
4    //We place the method that throws exceptions in a try block.
5
6    import javax.swing.*;   //for JButton, JFrame, JOptionPane
7
8    import java.awt.Container;
9    import java.awt.GridLayout;
10   import java.awt.event.ActionListener;
11   import java.awt.event.ActionEvent;
12
13
```

10

```
14     import javax.swing.JOptionPane;
15     import java.text.DecimalFormat;
16
17     public class ArrayExceptionDemo4 extends JFrame
18     {
19        double numbers [] = new double[5];
20
21        int howManyNumbers;
22        String sHowMany;
23        String title = "Array Exceptions Demo, 4th Version";
24
25        boolean ok;
26
27        JButton showButton  = new JButton("Show Numbers");
28        JTextField numbersField = new JTextField("");
29        JLabel howManyLabel = new JLabel("How many? (5 max)");
30        JLabel hereAreTheNumbersLabel = new JLabel(" ");
31
32
33        public ArrayExceptionDemo4()
34        {
35
36             this.setTitle(title);
37             this.setSize(450,150);
38             Container canvas = getContentPane();
39
40             canvas.setLayout( new GridLayout(2,2) );
41
42             canvas.add(howManyLabel);
43             canvas.add(numbersField);
44             canvas.add(showButton);
45             canvas.add(hereAreTheNumbersLabel);
46
47             //Use an anonymous class with the Action Listener.
48             showButton.addActionListener(   new ActionListener()
49             {
50                  public void actionPerformed(ActionEvent event)
51                  {
52                       fillArray();
53
54                       //Show the numbers if all is well.
55                       if(ok)showTheNumbers();
56                  }
57             } );
58
59             show();
60        }
```

10

```
61
62    public void fillArray()
63    {
64            //ok is set to true when user enters valid input,
65            //false if not.
66            try
67            {
68                    askHowManyNumbersAndFillIt();
69
70                    ok = true;
71            }
72            catch(NumberFormatException nfe)
73            {
74                    //Whoops, there's an error.
75                    //Clear the numbers out of the text field.
76                    hereAreTheNumbersLabel.setText("");
77
78                    JOptionPane.showMessageDialog(null,"Must enter integers! ",
79                    "Error in Input ", JOptionPane.ERROR_MESSAGE);
80
81                    ok = false;
82            }
83            catch(ArrayIndexOutOfBoundsException e)
84            {
85                    hereAreTheNumbersLabel.setText("");
86
87                    JOptionPane.showMessageDialog(null,
88                    "You have exceeded the array boundries!",
89                    "Array Out Of Bounds Error! ", JOptionPane.ERROR_MESSAGE);
90
91                    ok = false;
92            }
93
94    }
95
96
97    //This method might throw exceptions, which are sent back
98    //to the calling method and handled there.
99    public void askHowManyNumbersAndFillIt()
100           throws ArrayIndexOutOfBoundsException, NumberFormatException
101    {
102
103           //Obtain the user's value from the text field.
104           sHowMany = numbersField.getText();
105
106           //parseInt() throws NumberFormatException if it doesn't get an int.
107           howManyNumbers = Integer.parseInt(sHowMany);
```

```
108
109            //If we attempt to go beyond 5 elements, Java throws
110            //an ArrayIndexOutOfBoundsException.
111            for(int i = 0; i < howManyNumbers; ++i)
112            {
113                  numbers[i] = Math.random();
114            }
115     }
116
117     //Show the user his or her numbers!
118     public void showTheNumbers()
119     {
120            String output = "";
121            String temp;
122
123            DecimalFormat df = new DecimalFormat("0.000");
124
125            for(int i = 0; i < howManyNumbers; ++i)
126            {
127                  temp = df.format(numbers[i]);
128                  output += temp + "   ";
129            }
130
131            hereAreTheNumbersLabel.setText(output);
132     }
133
134     public static void main(String args[] )
135     {
136            ArrayExceptionDemo4 theApp = new ArrayExceptionDemo4();
137            theApp.setDefaultCloseOperation(JFrame.EXIT_ON_CLOSE);
138     }
139  }
```

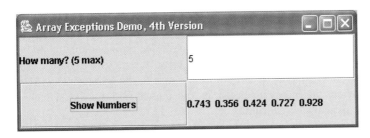

Figure 10-13
The frame window shows the four GUI controls for this array program. The user
requested that the program generate five random numbers. If the user happened to
enter a value greater than five or a noninteger value, the exceptions are caught and
handled in the program.

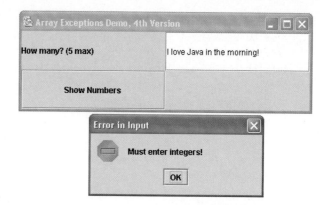

Figure 10-14
The user has entered invalid data and the error is caught and handled.

10.6
Summary

In this chapter we introduced the concept of a program run-time error. Java has classes incorporated into the language to alert the programmer to the various types of errors that a program may encounter. Java has both Exception and Error classes, and the language will throw an exception or an error when it encounters a run-time problem. Java uses the term *exception* to refer to a problem that it has encountered when the code may be able to recover and continue to execute. The term *error* is used when referring to a nonrecoverable problem. Error and exception handling should be written into programs to inform the user when a problem has been encountered and attempt a possible recovery instead of just letting the program crash ungracefully.

Java requires the programmer to use try and catch statements in his or her code. A try statement block encloses program statements that might produce an exception. Catch blocks identify the specific type of exception. When an exception occurs, Java throws a specific type of exception object, which is then caught in the catch statement. The programmer should write the error handling code in the catch statement. When the program throws an error, the program control jumps to the appropriate catch statement and does not return to the try statement. The Java language provides the finally block that is placed after the last catch statement, and the finally block is always executed.

The Java language provides exception and error classes for all of the possible language problems encountered in a program, such as not parsing a number from a String, not being able to locate a file, or attempting to access an illegal array element. Java also allows the programmer to write and throw his or her own exceptions by using the Exception superclass. These programmer-generated exceptions are specific to a certain condition found in the program.

The programmer may delay handling an exception or an error to allow it to be passed up the chain of calling methods in search of a try and catch block. Method calls can be placed within a try block. The programmer should use the throws keyword in a method definition line to indicate the type of exception that the method might throw. If an exception is thrown—and not caught in the method—the exception is passed up the chain of calling methods in search of a try and catch statement. If an exception is not caught, Java stops the execution of the program.

Many Java classes require that their methods be called within a try block with the associated catch block in the program. With this in mind, Java programmers should always be on the lookout for possible errors and write their code with error handling code included. Writing exeception handling code increases a programmer's work, but it allows the program to keep the user informed, may allow recovery from a run-time error, and provides a controlled exit if the program must halt execution.

10

11

Advanced Topic: Java Input/Output

KEY TERMS AND CONCEPTS

buffered character streams
BufferedReader
BufferedWriter
byte stream
character stream
FileInputStream
FileOutputStream
FileReader
FileWriter
InputStream class
Internet protocol
network socket
OutputStream class
packet
program input/output
token
stream
stream buffering classes
StringTokenizer
TCP/IP
wrapper classes

CHAPTER OBJECTIVES

Introduce Java's input/output classes and Java's three basic principles for program I/O.

Present Java's two types of streams: byte streams and character streams.

Illustrate reading data into a program as a byte stream from a file.

Demonstrate how stream buffering wrapper classes attach a memory buffer to an I/O stream and how they help the programmer work with character data.

Show several examples using String Tokenizer objects to parse pertinent data from an entire line of data.

Provide a brief introduction to networking, sockets, and TCP/IP.

Illustrate how Java treats network data as stream data.

Use a simple program to illustrate network sockets.

Reading and Writing

The vast majority of computer programs require information be entered into them, and programs usually provide some form of output information. In our first programs, we used the println() and print() methods of the java.lang.System class to write information to the MS-DOS Prompt window. We quickly graduated to using the JOptionPane class methods to ask our user questions, collect information, and report program results. Programs found in the latter portion of this text provide our user with GUI components, such as combo boxes, sliders, and buttons, for entering program data.

Many programs rely on input information being contained in a data file that the program must read and process. In turn, the program writes information to an output file. Java provides many classes to perform the program input (such as file reading) and program output (such as file writing). Program input and output is commonly referred to as **program I/O**. File input and output is referred to as file I/O. Java programs may require that the input information come from data files, network sockets, or the keyboard. A network socket can be thought of as an electrical socket, delivering network data instead of electricity.

program I/O
program input and output

The designers of the Java language constructed program I/O to be based on three principles: (1) the input and output is based on "streams" that have a physical device at one end, such as a disk file, and data streams into or out of the program in a flow of characters or bytes. We use classes to manage how the data comes into or leaves our program. (2) I/O should be portable and should obtain consistent results even though the platforms may differ. Because Java is designed to run worldwide, on any network and on any JVM, the I/O should ensure that the code runs everywhere. (3) Java provides many classes that each perform a few tasks instead of large classes that do many things. As we shall see, we use several classes to read and gather information from data files. This many-class approach may seem confusing at first, but as we perform different types of reads and writes, their utility becomes clear.

We will concentrate on the fundamental ways to read and write data files. However, the basic approach for data files is similar for other input or output devices, such as network sockets. Also, the adoption of the XML file within distributed computing has resurrected the need for Java programmers to understand file handling. XML file processing is crucial for the web services application. Lastly, we present a brief discussion of networking topics at the end of the chapter and run through an example that uses Java's Socket class.

Java provides classes for more advanced I/O techniques, including Random Access I/O, the means for working with directory structures, and an extensive Network Application Programming Interface. We do not present these more advanced Java I/O topics. For an explanation please refer to the references listed in the bibliography.

Note: This chapter uses Java Exception handling in all of the sample programs. The reader is encouraged to read and understand Chapter 10, *Exception Handling,* before tackling this chapter.

11.1
Streams

stream

a flow of data into or out of a program

byte stream

data flows into or out of programs as bytes

character streams

data flows into or out of programs as two-byte Unicode characters

A way to visualize data flowing into or out of a Java program is to envision a stream of characters or a data pipeline. This stream of data is linked to a physical device, such as a file stored on the hard drive or a network socket. Figure 11-1 illustrates a stream of data from a file named *GroceryList.txt* (stored on the hard drive).

There are two types of **streams** in Java, byte streams and character streams. **Byte streams** pump the data into programs and out of programs as bytes. Byte stream classes are used for handling these bytes. Binary data are stored as either 8-bit bytes or as an ASCII character code set. **Characters streams** are used for handling character data. Character streams use Unicode, which is composed of two-byte characters and can be used on an international basis. Original versions of Java provided only byte code stream support, but Java 1.1 added character streams. We present two examples using byte code stream classes. The majority of our examples

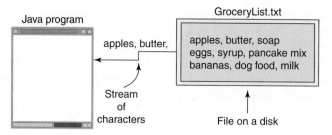

Figure 11-1
A stream of data from the *GroceryList.txt* file.

use the character streams classes, as they provide handy tools and consistent results when a Java program is handling character file data.

Reading and Writing Data Using Byte Stream Classes

Byte stream classes in Java use a two-class hierarchical structure, one for reading and one for writing. The top two classes are InputStream and OutputStream. Each of these superclasses has many subclasses designed for working with different devices such as files and network connections. Important methods include read() and write(). For reading and writing data files, we use the **FileInputStream** and **FileOutputStream** class objects. The simplest form of these classes reads and writes the data one byte at a time. When the data is read, they are treated as integers. If the FileInputStream object tries to read beyond the last character in the file, the read method returns a negative one (–1).

FileInputStream and FileOutputStream

Java classes that read and write data files one byte at a time

Byte Stream Methods

The FileInputStream class has several read() methods as well as other supporting methods. A partial listing of these methods are seen in Table 11-1. Notice how the data is treated as either integers or bytes.

The FileOutputStream methods are similar to the input methods. A partial listing of these methods is seen in Table 11-2.

TABLE 11-1
A partial listing of Java's FileInputStream methods.

Method	Purpose
int available()	Returns the number of bytes available that can be read in this file.
int read()	Reads one byte at a time and returns each byte as an integer.
void read(byte[] b)	Reads up to b.length bytes of data from the input stream.
void read(byte[] b, int offset, int length)	Reads *length* number of bytes from the input stream beginning at the offset of the data.
void close()	Closes the file and releases any resources associated with the input stream.
void skip(int n)	Skips *n* number of bytes in the stream. The *n* number of skipped bytes are discarded.

Note: Remember b is a Java array and b.length is the size of the array.

11

TABLE 11-2

A partial listing of Java's FileOutputStream methods.

Method	Purpose
void write(int b)	Writes the byte to the output stream. The input is a single integer and is converted to a byte. This relieves the programmer from having to cast it.
void write(byte[] b)	Writes up to b.length bytes of data into the output file stream.
void write (byte[] b, int from, int length)	Writes a portion of the byte array to the output file stream. The from variable indicates the starting index, and the length is number of bytes.
void close()	Closes the file and releases any resources associated with the output stream.

Read the Grocery List one Byte at a Time Program

The first program demonstrates how to read a text data file a byte at a time, and print each byte as a character. In Program 11-1, we create a FileInputStream object and pass in the name of our data file, *GroceryList1.txt*, to the class constructor. The file is located in the same directory as the *.java* and *.class* files. If Java cannot find the file, it throws a FileNotFoundException. Here is the data file we are going to read:

apples, butter, soap
eggs, syrup, pancake mix
bananas, dog food, milk

Once we create the FileInputStream object, we then query the object to determine the size. The available() method returns the number of bytes that can be read from this file. In the for loop we read one byte at a time and print it to the MS-DOS Prompt window. Notice that we use print() which does not add a linefeed (new line character). The linefeed characters are in the data file. When these \n characters are read and output via the print() method, we see a linefeed in the output. Figure 11-2 on page 676 shows the command window with our program results.

```
1    //Program 11-1
2    //File:  ReadFile1.java
3
4    /* This program reads a file using FileInputStream object.
5     * It reads the file a byte at a time and prints the char
6     * to the screen.
7     */
8
```

```java
 9    import java.io.FileInputStream;
10    import java.io.IOException;
11    import java.io.FileNotFoundException;
12
13    public class ReadFile1
14    {
15      public static void main( String[] args)
16      {
17            ReadFile1 app = new ReadFile1();
18            System.exit(0);
19      }
20
21      public ReadFile1()
22      {
23            //We create a FileInputStream object and pass the name of the
24            //data file into the constructor. If Java can't find the file,
25            //it throws a FileNotFoundException.
26
27            try
28            {
29
30                  FileInputStream fileIn = new FileInputStream( "GroceryList1.txt");
31
32                  //We ask the file object to tell us how many bytes are in the file.
33                  int size = fileIn.available();
34
35                  int oneChar;
36                  for(int i = 0; i < size; ++i)
37                  {
38                        //Read the file one byte at a time.
39                        //If a read error occurs, read throws an IOException.
40                        oneChar = fileIn.read();
41
42                        //print without linefeeds
43                        System.out.print((char)oneChar);
44                  }
45                  fileIn.close();
46            }
47            catch(FileNotFoundException fnfe)
48            {
49                  System.out.println("Can't find the file!");
50            }
51            catch(IOException ioe)
52            {
53                  System.out.println("Problem reading the file!");
54            }
55      }
56    }
```

```
C:\JPT\Ch11\ReadFile1>javac ReadFile1.java

C:\JPT\Ch11\ReadFile1>java ReadFile1
apples, butter, soap
eggs, syrup, pancake mix
bananas, dog food, milk
C:\JPT\Ch11\ReadFile1>
```

Figure 11-2
The *GroceryList1.txt* data is read one byte at a time using a FileInputStream object. The bytes are cast into characters as they are displayed by the System.out.print() method.

A second way that we could write this code involves checking each integer as we read it, to see if it is a negative one (–1). We do not obtain the number of bytes in the file, but just read until we read the last byte. This while loop could replace the for loop in the above code:

```
//The FileInputStream object returns a -1 when it can't read any more data from
//the file. Instead of reading the data in a for loop, we can use a while loop
//and stop reading when the fileIn object returns a -1.

int oneChar;
while( ( oneChar = fileIn.read() )  != -1)
{
        //print without linefeeds
        System.out.print((char)oneChar);
}
```

Read the Entire List into a Byte Array Program

In Program 11-2, we read the entire file into a byte array using one read statement. Just for fun, let's reverse the characters in the array ("apples, butter" would be reversed to "rettub ,selppa", etc.) and write the reversed data into an output file. In this program, we pass the write method the entire byte array. We use the same *GroceryList1.txt* file from Program 11-1 for the input and write a new file called YrecorgList1. Figure 11-3 on page 678 shows the results from this program. The *YrecorgList1.txt* file is created when the program executes.

```
1   //Program 11-2
2   //File:  ReadFile2.java
3
4   /* This program reads a file using FileInputStream object.
5    * It reads the entire file into a byte array in one read statement.
6    * We then reverse the elements and write it to an output file.
7    */
```

```
8
9     import java.io.FileInputStream;
10    import java.io.FileOutputStream;
11    import java.io.IOException;
12    import java.io.FileNotFoundException;
13
14    public class ReadFile2
15    {
16      public static void main( String[] args)
17      {
18            ReadFile2 app = new ReadFile2();
19            System.exit(0);
20      }
21
22      public ReadFile2()
23      {
24            //We create FileInputStream and FileOutputStream objects, passing
25            //the filename to each constructor.
26
27            try
28            {
29
30                  FileInputStream fileIn = new FileInputStream( "GroceryList1.txt");
31                  FileOutputStream fileOut = new FileOutputStream(
32                        "YrecorgList1.txt");
33
34                  //We ask the file object to tell us how many bytes are in the file.
35                  int size = fileIn.available();
36
37                  byte array[] = new byte[size];
38                  byte reversedArray[] = new byte[size];
39
40                  fileIn.read( array);
41                  fileIn.close();                    //done reading, close the file
42
43                  //print the original array
44                  System.out.println("\n The original array is: \n");
45                  System.out.print( new String( array));
46
47                  for(int i = 0; i < size; ++i)
48                  {
49                        reversedArray[i] = array[size - i - 1];
50                  }
51
```

```
52              //print the reversed array
53              System.out.println("\n\n The reversed array is: \n ");
54              System.out.print( new String( reversedArray));
55
56              fileOut.write( reversedArray );
57
58          }
59      catch(FileNotFoundException fnfe)
60      {
61              System.out.println("Can't find the file!");
62      }
63      catch(IOException ioe)
64      {
65              System.out.println("Problem reading the file!");
66      }
67   }
68 }
```

C:\JPT\Ch11\ReadFile2>javac ReadFile2.java

C:\JPT\Ch11\ReadFile2>java ReadFile2

The original array is:

apples, butter, soap
eggs, syrup, pancake mix
bananas, dog food, milk

The reversed array is:

klim ,doof god ,sananab
xim ekacnap ,purys ,sgge
paos ,rettub ,selppa
C:\JPT\Ch11\ReadFile2>

Figure 11-3
The *GroceryList1.txt* data is read into a byte array using one read statement. The array elements are written to a file in reverse order.

11.3
Buffered Character Stream File Input and Output

Reading and writing program data using byte stream classes is straightforward, but it presents problems for the Java programmer. The data comes into the program as bytes (integers) or in byte arrays. If the programmer wanted to work with each data item in the byte array, he or she would need to find a way to separate the individual data items. For example, if we wanted to list the items in our grocery list, we would need to go through the byte array, pulling out the letters, and starting a new item when we encountered a comma. If you are thinking that there has got to be a better way, you are right!

Wrapper Classes

Java provides many wrapper classes to help the programmer with his or her programming tasks. Let's clarify what we mean by a wrapper class. "Wrapper class" is a programming term that is part of the Java jargon. For example, when we refer to a program error as a "bug," this, too, is a programming term. If you look for Java classes with "Wrapper" in the name, you will not find them. **Wrapper classes** wrap one class in another class, thus improving the features of the first class. We have already seen and used the Integer, Double, and Float wrapper classes. Each of these classes wraps a primitive single data type value into a class, and provides useful methods for the programmer who is working with primitive values.

> For I/O, Java provides **stream buffering classes** that provide the programmer with a means to attach a memory buffer to the I/O streams. By having a memory buffer attached to the I/O stream, the memory buffer lets us work on more than one byte or one character at a time. There are buffered classes for both byte streams and character stream use. We will wrap the file readers and file writers in buffered readers and writers. Because we aim for maximum portability in our Java code, we concentrate on character stream I/O.

wrapper classes

wrap one class in another class, thus improving the features of the first class

stream buffering classes

wrapper classes that provide a means to attach a memory buffer to the I/O streams

File Input

Java's **FileReader** class allows you to read a data file as characters instead of bytes. We can wrap the FileReader in a **BufferedReader** class, which provides a readLine() method and the ability to read a data file one line at a time. Let's look at the two basic constructors for the classes we will be using. The BufferedReader constructors require a FileReader object. We create the FileReader object and then use it in the constructor for the BufferedReader, like this:

FileReader

a class that allows you to read a data file as characters instead of bytes

BufferedReader

a wrapper class that provides readLine methods to read a data file one line at a time

```
//The BufferedReader wraps the FileReader object.
//This allows us to read a data file one line at a time.

FileReader reader = new FileReader();

BufferedReader bufreader = new BufferedReader( reader );
```

The supporting methods for the BufferedReader class are shown in Table 11-3.

Method	Purpose
void close()	Closes the file and releases any resources associated with the output stream.
void mark(int readAheadLimit)	Marks the present position in the stream.
boolean markSupported()	Returns a true if this stream supports the mark() operation. The BufferedReader class supports this operation.
int read()	Reads a single character.
int read(char[] buf, int offset, int length)	Reads characters into a portion of an array.
String readLine()	Reads a line of text.
boolean ready()	Returns true if this stream is ready to be read.
void reset()	Resets the stream to the most recent mark.
long skip(long n)	Skips *n* characters in the stream. Returns the number of characters actually skipped.

Read the States Program

It's time to see the BufferedReader in action! When programming in any language, it is vital that the programmer knows exactly how the data file is designed. The programmer must write the corresponding read statements to match the file design in order to read the file accurately. The data file for Program 11-3 is set up so that the name of a state is listed on each line of the *StateList.txt* file. We read our data file one line at a time and write the name of the state to the screen. Here is the *StateList.txt* file.

Hawaii
Colorado
Alabama
Texas
Oregon
Alaska
New Jersey
Mississippi
Arkansas
New York
Maryland
North Carolina
Florida
Michigan
New Mexico
Arizona

Our Java code creates a FileReader object named *fr* and a BufferedReader object named *br*. In the program, we create objects on individual lines, like this:

```
//Class for reading character files.
    FileReader fr = new FileReader( "StateList.txt");


    BufferedReader br = new BufferedReader( fr );
```

The preferred way in Java is to perform these two instantiations in one line. Because we are never going to use the FileReader object directly, there is no need to make a reference to it. In later programs we will combine these two steps, like this:

```
//The preferred wrapper style:
BufferedReader br = new BufferedReader( new FileReader( FILE_NAME));
```

As with all the wrapper style classes, we put a new operator inside the constructor.

In the following code, we read the states one line at a time and add the name into a Vector object named stateList. A Vector is one of the many helper classes provided to us in the java.util package. Let's clarify what we mean by a helper class. "Helper class" is another programming term, and you will not see "Helper" in any class name. A helper class is a class that provides a helpful service to the Java programmer.

Vectors can be thought of as dynamic arrays that hold objects. In fact, many Java programmers believe we should never make an array of objects, but simply use the Vector class. Examine the Java documentation for Vector and see the many supporting methods, such as add(), clear(), remove(), get(), indexOf(), and isEmpty(). The stateList Vector object is filled when we read the state names, and then it is used to create and fill the JComboBox. (Refer to Chapters 7 and 8 for a discussion of GUI components. Line 79 shows an efficient way to handle GUI components without the use of intermediate objects.) Figure 11-4a shows the compilation and execution commands in an MS-DOS Prompt window, as well as the results using the println() command. Figure 11-4b shows the resultant combo box.

```
1   //Program 11-3
2   //Use a BufferedReader and FileReader to read a data file
3   //one line at a time.
4
5   import java.util.Vector;
6   import java.io.FileReader;
7   import java.io.BufferedReader;
8   import java.io.IOException;
9   import java.awt.event.WindowEvent;
10  import java.awt.event.WindowAdapter;
11  import javax.swing.JFrame;
12  import javax.swing.JComboBox;
13
```

11

```
14    public class ReadStateFile1 extends JFrame
15    {
16      //Create a Vector object, which is a dynamic array that hold objects.
17      private static Vector stateList = new Vector();
18
19      public ReadStateFile1()
20      {
21            super( "State List");
22      }
23
24      private void readStateList() throws IOException
25      {
26
27            // Class for reading character files.
28            FileReader fr = new FileReader( "StateList.txt");
29
30            /* Read text from a character-input stream, buffering
31             * characters so as to provide for the efficient
32             * reading of characters, arrays, and lines.          */
33
34            BufferedReader br = new BufferedReader( fr );
35
36            // Holds the entire line read by BufferedReaders
37            String line;
38
39            //The ready() method returns true as long as there are lines to read.
40            while( br.ready())
41            {
42                //Use the buffered reader to read the string till \n
43                line =  br.readLine();
44
45                System.out.println(line);  //print the line to the command window
46                stateList.add( line);               //add each line to the array
47            }
48
49            // close the Buffered Reader
50            br.close();
51
52      }
53
54      public static void main( String[] args)
55      {
56            ReadStateFile1 app = new ReadStateFile1();
57
```

```
58          try
59          {
60                  app.readStateList();
61          }
62          catch( IOException ioe)
63          {
64                  ioe.printStackTrace();
65                  System.exit( 1);
66          }
67
68          //add a listener
69          app.addWindowListener( new WindowAdapter()
70          {
71                  public void windowClosing( WindowEvent e)
72                  {
73                          System.exit( 0);
74                  }
75          });
76          app.setSize( 200,75);
77
78          //Get the frame's content pane and add the combo box to it.
79          app.getContentPane().add( new JComboBox( stateList));
80          app.show();
81
82     }
83 }
```

```
C:\JPT\Ch11\ReadStateFile1>javac ReadStateFile1.java

C:\JPT\Ch11\ReadStateFile1>java ReadStateFile1
Hawaii
Colorado
Alabama
Texas
Oregon
Alaska
New Jersey
Mississippi
Arkansas
New York
Maryland
North Carolina
Florida
Michigan
New Mexico
Arizona
```

(a)

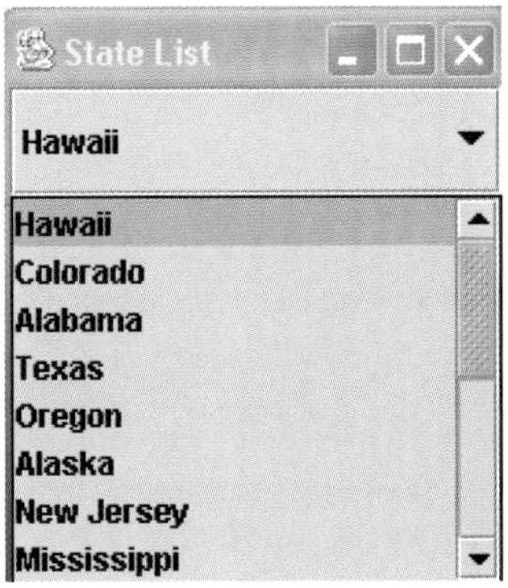

(b)

Figure 11-4
The state names are read from *StateList.txt* data file and written to the command
window as well as shown in a JComboBox. This program uses a Vector object to
store the names as we read them from the file.

Read Weather Data   The BufferedReader readLine() method is handy any time the data file is organized with data on individual lines. In Program 11-4, we read a weather file that is organized in this manner:

Date
Reporting Station
High temperature in Fahrenheit degrees
Low temperature in Fahrenheit degrees
Relative Humidity at 12 noon stated as percentage 0.xx
Rainfall total in inches

This file has a mixture of textual and numeric information, yet the readLine() method is used for all lines. We must keep track of what we have read in the file. Here is the *WeatherSummary.txt* data file we'll use in this sample program.

September 7, 2002
Albuquerque International Airport
85
64
0.20
0.00

The program output is shown in Figure 11-5 on page 686.

```
1    //Program 11-4 Read Weather Data
2    //We read the data on six lines using a separate read statement
3    //for each piece of data.
4    //File: ReadWeatherData
5
6
7    import java.io.FileReader;
8    import java.io.BufferedReader;
9    import java.io.IOException;
10   import java.io.FileNotFoundException;
11   import javax.swing.JOptionPane;
12
13   public class ReadWeatherData
14   {
15     public static void main( String[] args) throws IOException
16     {
17            final String FILENAME = "WeatherSummary.txt";
18            int exitCode = 0;
19
20            try
21            {
22                   //Preferred declaration:
23                   BufferedReader br = new BufferedReader( new FileReader( FILENAME) );
24
```

```
25              //The line holds the line read by BufferedReaders
26          String line, output;
27
28          String reportingStation, date;
29          double highTemp, lowTemp, humidity, rainfall;
30
31      //We have to make 6 separate read statements to gather the data
32      //from the file.
33      //The readLine throws IOException if there's a problem.
34
35          // first line is the data
36          date =  br.readLine();
37
38          // second line is the station
39          reportingStation = br.readLine();
40
41          // third line is the high temp
42          line = br.readLine();
43          highTemp = Double.parseDouble(line);
44
45          //fourth line is the low temp
46          //combine into one line
47
48          lowTemp = Double.parseDouble( br.readLine() );
49
50          // fifth line is the humidity
51          humidity = Double.parseDouble( br.readLine() );
52          humidity *= 100.0;
53
54          //last line is the rainfall
55          rainfall = Double.parseDouble( br.readLine() );
56
57          output = "Date: " + date + "\nStation: " + reportingStation +
58                  "\nTemp Range: " + highTemp + " to " + lowTemp +
59                  "\nHumidity at noon: " + humidity + "% (Rainfall = "
60                  + rainfall + " \")";
61
62          JOptionPane.showMessageDialog(null, output, FILENAME, 1);
63
64              br.close();
65
66      }
67      catch(FileNotFoundException fnfe)
68      {
69          JOptionPane.showMessageDialog(null, "Can't find the file!",
70              FILENAME, 2);
71          exitCode = 1;   //had a problem
72      }
```

```
73        catch(IOException ioe)
74        {
75              JOptionPane.showMessageDialog(null, "Trouble!", FILENAME, 2);
76              exitCode = 1;
77        }
78
79        System.exit( exitCode);
80    }
81 }
```

Figure 11-5
The weather data items are contained on six lines in the *WeatherSummary.txt* file.
We use the BufferedReader readLine() method to read each line from the file.

11.4
String Tokenizers

If our data file is structured so that we have one data item on each line, it makes our reading job simple. The BufferedReader's readLine() method returns each line as a String, and we can convert it to a numeric value if need be. But what about the case where we have more than one data item on the line? Maybe we have a series of text items or numbers separated by commas. Also, we may need to strip out characters that we do not want to process in our program.

StringTokenizer

a class that helps us separate individual parts of a String if the items are separated by one character, such as a comma

Java has a helper class, called **StringTokenizer**, which helps us to separate individual parts of the String. The StringTokenizer class helps us when our program reads textual data from a file. The lines that we read from the data file are read as Strings. StringTokenizer can be used on any String, such as the input from JOptionPane.show-InputDialog(), a String that you initialize in a program, or a String that is filled by a readLine() method. The StringTokenizer class has limited capabilities involving what you can pull out of the String. A good rule of thumb for programmers is that if a single character separates data items in the line, such as a comma or a space, the String-Tokenizer is the class for you. For more precise or complicated pattern matching, we can use the Pattern and Matcher classes from Java's java.util.regex package. We see

Pattern and Matcher objects in action in the last examples of this chapter. For now, let's concentrate on using StringTokenizer objects. We will introduce them next, with regards to reading files, because it is especially handy for this task.

Reading Strings

Grocery List   Remember our grocery list from Programs 11-1 and 11-2? The data file, *GroceryList1.txt* had three items on each line. For this example there are no spaces between the items—only commas.

apples,butter,soap
eggs,syrup,pancake mix
bananas,dog food,milk

If we wish to handle each of the items in our list separately, we must find a way to pull each item off when our program reads the line from the file. As we read the first line into a String, we must pull out "apples", "butter", and "soap", and place them in separate variables. A StringTokenizer object helps us perform this task.

When we create a StringTokenizer object in our program, we pass it the String we want it to work on, and we must tell it what delimits or separates each data item. In other words, we will read in a line from our grocery list, and the commas separate or delimit the items. We ask the tokenizer object how many **tokens** it finds in our line and then we loop through the object, extracting the strings that are delimited by the commas. Figure 11-6 illustrates this process. Figure 11-7 shows the output from Program 11-5 (contained in the folder ReadGroceryWithTokenizer).

tokens
the data of interest in a String of characters. They may be separated by a comma, a space, or one other special character

```
1    //Program 11-5 Use a StringTokenizer to separate data items
2    //from a String read by the BufferedReader.
3    //File ReadFileToken.java
4
5    import java.io.FileReader;
6    import java.io.BufferedReader;
7    import java.io.IOException;
8    import java.io.FileNotFoundException;
9    import java.util.StringTokenizer;
10   import javax.swing.JOptionPane;
11
12   public class ReadFileToken
13   {
14     public static void main( String[] args) throws IOException
15     {
16            final String FILENAME = "GroceryList1.txt";
17            int exitCode = 0;
18
19            try
20            {
21                   //FileNotFoundException thrown if we can't find the file.
22                   BufferedReader br = new BufferedReader( new FileReader( FILENAME) );
```

```
23
24              //The line holds the line read by BufferedReader
25              String line;
26
27              // The string tokenizer class allows an application
28              // to break a string into tokens.
29              StringTokenizer token;
30
31      //both ready and read might throw IOException
32              while( br.ready() )
33              {
34                      String storeItem;
35
36                      // use the buffered reader to read the string till \n
37                      line =  br.readLine();
38
39                      // construct with "," as the element delimiter
40                      token = new StringTokenizer( line, ",");
41
42                      int howManyTokens = token.countTokens();
43                      System.out.println("\nThe line: " + line + " has " +
44                              howManyTokens + " tokens");
45
46                      for(int i = 0; i < howManyTokens; ++i)
47                      {
48                              storeItem = token.nextToken();
49                              System.out.println(storeItem);
50                      }
51              }
52
53      // close the Buffered Reader
54              br.close();
55
56      }
57      catch(FileNotFoundException fnfe)
58      {
59              JOptionPane.showMessageDialog(null, "Can't find the file!",
60                      FILENAME, 2);
61              exitCode = 1;  //had a problem
62      }
63      catch(IOException ioe)
64      {
65              JOptionPane.showMessageDialog(null, "Trouble!", FILENAME, 2);
66              exitCode = 1;
67      }
68
69      System.exit( exitCode);
70  }
71 }
```

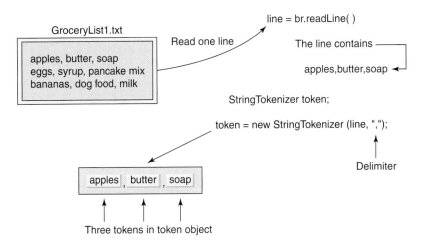

GroceryList1.txt

apples, butter, soap
eggs, syrup, pancake mix
bananas, dog food, milk

Read one line

line = br.readLine( )

The line contains ———

apples,butter,soap

StringTokenizer token;

token = new StringTokenizer (line, ",");

Delimiter

apples , butter , soap

Three tokens in token object

Figure 11-6
A line of data that contains items separated by commas is read from the data file and a StringTokenizer object is created. We ask the tokenizer object to tell us how many tokens it has, and then we loop through, extracting each token with the nextToken() method.

```
C:\JPT\Ch11\ReadGroceryWithTokenizer>javac ReadFileToken.java

C:\JPT\Ch11\ReadGroceryWithTokenizer>java ReadFileToken

The line: apples,butter,soap has 3 tokens
apples
butter
soap

The line: eggs,syrup,pancake mix has 3 tokens
eggs
syrup
pancake mix

The line: bananas,dog food,milk has 3 tokens
bananas
dog food
milk
```

Figure 11-7
The command window shows the lines of data and the resultant Strings as the StringTokenizer object separates the data for us.

Hardware Parts   The ReadParts program reads a list of hardware store items that are found in the *PartsList1.txt* file. In this file there are a different number of items in each line.

hammer, nails, wood screws, screw drivers
hack saw, blades
brass valve, teflon tape, copper fittings
sawhorse

11

This poses no problem for the StringTokenizer because, for each line, we can get the total number of tokens and run a for loop to extract each one. Another approach that we show in this example uses the hasMoreTokens() method, which returns true if there are more tokens in our tokenizer object.

Notice that there is a space after each comma in this data file. We want to strip out this leading space so that our data items are represented correctly. That is, when we extract "nails" from the first line, the tokenizer extracts " nails" because it extracts the data between the commas, including the leading space. We employ the String class's **trim() method** that returns a copy of the String with leading and trailing whitespace characters omitted. The strings are then stored in a Vector object named partsList. Remember that a Vector object is a dynamic array in which we can add objects (review the java.util.Vector class documentation to see all of the available methods).

Another very useful helper class is the Collections class. The Collections class provides many methods that are able to perform tasks on Java List objects. Three Java List object types are (1) Vector objects, (2) LinkedList objects, and (3) ArrayList objects. The Collections class contains many static methods, including ones for searching, sorting, shuffling, finding the max and min, and reversing the elements. Because we have stored our hardware items in a Vector object, we can call the Collection.sort() method to alphabetize the parts. The code is shown in Program 11-6 and the alphabetized parts are shown in Figure 11-8.

trim() method

a method in the String class that returns a copy of the String with leading and trailing whitespace characters (such as spaces) omitted

```
1    //Program 11-6 Use a StringTokenizer to separate data items.
2    //Add them into a Vector to be sorted into alphabetical order.
3    //File: ReadParts.java
4
5    import java.io.FileReader;
6    import java.io.BufferedReader;
7    import java.io.IOException;
8    import java.io.FileNotFoundException;
9    import java.util.StringTokenizer;
10   import javax.swing.JOptionPane;
11
12   import java.util.Vector;
13   import java.util.Collections;
14
15   public class ReadParts
16   {
17      public static void main( String[] args) throws IOException
18      {
19            final String FILENAME = "PartsList1.txt";
20            int exitCode = 0;
21
22            Vector partsList = new Vector();
```

```
23
24          try
25          {
26                  //FileNotFoundException thrown if we can't find the file.
27                  BufferedReader bufReader = new BufferedReader(
28                          new FileReader( FILENAME) );
29
30                  //The line holds the line read by BufferedReader
31                  String line;
32
33                  // The string tokenizer helps us separate the data items.
34                  StringTokenizer sepToken;
35
36          //both ready and read might throw IOException
37                  while( bufReader.ready() )
38                  {
39                          String part;
40
41                          // use the buffered reader to read the string till \n
42                          line =  bufReader.readLine();
43
44                          // construct with "," as the element delimiter
45                          sepToken = new StringTokenizer( line, ",");
46
47                          while( sepToken.hasMoreElements () )
48                          {
49                                  part = sepToken.nextToken();
50
51                  //Trim off the leading and trailing whitespace characters.
52                                  part = part.trim();
53
54                                  //add the part to the partsList array
55                                  partsList.add(part);
56                          }
57                  }
58
59          //The Collections class works on Vector objects.
60          //The static sort method sorts the elements found in the vector object.
61                  Collections.sort(partsList);
62
63                  String output = "";
64                  for(int i = 0; i < partsList.size(); ++i)
65                  {
66                          //We get each element from the list and tack on a \n
67                          output += partsList.get(i) + "\n";
68                  }
```

11

```
69              // close the Buffered Reader
70                  bufReader.close();
71
72                  JOptionPane.showMessageDialog(null,output, FILENAME,1);
73
74          }
75          catch(FileNotFoundException fnfe)
76          {
77                  JOptionPane.showMessageDialog(null, "Can't find the file!",
78                      FILENAME, 2);
79                  exitCode = 1;   //had a problem
80          }
81          catch(IOException ioe)
82          {
83                  JOptionPane.showMessageDialog(null,  "Trouble!", FILENAME, 2);
84                  exitCode = 1;
85          }
86
87          System.exit( exitCode);
88      }
89  }
```

Figure 11-8
The items in the *PartsList1.txt* file are read and stored in a Vector object called
partsList. The Collections.sort() method is called to alphabetize the partsList vector.

BufferedWriter

a wrapper class that
provides write()
methods to write data
to a file one line at a
time

File Output with the BufferedWriter Class

Now that we are familiar with the BufferedReader class, we will quickly see how
the **BufferedWriter** class works in a similar manner. We wrap a FileWriter object
in a BufferedWriter class, and we are then able to write Strings to an output file.
The BufferedWriter constructors require a FileWriter object. We create the

Chapter 11 ▌ Advanced Topic: Java Input/Output

FileWriter object and then use it in the constructor for the BufferedWriter:

```
//The BufferedWriter wraps the FileWriter object.
//This allows us to read a data file one line at a time.

FileWriter writer = new FileWriter();

BufferedWriter bufWriter = new BufferedWriter( writer );

//OR the preferred instantiation technique is:

BufferedWriter bufWriter = new BufferedWriter( new FileWriter()  );
```

The supporting methods for the BufferedWriter class are shown in Table 11-4.

TABLE 11-4
Java's BufferedWriter methods.

Method	Purpose
void close()	Closes the file and releases any resources associated with the output stream.
void flush()	Flushes any characters out of the output stream.
void newLine()	Writes a line separator into the output stream.
void write(char[] buf, int offset, int length)	Writes a portion of a character array, beginning at the offset. Writes *length* number of characters.
void write (char c)	Writes a single character.
void write(String s, int offset, int length)	Writes a portion of the String, beginning at the offset character. Writes *length* number of characters.

Find the Warblers   This next demonstration program reads the names of birds
from the *BirdsAtTheFeeder.txt* file and writes all of the warblers to the *Warblers.txt*
file. The input file is organized with a different bird on each line, as shown here:

Common Yellowthroat Warbler
English House Sparrow
Scrub Jay
House Finch
Rufous Hummingbird
Scott's Oriole
Pine Siskin
Grace's Warbler
Bullock's Oriole
American Redstart Warbler
Blackchinned Hummingbird

11

indexOf()

method of String class
returns the location of a
substring or −1 if the
substring is not found

We create BufferedReader and BufferedWriter objects and then read each line, searching it with String's **indexOf()** method. The indexOf() method returns the location of the substring in the String, and a negative one (−1) if it cannot find the substring. If we locate a bird that is a warbler, we write it to the output file using the BufferedWriter's write() method that accepts Strings as input. This write() method writes a portion of the String and requires the beginning position and number of characters. We want to write the entire String, so we use zero (0) as the offset (startWritingAt), and birdLine.length() for the number of characters. In our program, it has this form:

```
//inputs to write(String, startWritingAt, howManyChars
bufWriter.write(birdLine, 0, birdLine.length() );
```

The complete program is shown in Program 11-7. Figure 11-9 shows the *Warblers.txt* file that has been opened in Microsoft's Notepad.

```
1    //Program 11-7 We search through the list of birds that we read
2    //from the BirdsAtTheFeeder.txt file looking for Warblers.
3    //Write all the warblers to Warblers.txt file.
4
5    //File: FindWarblers.java
6
7    import java.io.FileReader;
8    import java.io.FileWriter;
9    import java.io.BufferedReader;
10   import java.io.BufferedWriter;
11   import java.io.IOException;
12   import java.io.FileNotFoundException;
13
14   import javax.swing.JOptionPane;
15
16   public class FindWarblers
17   {
18      public static void main( String[] args)
19      {
20           final String FILENAME = "BirdsAtTheFeeder.txt";
21           final String FILEOUT = "Warblers.txt";
22           int exitCode = 0;
23
24           try
25           {
26               //FileNotFoundException thrown if we can't find the file.
27               BufferedReader bufReader = new BufferedReader(
28                       new FileReader( FILENAME) );
29
30               //Create a BufferedWriter object to write our Strings
31               BufferedWriter bufWriter = new BufferedWriter(
32                       new FileWriter( FILEOUT) );
```

11

```
33
34                   //The line holds the line read by BufferedReader
35             String birdLine;
36
37             int warblerPosition;
38
39         //both ready and read might throw IOException
40             while( bufReader.ready() )
41             {
42                     // use the buffered reader to read the string till \n
43                     birdLine =  bufReader.readLine();
44
45                     warblerPosition = -1;
46
47 //The indexOf() needs exact String, returns the position if it finds it
48                     warblerPosition = birdLine.indexOf("Warbler");
49
50                     if(warblerPosition >= 0)        //we have a warbler
51                     {
52                             //inputs to write(String, startWritingAt, howManyChars
53                             bufWriter.write(birdLine, 0, birdLine.length() );
54
55                             //write a newline into the file
56                             bufWriter.newLine();
57                     }
58             }
59
60         // close the Buffered Reader and Writer
61             bufReader.close();
62             bufWriter.close();
63         }
64         catch(FileNotFoundException fnfe)
65         {
66             JOptionPane.showMessageDialog(null, "Can't find the file!",
67                     FILENAME, 2);
68             exitCode = 1;   //had a problem
69         }
70         catch(IOException ioe)
71         {
72             JOptionPane.showMessageDialog(null, "Trouble!", FILENAME, 2);
73             exitCode = 1;
74         }
75
76         System.exit( exitCode);
77     }
78 }
```

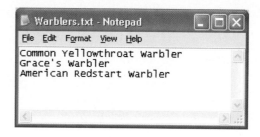

Figure 11-9
The output file written by a BufferedWriter object in the FindWarblers program.

The Trip Expenses Program   The Trip Expenses program demonstrates many of Java's coding techniques, including the use of buffered readers and writers, StringTokenizers, and exception handling. The purpose of this program is to read the file *TripExpenses.txt* and sum the various items. The total costs are written to the file *TripTotalCosts.txt*. Here is the expense file:

```
# denotes a comment and is ignored
# This lists the items and costs for a trip.
# Airline Tickets
$475.00
# Rental Car
$179.99
# Gas for the Rental Car
$18.00
#Hotel for 3 nights
$90.18  $90.18  $79.74
# Meals for 3 days
$46.75  $32.00  $48.22
# Parking fees
$8.50  $8.50  $2.50
# Toll fees
$3.75  $3.75
# uncomment the next line to cause error
# Water park tickets
```

The program reads a line at a time, and any line that begins with a "#" is not processed. The program assumes that if the line does not begin with a "#," then it is a line that contains expense items written with a dollar sign and numeric value, such as "$3.75". The StringTokenizer object is created with the "$" as the delimiter, and the object is searched for tokens. Remember that the $ is not part of the extracted part of the line, and the nextToken() method pulls the data from between the delimiters. Assuming that we now have extracted a String containing a numeric value, we perform parseFloat( ) to convert the value to a float. We sum the numeric values, and the total is written to the output file. If a line does not start with a "#," and we attempt to parseFloat a nonnumeric value, Java throws a NumberFormatException.

This program is organized so that the work is performed by these methods: openFileToRead(), readFile(), openFileToWrite(), writeTripTotal(), and close-Files(). As the program executes, we keep count of the successful method calls. All of these methods are within a single try block. If an error is encountered, then the exception is thrown in the method. Catch statements are grouped after the try block in one location, thus avoiding trys and catches being scattered throughout the program.

Program 11-8 shows the source code. The program sample on the text's CD includes JOptionPane message boxes after each method call. The message boxes provide feedback to the user as the program executes. The JOptionPane calls have been removed for clarity. We encourage you to obtain the source code and data file from the text's CD and play with this program. How many ways can you get it to throw exceptions? Figure 11-10 on page 700 shows the output file in Microsoft's Notepad.

```
1    //Program 11-8
2    //TripExpenses.java
3
4    /* Reads in the expense amounts from the file, strip off the
5     * $ and parse the float value from the String. If the line contains
6     * a # in the first character, we assume it is a comment and ignore it.
7
8     * This program has one try and many catch statements. The finally block
9     * reports the results of the program.
10
11    * We keep count of the successful methods and write a final report
12    * in the finally block.
13    */
14
15   import java.io.*;
16   import java.util.StringTokenizer;
17   import javax.swing.JOptionPane;
18
19   public class TripExpenses
20   {
21     BufferedReader reader;
22     BufferedWriter writer;
23     static int exitCode;
24     static final String FILENAME = "TripExpenses.txt";
25     static final String FILEOUT = "TripTotalCost.txt";
26
27     public static void main(String[] args)
28     {
```

```
29          TripExpenses app = new TripExpenses();
30          int successfulMethods = 0;         //if we get 5, all is well
31
32          try
33          {
34          //Step 1 Open the file for reading
35                  app.openFileToRead();
36                  successfulMethods++;
37
38          //Step 2 Read the file parsing out the $ and tally the bill
39          //If there is a problem with the read, we catch it here.
40                  float billAmount = app.readFile();
41                  successfulMethods++;
42
43          //Step 3 Open file for writing.
44                  app.openFileToWrite();
45                  successfulMethods++;
46
47          //Step 4 Write the total expense amount to the output file.
48                  app.writeTripTotal(billAmount);
49                  successfulMethods++;
50
51          //Step 5 Close the files.
52                  app.closeFiles();
53                  successfulMethods++;
54
55          }
56          catch(IOException ioe)
57          {
58                  JOptionPane.showMessageDialog(null,
59                      "File errors.\nExiting with error code 1.");
60                  ioe.printStackTrace();
61                  exitCode = 1;
62          }
63          catch(NumberFormatException nfe)
64          {
65                  JOptionPane.showMessageDialog(null,
66          "The file is not in the proper format.\nExiting with error code 2.");
67                  nfe.printStackTrace();
68                  exitCode = 2;
69          }
70
71          // report how many methods were called
72          finally
73          {
```

```java
74              if(successfulMethods == 5)
75                  JOptionPane.showMessageDialog(null,
76                      "Completed all method calls successfully.");
77              else
78                  JOptionPane.showMessageDialog(null,
79                      "Completed " + successfulMethods + " successful method
80                          call(s).");
81          }
82          System.exit(exitCode);
83      }
84
85      private void writeTripTotal(float total) throws IOException
86      {
87          //Use a DecimalFormat object to format our output numbers.
88          //We use the package.Class name here instead of importing it.
89          java.text.DecimalFormat currency = new java.text.DecimalFormat("0.00");
90          String howMuch = currency.format(total);
91
92          writer.write("Your total trip expenses amounted to $");
93          writer.write(howMuch, 0, howMuch.length());
94          writer.write(".");
95
96      }
97
98      private void openFileToRead() throws IOException
99      {
100         reader = new BufferedReader(new FileReader(FILENAME));
101     }
102
103     private void openFileToWrite() throws IOException
104     {
105         writer = new BufferedWriter(new FileWriter(FILEOUT));
106     }
107
108     private float readFile() throws NumberFormatException, IOException
109     {
110         // Holds the entire line read by BufferedReaders
111         String line;
112
113         float amount = 0.0f;
114
115         // The string tokenizer class allows an application
116         // to break a string into tokens.
117         StringTokenizer token;
118
119         while(reader.ready())
120         {
```

11

```
121              // use the buffered reader to read the string till \n
122              line =  reader.readLine();
123
124              //Line example:   # Toll Fees
125              //Line example:   $3.75   $3.75
126
127              //We want to pull out the lines with the costs.
128
129              if( line.charAt(0) != '#')
130              {
131                    //The $ is the delimiter and separates our tokens.
132                    //Our token will have XX.XX    form.
133                    //The parseFloat ignores the trailing spaces.
134
135                    token = new StringTokenizer(line, "$");
136
137                    // separate the elements
138                    while(token.hasMoreElements() )
139                    {
140                          amount += Float.parseFloat(token.nextToken());
141                    }
142              }
143          }
144          return amount;
145    }
146
147    private void closeFiles() throws IOException
148    {
149          reader.close();
150          writer.close();
151    }
152 }
```

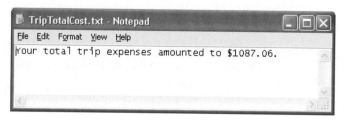

Figure 11-10
The output file written by a BufferedWriter object in the TripExpense program.

Chapter 11 ▌ Advanced Topic: Java Input/Output

11.5
A Brief Introduction to Networking and Sockets

Java I/O classes are written to handle streams of data. Recall that a stream has a physical device at one end such as a data file, the keyboard, or a network socket. We have already seen how files are read and written in Java; now let's examine sockets. The beginning programmer can visualize a **network socket** as the hook or connector at either end of a data pipeline. Data gets shipped from a server computer, located somewhere on a network or the Internet, to the user's computer. If you research Java Sockets in today's textbooks, they are found in the Java networking sections. Many fine texts present complete discussions of this advanced complex topic. For our purposes we'll show one program that uses Sockets with the intention of showing how Socket I/O is very similar to File I/O.

network socket

the connector at either end of a data or network pipeline

TCP/IP, Packets, and Sockets

The basic job of a computer network is to move bits of data from one location to another. Data bits are packed into groups, and additional data bits that say where the data is going—the data's destination address—are added. This group of data is called a **packet**, and the shipping process is referred to as **Internet Protocol (IP)**. If the data we wish to send does not fit into one packet, then we can divide the data into two or more packets and send the group of packets.

packet

a group of data bits that include the data's destination address

Every month when you drop off your bill payments at the post office, the post office reads the address on each envelope and delivers the letter to its destination. The post office has the procedures in place to route and deliver your letters across town or across the country. This post office analogy holds true for sending a packet across the network. The network IP routes and delivers the packet to the destination address that is included in the packet.

Internet Protocol (IP)

the process used to ship packets across a network

Suppose you mail several letters to the same address. You drop the letters into the slot at the post office. At that point, you do not know either when (or if) the letters arrive at their destination or the order of their arrival. If you want assurances that your letters arrived at their destination, you need to send your letters via registered mail. This procedure involves the postal carrier obtaining a signature from the receiver when the letters are delivered. The post office returns these signature cards to you. Registering your mail takes extra time when preparing your letters and requires additional postage.

For data traveling across a network, unreliable packet delivery or packets of data delivered haphazardly to their destination are unacceptable. Borrowing the registered mail idea from the post office, there is a similar procedure that insures your packets of data are delivered to their destination in the order they are sent. This protocol is the Transmission Control Protocol (TCP). TCP uses IP (hence the term **TCP/IP**) for routing and delivery, and acts as an end-to-end connection while your packets are being sent to their destination. The TCP connection is a dedicated

TCP/IP

a procedure that uses an end-to-end connection for routing and delivering data packets across a network

11

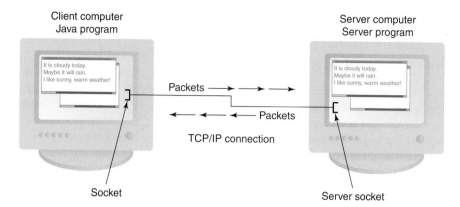

Client computer
Java program

Server computer
Server program

It is cloudy today.
Maybe it will rain.
I like sunny, warm weather!

It is cloudy today.
Maybe it will rain.
I like sunny, warm weather!

Packets ⟶ ⟶ ⟶

⟵ ⟵ ⟵ Packets

TCP/IP connection

Socket

Server socket

Figure 11-11
The TCP/IP network session has a socket at both the client and server ends. Data is sent in packets. TCP/IP provides data verification and order correctness for packets of network data.

connection that can be envisioned more like a telephone connection than registered mail at the post office. When you make a TCP connection, the client and the server are connected throughout the data transfer, and feedback is immediate.

When you visit a website on the Internet, you have a TCP/IP connection. At either end of the connection is a socket. Today, every operating system has adopted the use of sockets and IP. You, at your computer, are the client. The website you are visiting is the server. Both ends of the connection (the client and the server) have a socket. The client initiates a connection to a server and passes a request for data from the server. Figure 11-11 illustrates this relationship.

Java has a Networking Library Application Programming Interface which contains many classes. The two classes we are interested in are (1) the Socket class and (2) the ServerSocket class. The Socket class is for client sockets, which allow your Java program to open a connection to another computer on the Internet, assuming that you have permission. The ServerSocket class lets an application accept a TCP connection from other systems in order to exchange data.

Sockets must have an IP address, which is its network address. All computers on the Internet have an IP address. Sockets must also have a port number. A port is a software process that allows an incoming network connection to be directed to a process on the server computer. You can think of the IP address as a company's phone number and a port as an extension to a particular employee of the company.

Java's I/O for network activity is very similar to Java's file I/O. The data is handled as streams and we use Java's classes to help us work with the data. We are presenting a top-level overview of network basics and do not expect you to be a network programmer after reading this section! We'll leave that task for your advanced Java teacher. What is important here is to examine the following example and sit back and say, "Hey, these Java sockets remind me of Java's file I/O."

What Time Is It? Socket, Pattern, and Matcher Classes

In this program, we open a socket connection to port 13 of the National Institute of Standards and Technology (NIST) website. Port 13 has been designated to report official time and date information. We make a socket connection and pass the Uniform Resource Locator (URL), and port number. Most people recognize the URL as the website address, such as http://java.sun.com/ or www.prenhall.com. We call getInputStream() from our socket object to get time and date information from the NIST web site. We then read the data one character at a time by placing each character into a StringBuffer object. Does this remind you of our first program in this chapter? The complete program is seen in Program 11-9, but first let's examine the pertinent lines of code for our Socket object.

```
//In class variables we have:
        final String NIST = "time.nist.gov";



//The socket code is in the main()  method.
        //Make a Socket object and pass the URL and port.
        Socket socket = new Socket(NIST, 13);

        //Our inputStream is from the socket, not a file.
        InputStream inputStream = socket.getInputStream();

        //Read character by character the information from nist
        int character = 0;
        while(character != -1)
        {
                character = inputStream.read();
                buffer.append((char)character);
        }

        socket.close();
```

Once we have the data from NIST, we write it out to see what it looks like. One sample data String from NIST looks like this:

52582 02-11-04 03:16:38 00 0 0   2.8 UTC(NIST) *
?

Buried in the string of characters is the Universal Time Code (UTC) time, which in this example is 03:16:38. UTC is defined as the Greenwich Mean Time (GMT), located at the Greenwich Royal Observatory in London, England. Greenwich is where "East meets West," meaning that it is the location of the zero degree designation for the Earth's longitude. It is where the world's time is set. To learn more about GMT or NIST, visit their websites at http://greenwichmeantime.com/ and http://www.nist.gov/.

11

If we want to compare the NIST time to the time on your computer, you need to get your computer's time. This is accomplished by instantiating a Date object. When Java executes this instantiation, it automatically sets the time and date in the object. The data in the date object can be written to the screen by using the toString() method. These lines of code perform this task:

```
//obtain today's date and time
        Date today = new Date();


        String todaysDateTime = today.toString();
//let's see what we have
        System.out.println("\nLocal time from my computer: \n" + todaysDateTime );
```

Here is what we see:

Local time from my computer:
Sun Nov 03 20:16:38 MST 2002

The time on my computer, located in Albuquerque, New Mexico, is 20:16:38 Mountain Standard Time—which is 8:16:38 PM. England is seven hours ahead of New Mexico time—when it is 8:16 in the evening MST, it is 3:16 AM GMT.

In Program 11-9, we obtain the two Strings that contain the time in HH:MM:SS format. Just for fun, we wish to search both Strings for their time component and pull them out into separate Strings. Java's java.util.regex package contains **Pattern and Matcher classes** that work on regular expressions. These two classes can accomplish precise pattern matching operations. This example presents an overview to give you an idea of how Pattern and Matcher work together to find a given pattern in a String, but you should research this topic further to gain expertise.

In order to find the time components in our two Strings, we use a **Pattern** object that knows the pattern is HH:MM:SS, where H, M, and S are integers. First, we call the Pattern class's static method compile() and specify the pattern. It returns to us a Pattern object. This cryptic but powerful input sequence comes to us from the Perl language. To form the pattern, the square braces ([ ]) indicate a character in the String, and we can specify a range within them. For example, the first digit of our time may be a 0, a 1, or a 2, so we set the pattern [0–2] for our first digit. The second digit may be a 0, 1, 2, or 3, so we write this as [0–3]. The minutes and hours can range from 00 to 59, so we set those characters to [0–5][0–9]. There are more sophisticated ways to write this pattern, but because it is our first example, we will keep it simple sweetie. Here is how we designate our pattern:

```
Pattern p = Pattern.compile("[0-2][0-3]:[0-5][0-9]:[0-5][0-9]");
```

Now that we have our pattern, we obtain two **Matcher** objects: one for the NIST time and one for my computer's time. To obtain a Matcher object, we must

Pattern and Matcher classes

two classes that work together to determine if a character pattern is present in a String of characters

Pattern

an object constructed with a known character pattern. The pattern is built by using an input sequence based on the Perl language

Matcher

an object built by calling the Pattern's matcher() method and passing it the String, which might contain the desired pattern call the matcher() method of our Pattern object and pass it the String that might contain our pattern.

```
//Now we make Matcher objects by calling the Pattern's matcher() method.
    Matcher nistMatcher = p.matcher(buffer.toString());
    Matcher localMatcher = p.matcher(todaysDateTime);
```

The Matcher's find() method scans the input String and returns a true if it finds a match to our designated pattern. The group() method returns the matched sequence.

```
//We now use the Matcher find() method that scans a character sequence to
//see if it has the HH:MM:SS pattern.
//The Matcher group() method returns the "matched" sequence
    while(nistMatcher.find())
            NISTtime = nistMatcher.group();

    while(localMatcher.find())
            localTime = localMatcher.group();
```

The complete program is seen in Program 11-9 and the output is seen in Figure 11-12.

```
1   //Program 11-9
2   //File:  CheckTime.java
3
4   import java.util.regex.*;         //for Matcher and Pattern
5   import java.util.*;               //for Date
6   import java.io.*;                 //for InputStream, IOException
7   import java.net.*;                //for Socket
8
9   public class CheckTime
10  {
11    public static void main(String[] args)
12    {
13          final String NIST = "time.nist.gov";
14          String NISTtime = null;
15          String localTime = null;
16          StringBuffer buffer = new StringBuffer();
17
18          //Get a socket connection on port 13 at time.nist.gov.
19          //Port 13 is the designated port for time.
20          try
21          {
22                //Make a Socket object and pass the URL and port.
23                Socket socket = new Socket(NIST, 13);
24
```

```java
25              //Our inputStream is from the socket, not a file.
26              InputStream inputStream = socket.getInputStream();
27
28              //Read character by character the information from nist
29              int character = 0;
30              while(character != -1)
31              {
32                      character = inputStream.read();
33                      buffer.append((char)character);
34              }
35
36              socket.close();
37        }
38        catch(IOException e)
39        {
40              System.err.println("I/O Error");
41              System.exit(1);
42        }
43
44        //obtain today's date and time
45        Date today = new Date();
46        String todaysDateTime = today.toString();
47
48        //Let's see what we have.
49        System.out.println("\nLocal time from my computer: \n" + todaysDateTime );
50        System.out.println("\n\nThis is what we received from NIST: "
51                                      + buffer.toString() );
52
53
54        //We want to search both strings for the time component.
55        //It will be in the form  HH:MM:SS, such as 10:45:32
56
57        System.out.println("\n\nSearch for the HH:MM:SS pattern in both strings.");
58
59        //First we call the static compile() method which returns
60        //a Pattern object. We pass in the desired pattern.
61
62        Pattern p = Pattern.compile("[0-2][0-3]:[0-5][0-9]:[0-5][0-9]");
63
64        //Now we make Matcher objects by calling the Pattern's matcher() method.
65        Matcher nistMatcher = p.matcher(buffer.toString());
66        Matcher localMatcher = p.matcher(todaysDateTime);
67
68        //We now use the Matcher find() method that scans a character sequence to
69        //see if it has the HH:MM:SS pattern.
```

```
70        //The Matcher group() method returns the "matched" sequence
71        while(nistMatcher.find())
72              NISTtime = nistMatcher.group();
73
74        while(localMatcher.find())
75              localTime = localMatcher.group();
76
77
78        // prints the times found from the pattern
79        System.out.println("\nLocal Time: " + localTime);
80        System.out.println("\nNIST Time:   " + NISTtime);
81
82    }
83 }
```

```
C:\JPT\Ch11\TimeChecker>javac CheckTime.java

C:\JPT\Ch11\TimeChecker>java CheckTime

Local time from my computer:
Sat Dec 21 13:34:27 MST 2002


This is what we received from NIST:
52629 02-12-21 20:34:26 00 0 0 240.8 UTC(NIST) *
?


Search for the HH:MM:SS pattern in both strings.

Local Time: 13:34:27

NIST Time:  20:34:26

C:\JPT\Ch11\TimeChecker>
```

Figure 11-12
The UTC time from the NIST website and local time from my computer is shown in
the TimeCheck program output. The java.util.regex package's Pattern and Matcher
classes are used to search both Strings for the HH:MM:SS pattern. The time pattern
is pulled out of both Strings.

11.6
Summary

This chapter introduces Java's input/output classes and the three basic I/O principles.
Java was designed so that there are many classes involved with program I/O, each
class having a small set of methods for performing the input or output tasks. The language models the data flow into and out of programs as a stream of bytes or characters. This stream has a physical device, such as a disk file or network connection, at

one end. Java is designed for consistent execution on worldwide computers, therefore it is crucial for the I/O to run consistently across platforms.

Java can handle two types of data streams in the programs: 1) byte streams and 2) character streams. Reading and writing byte data can be accomplished either one byte at a time or by reading "blocks" or "chunks" of bytes. If the program processes its data one byte at a time, this works well. But for many Java programs, it is necessary to read and write data as characters or lines of characters. Java provides the programmer with stream buffering wrapper classes that attach a memory buffer to an I/O stream. Having the memory buffer makes it possible for the programmer to read and write data in terms of lines instead of bytes. The data file may be read (or written) one line at a time. Each line is stored in the program as a String variable.

In order to separate data items in a line of text (String) that are delimited by a single character such as a comma, a String Tokenizer may be used to parse pertinent data from a line of data. The String Tokenizer is created and is passed the String containing the line and the delimiter symbol. Various methods allow the programmer to determine the number of data items (tokens) in the line and pull them off one at a time. Java provides the Pattern and Matcher classes to perform more complicated String parsing activities.

This chapter provided a brief introduction to networking, sockets, and TCP/IP. Data is transmitted across a network wrapped in packets, and each packet contains routing information. Internet Protocol dictates how the packets are handled en route. Java programs use a Socket class in order to obtain stream data from the network. In the example in this chapter, we saw that the Socket read the data from the network stream one character at time.

Java programmers should have the basic understanding of program I/O, because the majority of computer programs perform some sort of I/O operations. I/O operations can take on many forms, including reading data from or to a file, database, or network. The adoption of the XML file within distributed computing has resurrected the need for Java programmers to understand file handling. XML file processing is crucial for the web services applications. Time spent working with program I/O, initially with data files, is time well spent for the beginning Java programmer.

11

Chapter 11 ▌ Advanced Topic: Java Input/Output

12

Advanced Topic: JAR Files

KEY TERMS AND CONCEPTS

compressed JAR file
HTML archive reference for JAR files
jar utility
java -jar command
Java ARchive files (JAR files)
Image Producer
jar command switches or options
manifest file
PKZip
uncompressed JAR file
URL

CHAPTER OBJECTIVES

Introduce the programmer to the Java ARchive (JAR) file.

Demonstrate how to use Java's jar utility to create JAR files.

Present the commonly used jar utility options.

Revisit several programs from the text's other chapters and bundle these programs into JAR files.

Illustrate several jar options, including the uncompress option.

Show how HTML files must reference JAR archive files and class files.

Present the correct way to write a manifest file for a Java application.

Write a manifest file and include it in an application's JAR file. This produces an executable JAR file.

Build an executable JAR file that contains an application program that includes several images. Show how to execute the program through this JAR file.

Wrap it up!

This chapter is intended to introduce the beginning Java programmer to "Java ARchive" files, better known as JAR files. We explain their use and show how they are created. A side benefit for our beginning programmers is that a JAR file can be used as a quick and easy way to run the program it contains. In other words, we are going to wrap up our application program files into a single file that we can execute on a Windows machine with a double click of a mouse. For non-Windows machines the program can be executed with the "java -jar jarFile.jar" command.

This chapter covers the basics of the jar utility. Once you feel comfortable with this, the next step is to explore how to bundle class files that have been placed into a package. The packaged classes can then be imported into a program. We cover how to create a package, import these packaged classes into a program, and bundle the package into a JAR file in Chapter 13, *Packages, Classpaths, and JARs*.

12.1
What is a JAR File?

The **Java ARchive file (JAR file)** is a file that contains a group of files in a compressed format. The JAR format is based on (and essentially is) the Zip format. In 1986, Phil Katz (a software engineer) developed the zip file format and **PKZip** program, which is a file compression utility program. PKZip includes the zip file format, a compression routine, and has the files named with the *.zip* extension. He placed the work in the public domain so that the PKZip program and *.zip* format are available to all programmers. It has been universally adopted as the industry standard tool for file compression. Java adopted the zip format for its JAR files and provides its own jar utility program. In fact, the Java programmer can create his or her own JAR files by using the jar program that comes with Java or the Windows WinZIP program.

There are several reasons that the Java programmer should be comfortable working with jar files. First, if you have a Java program that contains many files, it

Java ARchive file (JAR file)

a file that contains a group of files in a compressed format

PKZip

a file compression utility program written in 1986 by Phil Katz. Java's JAR utility is based on PKZip

is easier to bundle all of the files into a single file—for running the program, storage, handing off to other programmers, or sending in e-mail. If you are placing files on a web server, having the program files compressed into a single JAR file makes moving the program to the server a one-step operation. It also provides a faster download of applet resources.

JAR files should be used in web applications. Hyper-Text Transfer Protocol (HTTP), the protocol that is used between a web server and a client's browser, requires time and effort on both ends of the connection for data transfer. Sending one large file between a server and a client is more efficient than sending the same amount of data via several small files. The use of many small files requires the web browser to make repeated requests of the server in order to download all of the files—time is spent making the connections. Wrapping program files into a single JAR file benefits the server's throughput because it is able to handle more client requests over a given time period.

12.2
How to Make a JAR File

jar program

J2SDK's program that is used to create JAR files

J2SDK SE provides a **jar program** that has a similar command syntax to Unix's tar (tape archive) utility. However, Java's jar and Unix's tar use different format schemes, and tar files are not used in Java!

If you execute the jar program at the MS-DOS Command window, you will see the various usage information (see Figure 12-1). The switches that we routinely use are described in Table 12-1.

One thing to keep in mind as you work with JAR files: If you make a change in your source code, you will need to recompile the source code and rebuild your

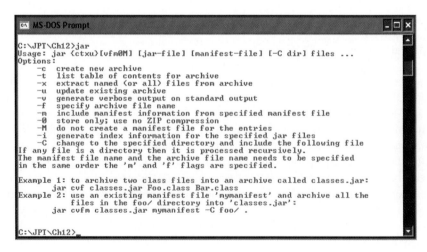

Figure 12-1
jar program usage information.

TABLE 12-1

A partial listing of Java's jar program options.

Option	Purpose
-c	Creates a new JAR archive file.
-f	Specifies the new JAR file name.
-v	Generates a verbose output as the jar program runs, describing the actions taken by the jar program.
-m	Includes the specified manifest file in the JAR file.
0 (zero)	Do not compress the jar file.

JAR file with the new *.class* file. The JAR file actually contains the *.class* files and it does not reference them. When you make a change in the *.class* file, that new file will need to be archived in the JAR file.

The jar Program and Applets

Let's examine how to make a JAR file using Java's jar program. The jar command requires the user to enter the option flags (letters) that dictate how to make the JAR file. For the JAR examples in this chapter, we borrow a few sample programs that we have built in the text—both applets and applications. These sample programs are found in the Chapter 12 source code section on the text's CD. You will find the source code, class, html for applets, and image files. The JAR files have been placed in the Test subfolder of each Chapter 12 sample program.

Recall the RandomLinesApplet from Chapters 4 and 6. Review the Chapter 6 version, found on page 309, and note how we built a LineGenerator class that is contained in the *LineGenerator.java* file. Our applet class, RandomLinesApplet2, instantiates a LineGenerator object so that it creates random sets of *x* and *y* coordinates for lines. Our HTML file references the *RandomLinesApplet2.class* file. The appletviewer program reads the HTML file and loads the applet class. It then draws fifteen random lines in the applet window.

Java programmers typically place the source code, which is intended to be distributed to other programmers, in a JAR file. Class files for applications or applets are usually packaged without the source files. In our first example, let's bundle the *.java* and *.class* files together in one JAR file. We have to modify the HTML file so that the appletviewer loads the JAR file. We place the *LineGenerator.java* and *.class*, and *RandomLinesApplet2.java* and *.class* in the same directory, then enter the following command sequence:

```
jar  cvf  Lines.jar  *.class  *.java
```

The "c" option says create a new archive. Because we create the *Lines.jar* file with the "v" (verbose) option, the jar program issues a line-by-line summary of each file that is placed in the *.jar* file. The "f" option says use the name we place on the command line for the name of the JAR file. Figure 12-2 shows the command and the resulting actions from the jar program.

```
C:\JPT\Ch12\RandomLinesJarDemo>
C:\JPT\Ch12\RandomLinesJarDemo>jar cvf Lines.jar *.class *.java
added manifest
adding: LineGenerator.class(in = 1016) (out= 597)(deflated 41%)
adding: RandomLinesApplet2.class(in = 935) (out= 617)(deflated 34%)
adding: LineGenerator.java(in = 1810) (out= 745)(deflated 58%)
adding: RandomLinesApplet2.java(in = 1456) (out= 723)(deflated 50%)

C:\JPT\Ch12\RandomLinesJarDemo>
```

Figure 12-2
The jar program issues a summary of all the files compressed and placed in the *Lines.jar* file because we used the "v" option in the jar command line.

compressed format

Java's jar program packs files into a JAR file. These files are smaller than the original size

Our *Lines.jar* file contains the *.java* and *.class* files in a **compressed format**. The amount of compression can be seen in Figure 12-2. For example, the *LineGenerator.java* file was compressed 58%; from an original size of 1810 to 745 bytes.

archive

HTML reference for a JAR file

If we modify the HTML file so that it references the JAR file as an **archive**, as well as our applet class, appletviewer can run successfully given the *Lines.jar* file. Here is the modified *RandomLinesJar.html* file:

```
<!-- RandomLinesJar.html for Program 6-5-->
<html>
<applet archive = Lines.jar
           code = "RandomLinesApplet2.class"
           width = 400   height = 200 >
</applet>
</html>
```

We can see our applet execute by entering the command:

```
appletviewer RandomLinesJar.html
```

It is possible to bundle only the *.class* files in a JAR file. In fact, in most cases, you will place only the *.class* files in the JAR file because you will not want your general users to have access to your Java source code. This task is easy enough. You just specify the class files using the *.class* wildcard format, or you can specify each class file by name. Both of these commands are shown here:

```
jar  cvf  Lines.jar  *.class
```

or

```
jar  cvf  Lines.jar  LineGenerator.class RandomLinesApplet2.class
```

```
C:\JPT\Ch12\RandomLinesJarDemo>jar cvf0 Lines.jar *.class
added manifest
adding: LineGenerator.class(in = 1016) (out= 1016)(stored 0%)
adding: RandomLinesApplet2.class(in = 935) (out= 935)(stored 0%)
```

Figure 12-3
The jar program normally compresses the files it contains. If the 0 (zero) option is used, the files are not compressed. Uncompressed JAR files load more quickly than compressed JARs, a consideration for web-based JARs.

You may wish to not compress the files in the JAR file. A browser program can load an **uncompressed JAR** file more quickly than a compressed JAR, because the need to decompress the files is eliminated. To build an uncompressed JAR file, the zero option should be added to the jar command as shown here. The messages from the jar program are seen in Figure 12-3.

uncompressed JAR
Java's jar program packs the files into the JAR file in their original size if the 0 (zero) option is used. Uncompressed JARs load more quickly than a compressed JAR

```
jar  cvf0  Lines.jar  *.class
```

Obtain the RandomLinesApplet2 code from the text's CD and practice making a JAR file. Test that the JAR file works correctly by placing it and the associated HTML file alone in their own folder. If you examine the Chapter 12 folder on the CD, you will see the source and class files in the *RandomLinesJarDemo* folder. The *Lines.jar* and *RandomLinesJar.html* files are contained in the *RandomLinesJarDemo\Test* subfolder.

Image Files and JARs   It is also possible to place image files (and other resource files such as *.wav* files) in the JARs. However, these files must be extracted and loaded into the program in a different way. The UFOApplet program in Chapter 4 requires the *AlbuquerqueAtNight.jpg* image. In the Chapter 4 version, we use the following code to assign the image data into our Image reference named pic.

```
public void init()
{
        canvas = getContentPane();
        pic = getImage(getDocumentBase(), "AlbuquerqueAtNight.jpg");

}
```

This works well as long as the image file itself is located in the same directory as the HTML file for the appletviewer. This approach does not work if the code and image(s) are bundled in a JAR file. There are a few ways to load resource files from a JAR file. One approach uses the new portion of code shown in Program 12-1.

Note: The start() and paint() methods are identical to Program 4-19 and are not shown here.

12

```
1    //Program 12-1
2    //File: UfoApplet.java
3    //Modified from Program 4-19 so that we can extract the image
4    //file from the JAR file.
5
6    //Note:  start() and paint() are not shown here.
7
8    //Non-code files, such as .jpgs are extracted from the JAR using
9    //a technique that creates a URL for files inside the JAR.
10
11   import java.net.*;
12   import java.awt.*;
13   import java.awt.image.*;
14   import java.applet.*;
15   import javax.swing.JApplet;
16
17   public class UfoApplet extends JApplet
18   {
19     Image pic;
20     Container canvas;
21
22     URL MyURL;
23     ImageProducer MyImageProducer;
24
25      boolean ranOnce;
26
27     public void init()
28     {
29           Toolkit tool = Toolkit.getDefaultToolkit();
30           MyURL = getClass().getResource("AlbuquerqueAtNight.jpg");
31           try
32           {
33                 MyImageProducer = (ImageProducer) MyURL.getContent();
34           }
35           catch( Exception ex)
36           {
37                 System.out.println(ex.getMessage() );
38           }
39           pic = tool.createImage(MyImageProducer);
40
41           canvas = getContentPane();
42
43     }
44   }
```

12

The idea behind this new code is that the class loader (JVM) knows where to find the JAR file, and there is a way for the code to create a URL for the image file inside the JAR. The image file is associated with a URL object. The image is eventually loaded through the combined efforts of a Toolkit and an ImageProducer object. This code is compiled and *UFOApplet.class* file is created.

We can create the *UFO.jar* file that contains the *UFOApplet.class* and image file by entering the command:

```
jar  cvf  UFO.jar  UFOApplet.class AlbuquerqueAtNight.jpg
```

or

```
jar  cvf  UFO.jar  *.class *.jpg
```

The jar compression summary for this command is seen in Figure 12-4.

```
C:\JPT\Ch12\UFOJarDemo>jar cfv UFO.jar *.class *.jpg
added manifest
adding: UfoApplet.class(in = 2479) (out= 1471)(deflated 40%)
adding: AlbuquerqueAtNight.jpg(in = 28997) (out= 28793)(deflated 0%)

C:\JPT\Ch12\UFOJarDemo>
```

Figure 12-4
The jar program can bundle image files into a JAR file. Here we create *UFO.jar*, which contains the class and image file for a modified version of the UFOApplet program from Chapter 4. Note that the order of option flags can vary for this type of JAR (cvf and cfv produce the same results).

We have moved the *UFO.jar* file into the *Ch12\UfoJarDemo\Test* directory with the *UfoAppletJar.html* file and verified that the JAR file does indeed run as expected. The associated HTML file that references the *UFO.jar* is:

```
<!-- UfoAppletJar.html for Program 12-1   -->

<html>
<applet        archive = UFO.jar
               code = "UFOApplet.class"
               width = 550  height = 400      >
</applet>
</html>
```

JARs and Applications

An application program may also be bundled into a JAR file. It is possible to run it without unpacking the contents. The command:

```
java -jar MyJarFile.jar
```

12

executes the application contained in *MyJarFile.jar*. On most Windows machines, double-clicking the jar file will also execute the program.

The jar commands work in the same manner for applications as they do for applets. You may bundle all of your *.java*, *.class*, and other resource files into a JAR. There is a key procedural difference in creating your application JAR if you wish to execute the program in the manner shown above.

Recall that the way we execute any applet is through a web browser program. The web browser can load and execute the applet programs that are contained in a JAR file. However, for an application program to execute from a JAR, we must include a **manifest** file that tells the Java interpreter where to find the class that contains the main() method. The manifest file is a text-based file and we include the manifest filename in the jar command when the JAR file is created.

manifest

a file that is bundled into a JAR file and tells the Java interpreter where to find the class that contains the main() method

> **Note:** Java makes its own manifest file when it creates a JAR file. When we include our own manifest, Java extracts the information from our manifest and places it into the JAR's manifest file. We will see this shortly.

We will revisit Program 3-8 and bundle this application into a JAR file named *Hello.jar*. The code for HelloFrame is shown below and the output is seen in Figure 12-5.

```
1   //Program 12-2 and 3-8 A JFrame that says hello.
2   //File: HelloFrame.java
3
4   import java.awt.Color;
5   import java.awt.Graphics;
6   import javax.swing.JFrame;
7
8   public class HelloFrame extends JFrame
9   {
10    public static void main( String[] args )
11    {
12          HelloFrame isaJFrame = new HelloFrame();
13          isaJFrame.setDefaultCloseOperation( EXIT_ON_CLOSE );
14    }
15
16    public HelloFrame()        //class constructor method
17    {
18
19          //Set the size and title for the window.
20          setSize( 300, 100 );
21          setTitle("Hello Frame Program");
22
23          show();                    //force a call to paint
24    }
```

```
25
26      public void paint( Graphics g )
27      {
28          g.setColor( Color.magenta );
29          g.drawString( "Hello from javax.swing.JFrame!", 25, 60 );
30      }
31  }
```

Figure 12-5
The output from the HelloFrame application.

When the programmer is bundling an application program into a JAR file, and he or she intends to execute the program from the JAR, there must be a manifest file that contains the name of the class that contains the main() method. The manifest file must contain this line, followed by an Enter Key:

`Main-Class: HelloFrame`

The manifest file can have a programmer-designated name, and the filename is used in the jar command. For example, we can create a manifest file named *WhereIsMain.txt* for the HelloFrame program (see Figure 12-6).

Recommendation: When you create your manifest file, be sure that you hit an Enter key after the Main-Class: MyClass line! If you do not have that Enter key, the JAR file will not execute correctly!

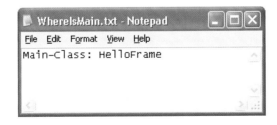

Figure 12-6
The JAR manifest file can be named however the programmer desires, but it must contain the class that has the main() method. (Be sure there is an Enter key after the class name.) Here is the *WhereIsMain.txt* file in Microsoft's Notepad editor.

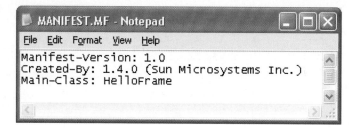

Figure 12-7
The information from the programmer-provided manifest file is incorporated in the *Manifest.mf* file generated by Java.

The jar command must include the "m" option, telling the jar program to include the specified manifest file. Java will write its own manifest file, named *Manifest.mf*, containing the main class information. Figure 12-7 shows a Java generated manifest file.

It is important to note the order of the option flags in the jar command. It is possible to specify the JAR filename and then the manifest file using the "cvfm" option ("f" before "m") or specify the manifest file and then JAR filename with "cvmf" option ("m" before "f"). Figure 12-8 illustrates this difference with the HelloFrame jar command. Figure 12-9 shows the command line steps with the two versions of the jar command and the messages from the jar program. We make a *Hello1.jar* and *Hello2.jar*. Both JAR files are identical.

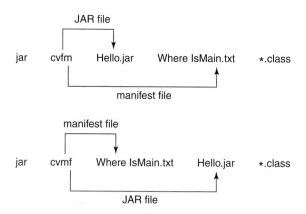

Figure 12-8
The "m" for manifest file and "f" for JAR filename can be interchanged on the jar command line. The JAR filename and manifest file must be listed in the same order as the "f" and "m" (or "m" and "f").

```
C:\JPT\Ch12\HelloFrameJarDemo>jar cvfm Hello1.jar WhereIsMain.txt *.class
added manifest
adding: HelloFrame.class(in = 794) (out= 500)(deflated 37%)

C:\JPT\Ch12\HelloFrameJarDemo>jar cvmf WhereIsMain.txt Hello2.jar *.class
added manifest
adding: HelloFrame.class(in = 794) (out= 500)(deflated 37%)

C:\JPT\Ch12\HelloFrameJarDemo>java -jar Hello1.jar
```

Figure 12-9
The two ways to create a JAR file with the HelloFrame program and *WhereIsMain.txt*
manifest file. Either set of commands creates valid, executable JARs. The java -jar
command is also shown.

Applications with Images   Application programs that use image files (or other
resources) that are bundled into executable JARs must load the images in the same
manner as we did with Applets and JARs. Let's look at another application from
Chapter 3: Program 3-9. In this application, we drew three shapes and placed an image
of gray rocks in the frame. Figure 12-10 shows the output frame from this program.

In the DrawShapesApp class, we accessed the image file and drew it into the
frame with the following code:

```
//code from the original Program 3-9

     Toolkit toolkit = Toolkit.getDefaultToolkit();
     Image myImage = toolkit.getImage("Rocks.jpg");

     g.drawImage(myImage, 300, 220, 150, 100, this);
```

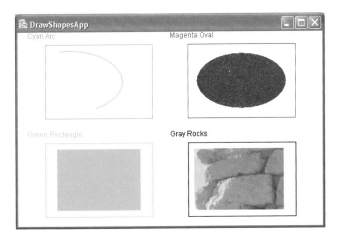

Figure 12-10
The output from the DrawShapesApp program in Chapter 3. This application
includes reading and displaying a JPG image.

If we bundle the class with this code and the *Rocks.jpg* image into a JAR file and execute it, the image is not seen in the frame.

Once again, we must rewrite this code so that it creates a URL for the files inside the JAR and the image file is loaded through the use of the Toolkit and ImageProducer classes. In Program 12-3, we load the image in the class constructor and draw it in the paint() method.

```
1   //Program 12-3 (modified Program 3-9)
2   //File: DrawShapesApp.java
3
4   import javax.swing.JFrame;
5   import java.awt.Graphics;
6   import java.awt.Color;
7   import java.awt.Image;
8   import java.awt.Toolkit;
9
10  import java.net.*;           //for URL
11  import java.awt.image.*;
12
13  public class DrawShapesApp extends JFrame
14  {
15    //We must have the Image as a class variable.
16    //We load the image in the constructor and draw it in paint().
17
18    Image myImage;
19
20    public void paint (Graphics g)
21    {
22          //set the background color to white
23          setBackground(Color.white);
24
25          // draw Arc
26          g.setColor(Color.cyan);
27          g.drawString("Cyan Arc", 20, 40);
28          g.drawRect(50,50,180,120);
29          g.drawArc(0,60,180,100,-60,160);
30
31          // draw oval
32          g.setColor(Color.magenta);
33          g.drawString("Magenta Oval ", 260, 40);
34          g.drawRect(290,50,180,120);
35          g.fillOval(305,65,150,90);
36
```

```
37          // draw rectangle
38          g.setColor(Color.green);
39          g.drawString("Green Rectangle ", 20,200);
40          g.drawRect(50,210,180,120);
41          g.fillRect(70, 220, 140, 100);
42
43          // draw image
44          g.setColor(Color.black);
45          g.drawString("Gray Rocks", 260, 200) ;
46          g.drawRect(290,210,180,120);
47
48          g.drawImage(myImage, 300, 220, 150, 100, this);
49      }
50
51
52  public DrawShapesApp()
53  {
54          //set the title of the window
55          setTitle("DrawShapesApp");
56
57          setSize(520,350);
58
59          //load the image in the constructor, not in paint()
60          Toolkit tool = Toolkit.getDefaultToolkit();
61          URL MyURL = getClass().getResource("Rocks.jpg" );
62          ImageProducer MyImageProducer;
63          try
64          {
65                  MyImageProducer = (ImageProducer) MyURL.getContent();
66                  myImage = tool.createImage(MyImageProducer);
67
68          }
69          catch( Exception ex)
70          {
71                  System.out.println(ex.getMessage() );
72          }
73
74          //show the window, this forces a call to paint
75          show();
76      }
77  public static void main(String args[] )
78  {
79          DrawShapesApp theApp = new DrawShapesApp();
80          theApp.setDefaultCloseOperation(JFrame.EXIT_ON_CLOSE);
81      }
82  }
```

12

Our manifest file for this program is named *MainIsHere.txt*, and it contains this line with an Enter key following the class name:

```
Main-Class: DrawShapesApp
```

The jar command for this application is:

```
jar cvfm  Shapes.jar   MainIsHere.txt  *.class *.jpg
```

This command executes the application contained in the JAR file:

```
java -jar  Shapes.jar
```

Figure 12-11 shows the compiler, jar, and java commands for this program. You will find the *Shapes.jar* file in the text's CD *\Ch12\DrawShapesJarDemo\Test* folder. A mouse double-click on this JAR also executes the program.

```
C:\JPT\Ch12\DrawShapesJarDemo>javac DrawShapesApp.java

C:\JPT\Ch12\DrawShapesJarDemo>jar cvfm Shapes.jar MainIsHere.txt *.class *.jpg
added manifest
adding: DrawShapesApp.class(in = 2052) (out= 1224)(deflated 40%)
adding: Rocks.jpg(in = 2148) (out= 1974)(deflated 8%)

C:\JPT\Ch12\DrawShapesJarDemo>java -jar Shapes.jar
```

Figure 12-11
The compiler, jar, and java commands for the DrawShapesApp program and the resultant output frame executed from the *Shapes.jar* file. The class and image files are contained in the JAR file.

Pond Pictures in a JAR   The last example shown in this chapter is Program 5-10, found on page 273. This program displays four images in a frame window. The images and filenames are stored in the program in arrays. We rewrite the program here using arrays for the URL and ImageProducer objects.

```
1   //Program 12-4 Modified from Program 5-10
2   //Use 2D Arrays for Images and Strings.
3   //We must create URLs for each image since this code will
4   //be executed from a JAR file.
5
6   //File: PondPicsFrame.java
7
8
9   import javax.swing.JFrame;
10  import java.net.*;          //for URL
```

```
11    import java.awt.*;
12    import java.awt.image.*;
13
14
15    public class PondPicsFrame extends JFrame
16    {
17      Image pictures[][] = new Image [2][2];
18
19      int ROWSIZE = pictures.length;
20      int COLSIZE = pictures[0].length;
21
22      String filenames[][] = {
23            {"YellowLilly2Small.jpg", "PinkLilly2Small.jpg"},
24            {"HungryFishSmall.jpg","TwoGoldenOrfesSmall.jpg"} };
25
26      String picTitles[][] = {
27            {"A yellow lilly", "A pink lilly"},
28            {"Feed us!", "Two Golden Orfes" } };
29
30      URL MyURL[][] = new URL[2][2];
31      ImageProducer MyImageProducer[][] = new ImageProducer[2][2];
32
33      public static void main( String[] args )
34      {
35            PondPicsFrame sb = new PondPicsFrame();
36            sb.setDefaultCloseOperation( EXIT_ON_CLOSE );
37      }
38
39      public PondPicsFrame()              //class constructor method
40      {
41            for(int i = 0; i < ROWSIZE; ++i)
42            {
43                  for(int j = 0; j < COLSIZE; ++j)
44                  {
45
46                        Toolkit tool = Toolkit.getDefaultToolkit();
47                        MyURL[i][j] =
48                              getClass().getResource(filenames[i][j] );
49
50                        try
51                        {
```

```
52                      MyImageProducer[i][j] =
53                          (ImageProducer) MyURL[i][j].getContent();
54                  }
55              catch( Exception ex)
56              {
57                  System.out.println(ex.getMessage() );
58              }
59              pictures[i][j] =
60                  tool.createImage(MyImageProducer[i][j]);
61
62          }
63      }
64      setSize( 450, 460 );     //set the window size
65      setTitle("Pond Pictures Program");
66      show();
67   }
68
69   public void paint( Graphics g )
70   {
71      int x = 0, y = 0;
72      for(int i = 0; i < ROWSIZE; ++i)
73      {
74          for(int j = 0; j < COLSIZE; ++j)
75          {
76              x = i * 210 + 20;    //offset to the right
77              y = j * 210 + 40;    //offset the y due to title bar
78              g.drawImage(pictures[i][j], x, y, this);
79              g.drawString(picTitles[i][j], x+10, y + 200);
80
81          }
82      }
83   }
84 }
```

The associated manifest file named *WhereIsMain.txt* contains the line:

```
Main-Class: PondPicsFrame
```

The *PondPicsFrame.class* file, four JPG images, and manifest file are all located in the same directory. (*\Ch12\PondPicturesJarDemo* on the text's CD). This jar command creates the Pond.jar file. It is located in the *\Ch12\PondPicturesJarDemo\Test* folder.

```
jar cvfm  Pond.jar   WhereIsMain.txt  *.class *.jpg
```

12.3
Summary

The Java language provides a powerful archive utility that is used for bundling program files into a single file. This file is referred to as a Java ARchive file (JAR file). The JAR file is based on the PKZip utility and the *.zip* file format. The jar utility has many options that the programmer may select when a JAR file is created. Java requires options to be placed on the command line when the command is issued.

Applets may be bundled into a JAR file and then loaded by the web browser program. The associated HTML file must refer to the archive file and the class file, such as we saw with the UFOApplet example:

```
<!-- UfoAppletJar.html for Program 12-1  -->


<html>
<applet        archive = UFO.jar
               code = "UfoApplet.class"
               width = 550   height = 400       >
</applet>
</html>
```

Application programs can also be bundled into a JAR file. If the programmer wishes to run the program via the JAR file, he or she must include a manifest file that states the name of the class that contains the main() method. For example, in the HelloFrame example, the manifest is named *WhereIsMain.txt* and it contained the line:

```
Main-Class: HelloFrame
```

The manifest file is included in the jar command:

```
jar  cvfm  Hello1.jar  WhereIsMain.txt   *.class
```

The *Hello1.jar* can then be executed by a double-click of the mouse or though the java command, such as:

```
java -jar Hello1.jar
```

Remember as you work with JAR files, if you make a change in your source code you will need to recompile the source code and rebuild your JAR file with the new *.class* file. The JAR file actually contains the class files and does not reference them. When you make a change in the class file, that new file will need to be archived in the JAR file.

Practice makes perfect! Work through the examples presented in this chapter and build your own JAR files.

12

13

Advanced Topics: Packages, Classpaths, and JARs

CHAPTER OBJECTIVES

Review the concept of a Java package.

Show the required steps to place classes in packages.

Demonstrate how the javac -d compile option should be used when compiling .*java* files that contain (and belong to) a package statement.

Execute a program that imports a package.

Introduce the CLASSPATH variable and explain how the operating system uses it to locate Java packages, classes, and JAR files.

Bundle a package into a JAR file and then use the JAR file as a source for a program to import a package.

Discuss package scope and show how class members that do not have access specifiers have package scope by default.

Demonstrate how a program that imports package classes using a JAR can itself be packaged and placed in a JAR file.

Packages and Imports

Up to now in our Java career, we have placed all of our *.java*, *.class*, and resource files in the same directory and we have only imported prebuilt Java classes to use in our programs. We use the javac compiler command to build class files. If our program is an applet, we execute it in a web browser or in Java's appletviewer program. If the program is an application, we use the java command to execute it.

We have been using Java's prebuilt classes since Chapter 2. These classes are grouped together in various packages, such as javax.swing (for JComponents), java.awt (for Windowing Toolkit classes), and java.util (for utility classes). If we wish to use one of Java's classes, such as JOptionPane, we must first import the package and class into our program with an import statement unless we wish to write the full package name each time we use it, such as javax.swing.JoptionPane.show Message Dialog (. . .).

How do we build our own package that contains our own classes? How do we place our package in a general location on the computer's disk instead of having the *.java* and *.class* files located right in the same folder? After all, Java's packages are not located in our folders. Is it possible to bundle our own packages into JAR files? Can the JAR file be placed in a different location on the disk? The goal of this chapter is to answer all of these questions and demonstrate how these tasks are accomplished.

If you have not yet discovered Java ARchive (JAR) files, now is a good time to read Chapter 12, JAR Files. JAR files give us a nice way to compress Java files into a single file. In Chapter 12, we learned how to use a JAR file in an applet and how to execute an application with a double-click on the JAR file. The latter portion of this chapter assumes that you are familiar with the basic steps for creating a JAR file.

▓▓▓ 13.1
A Simple Program

The TestShapes program is a simple application that includes a circle and a rectangle. The program presents a window that contains text fields for the two different shapes. Figure 13-1 shows an instance of this program's output window. There are

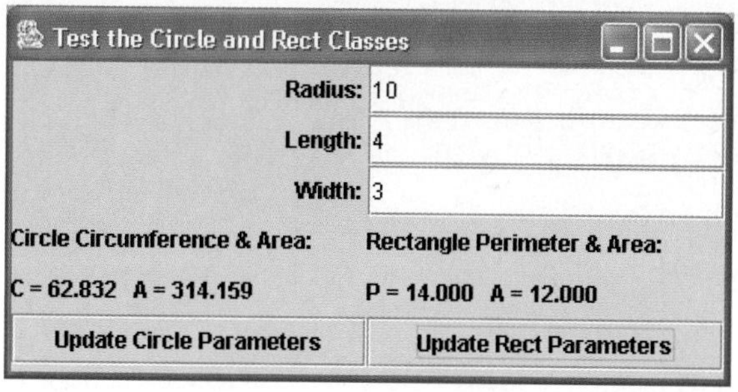

Figure 13-1
The TestShapes program frame allowing the user to enter values for a circle's radius and a rectangle's length and width. The update buttons show the calculated values.

text fields for a circle's radius and a rectangle's length and width values. There are update buttons for each shape—when pressed, the shape's parameter values are used to calculate two values for each shape. The circle's circumference and area values are based on the radius. The rectangle's perimeter and area values are based on its length and width.

In order to compile and execute this program, the three *.java* files are in the same directory. The three source files are compiled with javac and we use the java command with TestShapes because it is the class that contains the main() method. Examine these steps to compile and run the program in Figure 13-2.

The program code seen here in Program 13-1 is located on the text's CD in the *\Ch13\ShapesDemo1* folder. The Circle and Rect class constructors set the default values to 1.0 and call the doCalcs() method. In doCalcs() the circumference/perimeter and area values are calculated. The doCalcs() method is called whenever new values are set into the objects.

```
1    //Program 13-1
2    //File: \ShapesDemo1\Circle.java
3
4    public class Circle
5    {
6        double radius, circumf, area;
7
8        public Circle()
9        {
10               radius = 1.0;
11               doCalcs();
12       }
13       public Circle(double r)
14       {
```

13

```
15          radius = r;
16          doCalcs();
17      }
18
19      private void doCalcs()
20      {
21          area = Math.PI * Math.pow(radius,2);
22          circumf = radius * 2.0 * Math.PI;
23      }
24
25      public void setRadius(double r)
26      {
27          radius = r;
28          doCalcs();
29      }
30
31      public double getCircumference(){ return circumf; }
32      public double getArea(){return area; }
33  }
```

```
1   //Program 13-1
2   //File: \ShapesDemo1\Rect.java
3
4   public class Rect
5   {
6       double length, width, perimeter, area;
7
8       public Rect()
9       {
10          length = width = 1.0;
11          doCalcs();
12      }
13      public Rect(double l, double w)
14      {
15          length = l;
16          width = w;
17          doCalcs();
18      }
19
20      private void doCalcs()
21      {
22          area = length*width;
23          perimeter = length* 2.0 + width*2.0;
24      }
```

```
25
26        public void setLengthWidth(double l, double w)
27        {
28              length = l;
29              width = w;
30              doCalcs();
31        }
32
33        public double getPerimeter(){ return perimeter; }
34        public double getArea(){return area; }
35   }
```

C:\JPT\Ch13\ShapesDemo1>javac Circle.java

C:\JPT\Ch13\ShapesDemo1>javac Rect.java

C:\JPT\Ch13\ShapesDemo1>javac TestShapes.java

C:\JPT\Ch13\ShapesDemo1>java TestShapes

Figure 13-2
The compile and execution steps required for Program 13-1, TestShapes. All of the *.java* and *.class* files are located in the same folder, *JPT\Ch13\ShapesDemo1*. We could have compiled the *.java* files using the javac *.java command.

The TestShape class instantiates a Circle and Rect object along with the twelve JComponent objects we need for the user interface. We also instantiate a Decimal-Format object named fred. We'll ask fred to format our numbers to three decimal places. Here is the code:

```
1    //Program 13-1
2    //File: \ShapesDemo1\TestShapes.java
3
4    import javax.swing.*; //for JFrame, JButton, JTextField, JLabel
5    import java.awt.*;        //for Container, GridLayout
6    import java.awt.event.*;   //for ActionListener, ActionEvent
7    import java.text.DecimalFormat;
8
9    public class TestShapes extends JFrame implements ActionListener
10   {
11
12     //Yippee!!!  Here are our Circle and Rect objects!
13     Circle circle = new Circle();
14     Rect rect = new Rect();
15
```

```
16      //Here are all the GUI components.
17      JButton cirButton = new JButton("Update Circle Parameters");
18      JButton rectButton = new JButton("Update Rect Parameters");
19
20      JLabel radLabel = new JLabel("Radius: ", JLabel.RIGHT);
21      JLabel lengthLabel = new JLabel("Length: ", JLabel.RIGHT);
22      JLabel widthLabel = new JLabel("Width: ", JLabel.RIGHT);
23
24      JTextField radTextField = new JTextField();
25      JTextField lengthTextField = new JTextField();
26      JTextField widthTextField = new JTextField();
27
28      JLabel circleParamsLabel = new JLabel("Circle Circumference & Area: ");
29      JLabel rectParamsLabel = new JLabel("Rectangle Perimeter & Area: ");
30
31      JLabel circleResultsLabel = new JLabel("");
32      JLabel rectResultsLabel = new JLabel("");
33
34      //Let's not forget fred, our DecimalFormat object.  ;-)
35      DecimalFormat fred = new DecimalFormat("0.000");
36
37
38
39      double radius, circumf, sa, length, width, perimeter, area;
40
41      public TestShapes()
42      {
43              setTitle("Test the Circle and Rect Classes");
44
45              radTextField.setText("1.0");
46              lengthTextField.setText("1.0");
47              widthTextField.setText("1.0");
48
49              Container canvas = getContentPane();
50              canvas.setLayout( new GridLayout(6,2));
51
52              circleResultsLabel.setText( "1.000");
53              rectResultsLabel.setText("1.000");
54              canvas.add(radLabel);
55              canvas.add(radTextField);
56              canvas.add(lengthLabel);
57              canvas.add(lengthTextField);
58              canvas.add(widthLabel);
59              canvas.add(widthTextField);
60              canvas.add(circleParamsLabel);
61              canvas.add(rectParamsLabel);
62              canvas.add(circleResultsLabel);
```

```
63          canvas.add(rectResultsLabel);
64          canvas.add(cirButton);
65          canvas.add(rectButton);
66
67          cirButton.addActionListener(this);
68          rectButton.addActionListener(this);
69          setSize(400,200);
70          show();
71      }
72
73   public void actionPerformed(ActionEvent e)
74   {
75          if(e.getSource() == cirButton)
76          {
77                  //Fetch the radius from the text field.
78                  String s1 = radTextField.getText();
79                  radius = Double.parseDouble(s1);
80
81                  //Set it into the circle. It'll do calcs.
82                  circle.setRadius(radius);
83
84                  //Now get the goodies from the circle.
85                  circumf = circle.getCircumference();
86                  area = circle.getArea();
87
88                  //fred will format our number for us.
89                  String output =  "C = " + fred.format(circumf);
90                  output += "   A = " + fred.format(area);
91
92                  //Set the results label.
93                  circleResultsLabel.setText( output);
94
95          }
96          else if(e.getSource() == rectButton)
97          {
98                  String slen = lengthTextField.getText();
99                  length = Double.parseDouble(slen);
100                 String swid= widthTextField.getText();
101                 width = Double.parseDouble(swid);
102                 rect.setLengthWidth(length, width);
103                 perimeter = rect.getPerimeter();
104                 area = rect.getArea();
105                 String output =  "P = " + fred.format(perimeter);
106                 output += "   A = " + fred.format(area);
107                 rectResultsLabel.setText( output);
108         }
109     }
```

```
110    public static void main(String args[] )
111    {
112          TestShapes theApp = new TestShapes();
113          theApp.setDefaultCloseOperation(JFrame.EXIT_ON_CLOSE);
114    }
115  }
```

We will use this program throughout this chapter. We will package our Circle and Rect classes into our own shapes package, and import our shape classes into our TestShapes class. We will place our shapes package in various places on the disk. To top it off, we will wrap up our shapes package in a *shapes.jar* file and use it in our program. Isn't this exciting? I can't wait to get started. Here we go!

13.2
What is a Java Package?

Java uses the term **package** to mean a collection of logically related *.class* files. A package is intended to wrap classes together into a group with its own name. This grouping allows programmers to organize their code. A package can be thought of as a library of classes. A package is also a folder or directory structure. (Classes are files and packages are located within directories or folders.) Java allows source code to be "packaged" and stored in databases and other places as well, but for our purposes, we will just consider packages as directories.

package
a collection of logically related *.class* files wrapped together into a group with its own name

The Java language has made the mechanics of packaging your classes very simple. The package name is included in the source code of the class that will be in the package. The package statement should be the first "code" line in a *.java* file, like this:

```
//File:  MyClass.java

//The package statement has to be above the class definition line.
//It should be the first code line in the .java file.
package identifierName.identifierName...;

public class MyClass
{
      //class code
}
```

There can be one or many identifiers in a package name. The identifiers represent the directory structure in which the class file is located. When a class is contained in a package—there is a package statement in the source code file—it is saying, "This class lives in this package—or directory structure."

13

TestShapes Program and the johnston.shapes Package

For our TestShapes program we place the Circle and Rect classes into their own package called johnston.shapes. We build the package and then import our Circle and Rect classes into the TestShapes class by using an import statement. The text's CD's \Ch13\ShapesDemo2\ folder contains these modified files and the johnston.shape package. We are using the author's name for the examples in this chapter. Why don't you obtain the files from \ShapesDemo1\ and build your own package as you work through this section of the text? Use your own name for your package.

The Circle and Rect classes will be contained in the johnston.shapes package. Therefore, the package statement is required in the *Circle.java* and *Rect.java* source code files. In Program 13-2, we show the package statement on line 4 located above the class definition lines:

```
1   //Program 13-2
2   //File: \ShapesDemo2\Circle.java
3
4   package johnston.shapes;
5
6   public class Circle
7   {
8      //The code in the 13-2 Circle class has not been changed
9      //from the 13-1 Circle. The only difference is the
10     //inclusion of the above package statement.
11  }
```

```
1   //Program 13-2
2   //File: \ShapesDemo2\Rect.java
3
4   package johnston.shapes;
5
6   public class Rect
7   {
8      //The code in the 13-2 Rect class has not been changed
9      //from the 13-1 Rect. The only difference is the
10     //inclusion of the above package statement.
11  }
```

Now we must compile (and build) the package. In order to do this we use a new command option with the Java compiler. The **javac -d option** should be used by the programmer when he or she is building a package. When a *.java* file is compiled with the -d option, the compiler creates the directory structure as designated in the package statement and places the *.class* file within that package structure. The form of this compiler command is as follows:

```
javac -d . Circle.java
```

The . (dot) in the command is the location where the package structure should be built. The **. (dot)**, used when referencing a PATH, says "the current directory." When we compile our *Circle.java* file in the above manner, Java will create a folder named "johnston" in the directory where the *Circle.java* file is located. Within that folder there is a folder created by Java named "shapes." The *Circle.class* file is placed in the shapes folder.

Figure 13-3 shows the directory listing command (dir) of the *\Ch13\ ShapesDemo2* folder and the two javac commands. The Java compiler creates the package structure in the current directory and places the *.class* files in the *\johnston\shapes* folder. The class files can be seen in Figure 13-4.

javac -d option

should be used when a *.java* file contains a package statement. This command creates the package directory structure and places the *.class* file within that package structure

. (dot)

when used in a PATH statement, it refers to the current directory

```
C:\JPT\Ch13\ShapesDemo2>dir
 Volume in drive C has no label.
 Volume Serial Number is 407B-0467

 Directory of C:\JPT\Ch13\ShapesDemo2

12/21/2002  08:42 PM    <DIR>          .
12/21/2002  08:42 PM    <DIR>          ..
12/01/2002  02:14 PM               553 Circle.java
12/01/2002  02:14 PM               597 Rect.java
12/01/2002  02:17 PM             3,517 TestShapes.java
               3 File(s)          4,667 bytes
               2 Dir(s)  29,057,540,096 bytes free

C:\JPT\Ch13\ShapesDemo2>javac -d . Circle.java

C:\JPT\Ch13\ShapesDemo2>javac -d . Rect.java

C:\JPT\Ch13\ShapesDemo2>
```

Figure 13-3
The Java compiler commands showing the -d option. The compiler builds the package structure within the current directory.

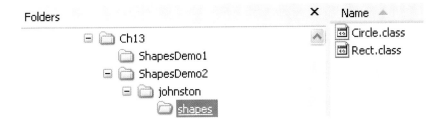

Figure 13-4
The directory structure of the package johnston.shapes. The Circle and Rect class files are placed in the package. The *.java* files remain in their original locations.

If we wanted our package structure to be placed in the root of the C:\ drive, we would use this form of the command:

```
javac -d c:\  Circle.java
```

The next step for us is to have our TestShapes program import the Circle and Rect classes. We use the import statements, as seen here on lines 9 and 10:

```
1   //Program 13-2
2   //File: \Shapes\Demo2\TestShapes.java
3
4   //Standard Java import statements are here.
5
6   //Now we import the Circle and Rect class for this program.
7   //We must use the package and class names
8
9   import johnston.shapes.Circle;
10  import johnston.shapes.Rect;
11
12  //We could have said import johnston.shapes.*;
13
14  public class TestShapes extends JFrame implements ActionListener
15  {
16     //This code does not change from Program 13-1.
17
18     //Yippee!!!  Here are our Circle and Rect objects!
19     Circle circle = new Circle();
20     Rect rect = new Rect();
21
22     //Rest of program.
23  }
```

The package statements (package johnston.shapes;) in the Circle and Rect classes and import statements (import johnston.shapes.Circle; and import johnston.shapes.Rect;) in the TestShapes class are straightforward. Building the package is simple too, because the -d option creates the package directory structure and automatically places the class files in the package. Now we are ready to compile and run our TestShapes program. Because the johnston.shapes package is located in the same directory as the *TestShapes.java* file, we are able to compile and run this in the usual manner. Figure 13-5 shows the compilation and execution commands. Figure 13-6 illustrates the packaging and import relationship.

> **Note:** If when you build your own package, your computer is unable to find the package and you get errors similar to those seen in Figure 13-8, read ahead in the CLASSPATH section. Chances are, your computer does not have its CLASSPATH set.

```
C:\JPT\Ch13\ShapesDemo2>javac -d . Circle.java

C:\JPT\Ch13\ShapesDemo2>javac -d . Rect.java

C:\JPT\Ch13\ShapesDemo2>javac TestShapes.java

C:\JPT\Ch13\ShapesDemo2>java TestShapes
```

Figure 13-5
The TestShapes program can be compiled and executed because the johnston.shapes package is located in the same directory as the *TestShapes.java* file.

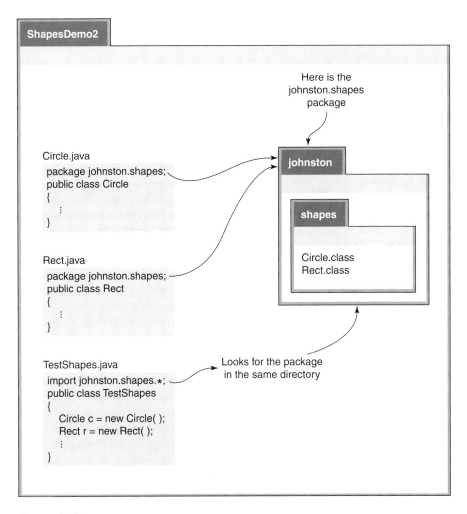

Figure 13-6
The package statement dictates the directory structure for the class files in the package. The *TestShapes.java* and package are located in the same folder and Java can find the package by using the normal javac and java commands.

Folders	✕	Name ▲
⊟ 📁 Ch13		📄 Circle.java
⊟ 📁 johnston		📄 Rect.java
📁 shapes		📄 TestShapes.class
📁 ShapesDemo1		📄 TestShapes.java
📁 ShapesDemo2		

Figure 13-7
The johnston.shapes package has been moved out of the ShapesDemo2 folder. The *TestShapes.java* imports the two classes in this package.

```
C:\JPT\Ch13\ShapesDemo2>javac TestShapes.java
TestShapes.java:9: package johnston.shapes does not exist
import johnston.shapes.Circle;
                      ^
TestShapes.java:10: package johnston.shapes does not exist
import johnston.shapes.Rect;
                      ^
TestShapes.java:17: cannot resolve symbol
symbol  : constructor Circle  ()
location: class Circle
          Circle circle = new Circle();
                              ^
TestShapes.java:18: cannot resolve symbol
symbol  : constructor Rect  ()
location: class Rect
          Rect rect = new Rect();
                          ^
```

Figure 13-8
Four of the ten compiler errors seen when we attempt to compile the TestShapes program. The johnston.shapes package has been moved out of the ShapesDemo2 folder.

Now, just for fun, what do you think happens if we move the package out of the *\Ch13\ShapesDemo2* folder? Look at Figure 13-7. Notice that the package is now in the *\JPT\Ch13* folder and not in the *\Ch13\ShapesDemo2* folder with the TestShapes files. If we attempt to compile the TestShapes program, the compiler will not be able to find the package or resolve the Circle and Rect classes. See the compiler errors shown in Figure 13-8. How do we solve this problem? We need to be able to place our package wherever we wish on our computer. How do we tell the Java compiler and interpreter how to find our package? Excellent questions. The CLASSPATH environment variable helps us solve this problem. Read on!

CLASSPATH
a computer operating system environment variable. Java looks at all of the CLASSPATH locations when it is searching for Java classes and packages

▊13.3
CLASSPATHs

The **CLASSPATH** is an environment variable of your computer's operating system and it tells Java all the possible places to look for Java packages, classes, and JAR files. In Appendix A we had to set the PATH variable so that our operating system

Chapter 13 ▊ Advanced Topics: Packages, Classpaths, and JARs

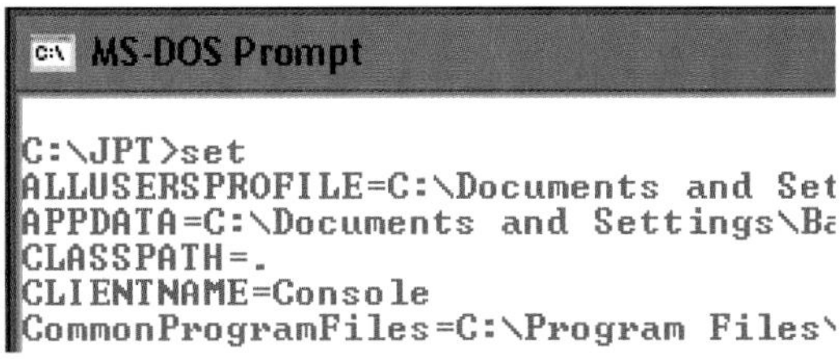

Figure 13-9
A partial listing of a computer's setting for environmental variables. This listing shows the CLASSPATH that is set to the current directory (.).

knows to look in the *j2sdk1.4.1\bin* folder to find the various Java programs (javac, java, jar, etc.). Now, we must use the CLASSPATH variable to help Java find imported packages.

For the examples in this text we will set our CLASSPATH variable to the "current directory," that is, a . (dot). This says we are telling Java to look for any packages in the current directory. First, you must determine if your system has the CLASSPATH set. If you type the word "set" in the MS-DOS Prompt window, you will see the settings for the various environmental variables. Figure 13-9 shows a partial listing of a computer's settings that include the CLASSPATH variable.

If you need to set your computer's CLASSPATH variable, refer to Appendix A and follow the guidelines shown for setting the PATH variable. The steps for setting the CLASSPATH are identical to those for the PATH. It is set in the *autoexec.bat* file (Windows 95, 98, ME), in the control panel (XP, NT, or Win2000), or in the shell initialization file for Unix. Once you have your CLASSPATH set, you should enter "set" at the command line. You should see the CLASSPATH in your setting—just as in Figure 13-9. As you progress in your knowledge of Java, you will add more items to the CLASSPATH. Remember that each entry in the CLASSPATH must be separated by a semicolon (;). There are no spaces in the statement.

TestShapes and CLASSPATHs

The TestShapes class imports the Circle and Rect classes that are contained in the johnston.shapes package. The program example in Program 13-2 was in the *ShapesDemo2* folder that contained the *johnston\shapes* directory structure (review Figure 13-6 again). The CLASSPATH is set to the current directory so that when the program was compiled and executed it could find the package. The CLASSPATH says, "Look in the current directory for any custom made packages that you need."

After we saw how Java could find the package as we compiled and ran the TestShapes program, we moved the johnston.shapes package from the *JPT\Ch13\ShapesDemo2* directory to the *JPT\Ch13* directory. Once the package was moved, javac could not find it when we compiled our *TestShapes.java* (review Figures 13-7 and 13-8). Now we have to use the CLASSPATH to help the Java compiler find our johnston.shape package.

javac -classpath
option

allows the programmer
to specify additional
CLASSPATH locations

The **javac -classpath option** allows the programmer to specify additional locations for the compiler to look for imported packages. The form of this javac command is:

```
javac  -classpath %CLASSPATH%;additionalPath    MyClass.java
```

-classpath tells the compiler that there are places to look for packages other than the one(s) set in the operating system's CLASSPATH variable. The %CLASSPATH% says to look in the default CLASSPATH initially. (If you leave out this portion, javac will not look in the default locations.) The additionalPath is the root location of the package. That is, the path of the folder that contains the package.

Using the above example, the path to our package is *C:\JPT\Ch13*. Our *TestShapes.java* is located in *C:\JPT\Ch13\ShapesDemo2*. We must tell the Java compiler and the java interpreter where our package is located by using the following javac and java commands. See Figure 13-10 for an illustration.

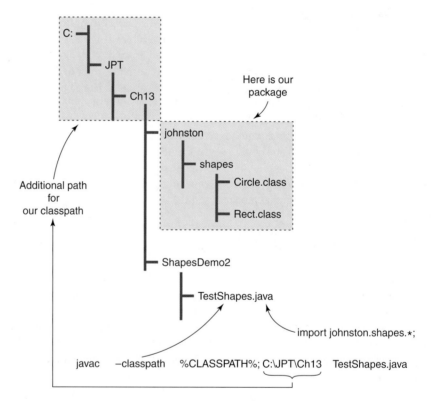

Figure 13-10
The directory structure showing the relationship between the package, the additional classpath information, and the *TestShapes.java* file.

Chapter 13 ▌ Advanced Topics: Packages, Classpaths, and JARs

```
javac  -classpath %CLASSPATH%;C:\JPT\Ch13     TestShapes.java

java  -classpath %CLASSPATH%;C:\JPT\Ch13     TestShapes
```

If we moved the johnston.shapes package to a different location on the computer's disk, then the additional information for the CLASSPATH would also change. Let's say we move the package to *C:\MyJavaPackages* and leave the *TestShapes.java* file where it is in *C:\JPT\Ch13\ShapesDemo2*. The compilation and execution commands are shown here. Refer to Figure 13-11.

```
javac  -classpath %CLASSPATH%;C:\MyJavaPackages     TestShapes.java

java  -classpath %CLASSPATH%;C:\MyJavaPackages     TestShapes
```

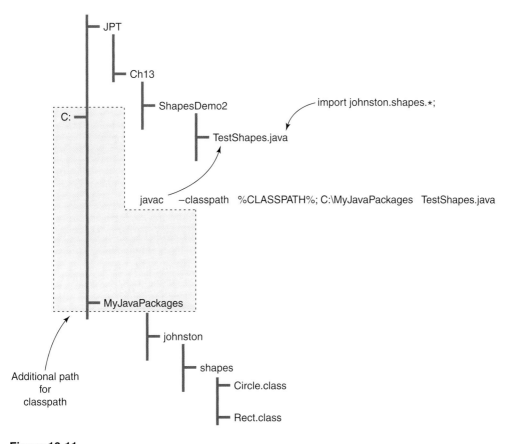

Figure 13-11
The johnston.shapes package is now in the *C:\MyJavaPackages* directory. The additional classpath information must contain the root directory of where the Java package is located.

13.4
Package Scope

In Chapter 6, we presented the concept of scope for variables. Scope describes the lifetime and visibility of variables and methods, i.e., what portions of the program can see and access the variables and methods. The scope of a variable is determined by where the variable is declared. Some variables exist for brief periods of time while others exist for the duration of the program.

We also showed the four types of scope for class or instance variables and methods using access specifiers. The three access specifier keywords in Java are: (1) public, (2) private, and (3) protected. In Chapter 6, we discussed public and private. We covered protected in Chapter 9 when we explored inheritance. The fourth type of scope is known as **package scope**, and it is now of interest to us.

package scope

when a class member does not have an access specifier (neither public, private, nor protected), it has package scope and only other members of the package can access it

If a class member does not have an access specifier (no public, private, or protected keyword by the class variable or method), then the member is said to have "friendly" access or package scope. Package access or scope is friendly because the class member is visible and accessible to other members in the same package, but private (and not visible) to any class outside of the package. The access specifier may be intentionally left off class members so that the member can be used only within the other classes of the package.

Forget a Specifier? A Package Scope Problem

A beginning programmer sometimes forgets to state the access specifier for his or her class members. Therefore, these class members have package scope. This is not a problem when we do not include package statements in our code. But suppose a programmer intends to build a package and forgets the access specifier on the class constructors. The programmer carefully builds and tests the code before packaging it, as we did in Program 13-1, where there are no package statements and all of the files are located in the same directory. The class members can see each other. Then, our programmer packages the classes by adding the necessary package statements and compiles them with the -d option. The package folder is left in the current directory. Remember that these class constructors do not have access specifiers—which means they have package scope. Refer to Circle's lines 15 and 20 and Rect's lines 12 and 17. Examine the two classes in Program 13-3.

```
1   //Program 13-3
2   //File: \ShapesDemo3\Circle.java
3
4   package johnston.shapes;
```

```
5
6     public class Circle
7     {
8       double radius, circumf, area;
9
10      //There are no access specifiers on the constructors
11      //therefore they have package scope. That means only
12      //classes in the package can see them. The constructors
13      //are private to the classes not contained in johnston.shapes.
14
15      Circle()
16      {
17          radius = 1.0;
18          doCalcs();
19      }
20      Circle(double r)
21      {
22          radius = r;
23          doCalcs();
24      }
25
26      //rest of class
27    }
```

```
1     //Program 13-3
2     //File: \ShapesDemo3\Rect.java
3
4     package johnston.shapes;
5
6     public class Rect
7     {
8       double length, width, perimeter, area;
9
10      //No access specifiers on the constructors, therefore package scope.
11      //Private to the non-johnston.shapes package.
12      Rect()
13      {
14          length = width = 1.0;
15          doCalcs();
16      }
```

```
17      Rect(double l, double w)
18      {
19            length = l;
20            width = w;
21            doCalcs();
22      }
23
24      //rest of class
25    }
```

The classes are imported in the frame class:

```
1    //Program 13-3
2    //File: \ShapesDemo3\TestShapes.java
3
4    //other import statements
5
6    import johnston.shapes.*;
7
8    public class TestShapes extends JFrame implements ActionListener
9    {
10
11      //This program has trouble seeing these classes because the
12      //Circle and Rect have package scope and are not public.
13      //The TestShapes class is not in the johnston.shapes package,
14      //so the Circle and Rect constructors are unresolved in TestShapes.
15
16      Circle circle = new Circle();
17      Rect rect = new Rect();
18
19
20      //rest of class
21    }
```

If the programmer compiles the frame class, many errors occur. Figure 13-12 shows these steps and a few of the errors. Often, this situation produces unique and puzzling errors for the new Java programmer. It is a good rule of thumb to always have access specifiers on your methods and class data unless your intention is for the member to have package scope.

```
C:\JPT\Ch13\ShapesDemo3>javac -d . Rect.java

C:\JPT\Ch13\ShapesDemo3>javac -d . Circle.java

C:\JPT\Ch13\ShapesDemo3>javac TestShapes.java
TestShapes.java:20: cannot resolve symbol
symbol  : constructor Circle  ()
location: class Circle
          Circle circle = new Circle();
                              ^
TestShapes.java:21: cannot resolve symbol
symbol  : constructor Rect  ()
location: class Rect
          Rect rect = new Rect();
                          ^
```

Figure 13-12
The constructor methods in the johnston.shapes package do not have access specifiers. Therefore they have package scope. The constructors are hidden (private) from
the world and the TestShapes program does not compile because the Rect and
Circle constructors are not available to it.

13.5
Packages, JARs, and the CLASSPATH

Perhaps you are now asking the logical question, "Can I put a package in a JAR
file?" Yes! Absolutely! In fact, Java programmers build packages of classes and
then bundle the package in a JAR file for ease of distribution. The JAR file can be
thought of as a Java library. Often, programmers place all of their JARs in a single
common directory so that the packages are accessible to the programmer or other
programmers' classpaths.

In order to import any classes that are bundled into a JAR file, the specific
path and JAR file must be listed on the CLASSPATH. It is not enough to have the
JAR file located in the current directory with the file that is importing the JAR
package, nor can the CLASSPATH be set to just the directory that contains the
JAR. There are three ways a programmer can ensure that their JAR is on the
CLASSPATH: (1) You may place the JAR file and path in the computer's
CLASSPATH environment variable, (2) You may compile and run your code with
the -classpath option, or (3) You may write a script that sets the CLASSPATH as
needed. We will see how these are accomplished in the following sections.

Package Your Package in a JAR

In Chapter 12, we presented the information for how to place your applet or application in a JAR file. For applets, you must modify the HTML file that references
the applet class so the HTML file also references the JAR file. For applications, the
programmer must include a manifest file that specifies the file that contains the
main() method. Some of our packages do not contain a main() method, such as our
johnston.shapes package, so we do not have to worry about providing a manifest

13

```
C:\JPT\Ch13\ShapesDemo2>dir
 Volume in drive C has no label.
 Volume Serial Number is 407B-0467

 Directory of C:\JPT\Ch13\ShapesDemo2

12/21/2002  09:04 PM    <DIR>          .
12/21/2002  09:04 PM    <DIR>          ..
12/01/2002  02:14 PM               553 Circle.java
12/21/2002  08:51 PM    <DIR>          johnston
12/01/2002  02:14 PM               597 Rect.java
12/21/2002  08:49 PM             3,666 TestShapes.class
12/01/2002  02:17 PM             3,517 TestShapes.java
               4 File(s)          8,333 bytes
               3 Dir(s)  29,052,940,288 bytes free

C:\JPT\Ch13\ShapesDemo2>jar cvf shapes.jar johnston/*.*
added manifest
adding: johnston/shapes/(in = 0) (out= 0)(stored 0%)
adding: johnston/shapes/Circle.class(in = 730) (out= 441)(deflated 39%)
adding: johnston/shapes/Rect.class(in = 726) (out= 436)(deflated 39%)

C:\JPT\Ch13\ShapesDemo2>
```

Figure 13-13

A directory listing shows the top level of the johnston.shapes package that is contained in the *\JPT\Ch13\ShapesDemo2* folder. The jar command creates the *shapes.jar* file.

with the Main-Class designation. Java will create its own manifest for the JAR file when the JAR is created.

The jar command for bundling a package in a JAR file is straightforward. It is necessary to bundle the class files in their directory structure for the JAR file. Remember that the package statement in a Java file is saying, "I live in this directory structure." The command should be issued in the directory that contains the top level of the package.

To see how to bundle a package in a JAR file, we will place the johnston.shapes package in a JAR file named *shapes.jar*. Once the JAR is built, we will have our *TestShapes.java* import the Rect and Circle classes from the JAR file. Before we perform these steps, let's review Program 13-2 and Figures 13-3, 13-4, and 13-5. We packaged the shape classes and created the johnston.shapes package by using the -d option with javac. This package was located in the *\Ch13\ShapesDemo2* folder. To create a JAR file for this package, we use the following jar command to create a JAR file named *shapes.jar*. We must be in the folder that contains the top-level folder of the package structure—which is *ShapesDemo2* folder in this example. Figure 13-13 above shows the directory listing for this folder and the jar command. The file *shapes.jar* is created successfully, as seen in Figure 13-14.

```
//This is the general form of the jar command:
//jar cvf jarName.jar  topLevelOfPackage/*.*


//Here is the command we need to use:
jar cvf shapes.jar  johnston/*.*
```

To compile and run our TestShapes program using the *shapes.jar* file, we must include the JAR filename on the CLASSPATH. Recall that our CLASSPATH is set to

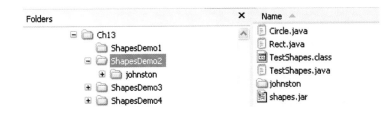

Figure 13-14
The *shapes.jar* file can be seen in the *ShapesDemo2*\\ folder.

the . (dot), which is the current directory. Examine Figure 13-15. We have removed all of the class files and package directory structure from the *Ch13**ShapesDemo2*\\ folder. This is verified by performing a "dir" command. We then compile and execute the *TestShapes.java* by placing the *shapes.jar* file on the CLASSPATH. The commands are:

```
javac  -classpath  %CLASSPATH%;shapes.jar  TestShapes.java
```

```
java  -classpath  %CLASSPATH%;shapes.jar  TestShapes
```

Please note that the java command allows the programmer to abbreviate the -classpath option to -cp. Equivalent valid commands for our TestShapes program are:

```
javac  -classpath  %CLASSPATH%;shapes.jar  TestShapes.java
```

```
java  -cp  %CLASSPATH%;shapes.jar  TestShapes
```

```
C:\JPT\Ch13\ShapesDemo2>dir
 Volume in drive C has no label.
 Volume Serial Number is 407B-0467

 Directory of C:\JPT\Ch13\ShapesDemo2

12/21/2002  09:14 PM    <DIR>          .
12/21/2002  09:14 PM    <DIR>          ..
12/01/2002  02:14 PM               553 Circle.java
12/01/2002  02:14 PM               597 Rect.java
12/21/2002  09:04 PM             1,619 shapes.jar
12/21/2002  09:12 PM             3,517 TestShapes.java
               4 File(s)          6,286 bytes
               2 Dir(s)  29,048,553,472 bytes free

C:\JPT\Ch13\ShapesDemo2>javac -classpath %CLASSPATH%;shapes.jar TestShapes.java

C:\JPT\Ch13\ShapesDemo2>java -cp  %CLASSPATH%;shapes.jar TestShapes
```

Figure 13-15
A directory listing shows the *shapes.jar* and *TestShapes.java* files. The javac and java commands are issued with the -classpath indicating the location of the *shapes.jar* file. This program executes successfully with these commands.

If we move the *shapes.jar* file to the folder *c:\MyJARs*, then the commands for compiling and executing the TestShapes program are:

```
javac  -classpath  %CLASSPATH%;c:\MyJARs\shapes.jar  TestShapes.java
```

```
java  -classpath  %CLASSPATH%;c:\MyJARs\shapes.jar  TestShapes
```

13

JAR in a JAR? No. Package in a JAR? Yes!

In the previous sections of this chapter we built two shape classes: (1) a Rect and (2) a Circle. We packaged these classes in johnston.shapes. We built an application program named TestShapes, which imported the johnston.shapes package. We then created a JAR file of this johnston.shapes package and we learned the steps necessary so that our TestShapes program could import johnston.shapes classes contained in the *shapes.jar*. This is summarized in Figure 13-16.

The next logical step in this process is to bundle our application program into another JAR file so that we may execute the TestShapes program by double-clicking it with the mouse on a Windows machine or with the java -jar command. In Java, it is a common occurrence to create a JAR file of classes that import packages found in other JAR files. You may ask if it is possible to simply bundle the *TestShapes.class* and *shapes.jar* file into a new JAR file, named *test.jar*, and provide a manifest that references the TestShape. The answer is no. Java does not allow you to do this. Figure 13-17 illustrates this concept and the skull and crossbones warn you that it will not work in Java.

As we have seen, Java allows us to place a package in a JAR. We will place our application in its own package and then make a JAR of this package. Because we wish to run this application from the JAR, we must provide manifest information so that the application JAR knows where to find main() and the classpath for the *shapes.jar* file.

The testshape Package and *test.jar* We place our TestShapes program in its own package and bundle this program in a JAR file named *test.jar*. The TestShapes program imports the Circle and Rect classes from the johnston.shapes

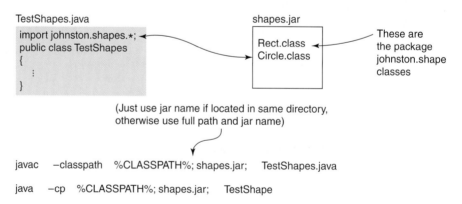

Figure 13-16
The *shapes.jar* contains the johnston.shapes package classes including *Circle.class* and *Rect.class*. Our *TestShapes.java* can import this package if we specify the location of the *shapes.jar* on the classpath.

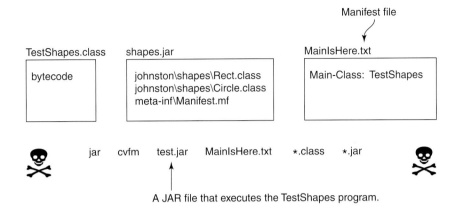

Manifest file

TestShapes.class

bytecode

shapes.jar

johnston\shapes\Rect.class johnston\shapes\Circle.class meta-inf\Manifest.mf

MainIsHere.txt

Main-Class: TestShapes

jar cvfm test.jar MainIsHere.txt *.class *.jar

A JAR file that executes the TestShapes program.

Figure 13-17
The next step is to create a JAR file that contains our TestShapes program. You might think a logical approach to this problem is to include the *shapes.jar* when you make testshape.jar. This in an incorrect approach.

package, which is bundled in a JAR file named *shapes.jar*. Do not panic at the sound of this! The steps are straightforward and once you've made one package and JARed it up, you can do any package. You will see that we have already performed all of these steps.

In order to package our TestShapes program, we need to add the package statement in the code and compile it with a -d option. Refer to line 6 in Program 13-4. The package name is testshapes. Program 13-4 is located on the text's CD in the \Ch13\ShapesDemo4\ folder. The TestShapes code is shown here:

```
1   //Program 13-4
2   //File: \ShapesDemo4\TestShapes.java
3
4   //We package our application in the testshapes package.
5
6   package testshapes;
7
8   import javax.swing.*; //for JFrame, JButton, JTextField, JLabel
9   import java.awt.*;        //for Container, GridLayout
10  import java.awt.event.*;  //for ActionListener, ActionEvent
11  import java.text.DecimalFormat;
12
13  //The johnston.shape package is contained in shapes.jar.
14  import johnston.shapes.Circle;
15  import johnston.shapes.Rect;
```

```
16
17
18   public class TestShapes extends JFrame implements ActionListener
19   {
20
21      //Yippee!!!  Here are our Circle and Rect objects!
22      Circle circle = new Circle();
23      Rect rect = new Rect();
24
25      //rest of class
26   }
```

Just to be sure our code executes, we place a copy of *shapes.jar* in the same directory as TestShapes, because TestShapes imports johnston.shapes. We must use the -classpath option stating the location of the *shapes.jar* file so that javac and TestShapes can find the package with the Circle and Rect classes. We are also building a package, so we must use the -d option (see Figure 13-18). The compile command for this program is seen here:

```
javac  -classpath  %CLASSPATH%; shapes.jar  -d .   TestShapes.java
```

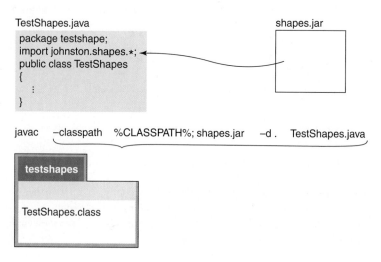

Figure 13-18
The *TestShapes.java* has a package statement in it and is compiled with the -d option. Because we are importing a package from a JAR file, we must use the classpath option to tell javac where *shapes.jar* is located.

After this statement is executed, there is a new folder named testshapes in our directory. It contains the *TestShapes.class* file. In order to run this program we must use the -classpath option again and reference the testshapes folder that contains our class. The statement to execute the program is:

```
java  -classpath  %CLASSPATH%;shapes.jar  testshapes/TestShapes
```

To create a JAR file of our testshapes package, we first create a manifest file with information concerning the class that contains main() and the classpath for the shapes.jar file. (The JAR file needs the same information that we had to provide in order to run this program from the command line.) The manifest information file is named *MainIsHere.txt* and it contains these two lines:

```
Main-Class: testshapes.TestShapes
Class-Path: shapes.jar
```

> **Note:** Be sure to have an Enter key after the last entry in the manifest file!

We create the JAR file with this command:

```
jar  cvfm  test.jar  MainIsHere.txt  testshapes/*.*
```

A double-click of the mouse verifies that our *test.jar* file executes the TestShapes program!

> **Note:** Class-Path: uses relative path URL format (relative path meaning relative to the *test.jar* file. This means that if the *shapes.jar* file was in a child directory of *testshapes.jar* named *MyJars*, then the *MainIsHere2.txt* file has this Class-Path statement.

```
Main-Class: testshapes/TestShapes
Class-Path: MyJars/shapes.jar
```

The associated jar command is:

```
jar  cvfm  test2.jar  MainIsHere2.txt  testshapes/*.*
```

If we place the *shapes.jar* in the *c:\JPT\JPTJars* directory, the *HereIsMain3.txt* manifest file must look like this:

```
Main-Class: testshapes.TestShapes
Class-Path: file://c:/JPT/JPTJars/shapes.jar
```

The associated jar command is:

```
jar  cvfm  test3.jar  MainIsHere3.txt  testshapes/*.*
```

The text's CD has these sample files in the *\Ch13\ShapesDemo4* folder.

13

More on CLASSPATHs

As your Java programs become more complicated and you begin using other Java Application Programming Interfaces, your CLASSPATH environment variable can become very long and unwieldy as it references many JAR files. Remember that each JAR file your program uses must be listed on the CLASSPATH.

In the previous examples we used the -classpath option to assist us in compiling and executing our programs. Appendix A shows the necessary steps for setting the CLASSPATH environment variable permanently. There is a third approach that allows us to set the CLASSPATH as needed using the command line "set" command. For example, in Program 13-2, once we created our *shapes.jar* file we had to use the -classpath to compile and run it (refer to Figure 13-15). We could have issued this command initially, from the command line in an MS-DOS Prompt window, setting our classpath to this directory:

```
SET CLASSPATH=C:\JPT\Ch13\ShapesDemo2\shapes.jar
```

Once accomplished, we can compile and run TestShapes without the -classpath option. This command sets the classpath to only the above path. We can preserve the operating system's CLASSPATH and place additional locations on it by entering:

```
SET CLASSPATH= %CLASSPATH%;C:\JPT\Ch13\ShapesDemo2\shapes.jar
```

▮13.6
Summary

This chapter reviewed the concept of a package in Java as we have used it (up to now) in our Java programs. Packages can be thought of a library of classes. In order to use a class from a package in our program, we must use the import statement with the package name at the top of our class file.

The new chapter material presented the required steps a programmer must take to place his or her classes in their own packages. Creating a package is straightforward. First, we include the package statement at the top of our source code containing the classes that are to be in the package. As it turns out, Java packages are also directory structures. The package statement tells the sequence about folders and subfolders that contain the package's *.class* files.

The package source code should be compiled with javac's -d option. Java automatically creates the package folder structure and places the *.class* files inside the correct folder. The javac's -d option allows the programmer to specify the location on the computer's disk for the places of this package. By using the . (dot), the programmer is telling Java to place the package in the current directory.

In order for another class to use a programmer-built class in a package, the package and class is imported—just like we did when we used prebuilt Java packages. The Java compiler (javac) and interpreter (java) must know where to look for the package. Java refers to the operating system's CLASSPATH environment

Chapter 13 ▮ Advanced Topics: Packages, Classpaths, and JARs variable to look for possible locations of classes and packages. (The CLASSPATH is configured in a similar manner to how we configured the PATH variable.) Normally, the CLASSPATH is set to the . (dot), meaning the current directory. If the package folder structure is located in the same folder as the code that is importing/using the package, and the CLASSPATH is set to the current directory, javac and java can find the package without problem. If the package is not located in the current directory, the programmer may use the javac and java -classpath option to tell Java where to find the package. The programmer may choose to edit the operating system's CLASSPATH variable to include the root of the package (a permanent solution) or use the SET CLASSPATH command at the command window (a temporary solution that is valid as long as that window remains open).

Java allows the programmer to bundle a package into a JAR file and then use the JAR file as a source for a program to import a package. The path and name of the JAR file (not just its location) must be referenced on the CLASSPATH. Also, a program that imports a package located in a JAR file can itself be packaged into a JAR file.

Lastly, we discussed the concept of package scope and showed how class members that do not have access specifiers have package scope by default. This means that class members within the package can all see and access other class member in the package, but package scope members are private to the world. This is a problem if programmers create classes, forget access specifiers, and then attempt to access these members from outside the package.

The concepts presented in this chapter cover the real-world situations encountered by professional Java programmers. Classes are written in packages, and packages are bundled into JAR files. JAR files are usually placed in a central location on a server and other programmers rely on their CLASSPATH settings in order to locate the packages. Whether you are writing small Java programs for a school project or a large engineering model, packages and CLASSPATHs will be in your Java future.

13

Getting Started with Java

Java Development Environments

We are going to build Java programs "from scratch" using the Java™ 2 Software Development Kit (J2SDK) Standard Edition 1.4.1_02 from Sun Microsystems, Inc. The source code for our programs will be written in a text editor such as jEdit or Microsoft's Notepad. (See Appendix B for installation and getting started with jEdit.) The source code files are saved to the disk and are compiled and run by typing commands in the MS-DOS Prompt window. Constructing programs from scratch enables the beginning Java programmer to understand every line of code and each step of the development process.

Appendix E references several Java Integrated Development Environments (IDEs). What is an IDE? An IDE provides the Java programmer with a complete set of tools; including a source editor, a compiler, a debugger, help, and documentation. The environment generates Java source code automatically and allows the programmer to execute the code with a push of a button. We neither include nor describe the use of any IDEs in this text because there are so many available it is hard to select just one. Once you become an expert at building programs from scratch, you are better able to judge these development environments. The source code produced by the IDE may be unfamiliar to the beginning Java programmer, because it uses a more efficient, yet more complicated approach in the way it organizes its classes. We prefer that the beginning programmer build his or her first programs from scratch before tackling a more complicated IDE.

We plan to start with simple programs. Our initial Java programs are written from the ground up by writing each line of Java code ourselves, compiling, and running the programs from the command line. The first tasks at hand are to install the J2SDK and set up our computer environment in preparation for writing and running Java programs.

The J2SDK SE

The J2SDK SE for Windows is provided on the CD that accompanies this text. The SDK contains all of the necessary files for a programmer to write his or her own Java programs and run these programs from the command line within an MS-DOS Prompt window. This executable file is located on the CD in the folder named Sun J2SDK. (The latest edition of the SDK can be found at Sun Microsystem's website: *java.sun.com.*) The associated documentation for this J2SDK can be found at *java.sun.com*, and we recommend that the programmer download and install this on his or her machine for easy reference.

Installation Procedures for the J2SDK on Microsoft Windows Platforms

Before we are able to write any Java programs, we must install the Java software and set up the computer's environment so it knows about the Java environment. These instructions assume your computer is running one of the Windows Operating Systems: Windows 98, Windows 2000, Windows NT, Windows XP, or Windows ME. For other operating systems on different hardware platforms, refer to the *java.sun.com* website for installation instructions.

1. On the text CD, in the folder named Sun J2SDK, locate the file *j2sdk-1_4_1_02-windows-i586.exe* on the CD accompanying this text. This file is the installation file for the J2SDK SE version 1.4.1.

2. For a safe installation, close all other programs (such as Word or Excel).

3. Double-click the *j2sdk* executable file. If you are running NT, 2000, or XP, you must have administrative rights in order to install the software.

4. Allow the software to install on your machine. In this appendix, we assume the software was installed into the *C:\j2sdk1.4.1* directory.

5. As the software installs on your computer, accept all of the software components presented in the checklist (regarding what to install) and select the appropriate browsers (Internet Explorer and/or Netscape). You will see a pop-up box with a message that reads "Setting up Java 2 Runtime Environment."

Open MyComputer or Windows Explorer and examine the new folders you now have on your computer. Figure A-1 illustrates what you should see.

Open the bin directory and examine the various files located there. Refer to Figure A-2. You should see *appletviewer.exe*, *jar.exe*, *java.exe*, *javac.exe*, and many other executable files.

These executable files are the files that we use to compile and run our Java programs from scratch. In order for us to build and run our programs from the

A

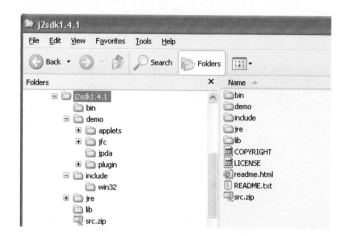

Figure A-1
The j2skd1.4.1 directory structure after the installation procedure is complete, as seen in a Windows XP environment.

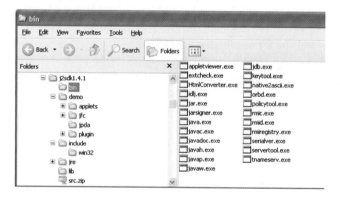

Figure A-2
The j2skd1.4.1\bin directory (as seen in a Windows XP environment) contains the executable files for compiling and running Java programs from scratch.

MS-DOS Prompt command line, we must (1) have access to, and (2) be able to execute the files located in the *C:\j2sdk1.4.1\bin* folder. Table A-1 summarizes each of the executable files.

The MS-DOS Prompt Command Line or Command Window

We use the Java compiler, *javac.exe*, the Java interpreter, *java.exe*, and the Java applet viewer utility, *appletviewer.exe* for our first Java programs. We perform these Java operations from the MS-DOS Prompt command window (the

TABLE A-1
A summary of Java bin directory executable files (partial).

File	Purpose
appletviewer.exe	The Java applet viewer utility. The appletviewer reads an HTML file and loads and executes the referenced applet *.class file.
jar.exe	The Java Archive utility. The Java archive utility creates and opens Java archive files. The *.jar files are similar to zipped *.zip files.
javac.exe	The Java compiler. The Java source code (stored in a file with extension *.java) is read by this compiler, which checks to see that the source code is grammatically correct and does not violate any rules of syntax. If there are no errors, the compiler produces bytecode in a *.class file. The compiler results are listed on the screen.
java.exe	The Java interpreter. The Java interpreter loads the bytecode (found in the *.class file generated by the Java compiler) and then executes the Java program.
javadoc.exe	The Java Docs program is used to generate Java documentation from the source code. Special comments /** */ are used by javadoc.

Command Prompt window). In Microsoft Windows operating systems, we open a MS-DOS Prompt window. This window allows us to enter the various Java commands at the prompt (blinking cursor). Figure A-3 shows examples of a MS-DOS window in Windows 98 and XP environments. There are different ways to find

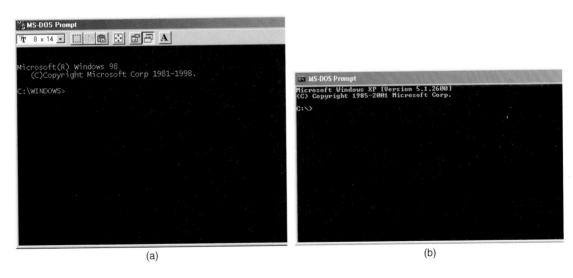

(a) (b)

Figure A-3
An MS-DOS Prompt window on (a) Windows 98 and (b) Windows XP machines.

A

Operating system	Window location
Windows 98	Start → Programs → MS-DOS Prompt
Windows XP, NT, and 2000	Some configurations may have an icon for the Command Prompt on the desktop. Look for the small black icon labeled MS-Dos Prompt or Command Prompt. It also can be found in the Start menu.

and open the command window (depending on which operating system your computer is running). Table A-2 presents information for locating a command window on your machine. For ease of use, place a shortcut to this window on your desktop.

MS-DOS Commands

Java programmers must be able to navigate their way around the file directory system from the command line—in whatever operating system they find on the machine. For our work on a Windows machine, we use the standard MS-DOS commands. (The UNIX operating system commands are similar, but the reader should refer to a UNIX reference for exact commands.) A partial listing of the standard MS-DOS commands are shown in Table A-3. These are a few commands we need for our Java work. The command examples are shown in bold type.

TABLE A-3
Partial listing of MS-DOS commands.

Command	Purpose and example
cd directory_name	Change the current directory. C:\Windows> **cd System** Here we change the current directory from the Windows directory to the C:\Windows\System directory
cd partial_directory_name*	Change the current directory using a partial name and *. You do not need to type the entire directory name as long as you give it a unique portion of the name. You can use the * to designate "the rest" of the name. For example, if the JPT folder had Ch2samples and Ch2problems directories, you could change into the sample directory by entering: C:\ cd **JPT** C:\JPT > **cd Ch2sam*** C:\JPT\Ch2samples>

(continued on page 761)

A

Command	Purpose and example
	or just enter this brief one-line command: C:\ **cd JPT\Ch2s***
cd ..	Change directory. Using the two dots (periods) takes you up one directory level higher. C:\Windows> **cd ..** will change the current directory to C:\
cd full_path\directory	Changes the current directory to the one shown with the complete path. C:\Windows> **cd C:\JPT** Here we change the current directory to be the C:\JPT directory.
md directory_name	Make a new directory. C:\> **md JPT** Here we create a new directory called JPT located at the root of the C drive. We could then move into that directory by typing C:\ > **cd JPT**
dir	Directory listing, shows the files in the current directory. This example shows all of the files in the JPT directory. C:\JPT>**dir**
dir /p	Directory listing, shows the files a page at a time, pausing so that the user may see all of the files. C:\JPT> **dir /p**
dir /w	Directory listing, shows the files in the wide format. C:\JPT> **dir /w**
dir *.extension	Directory listing using the wildcard and file extension. For example, using dir *.java command, will only show the files with *.java extension. C:\JPT> **dir *.java**
dir *.	Directory listing that shows all of the files without extensions as well as the directories within this directory. C:\> **dir *.**
Drive letter:	By entering a different drive letter, you change the current directory to the new drive. C:\Windows> **D:** D:\> Change the current directory to the D drive.

For practice, bring up a Command Window or MS-DOS Prompt window and navigate to the *C:\j2sdk1.4.1\bin* directory. Once there, type the command javac (Enter key), which executes the Java compiler. Notice that the current directory must be *C:\j2sdk1.4.1\bin* in order for the javac command to be executed. The command sequence (commands in bold) from a Windows 98 MS-DOS Prompt

A

for this exercise is:

```
C:\Windows> cd ..
C:\ > cd j2sdk1.4.1
C:\ j2sdk1.4.1 > cd bin
C:\ j2sdk1.4.1\bin > javac
```

After you have entered the javac command, you should see the usage and option switches for javac Java compiler. These options and switches are used by the programmer to give the compiler special commands. For example, if the programmer wished to use debugging information, he or she would enter the -g switch. (Do not worry about this now!)

Setting the Path to J2SDK's bin Directory

As we develop our Java programs, we want to organize them into appropriate folders on our computer's hard disk. We need to access J2SDK's bin directory from anywhere on our computer; therefore, we need to set the *path* in our operating system so that it knows where to find javac, java, appletviewer, or any of the other Java executable files. A path is a directive in the computer operating system that tells the computer to "go look in these other places" if it cannot find a program that it is trying to run. (Your computer may have many different directories on the path statement.) Figure A-4 illustrates this concept. Assume that we place our Java programs in a subdirectory of JPT (for *Java Programming Today*). We want to compile and run our programs inside this directory. The operating system needs to know where to find the J2SDK programs (javac, java, etc.) because they are not located in the JPT directory.

Setting the computer's operating system path is straightforward. The mechanics of setting the path depend on which operating system your computer is running. We need to add the *C:\j2sdk1.4.1\bin* directory into the computer's PATH command. Once this is accomplished, the computer's operating system knows to look in this directory for Java executable files.

Windows 98   There are several ways to set the path in Windows 98. We suggest that you run the *msconfig* program from the Start menu.

1. Start → Run (type in *msconfig* in the Open edit box)
2. Select the Autoexec.bat tab
3. Add the path **C:\j2skd1.4.1\bin;** in the PATH line. (Be sure to remember the semicolon if you place this statement within the path statement. The semicolon is a separator and is not required if you place this at the end of the path name.) Refer to Figure A-5.

While we are working with the System Configuration Utility for a Windows 98 machine, add the doskey statement into your Autoexec.bat. The DOS Key statement (doskey statement) is a convenient tool when the programmer is entering commands by typing them into an MS-DOS window. This command line utility allows

A

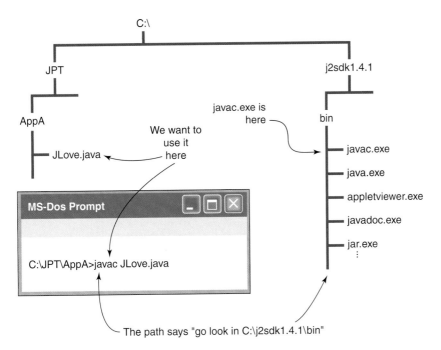

Figure A-4
The operating system path must include the C:\j2sdk1.4.1\bin directory so Java programs can be compiled and run from anywhere on our computer.

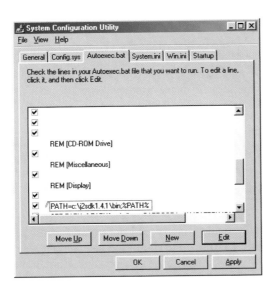

Figure A-5
The System Configuration Utility window in Windows 98 showing the Java bin directory in the PATH statement.

A

The J2SDK SE

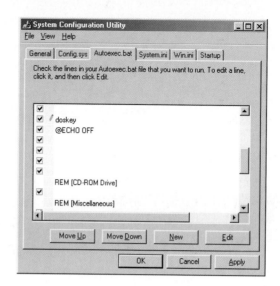

Figure A-6
The DOS Key program is added to the Autoexec.bat tab in the Windows 98 System Configuration Utility.

the user to make use of the arrow keys on the keyboard to repeat and edit command line commands. Pressing the up/down arrows causes the previous/next commands to be retyped automatically on the command line. Left/right arrows provide easy editing capabilities. Figure A-6 illustrates setting the DOSKey program in the Autoexec.bat tab for a Windows 98 machine. Reboot the computer for the changes to the autoexec.bat to become effective.

Windows 2000 and Window XP   The Windows 2000/XP path is set via an Environment Variable located in the Systems Properties window. You must have administrative rights in order to set the Environment variables.

1. In Windows 2000 and XP, go to Start → Control Panel → System
2. Double-click the System icon, which brings up the System Properties dialog box.
3. Click the Advanced tab.
4. Press the Environment Variables button.
5. In the System Variable window, select Path and then press the Edit button. Add **C:\j2sdk1.4.1\bin** at the end of the path variable. Refer to Figures A-7 and A-8. (If you place it within the command string, use a semicolon at the end, and remember—no spaces.)

The arrow keys in Windows XP and Windows 2000 are enabled to repeat command line commands, and it is not necessary to add the doskey program in these operating

Figure A-7
The Environment Variables input window in Windows XP.

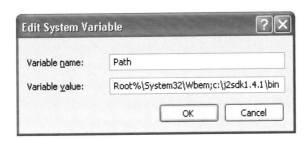

Figure A-8
The Edit System Variable input window showing the Path name and value in XP.

systems. Reboot the system to ensure that the changes to the environment variables are effective.

Test Your Path Setting Once your computer has been rebooted, you may now test that the path settings are in effect and that your operating system can find the C:\j2sdk1.4.1\bin directory. Open a command window and type the PATH command. You should see the c:\j2sdk1.4.1\bin in the path statement. Next, type the javac command. You should see the Java compiler usage and switch settings. Figure A-9 illustrates these two commands on a Windows XP machine.

A

Figure A-9

Verifying that the path contains c:\j2skd1.4.1\bin setting, and the operating system can execute the javac command. (Shown on a Windows XP system.)

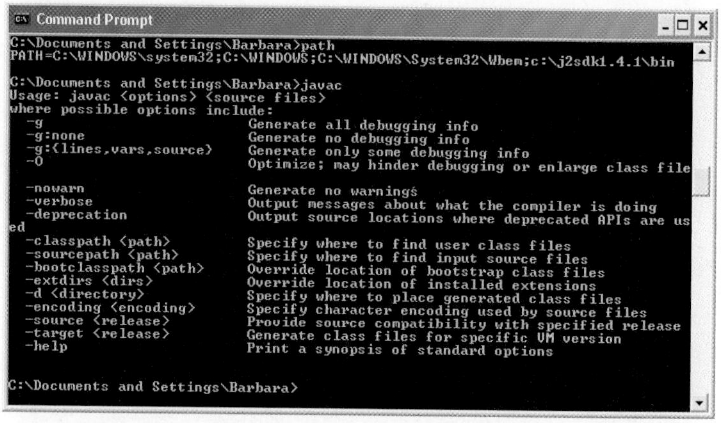

```
Command Prompt                                                              _ □ x
C:\Documents and Settings\Barbara>path
PATH=C:\WINDOWS\system32;C:\WINDOWS;C:\WINDOWS\System32\Wbem;c:\j2sdk1.4.1\bin

C:\Documents and Settings\Barbara>javac
Usage: javac <options> <source files>
where possible options include:
  -g                        Generate all debugging info
  -g:none                   Generate no debugging info
  -g:{lines,vars,source}    Generate only some debugging info
  -O                        Optimize; may hinder debugging or enlarge class file

  -nowarn                   Generate no warnings
  -verbose                  Output messages about what the compiler is doing
  -deprecation              Output source locations where deprecated APIs are us
ed
  -classpath <path>         Specify where to find user class files
  -sourcepath <path>        Specify where to find input source files
  -bootclasspath <path>     Override location of bootstrap class files
  -extdirs <dirs>           Override location of installed extensions
  -d <directory>            Specify where to place generated class files
  -encoding <encoding>      Specify character encoding used by source files
  -source <release>         Provide source compatibility with specified release
  -target <release>         Generate class files for specific VM version
  -help                     Print a synopsis of standard options

C:\Documents and Settings\Barbara>
```

Running Our First Java Programs

We are now ready to write and run our first Java program. We will write and run a Java application and a Java applet. Before we write the code, create a new folder for our Java files. In these examples, we use the folder C:\JPT. We write the code from scratch by typing the lines of source code in the Notepad editor.

Our First Java Application

The Java application program here is very simple. It writes the phrase I love Java!!! to the command window and then exits the program. Open the Notepad editor and enter the following Java code. Save the file with the name *JLove.java*.

```java
//File:  JLove.java
public class JLove
{
      public static void main(String args[] )
      {
            System.out.println("I love Java!!! ");
      }
}
```

> **Note:** Older versions of Notepad tack on a ".txt" extension when you perform the initial save operation. This results in the *JLove.java* file being saved as *JLove.java.txt*. Newer versions of Notepad, such as with XP, do not write this default extension. Be sure to check how your version of Notepad saves its files. If you add quotation marks around the filename (such as "JLove.java") when you save in Notepad, it will not add the ".txt" extension. Better yet, install and use jEdit!

A

Once the *JLove.java* file is located in the C:\JPT folder, open a command prompt window and change directory to the JPT folder. Check that the *JLove.java* file is in the folder (and named correctly). Now enter the command:

C:\JPT> **javac JLove.java** (Enter key).

If there are no compile errors, the command prompt is presented. (The directory command, dir, shows that we now have a JLove.class file in our directory.) Type the command:

C:\JPT> **java JLove** (Enter key)

This command executes the Java program, and we see the phrase I love Java!!! in the window. Figure A-10 illustrates these steps.

Our First Java Applet

Java applets run in web browsers (such as Internet Explorer or Netscape) and therefore need a HTML file. All web browsers read HTML files, and the HTML file references (by name) which Java class file should be loaded and executed. The HTML

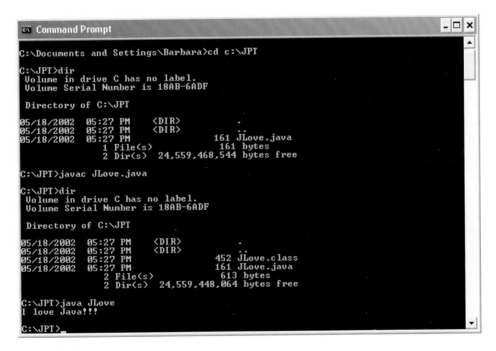

Figure A-10
Steps using the command prompt for compiling and running our first Java application program.

A

file also specifies the window size (and it can pass other parameters into the applet). J2SDK provides an applet viewer utility called appletviewer.

In this first Java applet, we "paint" the phrase "I love Java!!!" into an applet window at the position 25,25 (twenty-five pixels from the left edge of the window, and twenty-five pixels from the top. The window is 300 × 100 pixels.) Use the Notepad editor to enter the following lines of source code and save the *JLoveApplet.java* file.

```
//File:  JLoveApplet.java
//Load the javax.swing's JApplet
import javax.swing.JApplet;

//Load the awt.Graphics class for our use in this program
import java.awt.Graphics;
public class JLoveApplet extends JApplet
{
        public void paint(Graphics g )
        {
                g.drawString(" I Love Java!!! ", 25, 25);
        }
}
```

The JLoveApplet.java file must be compiled with the Java compiler. The command for compiling applets is the same as for application programs. Assuming the applet file is saved in the C:\JPT folder, the command is:

C:\JPT > **javac JLoveApplet.java**

The associated HTML file for this applet can be entered in Notepad and saved in the C:\JPT folder with the *JLoveApplet.html* filename. The HTML file dictates the size of the window. The *JLoveApplet.class* file and *JLoveApplet.html* file must be located in the same directory.

```
<html>
<applet code = "JLoveApplet.class"   width = 300   height = 100 >
</applet>
</html>
```

The appletviewer command references the HTML file:

C:\JPT > **appletviewer JLoveApplet.html**

Figure A-11 illustrates the commands to run this applet, and Figure A-12 shows the resulting applet running in the J2SDK Applet Viewer browser window.

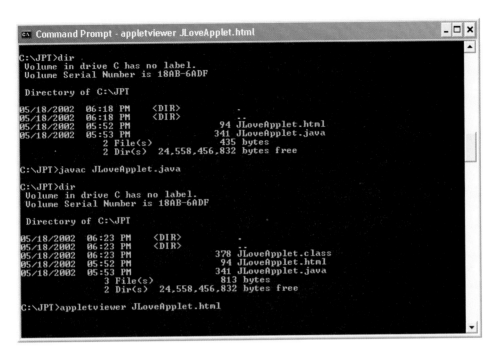

Figure A-11
Steps using the command prompt for compiling and running our first Java applet.

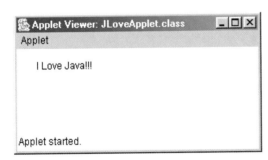

Figure A-12
Steps using the command prompt for compiling and running our first Java program.

J2SDK Documentation

There is a complete set of documentation for J2SDK, that is available (for free) from java.sun.com, and we encourage the reader to download and install the documentation on his or her Java development computer. Figure A-13 shows the opening

A

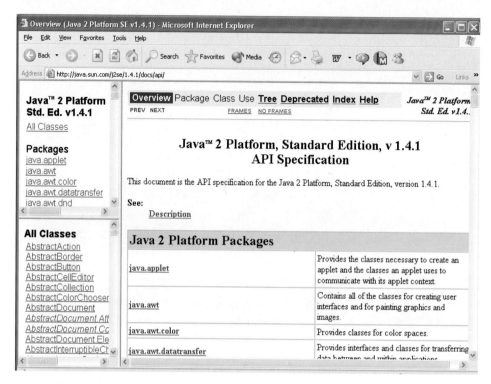

Figure A-13
The Java 2 Platform API Specification which contains complete documentation of the J2SDK.
Copyright 1993–2003 Sun Microsystems, Inc. Reprinted with permission.

page for this documentation, and we cover what the various items are (such as packages and classes) in the early chapters of this text. If you are planning to access this documentation directly using by the web, the address is http://java.sun.com/j2se/1.4.1/docs/api/

> **Note:** The J2SDK package that you installed on your computer contains a demo directory that includes sample programs. The *C:\j2sdk1.4.1\demo\applets* directory contains many examples that illustrate how many Java classes are used. Remember to check out these demo programs as you travel through the text's material.

jEdit, a Java Source Code Editor

One of the most important tools a software developer uses is the source code editor. A source code editor is a program that allows the programmer to enter and edit his or her source code by typing lines of code. *Java Programming Today* includes jEdit for our readers. It is located on the text's CD.

The jEdit software is a general-purpose source code editor written by a world-wide team of programmers led by Slava Pestov. The software is open source and free to users. The jEdit website is www.jedit.org, and is seen in Figure B-1. The reader is encouraged to visit the website and investigate the latest code and developments for jEdit.

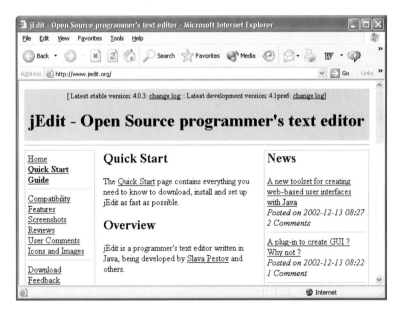

Figure B-1
The jEdit website, found at www.jedit.org, contains the latest software and news concerning the jEdit source code editor program.
Reprinted with permission.

We will be building our Java programs from scratch in this text, meaning that we will type in each line of code instead of using an IDE tool. The jEdit program is designed to assist the programmer as he or she edits the code. jEdit provides many wonderful editing tools, including automatic indentation, keyword highlighting, brace matching, line numbering, and formatted printing to name a few. The team of jEdit programmers continues to develop plugins for jEdit. Plugins are separate programs that are designed to work seamlessly with jEdit software, providing new tools and capabilities to the Java programmer. Although a new programmer may not understand why these features are nice (some may say essential), time and practice will convince you of jEdit's usefulness.

How to Install jEdit

In order to install jEdit, you must have already installed J2SDK and set your PATH variable as we described in Appendix A. On the text's CD, in the folder named "jEdit," you will find the *jedit403install.jar* and *jedit40manual-letter.pdf* files. The JAR file is an executable Java archive file that contains the jEdit software. The PDF file is the "jEdit 4.0 User's Guide" document. The User's Guide is an Adobe Portable Document Format (PDF) file and can be opened and read and printed by Adobe's Acrobat Reader software.[1] If your computer does not already have the Acrobat Reader software, it is free and available for download from www.adobe.com.

The jEdit software included with this text is for any operating system. The instructions below are for installing jEdit on a Windows-based machine. We refer the reader to the www.jedit.org website for installation instructions for MacOS X, Linux, Unix, or OS/2 operating systems.

The steps for installing jEdit on a Windows machine are straightforward.

1. Copy the *jedit403install.jar* file into a location on your hard disk, such as *C:\temp*.

2. Open an MS-DOS Prompt window and enter the following commands. Figure B-2 illustrates them.

   cd c:\temp
   java –jar jedit403install.jar

3. You will see the jEdit installation window, seen in Figure B-3. Fill out the requested information at each screen, clicking Next to move to the next step. Following these few steps installs jEdit on your machine.

4. When jEdit has successfully been installed on your machine, you will see a successful installation window and a jEdit icon on your desktop. Double-click this icon with your left mouse button and you are ready to go!

---

[1] Adobe Acrobat Reader® is free software from Adobe Systems Incorporated.

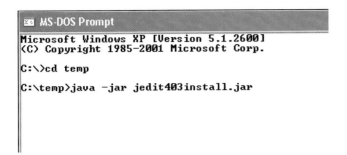

Figure B-2
The commands for installing the jEdit software from an MS-DOS Prompt window.
The *jedit403install.jar* file is located in *C:\temp*.

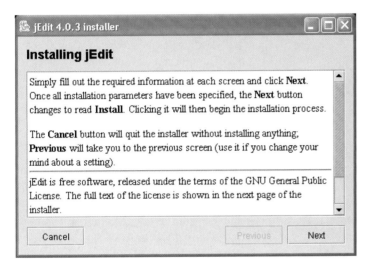

Figure B-3
The first of several windows shown to the programmer as the jEdit installation program executes. The programmer should answer the questions and press the "Next" button to proceed to the following installation step.

Using jEdit

A double-click on the jEdit icon begins the jEdit program. The first time you bring up the editor, the jEdit Help and Welcome window is presented. This window, shown in Figure B-4, is readily available to the jEdit user by pressing Help → jEdit Help on the menu (or the F1 key). Spend time going through the help windows to familiarize yourself with the jEdit's many features.

B

Figure B-4
The jEdit Help window provides full documentation for the jEdit user. It is available by pressing Help → jEdit Help on the menu (or the F1 key).

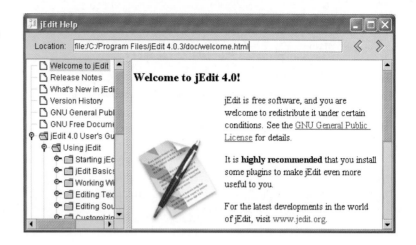

The menu and toolbar items are located at the top of the jEdit window. A portion of the window is seen in Figure B-5. Menu items are grouped by general purpose (File, Search, Utilities, etc.) and commonly used tools are found in the toolbar. Tooltips are provided to the user as he or she places the mouse cursor over a toolbar item.

A Brand New File: *jEditDemo.java*

Let's type in a brand new Java program. By doing so, we can see the basic mechanics of using jEdit. Opening the jEdit software, we see that the current file *is "Untitled-1 C:\Program Files\jEdit 4 0 3\."* This simple program we are about to write will pop up a message box that says "Hi from jEditDemo." As we begin entering the source code, jEdit shows the lines of code in black (see Figure B-6).

jEdit will help the programmer with the source code if it knows the type of file. For our use, we are building a *.java* file. Once we save the file with a *.java*

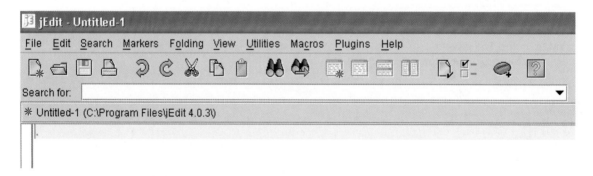

Figure B-5
The jEdit window has a full range of menu items and a toolbar with commonly used features.

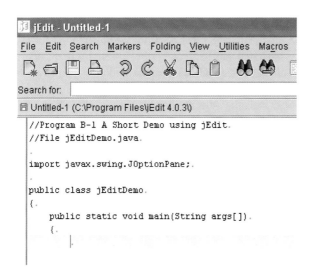

Figure B-6
As we begin entering code, all of the words and lines are shown in black. The file has yet to be saved.

extension, jEdit can now apply color coding for the various lines and keywords. We save our Java program file, named *jEditDemo.java* in the AppB directory (see Figure B-7). The comment lines are in a different color than the source lines and the Java keywords are shown in bold.

Figure B-7
Once a file has been saved with the *.java* extension, jEdit can now highlight and color code the various source code lines.

Two useful features of jEdit include an indicator of whether or not the file has been saved. There is a small red disk icon located beside the file name and path if the file has been changed but has not yet been saved. Often, beginning programmers will make changes in their source code and forget to save the file. A quick glance at the jEdit window and red disk icon provides the needed cue that the file has not been saved with the current changes. Press File → Save or the disk (save) icon on the toolbar and jEdit saves the file contents.

The brace-matching utility shows the associated open-close brace pairs in the source code. As your code becomes more complicated, it can be difficult to locate the sets of braces. If you do not have the correct number of opening/closing braces, the code will not compile. Examine the completed program code in Figure B-8. You can see the red disk indicator telling us that there are unsaved changes in this file. You can also see the angle bracket on the left margin showing the beginning and ending braces. It is possible to see this brace-pairing graphic by placing the cursor on the right side of the brace in question—jEdit then draws this angle bracket showing you what it believes to be the associated brace pair.

jEdit Allows You to Edit Many Files at Once

As you gain knowledge and expertise in Java, there are many times you will find yourself editing several Java source code files at once. jEdit allows you to see and edit several files at once by using the split horizontally and split vertically toolbar

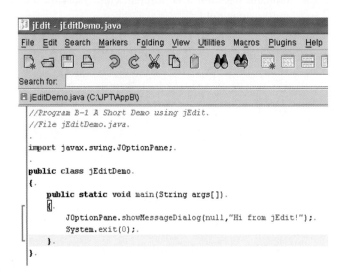

Figure B-8
The brace pairs can be seen by the automatic brace-matching utility in jEdit. Place the cursor on the right side of any brace and its pair will be identified by the angle bracket located in the left margin. The red disk symbol beside the file name indicates that the file has unsaved changes.

B

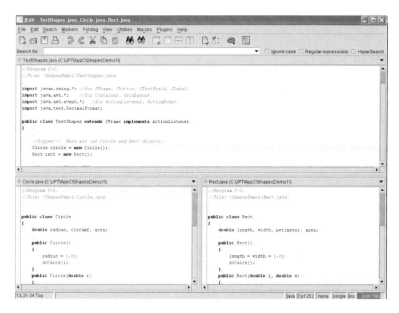

Figure B-9
Many files can be opened and displayed in jEdit by using the horizontal or vertical split toolbar controls. Here the three different files are shown in three edit windows.

controls. Figure B-9 shows the three Java files that constitute a Java program. This figure is small, and details of the code are not clearly visible. The important thing to learn from this figure is that you can see and edit many files at one time using jEdit. Simply open the desired file and press one of the split toolbar controls. Using the pull down list located at the top of each text area, you can select the file that appears in that editing window.

Explore jEdit

There are many more features in jEdit that the more experienced Java programmer will find useful. We leave the task of exploring jEdit to the new programmer but include a few hints here.

- jEdit's Utilities → Global Options provide a wealth of options for controlling your version of the jEdit software. Options provide you the ability to determine the appearance, color scheme, short cuts, and printing, just to name a few.

- jEdit provides line numbering for the current window in the View → Line Numbers menu item.

B

- jEdit Plugins are available at the www.jedit.org website. You may use the jEdit Plugin Manager to assist you in determining the purpose of each plugin. SpeedJava provides pick lists, a very handy tool for the Java developer! ThumbWheel, JCompiler, JarMaker, and SpellChecker are just a few of the other plugins available. The plugins are a continual work in progress by the jEdit team, who are improving and expanding the plugin capabilities with each release. Explore the jEdit website to learn more. You will need to be connected to the Internet in order to use the Plugin Manager.

- jEdit may also be used as an editor for other languages.

Bits, Bytes, Hexadecimal Notation, and Unicode™

Computer Memory and Disks

Computers store pieces of information in the form of bits, which are commonly referred to as 1s and 0s. Computer systems use several types of physical materials for storing and accessing data. Fundamentally, all these systems maintain the bits of data in one of two states, which are interpreted as 1s and 0s. For example, magnetic media such as floppy and hard disks are similar to old phonograph records, and the tracks are charged into positive or negative states. Random access memory (RAM) in personal computers is made up of computer chips that have digital logic with two distinct voltage states, often referred to as high and low. This two-state representation for data storage is known as binary. Table C-1 summarizes the two-state storage methods for computers.

TABLE C-1
Computer Media

Type of material	Where is it?	How does it work?	Note
Magnetic material	Floppy disk, zip disks, computer hard disks	Disk head sets the polarity on the media	Very important to keep magnets away from disks and computers because they can remagnetize them.
Digital logic	Random access memory (RAM)	Electronic chips have voltage values set high or low	Data in RAM is lost if the power is turned off.

C

Bits and Bytes

When data is read from a floppy disk, the positive and negative regions are interpreted as a series of 1s and 0s. This continuous stream of 1s and 0s is grouped into 8-bit sections, or bytes. Eight bits make up 1 byte of data, and 4 bits represent $\frac{1}{2}$ byte, or a nibble.

Byte Formats: ASCII, EBCDIC, and Unicode

In the days before Java, there were two standard conventions for interpreting the series of bits: the American Standard Code for Information Interchange (ASCII) and the Extended Binary Coded Decimal Interchange Code (EBCDIC). PCs use the ASCII notation for interpreting bits, whereas mainframes and some minicomputers use the EBCDIC format. Table C-2 illustrates four different bit patterns and their resultant character interpretation for ASCII and EBCDIC format. Notice how the bit pattern "01010000" represents the letter "P" in ASCII and "&" in EBCDIC.

Remember that Java programs are intended to be executed worldwide on many types of computer systems. It is impossible to expect the code to run consistently if the software bit patterns have different interpretations on different machines. To solve this problem, Java designers adopted the Unicode™ Standard[1] (www.unicode.org). The Unicode Standard describes the specifications to produce consistent encoding of the world's characters and symbols. The Unicode Standard is maintained by the Unicode® Consortium, a nonprofit organization made up of members from Adobe, Compaq, CISCO Systems, HP Invent, IBM, Apple, Sun Microsystems, Microsoft, and many others. You may see the list of consortium members at www.unicode.org/consortium/memblogo.html. Before

TABLE C-2

Byte Format Conventions

Bit pattern	Hex notation	In ASCII (on a PC)	In EBCDIC (on a mainframe)
0101 0000	0x50	P	&
0110 0001	0x61	a	/
0100 1100	0x4C	L	<
0110 1111	0x6F	o	?

---

[1]Unicode® Consortium is a registered trademark, and Unicode™ is a trademark of Unicode, Inc.

we examine Unicode characters, we must introduce the concept of hexadecimal notation.

Hexadecimal Notation

To read the series of 1s and 0s, computer scientists have adopted *hexadecimal (hex) notation* as a way to write and understand bit patterns in bytes. This *hex* notation provides an easy and efficient way to interpret bit patterns and is used when addressing computer memory. The Java programmer will see hex notation when he or she works with Unicode characters.

All programmers should have an appreciation of the complex science that underlies computer programming languages. The beginning Java programmer needs to know three facts concerning hexadecimal characters: (1) Computer memory is addressed and reported in hexadecimal notation. (2) Array and object references contain the hex address of where these objects are stored in the computer's memory. (3) The characters and symbols in Unicode are referenced by using hexadecimal notation.

As beginning Java programmers, we do not worry about seeing the memory addresses for our variables. The JVM handled that aspect of our programs for us. We do need to be familiar with hexadecimal notation when we are working with Unicode characters. Let's explore how hexadecimal notation works and see how the bit patterns can be written in shorthand by using hex characters.

Base 10 Decimal, Base 2 Binary, Base 16 Hexadecimal

We are all familiar with counting in decimal notation (base 10) because that notation is our normal counting method. The symbol *0* represents none and the symbol *1* represents one. We use the symbol *5* to represent the number of fingers on one hand. But when asked how many eggs in a dozen, we do not have one symbol to represent twelve. We need to use two of our symbols, a 1 and a 2, to represent twelve. Ten different symbols are used for writing numeric values. These symbols are 0, 1, 2, 3, 4, 5, 6, 7, 8, and 9. Our counting scheme has an individual symbol for representing zero through nine, but when we need to represent ten objects, we must use a combination of our symbols. We write ten using 10 (we have started reusing our symbols).

Because computer data is stored in bits, we have only two symbols, 1 and 0, with which to write all the information for the computer. (Our alphabet uses twenty-six symbols to represent the English language.) All computer data is written in this two-symbol language known as *base 2* or *binary*. Since binary notation is so cumbersome, computer scientists use *base 16*, also known as *hexadecimal*, as a shorthand notation for representing the binary data. Hexadecimal notation uses sixteen separate symbols, 0 to 9 and A, B, C, D, E, and F. Table C-3 shows the different base representations for the numeric values 0 to 20.

C

Numeric Values and Different Bases

Numeric amount	Base 2	Base 10	Base 16	Notes
Zero	0	0	0	
One	1	1	1	
Two	10	2	2	Base 2: start reusing symbols
Three	11	3	3	
Four	100	4	4	Base 2: we now use three symbols
Five	101	5	5	
Six	110	6	6	
Seven	111	7	7	
Eight	1000	8	8	
Nine	1001	9	9	
Ten	1010	10	A	Base 10: start reusing symbols
Eleven	1011	11	B	
Twelve	1100	12	C	
Thirteen	1101	13	D	
Fourteen	1110	14	E	
Fifteen	1111	15	F	
Sixteen	10000	16	10	Base 16: carry the 1 and start reusing symbols
Seventeen	10001	17	11	
Eighteen	10010	18	12	
Nineteen	10011	19	13	
Twenty	10100	20	14	Base 10: increment 1 to 2 and start the ones column at 0 again.

■ TABLE C-4
Hex and Bit Patterns

Hex pattern	Number of bytes	Details	Bit pattern
0xFF24	2	0xF = 1111, 0x2 = 0010, 0x4 = 0100	1111 1111 0010 0100 F F 2 4
0xFA1E	2	0xA = 1010, 0x1 = 0001, 0xE = 1110	1111 1010 0001 1110 F A 1 E

C

By combining the 8-bit byte and hexadecimal notation, computer scientists have a method where one digit (or symbol) can be used to represent 4 bits, and two hex digits (symbols) can be used to represent 1 byte of data. Decimal notation (0 to 9) would not be practical to use because it requires two digits to represent ten through fifteen.

Individual bit patterns can be obtained from hexadecimal notation. Two examples are shown in Table C-4. (Refer to Table C-3 for actual hex values shown in detail.)

Introduction to Unicode

The Unicode Standard has adopted the ASCII character set, providing the basic Western alphabet including A–Z, a–z, 0–9, and the symbols on the keyboard. Unicode provides tens of thousands of letters from any of the major languages in the world, including Greek, Arabic, Bengali, Thai, and Cyrillic. Unicode also describes mathematical, musical, Braille, and Dingbats symbols. Visit the www.unicode.org website for a complete list of the supported languages.

Java Programming Today presents four tables at the end of this appendix. They illustrate four sets of Unicode characters. These tables, reproduced with permission of the Unicode Consortium, are Controls and Basic Latin (Table C-6), Greek and Coptic (Table C-8), Mathematical Operators (Table C-9), and the programmer favorite, Dingbats (Table C-10). The reader should visit the Unicode website for the most up-to-date versions of these tables and references.

In Program C-1, we write a series of Unicode characters from each of the Unicode tables into a JFrame. In order to write these seven characters "J A V A" (four letters and three spaces), we first write the Unicode sequence for the letter "J." The "J" can be found in Table C-6 on page 787. Locate the letter "J" on this table. It is located in the column labeled "004" (read across the top of the table) and on the row labeled "A." Therefore, the letter "J" is 004A. Notice that there are 16 rows on this table, each row corresponds to a hex character.

To write a space, we need to find the Unicode sequence for a space. The Unicode sequence 0000–0020 (first two columns) represents the thirty-two various control sequences. Table C-7 shows the meaning for each of these control sequences. We can see that the hex sequence "0020" is a space. The letter "A" can be found at "0041" and the "V" is "0056."

In order to see our "J A V A" characters, we use the escape sequence "\u" for Unicode, and can write the sequence like this:

```
String output;

//Hardcode a space in the String using \u0020.
output = "\u004A\u0020\u0041\u0020\u0056\u0020\u0041";
g.drawString(output, x,y);
```

C

or like this:

```
String output;
output = "\u004A" + " " + "\u0041" + " " + "\u0056" + " " + "\u0041";
g.drawString(output, x,y);
```

Here is the complete program. Figure C-1 shows the output from this program.

```
1   //Program C-1
2   //File: UnicodeDemo.java
3
4   //Write a series of Unicode characters into a frame.
5
6   import java.awt.*;
7   import javax.swing.JFrame;
8   import java.awt.Color;
9
10
11  public class UnicodeDemo extends JFrame
12  {
13
14    public static void main( String[] args )
15    {
16          UnicodeDemo ud = new UnicodeDemo();
17          ud.setDefaultCloseOperation( EXIT_ON_CLOSE );
18    }
19
20    public UnicodeDemo()            //class constructor method
21    {
22
23          setSize( 375, 225 );      //set the window size
24          setTitle("A Demo of Unicode Characters" );
25          show();
26    }
27
28    public void paint( Graphics g )
29    {
```

```java
30          this.setBackground(Color.white);
31          g.setFont( new Font("Ariel", Font.BOLD, 18));
32          String output = "";
33          g.setColor(Color.magenta);
34
35          int x = 15, y = 50, yIncr = 22;
36          g.drawString("Here are some ASCII characters:", x,y);
37
38          //we use the \u0020 for a space
39          y += yIncr;
40          output = "\u004A\u0020\u0041\u0020\u0056\u0020\u0041";
41          g.drawString(output, x,y);
42
43          y += yIncr;
44          g.drawString("Here are some Greek characters:", x,y);
45
46          //we can just put a space like this " "
47          y += yIncr;
48          output = "\u0394" + " " + "\u03C8" + " " + "\u03C9" + " " +"\u03EA";
49          g.drawString(output, x,y);
50
51          y += yIncr;
52          g.drawString("Here are some mathematical operators:", x,y);
53
54          output = "\u2205" + " " + "\u2264" + " " + "\u2211" + " " + "\u222B";
55          y += yIncr;
56          g.drawString(output, x,y);
57
58          y += yIncr;
59          g.drawString("Here are some Dingbat characters:", x,y);
60
61          output = "\u2702\u0020\u2782\u0020\u270C\u0020\u27B4";
62          y += yIncr;
63          g.drawString(output, x,y);
64      }
65  }
```

C

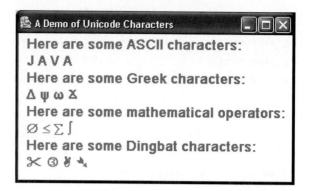

Figure C-1
Program output showing various symbols being written using their Unicode hexa-decimal sequences.

The four Unicode tables show the various symbols as well as their unique bit sequence. Because Java uses the Unicode Standard, there is no confusion as to what a bit sequence represents. Let's look at four different characters, the letter "J", Greek letter delta (Δ), the mathematical empty set (∅), and the Dingbats scissors (✂). Table C-5 shows these four characters and their hex and bit pattern sequence.

▍ TABLE C-5
Comparison of four Unicode characters including their bit pattern. Refer to Table C-3 for help with the hex-to-binary conversion.

Symbol	Unicode reference	Hex notation	Bit pattern
J	Controls and Basic Latin	0x004A	0000 0000 0100 1010
delta (Δ)	Greek and Coptic	0x0394	0000 0011 1001 0100
empty set (∅),	Mathematical Operators	0x2205	0010 0010 0000 0101
scissors (✂).	Dingbats	0x2702	0010 0111 0000 0010

C

TABLE C-6

0000   C0 Controls and Basic Latin   007F

	000	001	002	003	004	005	006	007
0	NUL 0000	DLE 0010	SP 0020	0 0030	@ 0040	P 0050	` 0060	p 0070
1	SOH 0001	DC1 0011	! 0021	1 0031	A 0041	Q 0051	a 0061	q 0071
2	STX 0002	DC2 0012	" 0022	2 0032	B 0042	R 0052	b 0062	r 0072
3	ETX 0003	DC3 0013	# 0023	3 0033	C 0043	S 0053	c 0063	s 0073
4	EOT 0004	DC4 0014	$ 0024	4 0034	D 0044	T 0054	d 0064	t 0074
5	ENQ 0005	NAK 0015	% 0025	5 0035	E 0045	U 0055	e 0065	u 0075
6	ACK 0006	SYN 0016	& 0026	6 0036	F 0046	V 0056	f 0066	v 0076
7	BEL 0007	ETB 0017	' 0027	7 0037	G 0047	W 0057	g 0067	w 0077
8	BS 0008	CAN 0018	(0028	8 0038	H 0048	X 0058	h 0068	x 0078
9	HT 0009	EM 0019	) 0029	9 0039	I 0049	Y 0059	i 0069	y 0079
A	LF 000A	SUB 001A	* 002A	: 003A	J 004A	Z 005A	j 006A	z 007A
B	VT 000B	ESC 001B	+ 002B	; 003B	K 004B	[005B	k 006B	{ 007B
C	FF 000C	FS 001C	, 002C	< 003C	L 004C	\ 005C	l 006C	| 007C
D	CR 000D	GS 001D	- 002D	= 003D	M 004D	] 005D	m 006D	} 007D
E	SO 000E	RS 001E	. 002E	> 003E	N 004E	^ 005E	n 006E	~ 007E
F	SI 000F	US 001F	/ 002F	? 003F	O 004F	_ 005F	o 006F	DEL 007F

Bits and Bytes

C

TABLE C-7

Control sequences for Unicode sequence 0000–0020.

Decimal	Hex	Octal	Symbol
0	0	0	NULL
1	1	1	Start of Heading control
2	2	2	Start of Text control
3	3	3	End of Text control
4	4	4	End of Transmission control
5	5	5	Enquiry control
6	6	6	Acknowledge control
7	7	7	Beep or Bell control
8	8	10	Backspace control
9	9	11	Horizontal Tab control
10	A	12	\n newline control
11	B	13	Vertical Tab control
12	C	14	Form Feed control
13	D	15	Enter Key or Carriage Return control
14	E	16	Shift Out control
15	F	17	Shift In control
16	10	20	Data Link Escape control
17	11	21	Device Control One control
18	12	22	Device Control Two control
19	13	23	Device Control Three control
20	14	24	Device Control Four control
21	15	25	Negative Acknowledge control
22	16	26	Synchronous Idle control
23	17	27	End of Transmission Block control
24	18	30	Cancel control
25	19	31	End of Medium control
26	1A	32	Substitute control
27	1B	33	Escape control
28	1C	34	File Separator control
29	1D	35	Group Separator control
30	1E	36	Record Separator control
31	1F	37	Unit Separator control
32	20	40	space

C

TABLE C-8

0370 Greek and Coptic 03FF

	037	038	039	03A	03B	03C	03D	03E	03F
0	▨	▨	ΐ 0390	Π 03A0	ΰ 03B0	π 00C0	ϐ 03D0	Ϡ 03E0	ϰ 03F0
1	▨	▨	Α 0391	Ρ 03A1	α 03B1	ρ 03C1	ϑ 03D1	ϡ 03E1	ϱ 03F1
2	▨	▨	Β 0392	▨	β 03B2	ς 03C2	ϒ 03D2	Ϣ 03E2	ϲ 03F2
3	▨	▨	Γ 0393	Σ 03A3	γ 03B3	σ 03C3	ϓ 03D3	ϣ 03E3	ϳ 03F3
4	ʹ 0374	΄ 0384	Δ 0394	Τ 03A4	δ 03B4	τ 03C4	ϔ 03D4	Ϥ 03E4	ϴ 03F4
5	͵ 0375	΅ 0385	Ε 0395	Υ 03A5	ε 03B5	υ 03C5	ϕ 03D5	ϥ 03E5	ϵ 03F5
6	▨	Ά 0386	Ζ 0396	Φ 03A6	ζ 03B6	φ 03C6	ϖ 03D6	Ϧ 03E6	϶ 03F6
7	▨	· 0387	Η 0397	Χ 03A7	η 03B7	χ 03C7	ϗ 03D7	ϧ 03E7	▨
8	▨	Έ 0388	Θ 0398	Ψ 03A8	θ 03B8	ψ 03C8	Ϙ 03D8	Ϩ 03E8	▨
9	▨	Ή 0389	Ι 0399	Ω 03A9	ι 03B9	ω 03C9	ϙ 03D9	ϩ 03E9	▨
A	ͺ 037A	Ί 038A	Κ 039A	Ϊ 03AA	κ 03BA	ϊ 03CA	Ϛ 03DA	Ϫ 03EA	▨
B	▨	▨	Λ 039B	Ϋ 03AB	λ 03BB	ϋ 03CB	ϛ 03DB	ϫ 03EB	▨
C	▨	Ό 038C	Μ 039C	ά 03AC	μ 03BC	ό 036C	Ϝ 03DC	Ϭ 03EC	▨
D	▨	▨	Ν 039D	έ 03AD	ν 03BD	ύ 03CD	ϝ 03DD	ϭ 03ED	▨
E	; 037E	Ύ 038E	Ξ 039E	ή 03AE	ξ 03BE	ώ 03CE	Ϟ 03DE	Ϯ 03EE	▨
F	▨	Ώ 038F	Ο 039F	ί 03AF	ο 03BF	▨	ϟ 03DF	ϯ 03EF	▨

Bits and Bytes

C

TABLE C-9
2200   Mathematical Operators   227F

	220	221	222	223	224	225	226	227
0	∀ 2200	∐ 2210	∠ 2220	∰ 2230	∾ 2240	≐ 2250	≠ 2260	≰ 2270
1	∁ 2201	∑ 2211	∡ 2221	∱ 2231	∿ 2241	≑ 2251	≡ 2261	≱ 2271
2	∂ 2202	− 2212	∢ 2222	∲ 2232	≂ 2242	≒ 2252	≢ 2262	≲ 2272
3	∃ 2203	∓ 2213	∣ 2223	∳ 2233	≃ 2243	≓ 2253	≣ 2263	≳ 2273
4	∄ 2204	∔ 2214	∤ 2224	∴ 2234	≄ 2244	≔ 2254	≤ 2264	≴ 2274
5	∅ 2205	∕ 2215	∥ 2225	∵ 2235	≅ 2245	≕ 2255	≥ 2265	≵ 2275
6	∆ 2206	∖ 2216	∦ 2226	∶ 2236	≆ 2246	≖ 2256	≦ 2266	≶ 2276
7	∇ 2207	∗ 2217	∧ 2227	∷ 2237	≇ 2247	≗ 2257	≧ 2267	≷ 2277
8	∈ 2208	∘ 2218	∨ 2228	∸ 2238	≈ 2248	≘ 2258	≨ 2268	≸ 2278
9	∉ 2209	∙ 2219	∩ 2229	∹ 2239	≉ 2249	≙ 2259	≩ 2269	≹ 2279
A	∊ 220A	√ 221A	∪ 222A	∺ 223A	≊ 224A	≚ 225A	≪ 226A	≺ 227A
B	∋ 220B	∛ 221B	∫ 222B	∻ 223B	≋ 224B	≛ 225B	≫ 226B	≻ 227B
C	∌ 220C	∜ 221C	∬ 222C	∼ 223C	≌ 224C	≜ 225C	◊ 226C	≼ 227C
D	∍ 220D	∝ 221D	∭ 222D	∽ 223D	≍ 224D	≝ 225D	⋇ 226D	≽ 227D
E	∎ 220E	∞ 221E	∮ 222E	∾ 223E	≎ 224E	≞ 225E	⋉ 226E	≾ 227E
F	∏ 220F	∟ 221F	∯ 222F	∿ 223F	≏ 224F	≟ 225F	⋊ 226F	≿ 227F

C

TABLE C-10
2700   Dingbats   27BF

	270	271	272	273	274	275	276	277	278	279	27A	27B
0		2710	2720	2730	2740	2750		2770	2780	2790	27A0	
1	2701	2711	2721	2731	2741	2751	2761	2771	2781	2791	27A1	27B1
2	2702	2712	2722	2732	2742	2752	2762	2772	2782	2792	27A2	27B2
3	2703	2713	2723	2733	2743		2763	2773	2783	2793	27A3	27B3
4	2704	2714	2724	2734	2744		2764	2774	2784	2794	27A4	27B4
5		2715	2725	2735	2745		2765	2775	2785		27A5	27B5
6	2706	2716	2726	2736	2746	2756	2766	2776	2786		27A6	27B6
7	2707	2717	2727	2737	2747		2767	2777	2787		27A7	27B7
8	2708	2718		2738	2748	2758	2768	2778	2788	2798	27A8	27B8
9	2709	2719	2729	2739	2749	2759	2769	2779	2789	2799	27A9	27B9
A		271A	272A	273A	274A	275A	276A	277A	278A	279A	27AA	27BA
B		271B	272B	273B	274B	275B	276B	277B	278B	279B	27AB	27BB
C	270C	271C	272C	273C		275C	276C	277C	278C	279C	27AC	27BC
D	270D	271D	272D	273D	274D	275D	276D	277D	278D	279D	27AD	27BD
E	270E	271E	272E	273E		275E	276E	277E	278 E	279E	27AE	27BE
F	270F	271F	272F	273F	274F		276F	277F	278F	279F	27AF	

Bits and Bytes

C

Nested Classes

In a completely object-oriented programming language such as Java, everything must be contained in a class. Even if you wish to write one general-purpose method, that method must be within a class. In the early stages of Java, every class had to be a top-level class, meaning that the class source code is contained in its own file named with the *.java* extension. As Java designers improved and expanded the language, Java JDK 1.1 provided nested classes. Nested classes are classes that are defined within the body of another class.

There are four types of nested classes in Java. Java's nested classes are summarized in Table D-1. For the first three types, refer to the individual sections that follow this table to see how these nested classes are written in Java programs. Anonymous classes are discussed in detail in Chapter 7.

TABLE D-1
Nested classes in Java.

Type of class	Definition
Nested Static Class	A nested static class has the keyword static in its class definition line. A nested static class is defined inside another class and works in the same manner as a top-level class. The name of the enclosing class must be used when a nested class object is instantiated.
Member Class or Inner Class	A member or inner class is a class that is contained inside another class. The inner class can reference any members in its parent class.
Local Class	A local class is also an inner class but it is contained inside a block of code in the top-level class. A local class is usually defined in a method. See the Thread examples in Chapter 8.
Anonymous Class	An anonymous class is a special variation of an inner class. The class is declared and instantiated within a single expression. See Chapters 7 and 8 for examples of anonymous classes.

Review: The Hello Class

Before we jump into nested classes, let's review two simple, top-level classes. In Program D-1 we have the Hello and TestHello classes. The Hello class is contained in the file *Hello.java*. A Hello object is instantiated in the TestHello class, which is contained in *TestHello.java*. Both classes are top-level classes because the source code is in two separate *.java* files. Examine the two pieces of code below and see if you can determine the sequence of JOptionPane message boxes that are shown as this executes. Then execute TestHello and double-check your list of messages.

```
1   //Program D-1
2   //File:  Hello.java
3
4   import javax.swing.JOptionPane;
5
6   public class Hello
7   {
8     public Hello()
9     {
10          JOptionPane.showMessageDialog(null,
11          "In the standalone Hello constructor.",
12          "Hello Constructor", JOptionPane.INFORMATION_MESSAGE);
13    }
14
15    public void howdy()
16    {
17          JOptionPane.showMessageDialog(null,"In Howdy!!!",
18          "Hello's howdy() Method", JOptionPane.INFORMATION_MESSAGE);
19    }
20    public void howAreYou()
21    {
22          JOptionPane.showMessageDialog(null,"How Are You?",
23          "Hello's howAreYou() Method", JOptionPane.INFORMATION_MESSAGE);
24    }
25  }
```

```
1   //Program D-1 This class instantiates a Hello object
2   //and calls its methods.
3
4   //File TestHello.java
5
```

D

```
 6   import javax.swing.JOptionPane;
 7
 8   public class TestHello
 9   {
10     Hello myH = new Hello();
11
12     public static void main(String args[])
13     {
14           JOptionPane.showMessageDialog(null,
15           "In TestHello's main() method.",
16           "TestHello main",
17           JOptionPane.INFORMATION_MESSAGE);
18
19           new TestHello();
20           System.exit(0);
21     }
22
23     public TestHello()
24     {
25           myH.howdy();
26           myH.howAreYou();
27     }
28   }
```

Nested Static Classes

A nested static class is a class that is defined within another class, and it is treated just like any other top-level class. The nested static class has the keyword static in its class definition line. In this example, we have the TopLevelHello class, which encloses the StaticNestedHello class. Program D-2 shows the source code for a nested static class.

```
1   //Program D-2
2   //This class contains a nested static class
3
4   //File: TopLevelHello.java
5   import javax.swing.JOptionPane;
6
7   public class TopLevelHello
8   {
```

```
9       private String name = "Bob";
10      public TopLevelHello()
11      {
12              JOptionPane.showMessageDialog(null,
13                      "In the TopLevelHello constructor.");
14      }
15
16      public void topHowdy()
17      {
18              JOptionPane.showMessageDialog(null,
19                      "This is a top-level howdy " + name);
20      }
21
22      //Here is the nested static class.
23      //This static class cannot access any non-static
24      //members of the TopLevelHello class.
25      //It cannot access the String name.
26      public static class NestedStaticHello
27      {
28              public NestedStaticHello()
29              {
30                      JOptionPane.showMessageDialog(null,
31                              "In the nested static Hello constructor.");
32              }
33
34              public void nestedHowdy()
35              {
36                      JOptionPane.showMessageDialog(null,
37                              "This is a nested static Howdy");
38              }
39              public void nestedHowAreYou()
40              {
41                      JOptionPane.showMessageDialog(null,
42                              "This is a nested static How Are You?");
43              }
44      }
45  }
```

When a nested static class object is instantiated, the name of the enclosing class
(the class that contains it) must be included in the declaration statement. Because
the nested static class is declared as static, the nested class has no access to the nonstatic class data of objects of the enclosing class. The TopLevelHello class has a
private String variable that contains the name "Bob." The static inner class cannot

access it. If the name variable was declared static, then it could be accessed by the NestedStaticHello class.

```
1    //Program D-2
2    //File: TestTopLevelHello.java
3
4    import javax.swing.JOptionPane;
5
6    public class TestTopLevelHello
7    {
8      //Create a TopLevelHello object
9      TopLevelHello topper = new TopLevelHello();
10
11     //Create a NestedStaticHello object
12     //We must use the top level class name and dot operator.
13     TopLevelHello.NestedStaticHello nested =
14                      new TopLevelHello.NestedStaticHello();
15
16     public static void main(String args[])
17     {
18          JOptionPane.showMessageDialog(null,
19                  "In the TestTopLevelHello main method.");
20          new TestTopLevelHello();
21          System.exit(0);
22     }
23
24     public TestTopLevelHello()
25     {
26          topper.topHowdy();
27          nested.nestedHowdy();
28          nested.nestedHowAreYou();
29     }
30   }
31
```

When the *TestTopLevelHello.java* file is compiled, the compiler generated two class files: the *TestTopLevelHello.class* and the *TestTopLevelHello$NestedStatic-Hello.class*. The name of the nested class follows the $ in the *.class* filename. Any time a nested class is compiled, the Java compiler generates a separate class file for this class.

D

Member or Inner Classes

Inner classes in Java are classes that are defined inside another class, in much the same manner as a method is defined. An inner class looks just like a nested static class except there is no static keyword. The inner class is contained in every instance of the class, and has access to all of the enclosing class data and methods. Typically, inner classes are contained in a class that will use it, and it is not expected that other classes will need the inner class.

Program D-3 contains the TestHelloInnerClass source code, which has the Hello class defined within it. The enclosing class, TestHelloInnerClass, has a member variable, name, which is written out in the inner class Hello's howdy() and howAreYou() methods. When the Java compiler compiles the *TestHelloInner-Class.java* file, it creates a *TestHelloInnerClass.class* and *TestHelloInnerClass$Hello. class* file.

```
1    //Program D-3    This class contains an inner class.
2    //File:  TestHelloInnerClass.java
3
4    //Use an inner class inside this TestHelloInnerClass.
5    //Only the TestHelloInnerClass needs to access the Hello class.
6    //The Hello class is private, hidden from the world.
7
8    import javax.swing.JOptionPane;
9
10   public class TestHelloInnerClass
11   {
12      //The Hello class is nested inside this class.
13      Hello myH = new Hello();
14
15      //The name variable is a member of the TestHelloInnerClass.
16      String name = "Gina";
17
18      public static void main(String args[])
19      {
20           JOptionPane.showMessageDialog(null,
21                "In the TestHelloInnerClass' main() method.",
22                "Called from TestHelloInnerClass",
23                JOptionPane.INFORMATION_MESSAGE);
24
```

D

```
25              new TestHelloInnerClass();
26              System.exit(0);
27      }
28
29      public TestHelloInnerClass()
30      {
31              myH.howdy();
32              myH.howAreYou();
33      }
34
35
36  //Here is the inner class definition.
37  //This inner class has access to the TestHelloInnerClass data,
38  //just like the TestHelloInnerClass methods do.
39      public class Hello
40      {
41              String output;
42              public Hello()
43              {
44                      JOptionPane.showMessageDialog(null,
45                          "In the Hello Constructor.",
46                          "Called from the inner class",
47                          JOptionPane.INFORMATION_MESSAGE);
48              }
49
50              public void howdy()
51              {
52                      //The inner class has access to the name variable..
53                      output = "This is an inner class howdy to " + name + "!";
54                      JOptionPane.showMessageDialog(null, output,
55                          "Called from the inner class",
56                          JOptionPane.INFORMATION_MESSAGE);
57              }
58              public void howAreYou()
59              {
60              output = "This is an inner class How Are You " + name + "?";
61                      JOptionPane.showMessageDialog(null,output,
62                      "Called from the inner class",
63                              JOptionPane.INFORMATION_MESSAGE);
64              }
65      }
66  }
```

Local Classes

A local class is a class that is defined within a block of code of another class. The local class is usually contained inside one of the enclosing class's methods. Program D-4 shows the TestHelloLocalClass, which has a sayHello() method. In the sayHello() method, a local class named LocalHello is defined. A LocalHello object is declared and its methods are called. When the Java compiler compiles the *TestHelloLocalClass.java* file, once again we see two class files as the result: *TestHelloLocalClass.class* and *TestHelloLocalClass$LocalHello.class*.

```
1   //Program D-4    This class contains a local class.
2   //File:  TestHelloLocalClass.java
3
4   //Use a local class inside this TestHelloLocalClass
5   //Only the sayHello method has the LocalHello object.
6   //The Hello class is private, hidden from the world.
7
8   import javax.swing.JOptionPane;
9
10  public class TestHelloLocalClass
11  {
12
13      public static void main(String args[])
14      {
15              JOptionPane.showMessageDialog(null,
16                  "In the TestHelloLocalClass' main() method.",
17                  "Called from main() in TestHelloLocalClass",
18                  JOptionPane.INFORMATION_MESSAGE);
19
20              new TestHelloLocalClass();
21              System.exit(0);
22      }
23
24      public TestHelloLocalClass()
25      {
26              sayHello();
27      }
28
29      public void sayHello()
30      {
31
```

```
32        // local class definition
33        class LocalHello
34        {
35              public LocalHello()
36              {
37                    JOptionPane.showMessageDialog(null,
38                    "In the LocalHello Constructor.",
39                    "Called from LocalHello()", 1);
40              }
41
42              public void howdy()
43              {
44                    JOptionPane.showMessageDialog(null,
45                    "This is a local class Howdy!!!",
46                    "Called from LocalHello' howdy()", 1);
47              }
48              public void howAreYou()
49              {
50                    JOptionPane.showMessageDialog(null,
51                    "This is a local class How Are You?",
52                    "Called from LocalHello' howAreYou()", 1);
53              }
54        }
55
56        LocalHello local = new LocalHello();
57        local.howdy();
58        local.howAreYou();
59    }
60 }
```

Anonymous Inner Classes

An anonymous inner class is a class that is defined inside another class (i.e. inner) and is not assigned a name (i.e. anonymous). Anonymous inner classes are used for writing user interface event handlers. They facilitate and simplify the code that a programmer writes. Anonymous inner classes are covered in detail in Chapter 7.

D

Java Integrated Development Environments

This appendix provides a brief reference for several Java Integrated Development Environments (IDEs). What is an IDE? An IDE provides the Java programmer with a complete set of tools, including a source editor, a compiler, a debugger, help, and Java documentation. The environment generates Java source code automatically and allows the programmer to execute the code with a push of a button.

IDEs provide tools for building user interfaces, working with databases, creating Java Server Pages, and creating web applications. It is important for the Java programmer to have a clear idea of what type of programs he or she wishes to write. There are many different Java IDEs and each one has its strengths and weaknesses. The best approach is for the Java programmer to search the web for "Java IDE" or "Java IDE evaluations." Several independent journals evaluate IDEs on a yearly basis and publish their results.

Table E-1 shows a summary of Java IDEs and their associated websites.

TABLE E-1
Java IDEs and their website addresses.

Java IDE	Website
Borland JBuilder	http://www.borland.com/jbuilder
Metrowerks CodeWarrior	http://www.metrowerks.com
BlueJ	http://www.bluej.org
Sun Microsystems Sun One	http://sun.com/software
Sun Microsystems NetBeans	http://www.netbeans.org
Oracle JDeveloper	http://www.oracle.com
IBM WebSphere Studio	http://www-3.ibm.com/software
Open Source Eclipse	http://www.eclipse.org
JetBrains Inc. IntelliJ IDEA	http://www.intellij.com

Troubleshooting and Debugging

Aside from learning the Java language, a new programmer must learn how to troubleshoot and debug his or her program. It is important to learn how to debug your program and use the debugging tools in your development environment. What do we mean by the term, **debug your program**? If your program is compiling and executing, but not providing the correct results, you need to have some way to determine where the error is occurring so you can fix the code.

debug your program

if your program is compiling and executing but not providing the correct results, you must examine your program to determine the cause of the error

First Write Test Cases

As a Java programmer, it is crucial for you to know your program's expected results! You must know when the program is working correctly and when it is not working correctly. This sounds simple, but some beginning programmers are happy just to have their code compile and run. These novices never check their results for correctness and accuracy. As you begin to build Java programs, always think about how you will test your program to ensure that it is working correctly.

As part of your development for any program, you should write a testing scenario that includes all possible types of input. These input values should exercise the different conditions in your software. Your test case "write up" need not be a formal document. Simply make a list of input values and perform pencil and paper calculations to determine the correct results. Once your program is running, input your test data and check the output. Take the time to test your software carefully. If possible, ask another person to run your program.

If you become a member of a software development team, such as in a university or business setting, a commercial software business, or for a military application, you will realize that testing your software is as important as writing it. In large system development projects, testing is always part of the design process. Test plans are written along with software architecture, and testing is always an integral portion of the development cycle.

Two Approaches for Debugging Your Program

Assume that you know the expected behavior of your program. While you are testing, you input data and see the wrong results. Do you have any idea where the problem is occurring? Sometimes the problem is obvious. Other times the problem is difficult to find. If you are lucky (this sounds funny), your program crashes. When a program crashes, there is an obvious starting point for debugging—the line that caused the crash! In order to troubleshoot your program, you need to be able to watch the program run in a step-by-step manner. It is necessary to examine the intermediate results along the way to ensure that things are working correctly or to determine the spot where trouble begins.

We will discuss two ways of troubleshooting your programs. The first approach is a tried and true, brute force way used by programmers everywhere. It is the "put print statements in the program and write information to the screen" approach. Although not elegant, the print statement approach often provides the clue you need to find your error.

The second troubleshooting approach involves exploring the debugging tool that accompanies the J2SDK. If you check in your *j2skd1.4.1\bin* folder, you will see the **jdb.exe** program. This is Java's debugging tool, which is part of the Java Debugger API. The jbd program is a simple command line debugger that works with Java classes (some Java IDEs provide their own integrated debugger that may be easier to use than this command line program).

jdb.exe
the Java Debugger program. *jdb* is a simple command line debugger that works with Java classes

Java's debugging tool, jdb.exe, allows you to execute your program, stopping at any given line of code. Once stopped, you may step through the code one line at a time, checking the values for any variables and objects in your program. Therefore, it is possible to follow how the code runs and see exactly which lines are executed and which are skipped. You write your software with certain expectations. The debugger gives you the means to verify that the code is performing as anticipated and to locate the point where logic or calculation failures occur.

This appendix shows debugging steps for several programs from the text. The first program examples are debugged by using the print statement technique and also by using jdb tool. By showing both techniques, the reader will see the strengths and weaknesses of each. Later examples are shown using only the jdb program. I hope

> **Note:** The System.out.println() statement approach and jdb work well for Java applications (programs that have a main() method). Debugging Java applets presents a different problem. Applets "play in the sandbox," meaning that they run within a web browser and are not allowed access to system resources. However, if you run your applet using Java's appletviewer, you are able to place print statements in your applet code, which write messages to the MS-DOS window. You may also run appletviewer in its debug mode, utilizing all of the jdb commands. We examine debugging applets later in this appendix, but for now, let's look at several applications.

F

that you spend plenty of time practicing these techniques as you develop your programs. Good debugging skills will assist you throughout your programming career.

Debugging Applications

There are two schools of thought on debugging programs. One school says that you should start at the beginning and follow your input data through your code until you spot the error. The other school of thought concludes that the best way to find your problem is to work your way backward from where you see the error. No matter which school of thought you believe in, programmers inevitably do a little of both when trying to find the cause of an error.

When trying to find an error in a calculation, it is best to check all the input values to ensure that they are correct, and then look at the intermediate results. Do not forget about the possibility of integer division causing problems in your calculations (review Chapter 2, arithmetic operators if you need a refresher on integer division).

Example 1: CoconutEstimator from Chapter 2

Our first debugging example uses Program 2-21, the CoconutEstimator program. This program assists you candy lovers in determining your chances of selecting a piece of candy that contains coconut. The program asks the user to enter the total number of pieces in a box of candy and the number of pieces containing coconut. Dividing the coconut pieces by total pieces gives us the odds of being happy with your choice.

CoconutEstimator and the Print Statement Approach   Using the System.out.println() method allows us to place print statements inside our source code, which writes information to the MS-DOS window. This approach allows the programmer to sprinkle println() calls throughout the code, writing an exact message and data to the screen. We are not able to stop the program while it executes, but we are able to see the intermediate results via these printed messages. Examine lines 35, 41, and 53 in Program F-1 to see the placement of the System.out.println() calls. Figure F-1 shows the resultant messages in the window when we entered 60 total pieces of candy and 15 coconut pieces.

```
1    //Program F-1, a modified version of
2    //Program 2-21 Practice with Math
3    //File:  CoconutEstimator.java
4
5    import javax.swing.JOptionPane;
6
7    public class CoconutEstimator
8    {
9      public static void main(String args[])
10     {
```

```
11          int total = 0,              //total number of pieces in box
12              coconuts = 0;           //how many pieces with coconut
13          double chance = 0.0;        //Chance of getting a coconut piece
14          int last=0;      //percentage amount
15
16          String strTotal,       //user input for total
17              strNuts;       //user input for coconut amount
18
19          String question = "\nWhat are your chances of getting a "
20              + "\ncoconut filled chocolate in a candy box?";
21
22          String explanation = "\nThis program will show you what your "
23              + "\nchances are of getting/avoiding the coconut piece.";
24
25          String title = "Coconut Estimator Program";
26          JOptionPane.showMessageDialog(null, question, title,
27                                  JOptionPane.QUESTION_MESSAGE);
28          JOptionPane.showMessageDialog(null, explanation, title,
29                                  JOptionPane.INFORMATION_MESSAGE);
30
31          //Read user's answers for total in box as string.
32          strTotal =
33          JOptionPane.showInputDialog("Enter number of pieces in box.");
34
35          System.out.println("strTotal entered by user " + strTotal );
36
37      //Read user's answers for number of coconut pieces as string.
38          strNuts =
39          JOptionPane.showInputDialog(
40              "Enter number of coconut pieces in box");
41          System.out.println("strNuts entered by user " + strNuts );
42
43          //convert answers to Integers
44          total = Integer.parseInt(strTotal);
45          coconuts = Integer.parseInt(strNuts);
46
47          //cast the integers into doubles to perform accurate division
48          chance = (double)coconuts/(double)total;
49
50          chance = chance * 100;      //get percentage amount
51                                  //could have used chance *= 100;
52
53          System.out.println("The chance is " + Double.toString(chance));
54
55          String strChance =
56          "Your chance of getting a piece of coconut candy is "
57              + chance + "%";
58          JOptionPane.showMessageDialog(null,strChance, title,
59                              JOptionPane.INFORMATION_MESSAGE);
60          System.exit(0);
61      }
62  }
```

javac –g option

causes the compiler to generate debug information for the class

breakpoint

tells the debugger the line where execution should stop

step

performs the current line, then stops at the next line of code. If we step a method call, we step into that method

step into

when you are at a method call and you use the step command, the debugger jumps to the first line of a method

step over

when you are at a method call and you use the next command, the debugger performs the method and stops at the line after the method call

```
C:\JPT\AppF>javac CoconutEstimator.java

C:\JPT\AppF>java  CoconutEstimator
strTotal entered by user 60
strNuts entered by user 15
The chance is 25.0

C:\JPT\AppF>
```

Figure F-1

The resultant messages are printed to the MS-DOS window by the System.out.println() method for the CoconutEstimator program. The programmer places the calls to println() wherever he or she wishes.

jdb Debugger Concepts   The Java Debugger program, *jdb.exe*, is a command-line debugger for Java classes. The concept for using the jdb program is simple. It allows the programmer to run his or her program, stopping its execution at break-points, in order to examine variable and object values. The programmer compiles the code with the **javac –g option**. The –g option causes the compiler to generate debug information for the class.

The programmer starts the debugger program and provides the name of a Java class. This approach requires this "containing" class to have a main() method, because jdb starts its own version of the JVM. The programmer sets a **breakpoint** on a line of code in the program. A breakpoint tells the debugger where to stop execution (which line). The programmer may then ask the debugger to print variable and object values, which are displayed in the MS-DOS window. The programmer may also **step** through the program one line at a time. When the debugger is stopped at a call to a method, the programmer may either **step into** the method by using the *step* command or **step over** the method by using the **next** command. Many break-points may be set in the program, and the programmer may run to each breakpoint examining program data along the way. Table F-1 shows a list of these new terms.

▌ TABLE F-1
Debugging Terminology

Term	Use
breakpoint	A breakpoint is placed at a line of code in a program where the programmer wants the program to stop so that he or she may examine variables. Also, you may set a breakpoint where you wish to stop so that you may begin to step through the code one line at a time. The line in which the breakpoint is set is not executed when the program stops at the breakpoint.
step	The step command advances the program execution to the next line, then executes that line. This may be the next line in the source code, or if you are stepping into a method call, the code will jump to the first line of the method.
watch	Some debuggers allow programmers to identify different variables that are to be "watched" as the program executes.
trace	Debuggers are able to provide a trace of the program execution steps.

F

Table F-2 shows a brief summary of the commands needed for running the jdb. We encourage the Java programmer to start the debugger and enter the *help* or *?* command to see the complete command list. Table F-3 provides a quick reference guide for setting and clearing breakpoints.

next
steps over the method call and executes the method

▍ TABLE F-2
jdb Debugger Reference

Purpose	jdb command
Compile the source code (see Note 1)	In order to display local variables of the containing class, you must use the javac –g option in order for the compiler to generate debugging information. `C:\JPT>javac -g   MyClass.java`
Start the debugger (see Note 2)	Use the jdb command with class name: `C:\JPT> jdb  MyClass`
help or ?	The jdb command that shows the complete command list.
run	Starts the program execution in the debugger. Once you have started the debugger, you normally set breakpoints before you start the program running.
cont	Continues the execution of the program after being stopped.
breakpoints	See Table F-3.
step (steps into methods)	When the program is stopped, step executes the following line. You either step to the next line, or if you are at a method call, you will step into the method.
step up	When the program is stopped in a method, step up executes the rest of the method and stops at the line where the method was called.
next (steps over methods)	When the program is stopped, next executes the following line. If the next line is a call to a method, the program executes the method but does not step into the method.
locals	Prints all of the local variables in a method.

print	Displays object and primitive values
	
	`print varName`
	`print ClassName.staticVar`
	`print myObject.myData`
	
	Object data is shown with the dump objectName command
	
	`dump objectName`

where	Tells where the debugger is currently stopped and shows a trace of the calls.
exit or quit	Stops and exits the debugger programmer.

Note 1: The containing class is the class that is referenced when you start the debugger. Typically it is the class that contains main().

Note 2: There are other ways to start the debugger. We only cover this direct approach. Refer to the jdb information at java.sun.com for more information.

F

TABLE F-3

jdb breakpoints commands.

Purpose	jdb command
Set breakpoint at a line	Provide <classname>:<line number>
stop at	`stop at MyClass:25`
Set breakpoint at the beginning of a method	Provide <classname>.<methodName(arg)> (see Note)
stop in	`stop in MyClass.methodName()`
	`stop in MyClass.methodName(int, int, double)`
Set a breakpoint at the first line of a constructor	Provide<classname>.<init>
	`stop in MyClass.<init>`
Clear breakpoint	Provide<ClassName>:<Line Number>
	`clear MyClass:25`
	To see all currently set breakpoints
	`clear`

Note: If the method is overloaded, the exact method and argument list must be provide.

jdb and CoconutEstimator   We can use Chapter 2's version of the Coconut-Estimator program, which does not contain extra print statements, to illustrate our first use of the jdb. Program F-2 shows the program and its associated line numbers that we will use as references for the debugger.

```
1    //Program F-2, which is also
2    //Program 2-21 Practice with Math
3    //File:  CoconutEstimator.java
4
5    import javax.swing.JOptionPane;
6
7    public class CoconutEstimator
8    {
9      public static void main(String args[])
10     {
11         int total = 0,              //total number of pieces in box
12             coconuts = 0;           //how many pieces with coconut
13         double chance = 0.0;        //Chance of getting a coconut piece
14         int last=0;      //percentage amount
```

```
15
16          String strTotal,     //user input for total
17                    strNuts;         //user input for coconut amount
18
19          String question = "\nWhat are your chances of getting a "
20              + "\ncoconut filled chocolate in a candy box?";
21
22          String explanation = "\nThis program will show you what your "
23              + "\nchances are of getting/avoiding the coconut piece.";
24
25          String title = "Coconut Estimator Program";
26          JOptionPane.showMessageDialog(null, question, title,
27                    JOptionPane.QUESTION_MESSAGE);
28          JOptionPane.showMessageDialog(null, explanation, title,
29              JOptionPane.INFORMATION_MESSAGE);
30
31          //Read user's answers for total in box as string.
32          strTotal =
33          JOptionPane.showInputDialog("Enter number of pieces in box.");
34
35      //Read user's answers for number of coconut pieces as string.
36          strNuts =
37  JOptionPane.showInputDialog("Enter number of coconut pieces in box");
38
39      //convert answers to Integers
40          total = Integer.parseInt(strTotal);
41          coconuts = Integer.parseInt(strNuts);
42
43          //cast the integers into doubles to perform accurate division
44          chance = (double)coconuts/(double)total;
45
46      chance = chance * 100; //get percentage amount
47                            //could have used chance *= 100;
48  String strChance = "Your chance of getting a piece of coconut candy is "
49              + chance + "%";
50
51          JOptionPane.showMessageDialog(null,strChance, title,
52                      JOptionPane.INFORMATION_MESSAGE);
53          System.exit(0);
54  }
55 }
```

F

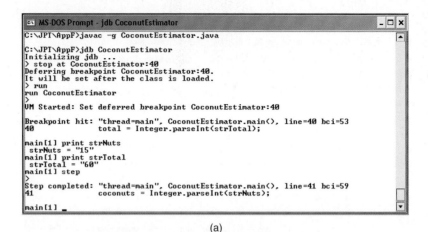

Figure F-2
The MS-DOS windows that show the Java debugger commands for the Coconut-Estimator program.

Figure F-2 shows the steps we take to compile, start, set breakpoints, and view various program variables in the CoconutEstimator code. Figure F-2a shows Steps 1–6, and F-2b shows steps 7–8. Refer to the figures, Program F-2 program code, and the following list of our steps to see how the jdb works.

Step 1: Compile the code with the –g option so that the local variables can be seen in the debugger.

Step 2: Start the debugger by using the jdb ClassName command. You can see that the debugger starts up and then provides us with the > prompt.

Step 3: Let's allow the program to run and the user to input the numbers for the candy. Then we can stop the program and examine the values. We put a breakpoint at line 40. We use the *stop at <classname>:<line number>* form of the jdb command. As you can see in Figure F-2a, jdb reports "Deferring breakpoint," which means it will set it once the program begins to run.

Step 4:   Start the program executing by issuing the *run* command. The program then pops up the message boxes for input (we enter 60 total pieces and 15 coconut pieces). The debugger then stops the execution at line 40.

Step 5:   We now ask the debugger to print the values for strNuts and strTotal. We see "15" and "60," respectively. The quotation marks (" ") indicate that values we see are String values.

Step 6:   We issue the *step* command so that the code executes the next line in the code, which is line 41.

Step 7:   We issue another *step* command (top of Figure F-2b). We see that jdb has stopped on line 44, but it has not yet executed it. This means that we have not yet calculated the value for the chance variable.

Step 8:   Print the chance variable. We see that it is 0.0.

Step 9:   Issue another *step* command. We have now executed line 44 and stopped at line 46.

Step 10:   Print the chance variable again. Now we see that its value is 0.25.

Step 11:   Stop the debugger by entering the *exit* command. We see the message box that reports our chance pop up, and we are then returned to the MS-DOS prompt.

The clear Command   It is possible to set and **clear breakpoints** as you are running the debugger. The clear command has two purposes. If the *clear* command is issued a line number of a breakpoint, such as *clear CoconutEstimator:10* it clears that breakpoint in the debugger. If the *clear* is issued by itself, the debugger then shows all of the currently set breakpoints. Figure F-3 shows these two commands, using the CoconutEstimator program.

clear breakpoints
remove the breakpoint at a given line of code in the debugger.

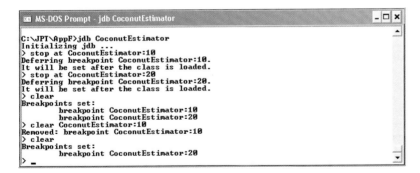

Figure F-3
The clear command will either clear a specific breakpoint or show the currently set breakpoints.

F

Figure F-4
The *locals* command shows a method's local variables and their values.

locals

debugger command
that prints the values of
all local variables in a
method

The locals Command   When your debugger is stopped inside a method, it is possible to see the values of that method's local variables by using the **locals** command. Class variables and class objects are not shown with the *locals* command. Figure F-4 shows the output from the CoconutEstimator program when a breakpoint is set at line 48.

Example 2: AccuracyDemo from Chapter 4

Program 4-10, AccuracyDemo, serves as our model for the second debugging example. Recall that in this program we sum the value 0.1 ten times, and then test to see if our summed value is 1.0. In Java, as in most programming languages, floating point arithmetic is carried on with double precision values. This means that our calculations are performed with 14–16 digits of precision. Our summed value is 0.99999999999999, not the expected 1.0.

AccuracyDemo and the Print Statement Approach   Programs that contain loops are sometimes challenging to debug. We do not wish to step through a loop that executes more than a few times, yet we need to see what occurs inside the loop. The System.out.println() method allows us to place print statements inside the loop, giving us a way to see each iteration of the loop. We avoid having to step through the code one line at a time. Of course, we may end up with a large output listing in our window! Another downfall with the print statement approach is seen when tracing our program in a series of if, else if statements because we need to place a call to System.out.println() in each block of code.

Examine Program F-3 and note the four separate calls to System.out.println(), including one in each section of the if else statement block. Figure F-5 shows the MS-DOS window with the resultant messages.

F

```
1    //Program F-3 is a modified version of
2    //Program 4-10 Demonstrate Java's Accuracy
3    //File:  AccuracyDemo.java
4
5    import javax.swing.JOptionPane;
6
7    public class AccuracyDemo
8    {
9       public AccuracyDemo()
10      {
11          String output = "Adding 0.1 10 times \n\n ";
12
13          int i;
14          double sum = 0.0;
15          for(i = 0; i < 10; ++i)
16          {
17              sum = sum + 0.1;
18              System.out.println("i = "+Integer.toString(i) +
19                        "  Sum = "+ Double.toString(sum) );
20          }
21
22          System.out.println("Done with for loop Sum = "
23                    + Double.toString(sum) );
24
25          output += "Sum = " + Double.toString(sum);
26          if(sum == 1.0)
27          {
28              output += "\n\nSum is the same as 1.0";
29              System.out.println("in true part of if statement");
30          }
31          else
32          {
33              output += "\n\nSum is not the same as 1.0";
34              System.out.println("in false part of if statement");
35          }
36
37          JOptionPane.showMessageDialog(null,output, "Accuracy",
38                    JOptionPane.INFORMATION_MESSAGE);
39      }
40
41      public static void main(String args [] )
42      {
43          AccuracyDemo theApp = new AccuracyDemo();
44          System.exit(0);
45      }
46  }
```

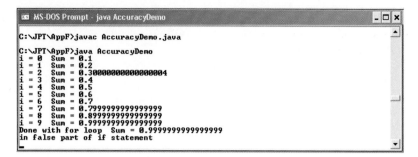

Figure F-5
The System.out.println() statements in the AccuracyDemo program write the intermediate sum values in each iteration of the for loop. We also write the sum after the loop. Calls to println() are placed in each section of the if else statement block. The false condition is met in this program.

AccuracyDemo and jdb   In debugging the AccuracyDemo program, we will not step through the for loop. We will stop at line 20 after the loop has executed, and print the sum value. We then step through the code, watching how the code jumps into the else portion of the if else block. Examine Program F-4 and the debugging steps shown in Figure F-6. Using the debugger to step through if else blocks is a much easier way to follow code execution than populating your code in println() statements.

```
1    //Program F-4 is
2    //Program 4-10 Demonstrate Java's Accuracy
3    //File:  AccuracyDemo.java
4
5    import javax.swing.JOptionPane;
6
7    public class AccuracyDemo
8    {
9      public AccuracyDemo()
10     {
11          String output = "Adding 0.1 10 times \n\n ";
12
13          int i;
14          double sum = 0.0;
15          for(i = 0; i < 10; ++i)
16          {
17                  sum = sum + 0.1;
18          }
```

```
19
20              output += "Sum = " + Double.toString(sum);
21              if(sum == 1.0)
22                      output += "\n\nSum is the same as 1.0";
23              else
24                      output += "\n\nSum is not the same as 1.0";
25
26              JOptionPane.showMessageDialog(null,output, "Accuracy",
27                          JOptionPane.INFORMATION_MESSAGE);
28      }
29
30      public static void main(String args [] )
31      {
32              AccuracyDemo theApp = new AccuracyDemo();
33              System.exit(0);
34      }
35  }
```

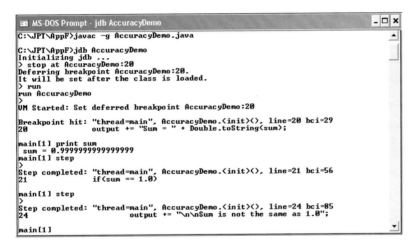

Figure F-6
Using the jdb program, we set a breakpoint at line 20 and print the sum value. We
then step through the code jumping into the else block of code. *Note:* Below the run
statement you may see *set uncaught java.lang. Throwable* and *set deferred
uncaught java.lang.Throwable.* For this example (and others) please ignore these
statements.

Just for fun, we reran this program in the debugger, stopping at line 26, and issued
the *locals* command. Figure F-7 shows the local variables of the AccuracyDemo()
constructor method, including the output String.

F

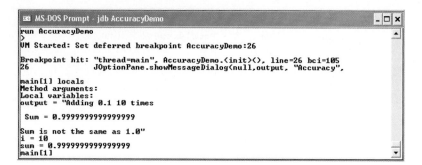

Figure F-7
The local variables of the AccuracyDemo constructor are seen in this figure. The program execution is stopped at line 26.

Example 3: step, step up, next, and the SevenDwarfs

For the Java programmer to become comfortable using the jdb, it is important for him or her to understand the different commands and how to use them to maneuver through the code. The *step*, *step up*, and *next* command are key. Review Table F-2. Recall that the *step* command steps us to the next line of code, and if it is a method call, we step into that method. The *next* command steps over the method call, executing the method. You would use the *next* command if you knew the method worked correctly and did not wish to step through it. The **step up** command should be issued while stopped inside a method. When the *step up* command is issued, the debugger executes the entire method, stopping at the line where the method was called.

We demonstrate these three commands, *step*, *step up*, and *next*, using Program F-5, which is Program 5-9, SevenDwarfsFrame, from Chapter 5. Recall that in the SevenDwarfsFrame, we have an array of Strings containing the names of the seven dwarfs. We call the bubblesort() method, which sorts the names into alphabetical order. After the sorting is finished, we show the frame that contains the names. Here is the code for you to review.

step up

issued while inside a method, it executes the entire method, stopping at the line where the method is called

```
1    //Program F-5 is
2    //Program 5-9  Use an array initialization expression for Strings
3    //File: SevenDwarfsFrame.java
4
5    import java.awt.Graphics;
6    import javax.swing.JFrame;
7    public class SevenDwarfsFrame extends JFrame
8    {
9       String dwarfs[] = { "Doc", "Sleepy", "Dopey", "Grumpy", "Sneezy",
10                                      "Bashful", "Happy" };
```

F

Appendix F ▊ Troubleshooting and Debugging

```java
11
12      public static void main( String[] args )
13      {
14              SevenDwarfsFrame hiho = new SevenDwarfsFrame();
15              hiho.setDefaultCloseOperation( EXIT_ON_CLOSE );
16      }
17
18      public SevenDwarfsFrame()            //class constructor method
19      {
20              bubblesort();          //sort the names into alphabetical order
21
22              setSize( 250, 175 );        //set the window size
23              setTitle("Seven Dwarfs Program");
24              show();
25      }
26
27      public void paint( Graphics g )
28      {
29              for(int i = 0; i < dwarfs.length; ++i)
30              {
31                      g.drawString(dwarfs[i],25, 60+15*i);
32              }
33      }
34
35      //this bubble sort routine sorts Strings in alphabetical order
36      public void bubblesort()
37      {
38              //we can obtain the size of a Java array like this:
39              int size = dwarfs.length;
40              int x, y;
41              String temp;
42
43              for(x = 1; x < size; ++x)
44              {
45                      for( y = 0; y < size - 1; ++y)
46                      {
47                              //String's compareTo returns an int
48                              //0 if the Strings hold the same value
49                              // < 0 for "A" < "B" situation
50                              // > 0 for "B" > "A" situation
51                              if( (dwarfs[y].compareTo( dwarfs[y +1] ) ) ) > 0 )
52                              {
```

F

```
53                              temp = dwarfs[y];
54                              dwarfs[y] = dwarfs[y+1];
55                              dwarfs[y+1] = temp;
56                          }
57                      }
58                  }
59          }
60  }
```

In order to compare how the *step*, *next*, and *step up* commands work, we run the debugger twice. In the first case, we set a breakpoint at the call to the bubblesort() method at line 20. When the debugger has stopped code execution we print the first name in the array. We see "Doc." We step over the bubblesort() method by using the *next* command. This allows the sort method to run but we do not watch the execution. The debugger stops at line 22. We print the first name again, and see "Bashful." Refer to Figure F-8 to see these commands in action.

The second method of debugging this program also stops at line 20. We then issue the *step* command, causing the debugger to jump to line 39, the first executable line of the bubblesort() method. We could continue to step through the method but instead we issue the *step up* command. The *step up* command causes the debugger to run the method and stop at line 22, which is the line after the call to bubblesort(). Figure F-9 shows these commands.

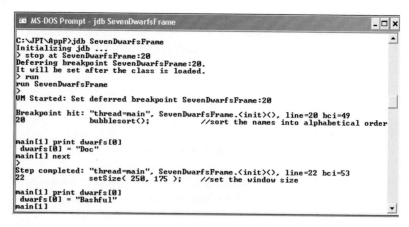

Figure F-8
We stop at line 20 in the SevenDwarfsFrame program and print the first name in the array. We then step over the bubblesort() method by using the next command. The sort method sorts the names into alphabetical order.

```
MS-DOS Prompt - jdb SevenDwarfsFrame                      - □ ×
C:\JPT\AppF>jdb SevenDwarfsFrame
Initializing jdb ...
> stop at SevenDwarfsFrame:20
Deferring breakpoint SevenDwarfsFrame:20.
It will be set after the class is loaded.
> run
run SevenDwarfsFrame
>
VM Started: Set deferred breakpoint SevenDwarfsFrame:20

Breakpoint hit: "thread=main", SevenDwarfsFrame.<init>(), line=20 bci=49
20                 bubblesort();          //sort the names into alphabetical order

main[1] step
>
Step completed: "thread=main", SevenDwarfsFrame.bubblesort(), line=39 bci=0
39                 int size = dwarfs.length;

main[1] step up
>
Step completed: "thread=main", SevenDwarfsFrame.<init>(), line=22 bci=53
22                 setSize( 250, 175 );   //set the window size

main[1]
```

Figure F-9

We stop at line 20 in the SevenDwarfsFrame program and *step* into the bubblesort()
method. Note that the debugger has now stopped at line 39, the first executable line
in the bubblesort() method. We then issue the *step up* command, which causes the
rest of the bubblesort() method to be executed. The debugger then stops at line 22.

Example 4: LoginUsersFrame, Objects, and the jdb

We should now spend time examining two more features of jdb. In this example, we
use the *stop in* command for designating breakpoints at methods—instead of the
stop at command, which uses line numbers. We also show how the jbd **dump** command displays an object's class data values.

Program F-6 is Program 6-11, the LoginUsersFrame. In this program we have
a ComputerUser class that represents a computer user's login name, password, and
access code. The code for this class is seen here:

dump

a jdb command that,
when issued with an
object, shows the
values for all of the
object data

```
1    //Program F-6 is
2    //Program 6-11 A class that describes a computer user.
3    //File: ComputerUser.java
4
5    public class ComputerUser
6    {
7        private      String userName, password;
8        private      int accessCode;
9        //0 = standard user, read/write own area, read group drives
10       //1 = write access to group drives
11       //2 = read/write access to entire system
12
13       public ComputerUser()
14       {
```

Debugging Applications   **819**

F

```
15            userName = "";
16            password = "";
17            accessCode = 0;
18      }
19
20      public ComputerUser(String name, String passwd, int code)
21      {
22            userName = name;
23            password = passwd;
24            accessCode = code;
25      }
26
27      public void setUser(String name, String passwd, int code)
28      {
29            userName = name;
30            password = passwd;
31            accessCode = code;
32      }
33
34      public String getUserName() {  return userName;  }
35
36      public String getPassword() {  return password;  }
37
38      public int getAccessCode()          {  return accessCode; }
39 }
```

The Login class has two important tasks. First, the askForLoginInfo() method asks the user to enter his or her user name and password. Secondly, that login information is then used to validate a known user. The Login's validateUser() method is passed the reference to an array of ComputerUsers. This method searches through the array to see if there is a user and password matching the login information obtained in the askForLoginInfo().

```
1   //Program F-6 is
2   //Program 6-11 A class that obtains computer user name and logic
3   //and validates the user by checking the infomation in an array
4   //of computer users.
5   //File: Login.java
6
7   import javax.swing.JOptionPane;
8
9   public class Login
10  {
11    private String loginName, loginPassword;
12    private String loginDetails;
13
```

```
14      public Login()
15      {
16              loginName = "";
17              loginPassword = "";
18              loginDetails = "No user and password has been obtained.";
19      }
20
21      public Login(String n, String p)
22      {
23              loginName = n;
24              loginPassword = p;
25              loginDetails = "No user and password has been obtained.";
26      }
27
28      public void askForLoginInfo()
29      {
30              loginName = JOptionPane.showInputDialog("Enter User Name");
31              loginPassword = JOptionPane.showInputDialog("Enter Password");
32      }
33
34      public boolean validateUser(ComputerUser userArray[])
35      {
36              //Return true if valid, false if not valid.
37              //Login details are written into the details String.
38
39              //search the userArray for the current login name
40              for(int i = 0; i < userArray.length; ++i)
41              {
42                      if(loginName.equals( userArray[i].getUserName() )  )
43                      {
44                      if(loginPassword.equals( userArray[i].getPassword() ) )
45                          {
46                          //we have a valid user, write details and return true
47                                  loginDetails = "Valid user and password.";
48                                  return true;
49                          }
50                          else    //valid name but passwords don't match
51                          {
52                          loginDetails = "Valid user but invalid password.";
53                                  return false;
54                          }
55                  }
56              }
57
58              //if we get to here, we don't have a valid user,
59              loginDetails = "User name not found in array of ComputerUsers.";
60              return false;
61      }
62
63      public String loginReport() { return loginDetails; }
```

```
64
65      public String toString()
66      {
67              String current = "User: " + loginName
68                      + "    (password: " + loginPassword +")";
69              return current;
70      }
71  }
```

In the LoginUsersFrame class, we have an array of five computer users for which we have set names, passwords, and access codes. The constructor calls the frame's loginAUser(), which in turn asks todd, our Login object, to askForLogin-Info() from our user. Once that method is performed, we ask todd to validate our user. The frame's paint() method obtains todd's login report data and displays the information in the window. Examine the LoginUsersFrame source code here:

```
1   //Program F-6 is
2   //Program 6-11
3   //File: LoginUsersFrame.java
4
5   import java.awt.Graphics;
6   import javax.swing.JFrame;
7
8   public class LoginUsersFrame extends JFrame
9   {
10     //We instantiate a Login object named todd.
11     private Login todd = new Login();
12
13     //We create an array reference called users.
14     //The array is sized to hold 5 users.
15     //NOTE: this is not ready to use until we allocate objects!
16     private ComputerUser users[] = new ComputerUser[5];
17
18     private String findings;
19     boolean bOK;
20
21     public static void main( String[] args )
22     {
23             LoginUsersFrame hal = new LoginUsersFrame();
24             hal.setDefaultCloseOperation( EXIT_ON_CLOSE );
25     }
26
27     //class constructor initializes values
28     public LoginUsersFrame()
29     {
```

```
30          setSize( 450, 200 );         //set the window size
31          setTitle("Login Users Program");
32
33          //Before we can use the User array, we must fill the array with
34          //ComputerUser objects!!!
35          for(int i = 0; i < users.length; ++i)
36          {
37                  users[i] = new ComputerUser();
38          }
39
40          //Now we set 5 users and their passwords.
41          users[0].setUser("BlueDog", "arfarf", 0);
42          users[1].setUser("KiowaTheWonderDog", "awooooooo", 0);
43          users[2].setUser("Doc","Irun4you",0);
44          users[3].setUser("Maddie","WhenDoWeGo",1);
45          users[4].setUser("HannahBanana","BarkBark",2);
46
47          loginAUser();           //now call LoginAUser
48     }
49
50     public void loginAUser()
51     {
52          //have todd ask for the login information
53          todd.askForLoginInfo();
54
55          //now todd validates the current login by checking it
56          //against the array of users
57          bOK = todd.validateUser(users);
58
59          //bOK would be checked and the user allowed to login if true
60
61          //now that we have a user, show the results
62          show();
63     }
64     public void paint( Graphics g )
65     {
66          String output = "Results ";
67          g.drawString( output, 25, 60 );
68          output = "Login Request for " + todd.toString();
69          g.drawString( output, 25, 90 );
70
71          findings = todd.loginReport();
72          g.drawString( findings, 25, 120);
73     }
74 }
```

F

We initially compile the three source files using the javac –g option. The first time we run the debugger we *stop in LoginUsersFrame.loginAUser()*. This action sets a breakpoint at the first executable line in the method (refer to line 53 in LoginUsersFrame). Issuing the *run* command, we stop at line 53. Remember that we have not yet executed the line that is the call to todd.askForLoginInfo() method. We ask the debugger to *dump* the data on todd, and we see that our Login object does not yet have any user information. Figure F-10a shows these debugging commands.

At this point we issue a *next* command seen in Figure F-10b. The debugger steps over (and executes) line 53, the todd.askForLoginInfo() method. The program pops up JOptionPane messages boxes for our user to enter the user name ("BlueDog") and password ("arfarf") and stops on line 57. Issuing one more *next* command causes

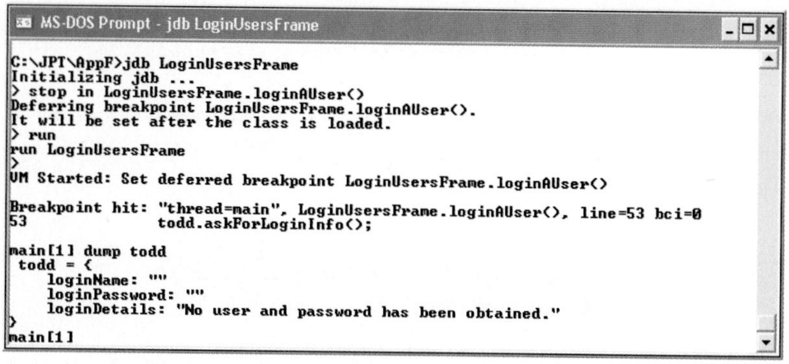

```
MS-DOS Prompt - jdb LoginUsersFrame                               _ □ ×

C:\JPT\AppF>jdb LoginUsersFrame
Initializing jdb ...
> stop in LoginUsersFrame.loginAUser()
Deferring breakpoint LoginUsersFrame.loginAUser().
It will be set after the class is loaded.
> run
run LoginUsersFrame
>
VM Started: Set deferred breakpoint LoginUsersFrame.loginAUser()

Breakpoint hit: "thread=main", LoginUsersFrame.loginAUser(), line=53 bci=0
53                 todd.askForLoginInfo();

main[1] dump todd
 todd = <
    loginName: ""
    loginPassword: ""
    loginDetails: "No user and password has been obtained."
>
main[1]
```

(a)

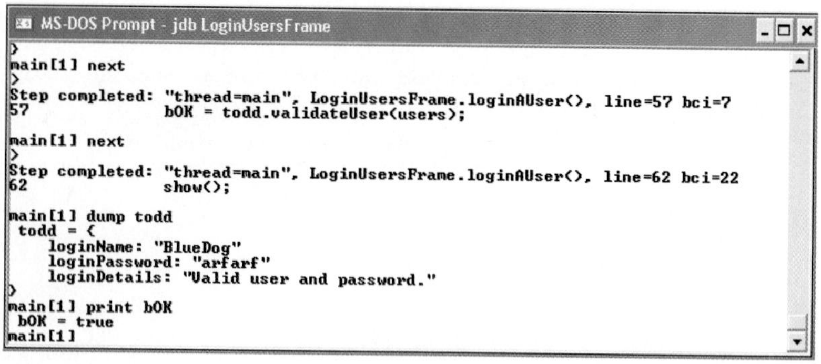

```
MS-DOS Prompt - jdb LoginUsersFrame                               _ □ ×
>
main[1] next
>
Step completed: "thread=main", LoginUsersFrame.loginAUser(), line=57 bci=7
57                 bOK = todd.validateUser(users);

main[1] next
>
Step completed: "thread=main", LoginUsersFrame.loginAUser(), line=62 bci=22
62                 show();

main[1] dump todd
 todd = <
    loginName: "BlueDog"
    loginPassword: "arfarf"
    loginDetails: "Valid user and password."
>
main[1] print bOK
 bOK = true
main[1]
```

(b)

Figure F-10
a) We stop in the LoginUsersFrame loginAUser() method and request that the debugger show us the data in the Login object todd via the jdb dump command. b) We issue two next commands, which execute the todd.askForLoginInfo() and todd.validateUser() methods. Examining the object data once again shows us the values we entered and results of login validation.

the debugger to run the todd.validateUser() on line 57 and we stop at line 62. We *dump* *todd* once again and we now see the Login's object.

Debugging Applets

Applets are executed in web browser programs, and typically do not have access to system resources. This means that applets are not allowed to read or to write files from the system's disk or to access the computer's memory. Applets "play in the sandbox," meaning that their execution is contained within the web browser. As a refresher on applets, please review Java Applets (section 3.2) in Chapter 3.

Once again, there are two approaches that the programmer may use for debugging applets. If the applet is being executed by the appletviewer program, messages written by System.out.println() statements are seen in the MS-DOS Prompt window. The appletviewer program also has a debug mode. The **appletviewer –debug** option initializes the Java debugger and provides all the jdb commands. These commands allow us to set breakpoints, step through the code, and examine variables. We concentrate on this option in this portion of the appendix.

appletviewer –debug initializes the Java debugger and provides all the jdb commands to debug an applet class

Example 5: AffirmationApplet

Program F-7 is the Program 4-16, the AffirmationApplet. In this applet, we ask the user to enter his or her name. The applet writes complimentary messages about the user's programming skills into the applet window. There are two while loops in the paint() method. The placement of the text in the applet window varies in each pass of the loop. The code is seen here for your reference.

```
1   //Program F-7 is
2   //Program 4-16 Write affirming statements about a programmer.
3   //File:  AffirmationApplet.java
4
5   import javax.swing.JApplet;
6   import javax.swing.JOptionPane;
7   import java.awt.*;   //for the Fonts, Color, and Graphics
8
9   public class AffirmationApplet extends JApplet
10  {
11    String name;
12
13    public void start()
14    {
```

F

```
15          //Obtain the Java Programmer's name.
16              name = JOptionPane.showInputDialog(null,
17              "What is your name? ","The Affirmation Applet",
18              JOptionPane.QUESTION_MESSAGE);
19      }
20
21      public void paint(Graphics g)
22      {
23              int x = 30, y = 30;
24
25      //Draw a filled rectangle so the window background is yellow.
26      //Could have said this.setBackground(Color.yellow);
27              g.setColor(Color.yellow);
28              g.fillRect(0,0,400,250);
29
30      //First we set the font to bold serif and write the name.
31      //We pass in a "new" Font. We don't have a font object here.
32              g.setFont(new Font("Ariel", Font.BOLD, 30));
33              g.setColor(Color.black);
34              g.drawString( name,x,y);
35
36          //Now we set the font to a new font.
37              g.setFont(new Font("Monospaced", Font.ITALIC, 14));
38              g.setColor(Color.blue);
39
40        //Next, find the font height and use it to increment the y position
41        //of the drawString method. Space the lines equally.
42        //We ask the Graphics object to tell us the font size.
43          FontMetrics size = g.getFontMetrics();
44          int h = size.getHeight();
45          y = 60;
46          while(y < 150)
47          {
48                  g.drawString( "You are a wonderful programmer!", x, y);
49                  y = y + h;
50          }
51
52          //Change the compliment and set a new font.
53          String last = name + " builds MARVELOUS code!!!!";
54
55          g.setFont(new Font("Serif", Font.PLAIN, 20));
56          g.setColor(Color.red);
57          size = g.getFontMetrics();
58          h = size.getHeight();
59
```

```
60        while(y < 225)
61        {
62                g.drawString( last, x, y);
63                y = y + h;
64        }
65    }
66 }
```

To run the debugger with our program, we must compile the applet source code with javac's –g option. The associated –debug option is issued when we start appletviewer. These commands can be seen in Figure F-11a. In this figure, you can see that we set breakpoints at lines 49 and 63, which are inside the two while loops,

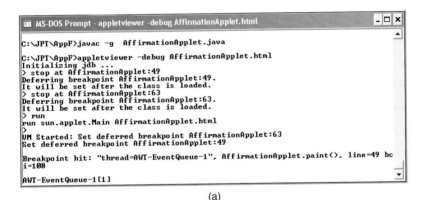

(a)

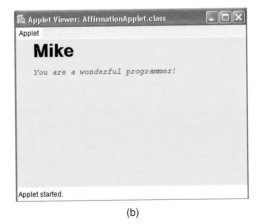

(b)

Figure F-11
a) We compile the AffirmationsApplet with the javac –g option and start appletviewer with the –debug option. This starts an associated jdb program. We set a breakpoint at lines 49 and 63. b) When we stop at line 49, we have painted the name and first complimentary message in the Applet Window.

F

Debugging Applets

and issue the *run* command. We enter the name "Mike" in the message box. When the appletviewer stops at the first breakpoint, Figure F-11b (see page 827) shows that the Applet Window has been drawn, the background has been set to yellow, and we see Mike's name and the first line of complimentary text. Examine the source code to convince yourself that we have executed through line 48 and the debugger has stopped in the first iteration of this loop.

We are able to issue the *cont* (continue) command—which continues running the debugger until it hits another breakpoint. Figure F-12 shows the Applet Window after we entered five *cont* commands. The first four *cont* commands stop us at line 49 as we iterate through the while loop. With each stop we see another "You are a wonderful programmer!" statement. The fifth *cont* command caused the program to run until line 63, writing "Mike builds MARVELOUS code!!!". As we stop at each breakpoint, we see another line of text in the window. Running an applet in appletwindow's debug mode allows you to watch the applet window being painted one line at a time!

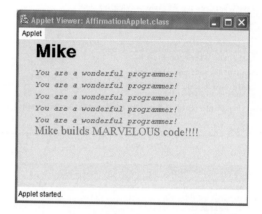

Figure F-12
We have issued five cont (continue) commands. We have executed the loop that writes, "You are a wonderful programmer!" five times. When we stop at the breakpoint on line 63, we have written "Mike builds MARVELOUS code" once.

Bibliography

General Java References

Deital, H. M. and P.J. Deital. *Java: How to Program.* 4th Ed. Upper Saddle River, NJ: Prentice Hall, 2002.

Eckel, Bruce. *Thinking in Java.* 2nd Ed. Upper Saddle River, NJ: Prentice Hall, 2000.

Gamma, Erich, Richard Helm, Ralph Johnson and John Vlissides. *Design Patterns: Elements of Reusable Object-Oriented Software.* Addison-Wesley, 1995.

Gosling, James, Bill Joy and Guy Steele: *Java Language Specifications.* 2nd Ed. java.sun.com.

Java™ 2 Platform, Standard Edition, v 1.4.0 and v 1.4.1 API Specification from Sun Microsystems, Inc.

Schlidt, Herbert. *The Complete Reference Java 2.* 4th Ed. Berkeley, CA: Osborne McGraw Hill, 2001.

van der Linden, Peter. *Just Java 2.* 5th Ed. Palo Alto: Sun Microsystems Press, A Prentice Hall Title, 2002.

Advanced Java References

Callaway, Dustin R. *Inside Servlets: Server-side Programming for the Java Platform.* 2nd Ed. Addison-Wesley, 2001.

Deital, H. M., P.J. Deital, and S.E. Santry. *Advanced Java 2: How to Program.* Upper Saddle River, NJ: Prentice Hall, 2002.

Goodwill, James. *Developing Java Servlets.* 2nd Ed. Same Publishing, May 2001.

Hall, Marty. *More Servlets and Java Server Pages.* Upper Saddle River, NJ: Prentice Hall PTR, December 2001.

Kurniawan, Budi. *Java for the Web with Servlets, JSP, and EJB: A Developer's Guide to J2EE Solutions.* Que Publishing, April 2002.

829

Glossary

abstraction   The process of selecting pertinent data describing the item we wish to model.

abstract class   A generalized "idea" or "blueprint" for a class of objects intended to be used as a superclass. The abstract superclass is then extended by concrete subclasses, and the abstract methods are overridden in these subclasses.

access specifiers or **access modifiers**   Java keywords that dictate the visibility and accessibility of class members, including private, public, and protected. These keywords are used with data, methods, and classes. Java provides a default specification if you forget, either intentionally or not, to provide one of the three modifiers.

anonymous inner class   A class that is defined inside another class (i.e. inner) and is not assigned a name (i.e. anonymous). Anonymous inner classes are commonly used for writing event handlers.

applet   A program that runs in a web browser. Typically, an applet is downloaded from a "server" onto the "client" machine and run in the client's web browser program.

application   A Java application is a stand-alone program that can be run from the command line on a computer.

Application Programming Interfaces (APIs)   A set of class libraries that provide existing classes available for use in programs.

ArithmeticException   Occurs during an illegal arithmetic condition or operation.

array   A group of variables of the same data type (primitives or object references) that is referenced with a single name. When the programmer creates the array, he or she must indicate the size of the array. Java array size cannot change once declared. Each of the array variables or elements is accessed using an array index or array subscript using the square angle brackets [ ]. An array index or subscript is an integer value.

array dimension   The size of the array.

array index or **array subscript**   An integer value.

array of arrays   An array that is composed of two subscripts that are often, but not always, used to represent a table of items. You can visualize the table organized in a row and column format. The elements in these multi-subscripted arrays are referenced with two numbers, the first representing the row number and the second referencing the column.

array variables or **elements**   An array element is an individual member of the array holding one value (primitive) or one object (array of objects).

ArrayIndexOutOfBoundsException   Occurs if the program attempts to access an array element that is out of bounds.

associativity   Dictates the priority of operations for operators with the same precedence found in the same statement. For arithmetic operators, the associativity is "left to right," meaning that the operator on the left *in the expression* gets performed first.

AWT (Abstract Windowing Toolkit) peer components   AWT components are termed "heavyweight" components and they rely on the target system's native or peer components.

bit   A bit is a unit of data that exists in one of two states. We often refer to a bit as being either a 1 or a 0.

block of code   A block of code is code that is enclosed in curly braces { }.

block scope   Any variable declared within a block of code has block scope and is only visible and accessible to code inside that block.

breakpoint   Used in debugging, a line of code, designated by the programmer where execution will halt.

bug   A general purpose term for an error in a program.

byte   A basic unit of computer memory. The byte consists of eight bits. A bit is a unit of data that exists in one of two states. We often refer to a bit as being either a 1 or a 0.

bytecode   Written by the Java compiler, bytecode is contained in a file that is named with the *.class* extension. A Bytecode file is read by the JVM. The JVM translates the commands into "native" instructions for the computer's processor.

bytecode verifier   Resides within the JVM. This verifier checks that the bytecode conforms to Java language specifications and checks to see if there are any violations of language. It examines each instruction and makes sure that the bytecode does not perform any illegal operations. Illegal operations include stack overflow or underflow, illegal accesses, or invalid paths.

cast   Casting a variable or a data cast is an operation in which the value of one type of data is transformed into another type of data.

catch   After an exception has been thrown, the exception is captured or caught and the error handling statements are executed. The program attempts to resolve the error by executing statements in the catch block of code. Catch is used in a block of code that specifies the type of exception it can catch.

ClassNotFoundException Thrown when an application tries to load a class but its definition is not found.

class definition The class definition line is the first line of a programmer-defined class. It usually begins with public class ClassName.

class Can be thought of as a job description. The term class is a keyword (reserved word with special meaning to the language).

class or **instance variables** Class or instance variables are declared after the class definition line and before any method definition lines. Class variables are "seen" by all of the methods inside the class and can be used by any of the class's methods.

class scope The same idea as block scope. Any variables that are declared within the class and outside of any method or block of code are in class scope and visible to the entire class.

classpath The classpath is an environment variable in the computer operating system. Java reads the classpath to determine other places in which to look for Java classes or packages.

client A user that downloads and uses information from a server. A client uses the resources provided by the server.

collection classes Include Java's ArrayList, Vector, List, and Map. In using these collection classes, the Java programmer instantiates an object of the collection class and uses methods to add, delete, or manipulate items in the object. These object-based collections are flexible in that they have no predetermined size and can grow or shrink dynamically as the program runs. Java also provides the Collection class, which can work on these different types of collection objects. The Collection class provides static methods for sorting, searching, shuffling, finding the max and min, reversing, and swapping items contained in the various objects.

comment Lines written by the programmer in the source file that convey information concerning the code, such as logic, author, run information, or special instructions.

compiler Reads the Java source code file and checks that the syntax (grammar) is correct. It issues errors when it finds them. If there are no errors, the Java compiler writes the associated *.class* file, which is bytecode.

computer programming language Allows a programmer to write instructions or commands that form a computer program. The programmer must build the program. When the program is run or executed, the commands found in the program make the computer perform tasks.

constructor method When the new keyword is executed in a Java statement, the class's constructor is run automatically. A special type of method that is written as part of the class and has the same name as the class. Java will execute whatever code is inside the constructor method when the object is created. Its job is to initialize the object's data to desired values. It does not have a return type. Perhaps a better name for a constructor is a memory allocator and initializer, as that describes the job of the constructor.

Container object   A Java component that holds other components.

crash   When a program halts execution in an ungraceful manner.

cross-platform   Java programs are cross-platform or platform-independent because you can write a Java program on one machine and run it on any machine.

DataFormatException   Thrown when a data format error has occurred.

debugger   A separate program that allows the programmer to execute his or her program to determine where problems exist. The debugger allows stopping at breakpoint so that the programmer may examine data values and step through the code a line at a time.

default constructor   The constructor method with no input values. Sets default values into the object's data when created.

early-binding   The ability of the compiler to determine which method to call is known as early-binding.

encapsulation   The process by which we bundle the data and the associated operations (methods) together and treat them as a single unit. When we write a class in Java, we bundle the data and operations together. Encapsulation also provides a wrapper that protects the code and data from being arbitrarily accessed or misused by outside sources.

Error   Serious problem in a program. It is not expected that the error may be resolved. At best, we tell the user about the error and exit the program gracefully.

escape sequence   An escape sequence is created when the backslash is combined with certain characters inside the string—telling Java to "escape from" the normal way to write the output. For example, combining the backslash with the letter *n* (\n) tells Java to go to a new line before it prints it.

Event-driven programs   Programs that wait for the user to issue a command of some sort, such as to click a button, select a menu item, or activate a variety of other controls. Programs that have GUIs are event-driven programs.

exception   An error that occurs while the program is executing. Also known as a run-time error.

final   Java provides the final keyword so that the programmer may designate that a variable cannot be modified. When used with classes, it says that this class cannot be extended.

finalize() method   The finalize() method is one of the methods in the java.lang.Object class, and is called before the memory occupied by that object is released. Programmers can write a finalize() method for any class. However, the finalize() method should be present in a class only if there are special reasons for needing access to an object when garbage collection occurs. The purpose of having a finalize() method is to provide the programmer a chance to free resources that we cannot free by some other means.

finally   The finally keyword designates a block of code, associated with a try block, that is performed whether or not an exception is thrown. There is only one finally block for each try (there may be many catch statements for each try), and the finally block is placed after the last catch statement. When the code executes, if no errors occurred in the try block, the catch blocks are skipped and the finally block is executed. If any errors occur and a catch statement is executed, the finally block is still executed.

garbage collection   A process that occurs sporadically during program execution. When there are no longer any references to an object or an array on the stack, Java assumes that the object is no longer needed and the memory is released from the heap.

"has a" relationship   The "has a" relationship describes the class relationship when one class is composed of another class. For example, the JFrame has JButtons.

heap   A portion of memory used to support the Java program. The memory for the actual data and methods for all objects and array data is allocated on the heap, never on the stack.

helper class   A programming term used to describe classes that provide useful services to the programmer. For example, the DecimalFormat class could be called a helper class because it helps us format our numeric output.

heavyweight components   AWT components are referred to as heavyweight components. They rely on the target machine's native components.

hexadecimal notation   Base 16 mathematical notation that uses sixteen symbols: 0–9 and A–F. Hex is used to describe byte patterns and computer memory.

HyperText Markup Language (HTML)   Language used to create web pages. Web pages are read by web browsers.

IllegalAccessException   Thrown when an application tries to create an instance, access a field, or call a method but the current method does not have access to the specified class.

inner class   A class that is contained inside another class.

identifier   In Java, the name provided by the programmer for a programmer-defined package, object, method, or variable. The language has specific rules for naming identifiers.

import statement   A statement that tells the Java compiler that the program is going to use the class specified in this statement and for the compiler to load this class to ensure we use it correctly.

implements   A Java keyword. See *interface*.

inheritance   The ability to create a new class from an existing class. The new class is referred to as the subclass, while the existing class is known as the superclass. The subclass inherits characteristics and methods from the superclass and has new, customized features not found in the superclass. For example, a SportsCar could be created from a Car class and could inherit all the necessary Car characteristics and features. The SportsCar also has customized features that the Car class does not, such as a specialized suspension. Inheritance represents an "is a" class relationship, the subclass is a superclass—the SportsCar is a Car.

instantiation   The creation process for an object. To use a Java class and its nonstatic methods, the Java programmer must create an instance (known as an object) of the class.

integrated development environment (IDE)   Contains a code editor, design tool, Java documentation, project management tools, and a debugger. The IDE provides the Java programmer with a complete development environment for Java. There are many different Java IDE packages available. Searching the WWW for "Java IDEs" produces a list of such tools.

interface   Defined by using the interface keyword instead of the class keyword, and it may contain public final fields and method signatures. The interface provides a list of method signatures—that is, method names and input and output values but no method bodies. When we need to use an interface, we implement it in a class by using the implements keyword. That class contains the completed interface methods. Java allows us to implement one or more interfaces in a class.

interpreted language   Java is said to be an interpreted language because running a Java program involves having the JVM read and interpret the Java bytecode, which then issues the appropriate processor instructions.

"is a" relationship   The "is a" relationship describes the class relationship between superclasses- and subclasses. The subclass is a superclass. For example, a Cat is a HousePet.

JAR file   Java Archive file based on the PKZip encoding method. Allows Java files to be combined and compressed into a single file. A JAR file can be configured so that the JVM can execute the program it contains.

Java   A completely object-oriented programming language originally developed by Sun Microsystems, Inc.

Java compiler   Reads the .*java* source code file and checks that the syntax is correct. It issues errors when it finds them. If there are no errors, it writes a .class file that contains bytecode.

Java Server Pages (JSP)   Modeled on ColdFusion technology. JSP and Microsoft's Active Server Pages (ASP) allow the programmer to embed programming statements, scripts, and other components into a web page on the server. When a server gets a request from a browser, the JSP sends HTML code to the browser. This HTML code may have been dynamically produced by the JSP. Information that changes rapidly, such as stock quotations, weather data, flight information, can be handled via a JSP on the web so that web data can be updated quickly.

Java Virtual Machine (JVM) A separate program that reads the bytecode found in the class file and translates the commands into "native" instructions for the computer's processor. The Java *.class* file does not "talk to" the computer's processor directly. The JVM "talks to" the processor, "telling it" what tasks to perform.

jEdit A Java source code editor developed and maintained by a world-wide team of Java programmers. It provides useful tools for the Java programmer as well as many plugins. Visit their website at www.jEdit.org.

keyword A word reserved by the programming language with specific meaning and syntax. The Java language has many keywords. These keywords may not be used by the programmer as identifiers (that is, names for classes, methods, or variables). Each keyword has specific syntax and actions associated with it.

late-binding Occurs if a Java program is compiled, and the compiler can not determine which of the methods will be called because they are identical. When the code is executed, the program examines which object is invoking the method and hence executes the correct one. This resolution occurs at runtime. The ability to choose the correct method during execution is called late binding.

Layout managers Dictate how the components are arranged in the window—such as in a grid or flow layout.

lightweight components Swing components that come equipped with everything they need to perform their job and do not rely on system components.

listener When an event occurs in a Java program, the event is received and handled by a Java listener. The listeners are provided to us as interfaces. The job of the listener interfaces is to "listen for" or be aware when an event occurs and to provide the necessary program control to perform the required tasks. We write our event handling code in the interface's method.

local class An inner class usually defined within the method of another class.

logical operator A logical operator in Java includes the && AND, || OR, and ! NOT operators. Logical operators require boolean operands and return a value of either true or false.

loop A loop is a fundamental tool for all programming languages. It involves the ability to have the program repeat the execution of a group of statements. This iterative process may be set up so that the loop is executed a predetermined number of times or until a certain condition is met.

machine dependent The JVM is machine dependent, meaning that it must be built specifically for whatever type of computer on which it is run. If you are running a Windows machine, you must have a Windows JVM, because the JVM translates the Java bytecode into Windows processor commands. If you have a Sun Microsystems UltraSPARC workstation, you must have a JVM for the Sun platform, as it must translate the bytecode into SPARC processor commands.

manifest file Required in a JAR file for applications. The manifest file tells Java what class contains the main() method.

method A discrete section of code that exists inside a class and performs a task or tasks for the class. The tasks are performed by the object and defined by the class. A method can have data passed into it and can return data if necessary.

method call or **call to the method** When a program invokes a particular method of a class, this is referred to as "calling the method."

method definition line A method definition line is the first line of a Java method. It contains return information, method name, and input information within the parentheses.

method overloading One type of polymorphism. Overloading occurs when a class has several methods with the same name.

method overriding A more complicated form of polymorphism. Method overriding is seen when a superclass and subclass have the same named method with the identical method inputs. The method in the subclass overrides the method in the superclass. The subclass method may call the superclass method by using super.methodName (inputs) format.

method signature Refers to the return type, method name, and input parameter list.

nested class A class that is defined within the body of another class.

NoSuchMethodException Thrown when an application attempts to call a method that cannot be found.

NumberFormatException Occurs when an illegal attempt is made to convert a String to a numeric data type.

NullPointerException Occurs when a program attempts to use a reference variable that contains a null value instead of a valid object reference.

object An instance of a class.

object-oriented A programming technique that requires programmers to write their code as classes.

object-oriented language A computer programming language that provides the ability for the programmer to write a program using classes and objects. Java programs are built using classes and objects.

one-dimensional array or **single-dimensioned array** An array that is sized with one value and represents a single list or column of values or objects.

operators Symbols that are part of the language that instruct the language to perform certain actions. For example, the "+" symbol adds numbers and the "*" symbol multiplies numbers.

OutOfMemoryError Occurs when the program attempts to allocate more memory than is available.

overloaded method See *method overloading.*

overriding method See *method overriding.*

package A technique that allows a group of classes to be organized and used in a logical manner. A Java package is a group of classes that are related in a logical manner and have been "packaged" or bundled together.

path An environment variable in the computer operating system that tells the operating system other places to look for executable programs.

peer components The Java AWT components are based on peer components. Peer components are also known as native components. When a Java program needs a button, the AWT button component code simply uses the operating system's native button. This means that if the Java program is running on a Windows machine, the program draws a Windows button. If the program is running on a Sun machine, a Solaris button is used.

platform independent A program that is able to work on a variety of computers, meaning it could be run on PCs, Sun workstations, Macs, etc. Java was originally designed for building software and embedding it in consumer electronic devices such as microwave ovens, washing machines, and remote controls. Java programs are platform-independent or cross platform because you can write a Java program on one machine and run it on any other machine!

polymorphism Many shapes or many forms. In object-oriented programming languages, it refers to one interface and many methods. Simply put, polymorphism is the ability to use the same name to refer to methods that perform different tasks or methods that have a variety of input values.

pop off the stack Removed a data item from the stack memory.

portable language Java is a highly portable language, meaning that it runs on many types of hardware. Java programs can run on all types of computers, and thanks to the way Java is designed, Java programs can run on other hardware such as cell phones, PDAs, embedded processors, microprocessors, and smart cards (credit cards with a microprocessor and memory). Java's source code can be written once and run on any machine with a JVM.

precedence of operations or **priority of operations** Which operation is performed first, which is performed second, and so on in a program statement.

primitive types or **primitives** The Java language provides eight "built-in" data types known as primitives for the programmer's use. A primitive data type is a nonobject "container" that can hold a specific kind of program data including int, float, double, char, boolean, short, long, and byte.

private A Java keyword and access specifier used to make data or methods hidden (made invisible) to all other classes. Private data and methods are not inherited by the subclasses.

protected A Java keyword and access specifier used for determining which class members are inherited by the class's subclasses. Protected members are hidden (invisible) to all other classes.

public A Java keyword and access specifier used to make data or methods visible to all of the other classes.

push on the stack Place a data item in the stack memory.

reference variables or **references**   Variables that refer to objects and arrays. References contain the memory location of an object or an array and not the actual data and methods. Arrays and objects must be allocated with the new operator. Objects contain both data and methods.

relational operator   Includes the $<, <=, >, >=, ==, !=$ operators. Relational operators evaluate variables or results from expressions and return a boolean result (either true or false).

return statement   Forces control of the program to exit the method and return to the calling statement. Return statements can be placed anywhere in a method.

return type   Indicates the type of data that is returned from a method. The data type may be a primitive, an array reference, or an object reference.

RuntimeException   The superclass of the exceptions that the JVM can throw during normal program operations.

scope   A programming term that describes the lifetime and visibility of variables. The scope of a variable is determined by where the variable is declared. Some variables exist for brief periods of time while others exist for the duration of the program. The scope of a variable determines where the variable can be referenced in the program.

servlet   A Java program that resides and runs on a web server. A servlet program responds to a request from a client. Typically, the servlet processes the request and posts that information back to the user/client.

single-dimensioned array or **a one-dimensional array**   An array that is sized with one value and represents a single list or column of values or objects.

source code   Lines of Java instructions written by the Java programmer.

source code file   The file that contains the lines of Java instructions. The file must be saved with a *.java* extension.

stack   The portion of memory that keeps track of certain information for Java methods. When a Java program calls a method, the address of the calling statement, copies of data that are being passed to the method, and the called method's local variables are pushed onto the stack. Pushing and popping are terms related to stacks. Being pushed simply means that we are placing that information in the stack's memory. When the program exits a method, information is popped off the stack (removed from the stack). The calling address is read and program control returns to the calling statement. The information that was stored on the stack has been popped off and is lost.

stack trace   A list of method calls that show the events leading up to where the exception occurred.

statement   A line of Java code that issues a command or performs an operation.

static   Static items in Java persist on a per-class basis, not a per-instance basis. There are four varieties of static items in Java: data, methods, blocks, and classes (described in Table 7-1).

static method Allows the programmer to use the class name to call the static method directly using the ClassName.staticMethod() syntax as opposed to making an object and calling the method using the object.

stream A flow of characters or bytes into or out of a program. For example, data input using data files can be envisioned as characters or bytes coming into the program one at a time.

String The String class is a class in Java designed to work with textual data. The String class provides many methods that are useful for manipulating and comparing textual data.

Super The way a programmer may call the superclass methods, (super.method-Name (inputs)) or superclass constructor (super (inputs)).

Swing components "lightweight" components that know how to draw themselves. They come with all the "know-how" to perform their jobs and do not rely on the target platform's native components.

syntax The grammatical rules required for writing in a programming language. Syntax rules include when and where semicolons and braces should be placed, spelling correctness, and the use of certain types of language components in certain places.

ternary conditional operator Requires three operands. This ? : operator set has similar functionality to the if, else statement with some restrictions.

text-based file A data file of characters without any special formatting symbols. Microsoft's Notepad and jEdit are text-based file editors.

this The *this* keyword contains the object reference or address value. The object reference is the location in the heap where the actual object data is stored. Each object contains a *this* reference which contains its address on the heap.

throw When an error occurs, the program "throws" an error or exception.

Throwable The superclass for all Java exceptions. Only objects of this class (or its subclasses) are able to be thrown by the Java run-time system or by using the throw statement.

try The Java keyword that is used to begin a block of code in which an error or exception may be generated.

top-level class A class whose source code is contained in its own file named with the *.java* extension.

Unicode The Unicode encoding system is used for coding data. In Unicode, every character and symbol has a unique byte representation. The Java language has adopted Unicode so that there is no confusion in character and symbol data for Java programs running on any hardware platform.

"uses a" relationship The "uses a" relationship describes the class relationship when one class provides a service to another class. For example, the Math class provides mathematical constants and methods for a class.

variable A variable is an actual location in memory that has been set aside for use by the program. It is referenced by a specific name. Variables contain values that may be modified by the program. The program must declare a variable by stating the type of data it is to contain and give the variable a name.

Vector class One of the many helpful collection-type classes provided by the java.util package. Vectors can be thought of as dynamic arrays that hold objects. When we refer to something as dynamic, it means that the size can grow and shrink as the program runs. In fact, many Java programmers believe we should never make an array of objects, but should use the Vector class instead.

web server A server is a computer with resources that are to be shared. It is attached to the WWW and has a specific web address.

whitespace characters Characters that are defined to be spaces, carriage returns, linefeeds (the Enter key), tabs, vertical tabs, and form feeds.

zero-indexed A term used for describing arrays. In arrays the first array element subscript is numbered starting at zero, not one.

Index

843